FISHING IN OREGON

Seventh Edition

by Dan Casali and Madelynne Diness

FLYING PENCIL PUBLICATIONS
Portland, Oregon

Published by Flying Pencil Publications
P.O. Box 19062
Portland, Oregon 97219

Manufactured in the United States of America.
2 3 4 5 6 7 8 9 10

Edited by Madelynne Diness

Cartography by:
Al Cardwell pp. 4, 12, 18, 19, 21, 26, 29, 47, 50, 62, 66, 76, 102, 124, 127, 129, 133, 134, 141
Dan Casali pp. 2, 10, 13, 22, 24, 30, 36, 45, 53, 55-58, 61, 96, 104, 113, 116, 118, 130, 137
"Two T" pp. 14

Photo Editing by Mary Stupp-Greer
Cover Photo by Steve Terrill
Photos by:
Mat Andrus p. 46
Tom Ballard pp. 38,189
Phil Bullock p. 166
Dan Callaghan p. 60
Dan Casali pp. 119, 145, 163
S. John Collins pp. 174, 184, 185, 186
Headlight Herald p. 26
Michael LeFors p. 20
Gerry Lewin pp. 6, 31, 65, 90, 180
Bill McMillan p. 143
Deke Meyer pp. 15, 72, 122, 128
Steven Nehl pp. 71, 97, 124, 137
Brian O'Keefe pp. 92, 136
Oregon Dept. of Fish and Wildlife pp. 37, 52, 64, 69, 115, 135
Oregon Dept. of Transportation pp. 42, 126, 161
Richard Paradzinski p. 15
Steve Terrill pp. *cover*, 7, 67, 101, 140, 172, 188, 158, 167, 169
Bill Wagner pp. 8, 35, 44, 52, 62, 68, 69, 87, 98
Veronica Walter p. 56

Library of Congress Number: 89-080880

ISBN 0-916473-03-1

CONTENTS

MAPS

ACKNOWLEDGEMENTS

Our sincere thanks to the men and women of the Oregon Department of Fish and Wildlife, who gave generously of their time and knowledge to help bring Fishing In Oregon up-to-date. It is always a delight to work with the district biologists, refreshing to share their enthusiasm for their home waters, and reassuring to know that our waters and fisheries are being monitored by folk who are sincerely devoted to their work. In particular, we would like to acknowledge the assistance of the following biolgists:

Jerry McLeod, ODFW, formerly of Siuslaw District
Bill Mullarkey, Reese Bender, ODFW, Coos-Coquille District
Dave Loomis, ODFW, Lower Rogue and South Coast District
David Liscia, Ray Perkins, Bill Metzler, ODFW Umpqua
Sam Hess,ODFW,Columbia Regional Office
John Haxton, ODFW, West Slope-Molalla District
Keith Braun, ODFW, Tillamook District
Bill Knox, ODFW, Wallowa District
Jim Newton, ODFW, Columbia District
Joe Wetherbee, Wayne Hunt , ODFW, Mid-Willamette District
Jay Massey, Pat Frazier, ODFW, Lower Willamette District
Gene Stewart, Jerry Butler, Jean Crae, ODFW, Lincoln District
Duane West, ODFW, LaGrande
Jim Phelps, ODFW, Umatilla District
Bill Hosford, ODFW, Southeast District
Errol Claire, ODFW, John Day District
Warren Knispel, ODFW, Astoria District
John Fortune, ODFW Klamath District
Ted Fies, Walt Weber, ODFW, Bend District
Greg Concannon, ODFW, Ochoco District
Jim Hutchison, ODFW, Upper Willamette District
Mick Jennings, ODFW, formerly of Upper Rogue District
Elaine Stewart, ODFW, Tillamook District
Lyle Curtis, ODFW, Salmon River Hatchery
Al Smith, ODFW, Portland

Thanks also to Carol Moon of the ODFW Portland Information Office, Terry Link of Warm Springs Indian Reservation, and Willamette Falls Lock Master John Wasson. And to Phil Hardison of Curry Anadramous Fishermen for verifying our Lower Rogue River information, Doc Foster of Roseburg (hope you don't get in trouble for sharing your favorite places on the Umpqua), John Judy of The Fly Fishers Place in Sisters and Deke Meyer for helping us get better acquainted with the Metolius, Scott Richmond for good advice on drifting the Deschutes, Randall Kaufmann of Kaufmann's Streamborn for various and sundry fly recommendations, and to Michael P. Stavenau who provided us with a delightful and informative account of fishing some of eastern Oregon's lesser known waters (we'll all watch out for the snakes!).

And to the following authors whose books and articles provided valuable information: Jack Webber, *Fishing Holes a Short Cast from Portland*; Stan Fagerstrom, *Catch More Steelhead*; Lewis A. MacArthur, *Oregon Geographic Names*; Clain Campagna, *A Fisherman's Guide to Central Oregon;*Patrick McGann, *Fishing and Hunting News*; Dwight Schuh, *Outdoor Life*; Tom McAllister, *The Oregonian*; Jed Davis, *Western Outdoors, Salmon Trout Steelheader.*

INTRODUCTION

What?! Your Copy of the Sixth Edition of Fishing in Oregon self-destructed just five years after purchase? And within days you learned that its authors had brought out a Seventh Edition? Sounds suspicious all right. But in truth, there have been enough significant changes in Oregon waters and fisheries since 1984 to impel us to issue a new edition. (The state went from flood to drought, to name but one.)

About that drought—all Oregon waters other than spring-fed were affected by drought conditions in 1987-88. A good snowpack in 1989 began to reverse the process, though in summer of 1989 many rivers and lakes were still lower than average (revealing their hidden channels and pools to those who were taking note), with fish still a little more wary than usual due to restricted cover.

Worst hit by drought were the southeastern reservoirs, including Phillips, Thief Valley, Chickahominy, Bully Creek, and Antelope. The Warner Valley Lakes were also severely affected, putting a temporary end to a terrific bluegill binge there. Most of these waters are expected to show good recovery by 1990, given another wet winter. At least one fishery, Brownlee Reservoir on the Snake, was positively affected by drought conditions, which stabilized its waters and encouraged better than average growth for its bass and panfish.

Steelhead and salmon hatchery programs are up to full production on Snake River tributaries, whose wild runs were decimated by dam construction. For the first time in many years there is a steelhead season on the Imnaha and Grand Ronde rivers (restricted to hatchery steelhead only). Salmon and steelhead returning to spawn on the upper Grand Ronde must negotiate 8 dams. We hope you agree that those hearty wild ones who make it through deserve to spawn, and will educate yourselves to recognize and (quickly and gently) release all wild steelhead caught in the Snake system, as prescribed by regulation.

On the Columbia River and throughout its system, salmon and steelhead returns have been much better than they were in 1984. In fact, 1988 was a record year for spring chinook returning to the Willamette system. This upturn is due both to successful hatchery production and to the effects of the U.S./Canadian Agreement to reduce offshore salmon harvests. This agreement (and the absence of the El Nino effect) has increased salmon returns to all Oregon coastal streams. The Rogue River recently experienced its highest ever recorded salmon run (over 90,000 chinook over Gold Ray Dam) as well as record-breaking steelhead runs. Summer steelhead returns over Willamette Falls have been as high as 40,000 since 1984, with the Santiam hatchery program producing especially good results.

While hatchery programs continue to be given high priority in the management of many Oregon rivers, there is a growing interest among anglers and within the Oregon Dept. of Fish and Wildlife in the protection and rehabilitation of the state's wild fisheries. The work of Oregon Trout, a non-profit organization, has been especially effective in steering public interest, management policy, and bureaucratic dollars toward wild trout, salmon, and steelhead enhancement. The Deschutes and Metolius rivers are fine examples of effective wild fish management, and of the positive results of citizen involvement in Oregon fishery policy. The 1989 Oregon State Legislature approved funding for the state's first natural fish production manager and for a staff geneticist.

Public involvement in Oregon's fishery policies and projects has never been stronger. ODFW's Salmon/Trout Enhancement Program (STEP) is going strong, with many districts making effective use of volunteer labor and enthusiasm, particularly in the southwest, Willamette, and Southeast zones. Individuals and organizations have reared salmon smolts, rebuilt spawning beds, and helped with other habitat enhancement projects that simply could not have been accomplished within the limited budget of Oregon's fishery program. (So limited, in fact, that the stocking of high trout lakes throughout the state has been reduced to every other year). What's more important, individuals and angling clubs are providing additional vigilance—keeping a watchful eye on their home waters, and sounding a warning (to ODFW, to Oregon Trout, to Northwest Steelheaders) whenever something doesn't seem right (increased erosion, unusual water withdrawals, riparian degradation).

Angler interest in Oregon's bass and panfish has been growing. In recognition of this, we have ferreted out and listed a number of bass and panfish waters that had previously escaped our attention, including a string of some 30 ponds adjacent to the Columbia River between Cascade Locks and the Deschutes (for which we provide a map that keys the location of the ponds to mileage on I-84). Speaking of bass, a new Oregon water has been added to the national bass tournament circuit—Lake Umatilla (one of the Columbia River dam pools), where smallmouth bass catches are reported to be on a par with the best in the country. Smallmouth are also thriving in the Umpqua River, and largemouth are now being caught with some regularity in Crane Prairie Reservoir. A complete listing of all bass and panfish waters can be found in the back of this book.

Oregon's sturgeon population is stable at this time, but there is growing concern for the state of the fishery. Since 1984, sturgeon angling has increased dramatically in the the Columbia, though sturgeon spawning grounds remain limited (sacrificed to Columbia River dams). To keep angler activity and sturgeon availability in balance, the minimum keeper size limit was increased from 36 inches to 40 inches in 1989, and anglers can anticipate additional restrictions during the next few years as ODFW biologists study sturgeon habitat and spawning needs.

Flounder have all but disappeared from Oregon's bays, though in 1988 flounder suddenly started appearing again in the Alsea Bay catch. The striper fishery on the south coast (Coos, Umpqua, and Smith rivers) is going, going. Everyone's sorry to see that fishery end. But Oregon always was an outer limit for comfortable striper habitat. For a brief moment there was rumor that stripers had been caught in the Willamette (summer, 1989), but they turned out to be wayward hybrids from the Tenmile stocking program that has (as a result of that tendency of the hybrids to roam) been discontinued.

Other stocking programs have been undertaken experimentally and, results in, abandoned. In some cases, the fish didn't bite readily enough to appease frustrated anglers, or failed to take advantage of the natural forage, or succumbed to mysterious disease. That's what happened to the big fish in Davis Lake. We are especially sorry about Davis Lake, one or our family favorites. And we appreciate the difficulty faced by biologists of the Oregon Dept. of Fish and Wildlife who must set up these gigantic aquariums by guess and by golly, working on such a grand scale, with so many variables. It isn't easy to play at Creator. Perhaps the new ODFW geneticist will be able to help.

We're sorry to report that there has been little enlightenment among Oregon landowners toward recognizing their responsibility as co-protectors of Oregon's streams. Cattle still trample fragile riparian vegetation, and excessive irrigation withdrawals continue to kill millions of fish and deny others access to spawning grounds. Keeping water in Oregon's rivers, particularly in eastern Oregon, will continue to challenge fishery activists. We urge you to speak up on this issue and others affecting the quality of fishing in Oregon.

It should come as no surprise to anyone that there are more campers in the forests, and more anglers than ever on Oregon waters. And more floaters and boaters on the rivers and lakes. Nevertheless, Oregon's fisheries are holding up pretty well, thanks to strict regulations and (in no small measure) to the vigilance of angler interest groups such as Oregon Trout and Northwest Steelheaders.

Also, it helps that more Oregon anglers are growing comfortable with catch and release philosophy, particularly in regard to wild fish, whether or not required by law. More anglers are fishing for recreation rather than consumption, and measuring the success of the outing by less tangibles rewards than a full freezer chest. We hope the trend continues, and that our readers catch many fine evening rises and return home with their heads full of images of Oregon's beauty and bounty, and with stories about the one that will live to thrill another angler, another day.

To those of our readers who are fishing Oregon for the first time, or coming here from other states or countries, we welcome you. In general, there are a few things you might appreciate knowing. Lodging is relatively sparse near even our most popular waters, except on the coast. Campgrounds, however, are very plentiful, particularly in the national forests. National forest and BLM (Bureau of Land Management) maps are an invaluable resource for locating waters and enjoying Oregon's abundant public lands. Several new 4-color BLM maps are now available (John Day, Lower Deschutes, Central Oregon). Many forest maps hav been revised to match new road numbering systems. To obtain maps of the forests and other public lands you plan to visit, see the map index in the back of this book.

Though we have seldom waxed eloquent about the campgrounds we list in Fishing in Oregon, it is not because they are unattractive. On the contrary, unless otherwise noted, you can generally assume that they are in an attractive natural setting, more often than not dust free, and with stunning views of the surrounding landscape. Most campgrounds in national forest are forested. BLM manages more of Oregon's wide open spaces, so the campgrounds are usually more sparsely shaded, though each BLM campsite usually boasts at least one fine old juniper tree.

Usual facilities in federally managed campgrounds include at least one piece of level ground suitable for a tent (though an awful lot of "campers" are sleeping in their rigs these days), a sturdy rough hewn picnic table with attached benches, a fireplace with grate, reasonably clean outhouses with toilet paper, and garbage bins. State park campgrounds are generally more spiffy, often with flush toilets, some even with showers and electrical hook-ups for RVs. These parks fill fast. A reservation service is available for state parks and for some campgrounds in the Umpqua National Forest.

Firewood is generally available for the gathering in national forest camps (especially in central Oregon, where lodgepole pine stands have just endured a devastating attack by beetles). Firewood is less available (no surprise) out in the sagebrush of eastern Oregon, and campfires are discouraged there throughout much of the year due to fire danger. Bring a Coleman stove. Firewood is sometimes available for a fee at state park camps.

Drinking water is available at most (though not all) fee-pay campgrounds (hand pump or spigot). The overnight fee at national forest campgrounds has increased to $4-6, but there are free campgrounds in all the forests. And it is legal to camp just about anywhere on public land. Just pull off the road. As for water, it is advised not to drink even the clearest water in the most pristine environments due to the sometime presence of the parasite giardia, which can cause gastro-intestinal discomfort. Plan to bring your own, boil stream or lake water for 10 minutes, or use filter systems or purifying tablets.

Most of Oregon's hike-in lakes have what we refer to in Fishing in Oregon as "natural campsites." Sometimes they are nothing more than the only relatively flat piece of ground within view of the water. Often, they are graced with something extra—a configuration of rocks ideal for sitting or turning into a camp shelf or reflecting the campfire's heat, a convenient placement of logs or tree stumps around a stone fire ring, a penninsula point that catches the breeze off the lake and keeps the mosquitoes at bay.

Wilderness campsites have no fire rings, and campers are urged to use no-trace camping methods. Use a backpack stove rather than a fire. To preserve fragile vegetation, camp well back from waters and on the edge of meadows. Degradation in Jefferson Park, Eagle Cap, and Sky Lakes Wilderness bear witness to the fragility of wilderness "view lots."

As for crowds, you can usually find a campsite at your chosen water, even at the most popular fisheries, except on holiday weekends (though you may have to settle for the back lot or uneven ground). Some campgrounds tend to be a little too crowded for our taste. Crane Prairie, for example, has probably exceeded its limit in terms of capacity to absorb car campers and provide a quality camping experience at the height of the summer season (despite the recent construction of a big new campground).

But there are always alternatives in Oregon. Thank goodness. If you need more elbow room, literally on the stream or figuratively, spiritually, for the good of your urban-dazed soul, you can still find it here with just a little thought, a manageable output of energy—and a map, a compass, a decent pair of hiking shoes, or a canoe. And perhaps a glance at Fishing in Oregon.

Good fishing to you.

HOW TO USE THIS BOOK

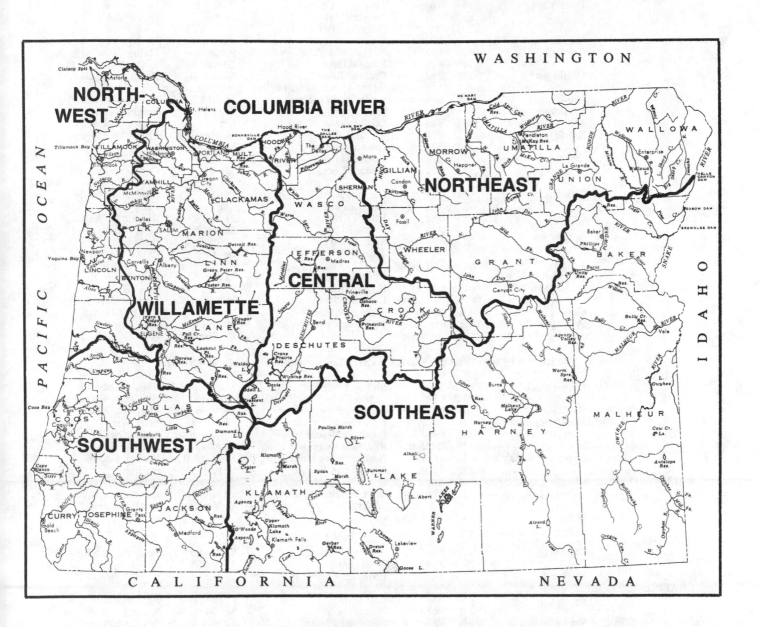

FISHING IN OREGON is presented in seven chapters corresponding to the seven angling zones of the Oregon Sport Fishing Regulations. Use the map above to determine the zone of waters that interest you. Waters within each zone are listed alphabetically. A complete Index at the end of the book provides a state-wide alphabetical listing of waters, with page references. There is also an index to bass and panfish waters, and an index to waters accessible to less-abled anglers.

The introduction to each chapter includes a zone map and a brief description of the zone's outstanding features, climate, road and trail conditions, and general availability of angler services.

Road and trail directions to each water listed in *FISHING IN OREGON* are generally given in the opening paragraphs. Angler services and facilities are listed near the end of each write-up. An Angling Information Sources Directory is provided following the Index.

Unofficial Oregon Cold Water Gamefish Records (April 1988)

TROUT

Brook	9 lb	6 oz	Deschutes River (below Little Lava Lake)	21 Jun 80	Burt Westbrook
	6 lb	12 oz	Hosmer Lake	13 Jul 77	Tad Walker
	5 lb	11 oz	Hosmer Lake	19 Sep 75	Jerry Odsather
Brown	35 lb	8 oz	Paulina Lake	3 Jul 65	Ike & Darrell Fox
	24 lb	14 oz	Wickiup Reservoir	1959	Donald Ivan LaDuke
Bull	20 lb	7 oz	Lake Billy Chinook	19 Mar 88	William E. Reid
Dolly Varden	20 lb	0 oz	Lake Billy Chinook	10 Oct 87	Bob Wehnert
	19 lb	0 oz	Candle Creek (Metolius System)	26 Aug 81	Don Miller
Searun Cutthroat	9 lb	8 oz	N. Fork Malheur River	9 Apr 86	Phillip Grove
	6 lb	4 oz	Siltcoos Lake	20 Aug 84	Kay Schmidt
Cutthroat	4 lb	9 oz	Crooked River (below Prineville Dam)	28 Apr 84	Blenn W. Raschke
Golden	7 lb	10 oz	Eagle Cap Wilderness	16 Jul 87	Douglas W. White
Mackinaw	40 lb	8 oz	Odell Lake	Sep 84	Ken Erickson
	36 lb	8 oz	Odell Lake	Jun 76	H. V. Hannon
Rainbow	28 lb	0 oz	Rogue River	19 May 82	Mike McGonagle
	24 lb	2 1/4oz	Lake Simtustus	Jun 74	Jerry Fifield
Steelhead	35 lb	8 oz	Columbia River	19 Sep 70	Berdell Todd
	31 lb	4 oz	Cascade Locks	Sep 63	Gus Hesgard

SALMON

Chinook	83 lb		Umpqua River	1910	Ernie St. Claire
	62lb (dressed)		Nestucca River	Oct 70	Craig Hansen
Chum	19 lb	0 oz	Kilchis River	11 Nov 83	Richard A. Weber
	15 lb	0 oz	Miami River	28 Nov 83	Steve Weeks
Coho	25 lb	5 1/4oz	Siltcoos Lake	5 Nov 66	Ed Martin
	23 lb		Tillamook Bay	Oct 63	Chuck Walters
Atlantic	no data on record				
Kokanee	3 lb	6 oz	Paulina Lake	22 Jun 79	Roy Mason
Stripe Bass	64 lb 8 oz **		Umpqua River	13 Jul 73	Beryl Bliss
	61 lb		Umpqua River	May 70	Don Carnfarth
Shad	4 lb	12 oz	Willamette River	5 Jul 77	Roy E. Kindrick
Whitefish	4 lb 0 oz		Mckenzie River	20 May 74	Todd Fisher

** World Record for Fly Rod

Unofficial Oregon Warm Water Gamefish Records (April 1988)

BASS

Largemouth	11 lb	5 oz*	McKay Reservoir	7 Sep 85	Ronald Campbell
	10 lb	15 oz	Selmac Lake	13 Apr 83	Butch Stauffacher
	10 lb	13 oz	Selmac Lake	25 Apr 81	Martin R. Bailey
Smallmouth	6 lb	13 oz	Brownlee Reservoir	17 Jun 78	Mark Weir
	6 lb	6 oz	Prineville Reservoir	Jun 77	Todd Close
	6 lb	2 1/2 oz	Brownlee Reservoir	17 Apr 77	Doug Hicks
Hybrid Striped	7 lb	11 oz	North Tenmile Lake	13 Aug 86	Paul M. George
	3 lb	12 oz	North Tenmile Lake	14 Jun 85	Michael J. Massingill

BULLHEAD

Yellow	3 lb	6 oz	Brownlee Reservoir	10 Jun 86	Loretta Fitzgerald
	3 lb	2 oz	Willamette River	15 Mar 61	Ted F. Schneider
Black	no data on record				
Brown	2 lb	4 oz	Eckman Lake	10 Jun 82	Joshua Spulnik

CATFISH

Channel	36 lb	8 oz	McKay Reservoir	17 Sep 80	Boone Haddock
	29 lb	4 oz	Devils Lake	20 Aug 71	Jim Overguard
Flathead	33 lb	8 oz	Brownlee Reservoir	28 Sep 73	Ray C. Gardner

CRAPPIE

Black	4 lb	0 oz	Lost River	1 May 78	Billy R. Biggs
	2 lb	12 oz	Pirate Pond	Sep 74	Victor Luey
White	4 lb	12 oz	Gerber Reservoir	22 May 67	Jim Duckett

YELLOW PERCH	2 lb	2 oz	Brownsmead Slough	5 Jun 71	Ernie Affolter III
STURGEON	(None - regulations limit catch size)				

SUNFISH

Bluegill	2 lb	5.5 oz	Farm Pond, Prineville	12 May 81	Wayne Elmore
	2 lb	2 oz	Farm Pond, Prineville	1 Jul 76	Dudley Nelson
Green	0 lb	9 oz	Holiday Motel Farm Pond	12 Jun 77	James L. Frick
Red-ear	0 lb	8 oz	Reynolds Pond	12 Jul 85	Charles Farley
Warmouth	1 lb	14.5 oz	Columbia River	27 Dec 75	Jess Nowell
	1 lb	13 oz	Columbia River	17 Sep 64	Roy Sams
WALLEYE	17 lb	9.4 oz	Columbia River	8 Sep 84	Peter P. Klick
	14 lb	14 oz	Columbia River	10 Apr 84	Ron Hillar

* A 12 lb largemouth bass was caught and released in Selmac Lake on 19 May 74 by Dave Kagley

NORTHWEST ZONE

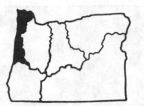

The Northwest Zone is all waters draining directly to the Pacific Ocean north of, but not including, the Umpqua River drainage; and those portions of Columbia River tributaries upstream from the railroad bridges near their mouths, northwest from the city of St. Helens.

Thanksgiving at Rockaway. It's easy to find a rental cottage at the coast in November, and the price is right. The little house fills with the aromas of the season, roasting turkey and potatoes, and with the din of children, dogs, and the family parrot in the overlapping space of the cabin.

The best thing about Thanksgiving at the beach is having a place to go after dinner. I am the main chef, so by family decree I do not have to clear and wash. As the children and men clatter in the kitchen, I pull on rubber boots, watch cap, and fingerless wool gloves. I take the big steelhead rod with level wind reel, a carton of sandshrimp from the fridge, and a pocket full of plastic worms as back up, some hooks and weights, a sampler of line, and head for the ocean.

I walk north toward the jetty where the Nehalem meets the Pacific. It's a good walk on a broad beach. Tide's about to turn, according to the tide card I picked up at the local Stop and Shop. That's the best time to fish for rockfish and perch. I scramble up the jetty rocks and walk the ridge to a just right spot. I bait up and cast, enjoying the sensation of the weight hurtling out over the foam, the drop, the slow reel in. Keep it away from the rocks. Is that a bite?

There are other walkers on the beach now, ambling toward the jetty. They stop to watch as I release a little bug-eyed rockfish. I am part of the scenery on the Northwest coast.

A dozen great rivers pour out of the Coast Range and into the Pacific off the Oregon coast. Many have sheltered bays with tidal flats rich with clams, and offer fishing the year around from boat, bank, dock, and jetty for varieties of perch, rock fish, cod, and crab. Surfperch, free biting and good eating, can be taken from any beach within a few miles of freshwater inlets—that's most of them. And then there are the salmon, also taken in the bay and just beyond the bars, and steelhead and sea-run cutthroat trout which move quickly through the bays to their home rivers.

Steelhead, salmon, sea-run. These are the great fisheries of the region. How long have these natural marvels repeated their fall migration to the cloud shrouded valleys of the northwest coast? The coastal Indians staked their lives on the rhythm of the great fish. Always they returned, fighting upstream against the rising waters to the very tributary of their birth to spawn and, for salmon to die. To repeat the grand cycle.

The northwest zone boasts many of the premier salmon and steelhead rivers of the state. They bear the names of the Native Americans who lived off their bounty. Nestucca. Alsea. Siuslaw. Siletz. Nehalem. Others carry the names of the first white settlers. Wilson, named for a founder of the dairy industry that still dominates the tidewater valleys. Trask, for a pioneer trapper and logger.

The Coast Range, a series of low mountains running north to south, separates this region from the Willamette Valley. Its slopes are thick with fir, cedar, and hemlock. Elk, deer, and bear still roam the hillsides, and beaver frequently dam the headwater creeks. Curiously, there are few lakes.

Highway travel across the range is limited. Primary routes from Portland are highways 26 (to Seaside), 6 (to Tillamook) and 18 (to Lincoln City). From Corvallis, Hwy. 20 leads to Newport. From Eugene, Hwy. 126 follows the Siuslaw to Florence. Over 150 miles of Oregon's rugged coastline are followed by scenic Hwy. 101.

Below Florence, huge sand dunes separate two exceptional coastal lakes, Siltcoos and Tahkenitch, from the Pacific. These lakes are among the best largemouth lakes in the state.

Unlike the rest of Oregon, most timberlands in the Northwest Region are in state or private ownership. An exception is the Siuslaw National Forest, which has large holdings between the Siuslaw and Yaquina Rivers (Florence to Newport). Private forest lands, criss-crossed by primitive logging roads, have traditionally been open to public access, though some of that may be changing as ownership moves out of local hands.

Water permeates the region. Armies of clouds sweep across the coast and release their moisture as the air is forced up the slopes of the Coast Range. A typical coastal town will receive 60 inches of rain a year; inland 5 miles you'll find *twice* the rainfall. The northwest region averages over 180 days with measurable rainfall each year.

A pleasant side effect of this deluge is moderate temperatures. Averages vary from about 40 degrees in winter to 60 degrees in summer, with a variance of 10 degrees or so. Summer warming is delayed at the coast, with seasonal highs occurring in late August.

The northwest region. Gray skies and strong silver fish. Pure Northwest.

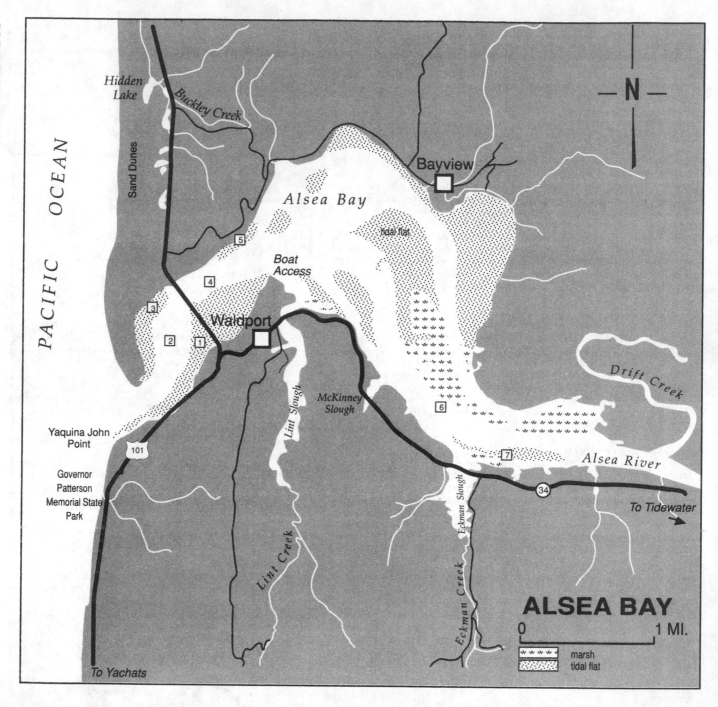

ALSEA BAY

0 | 1 MI.

marsh
tidal flat

1. LOWER BAY FLATS, SO. - Firm sand, not mud. Walk out at low tide and fish for coho and chinook in late Aug., perch all summer. Dig for cockles.

2. LOWER MAIN CHANNEL - Fish for fall salmon, crab.

3. LOWER BAY FLATS, NO. - Dig for clams, cockles, and gapers.

4. MID-CHANNEL - Hwy. 101 bridge to Waldport docks best area for perch; salmon and crab available.

5. OLD BRIDGE FLATS - Park below old bridge and walk out for cockles at low tide, perch at high and low.

6. MOUTH OF THE ALSEA - Troll for salmon July-Sept., jacks Sept.-Oct., Sea-run cutts June-Oct. No perch above Eckman Slough.

7. SOFTSHELL CLAMS. Park off road across Eckman causeway.

ACKERLY LAKE A small lake, about 2 miles north of Florence, one miles east of Hwy. 101. Privately owned at present, it contains cutthroat and largemouth bass.

ALDER LAKE A 3 acre trout lake 7 1/2 miles north of Florence. Alder is located on national forest land just west of Hwy. 101, about 1/2 mile north of Sutton Lake. The lake is stocked with legal rainbow twice yearly. Buck Lake is 1/4 mile north, and Dune Lake is 1/2 mile south, both similar to Alder in size and fishing. There is a campground at the north end of Alder Lake.

ALSEA BAY Lightly fished in early season, offering calm and productive waters close to its boat ramps. Alsea Bay is a good place to introduce family and friends to salmon fishing, especially during fine fall weather when the salmon and lively jacks are plentiful. Six miles long, with tidewater extending about 12 miles upriver, it can be reached in just over an hour from Corvallis by way of Hwy. 34. Hwy. 101 approaches it from north and south.

There are 8 moorages along the bay, from Waldport up to Tidewater, and almost all have launching facilities or rental boats. Most angling takes place right in front of the moorages, convenient to hot coffee.

Fishing for sea-run cutthroat is especially good at the mouth of the Alsea. Anglers are successful as early as June, with good fishing through September and peak catches in August. Most anglers troll with hardware and bait.

Alsea has no spring chinook, except for a few stragglers, but it has good runs of fall chinook, coho, and steelhead. Salmon are caught in the main lower channel and at the mouth of the Alsea. Some bank anglers work the lower bay flats at low tide. Chinook arrive in July and August and are fished until October. Jack salmon and coho are caught in late fall. Trolled herring, feathered spinners, Flatfish, and Hotshot lures will all take adult salmon. Cluster eggs drifted under a bobber attract the jacks

Perch fishing is good in the bay from spring through fall. Perch are caught from the Hwy. 101 Bridge to the public docks at Waldport and from the old bridge flats at high and low tide. There are no perch above Eckman Slough. Shrimp, clam necks, kelp worms, and sand crabs are all available locally for bait.

Crabbing has been very good here since 1984, with Best Catch On The Coast in 1987. The most popular area is the main channel below Lint Slough. Cockles are dug on the Lower Bay Flats (south shore), which are a comfortably firm sand rather than mud, and on the Old Bridge Flats above the 101 Bridge. Both cockles and gapers are dug on the smaller Lower Bay Flats north shore. Softshell clams are available in the flats above Eckman Slough.

Flounder are no longer plentiful in Alsea Bay, or in any other bay on the Oregon coast. Seals and sea lions are customarily blamed for this depletion. However, no scientific studies have identified them as the culprits, and it is noteworthy that encouraging catches of flounder did occur in Alsea Bay in 1988 for the first time in many years, *without* a corresponding drop in the marine mammal population.

Services and supplies are abundant along the bay, with motels and restaurants in Waldport. There is a Forest Service campground at Tillicum Beach, 5 miles south.

ALSEA RIVER A highly regarded steelhead stream, about 55 miles long, heading in the coast range west of Corvallis and entering the Pacific Ocean at Waldport. The main river provides excellent winter steelhead catches, as do its two main tributaries, Five Rivers and Drift Creek. The Alsea is closely followed by Hwy. 34 from its mouth to above the confluence of the North Fork. Good secondary roads follow all the major tributaries. The mouth is reached by Hwy. 101.

This stream has been a prize exhibit of the Dept. of Fish and Wildlife's steelhead program, with an annual catch for bay and river combined as high as 8,777 in 1984-85, dropping off to 4,926 in 1985-86.

Steelhead appear here in late November, and the run peaks in December and January. There's a lot of good water, with a fair share of snags and tackle grabbing boulders. Popular steelhead spots are at the head of tide, the Hatchery Hole, Barclay Drift, The Maples (at Lake Creek), and the Strawberry Patch. There's a lot of good accessible water for bank anglers.

Fall chinook and coho salmon are also available. The chinook run peaks in late September, and the coho in October. Most salmon are taken by trolling in the bay at Waldport and above, but casting will produce fish up to the forks. In 1986-87, a total of 2018 chinook were taken from Alsea Bay and River, and 2211 coho. Cutthroat are available in May and again in fall, when the sea-run return. Flatfish, Daredevils, red feathered hooks and spinners, and similar lures are popularly used.

Fly anglers have good success on the Alsea , especially when the water is low and clear. Sea-run fly anglers use the Borden Special (developed by Bob Borden of Monmouth), Alsea Pink, and Purple Joe. Several effective salmon and steelhead flies have been developed by Michael Gorman of the Scarlet Ibis fly shops, including the Red King, Green King, and Caballero. Hook sizes vary from #2-#6. The Silver Hilton is also popular for salmon and steelhead. Winter fly angling here, as on other Oregon streams, has been considerably enhanced by the development of a hybird line system (running line with shooting head) that helps get the fly down to the bottom.

Flood level on the Alsea is 18 cfs (cubic ft. per second). Best fishing is at 4 cfs, with acceptable levels from 3.6 to 5.4 cfs. Boat angling is allowed up to Mill Creek, just below the town of Alsea. There are a number of boat spots where boats can be launched, some of which have slight user fees. Rental boats, supplies and accommodations are available at Waldport, in the Alsea Bay area, and at several points upriver. There is a Forest Service camp 17 miles upstream from Waldport.

ALSEA RIVER, NORTH FORK A beautiful stream, well suited to fly angling, entering the main Alsea at the town of Alsea. It is easily accessed from county and logging roads running north and west from Hwy. 34.

Cutthroat trout fishing is generally good when the season opens, and holds up for several months. Several hundred winter steelhead are are usually taken each year in the lower water, as well as a small number of spring and fall chinook and coho. There is a trout and steelhead hatchery about one mile above Hwy. 34, and special regulations apply to salmon and steelhead angling above the Hwy. 34 Bridge. Angling from a floating device is prohibited throughout the North Fork.

ALSEA RIVER, SOUTH FORK An excellent cutthroat trout stream. This fair size fork of the Alsea, average width 40 feet, flows into the main river from the SW at the town of Alsea. County roads access it and many of its tributaries.

The South Fork offers good cover for trout, but limited food sources. If the water is clear, light leaders with single eggs, caddis worms, or small bits of crawfish tail will do the trick. Steelhead and salmon catches here are generally small. In 1986-87, anglers reported catching 83 fall chinook, 65 coho, and 23 winter steelhead. The nearest campground is 7 miles SE of Alsea.

ARCH CAPE CREEK A fair stream for sea-run cutthroat in spring and late fall. Only 4 miles long, it flows 6 miles south of Cannon Beach, which is on Hwy. 101. Arch Cape has some good pools and brush, but it's surrounded by mostly posted land, so be sure to ask permission. There's camping at Oswald West State Park.

BARK SHANTY CREEK A small stream that provides fair early cutthroat fishing. The creek enters the North Fork of the Trask River about 5 miles above its mouth. A logging road circles the headwater area. The lower end can be reached from the North Fork of the Trask Rd.

BEAVER CREEK (Columbia Co.) A good bass stream at its lower end, where it is known as Beaver Slough. Best fishing is in late summer. The stream flows about 25 miles west from near Ranier to the town of Clatskanie, and it is crossed many times by Hwy. 30.

A small stream fished mostly by local anglers, its upper waters offer poor early fishing for native cutthroat. It is not stocked. Hwy. 30 crosses it a number of times, and it is approached by many secondary roads. The creek is open to salmon and steelhead up to 200 ft downstream of the lower falls, but only a few are taken here each year.

BEAVER CREEK (Lincoln Co.) A short coastal stream, good for sea-run cutthroat, located about 6 miles south of Newport. Beaver Creek is followed by a county road which joins Hwy. 101 near its crossing of the creek. It is open to salmon and steelhead angling up to the bridge, about 3 miles upstream of 101.

Sea-run cutthroat are present in late summer and fall. Coho salmon enter in October and November, along with a few steelhead, but the catch is quite small. There is a boat ramp just off Hwy. 101. A state park at the mouth provides picnic facilities.

BEAVER CREEK (Tillamook Co.) A good sea-run cutthroat stream with lots of cover. This stream enters the main Nestucca River at the town of Beaver, about 15 miles south of Tillamook on Hwy. 101. It has an East fork and a West fork, for a total of about 15 miles of stream. A fair road follows each fork. The creek has many deep pools where spinner and bait work well. Crayfish tails are especially tempting here. A few salmon and steelhead are taken up to the West Beaver Creek deadline.

BEAVER SLOUGH COMPLEX (Columbia Co.) An extensive slough area in the lower Columbia River offering good fishing for bass and panfish. NE of the town of Clatskanie, boat access is available from the Columbia by Wallace Slough or from the Clatskanie River, with some bank access at road crossings. The entire slough offers good fishing for about 15 species, with crappie and perch most abundant. April and May are the best months for these fish, which can run to 5 pounds. Very small wobblers or weighted streamers can be used to catch them, and an abundance of rough fish here can be used for crappie bait.

BENEKE CREEK A good early season trout stream with some sea-runs showing in early fall if the water rises. This creek enters the Nehalem River at Jewell and is about 14 miles long if you include its tributary, Walker Creek. A good road parallels the stream. It is closed to salmon and steelhead angling.

BIG CREEK (Clatsop Co.) A good winter steelhead stream, with good fishing for native cutthroat above the hatchery in early season. About 15 miles long, Big Creek enters the lower Columbia sloughs near the town of Knappa. Followed by Hwy. 30 south from Knappa Junction, it is easily reached from the road for most of its length. The stream is stocked with sea-run

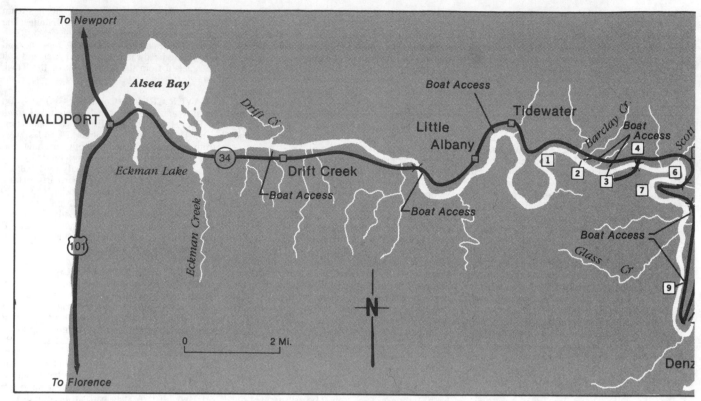

cutthroat below the hatchery.

A good number of steelhead and coho salmon ascend this stream. The peak months for steelhead are December and January, with fish caught in good numbers through March. The catch averages about 2000 fish per year. Coho show in October, but the catch has fallen off to about 600 fish per year. Fall chinook are present from August through November, but there is an angling closure in September, so check the current regulations. In 1986-87, anglers reported a catch of 318 chinook, 1,379 coho, and 53 summer steelhead, with 1055 winter steelhead reported in 1985-86.

Special regulations are associated with the hatchery on this stream, so check the regulations carefully, and stay 200 feet away from the hatchery fishways.

There is 1/2 mile of public access on the east bank, between the old highway bridge and the new one, but just about half the property along the stream is in private hands. Be sure to get permission.

BIG CREEK RESERVOIRS Two 20 acre reservoirs on the north edge of Newport, owned by the city and open for angling. Located just north of Yaquina Bay, they are accessible from Hwy. 101. by way of Big Creek Rd. just north of Hotel Newport and south of Agate Beach. Motors are prohibited, and only rafts and cartop boats can be launched from shore. Most anglers fish from the bank. The reservoirs are stocked heavily with rainbow in spring, and contain largemouth bass and brown bullhead. Bait or spinner/bait combinations seem to work best here.

BIG ELK CREEK A major tributary of the Yaquina river, with an on again/off again winter steelhead run that can be very good. Big Elk enters the Yaquina at Elk City and is reached from the coast by driving east on Hwy. 20 from Newport to Toledo, then crossing the main river and following it upstream on County Rd. 533

to Elk City. A county road at Eddyville follows Bear Creek down to its confluence with Big Elk, then follows Big Elk to Elk City.

This stream produces more steelhead than any in the Yaquina system, and in a good year the catch here exceeds 1000. It fluctuates considerably from the year to year, however. In 1986-87, only 206 steelhead were caught, though in 1984-85, the catch was 1256. Newport steelheaders like to bank fish here, with the best results in the lower few miles of the creek.

BLIND SLOUGH Offers opportunities to catch bass to 5 pounds, and large yellow perch on their spawning migration in March and April. Crappie and catfish are also available, with some fall fishing for chinook and coho. Covering 194 acres, it is reached by county roads heading north from Knappa Junction or Brownsmead Junction on Hwy. 30.

The slough can be fished from the north bank, which has a road paralleling it. In late fall, coho and chinook move through the slough, and a few are taken by trolling. Chinook show in September, and coho and jacks in October and November. There's a lot of private property here, so ask permission before you cross questionable land. Blind Slough connects to many other smaller sloughs, most of which are productive for bass and panfish.

BLUE LAKE (Tillamook Co.) Once a 3 acre cutthroat lake on the south side of the divide, Blue lost its fishery when the dam blew out. It's hardly even a pond now, with roads very deteriorated.

BRADBURY SLOUGH All the Columbia river bass and panfish species can be found in this good size slough, just west of Quincy, about 3 miles NE of Clatskanie on the lower Columbia highway. Two other sloughs, Johns and Deadend, are connected to it. Small boats can be launched, and there is some access from

bridges and the county road. It is only lightly fished.

BROWNSMEAD SLOUGH Offers good bass and panfish, just east of the community of Brownsmead. The Brownsmead junction on Hwy. 30 is 20 miles east of Astoria, and the town is located 5 miles north. The slough is over 10 miles long and holds good water levels with tide gates. Banks are steep, and bank access is limited except from county roads and bridges. One unimproved boat ramp near the middle of the slough is suitable for car-tops.

White and black crappie are abundant, and there are lots of yellow perch, and yellow, black, and brown bullhead. Bluegill and bass are occasionally taken. Bottom worm fishing is best for cats and perch. Bobber fishing with white meat or a spinner/bait combination works best for crappie and bass.

BURKES LAKE Just off Ridge Rd., one mile west of Warrenton, a 6.3 acre pond containing largemouth bass.

BUSTER CREEK A small early season cutthroat stream flowing west into the Nehalem River near Tidesport, about halfway between Elsie and Jewell. The middle stream can be reached by the Green Mt. Rd., which crosses both forks of the creek about 3 miles SE of Jewell. In early season this is a good cutthroat stream, but it is hard to fish because of the brush. A single egg or a small Indiana spinner with worm might work. Another trick that has produced here is to dribble a dark fly pattern off the brush.

CAPE MEARES LAKE An unusual lake, containing trout and bass, created several years ago by diking on the Cape Meares side of Tillamook Bay. It is about 10 miles from Tillamook off the Bay Ocean Rd. It covers about 65 acres with maximum depth of 6 ft. Aquatic vegetation is quite thick.

ALSEA RIVER

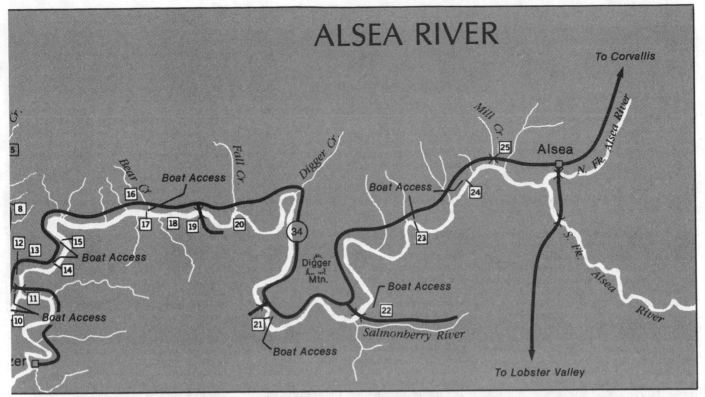

To Corvallis

To Lobster Valley

Salmonberry River

Digger Mtn.

Bear Cr.

Fall Cr.

Digger Cr.

Mill Cr.

Alsea

N. Fk. Alsea River

S. Fk. Alsea River

Boat Access

Previously stocked with a cutthroat and rainbow mix, the lake is now stocked fairly heavily several times each spring with legal rainbow. Largemouth bass are now an established population here. Nearby bay and beach offer alternative saltwater fishing opportunities. There is a campground 10 miles south at Cape Lookout State Park.

CARCUS CREEK A cutthroat stream tributary to the Clatskanie River, flowing from the south and meeting the Clatskanie about 8 miles SE of the town of Clatskanie near the Firwood School. It's lightly fished, but the beaver ponds have been known to make the trip worthwhile.

CARNAHAN LAKE A private 9 acre lake just west of Hwy. 101 about 5 miles north of Gearhart, and just north of Cullaby Lake. Maximum depth is 15 ft., and the lake is very weedy. It is closed to public access at this time.

CARTER LAKE A typical dune lake with fair trout fishing, one mile long and 200 feet wide. It is reached by Hwy. 101 about 9 miles south of Florence and about 12 miles north of Reedsport. The lake is on the west side of the highway.

A very brushy shoreline makes it difficult to fish from shore. Most anglers fish from boats. Carter is stocked with legal rainbow and occasional brood fish to 5 pounds. Catches are good for the first few months of the season.

There is a public campground at the lake, with concrete boat ramp, parking, and picnic facilities.

CEMETARY LAKE A 10.3 acre fishery for black crappie, warmouth, bluegill, largemouth bass, and yellow perch, connected by pipe to Smith Lake. Access is through the Astoria cemetery.

CHAMBERLAIN LAKE This 11 acre lake is located at the Scout camp just south of Cape Lookout State Park. It is not open to public angling.

CLATSKANIE RIVER Flows through the town of Clatskanie and enters the Columbia River about mid-way between St. Helens and Astoria. Do not confuse this with the Klaskanine River, which is

---

1. **SAND HOLE** - Head of tidewater; private property; boat fishing only.
2. **BARCLAY HOLE** - Good hole for plunking; good drifting when not crowded.
3. **BARCLAY HOLE PUT-IN** - Fish the channel.
4. **SCOTT CREEK HOLE** - Ledges & channels; fish just below the creek; bring lots of tackle.
5. **HELLION RAPIDS** - Deep hole just below rapids.
6. **HOOTENANY TRAIL** - Forest Service access trail up to Rock Crusher Hole; trail runs under edge of highway.
7. **ROCK CRUSHER HOLE** - Rocks, ledge, channels.
8. **MIKE BAUER WAYSIDE** - Popular for plunking; boat launch.
9. **BLACKBERRY CAMPGROUND** - Public boat ramp; deep holes; overnight camping with trailer spaces, nice forest trail.
10. **MAPLES HOLE** - Deep plunking water; boat ramp, parking, picnic area.
11. **FIVE RIVERS BRIDGE** - Productive fishing from bridge to Maples Hole; channels, ledges, rocks, holes.
12. **FIVE RIVERS BOAT RAMP**
13. **OLD PUT-IN HOLE** - Plunking hole just above Five Rivers put-in at bend of road.
14. **LOW WATER BRIDGE PUT-IN** - Good bank angling.
15. **TRANSFORMER PUT-IN HOLE**
16. **FOREST SERVICE CAMPGROUND**
17. **SWINGER BRIDGE PUT-IN** - Just below bridge.
18. **BEAR CREEK LODGE** - Bank fishing just above lodge.
19. **DIGGER MT. MILL BRIDGE** - Good fishing above & below, across stream from highway. *Private property; ask permission to fish.*
20. **PRIVATE PARK** - Access fee.
21. **MISSOURI BEND PARK** - Log skid, picnic facilities, lots of parking.
22. **SALMONBERRY BRIDGE** - Boat launch; good drifting and plunking.
23. **CAMPBELL PARK PUT-IN** - Fish just below.
24. **MILL CREEK BOAT RAMPS** - Upper limit for boats; fish the stretch from boat ramps up to Mill Cr. Accessible, good drifts all along here.
25. **ALSEA RANGER STATION**

---

near Astoria. About 26 miles long, it features cutthroat trout as well as a good steelhead run and a few coho salmon.

Roads parallel and cross the river in many spots and it has several good tributaries. The headwaters can be reached from the St. Helens-Vernonia Rd. by taking the gravel road north to Apiary. The lower stream is best reached from Clatskanie. Gravel and boulders make it an ideal fly stream.

In April and May, cutthroat are released into the stream, offering good early season fishing. They gradually move down into the Columbia and out to sea, to return in September as big sea-run cutts. There is a nice winter steelhead run here. The 1984-85 catch was 724, while 1986-87 was down to 187.

There's lots of private land along the lower river, but landowners continue to be generous about sharing access. Supplies are available in Clatskanie.

CLATSKANIE SLOUGH Very good bass and panfish water connected to the lower Clatskanie River, accessed by county roads just north of Clatskanie on Hwy. 30. The slough is controlled by tide gates. There are no boat ramps, and access is limited to a few auto and foot bridges. Good size yellow and black crappie and brown bullhead are plentiful. Perch, bluegill, and bass are present but not numerous. It is pretty much a still-fishing setup.

CLEAR LAKE (Clatsop Co.) An 8 acre largemouth bass fishery one mile north of Warrenton.

CLEAR LAKE (Lane Co.) About 160 acres, offering largemouth bass, yellow perch, and trout. Located about 3 miles north of Florence on Hwy. 101, just north of Munsel Lake, Clear Lake is quite prominent on maps. There is no public road to the lake, but there is some public access on the west shore, about a mile hike in.

CLEAR LAKE (Tillamook Co.) Not to be confused with Spring Lake, about a mile down the road. A small, poor cutthroat lake, about 3 acres and very shallow, it is located just south of Rockaway on the east side of Hwy. 101. It contains cutthroat trout, but isn't very productive. It is now surrounded by private land, and public access is doubtful.

CLEAWOX LAKE Popular because of its location within Honeyman State Park a few miles south of Florence. Stocked with rainbow trout and an occasional brood trout, the lake has also been a sleeper for largemouth bass and crappie, with yellow perch, brown bullhead, and bluegill available. It's a good bet in early season before the campers get too numerous. The lake covers about 82 acres, and boats with motors are allowed.

COFFENBURY LAKE A fair 50 acre rainbow trout lake within Fort Stevens State Park, about 2 miles west of Warrenton. The lake is long and narrow, in a deep depression between sand dunes. Maximum depth is 9 feet near the north end. The north end of the lake is easily reached by a good road.

Stocked annually with legal rainbow, it also contains yellow perch and brown bullhead. A poor producer, it provides fair fishing early in the season.

Ft. Stevens is one of Oregon's most extensive state parks, including a full service campground, bike and hiking trails through coastal forest, as well as access to some of the state's finest razor clam digging and surf fishing.

COLLARD LAKE A private 32 acre lake located about 3 miles north of Florence and one mile east of Hwy. 101. The lake contains yellow perch, bluegill, brown bullhead, and largemouth bass, but at present has no public access.

COOK CREEK A fair cutthroat and steelhead stream flowing SE into the lower Nehalem, about 7 miles from the town of Nehalem. The creek is about 18 miles long, including tributaries, and enters the Nehalem at a point shown as *Batterson* on most maps. A gravel road parallels the creek.

A good fly stream, with lots of boulders and gravel and not too brushy, it has quite a few cutthroat in early season. Open for winter steelhead up to the south fork, there are about 5 miles of good angling. Though only 69 steelhead were taken in 1986-87, the 1984-85 season produced 682. There are also small catches of fall chinook and occasional coho. The closest supply point is Wheeler.

CRABAPPLE LAKE A 22 acre lake in Ft. Stevens State Park. Fish it early in the season for largemouth bass and yellow perch before the weeds choke out access.

CREEP AND CRAWL LAKE A 5 acre pond in Ft. Stevens State Park, offering bluegill fishing in early season. By mid-summer the lake is usually weed-bound.

CRESCENT LAKE (Tillamook Co.) An 11 acre lake 5 miles north of Tillamook Bay on Hwy. 101 near Manhattan Beach. Just north of Lytle Lake (and connected to it), Crescent covers 11 acres, but has grown increasingly shallow due to siltation. Largemouth bass are available, and trout fishing holds up as long as the stocked rainbow and cutthroat last.

CRIMM'S ISLAND SLOUGH A Columbia River slough 6 miles NE of Clatskanie, with known populations of white and black crappie.

CRONIN CREEK A cutthroat stream that enters the Nehalem from the east, about 10 miles south of Elsie, on the lower Nehalem Rd. The cutts usually leave right after the first of the season, but show again in late fall. The stream can also be reached by coming up the Nehalem from Mohler. The lower mile provides most of the fishing.

CULLABY LAKE A good panfish lake and family fishing spot. It is just east of Hwy. 101 about 4 miles north of Gearhart and about 12 miles south of Astoria. Cullaby is a long and narrow 220 acres, about 1 1/2 miles from north to south and usually less than 1/4 mile wide. Its depth ranges 6-12 feet.

Cullaby usually provides excellent angling from spring through late fall for crappie, bluegill, perch, brown bullheads and largemouth bass. Bullhead fishing is excellent at the south end of the lake, especially in March. For nice bass, try working the snags on the east bank of the lake where the weeds aren't so thick. Better suited to bass and panfish, Cullaby is no longer stocked with trout.

A boat is essential to reach the fish later in summer when the lake chokes up with aquatic weeds. A county park extends half-way around the west side of the lake, with boat ramp and picnic areas.

DEADWOOD CREEK A trout stream, with a few steelhead and chinook, tributary to Lake Creek in the Siuslaw system. It joins Lake Creek from the north about 30 miles upstream from Florence, accessed from Hwy. 36 (Florence to Junction City) by a paved road that parallels its length.

There's good fishing for cutthroat in the early season. It's easy to fish, and bait is probably the best bet. A dozen or so fall chinook, coho, and winter steelhead are landed here every year. A few boats drift the lower 5 miles, which are primarily bedrock and boulder. The Closest campground is at Knowles, 4 miles east of Mapleton on Hwy. 126.

DEER ISLAND SLOUGH A large bass and panfish slough on the lower Columbia about 35 miles west of Portland. Access is from the town of Deer Island on Hwy. 30. Goat Island Slough connects to it. Boat access is only from the county road. About 15 species of fish are present, with crappie, perch, and brown bullhead most numerous. Some good size bass are taken on plugs and spinners. It is bordered by a lot of private property, but access permission is usually granted. The slough can also be reached from Shell Beach.

DEPOE BAY An excellent portal to the open sea. This is a very unusual salt water bay, located south of Siletz Bay and crossed by Hwy.101 about 10 miles south of Taft. It is about 100 miles from Portland by way of hwys. 18 and 101. The bay itself is very small, fed by two small streams, but it's a popular spot to take off for outside salmon and bottom angling. The entry into the ocean is through a narrow channel, and boats coming in and out usually have quite an audience on the highway bridge and at the State Park rest area on the bluff.

A fleet of commercial fishing boats make daily trips outside from June through October. There's no angling to speak of in the small bay, except for occasional catches of bottom fish and a few coho picked up late in the fall. For a quick way to get offshore, the bay is perfect. A large public boat ramp and parking area is located on the south side of the bay.

Although its access to the open sea is considered one of the least hazardous on the coast, normal safe boating procedures should be followed. If in doubt, check with the Coast Guard crew based in the bay. In any event, make sure

SURFCASTING THE PACIFIC BEACH
Gerry Lewin, Photographer

your boat is safety equipped, with a spare motor available, as on any ocean trip.

The salmon start showing well outside the bay in late June, with both coho and chinook taken on trolled wobblers or spinners, or on herring. At times the fish are right on top, but anglers often have to go deep for them. Most fishing takes place within a few miles of the buoys marking the channel entrance. There are about 40-50,000 angler trips out of Depoe Bay each year, and the average catch per trip is usually the highest on the coast. In 1986, 29,300 salmon were landed out of Depoe, topped only by the Columbia's offshore fishery that year. Following commercial trollers is an acceptable technique for locating the fish.

Charter boats make trips of two hours, four hours, and all-day. They can't guarantee your limit, but they have the equipment and know-how to locate fish, and you'll be in safe hands. Charter boats supply tackle and bait. Bring warm clothes and rain gear.

If the salmon aren't biting, you can still get a good haul of bottom fish using herring or jigs of several kinds. Coastal tackle shop provide gear and information. Rock fish, snapper, perch, lingcod, a rare flounder, or an occasional large halibut can all be taken in this area. One of the best bottom fishing spots out of Depoe Bay is Government Reef to the north.

DEVILS LAKE (Lincoln Co.) A large coastal lake with bass, panfish, and a fair trout fishery. Covering almost 700 acres, it is located on coast Hwy. 101 a few miles south of Lincoln City. Hwy. 18 through McMinnville offers the best route from the valley. The lake has a serious aquatic weed problem. In fact, grass carp have been introduced by the community as an experiment in weed control. It is illegal to fish for the carp.

Legal rainbow are stocked from spring into early summer, providing the bulk of the trout fishing here, with the average fish 11 inches. Carry-over rainbow reach 18-20 inches.

The lake's brown bullhead population is the best on the coast, and some channel cats have been planted. Black crappie to 13 inches and are present in good numbers. Yellow perch to 14 inches and largemouth bass to 5 pounds are also present.

In October, coho move through the lake and into the Rock Creek system to spawn. Trolling in the Rock Creek area and in the southern part of the lake can be productive for both coho and cutthroat.

Devils Lake State Park at the SE corner of the lake has a campground, boat ramp, and picnic area.

DIBBLEES SLOUGH A Columbia River slough west of Rainier. It is SW of the popular salmon beach known as Dibblees Beach, accessed by county roads and by boat from the Columbia at Rainier. It can aso be reached by the river road under the Longview Bridge. Crappie and brown bullhead are the main catch here, with bottom bait or bobber the best technique. The slough is used for log storage, and fishing under the log rafts often produce crappie.

DRIFT CREEK (Alsea area) A good size stream with native runs of salmon, steelhead, and cutthroat trout, opening into Alsea Bay about 3 miles east of Waldport. About 30 miles long and 30-60 ft. wide, it carves a nar-

DEPOE BAY
Steve Terrill, Photographer

row canyon through thick woods, including stands of old growth timber. Its lower waters can be approached from the north side of Alsea Bay by a road running east, and by boat from the bay itself. Logging roads bisect the upper stream, and several marked trails make the steep descent into the canyon. It's a 1200 ft. drop over 2 miles on the Horse Creek Trail, 1000 feet on the newer Harris Ranch Trail. This is a roadless area of old growth timber.

There are nice size cutthroat in the upper river, and several hundred salmon and steelhead are caught in the lower end, mostly by trolling. Chinook are available in October and November, coho in November and December, steelhead in December and January.

Boat moorages and ramps are available on nearby Alsea Bay. The lower end of Drift Creek is heavily posted against bank fishing.

DRIFT CREEK (Siletz area) A very good coastal cutthroat stream with a good winter steelhead run. Drift Creek enters Siletz Bay at Cutler City, right at Hwy. 101 one mile north of the Siletz River Rd. 229. It flows about 18 miles and averages 35 feet wide. About one mile north of Kernville a road heads west from 101 and follows Drift Creek more than 10 miles. Access within the first 8 miles requires a hike south to the stream. The upper water is reached by the Drift Creek Trail and by logging roads.

Native cutthroat trout are available here in the early season, and several hundred winter steelhead are taken each year. Summer steelhead, coho, and fall chinook are also landed in respectable numbers for such a small stream.

There are Forest Service campgrounds at stream mile 12 on Drift Creek, and about 5 miles up on Schooner Creek. Devils Lake State Park, north of Taft on Hwy. 101, also provides camping facilities. Supplies and accommodations are available in the Siletz Bay area.

ECKMAN LAKE A 45 acre lake adjacent to the lower Alsea River. It is beside Hwy. 34, about 2 miles east of Waldport.

There's fair fishing here early in the season for rainbow and cutthroat. A few largemouth bass are lurking in these waters, remnants of a less than successful stocking program. Brown bullhead are also present. There is a boat ramp but no camping.

ELK CREEK (Clatsop Co.,a.k.a. Ecola Cr.) A good sea-run and resident cutthroat stream, just 10 miles long including both forks, flowing directly into the ocean at Cannon Beach. Spinner and bait are popular in the lower half mile, though flies are effective when the sea-run are in. Try the tidewater areas. Elk Creek also has a small coho and steelhead run, best in November and December.

ERHART LAKE A small, very scenic rainbow lake on the west side of Hwy. 101, about 8 miles south of Florence near Siltcoos Lake. This is a beautiful little lake, reminiscent of those in the high Cascades. Stocked quite heavily with rainbow, it holds up well into summer. Fly anglers will lose less gear than hardware fishermen.

Erhart is heavily fished the first two or three weeks of the season, mostly from shore. A trail leads down to the lake from the highway. There is a little gravel road that goes around to the far shore where you can bank fish or launch a car-top boat. There are good camping areas nearby.

EUCHRE CREEK (Siletz area) A fair cutthroat stream entering the Siletz River about 24 river miles above the bay, 4 miles downstream from the town of Siletz. Hwy. 229 crosses it just above its mouth.

Not heavily fished, it affords good cover for trout, rich food sources, and fair cutthroat fishing in early season. It's easy on tackle, too.

Only about 10 miles long and about 25 feet wide, it has a good population of native cutthroat trout.

FIVE RIVERS A major tributary of the Alsea River, about 18 miles long with average width 75 ft. Five Rivers enters the Alsea from the south about 20 miles upstream from Waldport, 23 miles west of the town of Alsea off Hwy. 34. A good road follows the stream to its headwaters.

The stream has many nice pools and bedrock ledges, and offers good cutthroat angling well into the season. Crayfish tails, wet flies, or sandshrimp drifted under the ledges can produce nice size trout.

Coho are best in late October and November, and most winter steelhead are taken in January. The lower 13 miles, up to the confluence of Green River, are open to salmon and steelhead angling during the winter season.

The old Maples Forest Service Campground, about 4 miles by road upstream from the mouth, is no longer maintained, but there are still some sites among the blackberries. There is a developed campground on the Alsea toward Waldport.

FLOETERS POND A hike-in cutthroat lake, one of a group of small lakes originally built by Crown Zellerbach in their tree farm areas, now owned by Cavenham Forest Industries (CFI). Covering only about 3 acres and difficult to reach, it provides native cutthroat angling in spring and early summer. The lake is dominated by snags and fallen logs, and at times beavers have dammed the outlet.

The pond is about 5 miles SE of Vernonia and 3 miles north of the Columbia County line. To get there, take the trail south from the Vernonia-Scappoose Hwy., starting 1.5 miles east of the BLM picnic area on the East Fork Nehalem. It's a 1 1/2 mile hike south to the lake.

FOGARTY CREEK A small stream flowing into the ocean through Fogarty State Park, about 4 miles south of Siletz Bay on Hwy. 101. A few cutthroat are taken in the upper section, but its too small for much angling. Some perch and kelpfish are taken off the rocks at the outlet. There is a nice picnic area on the creek, but overnight camping is prohibited.

GOAT ISLAND SLOUGH A 55 acre slough on the Columbia River NE of Columbia City at Reichold Chemical Plant. Look for white crappie, brown bullhead, largemouth bass, bluegill, and yellow perch. There is public access at the south end only.

GNAT CREEK A fair cutthroat and sea-run stream, with good runs of steelhead and fall chinook for a stream of its size. It enters the lower Columbia by way of Blind Slough and crosses Hwy. 30 a few miles east of Knappa. About 9 miles long, it heads near Nicolai Mt. and has a lot of beaver ponds in its headwaters.

The Dept. of Fish and Wildlife hatchery stocks the stream with steelhead smolts, and there is some natural reproduction as well. It offers good fishing for steelhead from November or December on up to March. Try for chinook in late August or September. A small run of coho will also be in then. Check the regulations for deadline information.

GUNNERS LAKES A series of 3 small cutthroat lakes on tree farm land belonging to CFI. The lakes range from 1/2 to 3 acres in size. To get to them, turn south off the county road at

DRIFTING THE NECANICUM
Bill Wagner, Photographer

Chapman, then take the first left off Columbia Rd. About 3 miles west, you will cross the lower and largest lake at the dam. Keep track of the power line on your way in here, as it crosses one of the lakes. All are stocked annually with legal rainbow and have some fair size native cutthroat. It's pretty brushy, but almost any lure can be effective early in the year.

HEBO LAKE A 2 acre cutthroat lake 3.5 miles east of the Hebo Ranger Station on the Hebo Mt. Rd. The lake is shallow throughout and contains good feed. It is stocked with cutthroat through the spring. Still-fishing is the preferred method, although fishermen also troll. Fly fishing with streamers produces well in early season. Small boats can be launched, and there is a campground.

HULT RESERVOIR A warm water fishery located about 4 miles north of Horton. It provides fair angling for largemouth bass in spring. There is a good brown bullhead population (average size 9 inches), bluegill, and black crappie. A few cutthroat are also taken. The reservoir has a small boat ramp.

HUMBUG CREEK A fine cutthroat stream, about 9 miles long, entering the Nehalem just south of Elsie. Hwy. 26 parallels the creek and crosses both the east and west forks. It has some boulders and gravel, but is primarily a bedrock stream.

Try working a spinner and worm hookup along the ledges, though the best bait is probably the caddis larva found throughout stream bottom. Break open the pebbly case and thread the critter on a single egg hook or hook it on the ugliest sparse no. 12 fly you have. Cast to the riffles and slicks. This is a good bet even late in the season.

INDIAN CREEK A large tributary of Lake Creek, with rainbow, cutthroat, and a small run of salmon and steelhead. It joins Lake Creek

about 2 miles above that creek's confluence with the Siuslaw, about 2 miles north of Swisshome. The creek is about 20 miles long and averages 30-40 feet wide. A county road follows the stream north from Hwy. 36, about 40 miles west of Junction City.

Indian Creek offers good trout cover, with deep pools, bedrock ledges, and overhanging brush. It's a good bait stream for a month or so in early season.

KAUPPI LAKE One of CFI's lakes, 5 acres in size. It's no longer stocked due to weed problems, but a few native cutthroat are still taken. It's pretty hard to find. Leave Vernonia and go to the Cavenham Tree Farm office, then turn left. Take the Crooked Creek Rd. for 6 miles to Kauppi Rd., turn right, and continue 3.9 miles. The lake can be seen from that point. Weeds seal the lake in late summer, and there are lots of logs and snags. Deepest water (10 feet) is on the eastern edge.

KILCHIS RIVER A good winter steelhead, salmon, and sea-run cutthroat stream. The Kilchis enters Tillamook Bay just north of the Wilson River and the town of Tillamook. It's only about 20 miles long but offers a lot of fishing.

One of the first coast rivers to clear, the Kilchis heads in the Tillamook Burn, which was rededicated as an official forest in 1988. The upper stream is gravelly with scant cover, but the lower river has very good trout habitat.

Cutthroat angling is good, with the big sea-runs usually returning in August. Chinook and a very few coho are taken in season, and steelheading is excellent. A summer steelhead stocking program keeps production high, with steelhead showing up in May and available all summer. The winter steelhead run is still the strongest, however, with 500-1000 fish taken from November through March. The 1985-86 season's catch was 546 winter steelhead, 51 summer steelhead (though the summer catch is frequently close to 200).

The Kilchis has a good run of fall chinook, which sometimes arrives late. The 1986 run peaked in November, and the year's total catch was 281. The Kilchis is one of only two coastal streams with a strong chum salmon run. The chum season is now closely regulated to deter snagging. See Miami River for more details.

There's good access to this fine river. An improved public boat ramp, Park's Landing, is about 200 yds. above Hwy. 101 on Alderbrook Rd. The county maintains a picnic and recreational area about 5 miles from the mouth. Below the park most land is private, but the owner allows access for a modest fee. Note the coin box at Curl Road Bridge. Above the park the river flows thorugh Tillamook State Forest. There is a landing at Mapes Creek, with the lowest take-out at Park's Landing. Supplies and accommodations are available in Tillamook.

Flood level on the Kilchis is similar to taht of the Wilson River, 11 cfs (cubic ft. per second), with optimum fishing at 6 cfs, and acceptable levels beween 5.3 and 7 cfs. For current Wilson River reading, call ODFW Portland Information Line, or (503) 249-0666.

KLASKANINE RIVER A good winter steelhead stream, fair for salmon and cutthroat. Heading in the coast range west of Jewell, the Klaskanine flows about 20 miles into Young's Bay near Astoria. A paved road, Hwy. 202, follows the North Fork, and a gravel road follows the South Fork closely for several miles.

The Klaskanine provides good fish habitat—quite a few boulders and gravel bars. Some good but brushy holes are best fished with bait. The winter steelhead catch for both the main river and its (sometimes even better) North Fork fluctuates between one and two thousand fish annually, with some years closer to 3,000. The 1985-86 catch was 2,276. The South Fork catch is considerably smaller. Steelhead start arriving in numbers in early December, and the fishing holds up through February.

Coho and chinook returning to the hatchery have opened up a great fishery for jacks. This gets started in late September and continues through the winter. Sea-run cutthroat can be taken in late August or early September, depending on the rainfall.

The North Fork is open for steelhead up to 200 feet below the salmon hatchery. There is 3/4 of a mile of public access which begins at the first cement bridge above tidewater and continues (with the exception of two small private holdings) to the hatchery deadline.

The South Fork continues to be supplemented by a steelhead stocking program, with fair results. The catch fell to 111 in 1985-86 from a good showing of 348 in 1983-84.

To reach the South Fork, take the Green Mt. Road from the North Fork above Smiley's Hole, or take the Elk Mt. Rd. off Hwy. 202. The lower end of the South Fork flows through private land with restricted access, but the upper portions are open to public use courtesy of CFI. A road parallels the South Fork.

KLICKITAT LAKE A small lake in the headwaters of the North Fork of the Alsea River near the divide between Yaquina and Alsea. It has small native cutthroat in abundance. It's shown on most maps as a landmark.

LAKE CREEK (Lane Co.) A very good winter steelhead stream. Lake Creek is a major tributary of the Siuslaw River, joining the Siuslaw at Swisshome. The Siuslaw River Rd. from the upper river joins Hwy. 36 about 42 miles west of Junction City. Lake Creek is followed by 36

from just above Triangle Lake downstream to its mouth. It is an extremely clear stream, since Triangle Lake serves as a sediment trap. It really has to rain to muddy it up. A project is now underway to ladder the falls just below Triangle Lake, which will allow salmon to access an additional 100 miles of spawning ground.

A favorite of Eugene-Springfield drift fishermen, the creek has a winter steelhead run that often nets well over a thousand fish, with the run picking up in December and holding steady into March. In addition, a couple hundred coho and chinook salmon are taken each fall.

There are drift boat put-ins at Green Creek, the mouth of Indian Creek, and near the mouth of Deadwood Creek. About 1/2 mile below the mouth of Green Creek is an area called *The Horn* that is extremely dangerous and should *not* be run by drift boats. Take out 1/4 mile above this area at the highway gravel pile site.

This is an excellent trout stream in its upper stretch, heavily fished and stocked with good numbers of cutthroat for the first few months of the season. The creek above Triangle Lake near Blachly also offers good trout angling in early season.

It flows through a lot of private land, so beware of trespassing. The steelhead catch for boat fishermen is usually much higher than for bank anglers. Some guides are available in the area. There are no campgrounds nearby.

LAKE LYTLE A 65 acre coast lake with both bass and trout. Lytle is located just north of Rockaway, about 15 miles north of Tillamook on Hwy. 101. The lake is just east of the highway and is connected to Crescent Lake. Lytle is shallow and prone to heavy weed growth, particularly at the north end.

It contains both rainbow and cutthroat and is stocked each year. Since it is lightly fished, it might contain some surprises. Largemouth bass fishing is good, and black crappie have established themselves. Trout fishing is best in spring and early summer, bass in summer and fall.

Boats are not available for rent, but there is a public boat ramp on the NE shore. Supplies, facilities, and services are available at Rockaway.

LEWIS AND CLARK RIVER A pretty good coastal steelhead stream emptying into Young's Bay. It is reached from Astoria by way of Warrenton on the Miles Crossing. A road follows the stream to its headwaters near Saddle Mt. From 50 to 75 feet wide in many places, the stream has some good fly water.

The Lewis and Clark is stocked with a disease resistant strain of hatchery reared sea-run cutthroat, and there are natives as well. A good winter steelhead run hits the river in December and holds up through March. Over 900 fish were taken in 1980, but in recent years the river has been yielding closer to 400 annually. The river is currently receiving hatchery plants of steelhead smolts. It has a small showing of coho and fall chinook.

LILY LAKE (Lane Co.) A catch and release lake featuring native cutthroat. This small lake is located on the west side of Hwy.101, about 10 miles north of Florence. Take Baker Beach Rd. to the trailhead (unsigned). A 1/4 mile trail leads to the lake.

It is lightly fished for native cutthroat to 14 inches. The lake has a thick border of reeds and launching a boat is out of the question. A float tube angler might find the hike worth-while. Managed by the Forest Service, the lake is not

stocked, and is restricted to catch and release angling with barbless hooks.

LITTLE ELK RIVER A fair native cutthroat stream, tributary of the Yaquina River, joining the Yaquina near Eddyville on Hwy. 20, the Newport-Corvallis Hwy. Only 11 miles long and fairly small, it is followed by Hwy. 20 upstream from Eddyville. This stream is not currently stocked.

LOBSTER CREEK A good early season trout stream, major tributary of Five Rivers, which it joins about 3 miles above the junction of Five Rivers with the Alsea at Hwy. 34. Lobster Creek is about 20 miles long. A good road follows the creek upstream from its mouth. It has a healthy native cutthroat population and is a good bait fishing stream. A few steelhead are caught each year. It's open for steelhead and salmon up to Little Lobster Creek.

LOST LAKE (Columbia County) Formerly a small beaver pond lake with native cutthroat in the headwaters of the Clatskanie River, it was truly lost when its beaver dams were destroyed by persons unknown. Too bad.

LOST LAKE (Elsie area) A 15 acre rainbow lake east of Spruce Run Park on the Nehalem River. A badly deteriorated logging road currently runs east up Spruce Run Creek to the lake's north end, about 4-5 miles. The road is too deteriorated to allow the trout truck to pass at present, but reconstruction may take place within the next two years, at which time stocking will resume.

The lake is on private land and is sometimes blocked in spring by windfalls. The water is 20 feet deep at the deepest spot in the center of the north end. Rainbow fingerlings are stocked periodically, and some reach good size.

It's a fairly popular lake, but angling success tapers off after the first months of spring. It's difficult to get a boat in the water, but quite a few anglers troll, with spinner and worms favored. A few people fish it late in summer and get sizable fish on flies and bait. Small live crayfish fished near the bottom have produced some big ones. It's pretty snaggy, so bring plenty of tackle.

LOST LAKE (Lane Co.) An early season cutthroat lake, covering 6 acres, just east of Hwy. 101 about mid-way between Tahkenitch and Siltcoos lakes. The dirt access road off 101 just south of Carter Lake is now closed to cars, but anglers can park off the highway and walk in.

A good early season lake, it is stocked with cutthroat in spring. Boats can be slipped in (no ramp) but are not necessary. There are campgrounds north and south of on Hwy.101.

LOST LAKE (Westport Area) A small private lake with some bass, about 2 miles SW of Westport. A gravel road leads from Westport to the lake. It provides some early fishing for local anglers with permission from the owners.

MAGRUDER SLOUGH A good warm water fishery on the lower Columbia River. Magruder is located on Hwy. 30 about 3 miles east of Westport and is about 5 miles long. Most surrounding land is private, but bank fishing permission is usually given. County roads and bridges also provide access. Car-top boats can be launched in a few spots.

This is primarily a still-fishing show due to heavy vegetation. Crappie and bullhead are nu-

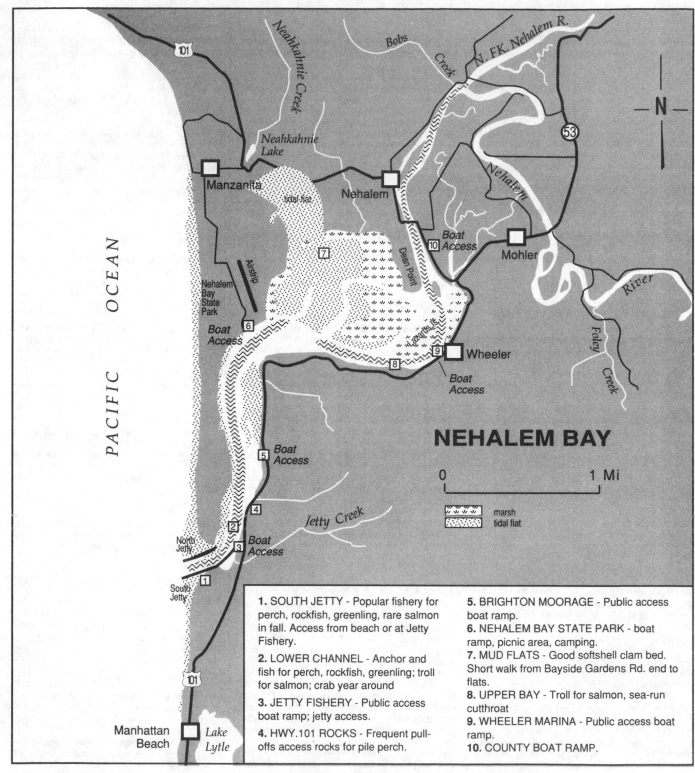

NEHALEM BAY

0   1 Mi

marsh
tidal flat

1. SOUTH JETTY - Popular fishery for perch, rockfish, greenling, rare salmon in fall. Access from beach or at Jetty Fishery.

2. LOWER CHANNEL - Anchor and fish for perch, rockfish, greenling; troll for salmon; crab year around

3. JETTY FISHERY - Public access boat ramp; jetty access.

4. HWY.101 ROCKS - Frequent pull-offs access rocks for pile perch.

5. BRIGHTON MOORAGE - Public access boat ramp.

6. NEHALEM BAY STATE PARK - boat ramp, picnic area, camping.

7. MUD FLATS - Good softshell clam bed. Short walk from Bayside Gardens Rd. end to flats.

8. UPPER BAY - Troll for salmon, sea-run cutthroat

9. WHEELER MARINA - Public access boat ramp.

10. COUNTY BOAT RAMP.

merous. Bluegill, perch, and a few bass are also present.

MAPLE CREEK A fair native cutthroat stream about 10 miles long, flowing into Siltcoos Lake from the NE. A county road parallels the stream to near its source. It can be reached from Hwy. 101 by several county roads in the vicinity of Siltcoos Lake. The creek provides fair native cutthroat in early season, and has a good largemouth bass population.

MARIE LAKE (Tillamook Co.) A little pothole just .6 acre at Twin Rocks, east of Hwy. 101. It contains largemouth bass.

MAYGER SLOUGH A Columbia River slough 3 miles NW of Downing, east of Crimm's Island. It contains white crappie and bluegill.

MERCER LAKE A good trout lake with lots of big, wiley bass. Mercer covers over 340 acres east of Hwy. 101, about 5 miles north of

Florence. A county road leads from the highway around the south shore.

Mercer's largemouth are plentiful, but are reputed to be very difficult to catch. The local bass clubs likes to fish the lake at night, but their success rate has been less than exceptional. If you find the secret, let us know. There are also several species of panfish in the lake, with yellow perch predominant. Perch to 14 inches are caught from bank and boat.

The lake is stocked with good numbers of rainbow each spring. Not heavily fished, it provides some good trout fishing from early spring well into the summer.

Mercer has a brushy shore that makes bank angling difficult. There is a resort on the lake where supplies and rental boats are available. The resort boat ramp is closed to general public use, but there is a public ramp about 2 1/2 miles around the lake. There are no campgrounds on Mercer.

MIAMI RIVER A good coastal river with a variety of fishing. Only about 14 miles long, entering Tillamook Bay just east of Garibaldi, it has a good native cutthroat population, fine shows of jack salmon and sea-run in fall, and good runs of salmon and steelhead. The river can be reached from Foley Creek Rd. upstream, and from Hwy. 101 near the lower end. A good road parallels the stream. The most popular stretch flows through agricultural land.

A fair steelhead run peaks early in January, and a run of larger steelhead (12-18 pounds) comes in late February and early March. Coho show in late October, and there is a fair fall chinook run. There are several miles of fishing in an forest setting above the old mill about 5 miles above Hwy. 101. This stretch is very good for early steelheading.

The Miami and a neighboring Tillamook stream, the Kilchis, have the largest chum salmon runs on the Oregon coast. Catches of over 2000 fish have been common, with best fishing in November. The fishery is now more tightly regulated, with catch and release in effect throughout a good part of the season. With the river often running shallow in late fall, the liberal regulations of the past tempted too many to snag. Chum are caught using normal drift fishing techniques with eggs, corkies, and small spinners (green lures are preferred by most anglers). Fly fishing for this big fish in the less congested areas is a real kick.

Much of the lower river is posted. Flood level on the Miami is similar to that of the Wilson River, 11 cfs (cubic ft. per second). Optimum fishing is at 6 cfs, and acceptable levels are between 5.3 and 7 cfs. Use the Wilson River as a gauge to determine the status of the Miami. For a current reading, call ODFW Portland Information Line, or (503) 249-0666.

MIDDLE LAKE (Clatsop Co.) Prominent on maps, this lake is located in the headwaters of Bear Creek in the Astoria watershed and is not open to the public.

MILES LAKE A small lake just west of the road between Woods, on the lower Nestucca, and Sand Lake, several miles north of Woods. Under private ownership at present, it contains rainbow trout and catfish.

MUNSEL LAKE A good trout and bass lake of about 93 acres, lightly fished. It is located about 2 1/2 miles north of Florence and about one mile east of Hwy.101. A good paved road leads to the lake.

Munsel is stocked with rainbow trout each season and has a good native cutthroat population. The lake occasionally gets a stocking of brood trout to 5 pounds. Fishing is good in the spring and holds up well into summer. Most anglers troll. A brushy shoreline limits bank fishing. Some big largemouth bass are taken on plugs and lures, and there's a good population of yellow perch. There is a county boat ramp at the lake, with camping about 4 miles north on Hwy.101.

NEACOXIE LAKE (a.k.a. Sunset Lake) See Sunset Lake.

NECANICUM RIVER A very pretty winter steelhead stream, about 22 miles long, flowing into the Pacific at Seaside. It is paralleled by paved roads through Coast Range forest for most of its length, heading near Saddle Mt. west of Elsie. It can be reached from the south by Hwy. 53 in the Nehalem area, and from the north by Hwy.101. It gets low in late summer. There's a lot of private land in the lower end, but it's fairly easy to fish at many points above.

The Necanicum has a fair native cutthroat population and is stocked in spring with hatchery cutthroat. There is some good fly water in the lower stream above tidewater, and fly fishing for sea-run cutthroat in late summer there can be terrific. Bait and spinner seem to work best on the hatchery trout.

Steelhead start to show in November, depending on water levels, and peak in December or January. The river is stocked with steelhead smolts and has been turning in catches of up to 2000 fish yearly. A few summer steelhead, coho, and fall chinook are also taken.

There is good bank casting in the lower river, a number of picnic areas, and some camping available.

NEHALEM BAY The fourth largest bay on the Oregon coast, with fair fishing both in the bay and offshore. To reach Nehalem Bay from Portland, drive west on Hwy. 26, then turn south on Hwy. 101. Or take Hwy. 6 to Tillamook, then Hwy. 101 north about 23 miles. It takes about 1 1/2 hrs. to reach the bay from Portland. Tidewater extends up to Eck Creek on the main Nehalem.

Angling activity in spring and early summer focuses on bottom and surf fish. Flounder are no longer abundant here, but good size perch, rockfish, and greenling are taken on shrimp, clam necks, and kelp worms. Good catches are made from the South Jetty and from the rocks off Hwy. 101. Best fishing is on the incoming tide. Anglers also anchor and fish for these species in the lower channel. Surf fishing from the beach both north and south of the bar can be excellent.

In early summer salmon appear at the Nehalem bar. They are fished on the bar and just outside. The Nehalem bar can be very dangerous, especially in high winds. Check with local moorage operators or the Coast Guard for a condition update. Offshore and bar salmon anglers usually troll or mooch herring. In 1986, the ocean salmon sport catch out of Nehalem was a low 781, though most years it is above 1000.

Salmon stay outside the bay until late summer. Jack salmon (juvenile males) are the first to enter after the early fall rains. They are taken on cluster eggs, small lures, and spinners. Chinook follow, sometimes as early as August, then coho. Salmon are caught in the bay until November. Early season catches are near the mouth, then the run and the action moves upstream. Bay anglers generally troll with spinners, herring, or Flatfish.

Crabbing is generally excellent throughout the year, with good catches even in late winter if you don't mind the cold. Best crabbing is in the lower channel. Rings and bait are available at most moorages. Softshell clams are easily dug in the flats about 3 miles up from the mouth. Follow Bayside Gardens Rd. to the dead end. There are about 400 acres of digging flats here. There are other small flats along both sides of the river, but the best spot is the large cove across from Wheeler.

Several moorages offer boat rentals, tackle, bait, and other supplies from Brighton upstream to Wheeler. Nehalem Bay State Park, just south of Manzanita, has pleasant sites for trailers and tents, picnic area, boat ramp, bike trails, and ocean access. There is also an airstrip within the park.

NEHALEM RIVER A good steelhead, salmon, and cutthroat stream, third longest river on the Oregon coast. It flows over 100 miles, entering Nehalem Bay at the town of Nehalem, easily reached from any direction.

The Lower Nehalem River Rd. follows the river from Nehalem Bay to Elsie. County Rd. 202 follows the upper river through Jewell, Birkenfeld, Mist, Pittsburg, and Vernonia. It is crossed twice by Hwy. 26.

A large stream, heavily fished and accessible, it is close to both the coast and the Portland area. Popular with steelheaders and salmon anglers, it's also an excellent cutthroat stream. Large cutthroat are taken in the lower river throughout the season.

Although most Nehalem salmon catches are made in the bay, there is a small spring chinook run that is lightly fished here in June and July. Coho are taken by bank casters above tidewater from late September on. Fall Chinook are usually in the river a little earlier, primarily taken in the lower river. In 1986, anglers reported a catch of 2,272 coho, and 1,227 fall chinook in the river and bay combined.

Best steelheading on the Nehalem is usually from December to March. The river has a lot of good steelhead water, though many of its best *drifts* are accessible only by boat. There is good bank fishing at Foley Creek, Batterson Riffles, and the Salmonberry Riffle. There is excellent steelhead water below the entrance of the Salmonberry River. There are also many good plunking holes on the Nehalem. Among the best known are Clover Patch, Sacrifice, and Freezeout. The 1986 winter steelhead catch on the Nehalem was 1417.

Drift boats are popular on the lower river, with the best boating from the Beaver Slide down. There are two boat ramps on the lower river, one at Roy Creek (rough ramp) about 3 miles upstream from Nehalem, and another (popularly known as the Beaver Slide) below Lost Creek on the county road about 100 yards downstream from the State Forest Guard Station. There are additional ramps in tidewater at Wheeler and at Nehalem below the bridge. Flood level on the Nehalem is 13 cfs (cubic ft. per second). Best fishing is at 4.5 cfs, with acceptable levels between 4 cfs and 5.2 cfs. The current river gauge reading is available from the ODFW Portland Information Line or by calling (503) 249-0666

Accommodations and supplies are available in the Nehalem Bay area. Watch for closure regulations at Nehalem Falls about 2 miles above Cook Creek. This is well marked.

NEHALEM RIVER, EAST FORK A small stream about 12 miles long. It is only a fair bait stream for native cutthroat. It flows into the Nehalem at Pittsburg, 2 miles north of Vernonia. A good road parallels the stream, and very little is private posted land. It can also be reached from Scappoose by the county road to Pittsburg.

NEHALEM RIVER, NORTH FORK A good salmon and steelhead stream. It is followed for about 7 miles NW by Hwy. 53. From that point a gravel road parallels the stream to the east. This private road is not open to cars, but anglers

NEHALEM RIVER

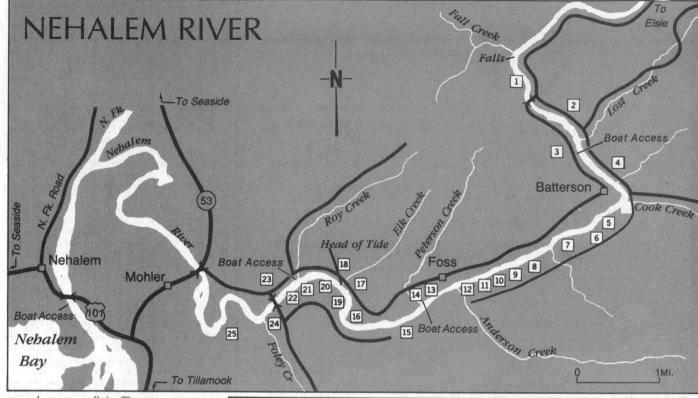

are welcome to walk in. The upper stream can be reached by road from Hamlet.

The North Fork is about 24 miles long and carries a good flow. The upper stream has good spawning gravel, and the lower stretch is a productive mix of boulder and gravel. There are some rich feeder streams in the lower end, notably Coal Creek and Soapstone Creek.

Coastal cutthroat are taken in good numbers in early spring, late summer, and fall. Fall chinook show in August and are taken through November. Jack salmon are available in September and October. A good run of coho usually appears in early November, followed by steelhead in December. Over 1500 winter steelhead were caught during the 1985-86 season, and more than 800 fall salmon were reported in 1986. There is a hatchery on the North Fork that stocks the stream with steelhead and coho. There are two fish ladders over the falls in the upper river. Anglers must stay 200 feet away from them.

NESKOWIN CREEK(a.k.a. Slab Creek) A fair coastal cutthroat stream about 7 miles long, entering the ocean at Neskowin, about 4 miles south of Nestucca Bay. Hwy. 101 follows most of the stream up from Neskowin.

A closure on salmon and steelhead fishing in the creek has recently been lifted to allow catch and release angling with barbless hooks. Check the current regulations for complete information.

There is a Forest Service campground about 5 miles south of Neskowin. Supplies and accomodations are available in town.

NESTUCCA BAY With its two big tributaries, one of the finest producers of salmon and steelhead on the Oregon coast. Over 5000 of each were caught in the system in 1981, and in 1986 the Nestucca complex was the Number One steelhead producer on the coast.

It's a quick trip here from the Willamette Valley. The bay is easily reached from any direction, located about 20 miles south of Tillamook

1. **NEHALEM FALLS** - Don't try it. Upstream there are drifts and holes, frequently far apart, for bank anglers and limited boating.
2. **LOST CR. HOLE** - Nothing between here and the next one except for pros; big boulders, some fish in pockets.
3. **BEAVER SLIDE** - Put-in only; slide drift boats down bank; park adjacent to county road.
4. **SACRIFICE HOLE** - A real tackle snatcher but good producer.
5. **BATTERSON RIFFLES** - Overhead pipeline about two-thirds way down.
6. **ROCK HOLE** - Strictly for plunking.
7. **CATTLE GUARD HOLE** - Plunker's paradise, both banks; drifters down the middle.
8. **STONE HILL HOLE** - Good drifting, brushy banks.
9. **CLOVER PATCH HOLE** - Excellent for plunking during high water; good drifting in low water; good drift water between here and Lindsay.
10. **LINDSAY RIFFLE** - Best for plunkers. Still eddy on north side holds fish; drift upper end at low water.
11. **ANDERSON CREEK HOLE** - Fish lie along south bank; boat drift only.
12. **FOSS DRIFT** - Fish below at piling close to brush.
13. **FREEZEOUT HOLE** - Sun never shines here, plunkers. Pretty water, drifters.
14. **MOHLER SAND & GRAVEL** - Pay to put in or take out at gravel bar; park along county road.
15. **UPPER WINSLOW DRIFT** - Long straight gravel bar drift; better slow down going through here.
16. **WINSLOW DRIFT** - Doesn't look as good as it is, though holding fewer fish than it used to.
17. **ROCK CRUSHER DRIFT**
18. **TWILIGHT HOLE** - Watch for jacks right after first fall rains, Sept. through Oct.
19. **MIDDLE EASOM DRIFT** - Slow water from here on down.
20. **EASOM DRIFT** - Just below big rock.
21. **WALKER HOLE** - Right across from Roy Creek.
22. **FENCE HOLE** - Good August, September fly fishing for cutthroat.
23. **STUMP HOLE** - Another good cutthroat spot early and late in day.
24. **FOLEY CREEK DRIFT** - Drift boats fish NW side; plunker access from south bank.
25. **LIVERPOOL** - Plunking in tidewater.

by Hwy. 101, or by the Tierra Del Mar Road. From the south its only 55 miles from Newport.

Nestucca Bay is created by the Big Nestucca coming in from the NW and the Little Nestucca from the SW, forming a wishbone shaped tidal area. Because it's a very shallow bay, boaters must be alert to depth and tide, or find themselves high and dry on the flats. Above Pacific City there's plenty of deep water.

Fishing is good for *something* year around here, but the main show is put on by salmon, steelhead, and sea-run cutthroat. June and July are best for spring chinook in the bay. Fall chinook follow a month or two later, accompanied by a small run of coho in September and October. Close to 3,000 fall salmon were taken in the bay and Big Nestucca combined in 1986.

To catch them, anglers drift and float eggs,

and use herring or trolled spinners. Bobber fishing with eggs has really produced in this area. The Airport Hole, across from the airport below the boat ramp is one of the hot spots. There's also good trolling down near the mouth, in the channel areas, and upstream from Pacific City.

For sea-run, a large spinner and bait combination is best. Trolled Flatfish also produce. The sea-run can exceed 18 inches..

The summer steelhead run developed by the Oregon Dept. of Fish and Wildlife continues to crank out fish, with 4,875 taken in the bay and Big Nestucca in 1985-86. Summers are taken from spring through October. In fact, you can catch a steelhead any month of the year in this bay. The winter steelhead catch for the bay and Big Nestucca was 4,875.

Perch are available in the shallows of the

1. UPPER TIDEWATER Troll for fall chinook, sea-run Aug.-Oct. Bank fishing at county park.

2. NESTUCCA RAMP Small public gravel ramp beside sporting goods store 2 mi. from Hwy. 101 on Pacific City loop. Limited parking. Drift down or motor up for fall chinook, coho, sea-run.

3. PACIFIC CITY RAMP Improved public ramp 2 mi. north of town. Accesses lower bay. Traditional Airport Hole has shifted to ramp side of river. Good fishery for fall chinook. Small early spring chinook fishery.

4. TROLL mid-bay for fall chinook.

5. FISHERY LANDING Unimproved public ramp. Bank angling from parking area slightly down bay for fall chinook (Guardrail Hole) Aug.-Oct. Limited parking.

6. MOUTH OF LITTLE NESTUCCA Fish for perch, sea-run, greenling in channel off rocky point.

7. LITTLE NESTUCCA FLATS Softshell flats. Marker on road indicates access trail. Limited parking.

8. SOFTSHELL FLATS Best digging on the bay for softshell clams.

9. LITTLE NESTUCCA/101 RAMP Improved ramp, bank access from bridge upstream. Fish for fall chinook Aug.-Oct., sea-run July-Sept. Accesses lower bay fisheries.

10. LITTLE NESTUCCA CHANNEL Troll for fall chinook, coho, sea-run, occasional perch in lower reach.

11. MOUTH OF BAY Can be productive *but dangerous* boat fishery for fall fish, perch, greenling, crab. Bank fishery accessed by hiking through park.

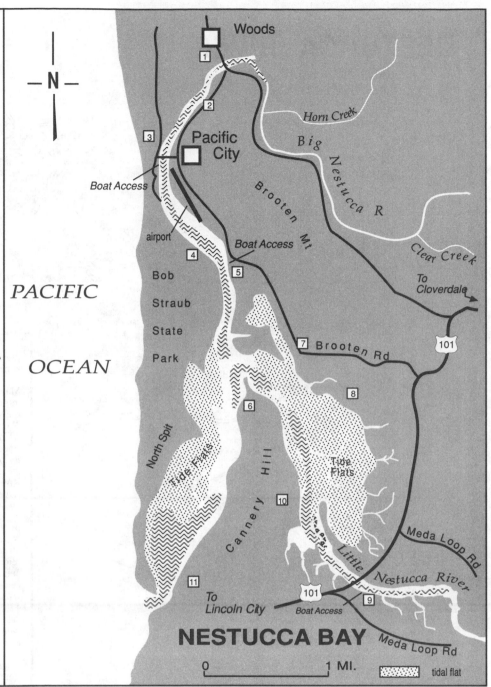

lower bay and in the Little Nestucca Channel, and surf fishing for perch is good anytime off the beach at Bob Straub State Park. Crab can be taken in the lower deep areas of the bay. For perch, time your fishing to the tide. Off the beaches, fish the last of the ebb and a few hours of the flood tide. Inside the bay, fish the high water.

There is a novel fishery for salmon and bottom fish off Cape Kiwanda just north of Pacific City. A fleet of dories launches from the beach and fishes 6-7 miles off shore. The skill of the dory operators is legendary, and their catch rate is very high for coho, ling cod, snapper, and halibut. Even if you don't go out yourself, it's interesting to watch the dories break through the surf. A good road leads to the dory launching area. It should be noted that launching through the surf should not be attempted by

novices. Charter dory rides are availble. In 1986, the salmon sport catch off Cape Kiwanda was a respectable 5,312. This is a summer fishery only.

The best softshell clamming in the bay is on the Little Nestucca Flats just off Brooten Rd., about 2 miles south of Pacific City. Almost any minus tide exposes the beds, and since you can't get out to fish the bay then anyway, dig in.

Supplies, facilities, and good advice are available in Pacific City. There's a gravel boat ramp beside the sporting goods store in town, and another public ramp a couple of miles south of town. You can also launch at Fisher Landing off Brooten Rd. and at the Little Nestucca Ramp off Meda Loop Rd.

If you are a flyer, the airport is less than 100 yards from the estuary, with marinas within

walking distance. Its only an 1800 ft strip, so be sharp. Best approach is from the south.

NESTUCCA RIVER (a.k.a. Big Nestucca) A real gem of an all-around stream. This big river flows 55 miles and runs 50-100 ft. wide in the lower stretch. Easily accessed, it is crossed and followed by Hwy. 101 from Pacific City to Beaver. County Rd. 858 follows the river upstream from Beaver into the Siuslaw National Forest. From inland, the Nestucca can be reached by a direct road west from Carlton.

Hatchery cutthroat are stocked in spring. Those that tarry are caught the first few weekends, and most of the rest go to sea, returning in August as big sea-runs, also known as *bluebacks*. Trolling for bluebacks in tidewater is popular, and the catch rate is high. Bank casting is good upstream for at least 25 miles. The Nes-

NESTUCCA RIVER

Fisherman's Map ©1981
by "Two T"
24643 NE Butteville Rd.
Aurora, OR 97002
Other maps available: Nehalem, Trask, Wilson

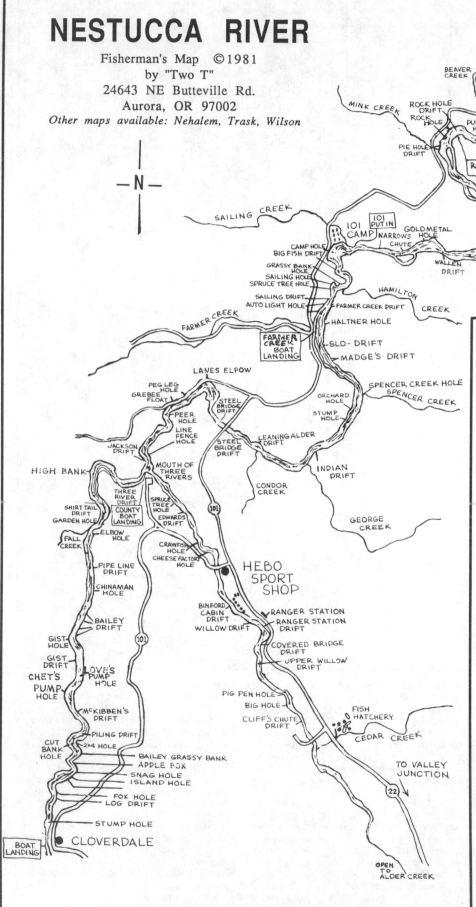

tucca is rich in natural feed, so rigged bait must appear natural to tempt the fish here.

A nice run of spring chinook starts in late May with the peak in June and July. A little more than 300 were taken here in 1986. The bigger fall chinook and coho runs begin in late August and reach the upper river in October when the rains begin. Salmon fishing is confined to tidewater until the fall rains. The majority of anglers fish the river below Hebo, since the salmon population thins out above Three Rivers and Beaver Creek. However, the upper river can be boated throughout most of the winter, and some good catches are made there.

Steelheading is superb year around. Scrappy 4-7 pound steelhead appear in tidewater in April, and by August they are nose to tail throughout a 20 mile section of the river. The return of hatchery reared summer steelhead continues to be excellent, with just under 5000 caught in the river and bay in 1985-86. The winter steelhead run averages 10,000 to 12,000, with a catch over 5,000 in 1985-86. They're taken on all types of lures, flies, and bait. Crayfish tails and sand shrimp are dependable. Fish the deep holes and stay out of sight if fishing from the bank. Morning and evening, when the sun is not on the water, are the best times.

Bank anglers pick fish out of even murky water here. There;s bank fishing access to the Cottonwood Hole, Pipeline Hole, Three Rivers Drift, Orchard Hole, and Lone Fir Hole. There are at least 40 well known holes, drifts, and riffles where steelhead have been known to linger. Check local tackle shops for an update on the progress of the run.

The Nestucca offers good boating from the 4th bridge down. Water above the bridge should be drifted by knowledgeable boaters only. Guides are available. Boat drifting is ideal when the water is about 3 feet above normal summer level. For best results, the river should not be too clear. It muddies quite rapidly after a good hard rain and doesn't clear quickly. Flood level on the Nestucca is 18 cfs. Best fishing is at 4.5 cfs, with acceptable levels between 3.6 and 5.4 cfs. A current river gauge reading can be obtained by calling the ODFW Portland Information Line or (503) 249-0666.

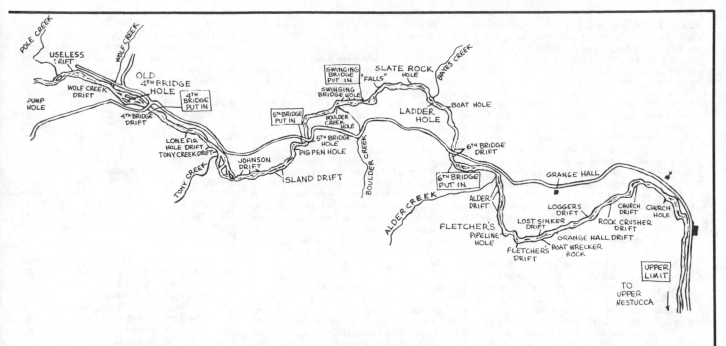

Tillamook County, the Dept. of Fish and Wildlife, the Highway Dept., and local sportsmen have all pitched in to make launching places available. There are public boat ramps at Pacific City, Cloverdale, Three Rivers, and Farmer Creek and put-ins (more and less developed) upriver.

There's a campground at Castle Rock on Three Rivers, and two camps 14 and 17 miles upstream from Beaver. Several boat rentals and moorages are available in tidewater. Accommodations and supplies are plentiful from Beaver to the mouth.

NESTUCCA RIVER, LITTLE A good winter steelhead stream. The Little Nestucca enters the Big Nestucca one mile above the ocean near Oretown, about 3 miles south of Pacific City. It heads in Yamhill County and flows past the community of Dolph on Hwy. 22, from which point a road follows the stream closely down to its mouth. This is a good native cutthroat stream and is stocked with trout in the area from Dolph downstream.

The Little Nestucca has a fall chinook run which usually returns in October with the rains. Some coho also show in October and can be taken both by bank casting and trolling in tidewater. Steelhead peak in December and January and are taken in good numbers. The steelhead run has improved due to increased stocking.

The entire stream is open during the winter season. Supplies and accommodations are available in the Nestucca Bay area. There is a public access area with parking facilities at the Hwy. 101 crossing, and bank access continues on National Forest land for 3 miles up. The 101 crossing is a popular place for bank casting.

NETARTS BAY A popular clamming and crabbing area. Netarts Bay is the sixth largest in the state in total area, but it is of little importance to anglers. It is about 7 miles long and quite shallow for the most part, with few channel areas more than 10 feet deep at high tide. No major rivers feed the bay, and of the dozen small streams that flow into it from the east, none harbor many salmon or steelhead. The bay does offer good crabbing and

clamming opportunities, however.

It's a quick hour and a half run to Netarts from the Willamette Valley. The bay is about 4 miles SW of Tillamook. The road follows the bay's eastern shore.

Netarts is one of five major crabbing bays on the Oregon coast. As in all bays, the winter rush of fresh water draws crab out into the open sea. They usually return in September, October, and November. In low water years, good catches of crab are taken in the bay year around. Both dungeness and red rock crab are found in Netarts. Crab rings and bait are available for rent, but you'll need a boat, as there are no piers here.

Clamming is really the main attraction at Netarts, with many good flats. The big flat off the spit at Cape Lookout State Park and the little flat on the north bayshore near the mouth yield tremendous numbers of cockle, butter, gaper, and littleneck clams and a few razors. Whiskey Creek Flats and Wilson Beach are less productive but worthwhile. Moorage operators make trips to these flats when the tides are favorable and will help you get started. Check current regulations for catch limits.

Kelp greenling and tomcod are caught in the bay from time to time. The north end and the area known as the Boiler Hole, just south of the county boat launch, are good for perch at times.

For these and other bottomfish, sand shrimp, clam necks, or kelp worms are good bait and can be purchased locally. Wind a few turns of pink thread or strands of fluorescent yarn around your baited hook to better secure it.

In summer and fall there are always a few bottom fish caught, but nothing exceptional. In October and November a few coho salmon are taken, usually on herring, spinners, or Flatfish on the flood tide. A few chum salmon also enter the bay, but they usually won't strike.

Netarts is a safe bay for family fun, as the water is so shallow that boat accidents are rare. Stay away from the Netarts bar, though, which is shallow and rough, a good spot to flip a boat if you are inexperienced. Veteran boaters do cross the bar in calm weather to fish the reef beyond Arch Rocks for rockfish,

halibut, and other bottom fish.

A word of warning—there are a number of privately owned oyster beds in the bay. These are off-limits to public harvest. There are *no* oyster beds in Oregon available to the public.

Several outlets on the bay rent boats and sell tackle and bait. There is a good county boat ramp and motel accomodations in Netarts. Lookout State Park, just south, offers camping facilities.

OLALLA RESERVOIR A reservoir on Olalla Creek, tributary to the Yaquina, a few miles east of Toledo. Owned by Cavenham Forest Industries, it covers 120 acres and is open to public use. It contains bass, panfish, and trout. It can be accessed from Toledo by a road off Hwy. 20.

Rainbow and cutthroat are stocked, with average catch 10 inches and some to 14 inches. Largemouth bass, brown bullhead, and bluegill are also in residence. The largemouth bass are in the mid-size range, but they are plentiful and a popular local fishery. Sportsmen have added submerged timber to the reservoir to provide additional bass habitat. There's a boat ramp on the lake, but motors are prohibited.

SUNRISE ON THE NESTUCCA
Richard Paradzinski, Photographer

PEBBLE CREEK A small tributary of the upper Nehalem, entering the river from the south at Vernonia. About 13 miles long, it is followed closely by roads. It is a fair early season cutthroat stream but doesn't hold up long and is not stocked.

PERKINS LAKE A 5 acre coastal lake stocked with rainbow, about 10 miles south of Florence on Hwy. 101 just west of the highway and a few miles north of Tahkenitch Lake. Park on the old Hwy. 101 shoulder. You can bank fish or launch a small boat from the old road along the north shore of the lake. It's very brushy around the shoreline, so a boat is helpful.

Some good catches are made fishing bait early in the season. Fly angling can pay off later when angling pressure drops. Large trout are sometimes taken. There's a campground at Carter Lake about one mile north.

PLYMPTON CREEK A small creek with native cutthroat, tributary to the Columbia in the vicinity of Puget Island. The mouth is near Westport on Hwy. 30. About 8 miles long, it heads near Nicolai Mt. and offers fair trout fishing in early season. Don't expect much excitement unless you get well away from the road.

PRESCOTT SLOUGH A 9 acre Columbia River slough off Hwy. 30 west of Trojan Nuclear Power Plant, featuring a smorgasbord of bass and panfish. West of Trojan and the entrance to Prescott Beach, the slough first appears as a narrow ditch paralleling the highway, then heads toward a grove of trees. You can slip a canoe or car-top boat into the water, or fish from the tall grass on the banks. Each tide brings new recruits of largemouth bass, with best fishing near the Columbia River outlet and along the base of the adjoining bluff. White crappie and brown bullhead are available in the channel, as well as yellow perch, bluegill, and warmouth bass.

QUARTZ LAKE A small but fairly deep cutthroat lake. It is located just south of Hwy. 26, about 2 miles east of the Jewell junction, some 50 miles west of Portland. Look for the highway gravel pit about 2 miles east of Jewell junction and just east of the high bridge crossing Quartz Creek.

The land has all been cut over, and the lake is brushy and hard to fish. There are lots of snags. About 4 acres, Quartz has produced some nice cutthroat.

RECREATION LAKE A 27 acre lake landscaped by PGE adjacent to the Trojan Nuclear Plant on Hwy. 30. The fishing is always *hot* here. Fantastic for giant mutant trout—2 inches head to head is average (we had pictures, but the film was fogged). Bring lots of lead.

RILEA SLOUGH At Camp Rilea, National Guard, about 3 1/2 miles SW of Warrenton. The public is allowed access to fish for yellow perch, white crappie, largemouth bass, and bluegill, except during Guard maneuvers.

RINEARSON SLOUGH A Columbia River slough, lightly fished but offering fair bass and panfish opportunities. The slough is NW of Rainier, some 45 miles from Portland. It can be accessed from the Columbia downstream from Longview Bridge. A number of side roads to the south cross or meet the slough. All the Columbia species are present, with crappie, perch, bluegill, and bass predominant. The only boat access is from the Columbia River. The banks are all privately owned, but permission to fish is usually granted.

ROCK CREEK (Columbia Co.) A very clear trout and steelhead stream, about 20 miles long, flowing into the upper Nehalem at Vernonia. It is a very popular stream, heavily fished in early season. A county road follows the creek from the NW side of Vernonia to Keasey. Private logging roads continue upstream and are accessible to the public when the gate is open (which it usually is). You can also reach the stream from the Sunset Rest Area at about milepost 30.

Rock Creek has a good native cutthroat population and is not stocked. It is open for steelhead in the winter to the former Keasey Dam site, which is about 15 miles up from the mouth. Best steelhead catches are in December and January. This is a good fly stream, very resistant to muddying. It does flow through a lot of private land, so ask for permission when you feel you might be intruding.

SALMON RIVER (Lincoln Co.) A fairly short coastal stream but a real producer. It heads in the coast range in northern Lincoln County and flows 24 miles to the ocean just north of Lincoln City. Followed by Hwy. 18 from McMinnville for most of its length, it is crossed by Hwy. 101 a few miles above its mouth.

One of the better small angling streams on the coast, it reliably produces good catches of fall salmon and winter steelhead. In 1986, almost 4,000 fall chinook and coho were caught here, and the 1985-86 winter steelhead catch was 4,875.

There is a salmon and steelhead hatchery above Otis, at about river mile 4, which releases thousands of smolts into the river annually, and attracts almost equal numbers of anglers during the return migration. The Salmon River is primarily a bank fishery, as most of the riffles are shallow gravel bars. Unfortunately, bank access is limited, with most salmon angling taking place just below the hatchery and at the Hwy. 101 Bridge downstream. The Dept. of Fish and Wildlife hatchery is on the North Bank Rd. at Otis. Anglers fish a 1/4 mile stretch down from the hatchery on both north and south banks. Park at the hatchery or pull off Hwy. 18 to fish the opposite bank.

At the Hwy. 101 Bridge, anglers park and fish from the bank both upstream and down. The land downstream from the bridge is public land, part of the Cascade Head National Scenic Research Area. Boat anglers launch at the ramp on Three Rocks Rd. below the bridge and motor up to popular holes. Few anglers boat higher than 3/4 mile. When the river is high enough to allow boating up to the hatchery, fishing is usually off.

Sea-run cutthroat are the first migrants to appear in the river, entering in late July. They are fished till September, when attention turns to Chinook, then coho. Peak fishing for fall salmon is September and October. Steelhead start crowding upstream in good numbers in December and are caught through March.

Both coho and steelhead are also taken in the Rose Lodge area off North Bank Rd. Anglers fish from the bridge at Rose Lodge and from roadside pull-offs.

Above Rose Lodge, the river passes through a corridor of state land (Van Duzer) where both steelhead and coho are taken. Sea-run cutthroat are also available there.

The Salmon River usually clears quickly after a muddy spell, and is even productive when roily. Eggs are probably the most popular bait, taking all species. Artificial lures will produce when the water is right, but the stream is brushy and a lot of gear is lost. Dry flies will work well in late spring when the water drops and warms. The stream is usually well stocked with hatchery trout in the spring.

The riverbank between Otis and Hwy. 101 is all privately owned, but some landowners do grant permission to fish. Be sure to ask before you wet your line. There are two privately owned RV encampments on the river. The one near 101 is operated by an RV membership organization without general public access. The Camp near Rose Lodge is available for public use, though space is limited. There are special angling rules in effect on the Salmon, so check the current regulations. Supplies are available at several service stations in the upper river. There are tackle stores on the lower river, and supplies and accommodations in the Lincoln City area.

SALMONBERRY RIVER A good winter steelhead stream. The Salmonberry is a major tributary of the Nehalem River. About 18 miles long, it enters the Nehalem about 11 miles south of Elsie on the Lower Nehalem River Road. The upper portion can be reached by logging roads from the east through Cochran, near Timber.

Best fishing is in February and March. The mainstem stream is open during the winter season, but not the tributaries. There's a good steelhead spot right at the point where the Salmonberry enters the Nehalem. Flyfishing is a popular method here.

This is a fair cutthroat stream in the spring. Sea-run appear after the fourth of July. During the regular trout season, angling is restricted to use of barbless flies and lures.

SAND CREEK A short stream that affords good fishing at times. Sand Creek is 6 miles long, with only about 2 miles fishable. The creek flows into Sand Lake about 20 miles south of Tillamook. From Hwy.101, take the Tierra Del Mar Rd. cutting west from Hemlock.

Sand Creek has a fair run of sea-run cutthroat which starts up in July and August. They remain in the river until late spring, when they run back to sea. Crayfish tails, and spinner and worms will produce some nice fish. There are rumors of a wild coho salmon run in late October (but no reported catches), and there may be some steelhead in February and March. Camping facilities are available at Sand Lake, Island Park, and at Cape Lookout State Park.

SAND LAKE Not really a lake, but a tidal basin at the mouth of Sand Creek, south of Tillamook. A popular recreation spot, it is reached by the county road leaving Hwy. 101 at Hemlock, or by going north from Woods on the Lower Nestucca Rd.

Cutthroat enter Sand Lake from the sea in July and August. Chum salmon come in during November and December, and steelhead enter in February and March, but few salmon and steelhead are taken here. Most of the angling is from boats or by bank casting on the east side of the island. A bridge crosses to the island from the county road, and boats can be easily launched.

Flounder fishing has fallen on hard times here as elsewhere on the Oregon coast, but a few are still taken. Fishing for them is concentrated mostly between the south side of the island and the outlet. Blue prawns, which can be purchased locally, make good bait for flounder as do mud shrimp and nightcrawlers. Surf perch fishing is possible on either side of the ocean outlet. Crabbing takes place just inside the inlet.

The county maintains a park on an island in the center of Sand Lake, and there is a campground on the NW shore near the ocean.

SANDY ISLAND SLOUGH A Columbia River slough north of Goble, with a known population of black crappie.

SANTOSH SLOUGH Good fishing for bass and panfish, a fine place for a family outing. This Columbia River slough is off Multnomah Channel near Scappoose. Take Hwy. 30 through town, turn right at the airport sign, then left on Honeyman Rd. The slough access is beyond the airport and gravel operation. At the metal dike gate, follow the dirt road. The Oregon Bass and Panfish Club helped develop the park and fishing area, which has 2000 ft. of grassy banks. Respect for the *Posted* signs will help keep this nice facility open to the public.

There are crappie, bass, perch, and bullhead catfish here, with some crappie to 3/4 pound and bass to 2 pounds. Rafts and canoes are best suited to the narrow waters, though boats occasionally squeeze in from Multnomah Channel.

SCHOONER CREEK A small stream with a fair salmon and steelhead run. It empties into the north end of Siletz Bay just east of Taft and is crossed by Hwy. 101 at its mouth. A county road follows the stream for most of its 10 mile length. The stream varies in width from 25 to 50 feet and has a lot deep pools and brushy banks. It's pretty snaggy. Winter fishing is restricted to the lower 4 miles.

Some chinook and coho are taken in September and October, but most salmon angling takes place in Siletz Bay. Steelhead are in the creek from December through February, but only a few have been taken each year for several seasons. Schooner is primarily a native cutthroat stream, with good early season catches and some large cutthroat in the lower end in August and September.

The upper deadline during the winter season is Erickson Creek. There's overnight camping at Devils Lake, about 4 miles south.

SEARS LAKE A small lake near Tierra Del Mar beach, between Sand Lake and Woods, located just east of the county road. This lake is privately owned at present. It contains a few cutthroat, but it is not open to the public.

SHAG LAKE A small lake, less than 5 acres, located near Fort Stevens State Park. Shag has been severely drained and is now weed choked. Very difficult to find, it is about 1/2 mile north of the gravel road from Warrenton to Fort Stevens Park, east of the paved road to Hammond. Shag is lightly fished for bass and panfish.

SILETZ BAY A lightly fished bay about 5 miles long from the jaws at Taft up to Kernville Bridge, used primarily by non-anglers, including a growing fleet of windsurfers. The Siletz River enters the bay at Kernville, while Drift Creek and Schooner Creek enter to the north. The bay has silted up considerably as a result of logging practices in the '30s and '40s. Not a good destination bay for anglers, but a pleasant place to clam or crab if you're vacationing at Lincoln City.

From early spring to summer, the chief angling here is for bottom fish, primarily perch and tomcod. Favorite baits are ghost or sand shrimp, kelp worms, and clam pieces. Perch to 3 pounds are caught up to the Kernville Bridge

starting in May. They leave well before the fall rains. In general, the best catches are made from boats anchored in the bay, but casting from shore near the bay mouth can be good. Flood tide is the preferred time.

Crabbing is excellent during the early part of the year. Rings and bait are available locally, and can be fished from public docks on the bay.

In late summer and fall, sea-run cutthroat arrive and are taken on trolled spinner and worm from Kernville upstream. Some anglers do well using shrimp as bait.

Salmon angling outside the bay starts as early as July with the arrival of chinook and coho at the jaws. In late fall, salmon are taken throughout the bay, though most catches are made in the Siletz River itself. The total catch for river and bay in 1986 was about 1300. A good number of big jacks also appear regularly with the run.

Chinook are usually caught in the upper bay. Coho are taken, usually with herring, near the jaws. Many anglers cast from the banks between Taft and the jaws. Be prepared to lose lots of terminal gear, as the bottom is rocky. Salmon anglers use spinners with feathered hook or Flatfish type lures. Steelhead pass through the bay, but are primarily taken in the river.

Bait can be purchased locally, but gathering your own is not difficult. Shrimp bait are easily found at low water in the flats all along the bay. Herring for bait (or eating) are taken intermittently through the summer months.

Surf casters can do well on the ocean side of the jaws. The beach drops off rapidly, and at low water there's easy casting for redtail and large dusky perch.

The tide flats between Cutler City and Kernville have good numbers of softshell clams. Any zero tide makes the flats accessible.

A number of reasonably priced moorages with rental boats and ramps are available along the bay and upriver. On weekends, it's a good idea to make reservations for your needs. A large state park is located at Devils Lake just north of the Bay, and there are other campgrounds further south on Hwy. 101. Siletz Bay

State Park in the Taft area of Lincoln City offers fine opportunities for viewing seals and shore birds, including brown pelicans in summer. Tackle shops, grocery stores, and motels are plentiful in the area. *The Siletz bar is dangerous. There are no jetties, and a number of lives have been lost in crossing.*

SILETZ RIVER A fine all around stream, one of Oregon's Top 10 coastal steelhead rivers. It enters Siletz Bay at Kernville, at the junction of Hwy. 101 with Hwy. 229, which follows the lower part of the river. It's accessible from the Corvallis area by way of Hwy. 20 and county roads to the Logsden area, and from the Newport-Toledo area by Hwy. 229.

The Siletz is outstanding for both salmon and steelhead and is an excellent trout stream as well. It is very fishable, with few snags. The main boating area is from the town of Siletz down through tidewater, although a lot of drifters put in upstream at Moonshine Park. The town of Siletz has a good ramp with parking and picnic facilities at the Hwy. 229 Bridge. The Siletz muddies easily, and eggs work best when the water's turbid.

Salmon start moving through the bay in late July or August, and fishing holds up well until late fall. Over a thousand fish are taken annually. They are fished throughout the river, some 70 miles of bank and drift boat fishing.

Steelhead are taken every month of the year in the Siletz, with a total catch in 1985-86 of 5,800. The winter run starts in November, and the summer run starts in late May.

The upper river is heavily stocked with hatchery cutthroat, many of which return as sea-run, appearing in the lower tidewater in July, with good catches until late fall.

The lower river and bay have many moorages where boats, bait, and tackle are available. Flood level on the Siletz is 16 cfs (cubic ft. per second). Optimum level for boating is 6.6, with acceptable levels from 3.9 cfs to 8 cfs. The current river gauge reading can be obtained by calling the ODFW Portland Information Line, or (503) 249-0666.

CAPE KIWANDA DORYMAN
Deke Meyer, Photographer

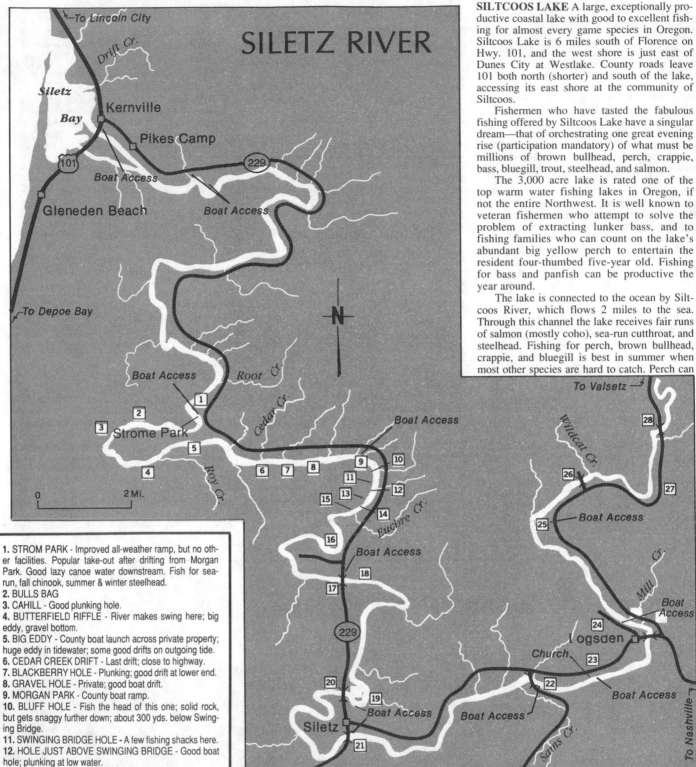

SILETZ RIVER

SILTCOOS LAKE A large, exceptionally productive coastal lake with good to excellent fishing for almost every game species in Oregon. Siltcoos Lake is 6 miles south of Florence on Hwy. 101, and the west shore is just east of Dunes City at Westlake. County roads leave 101 both north (shorter) and south of the lake, accessing its east shore at the community of Siltcoos.

Fishermen who have tasted the fabulous fishing offered by Siltcoos Lake have a singular dream—that of orchestrating one great evening rise (participation mandatory) of what must be millions of brown bullhead, perch, crappie, bass, bluegill, trout, steelhead, and salmon.

The 3,000 acre lake is rated one of the top warm water fishing lakes in Oregon, if not the entire Northwest. It is well known to veteran fishermen who attempt to solve the problem of extracting lunker bass, and to fishing families who can count on the lake's abundant big yellow perch to entertain the resident four-thumbed five-year old. Fishing for bass and panfish can be productive the year around.

The lake is connected to the ocean by Siltcoos River, which flows 2 miles to the sea. Through this channel the lake receives fair runs of salmon (mostly coho), sea-run cutthroat, and steelhead. Fishing for perch, brown bullhead, crappie, and bluegill is best in summer when most other species are hard to catch. Perch can

1. STROM PARK - Improved all-weather ramp, but no other facilities. Popular take-out after drifting from Morgan Park. Good lazy canoe water downstream. Fish for sea-run, fall chinook, summer & winter steelhead.

2. BULLS BAG

3. CAHILL - Good plunking hole.

4. BUTTERFIELD RIFFLE - River makes swing here; big eddy, gravel bottom.

5. BIG EDDY - County boat launch across private property; huge eddy in tidewater; some good drifts on outgoing tide.

6. CEDAR CREEK DRIFT - Last drift; close to highway.

7. BLACKBERRY HOLE - Plunking; good drift at lower end.

8. GRAVEL HOLE - Private; good boat drift.

9. MORGAN PARK - County boat ramp.

10. BLUFF HOLE - Fish the head of this one; solid rock, but gets snaggy further down; about 300 yds. below Swinging Bridge.

11. SWINGING BRIDGE HOLE - A few fishing shacks here.

12. HOLE JUST ABOVE SWINGING BRIDGE - Good boat hole; plunking at low water.

13. MITCHEL HOLE - Beautiful drift, best for boats.

14. FRENCH HOLE - Nice fishing for drifters and plunkers; walk down from road 150 ft.

15. EUCHRE CREEK HOLE - Mouth of Euchre Cr.

16. KUSYDOR DRIFT - Nice spot; calm edges with swift center.

17. SHOCK (OJOLLA) HOLE - Just below bridge. Good drift, fairly slow; fish both sides of river.

18. FIRST STEEL BRIDGE - Put-in just above bridge; you need a very long rope or cable to lower boat.

19. OLD MILL PARK BOAT RAMP - Just north of Siletz town center.

20. SECOND STEEL BRIDGE

21. HEE HEE ILAHEE PARK - Put-in for a 2-3 hr. drift. Take out at Old Mill Park, just a 15 minute walk across town.

22. SAMS CREEK BOAT RAMP - Mouth of Sams Creek.

23. MENONITE CHURCH - Put-in across from church.

24. LOGSDEN BRIDGE - Boat ramp above bridge; take road cross from store.

25. MOONSHINE COUNTY PARK - Boat ramp.

26. WILDCAT BRIDGE

27. LOWER GORGE - Road follows river accessing several miles of good fishing through mostly private property; avoid posted areas; *ask permission to fish when possible.*

28. STEEL BRIDGE

be caught throughout the lake, and yellow perch fishing, in particular, can be phenomenal.

The brown bullhead fishery is often very, very good. Although catfish are generally fished at night, this popular cat can be caught in large numbers in the early morning. Most bullhead anglers fish the bottom with worms. The best areas are only accessible by boat, including Butterfly Island, Goat Island, and the upper Fiddle Creek Arm.

Largemouth bass fishing varies with the weather and the month, but can be very good here. In 1988 no fewer than four bass tournaments took place on Siltcoos, including a Bass Classic. A lot of bass up to 8 pounds have been taken, particularly in the late winter and early spring with sculpin as bait. Plug fishermen wait until late spring, with early fall also good. The fishing is fine throughout the summer, though the size will not come up to early spring fishing. Bass angling is particularly good in the Booth Arm, Fiddle Creek Arm, and Harmony Bay.

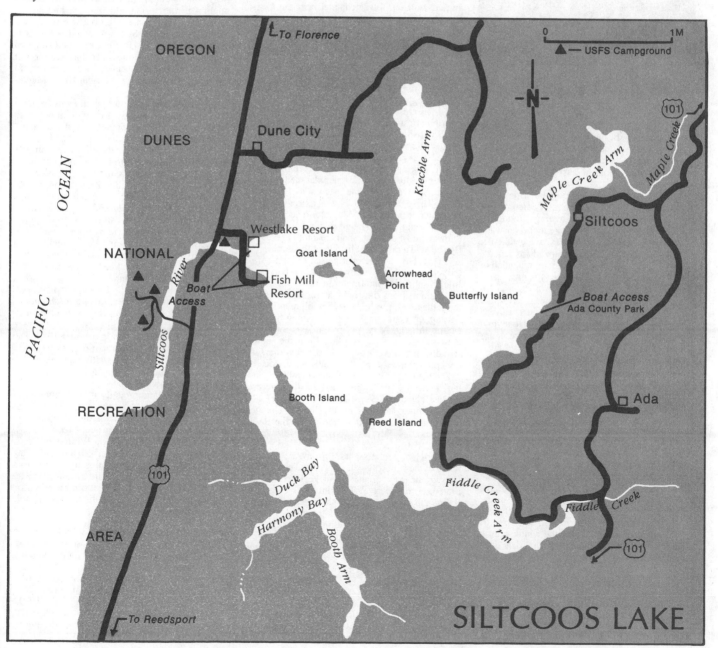

SILTCOOS LAKE

SIUSLAW WHARF
Michael LeFors, Photographer

Siltcoos is the best lake for native cutthroat in the area. In addition, 18,000 legal rainbow are stocked each spring. Six or seven pound holdovers aren't uncommon, and at least one 9 pounder has been taken in recent years. Best trout fishing is along the east shore and around Weber Island.

Trolling for coho is popular from mid-September through December. A catch of several hundred a year is the average, though in 1984 the catch in Siltcoos Lake and river was a whopping 1,091. Close to 400 were taken in 1986. A few chinook and steelhead are generally taken as well. These fish are apprehended on their spawning runs to tributary streams, usually in the Maple and Fiddle Creek arms.

There is a public boat ramp at Westlake, and another in a county park just north of Ada. Camping is available nearby at Honeyman State Park and at several forest service campgrounds on the Siltcoos River. There are a number of resorts on the lake, including Fish Mill Lodges and Westlake Resort, which offer cottage lodging, boat and motor rentals, tackle, supplies, and fishing tips. Fish Mill also has a trailer park with hook-ups. Supplies, good restaurants, and additional accommodations are available in Florence.

SILTCOOS RIVER The outlet stream of Siltcoos Lake, fished for sea-run cutthroat, salmon, and steelhead. About 7 miles south of Florence, and only 2 miles long, it carries a lot of fish traffic between the lake and the Pacific Ocean.

The Siltcoos offers good cutthroat fishing in early spring and again in fall. It's open for salmon and steelhead during the winter season, with coho showing the best. The fish don't come in until the water is high enough to breach the bar, usually around October. It's possible to fish by boat, but most anglers bank cast for coho.

There is a public boat ramp just north of Westlake. Westlake Resort and Fish Mill Lodges are situated on either side of the river's juncture with the lake. A large forest service campground complex is located along the river, with four separate campgrounds. The road into the campgrounds is a little over one mile south of the Westlake turnoff. These campgrounds generally support the dune buggy crowd. More camping is available at Honeyman State Park just north. There's good largemouth bass fishing in the river in late summer.

SIUSLAW BAY A good variety bay west of Eugene, providing fine clamming, crabbing, and fishing from late spring through fall. Hwy. 126 provides direct access from the Willamette Valley.

A lot of salmon are taken across the bar in season, with coho predominating. In 1986, the ocean sport salmon catch out of Florence was 13,692. Offshore fishing generally lasts from mid-June to October, whenever the bar is safe. The Siuslaw bar used to be a tough one, and even the current jetties don't guarantee easy passage. Bottom fish such as halibut and lingcod are sometimes taken by boat anglers just outside the bay. When the bar is closed, some anglers troll the lower channel near the Coast Guard lookout, but only the rare salmon is taken there.

In July the bay and tidewater come alive with sea-run cutthroat and jack salmon (both coho and chinook). These fish run to 18 inches, and the fishery holds up through August or September. Spinner and worm take most of the fish, but eggs drifted under bobbers work well, too. Flies are effective as the fish start moving up tributary streams.

Bay fishing for Coho and chinook is best in August and September. The best salmon angling in the bay is above Florence at the mouths of the North Fork and Siuslaw Rivers. Trolling with spinner and lure is the most popular method.

A good run of shad occurs in May and June. These are fished in the extreme upper tidewater area between Mapleton and Brickerville. Though trolling and jigging with small darts are most popular, shad are a lot of fun on a fly rod, and a tasty treat inspite of the bones.

This bay is the northernmost limit for striped bass. A few show up in February and March, following the smelt run in.

Fishing from the rocks along shore or off the jetties, will produce perch and greenling on shrimp or clam necks. Jetty fishing is best March through May, but rough seas may discourage access then. Angling from the jetties remains popular throughout the summer. A concrete pier east of the south jetty, locally called the Rock Dock, offers good crabbing and perch fishing. It was designed to allow access for less-abled anglers as well.

Crabbing is best in the lower channel around the coast guard station or off the Rock Dock, and is fair just above and below the Hwy. 101 Bridge.

For clam connoisseurs, Siuslaw Bay offers some of the best softshell flats on the coast. The flats to the west of the North Fork mouth are extremely productive. The flats to the east of the mouth produce fewer, but larger softshells. Cox Island, at the mouth of the Siuslaw, is a Nature Conservancy wildlife preserve, with good clam flats accessible only by boat.

At this writing there is only one boat ramp on the bay, near the 101 bridge at Florence. However, a ramp has been proposed for the mid-bay area north of Florence, just below the old marina. Good accommodations are available in the area, with many motels and campgrounds within a short distance. Several marinas near the bridge provide boat rentals, gas, tackle, bait, and other supplies.

SIUSLAW RIVER A good salmon and steelhead stream, heading in the Coast Range west of Eugene and Cottage Grove and flowing over 100 miles to the ocean near Florence. Not heavily fished, the Siuslaw produces from more than 2000 winter steelhead each year, along with a good number of fall salmon. A fish ladder at the falls on Lake Creek (a major tributary of the Siuslaw) is now under construction. Its completion will allow salmon access to an additional 100 miles of spawning ground above Triangle Lake, further enhancing the run.

The Siuslaw is approached from the Willamette Valley by driving west from Eugene on Hwy. 126 , which crosses the mainstem at Austa. From here one may turn downstream on a county road to Swisshome and the sea, upstream on a county road and a maze of logging roads that follow the river far into the hills, or continue on 126 to its intersection with Hwy. 36 at Mapleton.

The entire stream is open for trout during the regular season. The river is planted quite heavily with cutthroat. These fish provide good angling in the spring and fine sea-runs in the fall. The sea-run usually return in several runs during August and September, although occasionally they hit the river in one grand slug and scoot upriver before the word has time to get around. Angling for sea-run occurs mostly in the tidewater portion of the river (from Mapleton downstream).

Chinook and coho are taken from September through December. In 1986, more than 2,000 were caught, primarily in the area between Mapleton and the mouth of the Siuslaw.

The steelhead run gets into swing in late November and holds strong through February. Several good bank drifts and plunking holes are occupied by well chilled fishermen throughout the winter season. See the accompanying map for details. Drifting the lower river produces much of the catch. This stream is often murky in winter. If you get to the river and find this to be so, you might try fishing Lake Creek, which is usually clear and a good steelhead producer.

Shad run up the Siuslaw in respectable numbers in May and June. Most angling effort is concentrated between Mapleton and Brickerville, but the fish get as far up as Swisshome.

There are many boat ramps on the main river, including a new public ramp at Tiernan, scheduled for completion in summer 1989. The Siuslaw is a wide, fast stream requiring skillful and cautious boating, especially in the upper areas. Guide service is available in Eugene, Swisshome, and Florence.

There are campgrounds at Honeyman State Park on the coast, Knowles Creek (USFS) about 3 miles east of Mapleton, Linslaw Park (county) at Linslaw, Turner Creek (BLM) 2miles east of Richardson, Whittaker Creek (BLM) 1.5 miles south of Austa, and Clay Creek (BLM) about 10 miles upstream from Whittaker Creek. Supplies are available at Mapleton and Florence, and at several marinas on the lower river. Accommodations are available in Florence.

SIUSLAW RIVER, NORTH FORK A coastal trout stream with a fair run of winter steelhead. This good size tributary of the Siuslaw River enters Siuslaw Bay just east of Florence. The river is paralleled by a good paved road that runs north from Hwy. 126 about one mile east of Florence. The upper river can also be reached from Hwy. 36 at Firo on FS 5070, which crosses the river at the Minerva logging camp.

SIUSLAW RIVER

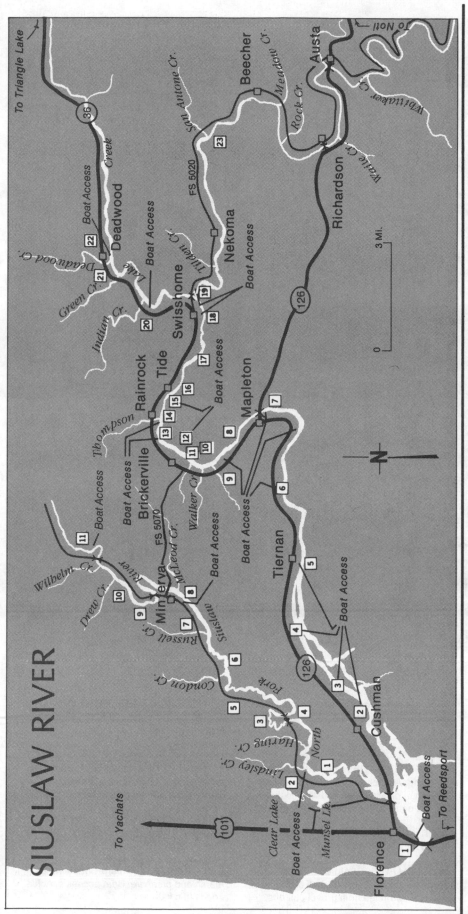

NORTHWEST

SIUSLAW NORTH FORK

1. WALKER BRIDGE - Two miles up North Fork River Rd. from Hwy. 126; mostly plunked from bridge.

2. BENDER LANDING - County park with concrete boat ramp. Good plunking from bank.

3. PORTAGE LOOP - River makes 2-mile loop about 5.6 miles above Hwy. 126. Good fishing, good walking. Road follows about one mile. *Respect private property; ask permission to fish.*

4. FUNKE BRIDGE - Good plunking hole beneath second bridge on Portage LOOP. Room for eight anglers on both sides of stream. *Respect private property; ask permission to fish.*

5. DAVIDSON RANCH - Easy fishing from bridge and for 2 miles above and below; 8 miles up N. Fk. Rd. *Respect private property; ask permission to fish.*

6. HUNTINGTON BRIDGE - Just above mouth of Condon Cr. Lots of open fishing above and below bridge. *Respect private property; ask permission to fish.*

7. CEDAR HOLE - Large deep plunking hole by big cedar tree. 9 miles up. *Respect private property; ask permission to fish.*

8. HOUGHTON LANDING - Just down from guard rail. Good plunking hole with public boat access 9.6 miles up.

9. SMITH CUT BRIDGE - First bridge above concrete (Meadow) bridge. Good plunking hole.

10. GARBAGE HOLE - First time you can actually see river after leaving Smith Cut Bridge. Next 10 miles is accessible, mostly good fast moving water. 13 miles up.

SIUSLAW MAINSTEM

1. HOLIDAY HARBOR - Paved public boat ramp.

2. SIUSLAW MARINA - Hoist facility 4 miles east of Florence.

3. CUSHMAN MARINA - Gravel ramp 3 miles east of Florence.

4. MIDWAY DOCK - Hoist facility.

5. TIERNAN BOAT ACCESS - ODFW ramp.

6. C&D DOCK - Hoist Facility.

7. MAPLETON LANDING - Paved public boat ramp.

8. DOLLAR HOLE - Head of tidewater.

9. FARNAM RIFFLE - Good drift from boat. Plunking just below Farnam Landing boat slide. Picnic area at Landing. About 2 miles above Mapleton.

10. WALKER RIFFLE - Good drift from boat, just down from guard rail, 2.5 miles above Mapleton.

11. GAUGING STATION HOLE - Good deep plunking hole 3 miles above Mapleton.

12. BRICKERVILLE - Primitive boat slide. Take trail to river just above last house above Brickerville. Good plunking hole; fish close to bank.

13. 4 VERY GOOD HOLES - Along edge of highway; includes fair boat access site. Good plunking; fast water above and below. From 4.2-4.6 miles above Mapleton.

14. RAINROCK HOLE - Extremely popular and productive plunking water. Watch for long, wide highway shoulder just below Thompson Creek. Fair boat access.

15. TIDE WAYSIDE - County park with boat ramp 5.9 miles above Mapleton, across from Big Red's Market.

16. RED HILL HOLE AND DRIFT - Just before railroad crossing. Several good holes and drifts, 6 1/2 miles above Mapleton.

17. MILL HOLE AND DRIFT - Walk back through mill to river, about one mile of fishing, 7 miles above Mapleton.

18. CHURCH HOLE - Turn off highway at Evangelical Church in Swisshome, keep to right after railroad tracks. Good drifts from boat and bank. Unimproved boat access. *Private property; ask permission to fish.*

19. SAND HOLE - Just below railroad bridge that crosses river at Swisshome, at mouth of Lake Creek. Sand bar a good place to put up wind break and build a fire. Boat slide on north side.

20. INDIAN CREEK - Hole just below creek; boat ramp.

21. GREEN CR. HOLE - Good drift from boat and bank.

22. DEADWOOD CR. BOAT ACCESS - Popular driftboat launch site; good holes for 5 miles upstream to greenleaf Cr.

23. SWISSHOME TO RICHARDSON BRIDGE - 12 miles of beautiful water, easily accessible; mostly bank fished, but some boat access.

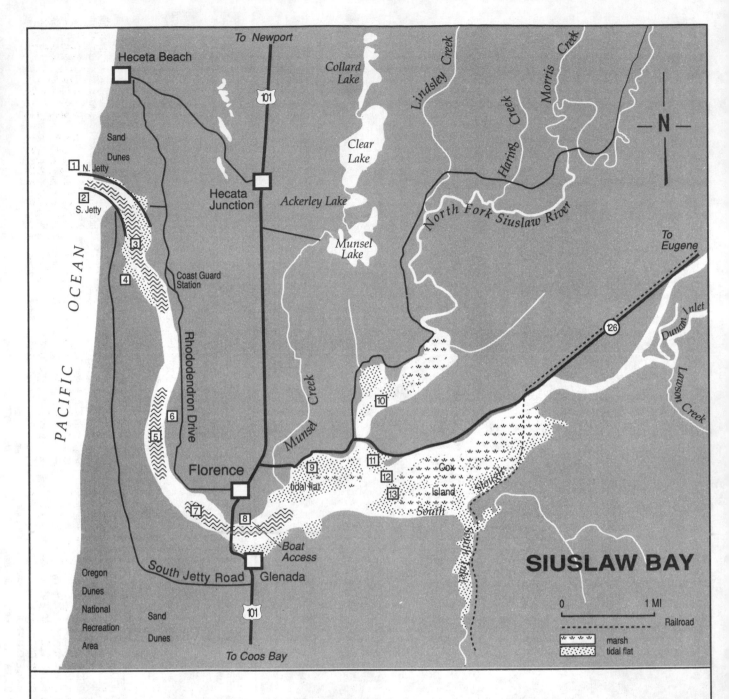

SIUSLAW BAY

0   1 MI

- - - - Railroad

marsh

tidal flat

1. NORTH JETTY - Fish for redtail perch, greenling spring and summer. Best Mar. through May, but rough seas may limit access.

2. SOUTH JETTY - Fish for redtail, greenling.

3. Lower Channel - Best crabbing in the bay on in-coming tide. Some perch fishing, rare salmon taken.

4. THE ROCK DOCK - Concrete pier popular for crabbing, some perch. Less-abled angler access.

5. FLOUNDER HOLE - Few flounder these days, but still a good hole for perch. Good crabbing in vicinity, too.

6. BEACH - Bank fishery for perch.

7. UPPER CHANNEL - Fair late sumer crabbing. Anchor among pilings and fish the run of pinkfin perch mid-May to July, striped perch and pile perch year around.

8. CITY DOCKS AND BOAT RAMP - Crab & fish for perch. Public campground.

9. NORTH FORK CLAM BED, West - Tremendous producer of softshell clams. Access below bridge from gravel pull-offs.

10. MOUTH OF THE NORTH FORK - Troll or cast lures to head of tide (3 miles to Portage) for sea-run July through Sept., salmon Aug. through Nov.

11. NORTH FORK CLAM BED, East - Dig for larger, but less numerous softshell clams. Access from pull-off below bridge.

12. MOUTH OF THE SIUSLAW - Troll to Mapleton for sea-run and salmon, Aug. & Sept.

13. COX ISLAND - Nature Conservancy marshland preserve. Boat access only for good clam flats.

About 25 miles long and 30-50 feet wide, it is not heavily fished. The bottom is primarily bedrock, sand, and gravel and there is little cover for fish. Nevertheless, between 100 and 500 winter steelhead are taken here each year, and about 200 fall salmon. The North Fork is a fair early season cutthroat stream for both wild and hatchery trout. A good number of sea-run turn in from the main river in fall. The North Fork is exclusively a bank fishery, as the river is to small for boats.

Camping facilities are available at Honeyman State Park just south of Florence, or at North Fork Siuslaw Campground about 3 miles upstream from Minerva.

SKOOKUM LAKE (Tillamook Co.) A small lake about 10 miles SW of Tillamook at the head of Fawcett Creek, in the Tillamook river watershed. It is a reservoir for Tillamook City Water and is closed to public fishing.

SLUSHER LAKE A 20 acre bass and panfish lake at Camp Rilea. The public is welcome to fish when the Guard is not holding maneuvers. The lake contains largemouth bass, yellow perch, and brown bullhead.

SMITH LAKE (Clatsop Co.) A long, narrow, shallow lake at the junction of the Hammond Rd. with Hwy. 101, about 2 miles south of Warrenton. It is on the west side of 101. It contains crappie, bluegill, brown bullhead, perch, and largemouth bass. Fish it early in the season, as it has a severe weed problem. In fact, weeds have diminished a very good bass fishery here. Bank access is limited. This is another lake to try while camping at Fort Stevens State Park. See also cullaby.

SMITH LAKE (Tillamook County) A fairly small lake north of Tillamook Bay on Hwy. 101, west of the highway just north of Barview. The lake covers 35 acres, and is relatively free of aquatic weeds. The central area of the lake averages 8-12 ft. deep.

Smith is occasionally stocked with legal rainbow in spring. It's a good prospect for early season angling with bait and lures fished from the bank. It also contains brown bullhead and largemouth bass. The bass haven't done well, but bullhead are plentiful and receive little pressure.

Boat launching is a problem, although a boat is not necessarily needed. A church camp located on the lake discourages use of motors because of children in row boats.

SOAPSTONE LAKE A small cutthroat lake in the North Fork of the Nehalem drainage, whose outlet is Soapstone Creek. To reach it (good luck), drive to the Necanicum junction on Hwy. 26, SW of Cannon Beach, then turn south on Hwy. 53. After about 8 miles and just before crossing the North Fork, turn NE onto Coal Ridge Rd. At about 1.5 miles you can spot the lake to the north. It's a 20 minute walk to lake.

Soapstone covers 10 acres and is over 20 ft. deep. Full of brush and snags, it can be fished for native cutthroat with flies, bait, or lures from the many logs that jut into the lake. It's usually a good early season lake.

SOUTH LAKE A 5 acre trout lake just south of Hebo Lake, about one mile from Hebo Ranger Station on the forest road west from the junction of Hwy. 14 and 101. Check at the sport shop at Hebo for exact location.

Occasionally stocked with rainbow catch a-

bles, it's not generally accessible until mid-May, as the road is usually full of mudholes. The lake has a lot of crayfish, which are a good choice for bait fishing. It's full of snags, so bring along plenty of tackle. It's a good lake to try along with Hebo Lake.

SPRING LAKE (a.k.a. Ocean Lake) A 13 acre put-and-take rainbow fishery and bass lake, about 1/2 mile north of Barview north of Tillamook Bay. It is just east of Hwy. 101 near Twin Rocks. You might be able to get a raft in, but most angling is done from the bank along the highway. Bass fishing is fair.

SPRUCE RUN LAKE A small lake south of Elsie in the coast range, about 70 miles from Portland. To get there see Lost Lake. Spruce Run is about 1/2 mile SE of it. Spruce Run heads Spruce Run Creek and has lots of small native cutthroat trout. Only 3 acres, it is brushy and hard on tackle.

SUNSET LAKE (a.k.a Neacoxie Lake) A very long, narrow lake, popular for bass, trout, and panfish. It is just west of Hwy. 101 in the resort area about 4 miles north of Gearhart. To get there, take the road west from Hwy. 101 just north of the Cullaby Lake junction. This road crosses over the north end of Sunset Lake.

Sunset is about 2 miles long and less than 500 ft wide. It covers about 110 acres, with lots of water over 15 feet deep, offering good early season fishing for stocked rainbow. Best trout catches are made from mid-lake to the south end, where the water is deepest.

Good size largemouth bass are also present. The best bass fishing is below the narrows, in the small pockets on the west shore. The lake also contains yellow perch, crappie, and brown bullhead. Spin casting from shore can net both crappie and trout. Boats can be launched at the county ramp on the north side of the bridge. Public parking is available on the west shore near the bridge. There's a resort near the bridge.

SUTTON LAKE Two fair size bodies of water connected by a narrow channel, with a total area of about 100 acres. It is located on the east side of Hwy. 101 about 6 miles north of Florence. Sutton has a few native cutthroat and is stocked heavily in spring with legal rainbow. It's a good panfish lake, with strong populations of yellow perch and largemouth bass. This is a nice recreational area, and the lake is not fished hard. There is a large Forest Service campground on Sutton Creek about 1/4 mile west of the lake, and a boat ramp off Hwy. 101.

SWEET CREEK A small stream with native cutthroat and steelhead, entering the Siuslaw River about 10 miles upstream from Florence. It can be reached by Hwy. 36 and a county road which follows it south. The creek is fair for cutthroat in early spring, and a few return as sea-run in the fall. It is not stocked. It has a fair steelhead run for a creek this size, with fishing from December to March. Over a hundred steelhead are caught some years, but 1985-86 saw only 11 taken, and the 1984-85 catch was 32. Sweet Creek does not have good public access, so ask permission to fish.

TAHKENITCH LAKE A good, large coastal lake 5 miles south of Siltcoos Lake, potentially as productive as Siltcoos, but less popular. It covers more than 1500 acres, located just east of Hwy. 101, about 13 miles south of Florence.

Everyone in the family can catch fish here, but you'll need a boat. The shore is too brushy for bank angling. Best fishing is for bluegill, yellow perch, and crappie, and there is a catch and release season for largemouth bass. Bluegill 5-7 inches are very plentiful. Kids love to fish for them on bobber and worm, and a fly rod with poppers can be fun. Yellow perch can be found along the shore line and on the bottom in deeper water.

Tahkenitch is a good largemouth bass lake, especially for the beginner. The fish are right where they should be, along the shoreline, around the weed beds, and near any structure. The lake has extensive weed beds around its perimeter. Weedless plugs and spinners produce well.

There's a small native cutthroat population, and legal rainbow are stocked each year. A few steelhead are also taken each winter. A small run of coho enters the lake in November and the salmon are taken on troll.

There are public boat ramps on the Hwy. 101 right-of-way and at Tahkenitch Landing Campground. A resort at the creek mouth provides rental boats, motors, and tackle. The lake is served by two good size campgrounds, one across the highway from the lake and one at Tahkenitch Landing.

TENMILE CREEK (Lane Co.) A good little stream for winter fishing. It is 15 miles south of Waldport, crossed at its mouth by Hwy. 101. The creek is about 11 miles long and runs from 15-30 ft. wide. There is plenty of cover for fish, but it can be hard on tackle.

The stream is no longer stocked, but remains a good producer of wild cutthroat early in season and late in the fall. This little stream actually had a run of over a thousand winter steelhead in 1972, but the catch has declined sadly. The catch in recent years has fluctuated between 50 and 200.

There's a lot of private land here, so ask permission before you fish. A good road follows the stream almost to its source and eventually ties in with Indian Creek Rd heading north from the Hwy. 36. There's a campground 5 miles upstream from Hwy. 101, and a state park with camping 4 miles south of the river mouth on 101.

THREE RIVERS A good salmon, steelhead, and cutthroat stream, tributary to the Big Nestucca. Three Rivers enters the Nestucca about 1/2 mile north of Hebo. A medium size stream, only about 14 miles long, it nevertheless carries a lot of water. The mouth is near the junction of hwys. 101 and 14, and Hwy. 14 follows it south towards Dolph.

Three Rivers is a good cutthroat stream in spring and is stocked with trout. Boulders, gravel, and undercut banks make it good fly water. It can be easily waded.

Fall chinook and coho come up river in October. The heaviest steelhead run is in late December and January, depending on water conditions. Easily fished from the bank, Three Rivers has some nice gravel drifts where yarn and eggs are effective. The mouth of Three Rivers is an ideal hole for all species and is very popular. The 1985-86 winter steelhead catch in Three Rivers was 1473, and the previous year's take was 2694. The annual fall salmon catch is considerably smaller, less than 200 total most years.

There is a public landing at the mouth of Three Rivers, but much of the lower area is private property, so get permission before you fish. Supplies and accommodations are available at Hebo, and there is a campground about 5 miles south of Hebo on Hwy. 14.

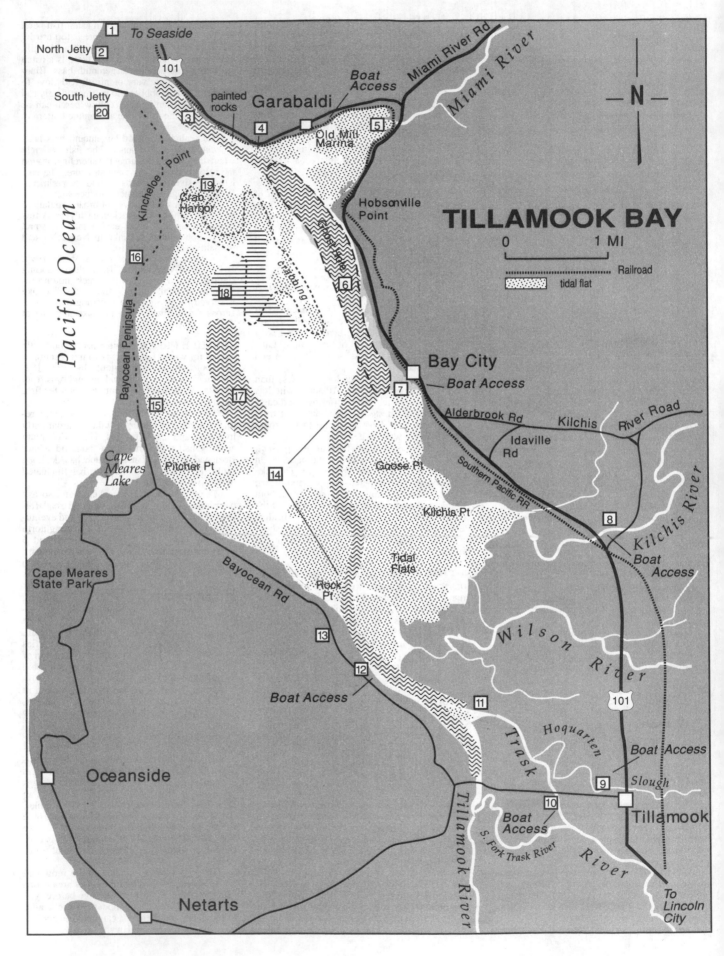

To Seaside

North Jetty

South Jetty

101

painted rocks

Garabaldi

Boat Access

Miami River Rd

Miami River

Kincheloe Point

Crab Harbor

Old Mill Marina

Hobsonville Point

TILLAMOOK BAY

0   1 MI

.... Railroad

tidal flat

crabbing

Goose Hole

Bay City

Boat Access

Alderbrook Rd

Kilchis   River Road

Idaville Rd

Southern Pacific RR

Kilchis River

Boat Access

Pacific Ocean

Bayocean Peninsula

Cape Meares Lake

Pitcher Pt

Goose Pt

Kilchis Pt

Tidal Flats

Wilson River

Cape Meares State Park

Bayocean Rd

Rock Pt

Oceanside

Boat Access

Trask

Hoquarten

101

Boat Access

Slough

Boat Access

S. Fork Trask River

Tillamook River

Tillamook

Netarts

River

To Lincoln City

1. **BARVIEW PARK** - County park with camping, RV hook-ups. Fish off the rock fill for perch.
2. **NORTH JETTY** - Fish for rockfish, some perch, salmon off furthest point.
3. **LOWER MAIN CHANNEL** - troll for salmon. Fish the rock outcrops for greenling and perch.
4. **OLD COAST GUARD PIER** - Dig the flats for clams. Fish for crab from the pier. Limited parking.
5. **MOUTH OF THE MIAMI** - Bank fishing below railroad bridge for fall chinook, chum salmon.
6. **GHOST HOLE** - Popular for salmon, perch, sturgeon at upper end, pile perch off Hobsonville Pt. Hole has 20-35 ft. depth.
7. **BAY CITY RAMP** - Unimproved public ramp with poor access at low tide.
8. **PARKS LANDING** - Improved ramp is lowest take-out on Kilchis. Provides bay access for car-top boats, but not at low water.
9. **HOQUARTEN SLOUGH** - Boat Ramp on First St. Accesses Hoquarten & Dougherty sloughs & lower Trask. Shallow at low tides. Fish sloughs for fall chinook in low water years.
10. **CARNAHAN PARK RAMP** - Improved ramp at end of 5th St., City of Tillamook, accesses lower Trask tidewater and upper bay. Heavily used.
11. **MOUTH OF THE TRASK** - Troll for sea-run; sturgeon hole.
12. **MEMALOOSE PT.** (Oyster House Hole) - Improved county ramp accesses mouth of Tillamook salmon fishery.
13. **BAY OCEAN RD.** - Bank fishing for fall chinook from pilings along main channel.
14. **UPPER MAIN CHANNEL** - Troll for salmon.
15. **MUD FLATS** - Hike across flats at low tide to fish for sturgeon. Beware of rising tide and soft mud.
16. **BAY OCEAN TRAIL** - 3 mile bike or hike on gravel road to South Jetty.
17. **OLD CHANNEL** - Sporadic sturgeon fishing; channel is 8-10 ft. deep.
18. **CLAM FLATS** - boat access.
19. **CRAB HARBOR** - Well sheltered, popular.
20. **SOUTH JETTY** - Less angling pressure, but more wind & rougher sea. Fish for perch, salmon, rockfish. Use bigger bait for ling cod. Night fish for sea bass.

THREEMILE LAKE A fair size dune lake that features good perch and cutthroat angling for the determined angler. The lake is in the Oregon Dunes National Recreation Area about one mile NW of the northernmost reach of Winchester Bay. It shows up quite well on the recreation area map available from the US Forest Service.

About 1 1/2 miles north of Gardiner on Hwy. 101, County Rd. 247 heads west along Threemile Creek (which does NOT flow from or into the lake). Follow the road to within 1/2 mile of the ocean, and hike north about .7 mile to the lake. Threemile has yellow perch which run to 14 inches and cutthroat over 14 inches, but it's a bear to fish without a boat. It's a good place for a raft or float tube.

TILLAMOOK BAY Oregon's second largest bay, exceeded in size only by Coos Bay. Fall salmon are the featured attraction, both off shore and in the bay, along with year around crabbing and perch. Garibaldi is the port town. One of the closest bays to Portland, it is surrounded by good roads, and almost any spot on shore can be reached by car and a short walk. Tillamook Bay is also home to one of the Northwest's largest concentrations of waterfowl.

From the Willamette Valley, the bay is about 1 1/2 hrs. drive. From Portland, follow Hwy. 26 west to Banks, then Hwy. 6 to Tillamook. Turn south on Hwy. 101, which skirts the bay on its east and north shores. Bay Ocean Rd. follows the south and west shores.

Garibaldi is a major port for Oregon's ocean salmon fishery, especially popular since ocean salmon angling has been restricted to the waters south of Tillamook Head. Ocean fishing for salmon starts in June and July and holds up through September. About 80% of the catch is coho, which are small in spring, going 5-7 pounds, but get up to 12-14 pounds by September. In 1986 the Garibaldi ocean salmon sport catch was 18,885.

Tillamook bar can be quite dangerous to cross, so keep your eye on weather conditions, and be extremely careful. Small boats can only expect to get outside about 25 percent of the time, even in summer. Charter boats operate out of Garibaldi regularly, both for salmon and ocean bottom fish. The best spot outside is usu-

TILLAMOOK BAY CHINOOK
Courtesy, *Headlight-Herald*, Tillamook

ally just south of the whistler buoy, about a mile beyond the bar.

First fishing in the bay in spring is for various surf and bottom fish, though even in January and February, casting from the rocks or jetties from the Barview area to Bay City can produce lingcod, rock fish, and perch. The North Jetty is the more protected of the two for early season outings. Later, perch and greenling are also fished from boats near the rock outcrops of the lower main channel, off the rocks at Barview Park near the mouth, and at the Old Garibaldi Coast Guard Pier, which is open for public angling. It extends 700 feet into the bay and is also used for crabbing and, at the end, a chance for salmon. South jetty anglers take ling cod on bigger bait, or night fish for sea bass. Ling cod are also taken in the Barview area by boaters drifting herring. Common bottom fish baits are shrimp, clam necks, and kelp worms.

Park-and-fish spots are available off Hwy. 101 from Bay City north to Hobsonville Point, an area that skirts the famous Ghost Hole, a popular salmon trolling area accessed by boats from the Bay City public ramp, and from Old Mill Marina.

Salmon angling in the bay usually starts in earnest in April, and for a month or two spring chinook are caught as they make their way toward the mouths of the Wilson and Trask. Five good size rivers empty into Tillamook Bay, the Wilson, Trask, Miami, Kilchis, and Tillamook. From 50 to 300 spring chinook are taken in the bay each year.

From August till late October, fall chinook then coho are available inside. In 1986, 4,776 fall chinook and 5,378 coho were taken in the bay itself. Boat anglers troll the lower main channel, the Ghost Hole, and the upper channel as well as the mouth of the Tillamook River. Herring, either whole or plug cut, is popular bait.

The Ghost Hole, just south of Hobsonville Point, is a favorite spot for large chinook. An occasional steelhead is picked up by lure trollers late in the season, but the prime quarry is the large fall chinook, which can weigh over fifty pounds.

Sturgeon angling has picked up in recent years, with best catches in the Ghost Hole, off the mouth of the Trask, and off the Bay Ocean Flats. These sturgeon are presumed to be migrants from the Columbia River, though old timers say there are stugeon in Tillamook Bay the year around. Best catches are made from mid-February to mid-April.

Crabbing is good year around with best catches in the winter. Most crabbers work in Crab Harbor off the Bay Ocean Peninsula. Crab rings are available for rent at Old Mill Marina, which also sells bait and keeps a crab cooker steaming.

For clamming, Tillamook Bay is hard to beat. Almost the entire perimeter of the bay has extensive clam beds. All the main species of clams can be gathered here, although razors are getting scarce. The tidal flats throughout the bay produce large numbers of gaper, cockles, and softshells on a zero or less tide. Littleneck clams and butter clams are generally found in the northern bay, while the gaper or blue clam is found all over. The southern bay has primarily softshell clams. Check the regulations carefully before digging, as its easy to get the limit.

Herring are plentiful in the bay at times from spring through fall. Fishermen use herring jigs to catch them for bait and eating. A shad run appears in June.

Moorages and supplies are plentiful around three sides of the bay. Free public ramps are located at Bay City, Parks Landing on the Kilchis, Hoquarten Slough and Carnahan Park in Tillamook, and Memaloose Pt. on the Bay Ocean Peninsula. The ramp at Old Mill Marina in Garibaldi is open to public use for a small fee and provides good access to the Ghost Hole and lower bay. The channel from Old Mill is dredged throughout the year. Old Mill main-

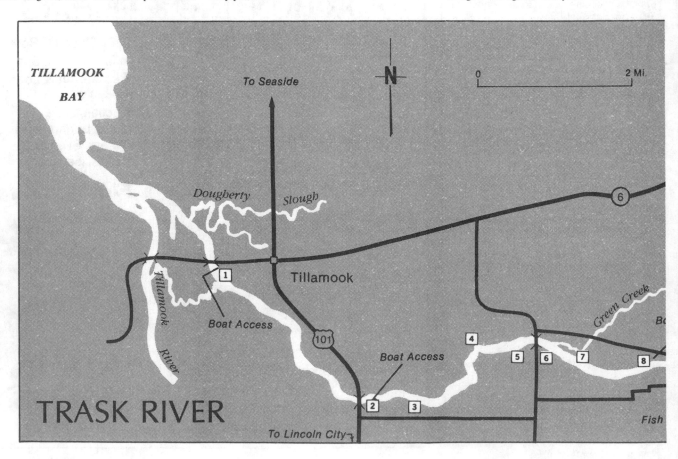

tains a fish cleaning station at its dock, open to public use. There is also a tackle and bait shop on the dock, and a restaurant that features chowder and fresh fish (yours or theirs). For campers, there is a big county park at Barview and another just up the Kilchis River. About 12 miles south, Lookout State Park has an excellent campground with lots of space. The RV park at Old Mill Marina is a membership park.

TILLAMOOK RIVER A tributary of Tillamook Bay, flowing from the south and entering the bay near the Trask River. It offers good plunking and trolling for sea-run cutthroat in tidewater. There is virtually no public access to the upper river except at the Hwy. 101 rest area, and a few fee-pay spots nearby. It is about 14 miles long.

The Tillamook can be good for native cutthroat trout and hatchery plants, stocked each summer. Sea-run provides a lot of action from July through September in the tidewater reach. The river is best for plunking, as it has very few riffles or boulder areas. A few white sturgeon are taken each year, usually by surprised cutthroat plunkers.

More salmon and steelhead are caught here than in the Miami, but less than in the Kilchis. Fall chinook show in late September and October. Coho move in about a month later. Cluster eggs work well, and there's always the chance of taking jack salmon. Steelhead fishing is best from late December to January.

Burton Bridge Boat Ramp on the Tillamook River Road provides access to the tidewater. Supplies and accommodations are available at Tillamook.

TRASK RIVER A very good steelhead and salmon river. The Trask is a large stream, about 50 miles long, entering Tillamook Bay at Tillamook just south of the Wilson River. It is crossed by Hwy. 101 at the head of tidewater, and both the mainstem and the north and south forks are followed by county and state forest roads.

It has lots of boulders and gravel stretches with some excellent fly water. The north fork is an exceptionally pretty fly stream. The south fork was ravaged by a forest fire in 1951 and was closed for a number of years but has now come back. In fact, the Tillamook Burn is officially healed, and the river reflects the forest's good health. Though the Trask still muddies, it clears quickly, and it no longer drops early now that the forest is holding.

---

1. TIDEWATER ACCESS - City of Tillamook boat ramp at end of Fifth St. near sewage treatment plant; accesses tidewater fisheries.

2. LOWER TRASK ACCESS - Paved ramp and bank angling at good salmon, steelhead hole. Drive in off Long Prairie Rd.

3. SLAUGHTER HOLE - Pay to fish good salmon hole below railroad bridge in fall. Park at slaughter house.

4. BEALER HOLE - boat fishery at big salmon hole.

5. HOLDEN DRIFT - Walk down from Johnson Bridge. *Private property; ask permission to fish from bank.*

6. JOHNSON BRIDGE DRIFT - Good salmon, steelhead drift just above bridge. *Private property; ask permission to fish from bank.*

7. ROCK HOLE - Bedrock chute drops into good salmon hole; anchor on south side; steelhead drift. *Private property; boat fishing only.*

8. LOREN'S DRIFT - ODFW public access boat ramp, slide, 1/4 mile bank access.

9. HANENKRAT DRIFT - Bank fish long stretch of good water off Chance Rd. just below fish hatchery. No longer a put-in. *Check for hatchery deadline and closures.*

10. MAPLE TREE HOLE - Good steelhead hole and two deep salmon holes. Trask River Rd. provides good access from here upstream. Steep bank demands sturdy legs. Good drift water.

11. CABLE CAR DRIFT - Overhead cable crossing. River widens and slows here; wade out and cast to opposite bank. *Private property; ask permission to bank fish.*

12. MOUTH OF CEDAR CREEK - Unimproved ramp, but useable. Drift down to Loren's.

13. WILDLIFE HOLE - Steep bank, good holes. About 1/4 mile of bank access.

14. DAM HOLE - Salmon and steelhead plunking. *Check for deadline and closures.*

15. LOWER PENINSULA BOAT LAUNCH

16. UPPER PENINSULA BOAT LAUNCH

17. STONE CAMP POLE SLIDE - Drift down to Upper or Lower Peninsula. Road leads in through Campfire camp opposite cut-off to Wilson River.

18. GIRL SCOUT BRIDGE

19. TRASK RIVER PARK

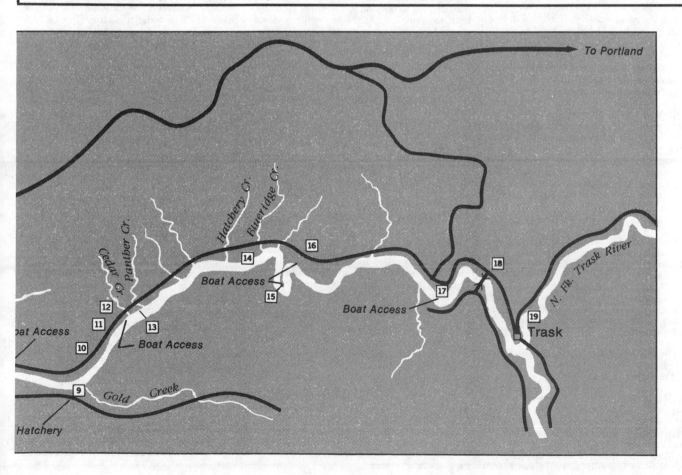

The Trask is managed primarily for wild steelhead. They are in the river year around, but the winter run is by far the larger. From 200-500 summer steelhead are caught each year (244 in 1986). The winter run begins building in December and holds through March, with annual catches often over 2000 (1245 in 1985-86).

There is a major fall chinook run on the Trask, with the annual catch almost always over 3,000. Spring chinook appear in the river in April, with the run peaking in June and annual catch around 500. the Trask is also a very good cutthroat stream. It is stocked lightly in early spring, and its sea-run return as early as July. A shad run usually appears in the lower river in June and July.

Flood level on the Trask is similar to that of the Wilson, 11 cubic ft. per second, with best fishing at 6 cfs, and acceptable levels between 5.3 and 7 cfs. Use the Wilson River as a gauge to determine the level of the Trask. The current Wilson River reading is available by calling ODFW Portland Information Line, or (503) 249-0666.

TRIANGLE LAKE Popular for bass, panfish, kokanee, and trout. This 290 acre lake is west of Blachly on Hwy. 36, about 23 miles west of Junction City. It can be r eached from the coast by Hwy. 36 from Florence.

A very popular lake because of its proximity to the Willamette Valley, it provides good numbers of bass and panfish throughout spring and summer. Bluegill are most plentiful, and there are brown bullhead, perch, and largemouth bass. Most fish are taken on simple bait, but evening fly fishing and plugging can produce some nice bass. Its tributaries supply a good population of native cutthroat. Kokanee are well established. Fish deep for these landlocked sockeye salmon.

There is a county boat ramp with plenty of parking. Water skiers abound in summer, so best fishing is early and late in the day, which suits the bass just fine anyway.

VERNONIA LAKE This popular 45 acre former mill pond is located at the south end of the town of Vernonia. It has a population of bluegill, largemouth bass, and perch. Currently perch and bluegill overpopulate the lake, with corresponding decreases in average size. The lake is stocked with legal size rainbow once a year to provide early season fishing. It has good bank access. Boats are allowed, but motors are prohibited.

WEST LAKE A fair bass and panfish lake just 3 miles north of Gearhart, east of Hwy. 101. The highway follows its western shore, and a county road follows the western shore. About 1/2 mile long, it is similar in character and fishing to Sunset, Cullaby, and South. It contains good size perch and crappie, and fair size bluegill. Largemouth bass are available, with a few 2 pounds or better.

WESTPORT SLOUGH An extensive slough area with over 15 species of bass and panfish, located just north and east of Westport on Hwy. 30, 10 miles west of Clatskanie on the lower Columbia. A number of bridges and county roads provide good access. The slough mouth can be reached by going north on the Columbia from Woodson Boat Ramp, or from the public ramp at Westport.

It has lots of white and black crappie, and fair numbers of bluegill, brown bullhead, and yellow perch. This is excellent largemouth bass water, with bass to 7 pounds taken on plugs and spinners.

WILSON RIVER Consistently one of the Top Ten producers of salmon and steelhead on the Oregon coast, a popular and accessible river that enters Tillamook Bay. It flows through Coast Range timberland then out across the bucolic Tillamook Valley, where black and white cows graze beside its banks. It is followed closely by Hwy. 6, also known as the Wilson River Rd., which runs west from Forest Grove west of Portland.

Salmon and steelhead are taken from the Wilson the year around. The winter run picks up in December and holds through March. The summer run picks up in May and carries through August. Close to 3000 winter steelhead were caught in 1985-86, and 800 summer run.

Chinook are available about 6 months of the year. The Wilson has both spring and fall runs, though the spring run is considerably smaller. Spring chinook generally enter the stream in April, and the catch peaks in June and July. A much larger fall chinook run begins in October and peaks in November. The 1986 catch was close to 3,000.

For sea-run cutthroat, the Wilson is a fly fisherman's dream. Riffles can be fished successfully with spruce fly, bucktail coachman, caddis, and practically any good streamer. Sea-run appear after the middle of July. Access is from pull-offs on Hwy. 6. The banks can be steep, with some bushwhacking necessary.

There is excellent access to bank fishable waters below the forks at Fall Creek, Herd Hole, Kansas Creek Bridge, Lee's Bridge, Mining Creek, Siskeyville, and Zig Zag Creek. Boat drifting is popular in the lower 10 miles from the ramp at Siskeyville, about 2 miles above Mills Bridge, with take-out at Solly Smith Bridge about one mile east of Tillamook. Supplies and accommodations are available at Tillamook and at several places along the river.

The South Fork Wilson River enters the mainstream 3-4 miles above Lee's Camp (on Hwy. 6). The South Fork Rd. keeps pace with the fork up to the South Fork Prison Camp. At this time, the South Fork is open only for trout fishing. Above the South Fork confluence, the mainstream Wilson is popularly known as the Devil's Lake Fork. It is restricted to fly fishing only. The Devil's Lake Fork is followed by Hwy. 6. Gravel pull-offs indicate popular river access points. All tributaries of the Wilson are currently open to trout angling after many years' closure. Check current angling regulations.

WOAHINK LAKE A large lake with fair fishing, whose shoreline forms the eastern boundary of Honeyman State Park, 3 miles south of Florence. Woahink is very popular for water sports and recreation, but the water isn't very productive for fishing. It covers 350 acres and receives plants of legal rainbow each spring. It also has native cutthroat and a fair largemouth bass population. There are two excellent boat ramps at the north end of the lake, and camping at the state park.

YACHATS RIVER Pronounced *yaw-hots*. A small coastal river with typical coastal fishing, entering the ocean just south of the town of Yachats, and crossed by Hwy. 101 near its mouth. Only about 15 miles long, it ranges from 30-50 feet wide. A good road, County Rd. 804, follows the main stream and both forks for most of their length.

The Yachats has a fair population of native cutthroat and some good sea-run angling in late summer and early fall. It produces up to a couple hundred steelhead in better years, along with some coho salmon and a scattering of chinook. Coho usually are best in late October and November, and steelhead are caught from late November through March. Most steelhead angling takes place in the lower few miles.

Nearby Beachside State Park, on the ocean about 4 miles north, is the site of a unique surf smelt fishery in the late spring. This is quite an occasion and the focus of an annual local festival. Smelt are caught with frame nets worked by hand in the flow over the sands.

There is lot of posted land on the stream. Camping facilities are available at state parks north and south on Hwy. 101, or in the Siuslaw National Forest at campgrounds near the headwaters.

YAQUINA BAY The outlet for the Yaquina River system, one of the most popular and productive bays on Oregon's Coast. Newport was Number One sport fishing port in the state for ocean salmon in 1986, with a catch of 51,338. The bay covers 1700 acres, and tidewater runs up about 13 miles.

The Yaquina enters the ocean just west of Newport, about 110 miles from Portland, and is easily reached by Hwy. 101 from north and south. From the Albany-Corvallis area, it's only an hour's drive on Hwy. 20 down the Yaquina River. The north bay shore is easily accessed by a road east to Toledo. Access on the south shore is limited to the stretch from Hwy. 101 east to Hinton Point. About half-way up the bay, Oysterville (on the south side) can be reached by a secondary road from Toledo.

Salmon is the focus of angling activity in the bay. A private salmon aquaculture facility in the lower bay contributes to the sport catch. Salmon are in the bay from June on, and the catch rate is excellent in most seasons, with an average of about one salmon per angler on all recorded trips. Coho outnumber chinook about 10 to 1, but the chinook are much larger, with many going over 20 pounds.

Fishing activity outside the bar centers around the whistler buoy, about 2 miles out. Halibut are also taken off the bottom near the whistler. Big lingcod are caught over reefs near the shore both north and south of the bay entrance and about 2 miles south of the whistler buoy. The Korean freighter that broke up on the jetties of Yaquina Bay in 1983 can be seen on low tides just north of the north jetty, providing a new reef for ling cod. The bar is usually safe to cross, but check with the Coast Guard if in doubt. Herring is the choice salmon bait, either mooched or trolled, and can be obtained locally or caught easily by jigging almost anywhere in the bay.

In late fall, salmon action moves further up the bay. Anglers anchor and fish, or troll from September to November. Spinners and Flatfish are popular lures. The South Beach Marina breakwater on the south shore of the bay is a good place to fish for aquaculture salmon, as is the bank just off the parking lot at the Marine Science Center. The Gas Plant dock on the north shore is also used to tap the aquaculture run, and provides access for less-abled anglers. The 1986 run was unusually large, with bay anglers taking almost 2000 fall chinook and over 4000 coho.

WILSON RIVER

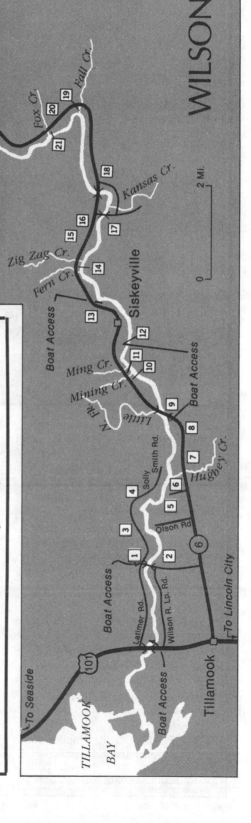

1. SOLLY SMITH PUBLIC ACCESS - Improved ramp, lowest public access, just above Solly Smith Bridge; used as take-out; some bank fishing.

2. TITTLE HOLE - Chinook only, no steelhead

3. LOWER JOSI - Good drift near center of Josi Farm; long drift at low end of hole.

4. UPPER JOSI - Salmon hole; tail-out for steelhead; pay to fish from bank.

5. DONALDSON BAR - Quarter mile steelhead drift; pay to put-in or take-out at gravel bar.

6. GUARD RAIL - Gravel bar and 1/2 mile drift; one of the popular spots on the river.

7. TRAILER PARK HOLE - Bank access for paying guests only.

8. MILLS BRIDGE BAR - County owned access to put-in/take-out at gravel bar; good bank fishing for steelhead and salmon.

9. JUST ABOVE THE BRIDGE - Public access from south shore.

10. SLIDE AREA - One-half mile of good steelhead drift downstream and up to Blue Hole.

11. MING CREEK PUBLIC ACCESS - Publicly owned bank angling access for steelhead and salmon; no boat ramp.

12. SISKYVILLE SLIDE - Improved ODFW boat slide, small parking area, about 1/4 mile below Siskyville.

13. VANDERZANDEN SLIDE (a.k.a. Herd Hole) - A quarter mile of north bank access on either side of public boat slide. Good hole, some parking.

14. YERGEN ACCESS - Public access upstream about 1/4 mile. Watch for small turn-out at about road mile 13.5. Trail to river starts 200 ft. downstream from parking area. Good steelhead water and access to salmon holding hole.

15. ZIG ZAG PUBLIC ACCESS - 1160 ft. of bank access.

16. KANSAS CREEK BRIDGE ACCESS - Access to 3/4 mile south bank, 1/2 mile north bank downstream. Good steelhead water.

17. KANSAS CREEK BRIDGE HOLE - Right under bridge; good for salmon, steelhead.

18. DEMOLAY CAMP HOLE - County park. Rough water here to swinging bridge; put-in not recommended. Good salmon hole, good steelhead drift upstream.

19. FALL CREEK PUBLIC ACCESS - Good winter steelhead water; drift 200 ft. above Fall Creek; fish pockets behind rocks 200 ft. downstream; no angling within 200 ft. of fishway at mouth of Fall Creek.

20. BIG NARROWS - Walk in on trail from turn-out just upstream of mile post 14; good summer steelhead and salmon hole.

21. FOX CREEK HOLE - Salmon and summer steelhead hole just below mouth.

22. OVERBANK - Good sea-run cutthroat hole; steep bank.

23. MUESIAL CREEK HOLE - Good for summer steelhead.

24. KEENIG BRIDGE HOLE - Salmon holding hole and summer steelhead right under bridge. County park with camping and picnic facilities on north bank.

25. JORDAN CREEK BRIDGE HOLE - Good for both winter and summer steelhead; stay below bridge.

26. HARRY SMITH HOLE - Good for salmon.

27. WOLF CREEK HOLE - Fish off steep bank.

28. TURN-OUT HOLE - Turn-out on north side of Hwy. 6.

29. CEDAR CREEK HOLE - Chinook holding area just below mouth of Cedar Cr.

30. CEDAR CREEK DRIFT - Good for summer steelhead.

31. COYOTE HOLE - Good for summer steelhead.

32. JONES CREEK BRIDGE HOLE - Fish right under bridge for salmon, steelhead. Park with camping across bridge from Hwy. 6.

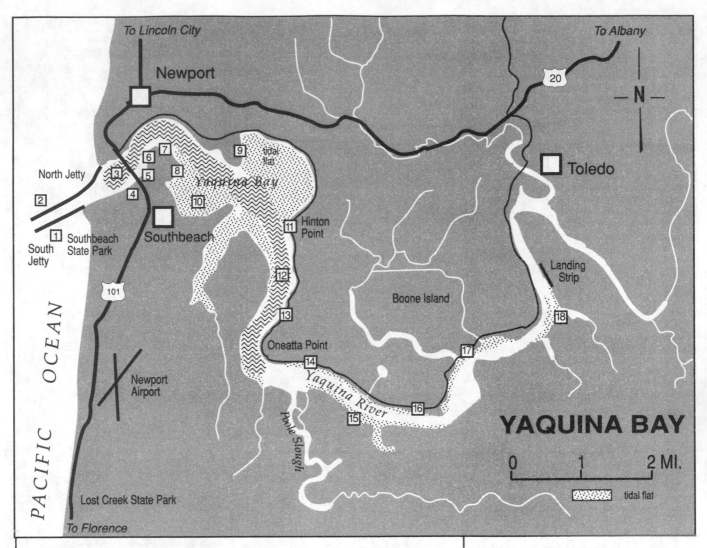

YAQUINA BAY

0   1   2 MI.

tidal flat

1. SOUTH JETTY - Fish for cabezon, striped perch, a few coho. Road directly to jetty.

2. NORTH JETTY - From State Park, take long stairs and rock hop to jetty. Fish for rockfish, greenling, cabezon, striped perch, some coho.

3. LOWER BAY - Anchor or troll for salmon Sept.-Nov. Also dungeness crab, lingcod, striped perch.

4. BRIDGE FLATS SO. - Dig for cockle and gaper clams.

5. PUBLIC DOCK - Dungeness crab

6. MARINA BREAKWATERS - Fish for aquaculture salmon. Public Access to South Beach Marina at Newport dock.

7. BREAKWATER FLAT - Dig on south side of flat only for gapers.

8. MARINE SCIENCE CENTER - Bank fish for aquaculture salmon off parking lot.

9. GAS PLANT DOCK - Public dock for less abled anglers. Drive up to dock. Fish from dock and west bank for aquaculture salmon in fall, perch

year around. Dig cockles at base of dock.

10. UP BAY FLATS - dig for cockle, gaper clams. Access from Science Center parking lot or Idaho Pt.

11. COQUILLE PT. - Fish the rocky area for perch (boat or bank?)

12. TROLL for salmon Sept.-Nov.

13. LAPAZ MARINA - Public access to decrepit wooden dock. Fish for perch.

14. MARKER 25 - From navigational marker 25. FISH FROM BANK for perch & sturgeon. From marker on up-intermittent bank access for perch, sturgeon. Dig flats for soft shell clams.

15. SOFT SHELL FLATS NORTH - Dig for soft shell clams.

16. SOFT SHELL FLATS - Best digging for soft shell clams.

17. MARKER 37 - Navigational marker on road marks the spot. Bank fish deep water for sturgeon.

18. CRIETSER'S IS. - Boat to island for good softshell clam digging. Access from Toledo public boat ramp.

Cabezon, striped perch, and a few coho are taken from the south jetty. The jetty is studded with rock breakwaters, which offer prime rockfish habitat. These, as well as rockfish and greenling, are fished from the north jetty. Bank anglers catch perch from the Gas Plant dock, at the old LaPaz Marina, and along the north shore around navigational marker 25. Boat anglers take perch in the lower bay and around the rocks off Coquille Pt.

Crab are taken the year around. Pots are available for rent, and bait can be obtained locally. Pots are used rather than rings to guard the bait against hungry seals. Check at the marina for current hot spots, or try casting pots about 1/2 mile above the bridge on either side of the channel.

Newport is a delightful coast town with all the flavor of a working fishing port. Just being at dockside when a big charter boat starts unloading its catch is a thrill. If you have a chance, stop by the Oregon State University Marine Science Center. This is a very fine aquarium complex, and admission is free. You'll long remember the octopus that greets you in the lobby.

Newport Marina at South Beach, operated by the Port of Newport, is near the Marine Science Center, with extensive public docks, charter boats, a full service public RV park, and other support facilities, including a fish clean-

YAQUINA BAY ANGLERS
Gerry Lewin, Photographer

ing station, crab cooker, grocery store, and marine information center.

YAQUINA RIVER The Yaquina is a large stream entering Yaquina Bay at Newport, fished primarily for fall salmon. County Rd. 515 follows the stream's north bank west from Hwy. 101 to Toledo. There one can cross the river and follow the south bank on County Rd. 533 to Elk City, and County Rd. 539 to Eddyville, where County Rd. 180 cuts north to follow the upper river to the Nashville area.

Most of the salmon angling takes place in the lower bay, but fish are taken up up to the salmon and steelhead deadline at Eddyville, about 2 1/2 miles upstream.

Early season trout angling is fair for native cutthroat in the upper river. Anglers troll for sea-run in the lower river on spinner and bait from July through the end of trout season.

Big Elk Creek, a major tributary entering the Yaquina at Elk City, sometimes provides very good winter steelhead angling. Between 500 and 1000 fish are taken in Big Elk, but few are caught in the Yaquina.

YOUNG'S RIVER The main stream entering Young's Bay, near Astoria. A high falls about 9 miles up, is impassable to salmon and steelhead. A few are taken in tidewater, but the river is closed to salmon and steelhead angling above the first highway bridge below the falls. Wild cutthroat are fished up to the falls and in the upper river, which is accessed by logging roads.

COASTAL FISHING

SURF FISHING Surf fish are available year around off virtually all Oregon's beaches. Redtail perch predominate, and are particularly plentiful April through June. But *anything* might show up in the catch.

Some anglers fish scientifically, using low tide conditions to identify channels and deeper pools on the beach, which they fish at high water. Others just fish to cover as much territory as they can, moving down the beach till they get results. Perch are a schooling fish, so where there's one, there are many.

Most anglers prefer a calm surf. Waders are a good idea, since the Pacific Ocean is almost always too cold for comfort here. Anglers wade knee deep when a wave is out, cast beyond the breaking surf, then back up to the shallows, letting out line. They retrieve slowly as the current washes bait or lure to shore.

Popular baits include mussels, sand worms, siphon tips from razor clams, and sand shrimp. Small white jigs are also used, and fly anglers tie on minnow imitations. Spinning, level-wind, and fly reels are all practical, with a long rod and 10 to 12 pound test line preferred.

Oregon has approximately 350 miles of shoreline, and all of it is open to public use. As always, when on an Oregon beach, keep an eye on the water for big waves, incoming tide, and large floating debris.

THE 10 BEST SURF FISHING BEACHES IN OREGON
(North to South)

1. Clatsop Beaches (Clatsop Co.) From the Columbia River South Jetty to Seaside, for redtail surfperch.

2. Short Beach (Tillamook Co.) Just south of Cape Mears, for redtail.

3. Beverly and Moolack Beaches (Lincoln Co.) Just north of Agate Beach, for redtail.

4. Yaquina Head (Lincoln Co.) On Agate Beach, fish the rocks for perch, greenling, rock fish.

5. Seal Rock (Lincoln Co.) Fish the large rocks extending into the ocean for perch,

6. Siuslaw Jettys (Lane Co.) Fish the adjacent beach.

7. Winchester Bay Jettys (Douglas) Fish the adjacent beach.

8. Horsefall Beach (Coos Co.) Just north of North Bend beyond 101 bridge, fish for redtail.

9. Nesika Beach (Curry Co.) Just north of Gold Beach, fish for redtail.

10. Myers Cr. Beach (Curry Co.) Just south of Cape Sebastian, fish for redtail.

OFF-SHORE SALMON Each year, sport fishermen harvest several hundred thousand salmon off the Oregon coast.

The majority of these fish are bound for the Columbia River system, but most are apprehended from Tillamook Head south due to the Columbia's limited off-shore sport fishing season. Salmon season from Tillamook Head south to California generally extends from May to September.

TOP 10 OREGON SALMON PORTS IN 1988

Port	Chinook	Coho
Newport	4,000	65,000
Pacific City	400	47,000
Winchester	5200	39,900
Depoe Bay	1400	35,700
Brookings *	21,600	14,800
Garibaldi	2,300	24,900
Florence	1,500	16,200
Coos Bay	1,400	14,900
Gold Beach	1,400	1,600

*Oregon's #1 small craft off-shore salmon port

SOUTHWEST ZONE

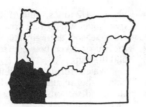

The Southwest Zone is all waters draining directly to the Pacific Ocean south of, and including, the Umpqua River drainage; and those portions of the Klamath River drainage in Jackson County.

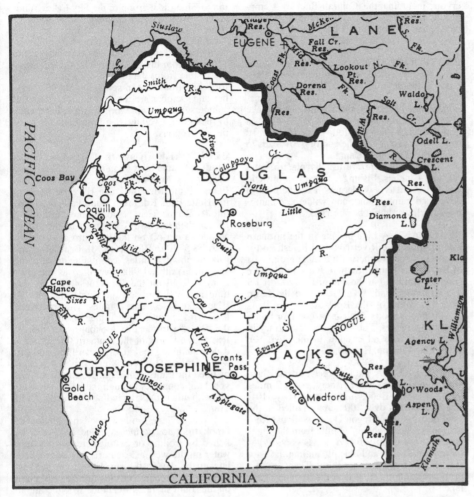

And Chetco Bay, safest bar crossing on the Oregon coast (I've heard you can do it in a canoe!). And there are the big striped bass, or what's left of them, in the Coos, Smith, and Umpqua rivers. And that's just the fish.

The region encompasses the entire southern Oregon coast, from the California border north to and including the Umpqua River estuary at Winchester Bay. Its extent is defined primarily by the Rogue, Coquille, and Umpqua watersheds. These major rivers reach inland almost 100 miles, draining the western slopes of the southern Cascades. The region includes most of the Siskiyou, Rogue, and Umpqua national forests.

There is a wide variety of terrain here, from rugged (and incredibly beautiful) coastal headlands,to peaceful harbor villages and coastal valleys, to alpine lakes in the Cascades over a mile above sea level. Coastal climate is similar to that further north, but somewhat warmer. Inland, the temperature extremes are greater than those of the Willamette Valley, with colder winters and hotter summers. Annual rainfall varies from over 100 inches per year in the western Siskiyou Mts. to less than 20 inches at Medford.

The ocean salmon catch in this region generally exceeds that of the north. The coastal areas offer similar angling opportunities to those of the northwest coast, but the angling pressure is a bit lighter. This is a long way from Willamette Valley population centers, though a growing attraction for California vacationers and retirees.

Access to the coast is by way of Hwy. 101. Only three major highways lead to the coast from inland. Hwy. 38, from I-5 at Cottage Grove, reaches Winchester Bay. Hwy. 42, from Roseburg, leads to Coos Bay and Bandon. Hwy. 199 connects Grants Pass with Crescent City, California, about 17 miles south of Brookings.

Both the Rogue and the Umpqua are deserving of their fame as steelhead rivers, and each supports a good summer run that can be tempted with a fly. The tributaries of the Rogue and Umpqua provide excellent trout angling.

Hiking anglers will find challenges in the waters of the lower Rogue within the Wild Rogue Wilderness, the Illinois River within the Kalmiopsis Wilderness of the Siskiyou National Forest, and the lake basins of Sky Lakes Wilderness of the Rogue River National Forest.

If you prefer big lakes, there are several good ones to choose from. Many of the valley reservoirs grow trophy size largemouth bass, as do the fine coastal Tenmile Lakes. Diamond Lake, in the northeast corner of the region, is one of the top trout producers in the state. Hyatt and Howard Prairie reservoirs put out good size rainbow.

Road conditions in the Rogue and Siskiyou National Forests are generally more primitive than those of the forests to the north. Good national forest maps are available and highly recommended. It can be a long way between gas stops, so check your gauge prior to taking any, 'short cuts'.

"Sometimes I just don't know how to call it," I complain to my partner. "I mean, people tell me things, places to fish, and I don't always know whether they've thought out what it might mean to share that information with 40,000 other anglers."

"Yeah, but it's not like you're telling them exactly where to go or what rock to stand on," he counters. "It's more like a treasure hunt. You give them a clue, and the rest is up to them."

I sigh. It was, after all, the Oregon Dept. of Fish and Wildlife that willingly gave me this information. We taxpaying anglers did pay for the fish that went into these waters—all stocked, none wild. And if I didn't tell, who would? How would anglers know there were fish there? Who would even think to look?

"Think of it as helping to spread out the crowds," he suggests.

"So you think I should tell?"

He nods. "We'd want to know if we were heading toward the Umpqua. And besides, how many people really read these chapter introductions anyway?"

"Are there many trout in the Umpqua River?" I asked ODFW Roseburg's most fanatic on-staff trout angler.

"No, but there are plenty of trout in the Umpqua National Forest." He leaned toward me, lowered his voice conspiratorially. "They're in places you might never think to look. Not many people know they're there." He spread open a forest map. "Every national forest has water holes, some big—some small, that are designated for fire fighting. There are roads almost right to them, though they're usually screened from view by brush. Most don't even have names. In the Umpqua National Forest, these water holes are signed on the road by a little marker, a W within a white circle. Not all, but some, quite a few, have been stocked with trout. They don't see much traffic, don't have much competition, just eat and grow..."

So there you are. Do with it what you will.

The southwest zone abounds in treasures. There's the Umpqua River and the Rogue, for starters, with their enormous summer steelhead runs. And the surprise of a really rich smallmouth bass fishery in the mainstem Umpqua.

AGATE RESERVOIR A good bass and panfish lake on Upper Dry Creek, NE of Medford. From Hwy. 62 in Medford, take Lake of the Woods Hwy. 140. Watch for signs. Agate covers 216 acres and is open year around, but fishing's best in spring. A good crappie population, largemouth bass, brown bullhead, and bluegill are available. A canoe, raft, or rowboat is useful here, but motors are prohibited. There's a picnic area, but no overnight camping.

ALTA LAKE A narrow, 32 acre hike-in lake in the Seven Lakes Basin of the Sky Lakes Area, Rogue River National Forest. The basin is accessed by several trails from the west with trailheads on FS Roads 3780, 3785, and 3790. The trailhead on FS 3780, leading to Trail 980 then Trail 979 is designated the Alta Lake Trail on the Sky Lakes Wilderness map.

Seven Lakes Basin is also approached by trails from the east, heading at Sevenmile Marsh. At Ft. Klamath on Hwy. 62, turn west on County Rd. 1419. At about 4 miles, when the county road bears right, continue straight then turn right onto FS 3334 to Sevenmile Marsh Campground. Follow Trail 3703. At its junction with the Pacific Crest Trail, take the left fork. The trail west to Grass and Middle lakes is less than 3 miles from the junction. About 1/2 mile further on the PCT, a trail leads west to Cliff Lake. To reach Alta, follow the Cliff Lake Trail past Cliff and South lakes. At the next trail junction, head north to Alta.

One of the last lakes in the area to thaw, Alta offers fair fishing for stocked brook trout. There is a natural campsite at the north end, and good trail access to other fishable lakes east in the basin. See MIDDLE, GRASS, CLIFF.

APPLEGATE RESERVOIR A full-service recreation area on the upper Applegate, varying from 990 to 360 acres. From Medford or Grants Pass, take Hwy. 238 south to the reservoir access road, which becomes FS 10. At the reservoir, the left fork leads to French Gulch and Stringtown campgrounds on the upper NE arm of the reservoir. The right fork leads to Watkins and Carberry camps at the southern end. A trail from French Gulch follows the east shore all the way to Manzanita Cr., about 4 miles.

The reservoir is annually stocked with 25,000 legal rainbow and 150,000 fingerlings. Largemouth bass and black crappie are also available, and smallmouth bass are present, though not well established. Fishing is best in late spring, while the lake is still full and cool. There is one boat ramp across the dam on the east side of French Gulch Rd.

APPLEGATE RIVER A major tributary of the Rogue River, entering the mainstem 2 miles above Whitehorse Rapids, 5 miles west of Grants Pass. Hwy. 199 and county roads access the lower river south of the city. A county road follows the south bank east from Wilderville, and another follows the north bank east from Jerome. There is a county park on the river about 5 miles south of Jerome. From Grants Pass, head south toward Murphy, and pick up Hwy. 238. From Medford, Hwy. 238 leads to the river road cut-off at the town of Ruch. The Applegate River Rd. follows the stream to Applegate Dam.

The Applegate produces a good run of late arriving winter steelhead that peaks in March. The annual catch is often between 500 and 1000, but drought years are always hard on the Applegate. In 1987-88 fewer than 400 steelhead were taken. Best steelheading is downstream from the mouth of the Little Applegate,

about 2 1/2 miles south of Ruch. Fishing for native rainbow and hatchery stock is good from early season through late spring, especially in the upper river between the Little Applegate and the dam.

Watch for the deadline at the dam, and check the regulations and special trout and steelhead seasons. Angling from a floating device is prohibited.

There are several camping and picnic areas on the upper river road before you get to the reservoir, including the Cantrall-Buckley Campground just about 6 miles east of the community of Applegate about a mile past the point where Hwy. 238 crosses the river.

BABYFOOT LAKE A popular 4 acre lake in a designated botanical area just inside the Kalmiopsis Wilderness of the Siskiyou National Forest, accessible from the east. From Cave Junction, in the valley of the Illinois River, take Hwy. 199 north about 4 miles to FS 4201, a gravel road, which you follow for roughly 10 miles. A dirt road near the end of 4201 leads to the trailhead at Onion Camp.

Brook trout here are usually plentiful and run to 14 inches. Fishing's best in spring and late fall. As it is a wilderness lake, there is no developed campground, and wilderness camping guidelines should be observed.

BEAL LAKE A hike-in lake in the northern half of the Rogue River National Forest, northernmost of the Northern Blue Lake group east of Butte Falls Ranger Station. It's a 4 mile hike from the trailhead at the end of FS 720, off FS 37. A shorter trail, 982, leads into the basin from the summit of Blue Rock Mt.

Fishing is spotty, but can be good for brook trout to 12 inches. This is a good lake to try in conjunction with other lakes in the area. See Blue, Blue Canyon, Horseshoe.

BEALE LAKE A hard to reach coastal lake with a good warm water fishery, about 7 miles north of North Bend, just west of Hwy. 101. The lake covers over 100 acres, cradled in the sand dunes of the Oregon Dunes National Recreation Area. It's about 1/2 mile from the highway by trail. Lightly fished, it has good largemouth bass, perch and bluegill angling. It is not stocked due to its inaccessibility. There are two primitive camping areas near the SW end of the lake.

BEN IRVING RESERVOIR A 100 plus acre lake west of Roseburg, created by Berry Creek Dam. From Roseburg, take Hwy. 42 west, then County Rd. 365, which joins 42 about 2 miles south of the town of Tenmile.

It is managed primarily for bass and panfish, but 2400 legal rainbow are stocked annually in March and April. Largemouth bass and bluegill are thriving. There is a boat ramp, and a posted speed limit, with motors prohibited at the upper end.

BIG BUTTE CREEK A very nice 30 mile tributary of the upper Rogue, entering the river at McLeod near Lost Creek Lake. To reach the lower stream from Medford, take Hwy. 62 north about 27 miles. To reach the upper waters, turn east off 62 onto the Butte Falls Rd. Crowfoot, McNeil, and Cobleigh roads cross the creek. Butte Falls Rd. reaches the creek at about mile 16 and follows the south bank for about 2 miles. A dirt road crosses the creek and follows it another 2 miles to Big Butte Spring. The upper waters are accessible by taking the Butte Falls-Prospect Rd. to the Rancheria Rd.

At about one mile, turn left off Rancheria. This road accesses the North Fork at about one mile and follows it for 4 1/2 miles.

A good trout stream, Big Butte features cutthroat to over 12 inches and stocked rainbow. About 3000 legals are supplied yearly from late April to mid-July. North and South Fork headwaters and some tributaries are spring fed, so fishing holds up well.

BLUE CANYON LAKE A small hike-in lake in the Blue Lake group of the Sky Lakes Wilderness Area, located about one mile south of Blue Lake. From Blue Lake, take the main Trail 982 for l/4 mile, then turn south and west on the Blue Canyon Trail. The lake is less than 1/2 mile from the fork, to the left of (and may not visible from) the trail. There's good fishing for brook trout here in spring and fall. September and October are the best months. Bait and spinners or lures will work anytime, but switch to flies in the evening. See Blue Lake for complete directions.

BLUE LAKE (Klamath Co. a.k.a. South Blue) A 15 acre hike-in, in the south Sky Lakes Wilderness Area of the Rogue River National Forest. From Medford, take Hwy. 62 north to the Butte Falls Rd. From Butte Falls head east into the Rogue River National Forest, following FS 30, then left on FS 37. Just past the Parker Meadows cut-off on the left, turn a hard right onto FS 3770 to Blue Rock Mt. Bear left at the fork at about 4 miles, continuing toward the summit. Trailhead 982, identified as the Blue Canyon Trail on the Wilderness map, is one mile past the fork, on the right. The hike to Blue Lake is less than 2 miles. The summit of Blue Mt., about a mile further up the road, is the site of a former fire lookout tower and offers a grand view of the southern Oregon Cascades, including the rim of Crater Lake and Mt. McLoughlin. The Blue Mt. Rd. is not recommended for trailer or RV traffic. The Blue Canyon Trail continues through the basin, connecting with other trails, including the Pacific Crest Trail.

A deep lake, with a good population of brook trout to 12 inches, Blue Lake can be fished by trolling or casting lures in the deep water on the west side. Fly fishing is excellent late in the day in the shoal areas on the east side, or by sinking wet flies off the rock point on the south shore. A float tube would come in handy. There are good campsites here, as at most lakes in the area. Other fishable lakes in the basin include Horseshoe, Pear, Blue Canyon.

Check for conditions at Butte Falls Ranger Station.

BLUEBILL LAKE A 35 acre lake at the southern edge of the Oregon Dunes National Recreation Area on Siuslaw Forest land north of North Bend. It contains largemouth bass. There is a small campground at the lake which is mercifully closed to off-road vehicle traffic.

BOLAN LAKE A small lake near the California border in the Siskiyou Mountains. It can be reached by turning east from Hwy. 199 onto County Rd. 5560 at O'Brien, 6 miles south of Cave Junction. Continue east on this road, which north of Takilma becomes 5828, to the border of the Siskiyou National Forest. Here the road becomes FS 48. Follow this road for 10 twisting miles to FS 4812, which leads 6 miles NE to the lake. The last section of road is rough and winding. It is usually snowbound until late spring.

Only about 12 acres, Bolan has both rainbow and brook trout, with fish to 14 inches. Fishing holds up well here throughout the season. Bait fishing is the most commonly used technique, but other methods work. There is a campground at the lake, and car-top boats can be launched.

BRADLEY LAKE A coastal lake of about 30 acres, west of Hwy.101, about 3 miles south of Bandon. It's about one mile west of the highway on the Bradley Lake Rd. China Creek flows into the lake and is crossed by 101 just east of the lake. Fished mostly for stocked rainbow trout, Bradley provides good catches in early spring and summer. Native cutthroat are also present, and there may be some largemouth bass.

BRUSH CREEK A classic little steelhead stream in Humbug State Park, which offers fine camping and picnic facilities in a magnificent south coast setting. The lower end of the creek is about 5 miles south of Port Orford on Hwy.101 and it's crossed by the highway a few times near Humbug State Park. It's a rich stream with lots of gravel and boulders, and two major forks.

A steelhead run here peaks in January. Migrating cutthroat may also be taken, but the salmon that used to come into this stream have about disappeared, despite efforts in the early '80s to build up a run.

BUCKEYE LAKE A fair, hike-in eastern brook trout lake in the Umpqua Divide Scenic Area, 1 1/2 miles south of Fish Lake about 35 miles east of Tiller. Buckeye is NW of Cliff Lake. For road and trail directions see Cliff Lake.

Tenacre Buckeye has good numbers of brook trout to 18 inches. Most of the catch is 7-12 inches. Bait, spinner, and fly all work. There are improved campsites at Buckeye and nearby Cliff Lake. Supplies are available at Tiller 35 miles west, or Clearwater, 30 twisting miles north. The lake is usually accessible in June.

BUTTERFIELD LAKE A small lake about 16 miles south of Reedsport, 1/4 mlie west of Hwy. 101. Roughly 50 acres, the lake is bisected by the railroad right of way and has walk-in access only. Cutthroat trout and bass are reported, but success is unknown. It is not stocked, and there is no camping nearby.

CALAMUT LAKE A good hike-in eastern brook trout lake 4 miles NE of Lemolo Lake just south of the Douglas/Lane County line. The road to the lake has been closed, but a trail leads in from Linda Lake, one mile south of Calamut.

Linda Lake is not shown on the Umpqua National Forest map. From Inlet Campground, at the east end of Lemolo Lake, take FS 999 east 2 miles to FS 60. Turn left on 60 and at about 2 miles, turn left on FS 700. Signs will direct you to Linda Lake. Trailhead 1494 is on the right. The hike to Calamut is just over a mile from Linda. The trail passes Lake Charlene on the way in. Linda and Lake Charlene were stocked with brook trout fingerlings for the first time in 1982.

Calamut has 18 acres and offers fair fishing in spring and fall. No inlets or outlets support spawning, so it is stocked every two or three years with fingerlings. The brookies have been running 6-12 inches, with average size 10 inches. It usually can be reached in June. There are improved campsites at the lake.

CALAPOOYA CREEK (Douglas Co.) A good-size tributary of the Umpqua River, about 40 miles long, entering the main river at the community of Umpqua about 10 miles downstream from the forks, 20 road miles north of Roseburg. It is crossed by Hwy. 15 just north of Sutherlin. Good roads follow the stream closely in both the lower and upper sections.

The stream has native cutthroat and rainbow trout, and receives annual plants of rainbow. It has a fair run of coho and steelhead along with a few fall chinook. For some time it has been closed to salmon angling, but it is currently open for steelhead. Be sure to check current regulations. There is a county park on the river at Fair Oaks east of Sutherlin. There are no camping areas in the vicinity.

CAMP CREEK (Douglas Co.) A fair size stream entering Mill Creek (outlet of Loon Lake) about 3 miles above its confluence with the Umpqua 4 miles west of Scottsburg. It can be reached by Hwy. 38 from Reedsport or Drain. The Loon Lake Rd. crosses Camp Creek at its lower end. A paved road follows it east for 15 miles.

It is primarily a trout stream, with native cutthroat and stocked rainbow available. Steelhead and salmon enter the creek, but angling for them is prohibited. There are several picnic areas just west of Scottsburg on Hwy. 38, but no camping.

CANTON CREEK A nice looking stream joining Steamboat Creek from the north, about a mile north of the junction of Steamboat and the North Umpqua. This stream is a sanctuary area for summer steelhead, closed to all angling.

CANYONVILLE POND See Herbert Log Pond.

CARBERRY CREEK A nice trout stream, one of the inlet streams of Applegate Reservoir, entering the reservoir from the SW. FS 10 follows the western shore of the reservoir to Carberry Campground, then follows the Carberry to its fork. Gravel roads parallel each of the forks, Sturgis and Steve.

Angling for native cutthroat trout can be good at times. Excess winter steelhead brood fish stocked in the reservoir are known to run up Carberry and are caught during regular trout season.

CHETCO BAY A small bay near the Oregon/California border whose good, safe bar contributes to its ranking as the Top Small Craft Port for Oregon's offshore salmon fishery. It draws anglers by the thousands from northern California, with an average annual catch of 27,000 fall salmon. Chinook and coho seem to be available in roughly equal quantities. The 1986 offshore salmon catch out of Chetco was 21,532.

Chetco is remote for most Oregonians, but real handy for Californians. From the Portland area it's about 340 miles on Hwy. 101, but only 24 miles from Crescent City, California. The section of the highway from Gold Beach south is now one of the best stretches on the Oregon coast.

The Chetco bar leads out into a sheltered cove that is shielded from the summer winds. Twelve foot boats, or even canoes, go to sea on good days. In June, most offshore fishing is for young, small coho on their way north. The offshore summer fishery is primarily for mixed chinook stock, bound for the Rogue, Klamath,

JETTY ANGLER
Bill Wagner, Photographer

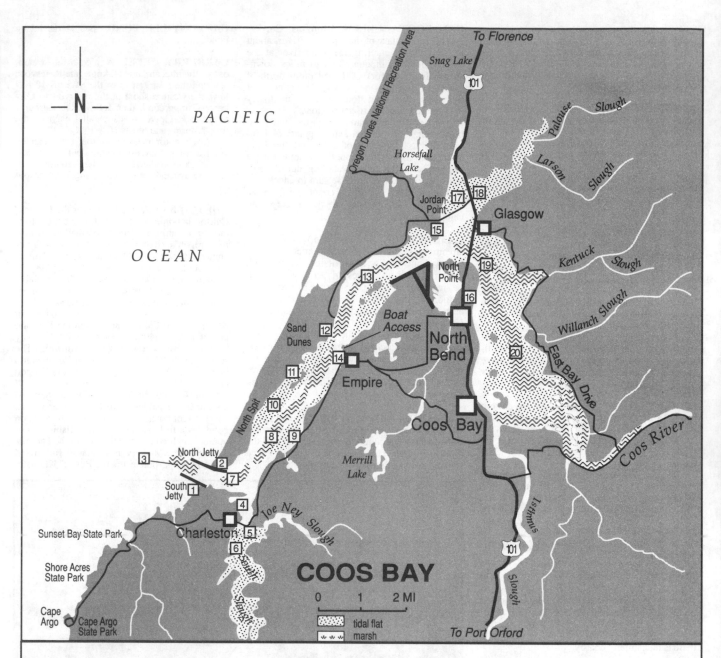

COOS BAY

0   1   2 MI

tidal flat
marsh

1. SOUTH JETTY - Park at Bastendorf County Park. Fish for redtail perch, greenling, ling cod, and occasional salmon.

2. NORTH JETTY - Fish for redtail perch, greenling, and lingcod.

3. LOWER BAY - Troll and mooch herring for salmon.

4. CHARLESTON WATERFRONT - Public access to extensive boat docks for perch Feb. through summer, smelt and herring jigged June - Sept., dungeness and rock crab.

5. CHARLESTON BRIDGE/Public Fishing Dock - From bridge or end of dock, jig for smelt and herring, fish for perch. Park near bridge to dig on Charleston Flats for cockles, gapers, some butter clams.

6. SOUTH SLOUGH FLAT - Fair digging for cockles, gapers, some butter clams. Park along primitive Port Access Rd. (watch the potholes!)

7. SUBMERGED ROCK JETTY - Good fishing at high tide for perch, rockfish, greenling, occasional lingcod. Identify by markers warning of hazard.

8. FOSSIL PT. TO PONY PT. - Natural rock structures provide good boat and bank fishing for perch; best on incoming tide. Bank anglers, respect private property.

9. PIGEON PT. FLATS - Popular digging for gapers, butter clams. Limited parking but accessible.

10. NORTH SPIT - Best digging on the bay for gapers, cockles, softshell. Walk out at low tide along entire bay side of spit.

11. CLAM ISLAND - fish for dungeness and some red rock crab off the island.

12. N. SPIT AQUACULTURE FACILITY - Home sweet home to many returning coho and spring chinook. Wade out on sand for extremely popular bank fishery. Good parking near T-dock at road's end.

13. AQUACULTURE SALMON - Popular boat fishery between N. Spit and Jordan Pt. aquaculture facilities. Chinook Mar. - Aug., coho Sept./Oct.

14. EMPIRE RAMP - Major access to aquaculture salmon fishery; beware of crossing bay during NW wind and incoming tide.

15. JORDAN PT. aquaculture facility - Up-bay destination for many returning coho and spring chinook.

16. HWY. 101 BRIDGE - Fish from bridge for perch.

17. MENASHA DIKE FLATS - Good digging for softshell clams on either side of causeway from Hwy.101 to Horsefall Beach.

18. HAYNES INLET BRIDGE - Fish from bridge for perch.

19. STURGEON HOLE

20. SHAD and remnant striped bass.

and Sacramento rivers. Fall chinook enter the bay mid-September to October. Trolling, bait fishing, and fly casting are all popular methods here. There is also an important jetty fishery for early fall chinook during the 6 weeks before the rains hit.

Many species of rockfish, flatfish, and other bottom fish are also available offshore. Charter operators begin bottom fishing trips in March, focusing on salmon after mid-July.

Perch fishing from the beach is excellent here most of the season, with best catches on the incoming tide. Jetty fishing for perch is only fair. There is good access to the jetty for less-abled anglers. There is a mostly untapped fishery for shrimp offshore, and local divers do well for scallops.

Accommodations are plentiful in the Brookings and Harbor area. Charter boats, and marine and fishing supplies are readily available. Harris Beach State Park 2 miles north of Brookings has a large camping area. Sporthaven Trailer Park, county run, is just south of town. Azalea State Park at Brookings is for picnicking only.

CHETCO RIVER A very good winter steelhead and salmon stream at the extreme south end of the Oregon coast. Scenic, flanked by myrtle trees, it enters the sea at Brookings after a 50 miles run. The whole river is accessible to driftboats (no jet sleds are used here), and there is good bank access. County Rd. 784 follows the north bank of the river up to Loeb State Park. Above Loeb, access roads lead to well-known gravel bars and holes such as Ice Box, Miller, Redwood, and So. Fork.

Fall chinook (and a few coho) are available from September through December, with peak catches in October and November. The total fall salmon catch for both river and bay in 1986 was 992.

Steelhead start showing well in December and hold up through March. In 1985-86, a total of 3,121 steelhead were caught—1,709 in January, 518 in December, and 613 in February. The Chetco is consistently among the 10 best Oregon coastal streams for winter steelhead.

The river also offers limited fishing for cutthroat trout in early season, and for sea-run in late summer. It is no longer stocked with trout, however.

The Oregon Dept. of Fish and Wildlife has acquired a number of fishing access areas for use by Oregon anglers. The furthest downstream is located about river mile 2 on the north bank and features a good salmon hole. The next is at Myrtle Grove, on the north bank just above Loeb State Park. The third, which includes a boat launch, is at Piling Hole on the south bank.

There is camping at Harris Beach State Park 2 miles north of Brookings and at Loeb State Park 8 miles up the river road.

CLEAR LAKE (Coos Co.) Don't confuse this with the large lake of the same name just south of Reedsport in Douglas County. This Clear Lake is about 14 miles south of Reedsport on the west side of Hwy. 101, a half mile north of Saunders Lake. To reach it you have to park along the highway and cross the railroad tracks. The north end of the lake is in the Oregon Dunes National Recreation Area. It offers very good fishing for yellow perch and supports a good population of cutthroat trout. About 15 acres and quite deep, it is primarily fished by local anglers. There are no camping facilities or improvements here.

CLEAR LAKE (Douglas Co.) A large coastal lake on the east side of Hwy. 101, 7 miles south of Reedsport. It covers 290 acres and contains cutthroat trout, but is closed to angling since it provides the water supply for Reedsport.

CLIFF LAKE (Douglas Co.) A rich 7 acre hike-in brook trout lake in the south Umpqua drainage, featuring the largest brook trout in the district, successfully fished by a knowing few. Cliff is adjacent to Buckeye Lake, about a mile south of Fish Lake in the Rogue-Umpqua Divide Wilderness just north of Grasshopper Mt., Umpqua National Forest. The Skimmerhorn Trail 1578 offers the most direct approach to Cliff, though other trails access the lake basin. At Tiller, on Hwy. 227, follow County Rd. 46 into the forest, where it becomes FS 28, the South Umpqua River Rd. Continue on FS 28 about 4 miles past South Umpqua Falls Campground where several roads branch off. Follow FS 2823 to the right about 2 miles, then FS 2830. Bear right at the first fork, left at the second fork. Skimmerhorn Trailhead is about one mile further at road's end. It is a designated saddle camp. The trail reaches Buckeye at about 1 1/2 miles, and Cliff 1/4 mile further.

Cliff Lake holds fish that exceed 4 pounds, but they can be cagey. Best fishing is in spring and fall. Trolling with spinner and bait produces well in spring. There are improved campsites here and at Buckeye Lake.

CLIFF LAKE (Klamath Co.) A nice hike-in brook trout lake in the Seven Lakes Basin of the Sky Lakes Wilderness, on the summit between the headwaters of the Middle Fork of the Rogue and Seven Mile Creek. The basin is about 10 miles south of Crater Lake National Park.

Cliff Lake is 1/4 mile west of the Pacific Crest Trail north of Devil's Peak. It's a 5 mile hike to the lake by trails from east or west. See Alta Lake for directions.

There are nice eastern brook trout in this 10 acre lake, with plenty of shoal area for fly anglers to work over. Dark patterns, sunk and fished with slow retrieve, do well. The trout population is maintained by air stocking of fingerlings. There are improved campsites at the lake. This is a picturesque area, and if the fishing is slow here there other lakes in the vicinity to try. See Alta, Middle, Grass.

COOPER CREEK RESERVOIR This 140 acre lake was built by the Soil Conservation Service as a multiple-use reservoir in the late '60s. It is stocked with rainbow trout and has been a good producer of largemouth bass, crappie, and brown bullhead. The reservoir is 2 miles east of Sutherlin, about 4 miles east of the I-5 exit. From Sutherlin, take the road east to Fair Oaks, 2 miles from Hwy. 99, and turn south onto a county road which leads to the reservoir in a bit over a mile.

Douglas County maintains two nice picnic areas here with excellent concrete boat ramps. The reservoir is popular with waterskiers, but a 5 mph speed limit is enforced in the fishing area.

Rainbow trout are stocked twice each spring. Respectable numbers of largemouth bass are taken. Crappie angling is very good in the arms of the lake during spring and early summer. Yellow, purple, or white jigs trolled through the shallows will produce. Bank angling is good, and an easy trail goes all the way around the lake. Camping is prohibited.

COOS BAY A large, tremendously productive bay with a great variety of angling the year around, and good public access. Coos Bay is a 4 hour drive from the Portland area and 2 hours from Eugene. Cut through the coast range at any of the major highways and follow Hwy. 101. From Roseburg, Hwy. 42 is still under construction, but will someday offer good access from I-5.

Salmon anglers will find chinook and coho outside the bay from May through September. Early in the year, most salmon fishing takes place outside the bar 1-10 miles offshore. The Coos Bay bar is a good one, but don't venture out under dangerous wind or fog conditions. Two of the hottest spots outside are about one mile west and 1-2 miles north of the north jetty, and between the bar and whistle buoy. In 1986, the offshore sport salmon catch out of Coos Bay was 18,093. Offshore anglers also take lingcod at times, with good catches inside as well.

In recent years, the biggest excitement in Coos Bay has been the salmon fishery in the bay itself, resulting primarily from the installation of salmon aquaculture facilities here. In 1986, Coos Bay ranked Number One on the Oregon coast for its coho catch of 6607, taken from an unusually large return. The spring chinook catch was 2364 in 1986, with a similar catch in 1987.

The chinook run lasts from March to August, peaking in May and June. The coho run takes place from late August through October. Most anglers fish off the North Spit near the lower aquaculture facility. Hundreds of anglers stand elbow to elbow daily, but manage to maintain an atmosphere of good fellowship, in the tradition of a social occasion rather than a sporting contest.

The runs are also fished from boats, launched primarily at Empire across the bay. Boaters should be wary of prevailing NW winds in summer, which can turn the bay very rough when they meet an incoming tide. Always wear life jackets when crossing Coos Bay. Most boaters anchor and cast lures. Blue Fox No. 5 has been popular here lately, as well as Rooster Tails. Bait is not used, due to the large number of thieving crabs. An occasional salmon is taken off the south jetty, and anglers troll and mooch herring for salmon in the lower bay.

The striped bass fishery has declined severely throughout Oregon's south coast during the past 5 years. The last good natural spawn took place in 1972. The Oregon Department of

COOS BAY STRIPER
Courtesy, Oregon Dept. of Fish & Wildlife

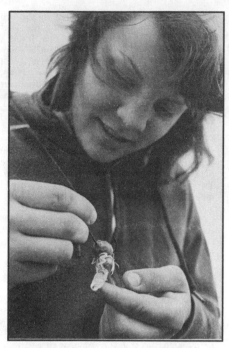

BAITING UP WITH SAND SHRIMP
Tom Ballard, Photographer

Fish and Wildlife's plans to enhance this fishery may be limited by funds, but not by commitment. There is general agreement that stripers, which can exceed 60 pounds, are worth the effort. Unfortunately, southern Oregon is the northern extreme of their successful range, with conditions for a good general spawn occurring less than once a decade.

Nevertheless, there are still some stripers out there, and determined anglers can catch them in the traditional places. From fall through May, look for stripers in the sloughs and upper tidewaters, where they seek spawning grounds, especially in the South Fork of the Coos River. From mid-June through mid-August they move to mid-bay, around the Hwy. 101 Bridge. This is when fishing activity for them is most active, as they are gorging on marine fish and will be tempted by a big, ugly plug or bait. Popular lures include the Rapala, Rebel, and Balino Eel. In the upper tidewater areas, trollers favor the Balino Eel. Stripers can also be taken on bait such as herring, and some of the locals use live mud cats. Stripers have also been caught on a fly. Check the current regulations for restrictions on this fishery.

Sturgeon catches, both white and green, have been good. Anglers use big gobs of bait and fish the deep holes. A favorite spot is above the Hwy. 101 Bridge off North Point in winter and early spring.

Redtail perch, greenling, and ling cod are fished from north and south jetties, and perch are caught from many docks and bridges throughout the bay, including the boat docks in Charleston, Charleston Bridge, 101 Bridge, and Haynes Inlet Bridge. There are also good perch catches by boaters around the submerged rock jetty in the lower bay (look for the hazard markers) and by both boat and bank anglers from Fossil Pt. to Pony Pt. This area has many submerged rock structures that make good perch habitat. Best catches are on the incoming tide. Bank anglers in this area should be considerate of private property.

Herring and smelt are jigged from the Charleston boat docks from June to September.

Dungeness and rock crab are also fished from Charleston docks and off Clam Island.

Best clam flats on the bay run the length of the North Spit. Walk out at low tide and dig for gapers, cockles, and softshell clams. Menasha Dike Flats also offer good digging on either side of the causeway from Hwy. 101 to Horsefall Beach. South Slough Flat offers fair digging for cockles, gapers, and some butter clams. Park along the Port Access Rd., but keep a sharp eye out for potholes.

Supplies and accommodations are available at Coos Bay, North Bend, and at Charleston, the little seaport town nearest the bar. Charleston has extensive, welcoming public docks and marinas, and is the gateway to two magnificent state parks, Shore Acres, for day use only, and Sunset Bay, which has a full service campground, including showers.

COOS RIVER The Coos River flows only a little over 4 miles from its major tributaries, the Millicoma River and the South Fork Coos, which split off about 2 miles west of Coos Bay. It is accessible from Hwy. 101. With the fading of the striped bass fishery, shad and salmon have become the main fisheries on the river.

The spring salmon that appear in the Coos in April and May are strays that avoided aquaculture ladders in the bay. The fall salmon run has improved significantly in recent years thanks to the efforts of local volunteers, coordinated by the Department of Fish and Wildlife's STEP program. The earliest fall chinook arrive in September, and coho follow in November. Steelhead are usually moving through in December and January. Trolling for sea-run cutthroat is fair in late fall.

Shad angling is very popular, though primarily a boat fishery due to limited bank access. Anglers use light tackle, and the shad put up a good fight. Extremely small spinners, small wobblers, and weighted streamer flies are all successful for shad to 3 pounds. This fishery usually takes off in May and June.

Tackle, supplies, and advice are available in Coos Bay. Boats can be launched at Doras and Rooke Higgins on the Millacoma, and at the Myrtle Tree Boat Ramp on the South Coos River.

COOS RIVER, SOUTH FORK A good south coast stream with a variety of angling. It meets the Coos River from the east about 4 miles above the bay, and about 6 miles east of the city of Coos Bay. County roads follow it throughout its length.

The stream has good populations of cutthroat, fall chinook, coho, steelhead, and a large shad run, as well as a few striped bass.

Fall chinook show well in October, and a smaller run of coho peaks in late November or December. The 1986 catch was a little better than average at 176 fall chinook and 109 coho. Steelhead are available from December through February with plunking very popular. The steelhead catch fluctuates considerably from year to year, from a high of 1,512 in 1984-85 to 683 the following season.

Wild cutthroat are taken early in the season and again in late fall. The river is no loner stocked with trout. Some anglers still catch striped bass in July.

In May and June, shad are in the South Fork, and anglers turn out in droves to cast or troll for them, using small spinners or weighted flies. Bank angling access is limited to the mouth of Daniels Creek across from the Myrtle Tree Ramp. Boaters take shad throughout the river.

COQUILLE RIVER A very good south coast stream with excellent access, entering the ocean at a small bay near Bandon. It is crossed by Hwy. 42S at Coquille, about 20 miles up from the mouth. Hwy. 42 from Roseburg follows the river downstream from the forks at Myrtle Point. The river offers a variety of freshwater, tidewater, and saltwater angling over its 30 mile run.

Coquille Bay is fished for salmon, a variety of perch, dungeness crab, and smelt. Both north and south jetties are well used by anglers, as are the Bandon City Docks, where large numbers of perch and crab are taken from April through August. Smelt are dipped from the docks in July. Softshell clams are dug primarily in the flats adjacent to the Bandon Treatment Plant.

A few spring chinook move into the river during summer, but salmon fishing begins in earnest with fall run chinook in September and coho in October. About 500 fall chinook are taken yearly from the river and bay, and half that number of coho. There's good trolling in the entire lower river, with herring and lures equally popular. Efforts to build up the Coquille salmon runs are being coordinated by the Dept. of Fish and Wildlife's STEP program. Volunteers help by rearing salmon fry, but releases are still small at this time.

Steelhead are taken in good numbers starting in late November and December in both tidewater and in the forks above. The 1985-86 steelhead catch was 702, down from 1815 in 1984-85. Trolling for sea-run cutthroat takes place in late summer and fall. Local anglers fish the lower river from Riverton to Myrtle for brown bullhead. Striped bass are rarely seen here anymore.

There are two boat ramps in Coquille, including an excellent new facility at Sturdivant Park which includes a fishing float. Other ramps are located at Rocky Point on South Bank Rd. 2 miles upstream, Bullard's Beach State Park, and at Bandon. There is also a ramp upstream at Riverton, mid-way up the South Bank Rd., at Arago, and at Myrtle Point.

COQUILLE RIVER, EAST FORK A good trout and steelhead stream meeting the North Fork of the Coquille at Gravelford, about 5 miles east of Myrtle Point on Hwy. 42, paralleled by a good road throughout its 30 mile length. The upper river has good trout water, with plenty of good pools and boulder areas.

The East Fork is no longer stocked with cutthroat. Fall chinook are numerous in October, and coho show well in November, but these fish are usually past their prime, as this fork of river has spawning beds. The first fish show in November after rains raise the river level. Best steelhead angling is in January, with a catch that fluctuates from less than a hundred, to more than 800.

COQUILLE RIVER, MIDDLE FORK A large fork of the Coquille, joining the South Fork just south of Myrtle Point. About 40 miles long, it is followed closely by Hwy. 42 throughout most of its length.

Angling is fair for native cutthroat trout. Fall chinook show up well in September, followed about a month later by coho. Steelheading peaks about January. The salmon and steelhead runs are fairly small and lightly fished.

COQUILLE RIVER, NORTH FORK A good steelhead and cutthroat stream, joining the mainstem just west of Myrtle Point after a 40 mile run. A county road follows the North Fork NE from Myrtle Pt. on Hwy. 42. The upper river can be reached by the Fairview Rd. from Co-quille.

It offers very good angling for wild cutthroat trout in early spring and for the returning sea-run in late fall.

Fall chinook appear here in October, and coho follow in November, with a total fall salmon catch around 200. Best steelheading is in January and February. Drift fishing takes most of the steelhead, 580 in the 1985-86 season.

COQUILLE RIVER, SOUTH FORK A very productive fork of the Coquille River, featuring the most consistent steelheading in the area. Over 50 miles long, it is followed closely by a paved road from Myrtle Point on Hwy. 42 to Powers, about 20 miles upstream.

Once offering some of the best trout fishing on the south coast, the South Fork is now heavily stocked with, and managed primarily for, winter steelhead. Trout are no longer stocked, but the river still offers good fishing for wild cutthroat in early season.

January and February are the prime months for steelhead. The annual catch rate is rarely less than 2500, and has been as high as 4800 (1984-85). Fall chinook are in the lower river in early October, with a total catch usually less than 100.

COW CREEK A large tributary of the South Umpqua, entering the river from the west about 8 miles south of Myrtle Creek. Over 80 miles long, it joins the South Umpqua between Riddle and Canyonville.

Cow Creek contains native cutthroat of good size, but they're hard to take. Rough fish populations are large, and the resulting trout angling is generally poor. It is open for winter steelhead downstream from the West Fork Bridge, but few are taken (only a hundred over the past 10 years). There are smallmouth bass in the lower creek up to Glendale. A dam has been proposed for the creek at river mile 6 at the upper end of salmon spawning beds.

There are several BLM picnic areas on the creek south of Riddle and a small campground on Cow Creek Rd. 18 miles upstream from Azalea at Devil's Flat.

CROOKS LAKE A cutthroat lake about 10 miles south of Bandon on Hwy. 101. About 50 acres, 1 1/2 miles west of the highway, it is privately owned, with no access to public.

DAVIDSON LAKE Prominent on some maps, this 25-acre lake is about 7 miles south of Bandon on Hwy. 101. It is between the ocean and highway, near the sand dunes. It contains black bass and good size trout, but is privately owned, without public access,

DENMAN MANAGEMENT AREA PONDS A Department of Fish and Wildlife angling and waterfowl development 6 miles north of Medford. The 20 small ponds here are managed for bass and panfish. The tract of land covers several thousand acres.

Most of the ponds are only an acre or two. Whetstone Pond #1, a 10 acre pond near the management headquarters, is very popular. The ponds contain largemouth bass, bluegill, crappie and catfish. Bass have been taken up to 17 lbs (they say). Early spring fishing produces brown bullhead to 2 pounds. Check with the resident manager for the best spots and for special regulations.

DIAMOND LAKE (Douglas Co.) A large, popular rainbow lake in an attractive setting, 15

miles north of Crater Lake. The lake is at elevation 5100 ft. The eastern skyline is dominated by nearby plus Mt. Thielsen, elevation 9000 ft. The Dept. of Fish and Wildlife estimates 300,000 trout are caught here annually, and many of exceptional size. Trout to 10 pounds are caught, with 6-8 pounders business as usual. The average fish taken here weighs over one pound.

Diamond Lake is part of the Umpqua system but is more easily reached from the east. From Hwy. 97 in central Oregon, paved Hwy. 138 leads 20 miles west directly to the lake. The same highway can be taken east from Roseburg, following the North Umpqua about 90 miles to the lake. From the south, Diamond Lake is 108 miles NE of Medford by way of hwys. 62, 230, and 138. Roads to the lake are usually open by late May.

Diamond is one of the larger natural lakes in the state, over 2800 acres in the Umpqua National Forest. The lake is rich in natural food, and trout put on weight fast. Fishing is sustained primarily by large plants of fingerling rainbow, made right after ice out. These fish are usually not caught during their first summer, but have a good heft come ice out the following year.

Angling holds up throughout the season, but the most exciting time to be here is the first month after ice out. For some reason the fish in Diamond Lake prefer to spawn in spring, swarming the inlets right after ice out. Smaller fish follow the large spawners for the eggs. In addition, a very heavy midge hatch takes place simultaneously, giving an edge to fly anglers who can fish a chironomid nymph. This jamboree usually occurs in May, but can vary from spring to spring. Call the Forest Service Information Station at the lake for an update. The phone number is (503)793-3310.

All methods of angling are used here, and all will produce at times. Bait angling takes fish in the shoal areas in 10-30 feet of water. Single eggs and worms work well, and cheesebait on no. 14 or 16 cheeseholder treble hooks is very popular. Use the soft packaged cheese and mold it on the hook. Gourmet varieties are usually too crumbly. The north end of the lake is heavily worked by cheesebait anglers and has picked up the name *Velveeta Hole*. The fish here have a reputation for leader shyness. Use the lightest line you can handle. Four pounds can be too heavy for still-fishing here.

Drifting worms through the weed beds at the south end produces the largest fish. Trolling in the deep areas near the center of the lake and parallel to the west and east shores near drop-offs can be profitable. Ask at the resort for hints and current hot spots.

Fly anglers who can work small dark nymphs will always take fish here. Trolling with sunken wet flies can also be effective. The west shore, in 10-20 feet of water, is a good trolling area. Flies should be trolled very slowly with lots of line out. Small dry flies work well early and late in the day. *Hint:* when the lake water warms in late summer, the trout seek the cooler waters of the inlets at the south end of the lake. A long fine leader and a small dead drifted nymph can do the trick.

Hearty anglers who enjoy breaking their own trail and getting away from the crowds might consider hiking and fishing Lake Creek, which flows from Diamond Lake to Lemolo (a good two day hike-and-fish). This adventure can be especially profitable in fall.

There are many facilities at the lake, including a resort at the NE end, several stores, boat and motor rentals, a boat ramp, lodging, and a

restaurant. There are two Forest Service fish cleaning stations at the north and south ends by the boat ramps. The cleaning station at the lodge is also open to public use. Three of the four forest service campgrounds around the lake also have boat ramps. Boat users should keep a weather eye out for high winds which sometimes rough up the lake in mid-day. Be sure to have safety equipment aboard. Speed limit on the lake is 10 MPH during angling season.

EEL LAKE A large coastal lake managed for cutthroat, rainbow, coho, and largemouth bass. Black crappie have been illegally introduced. Eel is about 10 miles south of Reedsport on Hwy. 101. The western arm of the lake is within William M. Tugman State Park.

Eel is a narrow, deep lake, shaped like a giant U about 2 miles long. It is 350 acres and 60 feet deep in the center channel. The water is fairly clear. It is drained by Eel Creek at the SW end of the lake near the bottom of the U.

Coho are stocked, and catches have been good. Increasing numbers of these fish run to 15 inches. A handful of seagoing coho enter the lake in November.

Eel provides some good trout fishing in spring and summer for wild and stocked fish. Fly fishing can be good and saves on tackle. Bait fishing also produces consistently. A good population of largemouth bass are established in the lake. Fish for them along the shoreline.

There is a campground and boat ramp in the state park at the SW end of the lake. Supplies are available in Lakeside. The Lakeside airstrip is within a half hour hike of the State Park camp.

ELBOW LAKE A 13 acre Forest Service lake with stocked rainbow and panfish, located on the west side of Hwy. 101, about 13 miles north of Reedsport. Elbow receives a fair stocking of legal rainbow each spring, and fishing pressure is moderate. There is a paved boat ramp and picnic facilities at the lake.

ELK CREEK (Douglas Co.) A good, accessible stream, flowing about 35 miles into the Umpqua River at Elkton. It is followed closely by Hwy. 38 from Elkton to Drain, about 13 miles. The upper stream east of Drain turns SE and is crossed by I-5. The upper area is reached by several roads east from Scott's Valley.

Elk offers good early season fishing for both native cutthroat and rainbow. The stream is closed to steelhead and salmon angling. There are no campgrounds on the stream.

ELK RIVER (Curry Co.) A south coast stream with fair steelhead and excellent salmon runs. The river flows west about 30 miles, entering the ocean north of Port Orford, just south of Camp Blanco. It's crossed by Hwy. 101 about 3 miles north of Port Orford. A paved road follows the south bank all the way up to the steelhead deadline at Bald Mt. Creek just above the hatchery.

Fall chinook fishing is very good in the lower section in October, or as soon as there is enough water for the stream to breach the dune at the mouth. The earliest fishing possible is actually a surf fishery on the beach. Walk south along the beach from Cape Blanco State Park, about a mile to the mouth. Fishing here can be fantastic, with some big fish taken through December. The runs are often late due to insufficient rainfall. The 1986 fall salmon catch was 1368.

Elk River is a good winter steelhead producer for its size, though the catch has fallen to about half of what it was in the '70s, as has the salmon catch. January and February are the best steelheading months, with an average annual catch around 500.

Most steelhead and salmon angling takes place in the lower river. Unfortunately, access is a problem here, as most of the river flows through private land. The only public bank access is at the Hwy. 101 Bridge, and at the hatchery (be sure to observe the hatchery area closure). There are some pay-to-fish landowners, but they seem to change their mind from year to year. Boat angling is the method of necessity. There are some excellent drifts in the lower river, with a minimum of snags and brush. The only put-in is at the hatchery, and the only take-out is at Hwy. 101, a 9 mile drift.

There are native cutthroat in the upper river, which flows through the Siskiyou National Forest, but the roads are steep, narrow, unpaved, and poorly marked (got the picture?). Carry a current Siskiyou Forest map if you venture far. There are campgrounds in the forest.

EMIGRANT RESERVOIR A large reservoir with bass and panfish in the Talent Irrigation complex, Jackson County. The reservoir is north of Hwy. 66 about 5 miles SE of Ashland. It can cover 800 acres, but actual size fluctuates due to irrigation use.

Smallmouth bass fishing is popular here, with catches to 12 inches. Best fishing is around the dam rockface. There's good fishing for crappie, largemouth bass, and bluegill. Largemouth bass to 5 pounds are caught around the willows in spring. A few brown bullhead are taken. Rainbow are caught in the arm where Emigrant Creek flows into the reservoir. The county run campground on the lake is comfortably situated within a natural oak grove, and provides trailer and tent spaces, a boat ramp, and elaborate sanitary facilities (including hot showers). It's an exzcellent place to camp if you're planning to spiff up after the evening rise and take in a little Shakespeare.

EMPIRE LAKES These are two artificial lakes which have been improved for angling by the city of Empire with help from the Dept. of Fish and Wildlife. Located north of the road that runs from Coos Bay to Empire, they fluctuate with water use from a maximum 50 acres.

The lakes are stocked with rainbow trout and have sustaining populations of bluegill and largemouth bass. There is a park on the upper lake.

EUCHRE CREEK (Curry Co.) A small coastal stream that enters the ocean about 20 miles south of Port Orford at Ophir. It is crossed by Hwy. 101 near the mouth. A fair road follows the stream for about 7 miles. Another road follows a large tributary, Cedar Creek, to the south. Cedar Creek offers fair trout fishing.

The salmon runs on Euchre continue to be depressed, but enhancement efforts (coordinated by the STEP program) continue. The thrust of the program is a mix of stocking and habitat improvement. The program began in 1980. Nearest camping is at Humbug Mt. State Park, about 10 miles north on Hwy. 101.

EVANS CREEK A fair size tributary of the Rogue River, entering from the north about 20 miles east of Grants Pass at the town of Rogue River. About 20 miles long, it furnishes some trout fishing in early season. It is followed north from Hwy. 99 by a paved road for about 7 miles, and by secondary roads upstream. The upper east fork is the best bet. Private property along the stream severely reduces access.

FISH CREEK (Douglas Co.) A fair trout stream high up the North Umpqua River, above an impassable barrier to salmon and steelhead. It enters the North Umpqua from the south one mile below Toketee Falls, about 40 miles upstream from Glide on the North Umpqua Highway. Several fair logging roads hit the upper stream, one heading south from the Toketee Generator Plant, and the other following Copelands Creek near Eagle Rock.

The stream offers good early fishing for wild trout. Don't neglect the impoundments on the creek. Follow Watson Creek Rd. to the Fish Creek forebay for rainbow to 17 inches. There are forest campgrounds at Fish Creek and Camas Creek about 5 miles south of the highway.

FISH LAKE (Douglas Co.) A big, beautiful trout lake beneath Grasshopper Mt. in the Umpqua-Rogue Divide Wilderness. This 95 acre hike-in rainbow and brook trout lake is at elevation 3500 ft., 1 1/2 miles (and 800 ft.) below, Buckeye and Cliff Lakes. Trail bikes are no longer allowed on the Fish Lake Trail.

At Tiller on Hwy. 227, follow County Rd. 46 into the forest, where it becomes FS 28, the South Umpqua River Rd. Continue on FS 28 about 4 miles past South Umpqua Falls Camp, where several roads branch off. Follow FS 2823 to the right about 2 miles, then FS 2830. Bear left at the fork. The Fish Lake Trailhead 2840 is a little over 2 miles further, at the next fork on the right. It's about a 3 mile hike to the lake.

Fish Lake has both rainbow and eastern brook trout, with fish up to 20 inches caught each season. It is stocked from time to time, but wild fish make up most of the catch. It can be fished from shore, but a raft or float tube will increase your chances. All methods will take fish. There's an improved camp at the lake, and good camping at Camp Comfort Campground on FS 28 about 2 1/2 miles beyond your first right.

FISH LAKE (Jackson Co.) A large, very popular lake about 37 miles NE of Medford on Hwy. 140, head waters of the North Fork of Little Butte Creek. Take Hwy. 62 north from Medford, to its junction with 140. From Ashland, take Dead Indian Rd. (east of the municipal airport), about 4 miles past Howard Prairie Lake to Big Elk Rd., a northbound gravel road which joins Hwy. 140 near Fish Lake. From Klamath Falls, take Hwy. 140 north past Lake of the Woods.

Covering 440 acres, Fish Lake has provided good fishing for stocked rainbow and brook trout. The lake does have a continuing rough fish problem which past treatments have failed to eradicate.

The Pacific Crest Trail comes to within 1/2 mile of Fish Lake, and with good campgrounds and a fishing village-like resort, it is a popular stopover for hikers. There are two campgrounds at the east end of the lake, Doe Point and Fish Lake. North Fork Camp on FS 3706 is about 3/4 mile west of the lake. There is a boat launch at Fish Lake Camp. The resort on the west shore has cabins, boat rentals, restaurant, and supplies.

FLORAS CREEK A short south coast stream with good steelhead and fair chinook runs. Hwy. 101 crosses it about 15 miles south of Bandon. The upper stream is followed by road for about 5 miles, but the stream is usually in a gorge well below the road. The stream below the highway can be reached in several spots by car, but the area is swampy.

It offers good early fishing for native cutthroat. Chinook show up in October or later, depending on the breaching of the outlet dune by high water. A few coho are also caught. Steelhead show in December and are caught through March. The creek is lightly fished due to difficulty of access, but it produces a fair catch.

FLORAS LAKE A large, popular lake west of Hwy. 101, about 17 miles south of Bandon. A good road just south of Langlois runs 2 miles west from 101 to the lake. The lake covers 250 acres and in places reaches a depth of 50 feet.

Rainbow trout are stocked, and wild cutthroat are caught in good numbers if the spring opening is not too late for the usual spring run.

The lake has a few largemouth bass 7-8 pounds, but it's slow fishing. There are quite a few weed beds. Try plugging into the open water near the beds to tempt these bass.

Chinook, coho, and steelhead all move through the lake into the upper tributaries. The combined winter steelhead catch for Floras Lake, New River (the outlet to Floras Creek), and Floras Creek fluctuates considerably, from 100 to over 600. Over 100 fall chinook and a few coho are also taken each year.

Biocope County Park is located on the lake road and provides camping and a boat ramp. It can get real windy here, so keep a weather eye out if you're boating.

FORDS MILL POND A large pond with bass and panfish on Hwy. 225 near Sutherlin, about one mile west of the junction of hwys. 225 and 99. About 100 acres, the pond is owned by Roseburg Lumber Co. They allow angler access during non-working hours.

East, south, and west banks are accessible. A number of species are present in good numbers, including bluegill, crappie, perch, brown bullhead and bass. Four pound bass are not uncommon, and buckets full of fine crappie are taken in spring. Yellow jigs and cut bait are best for the crappie. Motorboats are prohibited, but shore fishing is easy anywhere. Accommodations and supplies are available at Sutherlin, 2 miles east of the lake.

GARRISON LAKE A large 134 acre lake with trout, a small number of bass, and abundant small yellow perch, just west of Port Orford off Hwy. 101. Up to 30 ft. deep in places, the lake is typical for the coast area, with partly sandy shores and a severe weed problem.

The trout catch is good, although the lake is hard to fish. It is stocked with hatchery trout and has some wild cutthroat. It has been stocked with bass several times, but the population is at a low level.

Nearest camping is at Battle Rock State Park in Port Orford. There is a boat ramp and parking area provided by the state at the south end of the lake, and another provided by the county at the north end.

GALESVILLE RESERVOIR A 640 acre impoundment on Cow Creek, tributary to the South Umpqua. Created in 1986, it contains largemouth bass, crappie, trout, and coho. At this writing, after 2 years of drought, it has yet to fill. However, it should provide good fishing in the future. The submerged trees along the NW edge were cut high to create artificial reefs for the bass and crappie. The reservoir has spotty bank access along the road, but a good boat ramp.

GOLD RAY FOREBAY The 80 acre forebay to Gold Ray Dam on the Rogue River. Access is a problem due to the railroad tracks. There is no official boat access due to the danger of boats going over the dam *(some have)*, however anglers do launch boats to fish for largemouth bass and bluegill. Kelly Slough is a popular fishing area.

GRASS LAKE A rich, self-sustaining brook trout lake in the Seven Lakes Basin of the northern Sky Lakes Wilderness, headwaters of the Rogue River Middle Fork, offering very good fly fishing opportunities. It is accessible from east and west. See Alta Lake for detailed directions.

Trail 981 accesses the basin from FS 344, continuing past the cut-off to Alta, to the cut-off to Middle then Grass Lake. Trail 3703 approaches the basin from FS 3334 on the east at Sevenmile Marsh Campground, joining the Pacific Crest Trail after about 2 miles. The trail to Grass cuts off the PCT after about 2 miles.

Covering 30 acres, Grass supports an excellent brook trout population with fish to 15 inches, averaging 9 to 12 inches. Usually the most productive of the Seven Lakes group, it is quite shallow, and fly fishing is effective. There is an improved camp at Grass and other nearby lakes. See also Cliff, Middle, Alta. For trail information, check with the Butte Falls Ranger Station.

GRAVE CREEK A fairly large tributary of the Rogue River, entering from the east, about 6 miles north of Galice. It is followed by secondary roads for most of its 30 miles. I-5 crosses the middle stretch of stream about 14 miles north of Grants Pass at Sunny Valley, where secondary roads lead upstream and down. The creek is lowered by heavy irrigation in summer. It provides fair trout fishing in early season only and is closed to angling for salmon and steelhead, which use it as spawning ground.

HALL LAKE A small lake about 10 miles south of Reedsport on Hwy. 101, which is gradually being filled in by sand dunes. Private property surrounds the lake. It has a good population of cutthroat.

HERBERT LOG POND (a.k.a. Canyonville Pond) A good l0 acre mill pond purchased by the state for angling. It is located on Hwy. 227 in a county park about one mile east of I- 5 at Canyonville.

The pond produces a good number of largemouth bass, black crappie, and brown bullhead catfish. Bank fishing is easy, and it's ideal for youngsters. Motorboats are prohibited, but car-top or rubber boats will help you reach the larger bass. Supplies and accommodations are available at Canyonville.

HOOVER PONDS A series of four artificial ponds visible from Hwy.140 north of Medford. These ponds have been stocked with largemouth bass, bluegill, crappie and brown bullhead, and all species are reproducing naturally now. The ponds are small, 4-10 acres each, and most fishing is from the bank. Jackson Pond, at the County Sports Park, is just east of these. It has been stocked with bass and bluegill.

HORSESHOE LAKE (Klamath Co.) A good hike-in brook and rainbow trout lake in the Blue Lake Basin of the Sky Lakes Wilderness, Rogue River National Forest. See blue lake (klamath co.). for road and trail directions.

Horseshoe is about 1/2 mile SE of Blue Lake. Bear left at the trail fork. Other good lakes nearby include Blue Canyon, Pear, Casey.

Horseshoe Lake is about 20 acres, with good shoal areas and cover for fish. The lake has good numbers of brook trout to 18 inches, and a smaller population of rainbow about the same size. Fish this large provide exciting fishing but can be hard to catch. Fly fishing is most productive here, while bait fishing is difficult. Casting small lures from shore with a slow retrieve can also be effective.

There are good natural campsites at the lake. Improved sites are available at nearby lakes. The Blue Rock Mt. Rd. usually opens in June.

HORSEFALL LAKE A 250 acre lake within the National Dunes Recreation Area north of North Bend. From Hwy. 101, cross the Haynes Inlet of Coos Bay, turning onto the Bluebill Lake Rd. about half-way across the inlet. Horsefall Lake is NW of Little Bluebill Lake, part of a lake complex that includes adjacent Spirit Lake and Sandpoint Lake to the north. Horsefall contains yellow perch, largemouth bass, and brown bullhead.

HOWARD PRAIRIE LAKE One of southern Oregon's most popular lakes, a large irrigation reservoir in an alpine setting east of Ashland. Howard Prairie grows fish very well. Depending on irrigation needs and rainfall, the reservoir varies from 2000-1500 acres. From Ashland take Hwy. 66 to Dead Indian Rd. just past the municipal airport. Follow this paved road 22 miles to the reservoir. The route from Medford is circuitous but possible. Take Hwy. 62 to Hwy.140, Lake of the Woods Hwy. Turn south at Lake Creek, following Little Butte Rd. to Soda Creek Rd., then Conde Creek Rd. to Dead Indian Rd., emerging just west of Howard Prairie.

Stocked annually, the rainbows here range 10-18 inches, and most weigh over one pound, with 4 and 5 pounders not uncommon. Worms and eggs fished just off the bottom take fish in early season, and trolling with spinner/bait combinations works well. The best trolling area is the deep water in the east inside channel. Fly anglers might try streamers on a slow troll, or cast to the shallows. A lot of the larger rainbow are taken late in the day on flies slowly trolled just under the surface. While trolling is very popular, the lake can successfully be fished from its banks. If you enjoy brown bullhead, there's plenty of them here. These fish average 8 inches and run to 11 inches. Worms are the favored bait. Pumpkinseed sunfish are also present.

There are three county campgrounds on the lake, each with a boat ramp. A private resort provides accommodations, supplies and advice. It is open only during trout season.

HUNTER CREEK A small coast stream that empties directly into the ocean just south of the Rogue River Estuary. Hwy. 101 crosses its mouth about 2 miles south of Gold Beach. Hunter once supported nice runs of winter steelhead and fall salmon. Anglers also fished for sea-run cutthroat. But poor logging practices and angling pressure related to its easy accessibility have severely depleted its fisheries. The entire stream is now closed for rehabilitation until 1991.

HYATT RESERVOIR A large reservoir of about 9000 acres, north of the Green Springs summit on Hwy. 66, which leads from Ashland

to Klamath Falls. It is 5 miles from Green Springs, which is about 13 miles east of Ashland. Dead Indian Rd. accesses the reservoir from the north.

Managed for stocked rainbow and largemouth bass, the reservoir has recently become overpopulated by illegally introduced brown bullhead catfish, which compete with the rainbow for food. It is scheduled for treatment in 1989. The bass will be salvaged and reintroduced, and rainbow restocked. Complete recovery could take 2 years.

Traditional fishing methods on the lake include trolling the west shore and NE cove.

A BLM campground with boat ramps is at the south end of the reservoir. The reservoir is accessible in winter, and there is some ice fishing.

ILLINOIS RIVER A major tributary of the lower Rogue River, joining it from the south at Agness, about 25 miles upriver from Gold Beach. Headwaters of the Illinois are in the Siskiyou National Forest east of Cave Junction, but the main fishery is for winter steelhead in the 25 miles from Pomeroy Dam at Cave Junction to Oak Flat. A few anglers boat the 5 mile section between Kerby Bridge and Pomery Dam using small sleds, but the Illinois is primarily a bank fishery.

To access a popular section of the river, follow Hwy. 199 north from Cave Junction to Selma, then turn left on County Rd. 5070, which becomes FS 4203. This road leads to Kerby Flat, then follows the river to Oak Flat, ending at Briggs Cr. Watch for roadside pull-offs, indicating favorite river access points. At Briggs Cr., a Forest Service trail leads down to the river and follows it for about 5 miles to the Weaver Ranch, just beyond Pine Cr. This portion of the river is designated Wild and Scenic and is included in the Kalmiopsis Wilderness. There is no boat access here. There is boat angling in the lower river, from a ramp at Agness.

The fishery in the Illinois and its tributaries continues to be severely affected by water withdrawals for irrigation. The Illinois once yielded annual steelhead catches close to 3000, but now fluctuates between 500 and just over 1000. Salmon catches in the Illinois are rare. There is good early spring fishing for wild trout in the upper river.

JORDAN LAKE A 10 acre pond in an industrial waste pond area west of Jordan Point on Coos Bay. It contains yellow perch, largemouth bass, and brown bullhead.

JUMP OFF JOE CREEK A 20 mile tributary of the Middle Rogue River, entering the Rogue in the Merlin area NW of Grants Pass. It is crossed by Hwy. 99 about 10 miles north of Grants Pass and followed east by paved road for a good distance. It's not open for salmon or steelhead, but provides good early angling for wild trout. Fishing peters out with low water later in the season.

KLAMATH LAKE See Upper Klamath Lake.

LAKE CREEK (Klamath Co.) The outlet stream of Diamond Lake, headwaters of the North Umpqua. The creek runs l0 miles north from the lake to Lemolo Reservoir. Roads follow within a mile throughout its length. Hwy.138 crosses about 5 miles downstream from the lake at Thielsen Campground. The Umpqua National Forest map shows a rough track (FS 4792) leading south from the FS 60 junction with 138 near Thielsen, following the creek for almost 4 miles. North from Thielsen Camp, FS 2610 to Lemolo Lake stays within a mile of the creek, though the creek runs through a deep canyon there.

The upper end of the creek near Diamond Lake contains good size rainbow to 2 pounds. The beaver flats below yield more brown and brook trout in a series of pools. Hearty anglers might like to try a 2 day hike-and-fish from Diamond Lake to Lemolo for the chance of a catch worth bragging about, especially in fall.

There are camping facilities at Diamond Lake, Lemolo Lake, and Thielsen Campground.

LAKE IN THE WOODS A small but easily reached lake in the Umpqua National Forest due east of Roseburg. It's about 24 miles to the lake from Glide. Take the North Umpqua Rd. to Glide, and the Little River Rd., FS 27, to the lake.

The lake is at elevation 3000 ft. and is accessible early. Only about 4 acres, it provides fine fishing for rainbow averaging 10 inches, but fish to 19 inches have been caught. The biggest fish respond to bait, but fly casting can be effective. It is easily fished from shore. There's a nice campground here.

LAKE MARIE A 5 acre cutthroat lake within Umpqua Lighthouse State Park, about 2 miles south of Winchester Bay on Hwy. 101. There's fair fishing for cutthroat early in the season, and fly anglers do well. The lake is stocked with hatchery trout. Largemouth bass and yellow perch are also present.

There is no boat ramp, and motor boats are prohibited. The state park has picnic and camping facilities.

LEMOLO LAKE The largest reservoir in the upper North Umpqua power development, covering 415 acres when not drawn down. Lemolo is lightly fished, probably because it is positioned between Diamond Lake and Toketee Reservoir, both outstanding waters. It's a scenic spot, though, situated among the pines with Mt. Thielsen looming above.

From Diamond Lake take Hwy. 138 north about 7 miles to FS 2610, which leads north about 5 miles to the reservoir. From Roseburg, FS 2610 is about 80 miles east by way of Hwy. 138.

There's fair angling for brown trout from opening day through fall. Angling success usually falls off during midsummer. Drawdown in the fall reduces the pool to about 140 acres and severely limits angler success.

This reservoir is currently managed for wild brown trout. An effort by the state to develop a trophy fishery here failed, probably due to heavy angler harvest of trophy size trout, and the impact of the annual 40 foot drawdown. Nevertheless, there is a healthy population of browns here. The typical catch averages 12 inches, and much larger fish are present. A few monster browns to 15 lbs. have been taken, and there are rumors of much larger fish. It takes a substantial lure to interest these big old carnivors.

There are also brook trout and a few rainbow here, with brook trout to 12 inches near the dam and inlet. A few kokanee are also present, remnants of a stocking effort that failed.

Best catches are made from boats, but bank anglers can do well. Boats are not allowed in the upper end beyond markers which can be plainly seen. Boat ramps are located at Poole Creek Campground and at the resort.

There are 4 campgrounds on the Lake. The

LEMOLO FALLS, N. UMPQUA RIVER
Courtesy, Oregon State Highway Dept.

Forest Service also maintains a group campsite, available for reservation at Poole Creek. There is a resort on the NW end of the lake south of the dam. It features a lodge, groceries, tackle shop, dining room, cabins, boat and motor rentals, and a service station. Lemolo is no longer open for ice fishing, as it is heavily drawn down in winter.

LIBBY POND A 10 acre pond about 7 miles east of Gold Beach beside the south bank of the Rogue River, off County Rd. 595. It contains brown bullhead.

LITTLE APPLEGATE RIVER A long trout stream flowing into the Applegate River about 3 miles south of Ruch. Ten miles of good road follow the 20 mile stream, and primitive roads continue to its source near the California border. From Medford or Grants Pass, take Hwy. 238 to the upper Applegate River Rd. cut-off at Ruch. Early season bait fishing is often good. Campsites are available at the BLM's Tunnel Ridge Recreation Area about 8 miles upstream.

LITTLE RIVER A very nice tributary of the North Umpqua, joining the Umpqua at Glide,

about 20 miles east of Roseburg on Hwy.138. It is followed east from Glide by paved road for about 15 miles, and by gravel road another 15 miles to the headwaters.

Little River has good fishing for native cutthroat and stocked rainbow. Fishing usually holds up until mid-summer. The upper river has some good fly water. Check the current regulations for information related to Little River's salmon and steelhead runs. At this time the river is open for steelhead and has a limited salmon season.

LOON LAKE A large, deep lake, draining into the lower Umpqua River. Loon Lake offers good angling for trout in spring and fall, and fair angling for largemouth bass throughout the season. From Hwy. 38 (Reedsport to Darwin), a county road leads south about 6 miles to the lake. The turn-off is about 3 miles west of Scottsburg. Driving south on I-5, take the Drain Exit. The lake can also be reached from Coos Bay by very poor roads up the Millicoma River.

Loon Lake covers 275 acres and is very deep with little shoal area. Native cutthroat are present in good numbers, and rainbow are stocked. Rainbow fishing holds up for several months, with catches to 18 inches.

Largemouth black bass provide fair angling throughout the season. Anglers cast lures and plugs, and use bait for bass to 8 pounds. The average bass is 2-4 pounds. Crappie to 12 inches are caught on bait or spinner combinations. Brown bullhead to 16 inches are available in fair numbers. Nice size bluegill are also present.

There are two resorts on the lake, and angling information and supplies can be obtained from them. Boats and motors are available. Loon Lake Recreation Site, an excellent BLM campground and boat ramp, is at the north end of the lake just south of the outlet crossing. There's also camping at the resort as well as overnight accomodations, and several picnic areas are nearby on Hwy. 38.

LOST CREEK RESERVOIR A 3500 acre reservoir built by the Army Corp of Engineers on the Rogue at r.m. 157 just upstream from Cole Rivers Hatchery. The reservoir offers good fishing for a variety of trout, bass, and panfish. Located about 30 miles NE of Medford on Hwy. 62, it was first filled in 1977. The reservoir was built for flood control and to enhance downstream waterflow for anadramous fish.

Bass are a big fishery here. Lots of bass to 5 pounds have been taken, and the success rate has been very good. In the spring, anglers work the shoal areas on the south side of the reservoir. The trick is to get a lure under the overhanging brush. Largemouth bass fishing has been best when the reservoir is holding maximum water. There are also smallmouth bass, bluegill, crappie, pumpkinseed sunfish, and bullhead.

The reservoir is stocked annually with legal and fingerling rainbow which reach 16 inches. It also has wild populations of cutthroat, brook trout, and brown trout. The reservoir is over 300 feet deep, and still fishing is limited to a few shoal areas. Trolling with spinner and worm or lures works best, particularly at the upper end at the junction of north and south forks. Cold sunny days in December, January, and February can produce surprisingly good fishing on a troll here.

Camping facilities are available at Stewart State Park on the south shore. Boat ramps are located in Stewart Park and near the north abutment of the dam. There is a privately run moorage with store and boat rentals in the state park. Additional supplies are available at Prospect, Shady Cove, or Trail on Hwy. 62.

LOST LAKE (Douglas Co.) An 8-10 acre beaver pond in the Callahan Mts. near the town of Umpqua, with fine flyfishing for native cutthroat. Take the Hubbard Creek Rd. from Umpqua into the mountains, following the ridge crest. Turn right, and at about 100 yds. turn left to the creek. As you cross the creek, a trail leads off to the left, about 300 yds. to the lake. Good luck!

LUCILLE LAKE An 8 acre hike-in lake, in the Umpqua National Forest about 8 miles west of Lemolo Lake, 1/2 mile due west of Maidu Lake. The lake has very little cover and has consistently winterkilled. The Dept. of Fish and Wildlife has discontinued stocking.

MAIDU LAKE A good eastern brook trout lake in the headwaters of the North Umpqua just off the Pacific Crest Trail. It's an 8 mile hike from FS 958 west of the Bradley Creek

Arm of Lemolo. A shorter hike begins at Miller Lake in the Winema National Forest. Take Trail 1446 (which follows the north shore of Miller) up to the Pacific Crest Trail. It's about one mile to the junction, and less then a mile further NW to Maidu.

At 20 acres, Maidu has good size brook trout to 16 inches, with a few larger. Any method takes fish, but fly fishing really pays off in the evening. The lake is stocked every year or two, and has natural reproduction. It is usually accessible in late June.

MATSON CREEK A good trout stream, about 10 miles long, tributary to the East Fork Millicoma River. Matson joins the east fork about 10 miles east of Allegany, which is about 10 miles east of Coos Bay. Roads here are primitive logging tracks. This is Weyerhauser timber country, and access is limited. There are several high falls in the upper stream and real rough going.

However, the upper stream offers good cutthroat fishing and, surprisingly, eastern brook trout, which were stocked years ago. Bait fishing is the usual method.

MEDCO POND An old 70 acre log pond between Prospect and Butte Falls, on the Prospect-Butte Falls Hwy. NE of Medford. From Medford, follow Hwy. 62 east to the Butte Falls Hwy. Follow this past Butte Falls to the junction with Prospect Road. Head north 15 miles. The lake is on the east side of the road.

Medco is owned by the Medford Lumber Co., which allows public use. It is stocked with legal rainbow and has a good population of bass and bluegill. The bass run to 5 pounds, and bluegill to 8 inches.

MIDDLE LAKE (Klamath Co.) A good fly lake in the Seven Lakes Basin of the Sky Lakes Wilderness, accessible from east or west. For directions, see Grass Lake, Alta Lake. Middle Lake is between Grass and Cliff lakes, less than 1/4 mile from each.

Middle Lake is stocked annually with fingerlings and has native brook trout. The fish run to 16 inches and better, and angling holds up well all season. The west end seems to offer best fishing. Try wet bucktails and streamers in the morning and evening. There are good campsites here, as at other lakes in the basin.

MILLICOMA RIVER (NORTH FORK OF COOS RIVER) A major tributary of the Coos River, with a good run of shad, and good salmon angling. The main river is only about 7 or 8 miles long from Allegany to its confluence with the Coos. Above Allegany (which is head of tide) the river splits into East and West Forks. Access is by paved county roads off Hwy. 101 near Coos Bay.

Shad fishing is excellent at times, with best fishing in May and June. Best shad catches seem to be around the mid-section of the river near the tavern, especially on hot, sunny afternoons. It's a pretty stream, and a nice place to spend a summer day.

Trolling for fall chinook and coho occurs in September, October and November. The average year sees a couple hundred fall salmon landed. Most of the good steelhead angling takes place in the upper forks. Sea-run cutthroat angling is usually good from August through October.

Boat can be launched at Doras Ramp, 1/4 mile upstream from the confluence, and at Rooke Higgins, a newly refurbished facility with plenty of parking, about 3 miles further up-

stream. Log rafting, which was sometimes a problem to anglers, was discontinued tin 1988 with the completion of old growth logging in the area. Anglers can expect clearer water and perhaps less floating debris than in the past.

MILLICOMA RIVER, EAST FORK The East Fork is a good size stream with a fair steelhead run and cutthroat trout. About 25 miles long, it joins the main river at Allegany, about 10 miles east of Coos Bay. A road follows the East Fork another 10 miles, with logging roads branching off to follow the various tributaries.

A very good trout stream in early season, it is heavily fished for wild cutthroat by local anglers. Glen Creek, joining from the east about 6 miles upstream, has lots of cutthroat, too. The winter steelhead run has picked up in recent years due to a stocking program. The 1985-86 catch was over 400. The East Fork is also now open for salmon in summer, to take advantage of spring chinook strays associated with the aquaculture facility in Coos Bay.

MILLICOMA RIVER, WEST FORK A very good winter steelhead stream about 30 miles long, joining the main Millicoma River at head of tidewater at Allegany. Allegany is about 10 miles east of Coos Bay, reached by paved county road from Hwy. 101. A paved forest road continues upstream following the river. The road ends at Stall's Falls, which is about 10 miles above Allegany. Headwaters are reached by a detour through Elliot State Forest.

The upper stream, an area called the *Elkhorn Ranch*, affords very good angling for native cutthroat and is reached by hiking or pack trips. The fishing around Elkhorn Ranch provides a real quality angling experience. The fork provides outstanding cutthroat fishing starting as early as August.

The Dept. of Fish and Wildlife is currently stocking 35,000 steelhead smolts yearly in the fork, and anglers have reaped good returns. The 1985-86 catch was over 500, and over 1500 steelhead were taken the preceding year. The run hit its stride in December and holds through February. The West Fork has a high angler success rate for a small stream. It is open for salmon angling in summer to allow anglers to pick up strays from the aquaculture facility in Coos Bay.

Bank access is limited along the lower river due to private property. A storm in 1989 took out the public boat ramp at the county bridge, 5.5 miles upstream from the confluence.

MYRTLE CREEK (Douglas Co.) A good size tributary of the South Umpqua, actually two forks, each about 20 miles long, entering the South Umpqua at the town of Myrtle Creek on Hwy. 99. A paved road follows both forks to the east for 8 to 10 miles, and gravel roads continue up from there to the headwaters. The south fork road follows all the way into the Little River drainage to the NE. The upper north fork can also be reached by cutting south off the North Umpqua Rd. about 5 miles east of Roseburg.

The stream has a fair native cutthroat population and small steelhead. Most of the steelhead or young salmon are just barely six inches long and should be returned to the water so they can migrate to the ocean. The cutthroat are usually larger and can be easily identified by their heavy spotting. Single eggs or crayfish tails will work well in most areas. This stream is not open at present for salmon or steelhead angling. There is no camping in the vicinity, although picnic areas are available. Most of the property along the lower stream is privately owned. The upper portions are in BLM and private timberland.

NATIONAL CREEK A small but scenic tributary of the upper Rogue, entering the river west of Crater Lake National Park, about 4 miles north of the junction of hwys. 62 and 230. About 5 miles north of the junction on Hwy. 230, take FS 6530 to the right, which follows the stream for most of its 5 mile length. There's fair early trout fishing for brook trout and rainbow, with best fishing in June.

Union Creek Campground, just south of the Hwy. 62/230 junction, is a popular camping spot beside the scenic Rogue Gorge. For other good nearby trout streams see Copeland Creek, Wizard Creek.

NEW RIVER The short but interesting outlet stream for Floras Lake, Floras Creek, and other feeder creeks, New River has been known to reverse its flow from year to year, breaching the dunes in new locations to empty into the ocean. At this time, public access to the river has been denied by the current landowner. When accessible, New River provides bank angling for sea-run cutthroat, salmon, and steelhead. The stream parallels the beach and connects Floras Lake to Floras Creek. It is approached by a road just north of the Curry/Coos County line.

The river offers one mile of pretty good chinook bank angling from September through October. Some coho follow the chinook, and a fair winter steelhead run takes place in December. Sea-run are taken from July through fall.

The BLM has large holdings along the stream and is trying to preserve the natural scenic values of the sand dunes. There's excellent surfperch fishing along the beaches across the dunes, all in all, a wonderful coastal nature study area.

SURFFISHING AT SUNSET
Bill Wagner, Photographer

NORTH UMPQUA See umpqua river, north.

OPAL LAKE (Douglas Co.) A fairly good trout lake in the Willamette National Forest just west of the southern boundary of Diamond Peak Wilderness. Follow FS 211 from the SW end of Crescent Lake, then turn left on FS 398. Opal is about 13 miles from Crescent Lake. Timpanagos Lake is just south of Opal.

About l5 acres, the lake supports both rainbow and brook trout. The rainbow average 9 inches and run 6-l3 inches. Brook trout predominate, averaging 8 inches. All methods are used here. The lake can be fished from shore. There's a small campground here and another at Timpanogas Lake, one mile south.

PEAR LAKE A good brook trout lake in the Blue Lake group of the southern Sky Lakes Wilderness. A long narrow lake, it is just east of Horseshoe Lake on Trail 982. See Blue Lake for complete directions from the west. It's a 4 mile hike, past Blue and Horseshoe lakes, to Pear.

To access the basin from the east, take Hwy. 140 (Lake of the Woods Rd.) to FS 3651, about 6 miles NE of Lake of the Woods and 4 miles west of the junction of Hwys. 140 and 62 near Upper Klamath Lake. Turn left on FS 3659 toward Big Meadows about 1 1/2 miles north of the junction of FS 3651 and 3458. Trailhead 3712 is at the apex of the hairprin curve on FS 3659. On Trail 3712, cross over the Pacific Crest Trail at about one mile, and continue on 3712 to the basin. At the next fork, follow Trail 982 SW around the south end of Island Lake to Pear. It's less than a 4 mile hike to Pear.

Stocked with fingerlings annually, this 25 acre lake supports a good population of native brook trout to 14 inches. Catches are good in spring and fall. During the day, fish the deep water in the north end. In the evening the fish school and feed in the shallower southern end of the lake. A float tube or rubber raft would come in handy. Pear is usually accessible in early June.

PISTOL RIVER A south coast stream, quite small, with a fair winter steelhead run and a modest show of fall chinook. It flows into the Pacific about 15 miles south of Gold Beach and is crossed near the mouth by Hwy.101. Only 20 miles long, it is followed east by a good road about 8 miles upstream. Above that the only access is by logging roads or trails.

The Pistol has fair trout, steelhead and salmon populations, but is not as productive as Chetco, Sixes, and Elk rivers. It is no longer stocked with cutthroat, but sea-run can be taken here when the bar is breached in fall. The Pistol mouth is bar bound in the summer, and returning cutthroat are held out until late August or September most years. Check with the Department of Fish and Wildlife at Gold Beach for an update. Fishing takes place primarily within the lagoon area of the stream.

PLAT 1 RESERVOIR A very productive 140 acre lake, 4 miles east of Sutherlin by the Plat 1 Rd. Built for flood control and irrigation in the late '60's, it now supports good populations of rainbow, crappie, bluegill, largemouth bass, and brown bullhead.

Bank fishing is easy, with no brush or trees to interfere with casting. A fine spot to take youngsters. Water levels drop during the summer and stay pretty low in winter. Spring and early summer are the best times to fish. It is stocked with catchable rainbow twice in spring. Bass to 6 pounds are common in the shallows on the east side. Plastic worms, nightcrawlers, and streamer flies are all effective. There is a good boat ramp, but a light boat with a short shaft motor will get you into the shallows where the bass tend to lurk. There's no camping at the lake.

POWERS LAKE City park fishing in the town of Powers. Located in a very nice family recreation area, the lake features stocked rainbow trout(best fished in March, April and May before the water warms) and brown bullhead catfish, .

POWERS POND An old mill pond at the edge of the community of Powers that has been purchased by the county as a fishing recreation area. It covers about 10 acres and is stocked with legal rainbow, largemouth bass, and black crappie. The park has RV facilities, showers, and a picnic area.

ROCK CREEK (Douglas Co.) Good native cutthroat in this 20 mile tributary of the North Umpqua. The creek enters the river from the north, about 27 miles east of Roseburg. From Roseburg, take Hwy. 138, which meets and follows the North Umpqua just west of Glide. A paved road, about one mile from Idleyld Park, follows Rock Creek's west bank for about 14 miles.

There's good trout fishing here from early spring into summer. Native cutthroat are caught to 14 inches. Expect to lose a little tackle, however, as the stream is wide and rough. Rock Creek Hatchery is about 1/4 mile upstream from the mouth.

BLM maintains 2 nice campgrounds on the stream, and there are several county parks on the North Umpqua upstream. Susan Creek State Park, about 8 miles east of Rock Creek on the North Umpqua Hwy., has plenty of camping space.

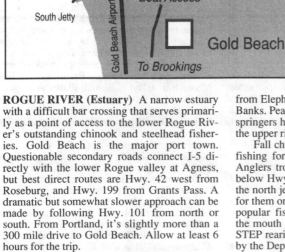

1. NORTH JETTY - Preferred to south jetty for ling cod, perch in spring, and chinook July through Sept. Home to a noteworthy colony of ground squirrels.

2. SAND SPIT - Bank fishery for fall chinook July through Sept. Use spinners or herring or anchovy.

3. TROLL for fall chinook.

4. Doyle Pt. - Best dungeness crabbing in bay.

5. INDIAN CR. - Fish the mouth for fall chinook. Bank fish off flat at low tide.

6. ELEPHANT ROCK - Chinook hole near down-bay side of rock.

7. JOHNS HOLE - Rocky point creates chinook hole.

8. CLAY BANKS - Gravel bar access to flyfish for chinook at lower end, hog lines at upper just below riffle.

9. FERRY HOLE - Drive onto gravel bar to launch drift boats and prams for chinook.

10. WILLOWS - bank fishery for winter steelhead; unsigned gravel access road.

ROGUE RIVER (Estuary) A narrow estuary with a difficult bar crossing that serves primarily as a point of access to the lower Rogue River's outstanding chinook and steelhead fisheries. Gold Beach is the major port town. Questionable secondary roads connect I-5 directly with the lower Rogue valley at Agness, but best direct routes are Hwy. 42 west from Roseburg, and Hwy. 199 from Grants Pass. A dramatic but somewhat slower approach can be made by following Hwy. 101 from north or south. From Portland, it's slightly more than a 300 mile drive to Gold Beach. Allow at least 6 hours for the trip.

The Rogue River bar is not an easy one to cross. Small boats cannot get outside safely. The total ocean salmon sport catch out of Gold Beach is small in comparison with other south coast bays, just abut 2000 annually.

Spring chinook enter the bay in late March, but the major fishery for them begins up-bay, from Elephant Rock to head of tide at The Clay Banks. Peak catches are in May. By July, all the springers have moved through the bay and into the upper river.

Fall chinook first enter the bay in July, and fishing for them usually picks up in August. Anglers troll or mooch herring and anchovies below Hwy. 101 Bridge. A few are caught off the north jetty, and there is a good bank fishery for them on the sand spit near the south jetty. A popular fishery in September and October at the mouth of Indian Creek is associated with a STEP rearing facility on the creek, coordinated by the Dept. of Fish and Wildlife and the Curry Anadramous Fishermen, a volunteer organization. At low tide, anglers can bank fish off the flats at Indian Creek. Other popular holes are below Elephant Rock, at Johns Hole in the lower river, and the Ferry Hole above the Clay Banks. The Clay Banks, head of tide, is a popular gravel bar access, with hog lines at the upper

end just below the riffle, and fly fishing for chinook at the lower end.

Summer steelhead hit the bay in good numbers in late July, and winter steelhead in November, but angling for them takes place upriver.

Perch and ling cod are caught off the north jetty in spring, and crab are available. Best crab catches are off Doyle Pt.

Boats can be launched on the south side of the bay at the Port Commission Ramp in Gold Beach below the 101 Bridge. Boats and equipment are available for rent nearby. On the north shore, small boats can be slipped into the river at the Ferry Hole, about 3 1/2 miles upstream, and at Canfield Riffle, 1 1/2 miles miles further up County Rd. 540. Private ramps with public access are numerous in the Gold Beach area, including Champion International's Huntley Park, about 6 miles upstream on the south bank. The lower river is broad and provides easygoing boating.

ROGUE RIVER SALMON
Matt Andrus

Restaurants, motels, trailer parks, and full-service resorts are plentiful in the Gold Beach/Wedderburn area. The nearest public coastal campground is about 20 miles north at Humbug Mt. State Park, but there's a large campground at Huntley Park, and there are Forest Service campgrounds at Lobster Creek and Quosatana upriver.

ROGUE RIVER (Clay Banks to Grave Cr.)
Always among the Top Ten producers of salmon and steelhead on the Oregon Coast. This portion of the Rogue includes 35 river miles that have been federally designated Wild and Scenic, including that portion that flows through the Wild Rogue Wilderness. Much of the lower Rogue runs through deep canyons, far from the nearest road. This challenging terrain limits accessibility, but helps to maintain outstanding angling the year around.

Between tidewater and Agnes, the south bank road offers the only improved boat ramps,

at Lobster Creek and Quosatana campgrounds below Copper Canyon, and at Agnes above. Huntley Park, on the south bank road about 2 miles above tidewater, provides 1/2 mile of gravel bar from which bank casters take chinook and steelhead, or launch riverboats to fish Coyote Riffle and the Ferry Hole downstream. Boaters also launch off the Gold Beach Plywood gravel bar below Huntley. From Lobster Creek (about 3 miles further upstream), boaters drift down or jet up to Coal Riffle, about 5 miles upstream. Quosatana Boat Ramp is a popular jet boat access to the Copper Canyon fisheries that are half-way to Agnes. Above Quosatana, the south bank road is carved out of canyon wall, and there is no further bank access until Agnes. A bridge connects the south bank and north bank roads at Lobster Creek.

From the north bank road out of Wedderburn on the coast, anglers can access Coyote Hole and the Ferry Hole right below it. Riverboats are launched off the gravel bar at Coyote,

or from the old concrete ferry ramp (at high water only). Anglers also fish from highway turnouts off the Wedderburn Rd. as far as Coyote Riffle.

The north bank road crosses Lobster Creek at river mile 11 and continues about 7 miles to the trailhead near the lower end of the Wild and Scenic section of the Rogue. Be warned, however, that the bridge across Lobster Creek occassionally washes out, so check with the Siskiyou Forest Service before planning a trip. The trail itself is about 10 miles long and is suited more to scenic enjoyment than to angling. Though well maintained, it remains high above the river all the way to Agnes (and is cursed with rampant poison oak off-trail).

Agnes is at the confluence of the Rogue and Illinois rivers. Below the confluence, the Rogue is suitable for novice riverboaters. Above, even experienced boaters would benefit from following a lead boat familiar with the Rogue's whitewater. At Agnes, boaters can launch at the improved public boat ramp below the Illinois confluence, or from the camp at Hog Eddy Cr. just north of town. There is also gravel bar access at Cougar Lane Lodge (ask permission before you launch) to fish Hog Eddy and the Hotel Riffle around the bend, which are both good for steelhead.

Above Agnes, the next improved boat ramp is at Foster Bar. Foster Bar to Quosatana is a popular long day drift for winter steelhead. At low water, Two-mile Riffle below Foster is Class 2 whitewater, for experienced boaters only.

Between Foster Bar and Grave Creek, a 35 mile flow, no roads access the Rogue. This section contains a string of superior riffles and bars, most of which are popularly named. A riffle on the Rogue is a place where the river drops, usually in the presence of big boulders. The result is water that is both fast and white. Below a riffle, the tail-out offers good holding water for salmon and steelhead as they pause before the upstream challenge. Above the riffle is the head and pool, where salmon and steelhead rest. Some anglers use an anchor on a quick-release pulley to stop mid-stream in order to fish the waters at the head of a riffle. Experienced rowers can also hold a driftboat in the water at the head of a riffle just by oar power, while fellow anglers fish the head and pool.

Some anglers reach this stretch of the Rogue by jet boat from the lower river, but jet sleds are only allowed as far as Blossom Bar, about 18 miles above Agnes. This does provide access to a number of handsome back-country lodges, including Marial, Paradise Bar, Half Moon Bar, Clay Hill, and Illahe. A popular five-day drift from Grave Creek to Foster Bar also includes a stop at Black Bar Lodge, about half way between Grave Creek and Marial. The most popular boat fishery here is for summer steelhead in the fall.

There is a hiking trail from Grave Creek to Illahe at Foster Bar. Unlike the trail below Agnes, this one offers many angling opportunities, climbing high above the river in the canyons, but dropping down to riverside at the bars. The hike most popular with anglers is a 2 mile trek from Grave Cr. to Rainie Falls, where salmon and steelhead hold for long periods. Many anglers also hike the additional mile to Whiskey Creek. There is an unmaintained trail on the south bank from Grave Creek to Rainie Falls. At Ranie Falls, anglers take spring chinook, steelhead, fall chinook and shad. About July 4, an excellent shad run reaches the falls, which is an impassable barrier to them.

To reach Grave Creek from I-5 north of

LOWER ROGUE RIVER

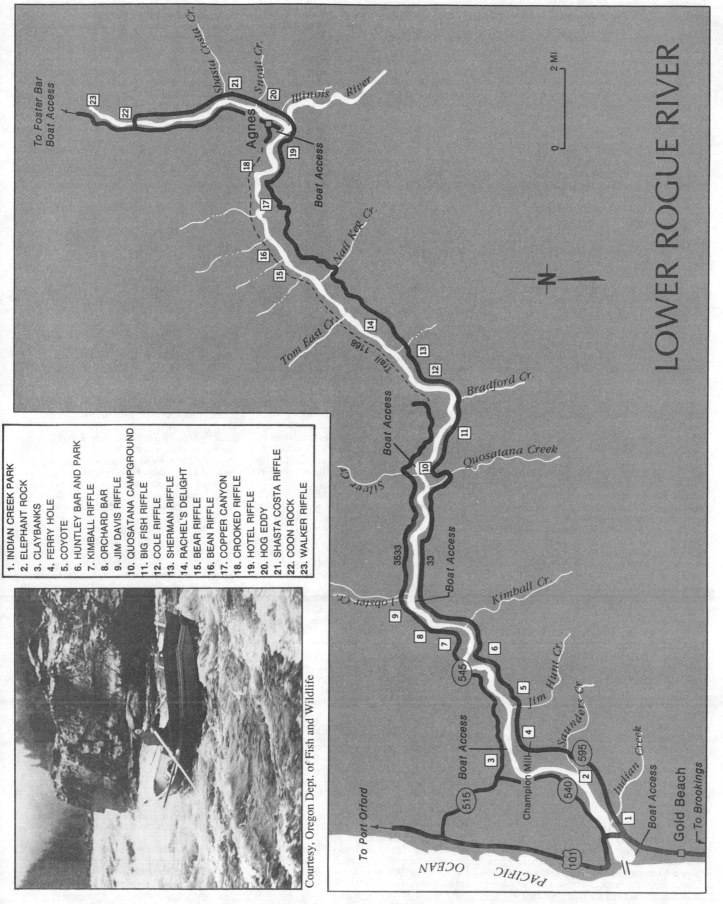

1. INDIAN CREEK PARK
2. ELEPHANT ROCK
3. CLAYBANKS
4. FERRY HOLE
5. COYOTE
6. HUNTLEY BAR AND PARK
7. KIMBALL RIFFLE
8. ORCHARD BAR
9. JIM DAVIS RIFFLE
10. QUOSATANA CAMPGROUND
11. BIG FISH RIFFLE
12. COLE RIFFLE
13. SHERMAN RIFFLE
14. RACHEL'S DELIGHT
15. BEAR RIFFLE
16. BEAN RIFFLE
17. COPPER CANYON
18. CROOKED RIFFLE
19. HOTEL RIFFLE
20. HOG EDDY
21. SHASTA COSTA RIFFLE
22. COON ROCK
23. WALKER RIFFLE

Courtesy, Oregon Dept. of Fish and Wildlife

Grants Pass, take the Merlin Exit to the Merlin-Galice Rd. Grave Creek is about 7 miles north of Galice.

About 2500 summer steelhead were taken in the lower Rogue in 1986, but other years have seen catches as high as 5000-10,000. Summer steelhead are in the river all year, but fishing for them is best from September through January, with peak catches in October. About 4600 spring chinook were taken in the lower Rogue in 1986, 4500 winter steelhead and 5000 fall chinook.

Most drift trips from Grave Creek are 3-4 days. Anglers wishing to book guides and rooms at the back-country lodges would be well advised to make reservations early in the year. Fishing guides can be located through the Oregon Guides and Packers Assoc., or through the lodges. TuTuTun Lodge and several private RV parks provide the only overnight facilities on North Bank Rogue Rd. Camping is available on the south bank road at Huntley Park, Lobster Creek, and Quosatana below Foster Bar, and at Brushy Bar within the Wild Rogue Wilderness. Unimproved sites are plentiful all along the trail to Grave Creek, which passes through a forested terrain of mixed Douglas fir, madronne, and maple.

ROGUE RIVER, Grave Cr. to Lost Creek Dam. Spring chinook offer the largest fishery on the Upper Rogue, which is frequently the Number One salmon producing water on the coast. Summer steelhead and half-pounders are also popular, with smaller numbers of winter steelhead, fall chinook, and coho taken. This portion of the Rogue includes 27 miles of Wild and Scenic river.
Spring Chinook are in the river from May through July, and are fished all the way to Lost Creek Dam. The run has been growing steadily since 1984 when the combined effects of *El Nino* and heavy ocean fishing reduced the catch in upper and lower river combined to barely more than 1000. The 1987 catch in the upper river alone was more than 8500.

Summer Steelhead are in this section of the river the year around, but fishing picks up in September, with peak catches in October, and good angling through February and March. The 1986 catch was 1160, not including half-pounders. Winter steelhead overtake the summer run by December, with good catches into April. About 550 winter steelhead were caught in 1985-86.

There are also about 200 coho and 50-200 fall chinook taken in the upper Rogue each year. The fall chinook fishery here is relatively new, created by improved water flow following the construction of Lost Creek Dam in the late 1970s.

Trout are a put-and-take fishery in the Upper Rogue, confined to waters around boat ramps and parks, where they are stocked weekly throughout spring and summer, or as long as the water remains below 70 degrees. Bass and panfish are available only in Gold Ray Dam Pool and the adjacent slough.

From Foster Bar to Grave Creek there is no road access to the Wild and Scenic Rogue. But access picks up again from Grave Creek upstream, with roads following or crossing the river all the way to Lost Creek Lake, except in the deep canyons.

One of the most popular boat fisheries in this section of the river is at Galice, where there's an improved boat ramp and a store with fishing supplies. Anglers drift to Rand or Almeda, a day's trip. Rocky Riffle, immediately below Galice, and Galice Riffle, immediately

above, are very popular steelhead and half-pounder fisheries. This is as far as half-pounders go. Anglers follow the adult run toward Grants Pass in November and December. There is also a growing fishery at Galice for fall chinook. The fall chinook run has been increasing yearly, ever since ocean salmon fishing began to be heavily regulated. The river from Almeda to Grave Cr. is only lightly fished, primarily drift fishing for summer and winter steelhead.

To reach Galice from I-5 north of Grants Pass, take the Merlin Exit and follow the Merlin-Galice Rd. NW. At Merlin, a county road also heads SW to Robertson Bridge.

Robertson Bridge to Galice is a long day's drift (about 11 river miles), accessing some good gravel bars and drift water. The trip includes a float through Hellgate Canyon. Some anglers do shorter trips from the bridge, mounting small kicker motors on their drift boats to enable them to motor up to a favorite water and drift down again. This is a practical technique in the slower, quiet stretches of the river above and below the bridge (between Ferry Park on the east bank and Griffin Park on the west.) From Grants Pass, the Lower River Rd. offers a pretty drive to Robertson Bridge.

Whitehorse is the last riffle before the upper end of the Wild and Scenic Rogue. It's a good steelhead producer, with bedrock shelves and channels that hold the fish. There's an unimproved ramp at Whitehorse Park on the east bank. Whitehorse to Ferry Park is a good short drift.

Anglers also fish the mouth of the Applegate, especially for fall chinook, many of which are returning to the Applegate to spawn in late August and early September. These salmon are not in prime condition, but are still acceptable keepers. The Applegate marks the end of heavy recreational activity on the Rogue west of Grants Pass.

There's a lot of good bank access throughout the river between Grave Creek and the Applegate. Anglers park and fish all along the Merlin-Galice Rd. from Galice to Grave Cr. Argo Riffle is a popular fishery, about 2 miles above Grave Cr. Almeda Park offers 1/2 mile of good beach fishing, with plentiful parking a mile above Argo. Anglers also fish at Rand, and at the Chair Riffle just above. Rock Riffle above Galice is accessible to bank anglers, but there is little access at Galice itself. Ennis Riffle about 2 miles above Galice includes two gravel bars.

Indian Mary Park, just below Taylor Cr. Gorge offers quiet water for trout fishing. The river here is stocked with legal rainbow weekly until the water warms to 70 degrees, usually in late July. Indian Mary is a popular tourist spot, with camping in a pleasant setting. Bank anglers also fish above and below Hellgate Bridge for steelhead. And there is plenty of bank access at Ferry and Griffin parks.

About 10 miles east of Grants Pass, the river opens into a broad valley with gravel bars, its banks lined with cottonwood and willow. The Rogue meanders through this valley for the next 20 miles to Shady Cove, where the valley begins to narrow and confine the diminished river flow. Another 10-12 miles up is Lost Creek Dam, the end of the mainstem Rogue.

Spring chinook move through the Upper Rogue from May through July. The first fishery for them east of Grants Pass is in May at Pierce Riffle, about 3/4 mile below Savage Rapids Dam. Boats launch at Pierce Riffle County Park off Foothill Blvd. on the north bank. Jet sleds motor up through the riffle to fish the deadline

below the dam. Drift boat anglers row up to Pierce Riffle. There is a bank fishery for springers at the dam deadline, accessed only through property owned by We Asku Inn, on the south bank off Hwy 99. Ask permission before you fish.

Above Savage Rapids, river access is limited to the parks. Boaters put in at Coyote-Evans Park in the community of Rogue River on Hwy.99, and take out at the Savage Rapids pool. There is also a boat ramp at Valley of the Rogue State Park. The drift from here to Coyote-Evans, about 2 1/2 miles, is good for beginners (more current than whitewater). Anglers primarily drift fish for steelhead through this stretch. There is also bank fishing at Valley of the Rogue for steelhead and stocked legal trout.

About 4 miles upstream there's bank angling at Rock Point Bridge on Hwy. 99, and at Sardine Creek near the junction of the Gold Hill and Sardine Cr. roads. At Gold Hill, on Hwy. 234, there is an improved boat ramp at Gold Nugget Park, though the primary fishery at the park is for stocked rainbow.

Gold Ray Dam is a popular spot for spring chinook and summer steelhead. Boaters launch sleds and drift boats with motors at an unimproved boat ramp off a dirt road between the dam and Gold Hill on the south bank, then motor up to the deadline. The road also offers about 1 1/2 miles of bank access.

The Gold Ray Pool and adjacent Kelly Slough provide fishing for largemouth bass, crappie, and bluegill. Boaters jet down to the pool from Tou Velle Park, as there is no good take-out in the pool area. Kelly Slough is a good place to explore by canoe. Canoes can be launched off the dirt road NW of Tolo by carrying the canoe across the railroad tracks, putting in at Gold Ray Pool. A nearby gravel area can be used for parking. Kelly Slough is lined with cottonwoods, home to many waterfowl and a small heron rookery. To access the slough, canoes must first head into the pool, then bear immediately right. Though you can hear the dam water thundering at that point, the current in the pool is slow enough to permit the short upstream paddle necessary to enter slough water. *WARNING: keep your wits about you. Unwary boaters have been known to go over the dam.*

The water above Gold Ray Pool is especially productive for spring chinook. Boaters launch jet sleds at Tou Velle Park on the south bank of the Rogue north of Medford. Anglers also bank fish for trout at Tou Velle. High Banks, just below Tou Velle, is a popular fly fishing spot for summer steelhead (boat access only).

Dodge Bridge Park, near the Hwy. 234 crossing of the Rogue, offers a nice long day's drift to Tou Velle, about 8 miles. There's good still water fishing for spring chinook and summer steelhead in this stretch, but there are rapids that should be scouted first, and attempted only by experienced boaters. Stocked trout and an occasional chinook and steelhead are available from the bank at Dodge Bridge. There's also a fishing ramp accessible to less-abled anglers.

Above Dodge Bridge on the west bank road to Shady Cove, Takelma Park offers a boat ramp and good bank access for spring chinook, steelhead, and trout. There's also a boat ramp at Shady Cove County Park, but bank access is limited to the area above Shady Cove Bridge. From Shady Cove to Lost Creek Dam, Hwy. 62 runs close to the river, with good access for bank anglers. Spring chinook are fished in this stretch from May 15 through July.

The mouth of Trail Creek is a popular bank access area. Anglers pull off and fish near the junction of hwys. 62 and 227. Rogue Elk County Park on Hwy. 62 is popular with boaters in pursuit of spring chinook and early summer steelhead. There is also a bank fishery for trout. Casey State Park, just west of the dam, has a boat ramp and excellent bank access for spring chinook, summer steelhead, and trout. Casey has a full service campground, and anglers will find it a little crowded here during spring chinook season. Between Casey State Park and the dam the river runs through public land where bank access is plentiful.

West of Grants Pass, camping facilities are available at Indian Mary County Park on the Merlin-Galice Rd. East of Grants Pass, there are campgrounds at Valley of the Rogue State Park on Hwy. 99, and at Rogue Elk County Park and Casey State Park on Hwy 62.

ROGUE RIVER, MIDDLE FORK A fair spring and summer trout stream, flowing into the upper Rogue above Lost Creek Lake. From Medford take Hwy. 62 north to Prospect, about 45 miles, then follow FS 37 from Prospect to the Middle Fork. Or follow the Butte Falls Rd. to its junction with the Middle Fork at FS 37. About 3 miles after 37 crosses the Middle Fork, a forest road on the left (before Imnaha Campground) leads to Trail 978, which follows the upper Middle Fork into its headwaters in the Seven Lakes Basin of the Sky Lakes Wilderness.

The upper portion of the stream is lightly fished for native trout and migrants from the high lakes. See alta, middle grass, cliff.

Campgrounds near the Middle Fork include a large campground at Joseph Stewart State Park on Lost Creek Lake, and three campgrounds just south of the Middle Fork on FS 37 (Imnaha, Sumpter Creek, and South Fork).

ROGUE RIVER, NORTH FORK Forty-seven miles of premium trout water, flowing into Lost Creek Lake. Hwys. 62 and 230 more or less follow the river to its headwaters south of Diamond Lake, near the northern boundary of Crater Lake National Park. Forest roads access the mainstream at the mouths of many fine tributaries, and the Upper Rogue River Trail 1034 follows it from Prospect through the scenic Rogue National Forest almost to the very end. Early season road access is often limited by heavy snow, so check with the ranger station at Prospect. Roads are usually open by late May.

The North Fork supports good populations of native rainbow, cutthroat, and brown and a few brook trout. Fish average 6-12 inches, with an infrequent brown taken in the 5-10 pound range. Beginning in late May, about 1500 legal rainbow are stocked weekly between Natural Bridge Campground and Hamaker Meadows. Fish are released near all access points, including the campgrounds at Union Creek, Farewell Bend, and Hamaker Meadows, and near the Jackson/Douglas County Rd.

There's good fishing near the mouths of the North Fork's many tributaries, including Mill, Abbot, Union, Wizard, National, Foster, and Minnehaha. Most of the tributaries are best fished in early season before they get low, though Union and Mill are good all summer.

ROGUE RIVER, SOUTH FORK A nice trout stream flowing into the main river at Lost Creek Lake, best in mid-summer. From Medford take Hwy. 62 north to the Butte Falls Rd. Head north on the Butte Falls-Prospect Rd.,

turning onto FS 34 toward Lodgepole, crossing the upper stream at South Fork Campground. Trail 988 follows the stream to Rogue Head Camp in the Blue Lake Group of the Sky Lakes Area. The upper stream is also accessible by forest roads from Prospect.

The upper portion is lightly fished and supports a native population of rainbow, cutthroat, and brook trout. A number of beaver ponds in the headwaters contain surprisingly big trout. Campgrounds near the South Fork include a large camp at Joseph Stewart State park on Lost Creek Lake, Imnaha and South Fork camps off FS 37, Parker Meadows Camp, and Upper South Fork camp.

SAUNDERS LAKE A coastal lake of about 55 acres west of Hwy. 101 about 15 miles south of Reedsport. The lake is stocked three times annually and provides good rainbow angling in the spring and early summer.

Bait fishing takes most of the trout, but a good mayfly hatch in spring provides an opportunity for good fly fishing. There are also a few bass and yellow perch.

There is a public boat ramp at the south end of the lake, but there is a lot of private property around the lake and no camping areas. Camping, accommodations, and supplies are available at Lakeside, 4 miles north.

SELMAC LAKE a record-breaking producer of largemouth bass, 23 miles SW of Grants Pass, with excellent facilities for family outings. Take Hwy. 199 to Selma, and turn east. It's 4 miles to the lake. Covering about 160 acres, this artificial lake provides lots of angling opportunity. The state record bass, a 10 lb. 15 oz. largemouth, was caught here in 1983. (An unofficial 12 pounder was caught and released in 1974). Rainbow trout are stocked in early spring, and there are many fair crappie, bluegill, and brown bullhead.

There is a county park here with boat rentals and ramp, tent sites, water, and picnic facilities. Finger-like dikes have been constructed into the lake to provide better bank access.

SIXES RIVER A fairly good steelhead and salmon stream, entering the ocean just north of Cape Blanco. It is crossed by Hwy. 101 about 5 miles above the mouth, 22 miles south of Bandon. The stream is about 36 miles long, with a good road east to its headwaters. The lower section of the stream is reached by several secondary roads. Tidewater extends to 2 miles below Hwy. 101 Bridge.

There is some trout fishing early in the season, but low water usually slows it down in June. After the fall rains, some sea-run cutthroat are taken in the lower section by trolling or casting.

Steelhead angling starts in November and continues into March. Some good size fall chinook are taken. The fish usually appear in numbers in November. About as many salmon are caught as steelhead.

The south bank of the estuary is publicly owned, as well as an additional 1/2 mile of access about 3 miles upstream from Hwy. 101 Bridge. This area contains two good salmon holes and a good drift. Boats can be launched at the county park at Edson Creek, and taken out at Hwy. 101 Bridge.

Summer camping is available at Humbug State Park, just south of Port Orford.

SKOOKUM LAKE (Douglas Co.) A 3/4 mile hike for brook trout in the Skookum Prairie area, about 10 miles west of Diamond Lake.

From Hwy. 230, just south of Diamond, take FS 3703 about 2 1/2 miles, then FS 200 (a primitive track) to the right. Skookum is less than 1/4 mile from road's end.

Covering about 15 acres, Skookum provides good catches of brook trout to 10 inches, and quite a few to 18. The outlet, Skookum Cr., produces small(but mature) rainbow and browns. The lake is usually inaccessible until late June. There are natural campsites.

SKOOKUM POND An artificial pond in the Umpqua National Forest, created in the mid-'70s and managed for rainbow trout. Take Jackson Cr. Rd. (FS 29) then FS 2924 about 2 1/2 miles, and follow FS 200 about 2 1/2 miles to the pond. There is no sign on the road indicating that the pond is there, so watch your odometer. The pond has a lot of submerged snags and an old clear cut which provide good habitat. Aquatic vegetation is heavy, but there is room for a small boat. Largemouth bass have been illegally introduced and will ultimately hurt the trout fishery there. There is an excellent population of crayfish.

SMITH RIVER A major tributary of the Umpqua River estuary, with fair runs of steelhead, salmon, and searun cutthroat, a good size shad run, and opportunities for striped bass. After a 75 mile tumble through the Coast Range, the Smith enters the Umpqua at Gardiner, just 9 miles from the sea.

From Gardiner, on Hwy. 101, a paved county road heads east to the river and follows it closely for 30 miles. A variety of gravel roads access its headwaters. The river can also be approached from the Eugene area by taking Hwy. 99 south to Drain, and Hwy. 38 west. County roads cut north to the Smith about 8 miles west of Elkton (just upstream of Sawyers Rapids on the Umpqua), and from the Wells Creek Guard Station about 3 1/2 miles upstream from Scottsburg.

Cutthroat trout are stocked for the spring opening, and most fishing for them takes place the first weekends in spring. Trout remain in the Smith throughout the summer, but the bite is off once the water warms (the Smith can get up to 70 degrees). Best summer trout fishing is in the cooler tributaries for smaller, but hungrier, fish. A hatchery produced sea-run cutthroat migration provides fall angling. Started in 1981, the program augments a small remnant native run. Most sea-run are caught by anglers trolling in tidewater, which extends to Spencer Creek, about 20 miles upriver. About 1000 sea-run are taken annually.

Coho and steelhead hatchery programs are also in effect, with the runs now balanced equally between hatchery and native stock. Coho catches have been good for several years, with close to a thousand taken in 1986. The fall chinook catch, which has been building steadily since 1981, was above average in 1986 at 249, and the 1988 catch is estimated to have been the largest in many years. One factor in the growing chinook fishery is a continuing habitat improvement program undertaken by the Forest Service. The Forest Service has dedicated over a million dollars to re-building gravel bars, necessary for salmon spawning, which were diminished by past logging practices. About 1500 winter steelhead were taken in the 1985-86 season in the lower and upper river.

A population of striped bass has been reproducing modestly in the lower Smith, migrating seasonally between the river and Winchester Bay, following the food supply. In March, April, and May, striped bass are upstream in

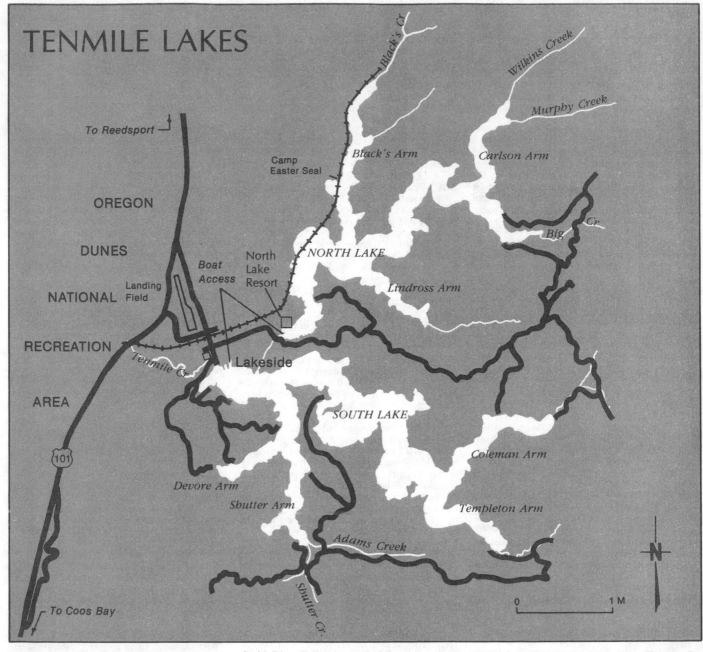

TENMILE LAKES

To Reedsport

OREGON

DUNES

NATIONAL

RECREATION

AREA

Boat Access

Landing Field

North Lake Resort

101

Tenmile Cr.

Lakeside

Camp Easter Seal

NORTH LAKE

SOUTH LAKE

Black's Cr.

Wilkins Creek

Murphy Creek

Black's Arm

Carlson Arm

Big Cr.

Lindross Arm

Coleman Arm

Templeton Arm

Devore Arm

Shutter Arm

Adams Creek

Shutter Cr.

To Coos Bay

0   1 M

N

tidewater, where anglers take them on trolled plugs and a variety of baits including herring, anchovies, and sea and mud worms. Stripers return to the bay in late spring, summer, and fall to feed on marine fish, then return to the river in September and October, when the best striper catches of the year are made. As elsewhere on the southern Oregon coast, the striper fishery here is down considerably from the 1970's. Most catches are in the 16-20 inch class, but some adults to 35 pounds are still taken here.

The Smith has a good shad run in May through June, which extends up to head of tide. Local anglers seem to fish the run only lightly, but there's potential here for excellent sport. Just ask the folks down at Coos Bay, for whom shad have become a passion. Shad are available to both boat and bank anglers, caught on troll and cast. A favorite shad spot at this time is the Noel Ranch Boat Ramp at about river mile 8.

The Smith is very accessible to boat and bank anglers, primarily from the north bank road. The highest put-in on the lower river is at

Smith River Falls (river mile 26), with a popular drift down to Dailey Pole Slide (river mile 11), a take-out *only* at the upper end of Dailey Ranch. Other boat ramps are at Wasson Creek Bridge about 20 river miles upstream (a primitive ramp, but suitable for drift boats and cartoppers), Art Moss Boat Ramp (locally known as the Schoolhouse Ramp, a very good facility), a natural site about 6 miles below Schoolhouse with launching from the beach off a gravel pulloff, and at Bolon State Park at Gardiner.

Above the falls, there is bank fishing and drift boat launching from several access roads that were once low water crossings for logging operations, now closed for crossing but open to north bank access.

SMITH RIVER, NORTH FORK A large, productive tributary of the Smith River, joining the Smith 13 miles above its confluence with the Umpqua. A good county road cuts off from the Smith River Rd. at the community of North Fork, about 15 miles from Gardiner, and

follows the Fork for about 8 miles. The paved Smith River Rd. is accessible from Hwy. 101 north of Gardiner, and from Hwy. 38 by way of a cut-off about 2 1/2 miles NE of Scottsburg near the Wells Creek Guard Station.

Steelhead is the most popular fishery on the river, with about 350 landed in the 1985-86 season. The run usually peaks in December and January. Most anglers plunk for steelhead downstream from Culvert Hole, a treacherous waterfall at about river mile 6. Drift fishing from bank or boat is the favorite method above the falls. Bank access is very good, with most landowners granting permission to fish when asked. *Be sure to ask.* Several primitive roads approach the river above Culvert Hole, with drift boat launching adjacent to the bridge crossings. There is a primitive take-out right above the Hole (don't boat it). When the mainstem is turbid, anglers will often find the North Fork clear.

The coho run reaches the North Fork Smith late in the spawning run, and most are not in prime condition, or eager to bite. About 100 coho were taken in the North Fork in 1986.

There's fair fishing for sea-run cutthroat here, especially in the lower tidewater area. Sea-run get up as far as a very high falls about 15 miles beyond the point where the road leaves the stream. These falls are approachable from Mapleton, a community on Hwy. 126, the Siletz River Rd.

SMITH RIVER, WEST FORK A beautiful trout stream, joining the mainstem Smith about 5 miles above Smith River Falls. Only about 10 miles long, the stream is paralleled by BLM Rd. 27.1 along its north bank almost to the headwaters. Closed to steelhead and salmon angling, it offers excellent fishing for native cutthroat. It is best fished early in season while the water is cool.

SNAG LAKE About 30 acres, west of Hauser. It contains largemouth bass, yellow perch, and brown bullhead.

SODA SPRING RESERVOIR A small reservoir on the North Umpqua River, about 7 miles downstream from Toketee Lake. It is on the north side of Hwy. 138, about 40 miles east of Glide. Approach from Roseburg on 138, or take County Rd. 200 from Hwy. 99 at Wilbur. No longer stocked, it is rainbow to 12 inches, brown, and brook trout. It is lightly fished and has a winter boat closure, due to danger from the spillway.

SOUTH UMPQUA RIVER See umpqua river, south.

SQUAW LAKE (Coos Co.) A 2 acre lake on the South Fork Coquille River road, about 22 miles south of Powers. The river road leaves Hwy. 42 about 3 miles south of Myrtle Point and is paved to the lake.

The lake provides good angling for rainbow trout, and it is usually stocked each season. The Forest Service maintains a campground at the lake. Other camping areas are located 3 and 5 miles back on the road toward Powers.

SQUAW LAKES (Jackson Co.) A good family recreation area in the upper Applegate drainage, about 4 miles east of Applegate Reservoir, 3 miles north of the California line. From I-5 or Hwy. 99 take Hwy. 238 south to Ruch, then follow the Applegate River Rd. south to Applegate Reservoir. Cross the dam face to FS 1075, which follows Squaw Creek to the lakes. Big Squaw covers about 50 acres. Little (or upper) Squaw Lake is about 1/4 that size, located about one mile SE of the large lake. There's no vehicle access to the lake shores, and motors are prohibited on the lake. There is a parking lot about 1/4 mile from Big Squaw. The road in can be rough in early spring.

The lakes are stocked with cutthroat and have good native populations as well, averaging 9 inches. There are lots of crappie and brown bullhead to 10 inches. Fair size largemouth bass are now well established. The Forest Service is planning to provide additional structure in the lake to enhance the bass population. The lakes are very popular and are fished heavily. Catches are good, especially in fall and early spring. Bait fishing is most popular, but trolling and casting will produce.

Camping is by reservation only. Contact the Star Ranger District at the town of McKee on the Applegate River. Additional camping is available at Applegate Reservoir.

STEAMBOAT CREEK A scenic and revered tributary of the North Umpqua River, entering the mainstream at Steamboat Ranger Station about 21 miles east of Glide. Closed to all fishing, it is a designated sanctuary for Umpqua summer steelhead. Camping is available at Canton Creek and Steamboat Island.

STEWART PARK POND City park fishing in Roseburg. Lightly fished, this 2 acre pond contains largemouth bass and black crappie.

STUMP LAKE A 30 acre reservoir on Clearwater Creek 7 air miles NW of Diamond Lake. The lake is on Hwy. 138, 11 miles NW of Diamond Lake Resort.

Not a scenic lake, but it has plump brook rainbow trout to 15 inches. Snags and stumps make trolling or spinning difficult. Still fishing with bait saves tackle. There's good fly action in the fall. There are improved campgrounds at Clearwater Falls, about 3 miles east, and at Whitehorse Falls 1 1/2 miles west.

SUCKER CREEK A popular trout stream in the Cave Junction area near Oregon Caves National Monument, about 24 miles long. Take Hwy. 199 south from Grants Pass about 40 miles. The creek flows into the Illinois River a couple of miles SE of Cave Junction, at the junction of Hwys. 199 and 46. Hwy. 46 follows the Creek quite closely to its headwaters near the caves. A network of secondary roads cross the main stream and its tributaries.

There's fair angling here for native cutthroat. Most fish are taken on bait, but fly fishing can be effective. Cave Creek, which flows out of the caves and into Sucker Creek, has some nice native rainbow. A large forest camp called Grayback is on Hwy. 46 about 15 miles east of Cave Junction.

TANNEN LAKE An 8 acre hike-in lake in the Siskiyou Mountains quite near the California line. The lake is just NW of Tannen Mountain and can be reached hiking 1/4 mile by trail from FS 041 south and east of Bolan Lake. From Cave Junction it's about 21 miles to Bolan Lake, following Hwy. 46 to Holland, and FS 4703 to a gravel road access to Bolan. The lake can also be reached by hiking the Thompson Creek Rd. north from Happy Camp, California. The hike in is less than one mile.

Tannen is stocked annually. Fishing holds up well in spring and fall with brook trout to 15 inches. There's a primitive campground at the lake. A one mile trail leads up to East Tannen Lake, elevation 5400 ft., which is also stocked but fairly brushy on three sides. The Tannens are usually accessible by early June.

TEAL LAKE A one acre lake 8 miles south of Reedsport near Hwy. 101, several hundred yards south of Clear Lake. The lake has cutthroat trout, but is closed to public access.

TENMILE LAKES Two large and varied coastal lakes, locally called North Lake and South Lake, offering some of the finest largemouth bass fishing in Oregon as well as bluegill, catfish, coho, rainbow trout and cutthroat. A striped/white bass hybrid is also present and open to angling.

Many-armed, the lakes sprawl invitingly east of Hwy. 101 at Lakeside, about 12 miles south of Reedsport. North Tenmile is a bit under 1000 acres, and South lake is several hundred acres larger. Average depth is about 15 feet, and neither lake has any real deep areas. Current management of the bass fishery here emphasizes high yield over trophy size, but some big bass are available. In fact, the state record hybrid bass was caught here in 1988, weighing 11 lbs. 4 oz.

Hybrid bass were stocked here starting in 1982 to help control the bluegill population and to introduce a new fishery. The Hybrid is a cross between striped bass and white bass, both very big fish. It is a handsome, deep bodied fish with an obvious resemblance to stripers.

These are good family fishing lakes, with enough bluegill to entertain the kids. Trout fishing is good in April and May. Some hold-over trout have been taken to 20 inches. Coho usually come in on a water rise in late October, but November and early December are the most productive periods. Trolling with spinners, wobblers, Daredevils or Flatfish produce salmon 5-6 pounds. About 100 coho were taken here in 1986.

Steelhead returns vary from year to year, with 1500 taken in 1985, 900 in 1986. Bluegill overpopulation continues to be a concern.

There's a resort with RV park on North Tenmile, public camping across the highway from Lakeside in the Dunes National Recreation Area, and another campground 2 miles north at Eel Lake. Flying fishermen will appreciate the airstrip at Lakeside, a 10 minute walk from the South Lake.

TOKETEE RESERVOIR One of several power system reservoirs on the upper North Umpqua, occupying several hundred acres when full. It is successfully managed for German brown trout.

Located about 60 miles east of Roseburg, 40 miles east of Glide, it can be approached from both east and west on the North Umpqua River Rd., Hwy. 138. From the east, take Hwy. 97 to the 138 (Diamond Lake) cut-off. Toketee

TENMILE LAKE
Courtesy, Oregon Dept. of Fish and Wildlife

is about 23 miles west of Diamond Lake.

The reservoir has good numbers of brown and rainbow trout, with a few eastern brook. The browns run to 21 inches and are best taken on bait and Flatfish-type lures. Rainbow average 11-12 inches and make up about half the catch. Fishing is good in spring, tapers off in summer, and picks up again in fall. Boat anglers usually catch the biggest fish.

There are two Forest Service campgrounds at the north and south ends of the lake and a boat ramp on the eastern shore. Good forest camps are also available up and down river on the North Umpqua Rd.

TRIANGLE LAKE 293 acres, east of Florence on Hwy. 36. It contains largemouth bass, bluegill, yellow perch, brown bullhead, and pumpkinseed sunfish.

TRUMIS & BYBEE PONDS Four small artificial ponds owned by the Jackson County Fair Board. The ponds are adjacent to the freeway at the community of Central Point, and contain bluegill, largemouth bass, and crappie. A few bass as large as 6 pounds have been taken here.

TWIN LAKES (Douglas Co.) Two nice brook trout lakes between the North and South Umpqua drainage systems, just 1/2 mile hike from the road. Take the North Umpqua Hwy. 138 about 32 miles east of Glide to the Wilson Creek Rd. FS 4770. Bear right at the forks. The trailhead is on the west side of the road, about 7 miles in. The lakes are also approachable by trail from Twin Lakes Mountain, by way of the Little River Rd.

The larger, lower lake is about 12 acres, and the smaller twin is half that. Both have brook trout to 15 inches and are stocked with fingerlings. Bait or spinner should work well in early season, with flies good in late summer and fall.

The Twins are among the last to thaw in the Umpqua drainage, and the smaller Twin sometimes winterkills. They are usually accessible by late June.

UMPQUA RIVER ESTUARY/ WINCHESTER BAY (Winchester Bar to Scottsburg Park) With the lower 10 miles of the mainstem Umpqua, one of the most productive salmon fisheries in the state. Winchester Bay, on the central coast, is one of Oregon's Top Ten offshore salmon ports, and the bay itself offers excellent fishing for spring and fall chinook and coho, striped bass, sturgeon, perch, and rockfish as well as crabs and softshell clams. There is also an offshore fishery for halibut. There are three port towns on the bay—Winchester Bay (which is closest to the bar), Reedsport, and Gardiner. The bay is reached by a good road, Hwy. 38, which cuts through the Coast Range south of Cottage Grove. From Eugene on I-5 it's about 90 miles to Reedsport. From Florence on the coast it's 15 miles south by Hwy. 101.

Salmon landings across Winchester bar were third highest in the state in 1986, just behind Astoria, at 35,238. Most salmon angling here takes place offshore, with a safe crossing dependent on favorable winds. But fishing in the bay itself and upriver to the mouth of the Smith can be good. Spring chinook arrive as early as March and are fished through September. Peak catches in the bay in 1986 were in April and May, with momentum picking up again in August.

Coho often arrive in time to celebrate the fourth of July with explosive angling. They make up about 90% of the total salmon catch. In September and October, fall chinook are taken along with some native coho. Chinook aver-

age 14-18 pounds, with coho at 8-9 pounds. There is some trolling for jacks and cutthroat in the fall, especially in the lower Scholfield River, but they are usually caught incidental to the salmon. The 1986 salmon catch in the bay and lower river was 725 spring chinook, 1205 coho, and 306 fall chinook.

Salmon are caught by boat anglers between the jetties below the town of Winchester Bay, and up-bay in the main channel north of Steamboat Island between Gardiner and the Point. There are also salmon fisheries off the mouths of the Smith and Umpqua. Bank fisheries for salmon include the south jetty, Training Jetty and extension, and the public docks in Reedsport. Coho are taken in tidewater in July, August, and September. There is also a modest fishery for fall chinook in Umpqua tidewater in August and September. The local Fishermen's Association, working to restore the fall chinook run in the lower river, recalls when the fall chinook population in the Umpqua supported a thriving commercial fishing industry here.

A population of striped bass continues to produce modestly in the lower Smith, migrating between the Smith and the bay, following the food source. These large bass live and grow a long time (up to 27 years), and thrillers to 45 pounds have been taken. In the bay, stripers are primarily caught on trolled plugs or bait from June to October, with best catches in September and October. Popular baits include herring, anchovies, and sea and mud worms. In late summer, surface plugs and flyfishing can supply a heart-stopping thrill. Stripers are fished by boat anglers in Social Security Bay south of the town of Winchester Bay, in the main channel below Gardiner, just below the mouth of Scholfield River near Reedsport, from the docks at Reedsport, and at the mouths of the Smith and Umpqua.

In the lower river, prime striper season is March, April, and May. Anglers use a backbounce troll with fresh or frozen smelt, or Rapallas in blue or black. Best catches seem to be made when there is a lot of sediment in the river after freshets. Stripers are generally found holding behind big boulders and in holes.

Perch and rockfish are available to anglers boating the lower bay, and there are good bank fisheries for them at South Jetty, the Training Jetty and extension, the Coast Guard Dock south of Winchester Bay, Winchester Point gravel fill, and the public docks and Coast Guard Park in Winchester Bay.

Softshell clams can be dug in many of the coves and flats on both sides of the bay. The

CLAMMING
Bill Wagner, Photographer

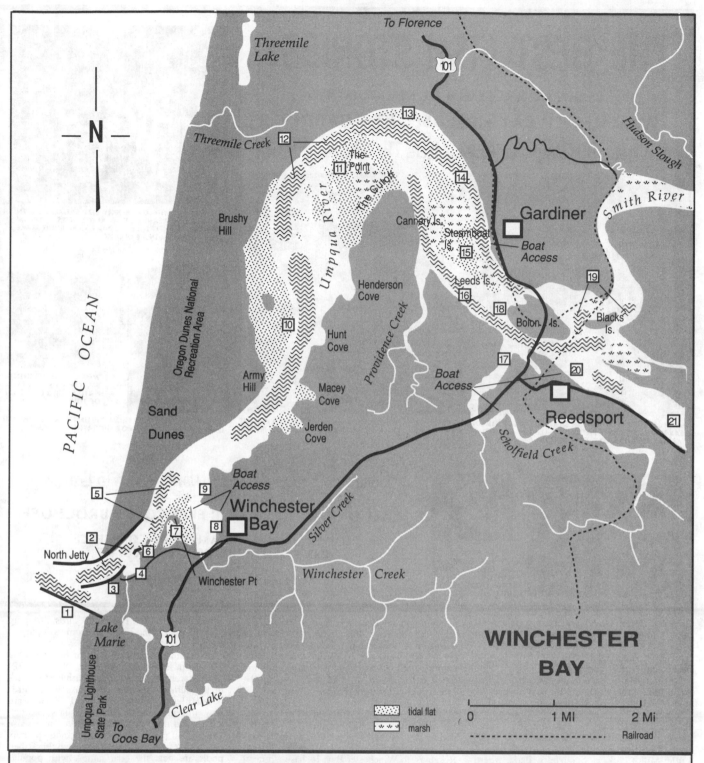

tidal flat
marsh

0   1 MI   2 Mi

Railroad

**WINCHESTER
BAY**

1. SOUTH JETTY - fish for salmon, perch, rockfish
2. BANK AND BOAT FISHING for salmon, perch, rockfish
3. TRAINING JETTY and extension - public access for salmon, perch, rockfish, crab
4. SOCIAL SECURITY BAY - Shore access for perch, striped bass
5. CRABBING
6. COAST GUARD DOCK - Public access for perch, rockfish, dungeness crab
7. WINCHESTER PT. - Gravel fill access

to bank fishing for rockfish, perch
8. PUBLIC DOCKS - Charter boats, public moorage, and dock fishing for tomcod, perch, rockperch.
9. COAST GUARD PARK - bank fishing from rock crib for perch and rockfish
10. NORTH SPIT - softshell clams; shad in channel (May - June)
11. THE POINT - softshell clams
12. SALMON, STRIPED BASS, STURGEON, pinkfin perch (July & Aug.); shad (May - June)
13. THREE MILE FLATS- softshell clams

14. STURGEON
15. STEAMBOAT IS. - softshell clams
16. STRIPED BASS
17. SEA-RUN CUTTHROAT
18. BOLON IS. - most popular area for softshell clams
19. MOUTH OF THE SMITH - Striped bass, salmon, sea-run cutts
20. REEDSPORT BOAT RAMP and Docks - striped bass, sturgeon, salmon
21. MOUTH OF THE UMPQUA - Striped bass, salmon, sturgeon

flats off Bolon Island are most popular, but good numbers are also dug in the North Spit Flats, off the Point, and above Steamboat Island. Crabs are available in good numbers, with best catches off Winchester Point.

Sturgeon are also present in the bay, fished from June through May, with peak catches in mid-March. Earliest catches are in the Big Bend area just below Gardiner, followed by a fishery at Reedsport beneath the 101 Bridge and at the bluff about 1 1/2 miles above Reedsport. The fishery then moves upstream toward Little Mill Creek at Scottsburg Park, where sturgeon are fished from boat and bank. Bank anglers access the river from pull-offs on Hwy. 38, at the junction of the road to Loon Lake (2nd highway bridge), and downstream from Mill Cr. Anglers fish the bottom with mud shrimp, smelt, herring, and sand shrimp.

Public boat ramps are in Gardiner, in Reedsport at the mouth of the Umpqua and on Scholfield River, at the docks in Winchester Bay, and at Scottsburg Park about 12 miles above Reedsport.

Overnight camping is available at Windy Cove in Winchester Bay, Lake Marie just south of the lighthouse, at William Tugman State Park south at Eel Lake, and at forest service campgrounds at Eel Creek just south of Tugman Park on Hwy. 101. Seven miles north of Gardiner at Tahkenitch Lake and also at Siltcoos Lake there are additional forest service campgrounds. RV parks, motels, moorages and other accommodations and supplies can be found throughout the bay area.

UMPQUA RIVER (Scottsburg Park to the Forks) A handsome and productive river, second largest on the Oregon Coast. It flows over 100 miles from The Forks 10 miles NW of Roseburg to Winchester Bay. Its base is gravel and bedrock, carved into underwater channels and shelves that provide ideal fish habitat suited to classic angling techniques. It's a top producer of winter steelhead, with good runs of spring and fall chinook, coho, and summer steelhead as well as one of the largest shad runs on the coast, and a large population of smallmouth bass.

Hwy. 38 follows the river from Reedsport east about 36 miles to Elkton. Gravel and paved county roads follow the river closely to the town of Umpqua, where paved roads continue to The Forks. The lower Umpqua meanders through relatively flat land, bordered by a mix of BLM timber and private ranchland. The river varies in width from 100 to 200 yards, dropping only 400 feet in the 100 miles from Roseburg to the bay.

Smallmouth bass are a major fishery in the river from Elkton to Tyee (r.m. 48 to r.m. 80) from March through October, with best catches in the summer months. The bass were introduced illegally sometime after 1970, and are now thriving among the Umpqua's bedrock ledges and deep pools. Most bass anglers use worms, but plugs, rubber worms, and spinners are also effective. The most heavily fished pools are near the boat ramps, with popular floats from just below Tyee to just above Kellogg Bridge. Below Kellogg the river bank is private with no public access, but bass fishing may actually be best there. To fish Tyee to Elkton, anglers put in at Yellow Creek Boat Ramp, or at Hutchison Wayside State Park where there is a natural gravel bar put-in at r.m. 72 just above Kellogg. Get permission from the landowners to access private land there. Boaters also launch at Mack Brown County Park to access good smallmouth bass water. Catch rate for smallmouth bass is about 3 per angler.

Spring chinook are in the mainstem Umpqua from mid-March to September, with high-

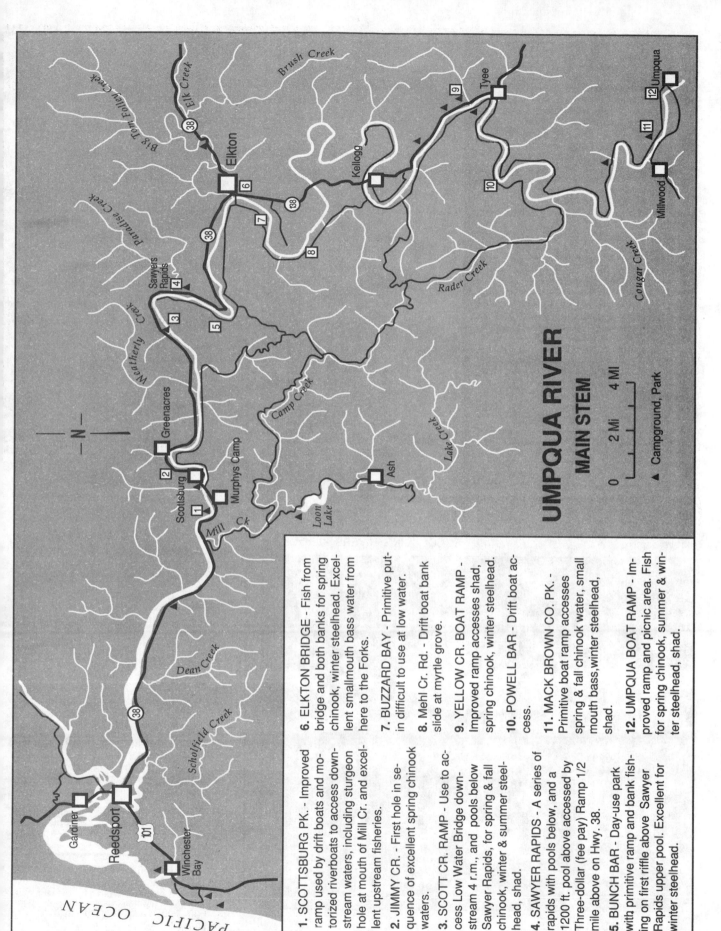

UMPQUA RIVER
MAIN STEM

0 2 Mi 4 MI

▲ Campground, Park

1. SCOTTSBURG PK. - Improved ramp used by drift boats and motorized riverboats to access downstream waters, including sturgeon hole at mouth of Mill Cr. and excellent upstream fisheries.

2. JIMMY CR. - First hole in sequence of excellent spring chinook waters.

3. SCOTT CR. RAMP - Use to access Low Water Bridge downstream 4 r.m., and pools below Sawyer Rapids, for spring & fall chinook, winter & summer steelhead, shad.

4. SAWYER RAPIDS - A series of rapids with pools below, and a 1200 ft. pool above accessed by Three-dollar (fee pay) Ramp 1/2 mile above on Hwy. 38.

5. BUNCH BAR - Day-use park with primitive ramp and bank fishing on first riffle above Sawyer Rapids upper pool. Excellent for winter steelhead.

6. ELKTON BRIDGE - Fish from bridge and both banks for spring chinook, winter steelhead. Excellent smallmouth bass water from here to the Forks.

7. BUZZARD BAY - Primitive put-in difficult to use at low water.

8. Mehl Cr. Rd. - Drift boat bank slide at myrtle grove.

9. YELLOW CR. BOAT RAMP - Improved ramp accesses shad, spring chinook, winter steelhead.

10. POWELL BAR - Drift boat access.

11. MACK BROWN CO. PK. - Primitive boat ramp accesses spring & fall chinook water, small mouth bass, winter steelhead, shad.

12. UMPQUA BOAT RAMP - Improved ramp and picnic area. Fish for spring chinook, summer & winter steelhead, shad.

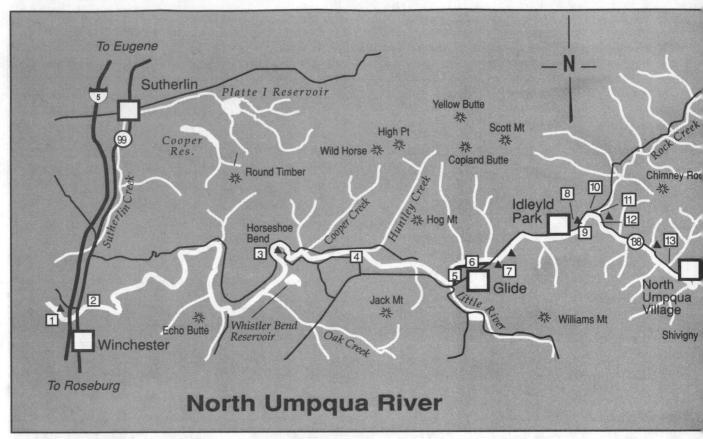

North Umpqua River

1. AMACHER PARK - To just below Winchester Dam, most popular fishing on the river. Productive bank access for 1/4 mile above boat ramp.

2. PAGE RD. TAKE-OUT - Pole slide above dam.

3. WHISTLER'S BEND - County park with boat ramp, camping. One mile of good bank fishing.

4. ROCK PIT BOAT ACCESS - Drift boats only.

5. COLLIDING RIVERS - Boat ramp -

good steelhead holes downstream.

6. BARN HOLE - One major hole in two miles of good water, accessed by the old Glide Rd. off Hwy. 138. Bank fishing along road.

7. LONE ROCK - Pole slide boat ramp. **DEADLINE: NO BOAT ANGLING ABOVE THIS POINT.**

8. NARROWS - This chute is one of the best spring chinook holes on the river.

9. MAC PLACE - Drift fishing for spring chinook, summer and winter steelhead, coho.

10. BRIDGE TO NOWHERE - Fish 200 yds. of good water on north and south banks.

11. ROCK CR. - Huge pool where fish congregate prior to running up to hatchery. Summer steelhead and stocked trout only available from here upstream. **DEADLINE: FLY FISHING ONLY ABOVE THIS POINT.**

12. FAMOUS - Bedrock tail-out.

13. LOWER HONEY - Pocket water and some gravel.

14. SUSAN CR. - Long classic steelhead run: tail-out, riffle, bedrock, shelf. BLM full-service camp.

LOWER UMPQUA CHINOOK
Veronica Walter, Photographer

est catches in April and May, and again in August. Most fishing is from anchored riverboats (flat bottoms only are suitable for the Umpqua), with anglers running spinners or herring. Earliest fishing for spring chinook takes place at Jimmy Creek, the first rapids above Scottsburg Bridge, featuring an excellent chinook hole.

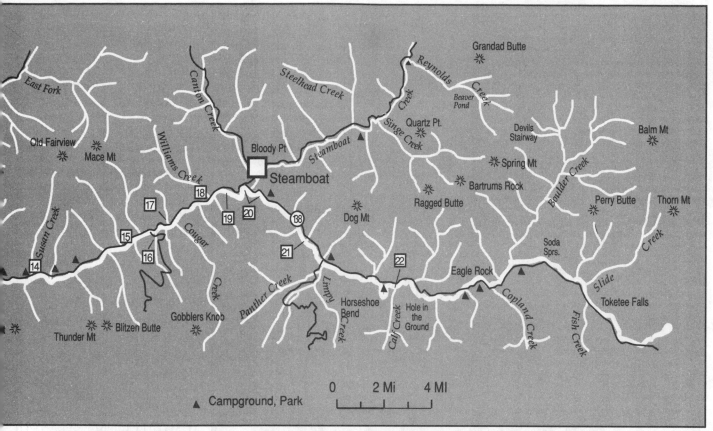

15. FAIRVIEW - Dead drift through a deep chute and around big boulders.

16. WRIGHT CREEK - Wide tail-out of bedrock ledges where steelhead rest above major rapids.

17. LOWER & UPPER ARCHIE - Two 20 ft. deep pools between major rapids.

18. WILLIAMS CR. - Half-mile classic run.

19. THE LEDGES - Shallow water featuring series of ledge slots where steelhead lie.

20. STEAMBOAT CR. *(Camp Water)* - At least 25 named holes where steelheaders and summer steelhead congregate. Bridge accesses south bank. **STEAMBOAT CREEK IS CLOSED TO ANGLING.**

21. REDMAN CR. - Gravel tail-out above a major rapids.

22. CALF CREEK - Pocket water.

Anglers launch at Scottsburg Park and motor up about 3 miles to the rapids, or launch at Scott Cr. Boat Ramp and drift down. Scott Cr. Ramp is also used to access Sawyer Rapids about a mile upriver. Sawyer is a series of rapids with pools below, and a large pool above accessed from the Three-dollar (fee-pay) ramp 1/ 2 mile further up on Hwy. 38. Bank anglers can fish the Sawyer Rapids upper pool from Bunch Bar, a day-use park about 5 miles west of Elkton. Other popular spring chinook access points are Elkton Bridge, Yellow Cr. Boat Ramp, Mack Brown Park, and Umpqua Boat Ramp. The total spring chinook catch in the lower river in 1986 was 725, with 1000 fish taken the previous year.

Summer steelhead is a very popular fishery on the mainstem, though nothing to compare with the North Fork. The fish are present in numbers in May, June, July, and August. Peak catches are taken in June and July, and boat and bank anglers use everything to catch them from flies to nightcrawlers. Most popular boat launches for summer steelhead are at Yellow Creek, Umpqua, and at The Forks. Bank anglers find best access above Yellow Creek, where there is a better mix of BLM to private land. Look for turn-outs off County Rd. 33 below Tyee. The 1986 summer steelhead catch was only about 200, down from catches above 500 the previous two seasons.

A very large run of shad appears in the river in May and June from Scottsburg to the forks. Popular fishing spots include the areas around Yellow Creek Boat Ramp, Umpqua, and The Forks. Yellow Creek attracts a large number of bank anglers. But any of the winter steelhead drifts can also be fished for shad in season. Shad anglers use light tackle with small spinners, darts, or shad flies.

Winter steelheading in the mainstem begins after the first fall freshets, usually in October, and lasts through March. Scottsburg to Elkton is the first fishery, with high quality catches to 20 pounds. Below Sawyer Rapids there's a good bank fishery accessed through private land, open to public use by the landowner. The Elkton area offers good bank access from Mehl Canyon Rd., and there is drift boat fishing throughout the stretch. Popular day drifts include Buzzard Bay at Elkton to Sawyer Rapids (a fee-pay take-out), the Myrtle Grove dirt skid on Mehl Canyon Rd. to Buzzard Bay, Yellow Creek Boat Ramp to Kellog Christian primitive ramp at milepost 9 on Hwy. 138W, Umpqua to just below Mac Brown Park on the Tyee Rd., and The Forks to Umpqua. The standard method is to run plugs in front of the drift boat. These same drifts can be used to fish summer steelhead. The annual catch of winter steelhead on the mainstem Umpqua usually fluctuates from 3000-5000. The 1985-86 reported catch was 2,837.

The only campground on the mainstem is the Tyee BLM camp on County Rd. 57 between Elkton and Umpqua.

UMPQUA RIVER, NORTH One of Oregon's most treasured streams, beloved for its pristine quality and picturesque setting, and for its enormous run of summer steelhead. The North Umpqua is unique among coastal rivers in supporting a very good spring chinook run in addition to its summer steelhead. Also unique is the closure to all but fly angling throughout a significant and productive stretch of the river. Coho and a run of wild winter steelhead are also available, with smallmouth bass and shad taken in the lower river. Native cutthroat trout and some nice browns can be found above Rock Creek, and catchable rainbow are planted throughout the river.

The North Umpqua originates high in the Cascade Mountains at Maidu Lake, and is fed by the outflow of big Diamond Lake and by snow melt and springs on a tumultuous 100-mile journey through a steep forested canyon. It joins the South Umpqua just NW of Roseburg to form the mainstem Umpqua.

For anglers, the North Umpqua offers a pleasant lesson in how big fish navigate their

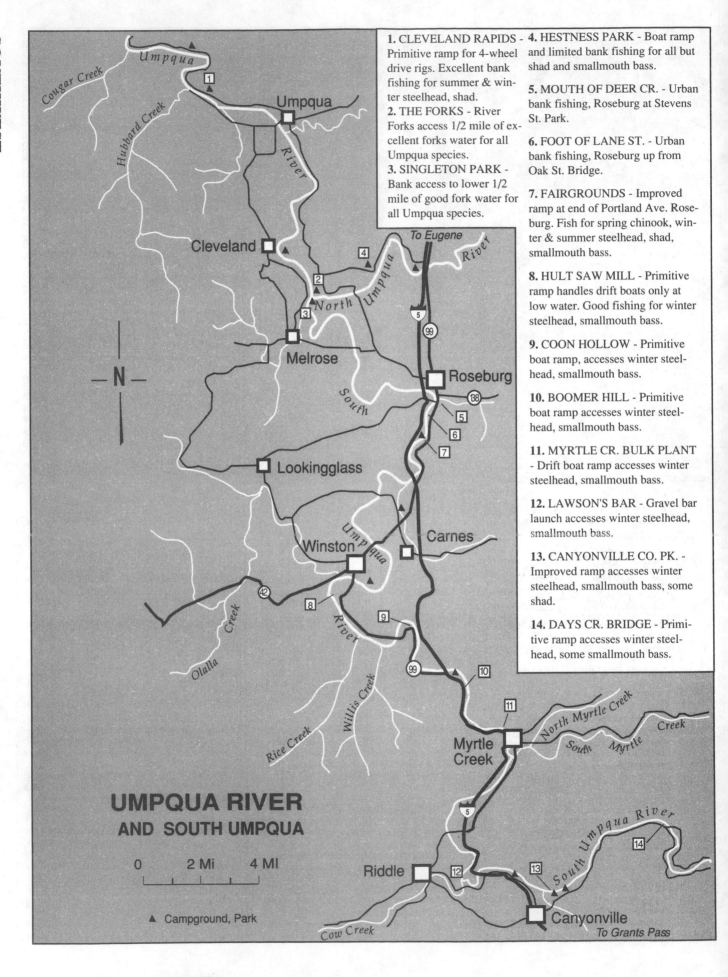

1. CLEVELAND RAPIDS - Primitive ramp for 4-wheel drive rigs. Excellent bank fishing for summer & winter steelhead, shad.

2. THE FORKS - River Forks access 1/2 mile of excellent forks water for all Umpqua species.

3. SINGLETON PARK - Bank access to lower 1/2 mile of good fork water for all Umpqua species.

4. HESTNESS PARK - Boat ramp and limited bank fishing for all but shad and smallmouth bass.

5. MOUTH OF DEER CR. - Urban bank fishing, Roseburg at Stevens St. Park.

6. FOOT OF LANE ST. - Urban bank fishing, Roseburg up from Oak St. Bridge.

7. FAIRGROUNDS - Improved ramp at end of Portland Ave. Roseburg. Fish for spring chinook, winter & summer steelhead, shad, smallmouth bass.

8. HULT SAW MILL - Primitive ramp handles drift boats only at low water. Good fishing for winter steelhead, smallmouth bass.

9. COON HOLLOW - Primitive boat ramp, accesses winter steelhead, smallmouth bass.

10. BOOMER HILL - Primitive boat ramp accesses winter steelhead, smallmouth bass.

11. MYRTLE CR. BULK PLANT - Drift boat ramp accesses winter steelhead, smallmouth bass.

12. LAWSON'S BAR - Gravel bar launch accesses winter steelhead, smallmouth bass.

13. CANYONVILLE CO. PK. - Improved ramp accesses winter steelhead, smallmouth bass, some shad.

14. DAYS CR. BRIDGE - Primitive ramp accesses winter steelhead, some smallmouth bass.

UMPQUA RIVER
AND SOUTH UMPQUA

0   2 Mi   4 MI

▲ Campground, Park

home stream, where they pause before attempting a chute, where they rest after they've made it to the upper pool. Here, more often than not, the fish are where the books say they should be. And each riffle, tail-out, chute, and pool seems to have been lovingly (or ruefully) named by local anglers.

Hwy. 138 follows the river all the way from the forks to Lemolo Lake. Above Lemolo, as 138 swings south toward Diamond Lake, FS 60 leads to the Kelsay Valley Trailhead, which tracks the North Umpqua to its headwaters at Maidu. West of the trailhead, forest roads follow the North Umpqua inlet of Lemolo Lake, including a stretch between Crystal Springs and the Lake that offers excellent opportunities for late season fishing for brook trout and browns to 1 1/2 pounds.

The lower 35 miles of the North Umpqua are less accessible, fished primarily by riverboat, since the surrounding land is mostly private. From The Forks County Park, about 6 miles north of Roseburg, anglers boat about 1/2 mile upstream. Jet sleds can navigate the 5 miles up to Winchester Dam (few jet the river beyond the dam). There is also a productive bank fishery at The Forks for salmon, steelhead, smallmouth bass, and shad. The most popular stretch on the lower river is from Amacher Park to just below Winchester Dam for stocked rainbow, steelhead, and salmon. There is 1/4 mile of good bank access at Amacher.

Above Winchester, Whistler's Bend County Park offers a mile of good bank fishing for salmon and steelhead in a fine stretch of classic water, including tail-out, riffle, bedrock chutes, and pockets.

Boat and bank access picks up from Glide east, with a boat ramp at the confluence of Lit-

tle River (Colliding Rivers) accessing a string of good steelh holes downstream. Anglers bank fish off the Old Glide Rd. off Hwy. 138, with the Barn Hole just one of many in a 2 mile string of good water. The deadline for boats on the North Umpqua is at Lone Rock Boat Ramp, about 3 miles west of the community of Idleyld Park. There's much good water in the Idleyld area, but not a lot of bank access. A 200 yd. stretch is accessible to bank anglers from north and south banks at Bridge to Nowhere, off Hwy. 138. Rock Creek joins the river about one mile east of Idleyld. There is a hatchery about 3/4 mile up the Rock Creek Rd., and fish congregate in a huge pool at the confluence prior to running up. A large concentration of stocked legal rainbow are also available here.

From Rock Creek up to Lemolo Lake, only flyfishing is permitted. Fly anglers in pursuit of steelhead use heavy gear in order to make long casts, and to break through the canyon winds. Named holes follow even more closely upon one another, many of them associated with the North Umpqua's plentiful tributaries. Among them are Susan Creek, *Fairview, Wright Creek, Lower & Upper Archie, Williams Cr., The Ledges,* and *Steamboat.* Steamboat Creek itself is a steelhead spawning ground, closed to angling. But the bend of river that includes the Steamboat confluence attracts anglers from throughout the world. Called *the Camp Water* by familiars, this 400 yard stretch of pocket water includes at least 25 named holes where summer steelhead and steelheaders gather under the protective eye of an organization of fly anglers called the Steamboaters.

The Umpqua's summer steelhead run now far surpasses historical numbers. Native summer steelhead, supplemented by stocked fish,

enter the North Umpqua in June and provide excellent fishing through October. The 1986 catch was over 6,000, with all but 700 taken in the river above Winchester Dam. The North Umpqua was Number One on the Oregon coast for summer steelhead. Spring chinook are in the river from April through October, with peak catches in May, June, and July. The total 1986 catch from the North Umpqua was 1479. The winter steelhead catch almost always exceeds 1000. Catchable hatchery reared rainbow trout are planted from Amacher Park on up from just before opening season until July 4, or until the river warms above 70 degrees. Contact the Dept. of Fish and Wildlife at Roseburg for a calendar of stocking dates and locations.

Whistler's Bend County Park offers the only camping facilities on the lower river, but camps are plentiful east of Idleyld on Hwy. 138 and at the reservoirs. At Susan Creek there is a long, classic steelhead run—tail-out, riffle, bedrock, shelf, as well as a full-service BLM camp. Other large facilities are at Bogus Creek, and Island. There are two small camps on Steamboat Creek (Canton Creek and Steamboat Falls) There are large camps at Apple Creek, Horseshoe Bend, and Eagle Rock; a small camp at Boulder Flat; and large camps at Toketee and Lemolo. There are also two BLM campgrounds on the Rock Creek Rd. (County Rd. 78) about 5 miles above the hatchery. Camping is free at Steamboat Creek, Apple Creek, Boulder Flat, and Toketee.

UMPQUA RIVER, SOUTH A big river, flowing over 95 miles from headwaters in the Rogue-Umpqua Divide Wilderness, joining the North Umpqua at The Forks about 10 miles NW of Roseburg to form the mainstem Umpqua. The South Umpqua fea-

tures some of western Oregon's best small-mouth bass water, and maintains a good winter steelhead run. Trout fishing is primarily for hatchery rainbow.

South of Roseburg the river is flanked by I-5 and accessed by county roads from Winston to Canyonville. From Canyonville, where the river bends east, it is followed by Hwy. 227 to Tiller, then by County Rd. 46 into the Umpqua National Forest. FS 28 continues along the stream past South Umpqua Falls to Camp Comfort.

Forest land along the South Umpqua was heavily logged in the 1950s and '60s, with maintenance of the river's fisheries a low priority. Today, reforestation, better logging practices, and sensitive management within the several impacting agencies have allowed the South Umpqua to stage a comeback. The construction of Galesville Dam has also helped, providing a better summer stream flow for salmon and steelhead.

The lower 30 miles offer the best angling for smallmouth bass, though bass are present up to Days Creek east of Canyonville. Good bass angling begins whenever river temperature hits 65 degrees, generally from March through October. Above Canyonville, the smallmouth population decreases and is lightly fished. Anglers access the best bedrock pockets from driftboats in spring, and fish from the banks and bridges around the boat ramps when the river drops too low for drifting in summer. Urban anglers can fish the mouth of Deer Creek from the banks at Stevens St. Park in Roseburg, or at the foot of Lane St. up from the Oak St. Bridge. The Fairgrounds south of town also offers opportunity for smallmouth bass as well as spring chinook, shad, and both winter and summer steelhead. The area around Winston, including the vicinity of Looking Glass Creek, is popular with smallmouth bass anglers. Coon Hollow and Round Prairie, off Hwy. 99, both have good bedrock bass pools.

The South Umpqua has both early and late arriving winter steelhead runs. The first run usually appears in the river in late November (depending on the arrival of fall freshets) and continues into December. The late run shows in late December with good catches till tax time. The river is open for steelhead up to Dumont Creek, and a lot of angling takes place in the area right below the deadline. The 1986 winter steelhead catch was close to 1000, but the previous year's take was double that number.

Trout are available from Dumont Creek (about 7 miles NE of Tille) to the Forks. These are primarily stocked rainbow, but native cutthroat are in the river. The South Umpqua is heavily stocked in spring and summer until the river warms above 70 degrees. Several of its good size tributaries, including Days, Elk, and Jackson creeks, offer good trout fishing. Elk Creek is accessed by Hwy. 227 south from Tiller. A few rattlesnakes are present around the river above Tiller.

There are also salmon in the South Umpqua, but the angler success rate is low. A few coho are caught by local anglers from the mouth of Cow Creek down. A small number of chinook are also caught. Check current regulations for special rules related to the salmon fishery.

Camping facilities are available at Dumont Creek about 7 miles above Tiller, at Boulder Creek, and at Camp Comfort, about 7 miles above South Umpqua Falls. These campgrounds are all free.

UNION CREEK A very good trout stream, extremely popular among anglers of the North Fork Rogue, of which it is a productive tributary. About 15 miles long, it enters the North Fork from the east about 10 miles north of Prospect, upstream from Natural Bridge. From Medford, follow Hwy. 62 about 58 miles north and east. Hwy. 62 crosses the lower end of the stream about one mile south of the junction of 62 (to Crater lake) and Hwy. 230 (to Diamond Lake). FS 6230 follows the creek for about 7 miles from Rt. 230, and FS 900 continues to its headwaters. There is a trail along the creek for several miles upstream from Union Creek Resort.

Fishing's best in late spring through July, but the creek does hold up all summer. There are native brook trout, cutthroat, rainbow, and browns. Browns to 10 pounds are rare but not unknown. The stream is heavily stocked with rainbow trout from late May through the end of August.

The actual opening of trout season here is often delayed following winters with heavy snowfall. Tributaries of the North Fork Rogue are usually accessible by late May. There is a large Forest Service camp at Union Creek and campgrounds upstream and down, at Farewell Bend and Natural Bridge.

VINCENT CREEK A very good native trout stream in the lower Umpqua area, heading north of the main Umpqua and flowing north to join the Smith River. The upper end can be reached by road from Hwy. 38, 1 1/2 miles east of Scottsburg. Take the road leading north from Wells Creek Guard Station and follow it over the ridge to the Vincent Creek watershed. The lower end of the creek is reached by the Vincent Cr. Rd., about 4 miles above Smith River Falls.

The stream is about 12 miles long and has good angling for native cutthroat. A spinner/bait combination in early season will usually work, and flies work well when the water drops and warms. There are no camps on the stream. This area suffered terribly from forest fires in 1967, but is healing nicely.

WASSON LAKE A small remote cutthroat lake in the west end of Douglas County north of the lower Umpqua River and south of Smith River. The lake is on government land and is the source of Wasson Creek, a tributary of Smith River. The lake is best reached from the Vincent Creek Rd. See vincent creek. But the new sections of the road are not usually passable until midsummer. A paved road now passes immediately beside Wassen Lake.

Only about 5 acres, it offers good fishing for native cutthroat. They average about 8 inches and run to 15 inches. Spinner and bait work well, but the lake is snaggy, and a lot of gear is lost. A fly angler can do well here.

WILLOW CREEK RESERVOIR (Jackson Co.) A very popular reservoir of 340 acres located about 9 miles SE of Butte Falls on Willow Creek, and about 41 miles north and east of Medford by way of Hwy. 62. From Ashland, later in the season when the roads are passable, it can be reached by the Fish Lake Rd. then about 8 miles of dirt road north from Fish Lake.

The reservoir has natural reproduction of rainbow trout and is stocked yearly with catchables. A population of kokanee was established years ago and still makes up a portion of the catch. Black crappie go to 10 inches, and the rainbow get up to 18 inches, occasionally larger. Fishing holds up well throughout the season, with May and September the best months. Trolling is common, but bait fishing accounts for most of the catch here. Flyfishing in the upper shoal areas can produce some nice rainbow. Fish nymphs with a sunken line, and use a slow jerky retrieve.

Largemouth bass are present in good numbers. The lake's elevation limits the growing season for the bass, but while they rarely get over 4 pounds, angler success rate for them is good.

Boats can be easily launched. A resort here has supplies and rents boats and motors. There are several nice picnic areas around the lake.

WINCHESTER BAY (See UMPQUA RIVER ESTUARY)

WOLF LAKE An 8 acre hike-in brook trout lake in the headwaters of the South Umpqua River. It is about a one mile hike SE from Black Rock, which is reached by FS 2780. Follow FS 28 NE from Camp Comfort about 10 miles to FS 2780, which leads about 2 miles to Black Rock. The trailhead is just south of the junction with FS 2716.

It offers good angling for brook trout to 16 inches. Fishing can be great in early spring if you can get in. The roads are usually accessible in mid-June. There are no improvements at the lake.

YANKEE RESERVOIR Prominent on maps of the area, a privately owned 30 acre impoundment on Yankee Creek, closed to public access. It is one mile upstream from Antelope Creek Rd. about 6 miles from White City.

NORTH UMPQUA ANGLING
Dan Callaghan, Photographer

COLUMBIA RIVER ZONE

The Columbia River zone is all waters of the Columbia River upstream from a north-south line through buoy 10 at the mouth, and includes those portions of tributaries downstream from the main line railroad bridges near their mouths except for the Willamette, Sandy, Hood, Deschutes, and Umatilla River systems.

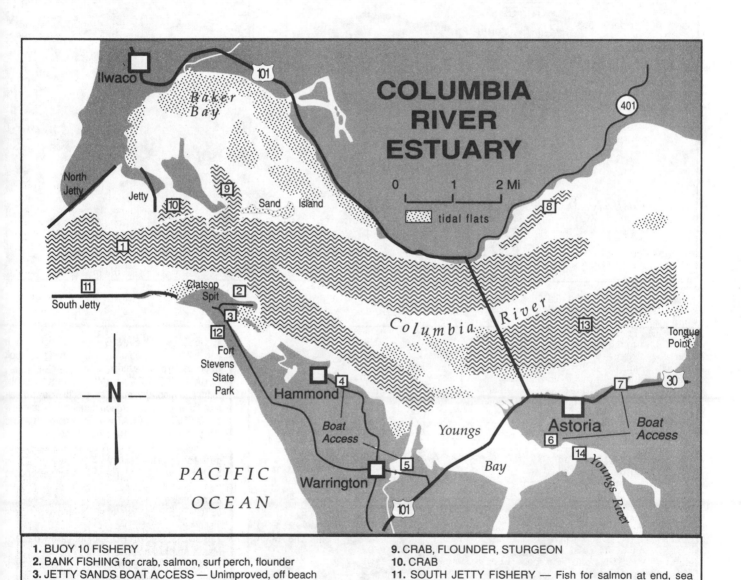

1. BUOY 10 FISHERY
2. BANK FISHING for crab, salmon, surf perch, flounder
3. JETTY SANDS BOAT ACCESS — Unimproved, off beach
4. HAMMOND BOAT RAMP — Improved ramps
5. WARRENTON BOAT RAMP — Improved public ramp
6. YOUNGS BAY BOAT ACCESS — Improved ramp
7. EAST END BASIN — Improved ramps
8. STURGEON
9. CRAB, FLOUNDER, STURGEON
10. CRAB
11. SOUTH JETTY FISHERY — Fish for salmon at end, sea bass and bottomfish mid-jetty, surf perch nearest spit
12. CLATSOP SPIT — Fish the surf for perch; most productive beach for razor clams in Oregon
13. STURGEON
14. STURGEON

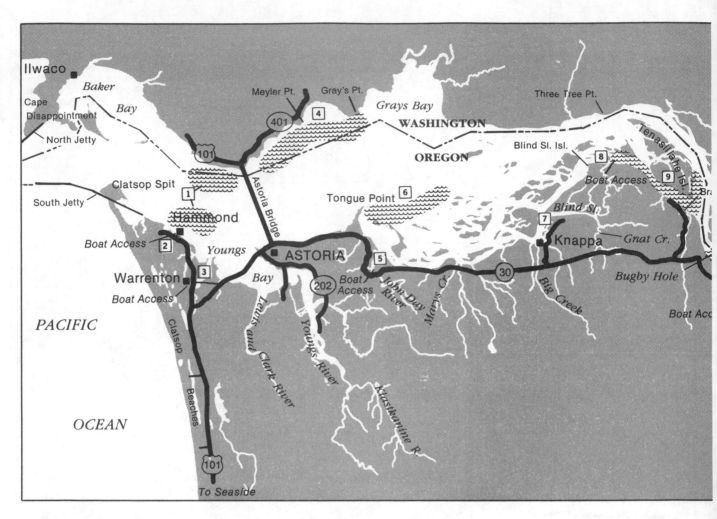

SOUTH JETTY FISHING FAMILY
Bill Wagner, Photographer

1. **DESDEMONA SANDS** - Fish troughs north and south of sandbar for early spring chinook when anchovies are running.
2. **HAMMOND BOAT RAMP** - Improved public ramp and moorage; major access to Buoy 10 salmon fishery and to sturgeon throughout summer.
3. **WARRENTON BOAT RAMP** - Improved public ramp accesses Buoy 10 salmon fishery.
4. **MEGLER PT. TO GRAY'S BAY** - Best sturgeon fishing in the estuary.
5. **JOHN DAY BOAT RAMP** - Improved public ramp is major access to sturgeon in estuary above bridge.
6. **TONGUE PT.** - Fish for sturgeon along islands just off shipping channel.
7. **BLIND SLOUGH** - Hot spot for yellow perch in Mar. & April when anchovies run.
8. **ALDRICH PT. BOAT RAMP** - Take Brownsmeade turn-off to improved single ramp to access Clifton Channel and Blind Slough.
9. **CLIFTON CHANNEL** - Fish through Mar. for spring chinook when water is clear and low.
10. **WESTPORT BOAT RAMP** - Improved single ramp accesses lower Clifton Channel.
11. **SEINING GROUNDS** - Fish wing jetties for salmon to just above Wallace Is.
12. **WALLACE TO CRIMMS IS.** - Spring chinook along Oregon shore; bank access at Jones Beach.
13. **BARLOW PT.** - Fish for coho jacks, sea-run cutthroat, some sturgeon.

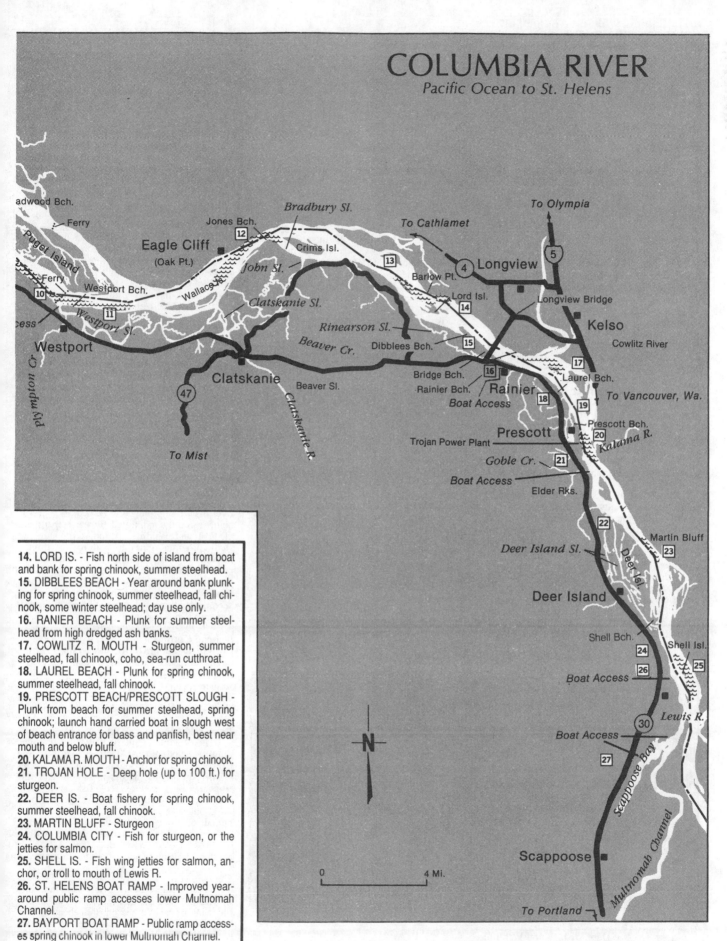

COLUMBIA RIVER
Pacific Ocean to St. Helens

adwood Bch.
Ferry
Puget Island
Ferry
Westport Bch.
cess
Westport
plympton Cr.
Westport Sl.
Wallace Is.
John Sl.
Clatskanie Sl.
Beaver Cr.
Beaver Sl.
Clatskanie
To Mist
Clatskanie R.
47

Eagle Cliff
(Oak Pt.)
12
Jones Bch.
Bradbury Sl.
Crims Isl.
13
To Cathlamet
Barlow Pt.
Lord Isl.
14
Rinearson Sl.
Dibblees Bch.
15
Bridge Bch.
16
Rainier Bch.
Boat Access
Rainier
18

To Olympia
5
4
Longview
Longview Bridge
Kelso
Cowlitz River
17
Laurel Bch.
To Vancouver, Wa.
19
Prescott Bch.
20
Kalama R.
Prescott
Trojan Power Plant
Goble Cr.
21
Boat Access
Elder Rks.
22
Martin Bluff
23
Deer Island Sl.
Deer Isl.
Deer Island
Shell Bch.
Shell Isl.
24
25
Boat Access
26
Lewis R.
30
Boat Access
27
Scappoose Bay
Scappoose
Multnomah Channel
To Portland

N

0   4 Mi.

14. LORD IS. - Fish north side of island from boat and bank for spring chinook, summer steelhead.

15. DIBBLEES BEACH - Year around bank plunking for spring chinook, summer steelhead, fall chinook, some winter steelhead; day use only.

16. RANIER BEACH - Plunk for summer steelhead from high dredged ash banks.

17. COWLITZ R. MOUTH - Sturgeon, summer steelhead, fall chinook, coho, sea-run cutthroat.

18. LAUREL BEACH - Plunk for spring chinook, summer steelhead, fall chinook.

19. PRESCOTT BEACH/PRESCOTT SLOUGH - Plunk from beach for summer steelhead, spring chinook; launch hand carried boat in slough west of beach entrance for bass and panfish, best near mouth and below bluff.

20. KALAMA R. MOUTH - Anchor for spring chinook.

21. TROJAN HOLE - Deep hole (up to 100 ft.) for sturgeon.

22. DEER IS. - Boat fishery for spring chinook, summer steelhead, fall chinook.

23. MARTIN BLUFF - Sturgeon

24. COLUMBIA CITY - Fish for sturgeon, or the jetties for salmon.

25. SHELL IS. - Fish wing jetties for salmon, anchor, or troll to mouth of Lewis R.

26. ST. HELENS BOAT RAMP - Improved year-around public ramp accesses lower Multnomah Channel.

27. BAYPORT BOAT RAMP - Public ramp accesses spring chinook in lower Multnomah Channel.

COLUMBIA RIVER, ESTUARY (Astoria Bridge to the Pacific Ocean) Oregon's Number One port of entry for salmon and steelhead. These anadramous fish are bound for home waters in Oregon, Washington, and Idaho—including the Willamette, Deschutes, and Snake River Systems among others. Sturgeon, sea-run cutthroat, bottom fish, and clams are also available here.

Offshore Fisheries

The mouth of the Columbia was once famed as an access to the offshore salmon fishery. Experienced anglers and charter boats out of the ports of Hammond, Warrenton, and Astoria would locate and start taking big chinook just beyond the bar as early as late May. The most intense fishing off the Columbia River bar was mid-August through Labor Day, when fall chinook gather to move upriver.

There are now severe constraints on the ocean salmon sport fishery off the Columbia bar, in an effort to protect weak salmon stocks. The waters directly west of, and between, the jettys (an intensive salmon feeding area) are permanently closed to fishing. In 1988, the off-shore season between the South Jetty and Cape Falcon was limited to July 11 through July 24, with a reported catch of 500 chinook and 9800 coho.

However, the Port of Astoria is still home to a highly respected fleet of charter fishing boats, and continues to be a popular starting point for ocean salmon trips, with destination waters beyond the heavily restricted area. In 1986 the ocean salmon sport catch out of Astoria was still second highest on the Oregon coast at 38,859. The 1987 catch was down due to poor coho returns (25,300 coho caught, 4000 chinook).

Some bottom fishing occurs offshore around the south jetty, but most offshore sport fishing in Oregon takes place from Cape Falcon (near the Port of Garibaldi) south, where the salmon season is generous, bottom fishing excellent, and (incidentally) the bars provide easier crossing.

A powerhouse throughout its long run (literally, alas), the Columbia rushes toward the ocean on an average summer day at a rate of 400,000 cubic feet per second. Its meeting with the ocean is *not* pacific. The Columbia River bar is the most dangerous on the Oregon coast. Only 25 feet deep, though dredged to 60 feet in the channel, and relatively narrow, it is subject to swells that can rise higher than the average water depth. More often the exchange of fresh and salt water takes place beneath a smooth surface, but boaters must be ever alert, mindful of the tide, time, and weather. A craft at least 18 ft. long is recommended for bar crossings, and boaters are urged to cross in flood and slack tides only, and to beware of the ebb tide.

Buoy 10 Salmon Fishery

As the Columbia's offshore salmon season has diminished, the importance of the estuary fishery has increased. Since 1982, growing numbers of charter and private boats have gathered to fish the waters upstream of the Buoy 10 line, which officially separates ocean and estuary fisheries about 2 miles upstream from jetty's end. Salmon angling takes place from Buoy 10 to Buoy 14 (about 12 miles up), with the majority of boats fishing as close as possible to the Buoy 10 line.

The Buoy 10 season usually opens mid-August and extends through Labor Day. Anglers should be aware that the salmon fishery here is subject to sudden in-season restrictions. Regulation updates are printed in local newspapers or available by calling the Dept. of Fish and Wildlife information line or the Columbia Regional Office. Check the synopsis for special regulations that apply to the estuary.

On the busiest weekends, over 2,000 boats have been known to gather along the buoy line, drifting or trolling herring or anchovies through the flood tide. Anglers fish coho closer to the surface, while chinook travel somewhat deeper. Many boats use electronic gear to locate salmon, but the presence of rips (the meeting of conflicting currents), and concentrations of bird activity are also good detectors.

Hundreds of bank anglers also participate in the Buoy 10 carnival, fishing off Clatsop Spit, where coho catches predominate.

In 1988, 185,500 angler trips to the estuary took a catch of 143,800 coho and 30,700 chinook, or approximately one salmon per angler.

Charter boats for the Columbia's estuary fishery are available in Warrenton, Hammond, and Astoria in Oregon, and in Ilwaco, Chinook, and Westport in Washington. Charter services provide everything from expert navigational skills to tackle, advice, and (sometimes) on-shore canning facilities.

Sturgeon

The Columbia River is host to one of the world's largest sturgeon populations. Both white and (less common) green sturgeon are present in the system. Fished commercially in the Columbia almost to extinction in the late 1800s, this ancient species has staged a come-back, offering Oregon anglers an outstanding fresh water fishing experience during the past 10 years.

With an estimated life expectancy of 100 years or more, sturgeon have been known to reach lengths of up to 20 feet, and the largest caught in the Columbia system weighed 1,500 pounds. Today, the average catch is about 41 inches. Minimum catch length is 40 inches, and sturgeon over 72 inches must be released immediately unharmed. Minimum handling of these often pregnant behemoths is urged.

The Columbia River estuary includes some of the most productive sturgeon water in the river. In 1988, sport anglers reported an estuary catch of 23,000.

Though the sturgeon fishery has been open year around, the spring and summer seasons are most popular with anglers. Increased catches generally coincide with the appearance of anchovies in the river from April to August, with peak catches in June and July. Check with local bait shops to determine when the anchovies have arrived, and to place your order for bait. Fresh bait is essential for this fishery, and should be ordered at least one day in advance to insure a supply. Normally 12 to 18 baits per person will suffice.

During the peak season, several hundred boats may gather on a single day in the area from Desdemona Sands to Grays Bay Point, with the best bite occurring from low slack to several hours into the flood tide. Tides and the persistence of sculpin at stealing bait often drive anglers to try several locations per trip.

The population of white sturgeon in the river is currently judged to be healthy, but it is being carefully monitored by the Department of Fish and Wildlife. A long-term sturgeon study program hopes to add to our limited knowledge of the biology, habits and habitat needs of the species. As participation in this sportfishery continues to increase, anglers should be prepared for tighter regulations. Conservation will insure continuation of the fishery for generations to come.

Sea-run Cutthroat

Sea-run cutthroat trout are available at the mouths of estuary tributaries, from July to October, but most angling for them takes place further up the tributaries. Ideal tide, time and conditions would be low water at dawn with cloud cover, light rain, and a breath of wind.

Bottom Fishing

The Columbia Estuary offers varied opportunities for bottom fishing from both boat and bank. The jetties on both north and south sides of the bay provide access to bottom and surf fish such as greenling, rock fish, surf perch, and ling cod. Ling cod may weigh in at over 20 pounds, and the perch sometimes reach 3 pounds or better. Best catches occur during incoming tide, using cut herring, shrimp, or clam necks. The surf along the Clatsop beaches south of the estuary are also very productive.

Clams

The Clatsop beaches, from the south jetty to Seaside, have the best razor clam digging in the state. There is a season, though, and catch rules, so check the regulations before you plan a trip. You'll also want to check the tide tables.

BUOY 10
Courtesy, Oregon Dept. of Fish and Wildlife

CLATSOP SPIT CLAMMING
Gerry Lewin, Photographer

Minus tides of below one foot at low water are usually necessary for good digging, and spring minus tides are best for razor clams. Clamming in Oregon is free, and beaches throughout its 300-mile length are open to the public.

Tidal information is published daily in the newspapers, and tables for the year are available free at many tackle shops. The Longbeach Peninsula north of Ilwaco, Washington is also famous for razor clams, but Washington regulations are changeable, and a non-resident license is required.

When the fishing season is open in both Oregon and Washington, a license of either state is valid for Columbia River angling except on the other state's shore. Anglers must follow the rules of their licensing state. When the Oregon season is closed, a Washington fishing license is not valid on the Oregon side of the state line (mid-channel), and vice-versa. The rules do vary between the states, so check on bag and maximum size limits.

Oregon salmon, steelhead, and sturgeon anglers are required to purchase a special angling tag in addition to the state license, and are asked to record their catch on a card, to be turned in before the beginning of the next fishing season. Statistics gathered from this record help monitor the state of the fisheries and shape management policy.

Downstream from Astoria-Megler Bridge ocean catch and length limits apply. Oregon and Washington usually adopt the regulations determined annually by the Federal Pacific Fisheries Management Council. The Council has jurisdiction over waters from 3 miles to 200 miles offshore. These are established in April each year by the Federal Pacific Fisheries Management Council. Check with the Department of Fish and Wildlife, or watch the local newspapers for announcements.

COLUMBIA RIVER, LOWER (Astoria Bridge to St. Helens) The lower Columbia River from Astoria Bridge to St. Helens offers 73 miles of outstanding fishing. The seasonal variety includes sturgeon, spring and fall chinook, summer and winter steelhead, cutthroat trout, and shad in the main river, and a rich variety of bass and panfish in adjacent slack water.

Highway 30 parallels the entire lower river, and the river is easily accessible for both boat and bank angling along most of its length. The river here is about one mile wide. Boats, moorage, bait, and tackle are available at St. Helens, Goble, Rainier, Astoria, and many points in between.

Sturgeon

The lower Columbia from Astoria to St. Helens contains some extremely productive sturgeon water. The fishery is primarily concentrated on the Washington side and at Tongue Point, on the Oregon Side. But other popular spots include the entire St. Helens area, Deer Island, Martins Bluff, Elder Rock, the Longview area, Oak Point, Bugby Hole, Three Tree Point, and Gray's Bay.

Sturgeon fishing is primarily a boat show. Anglers use depth finders (and the concentration of other boats) to locate sturgeon lays, then anchor and fish the bottom. Most popular baits are herring, and fresh anchovy and smelt. The most productive months are May through August, with peak catches in June and July. In 1988, the total reported sport catch between the estuary and mouth of the Willamette was 6,000.

Salmon

Spring chinook enter the lower Columbia in mid-February, with the run peaking in March. In an effort to rebuild the depleted upriver spring chinook run and to honor Indian treaty rights above Bonneville Dam, seasons have not extended beyond March, and in-season closures are always a possibility. Watch the newspapers or check with the Dept. of Fish and Wildlife before you plan your trip.

Salmon use the shoreline to navigate, so boat angling for these 3 to 6 year olds occurs along both sides of the shore, in 10 to 20 feet of water. Favorite spots include the waters just off Shell Island, Shell Beach, Deer Island, Sandy Island, Prescott Beach, Lord Island, Crim's Island, Westport Beach, Puget Island, Tenasillahe Island, and the mouths of the Lewis, Kalama, and Cowlitz Rivers.

Bank angling (often called *bar fishing* here) is most popular at the following beaches: Shell, Prescott, Laurel, Ranier, Bridge, Diblee, Jones, Westport, and Bradwood. An overwhelming percentage of bar anglers use No. 4 Spin-N-Glo lures. In low water years, angling for spring chinook may be excellent from St. Helens to Clifton Channel for boat and bank fishing. Most boat anglers troll herring, or anchor and use Flatfish. Prawns have also been used productively, both trolled and anchor-fished.

The fall chinook and jack salmon season in the lower Columbia is in August and September. It is primarily a boat fishery. Hog lines (regimental formations of anchored boats) form at the mouths of the Lewis, Kalama, and Cowlitz Rivers on the Washington side, with anglers preferring either flatfish or some kind of spinner. The water just off Shell Island is also productive, as is the area off Barlow Point just below the Cowlitz mouth. A successful bar fishery for jacks occurs at Prescott, Laurel, and Diblee beaches.

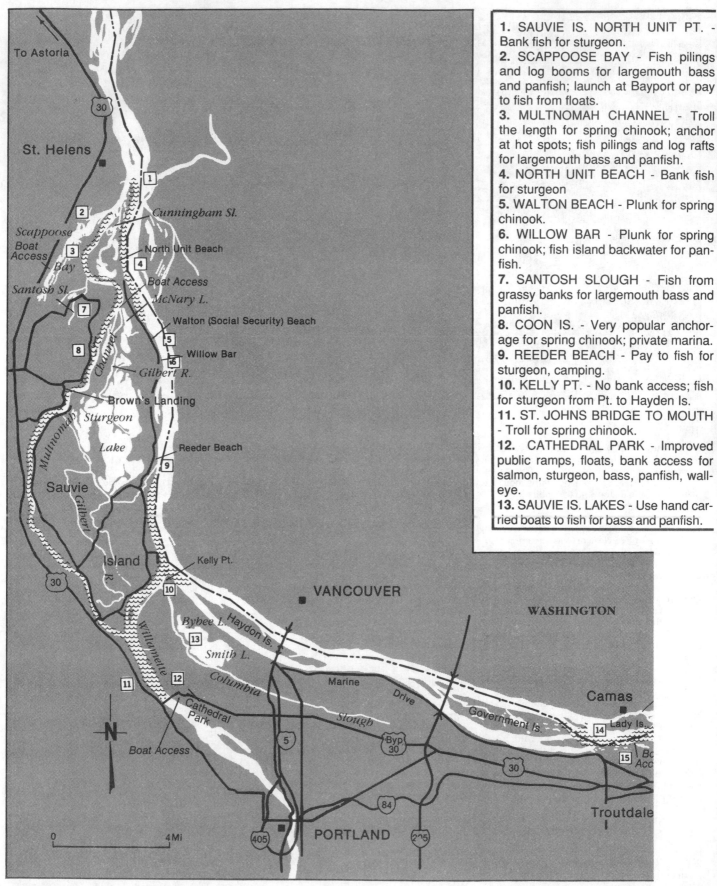

COLUMNA

1. **SAUVIE IS. NORTH UNIT PT.** - Bank fish for sturgeon.
2. **SCAPPOOSE BAY** - Fish pilings and log booms for largemouth bass and panfish; launch at Bayport or pay to fish from floats.
3. **MULTNOMAH CHANNEL** - Troll the length for spring chinook; anchor at hot spots; fish pilings and log rafts for largemouth bass and panfish.
4. **NORTH UNIT BEACH** - Bank fish for sturgeon
5. **WALTON BEACH** - Plunk for spring chinook.
6. **WILLOW BAR** - Plunk for spring chinook; fish island backwater for panfish.
7. **SANTOSH SLOUGH** - Fish from grassy banks for largemouth bass and panfish.
8. **COON IS.** - Very popular anchorage for spring chinook; private marina.
9. **REEDER BEACH** - Pay to fish for sturgeon, camping.
10. **KELLY PT.** - No bank access; fish for sturgeon from Pt. to Hayden Is.
11. **ST. JOHNS BRIDGE TO MOUTH** - Troll for spring chinook.
12. **CATHEDRAL PARK** - Improved public ramps, floats, bank access for salmon, sturgeon, bass, panfish, walleye.
13. **SAUVIE IS. LAKES** - Use hand carried boats to fish for bass and panfish.

14. GOVERNMENT IS. to mouth of Sandy R. - Anchor and spinfish for coho and chinook jacks in fall; summer steelhead, fall chinook, coho.

15. SUNDIAL BEACH - Improved private ramp popular access to summer steelhead, sturgeon, fall chinook.

16. WASHOUGAL REEF - Fish the rocks for walleye.

17. CAPE HORN - Popular sturgeon hole (especially in winter) beneath rocky cliff.

18. OUTLAW IS. - Fish around for sturgeon and walleye.

19. DODSON - Most popular sturgeon fishing on the river.

20. WARRENDALE - Plunk from beach for summer steelhead, fall chinook.

21. IVES IS. - Anchor for shad on south side of island.

22. HAMILTON IS. - Fish both sides of channel for fall chinook, summer steelhead.

23. TANNER CR. - Fish cautiously in heavy water from Bradford Is. to mouth of Tanner for sturgeon, summer steelhead, shad; bank access at mouth.

24. BRADFORD IS. - Fish lower end for sturgeon; only known shad bank fishery.

HEAVY TACKLE AT BONNEVILLE
Steve Terrill, Photographer

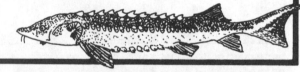
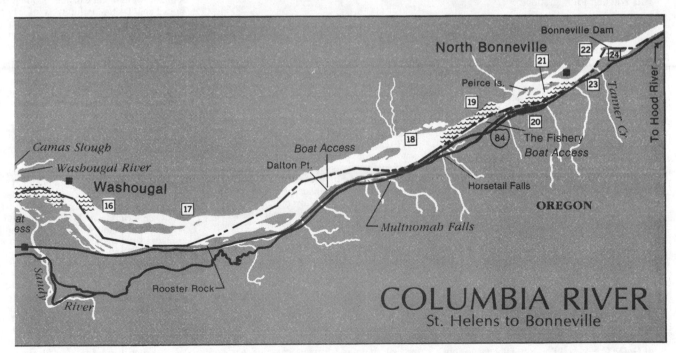

COLUMBIA RIVER
St. Helens to Bonneville

PELICANS FISHING IN COLUMBIA ESTUARY
Bill Wagner, Photographer

In 1988, anglers took home a total of 4,400 fall chinook, 4,600 spring chinook, and 2,000 coho (including jacks) from these waters.

Steelhead

The returns of summer steelhead in the Columbia river during the last 5 years have been outstanding. The reported catch in the lower river for 1988 was 10,400. Most boat anglers anchor to fish, using Flatfish and rainbow blade spinners. Bank anglers seem to prefer the old standard, Spin-N-Glo. Throughout the summer steelhead season on the river, only adipose fin-clipped steelhead may be kept.

Winter steelhead run up the lower Columbia from November through March. However, the fishery for them here is minor. Most anglers intercept them higher in the river system. Most successful winter steelheaders here fish from the beaches, including Shell, Prescott, Laurel, Ranier, Bridge, Diblee, Jones, Westport, and Bradwood.

Sea-run

Sea-run cutthroat trout are fished here July through November, with a peak in August through October. The majority of the catch is taken from the Washington shore, but good Oregon spots include Shell Beach, the mouth of Goble Creek, and Prescott, Diblee and Jones beaches. Over 50% of the Oregon catch is taken at Jones Beach. Anglers plunk worms and use the incidental catch of chub and squawfish as bait, sliced into strips.

Shad

Shad migrate through the lower Columbia on their way upriver, mid-May through June. But so far, anglers in this stretch have only tapped the run as it passes Shell Island. Average annual catch here is 2000. Other good spots are waiting to be discovered.

Because it is the Interstate of Northwest waters, and its salmon and steelhead are bound for home waters elsewhere in Oregon, Washington, and Idaho; because the salmon runs were so horribly decimated by dam construction; and because of treaty obligations to Native American tribes above Bonneville Dam—the Columbia is very heavily regulated throughout its length. Anglers for all fisheries on the Columbia are urged to check the current Sport Fishing Regulations prior to wetting a line.

Navigational charts of the Columbia River, produced by the National Oceanic and Atmospheric Administration (NOAA) are available through retail map outlets. An up-to-date chart (in hand) is a must for all boaters of the Columbia. In addition to helping anglers avoid commercial shipping channels, running aground, and losing the way back to the parking lot, the charts also provide a comprehensive presentation of the river's many backwater fishing opportunities.

Bass and Panfish

The Columbia River is home to an enormous population of bass and panfish, which inhabit its hundreds of sloughs and intertidal marshlands. Largemouth and smallmouth bass, white and black crappie, bluegill, yellow perch, channel cats, and brown bullhead are all richly represented.

For regulation and management purposes, these backwater adjuncts to the Columbia are not included within the Columbia Regulatory District, but rather, within the Northwest District. The following Columbia backwaters are described in the Northwest section of this book: Beaver Slough, Blind Slough, Bradbury Slough, Brownsmead Slough, Clatskanie Slough, Deer Island Slough, Diblees Slough, Goat Island Slough, Magruder Slough, Mayger Slough, Prescott Slough, Rinearson Slough, Sandy Island Slough, Westport Slough.

COLUMBIA RIVER, MIDDLE (St. Helens to Bonneville Dam)

A 58 mile stretch of mile-wide water, the most heavily fished in the river, providing the greatest variety of angling. Hwy. 30 follows closely along the south shore to Sauvie Island, where there is access from the island's north shore up to the mouth of the Willamette (an 18 mile stretch). From Portland east, I-84 follows the river, and many freeway exits offer access opportunities.

Boat moorages are located at frequent intervals along the waterfront. Some offer free launching and sell fuel and bait. Brown's Landing, on Multnomah Channel south of Scappoose, also has boat rentals, a restaurant, and an RV park. The Fishery, at the opposite end of this stretch (5 miles below Bonneville at Dodson), also provides camping facilities and is an informal angler's information center for the salmon, sturgeon, walleye, and shad fisheries in the upstream portion of this section.

There are public boat ramps at Clatskanie, Rainier, Multnomah Channel, Corbett, Rooster Rock, and Dalton Point west of Multnomah Falls. Marine sales, service, and fishing supplies are plentiful in the metropolitan waterfront areas, particularly on Marine Drive.

Sturgeon

The sturgeon catch in this section of the river continues to be down from its pre-Mt. St. Helens eruption days (perhaps due to silting), but catch numbers are still high, and sturgeon are successfully fished here the year around. The most productive angling in the Bonneville area occurs from February to March in conjunction with the arrival of smelt.

Boat angling for sturgeon begins at the boating deadline below Bonneville Dam and extends to Rooster Rock, about 12 miles down. Other favorite spots include Lady Island at Troutdale, near the I-5 bridge, the mouth of the Willamette, and the Washington side of the river across from Sauvie Island (between navigation lights 15 and 23).

Bank angling for sturgeon is best below Bonneville Dam at Bradford Island and the mouth of Tanner Creek, and off Sauvie Island beaches, particularly Reeder Beach (privately owned, fee required to fish) and North Unit Beach at the very end of Reeder Rd. (public property about 3 miles beyond the end of pavement).

Sturgeon bank angling demands sturdy gear: a 9-12 ft. rod, size 4/0+ reel, and 40-80 lb. line. Lamprey eel and sand shrimp are the

COLUMBIA RIVER STURGEON
Courtesy, Steve King, ODFW

favored bait. They stay on the hook well and are the natural bait below the dam. Smelt are also used. Boat anglers from Bonneville to Lady Island use smelt, lamprey eel, sand shrimp, salmon, pickled herring, and shad strips. From Lady Island down, smelt is most popular. Lighter gear is suitable for boat angling, except in the fast water just below Bonneville Dam.

Salmon and Steelhead

Angling for spring chinook in these waters is tightly regulated and requires a close reading of the rule book. The main salmon fishery in this section takes place in March off the Sauvie Island beaches. Most popular are Reeder Beach (private, fee required), Willow Bar, and Walton Beach (at the end of the pavement on Reeder Rd).

The fall salmon season (chinook and coho) is more generous. Catches are particularly good in August and September in the Sundial district and near the Sandy River mouth. The steelhead season is also liberal (for adipose fin clipped fish only). In 1986, the total reported catch of coho in the Columbia below Bonneville Dam was 33,446; The fall chinook catch for the entire stretch was 6,380. The reported steelhead catch for the entire lower river was 7,421 summer and 922 winter steelhead.

Shad

Shad migrate into this section of the Columbia from May through early July. Most angling occurs from the bank at Bonneville, off Bradford Island, and at the mouth of Tanner Creek. A record number (27,500) were taken from the Columbia in 1988—mostly from this area. Anglers use shad darts and small wobblers and spinners. Both plunking and casting are successful.

Boat anglers favor the waters off Ives Island (3 miles below Bonneville on the Washington side), and in Camas Slough at the mouth of the Washougal River.

Walleye

Walleye are increasingly available in the Columbia below Bonneville. Some of these large perch are landed by bank anglers just be

low the dam, but more are taken from boats just off Multnomah Falls, inside Ives and Pierce Island, at the mouth of Tanner Creek, and at the mouth of the Sandy River. Lures and worms are fished on the bottom in shallow water and rocky areas.

Bass and Panfish

Most angling for bass and panfish in this section of the river occurs in Scappoose Bay, Santosh Slough, Multnomah Channel, and the lakes and sloughs of Sauvie Island, including Cunningham Lake, Cunningham Slough, the Gilbert River, Haldeman Pond, Big and Little McNary, Pete's Slough, Pope Lake, and Sturgeon Lake. Columbia Slough in Portland also contains bass and panfish. These waters are described in the Willamette section of this book.

COLUMBIA RIVER, UPPER (Bonneville to Lake Wallula)

Four dams obstruct the flow in this portion of the Columbia, transforming the mighty river into a string of reservoirs 147 miles long—Bonneville Pool (Bonneville Dam), Lake Celilo (The Dalles Dam), Lake Umatilla (John Day Dam), and Lake Wallula (McNary Dam). As the character of the river has changed here, so has the life within it.

Salmon runs declined drastically following dam construction. For years, salmon that escaped death at the dams were strictly allocated to Native American tribes, whose rights to Columbia River fish were specified by treaty. Years of mitigation efforts have followed, involving enhancement of fish passage at the dams, hatchery production, and strict regulation.

Though spring chinook and coho populations are still years away from anything like restoration, the fall chinook run appears to be gaining ground. In 1985, fall chinook sportfishing recommenced in this portion of the river. In 1988, an estimated 114,700 adult chinook and 54,100 jacks made it past McNary Dam.

Hatchery reared steelhead runs are in fairly good shape as far up as the John Day River, but naturally spawned steelhead continue to be in the minority throughout the system, and even hatchery returns are still low on the Umatilla, Grande Ronde, and Imnaha rivers.

The sturgeon population behind the dams is currently under study. Biologists hope to determine whether or not the population is viable without its historic access to the sea. Walleye, smallmouth and largemouth bass, and a variety of panfish are flourishing in this section of the river and its adjacent ponds and backwaters.

For a complete description of angling opportunities in each of the dam pools, see bonneville pool and celilo, lake in the Central section of this book; umatilla, lake and wallula, lake in the Northeast section. A string of 31 bass and panfish ponds adjacent to the Columbia River between Bonneville Dam and the Deschutes River are mapped and described as columbia river ponds in the Central section.

YOUNGS RIVER FALLS
Bill Wagner, Photographer

WILLAMETTE ZONE

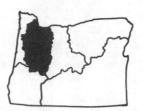

The Willamette Zone is all waters draining to the Columbia River between the city of St. Helens and Bonneville Dam, except for those portions of the Sandy River which are downstream from the Union Pacific Railroad line. Includes all waters on Sauvie Island except the Columbia River.

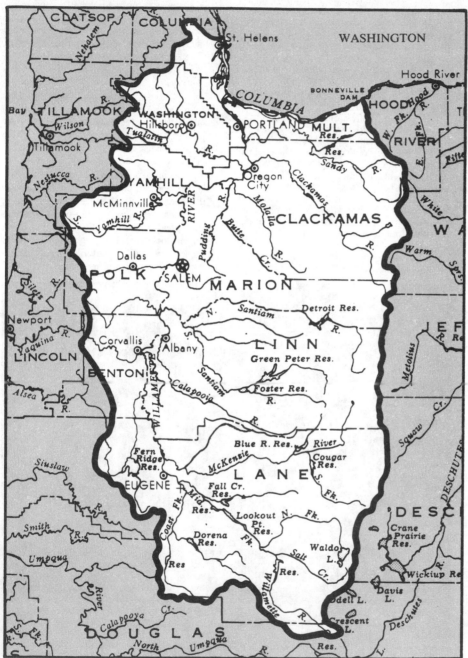

"Primitive Road," the sign said. What road, I thought. Ooof. Hope that crunching wasn't the oil pan. Can't be much farther up here. Finally, Irish Lake, high in the Cascades, actually on the Pacific Crest Trail. Allegedly big brook trout in here. But where?

Not a big lake. You can circle it in a canoe in 15 minutes. Clear water, with much of the bottom in plain view. Where are the fish? No rises. Sunset. No rises.

The next day, while canoeing the west shoreline, I notice an interesting feature. In places, the marl bottom has been disturbed, the marl blown away and gravel revealed. Why? Gliding slowly by another disturbance, I look more closely. Oh my. Big fins can sweep a bottom clean. A four pound brookie lies snug against the bottom, dead center in the cleared spot.

Four out of five Oregon anglers live within the Willamette zone. It includes the watershed of the Willamette, which itself drains other powerful river systems. The region spans over 150 miles from north to south, from the Coast Range Mountains on the west to the glacial crests of the Oregon Cascades on the east.

Western Oregon is blessed with an abundance of water—a mixed blessing, to be sure—and this abundance (rain, rain, rain) has created for valley anglers a tremendous variety of fishing opportunities.

Salmon and steelhead anglers claim the great inland rivers: the Sandy, Clackamas, Santiam, McKenzie, and lower Willamette. Trout anglers work the coast range streams in early season and move into the lower Cascades as the run-off slows. The Willamette River is a fine and underutilized trout water upstream from Corvallis. Valley bass anglers do very well in the river's oxbow lakes and sloughs, and those of the Columbia to the north.

By mid-summer, trails into the Cascade lakes are clearing of snow and the lakes turn on with hungry brook trout. You can drive to many of the lakes south of Mt. Hood, or hike to alpine angling adventures in Mt. Jefferson or Three Sisters wilderness areas. South of Eugene, the Taylor Burn and Mink Lake basins offer additional high country lakes of every size and shape.

The Willamette region.   A world of angling practically in our backyard.

ABERNATHY CREEK A very accessible cutthroat stream with a small run of coho. Abernathy joins the Willamette River on the east side of Oregon City. About 12 miles long, it flows from the Highland Butte area, SE of Oregon City. In Oregon City the creek is crossed by several bridges right in town and is followed and crossed by county roads throughout its mid-section. The upper waters are reached from Hwy. 213 by turning east through Beaver Creek.

This is a native cutthroat stream and is usually fished down in a month or two. In 1980, 101 coho were taken in the stream in early summer, but in recent years only a few dozen all total have been caught. A few steelhead are also caught in Abernathy each year. Except for road right-of-ways and bridges the creek flows through private land, so ask permission before you fish.

ABERNETHY LAKES A couple of good brook trout lakes 2 miles NW of Odell Lake, reached by a one mile hike. Take FS 5899 NW from West Bay, at the west end of Odell Lake. This road follows the railroad track to a derail station called Abernethy, a little over 2 miles from Odell. Follow Deer Creek Trail 3670 south and watch for the sign to the lakes. The trail is well blazed, and the upper lake is just NW of the lower.

Both lakes have naturally reproducing brook trout. The lower lake covers about 2 acres and is fairly shallow. It loses fish during hard winters. The upper lake is about 16 acres and 20 feet deep. Its brookies run to 13 inches. Both lakes are at elevation 4950 ft. You can camp at the lakes, but there are no facilities. There are campgrounds and supplies at Odell Lake.

ABIQUA CREEK A very nice trout stream with a fair winter steelhead run. The stream heads in the Cascades east of Silverton and flows into the Pudding River. It is crossed by Hwy. 213 about 24 miles south of Oregon City, just 2 miles north of Silverton. The mouth is about 3 miles to the west.

Abiqua flows about 30 miles, but gets pretty low in the upper stretch in summer. A good road follows the stream east for 9 miles, then leaves the stream, staying on the ridges.

Angling is good in early season until June, and there are fish later for anglers willing to work hard. Abiqua is lightly stocked with rainbow trout, that make up most of the catch. These will run 7-11 inches, and the cutthroat, which are about 1/4 of the catch, go 6-12 inches.

Every few years there is a good catch of winter steelhead here, with the fishing best from February through April. March is usually the big month. Over 200 steelhead were caught here in 1980, but most years since have netted fewer than 50. The creek is open for salmon and steelhead only up to the Silverton Water Supply Dam.

Abiqua flows through private land throughout its run, with public access at road crossings only.

AERIAL LAKE A hike-in brook trout lake in the Horse Lake area west of Elk Lake off Century Drive. The trailhead is across from Elk Lake Ranger Station on the the north end of Elk Lake, 35 miles from Bend. From the Elk Lake Forest Service Station on the west shore, follow the trail west to Horse Lakes. At the trail junction about 4 miles in, turn south. In less than 1/4 mile two side trails join the

TRILLIUM LAKE, MT. HOOD NATIONAL FOREST
Steven Nehl, Photographer

main trail. Take the right fork to Aeriel, less than one mile further. The left trail leads to Sunset Lake.

Aerial Lake is only about 3 acres, but fairly deep and lightly fished. Its brook trout have been known to show some size. The lake is usually accessible in July. Bring mosquito repellent.

AGENCY CREEK A fair size trout stream, tributary to the South Yamhill River. It flows into the Yamhill at Grande Ronde Agency, about 3 miles NW of Valley Junction on Hwy. 18. A BLM road parallels the creek upstream from Grande Ronde Agency and provides good access. It can also be reached from Hwy. 22.

Agency is stocked with legal rainbow in spring and has native cutthroat to 10 inches. It's a good early season stream but gets low quickly in summer. It can be fished at several bridges, and there is some streamside public right-of-way.

ALDER CREEK A native cutthroat and rainbow stream. Alder is a tributary of the Sandy River, joining it from the south at the community of Alder Creek, 9 miles east of the city of Sandy. It is crossed by Hwy. 26 at its mouth. Only about 5 miles long, it doesn't produce very long in the spring. Several dirt roads from the Cherryville area access the upper reaches of the stream.

Not stocked, it has some nice native cutthroat and a few rainbow. The fish run 6-10 inches, averaging 8. The banks are brushy, with bait producing best.

ALFORJA LAKE A consistent producer of fair size brook trout in the headwaters of the North Santiam near Duffy Butte, Mt. Jefferson Wilderness. A 4 acre lake, not very well known, it is off the trail and lightly fished. See Duffy Lake for directions into the basin. Alforja is about 3/4 mile SW of Duffy. Cincha Lakes is north of Alforja.

The brook trout back here run to 13 inches and will usually hit anything early in season. In late summer and fall, flies work best in morning and evening. The lake is brushy, but not hard to fish.

ALICE LAKE This is a tiny lake, about an acre, right on Trail 3422, 1 1/2 miles north of Duffy Lake just south of Red Butte. See Duffy Lake for directions. There are usually lots of fair size brook trout here in early season, but fishing tapers off in fall because the lake's so small. There are good campsites all along this part of the trail.

AMOS AND ANDY LAKES Two small high lakes in the southeastern tip of the Willamette National Forest, a bushwhack from Indigo Lake. See Indigo Lake for directions. From Indigo, cross country 1 1/4 miles NE, skirting a butte which projects NW from Sawtooth Mt. and divides the Indigo basin from the basin holding Amos and Andy. Hold your elevation, as Amos and Andy are just slightly higher than Indigo.

Is it worth it? The lakes are stocked by air from time to time, but at 6000 ft. and only 10 ft. deep, they frequently winterkill. On the other hand, a lot of 6-10 inch brook trout might just be hungrily awaiting your morsel.

ANN LAKE A good brook trout lake of about 20 acres just north of Marion Lake. See Marion Lake for road and trail directions. Ann is on the Marion Lake Trail about one mile in, on the left.

It provides excellent angling for eastern brook trout to 15 inches. A good fly lake, it usually holds up well throughout the season, though it may go slack in late summer. A rubber boat would come in handy. There are no improved campsites. It is usually accessible by late May.

AVERILL LAKE A good 4 acre brook trout lake in the western portion of the Olallie Lakes group about 95 miles SE of Portland. Quickest route is by trail from the west. Follow the Breitenbush River Rd. FS 46 from Detroit Reservoir to the Mt. Hood National Forest boundary. Turn east onto Breitenbush Lake Rd., FS 42, then go left at the fork onto FS 380 about 1/2 mile further. About 1/4 mile from where 380 passes under the power transmission lines, pick up Trail 719, which leads east about 1 1/2 miles to the lake. The trail first passes Red Lake,

FROG LAKE ANGLERS
Deke Meyer, Photographer

Averill can also be reached by way of trails leading into the basin from Olallie Lake on the east.

Averill is an excellent flyfishing lake, but other methods will work. Brook trout here run 6-12 inches. There are fair unimproved campsites at the lake. It's usually not accessible until late June. Be prepared for mosquitoes.

BAKER CREEK A small trout stream, about 9 miles long, located just north of McMinnville. It flows into the North Yamhill River from the west. Baker Creek is crossed just above its mouth by the paved Carlton-McMinnville Rd. Several good roads follow and cross the creek. These are reached by going west from the north end of McMinnville. Private property severely restricts access to this creek, so watch trespassing.

It contains native cutthroat to 12 inches and is not stocked. Baker is fished heavily in early season and doesn't hold up long.

BAYS LAKE A 10-acre brook trout lake in the picturesque and popular Jefferson Park of the Mt. Jefferson Wilderness. This natural alpine parkland of meadow and wooded hummocks is on a saddle dominated by Mt. Jefferson to the south.

There are several approaches to Jefferson Park, all at least a 5 mile hike. One approach is from the north by way of the Pacific Crest Trail from Breitenbush Lake. It's about a 4 hour hike with fair elevation gain, but the view is great all the way in. Another popular approach is from the west by a trail which follows Woodpecker Ridge to the PCT, and the PCT north to the Park. Take North Santiam Hwy. 22 to Pamelia Creek Rd. 2246, about 7 miles south of Idanha. At the first fork, bear left onto FS 040 and follow it about 4 miles to its end. A trail leads east 1 1/2 miles to the Pacific Crest Trail. Follow the PCT north to Bays.

Bays Lake is quite deep and easy to fish, with a rocky shoreline and many arms or bays. It offers good fly angling, particularly along the western shore. The lake is stocked by air with brook trout. This area is high, and the fish don't

put on a lot of size, but by August they come readily enough. Scout Lake to the east holds some good size brook trout, but you'll work harder for them.

There are several excellent campsites near the lake. Unfortunately, the beauty and accessibility of this area has lead to heavy use, especially on weekends. This is a wilderness area, and campers are urged to use no-trace methods and to camp well back from the water in order to assist in the regeneration of fragile plant life.

BEAR CREEK (Lane Co.) A small native cutthroat stream, about 8 miles long, joining the Long Tom River about 3 miles west of Junction City at Hwy. 99. It flows from the west and is followed and crossed by Hwy. 360 as well as by several county roads. Bear Creek is not stocked but has some fair spring angling for native cutthroat. It is usually fished down by June. Bait or spinners will work best. It is mostly fished by local anglers, and there is quite a bit of private property.

BEAR LAKE (Mt. Hood National Forest) A 2 acre hike-in brook trout lake in the Mt. Hood Forest SW of Hood River. The lake is about 2 miles NE of Rainy Lake, with the trailhead on the Rainy Lake Rd. From the community of Dee drive north about 2 miles towards Punchbowl Falls, and pick up FS 2820, which twists and winds its way west. The trailhead is on the north side of the road about 2 miles beyond the intersection of FS 2821. If you get to Rainy Lake, the trail's a mile behind you. The lake is on a spur trail off the Defiance Mt. Trail 413. The trailhead described here leads north under 1/4 mile to Trail 413, which you take to the east. A bit over 1/4 mile brings you to the Bear Lake Trail, cutting off to the north and leading 1/2 mile to the lake.

Though small, Bear Lake is fairly deep and hardly ever winterkills. At elevation 3800 ft., it is stocked by air with fingerling brook trout. The catch ranges in size from 8-12 inches. The road in usually opens by late June.

BEAR LAKE (Willamette National Forest) Across the ridge from Firecamp Lakes, one mile south of Slideout. See Slideout Lake for directions. Bear covers 9 acres and is 24 ft. deep. It is stocked every other year with brook trout.

BENSON LAKE (Lane Co.) A nice brook trout lake of about 25 acres, 1 1/2 miles by trail from Scott Lake on McKenzie Pass Hwy. 242. The McKenzie Hwy. is usually the last Cascade crossing to open each spring. The trailhead is at the Scott Lake campground, and the trail leads NW to Benson Lake then on to Tenas Lake and Mt. Scott.

Angling is usually good in early season as soon as the road is open, with angling primarily for stocked brook trout from 7-11 inches, though larger ones have been taken. There is no improved camp at the lake, but there are good campgrounds at Scott Lake and along the highway close by.

BENSON LAKE (Multnomah Co.) A 23 acre lake in Benson State Park, adjacent to the Columbia River on the south side of I-84 just before Multnomah Falls. The lake has populations of brown bullhead, white crappie, pumpkinseed sunfish, and largemouth bass. It is stocked each spring with catchable rainbow.

There is no boat ramp, but anglers can hand launch rafts and car-tops. The banks are quite flat, offering unimproved access for less-abled anglers. The lake itself is open for year around fishing, but the park closes after Labor Day. Anglers can park on the access road and hike in.

BERLEY LAKES Two small trout lakes north of the Santiam Hwy. near the summit. Take the Pacific Crest Trail north from Santiam Pass at Hwy. 20, and hike 1 1/2 miles north to the junction of Trail 3491, which ultimately leads to Duffy Lake. Follow 3491 two miles north to Lower Berley Lake. Upper Berley is off the trail about 1/8 mile NW of Lower.

The lakes are both about 7 acres. They are air stocked with either cutthroat or brook trout every other year. Any method will take fish here. There are no improved camps at the lakes.

BETH LAKE An interesting lake to find and to fish. It's located near the upper Collawash River in the Bull of the Woods area, some 50 miles SE of Portland. Five acres and 35 ft. deep, it sits at an elevation of 4450 ft.

Follow the Clackamas River Hwy. 224 to Ripplebrook Ranger Station, then take FS 63 south along the Collawash River. About 10 miles south, in the Toms Meadow area, take FS 6340 SW to where FS 6341 forks off to the right. Take 6341 and about 5 miles south, and where the road crosses Pansy Creek and switches back to the north, you'll hit Trail 551. In about 1/2 mile, Trail 549 intersects from the left (east). Follow 549 to its junction with 550, then cross over 550 and head up the ridge. Keep bearing NE, and you'll hit a small stream which enters the lake.

There are wild brook trout to 13 inches here, and the lake is easy to fish from the bank. Caddis, coachman, bucktail, or Mickey Finn will take fish if you sink them. There's one good campsite on the NW side.

BETHANY LAKE A fair size lake with a warm water fishery just west of Portland at the community of Bethany. Cut north off Sunset Hwy. just before the Cornelius Road junction, or take Cornelius Road to West Union, then go east to Bethany.

The lake is about 500 ft. wide and 1/2 mile long. It features bluegill, largemouth bass, and large brown bullhead. The bass grow to respectable size, with some to five pounds. There has been a charge for access at times. Check locally for details.

BETTY LAKE A 40 acre rainbow lake high in the Cascades that is lightly fished and offers nice angling. The lake is at an elevation of 5500 ft. one mile SE of the south end of Waldo Lake.

Take Hwy. 58 from Oakridge about 20 miles SE to Waldo Lake Rd. 5897. At 5 miles NE on this road there is a sign for the Betty Lake Trail 3664 on the west side. It's an easy 1/2 mile hike to the lake.

The rainbow run 6-14 inches, averaging about 10 inches. A rubber boat comes in handy here. Bait or lures will work well anytime, and flies will take large fish early in the day and near dusk. There are no improved campsites. Remember the slogan, *Waldo Lake, Famous Mosquitoes.* There are several other small lakes within a mile of the lake, and many hold fish.

BIG CLIFF RESERVOIR About 150 acres on the North Santiam River, built about the same time as Detroit Reservoir. The dam is located several miles below Detroit Dam.

Eclipsed by the popularity of Detroit, Big Cliff is lightly fished, but offers good catches of rainbow, and very large whitefish (up to 33 inches). There is a poor boat ramp near the Detroit Reservoir Dam. Nearest campgrounds are upriver along Hwy. 22.

BIG LAKE Over 225 acres, south of Santiam Hwy. 20 near the summit of the Cascades. The area is about 40 miles NW of Bend, and about 8 miles SE of the junction of North and South Santiam highways. The lake is 4 miles down FS 2690, which leads south from Hwy. 20 near the Santiam Lodge. Continue south past Hoodo Ski Bowl.

Speed boaters and waterskiers offer fisherfolk plenty of competition here. But Big Lake has some large brook trout, as well as a recent addition of kokanee and stocked rainbow. The lake gets rough during the day at times, so plan to fish early or late. There are several nice campgrounds on the lake, and good boat ramps. Open all year, it is a popular place for ice fishing.

BIG SLIDE LAKE, UPPER A small, hike-in brook trout lake in the headwaters of the Collawash River. Located in the Bull of the Woods area, it is at least a 3 mile hike in from the nearest road. Several trails will get you there. The lakes are less than 1/2 mile NE of the Bull of the Woods Lookout.

From Estacada drive up the Clackamas River on Hwy. 224 to Ripplebrook Ranger Station, then take FS 63 south along the Collawash River. About 10 miles south, in the Toms Meadow area, take FS 6340 SW several miles to Trailhead 550 near the end of the road. Three miles on this trail south will take you to Bull of the Woods Lookout. Slide Lake is 1/2 mile NE on Trail 555. The lake is at an elevation of 4300 ft.

Stocked periodically by air, the brook trout here average 9 inches with a range from 6-11. It's easy to fish, and any method works when they're hitting. Fly angling is good late in the season in the late hours of day. There are three nice campsites here. Supplies are available at Estacada or at Detroit if you come in from the south. Other lakes nearby are stocked with brook trout. See Welcome, Pansy, and Lenore.

BINGHAM LAKE (Linn Co.) A small bushwhack cutthroat lake in the Mt. Jefferson Wilderness Area 1/2 mile west of the Pacific Crest Trail in the Bingham Basin, south of Mt. Jefferson. It is about a 6 mile hike from Marion Lake and about 5 miles south from Pamelia. There is no blazed trail. The lake feeds Minto Creek, a tributary of the North Santiam River.

Bingham is about 4 acres and has cutthroat to 15 inches. It is lightly fished (rarely found?) and can provide good fly fishing for the pathfinding angler.

BINGO LAKE A shallow lake 1/2 mile west of the southern tip of Waldo Lake at the head of Black Creek, reached best by boat from Shadow Bay Campground on Waldo. It can also be approached by trails leading from Waldo Lake, and from the north off Black Creek or Salmon Creek roads out of Oakridge. About 4 acres and shallow, it frequently winterkills. Nevertheless, it is stocked periodically with brook trout. Bongo Lake is about a 3/4 mile bushwhack NW. Bongo covers 9 acres and holds brook trout. This here's 'skeeter country in late spring to early summer, so be prepared.

BIRTHDAY LAKE A small hike-in brook trout lake 3 miles south of Waldo in the Island Lakes Basin. See Island Lakes for the best trail route to the basin. Birthday Lake is less than 1/2 mile south of Lower Island Lake, reached by Trail 3674.

Birthday is about 3 acres, just north of the trail. Its brook trout are small, from 6-10 inches, but usually hit well in spring and fall. Fly angling here is usually good. An occasional lunker is taken. There are natural campsites here, with good campgrounds at Gold and Waldo lakes. The roads up are usually accessible by late June. Other lakes within 1/2 mile of Birthday are stocked. See Verde, Island Lakes, and Lorin Lake.

BLAIR LAKE A 35 acre trout lake in the Willamette National Forest at the head of Salmon Creek, NE of Oakridge on Hwy. 58. From Oakridge, take the Salmon Creek Rd., FS 24 (look for the salmon hatchery signs) about 9 miles NE to the signed Blair Lake turnoff. Follow FS 1934 north about 8 miles to the lake.

The brook trout at Blair run 6-16 inches, averaging 10 inches, and there are plenty of them. The lake is stocked with brook trout and cutthroat. There are several nice campsites near the lake outlet a very short hike from the road. Evening fly angling is generally excellent, with mosquitoes, blue uprights, caddis and gray hackles good bets. The lake is closed to angling from a motorboat.

About 1 1/2 miles east is Devil's Lake, which has no trail access. It is only about 5 acres but has nice brook trout to 14 inches.

The Blair Lake Rd. takes you past the small but pleasant Wall Creek Warm Springs, suitable for a soak on a summer day. The springs show up on the Forest Service map and are located about 1/4 mile in on a trail which follows Wall Creek. The trailhead is on the first hairpin turn, about 1/2 mile from the junction of FS 1934 with the Salmon Creek Rd. There are good camps along the Salmon Creek Rd.

BLOWOUT CREEK A good trout stream in the North Santiam area of Willamette National Forest. Take Hwy. 22 to FS 10, about 3 miles south of the community of Detroit. FS 10 crosses the North Fork of the Santiam River and follows the south shore of the reservoir to Blowout Creek, then follows the creek to its headwaters.

Blowout has a population of native rainbow and cutthroat. Bait and spinner work best in early season, and fly angling is productive when the water warms in late spring. There are no camps on the upper stream, but there is a good camp at Stahlman Point on Detroit Reservoir, and there are other camps on the north shore along Hwy. 22.

BLUE LAKE (Lane Co.) A good isolated brook trout lake on the western border of the Diamond Peak Wilderness Area, Willamette National Forest. From Oakridge, drive south on Hwy. 58 a mile or so to the Hills Creek Reservoir turn-off. Follow FS 21 around the west shore of the reservoir and up the upper Middle Fork of the Willamette, about 26 miles (from the dam) to where FS 2145 forks NE. Take 2145 about 5 miles to a fork where FS 2149 turns east then south. Follow 2149 about 4 miles to the Blue Lake Trailhead. It's a 1/2 mile hike east to the lake on a well marked trail. The roads usually open in late June.

Blue Lake covers 20 acres and is 33 ft. deep. It has naturally reproducing brook trout that run 6-16 inches, with a few larger taken at times. The average size is 10-12 inches. Bait and lures are best during the day, and fly angling is effective in early morning and evening.

BLUE LAKE (Marion Co.) A 12 acre brook trout lake in the Eight Lakes Basin of the Mt. Jefferson Wilderness. Blue Lake is 1/4 mile NE of Jorn Lake in the northern part of the basin, south of Marion Lake.

Blue Lake is over 40 ft. deep, and though its fish tend to be short, they are usually deep bodied. They average 6-11 inches, with most on the small side. Any method will take fish. Several other lakes are close by, and all are fishable. See Jorn, Bowerman, Teto and Chiquito.

BLUE LAKE (Multnomah Co., Mt. Hood NF) About 50 acres at the head of the Bull Run River, in Portland's water supply reserve. Closed to all recreational use.

BLUE LAKE (Multnomah Co. near Troutdale) A 62 acre lake east of Portland, 3 miles west of Troutdale. The lake is north of Hwy. 30 and 1/2 mile south of the Columbia River. A paved road leads to the north end, where there is a county park. The rest of the lakeshore is privately owned.

Blue Lake has good size largemouth bass that are taken on bait and lures, and crappie angling can be very good. In spring and summer the lake is stocked with catchable rainbow. The park is large and has a lot of picnic facilities but no camping. Rental boats are available in summer, with private boats permitted access in winter only and restricted to no larger than 14 ft. in length, 17 ft. for canoes, and maximum 3 hp motors. Effort has been made to provide a fishing area suitable for access by less-abled anglers. The water nearby will be regularly stocked with catchable rainbow.

BLUE RIVER A good sized tributary of the McKenzie River in the Willamette National Forest, flowing into the Blue River Reservoir about 43 miles east of Eugene off Hwy. 126. A good road, FS 15, leaves the highway about 5 miles east of the community of Blue River and follows the middle and upper stream more than 10 miles.

The main catch consists of stocked rainbow trout in the first 5 miles above the reservoir, although wild cutthroat and rainbow are present in small numbers. The catch rate for bank angling is on a par with the main McKenzie. The fish usually run 8-12 inches, but a few larger are taken. Bait is best in early season, and later there is fair fly angling.

Camping is available at Blue River Reservoir, and there are numerous camps near McKenzie Bridge on the highway to the east.

BLUE RIVER RESERVOIR A 935 acre flood control lake on a major tributary of the McKenzie River, offering fair to good angling for stocked rainbow. It's located north of Hwy. 126, about 45 miles east of Eugene in the heart of the McKenzie Recreational Area. The dam is about 2 miles above the mouth of Blue River.

The 14 inch McKenzie size limit applies below the dam, but not in the reservoir. This allows anglers to keep some lunker rainbow to 24 inches. By mid-August the reservoir is drawn way down, driving the fish to sulk in the depths and limiting boat ramp accessibility. (Few things are uglier than a drawn down reservoir).

There is a ramp and campground at the NE end of the lake. To get there, follow Hwy. 126 east past Blue River Ranger Station, about 3 miles to the FS 15 cut-off on the left.

BLUEGILL LAKE A lightly fished 7 acre bass and panfish pond on the eastern edge of Salem. It is located in Cascade Park, across the creek from Walter Wirth Lake, which is also in the park. The lake is just west of I-5, between the airport road and Turner Rd.

It has good populations of crappie and bluegill, and a fair number of largemouth bass. Bait fishing is the most popular method.

BLUE STAR POND A 6 acre pond north of Eugene. It is situated on the west side of Hwy. 99W 2 miles north of Airport Rd. and about 8 miles north of the city. It contains bluegill and white crappie, and may contain largemouth bass.

BOND BUTTE POND A 35 acre pond south of Albany. The lake is east of I-5 at Bond Butte Overpass, 15 miles south of town. It contains channel cats and white crappie.

BOOT LAKE Usually a good brook trout lake in the Mink Lake Basin, about 1/2 mile due east of Cliff Lake. See Cliff Lake for directions from the Bend area by the way of Elk Lake. From Cliff Lake you can test your compass skills on this 5 acre target.

Boot Lake is quite deep for its size, a good lake for lure, spinner, or bait, as the bottom drops off quickly in most spots. Flyfishing is best at dusk. There are nice campsites at the lake, but no facilities. The early summer mosquitoes up here are legendary.

BOWERMAN LAKE Usually a good producer of brook trout, at the north end of the Eight Lakes Basin. It is reached by 6 miles of trail from the Duffy Lake Trailhead, just 3 miles off Hwy. 22. Bowerman is just east of Jorn Lake. It can also be approached from the north by a 5 mile hike from Marion Lake.

Bowerman is shallow and covers only about 6 acres. The lake is a consistent producer of brook trout 6-12 inches, averaging 8-9. The outlet runs into Little Bowerman Lake, which is only several acres and not stocked, since it winter-kills. Flyfishing is usually good, although bait and lures will take fish, too. There are good campsites throughout the area. This is a scenic spot, and there are many other lakes to explore.

BREITENBUSH LAKE, (Warm Springs Indian Reservation) A large lake at the southern end of the Olallie Lake area north of Mt. Jefferson. The lake is about 105 miles from Portland. Take Hwy. 26 about 8 miles south of the Hwy. 35 junction to FS 42, which cuts south. Stay on 42 until you reach FS 4220, following signs to Olallie Lake. Continue past Olallie to Breitenbush Lake, about 3 miles south. It can also be reached from Detroit Reservoir by following FS 46 up the North Fork of the Breitenbush River to FS 4220. Watch for signs to the lake. Neither road is usually open before late June, so check with the Forest Service for conditions. Both approach roads are rough, with the way in from the north either muddy or dusty, and from the west, rocky.

Breitenbush is on a plateau area near the western boundary of Warm Springs Reservation. Tribal permits are generally required to fish waters on reservation land, however a permit is not currently required to fish Breitenbush. Other good lakes off the road to the north, not on the reservation, include Olallie, Monon, and Horseshoe.

Breitenbush is a nice family lake and has excellent fishing at times. The lake is stocked from time to time, and has natural reproduction of brook trout and rainbow. About 75 acres with quite a bit of shoal area, it offers good flyfishing in fall. August and September are the best months. The fish usually run 6-12 inches with a few larger. There is a campground at the north end of the lake. Boats can be easily launched, but motors are prohibited.

BREITENBUSH RIVER An excellent trout stream in Willamette National Forest, flowing down the slopes of Mt. Jefferson some 30 miles to Detroit Reservoir. The lower stream is crossed by Santiam Pass Hwy. 22 at the point where it enters Detroit Reservoir just north of Detroit. A good road, FS 46, follows the stream NE to the Mt. Hood Forest boundary. A poor road, S42, branches off and follows the North Fork to its source, Breitenbush Lake.

The lower 12 miles are stocked with rainbow, and there are a few wild cutthroat and rainbow. The rainbow run 7-12 inches, though good fly anglers can taker larger rainbow in the lower river late in the season. There are also whitefish present.

The lower end of the stream in the Breitenbush arm of Detroit Reservoir can be fished by boat until the water drops. All of the stream above can be reached from the road, but the bank in most areas is steep and brushy. Worms and eggs usually work well throughout the season, and there is good fly water available. There are four good campgrounds between the reservoir and Breitenbush Hot Springs (private), about 12 miles upstream.

BRICE CREEK About 16 miles long, joining Laying Creek to form Row River about 22 miles SE of Cottage Grove. From Cottage Grove take Hwy. 99 SE past Dorena Reservoir to Disston, where a gravel road follows the stream to its head.

The creek is not stocked, but native cutthroat are present. Most angling is confined to the lower 8 miles, but some fish are taken in the upper stretch. There is a campground at Cedar Creek about 4 miles up from Disston. Another park area is located a few miles upstream.

BRIDAL VEIL CREEK A nice little stream for native cutthroat in the Columbia Gorge area, about 7 miles long. It flows into the Columbia at Bridal Veil, 29 miles east of Portland, and is crossed by Hwy. 30 and the scenic route. Angling is confined to the stream above the falls. A poor dirt road follows the creek south, and the upper end is accessed by branch roads from the Larch Mountain Rd.

A 10 inch fish is a whopper in this little stream, but Bridal Veil has some feisty little wild cutthroat. Bait angling is the best bet, but flies should work well in late summer and fall using sneak tactics. State Park picnic areas are located on Hwy. 30 near the mouth, but there are no campgrounds.

BRITTANY LAKE A small but deep hike-in brook trout lake in the Taylor Burn area north of Waldo Lake. From North Waldo Campground at the NE end of Waldo, take Trail 3590 west. At slightly over one mile, a trail cuts north and reaches Rigdon Lakes in one mile. Brittany is about 1/4 mile bushwhack NE of Lower Rigdon.

Though only about 4 acres, Brittany is almost 30 feet deep. It is at elevation 5600 ft., a good little lake that's lightly fished. Any method works, but flies are always productive.

BROOK LAKE (Warm Springs Indian Reservation) A small brook trout lake just east of Olallie Meadows Campground, 3 miles north of Olallie Lake. See Breitenbush Lake for road directions. One of a group of three good lakes, including Jude and Russ, in a line 1/2 mile SE of the camp by easy trail.

About four acres, Brook has brook trout from 7-16 inches, averaging 10 inches. It's pretty brushy for shore fishing. A rubber boat comes in handy here. Bait or bait and spinner will usually take fish. Fly angling is good in evenings, especially in the fall. Brook and its two neighbors are on reservation land, but tribal fishing permits are not required at this time. It is usually inaccessible before early June. Camping at the lakes is prohibited due to fire danger.

BROWN-MINTO ISLAND COMPLEX On the Willamette River south of Salem, a network of borrow pits and sloughs near the east bank that contain largemouth bass, white crappie, bluegill, and brown bullhead. The closest public boat ramp is at Wallace Marine Park in Salem on the west bank, just north of the Hwy. 22 Bridge.

BUCK LAKE A 9 acre brook trout lake off the upper Clackamas Rd. just west of Timothy Lake, about 42 miles south of Estacada. It can be reached from the Shellrock Creek Rd., FS 58, by turning right onto FS 5810 about one mile north of Shellrock Campground. Drive 5 miles to FS 210. Trailhead 728 is about one mile up this road on the left. It's 1/4 mile hike south to the lake. If you are at Timothy Lake, head west on 5810 to reach the spur.

Buck is stocked with eastern brook trout that generally average 9-10 inches with some to 12. All methods are used, but fly angling produces consistently after the first month or two. Though accessible in early June, there may still be some snow here since the lake is at 4000 ft. Supplies are available at Estacada or Government Camp.

BULL RUN RIVER A large tributary of the lower Sandy River flowing in from the east about 16 miles up from the mouth, crossed by the east side Sandy River Rd. about 1 1/2 miles above its mouth. The upper stream is in the Bull Run watershed reserve. Not much angling takes place below in the open area because of water level fluctuations. A few trout are taken in this stretch, but it is not stocked. The lower 1 1/2 miles are also open during winter season, but very few steelhead or salmon are taken. After many years of being blocked from the upper stream, only a few stray fish enter.

BUMP LAKE A 3 acre drive-in lake at 4300 ft. in the Olallie Lakes group. The road is accessed by a series of spur roads off FS 46 north of Breitenbush. It is stocked with brook trout. Check the Mt. Hood National Forest Map for directions.

BURNT LAKE This is a favorite lake of many hiking anglers, as it is fairly accessible and close to Portland. The lake is about 8 acres and contains brook trout. Take Hwy. 26 east from Zigzag to an unnumbered forest road heading north about one mile east of Tollgate Campground. At about 4 miles, the road ends at Trailhead 772. Burnt Lake is 3 miles NE by trail, just to the east of East Zigzag Mountain. The trail passes 2 acre Devil's Lake about halfway. There are also brook trout in Devil's.

The brookies in Burnt average about 9 inches, with a size range 6-14 inches. Some years the fish run generally large, but there are off seasons. All methods are used, with flies working well in summer and fall. The lake is at 4100 ft. and is usually inaccessible until early June. There are no improved campsites at the lake.

BURNT TOP LAKE (a.k.a Top Lake) A fairly good 20-acre lake in the Three Sisters Wilderness, north of the Horse Lake area on the west side of the Cascade summit. It's a long hike from the west side McKenzie drainage. Best way in is from the east. From Bend, take the Cascade Lakes Hwy. south toward Bachelor Butte. About 5 miles past the ski resort and just past the Devil's Lake Campground, a trail leads west to Sister's Mirror Lake. Burnt Top is 1 1/2 miles west, 1/2, mile east-northeast of Burnt Top Peak. This last stretch is a bushwhack.

There are eastern brook trout in the lake, a good spot for flyfishing, though lures and bait can be worked easily from shore as well. Angling is consistently good due to light pressure, with trout 8-11 inches. There are pretty campsites here and one mile east at Sisters Mirror Lake. It is usually accessible by early July.

BUTTE CREEK (Marion Co.) A good size native cutthroat stream that offers good access and is close to population centers in the Willamette Valley. Fair roads follow both sides of the stream, but in the upper reaches the roads are not close to the creek.

Butte Creek forms the boundary between Clackamas and Marion counties, about 20 miles from the Salem area and 40 miles south of Portland. It flows NW over 30 miles from the lower Cascade range into the Pudding River near Woodburn. Hwy. 213 crosses it about 5 miles north of Silverton.

The creek supports a fair population of native cutthroat. Fishing is pretty much confined to the area above Scott's Mills, just 2 miles east of the highway. It has a small native winter steelhead run from January thru April.

BYBEE LAKE A 200 acre lake just north of Portland city limits, featuring largemouth bass, crappie, bluegill, and bullhead. Bybee is on a peninsula between the Willamette and Columbia rivers.

The lake is surrounded almost entirely by private land, so the best way to get to it is by boat from the Columbia Slough, which cuts in

from the Willamette 1/2 mile above the Willamette River mouth. Like all the lakes in this area, Bybee is subject to spring flooding and can be reached by boat from the river three or four months in spring and summer. Small boats can put into the Columbia Slough from several rights-of-way off North Portland Rd. The lake can also be reached from Rivergate Park, or from a dirt access road off Montgomery Ward's driveway on Kelley Point Rd. (park on the hard sand).

Bybee is a little wilderness in the heart of Portland's industrial sector. Dress appropriate to blackberry brambles and nettles. Car-top boats and canoes can be launched near the Ward's access road and portaged from one slough to another. Bass to 4 pounds have been taken here.

CALAPOOIA RIVER Flows 65 miles into the Willamette at Albany from its head in the Cascade range between South Santiam and McKenzie rivers. Trout fishing is confined to the upper half of the stream, with a run of wild steelhead available though lightly fished, and largemouth bass and panfish available near the mouth.

The Calapooia is usually well stocked with rainbow trout from just above Brownsville to just above Dollar, and native cutthroat are well represented in the total catch. Trout average about 9 inches with a range of 7-12. The upper stretch is usually a good bet in late season, with larger fish, if fewer, available. From Holley, which is south of Sweet Home on Hwy. 228, a good road follows the stream for 9 miles to Dollar, and a fair road continues upstream another 12 miles to the North Fork.

Bass and panfish are available in the lower river, with best catches near the Willamette confluence. The lower river is followed and crossed by many roads from Holley to Albany.

The Calapooia is managed for wild steelhead, and has netted as many as a 100 fish per year. However, the high yield of nearby Santiam River in recent times has decreased pressure on the Calapooia. Steelhead are generally in the river from February through April. The steelhead closure is at Hwy. 228 near Holley. There are also salmon in the river, but salmon angling is prohibited in an effort to rebuild the run.

CAMP CREEK (Clackamas Co.) A tributary of the upper Sandy River in the Mt. Hood National Forest. Though only 7 miles long, it provides good trout fishing. Camp Creek joins the Zig Zag River one mile east of Rhododendron. Hwy. 26 parallels the creek to the north from Rhododendron to Government Camp, but access is good only in the lower stretch.

Rainbow trout of legal size are stocked in the lower half of the stream in spring and summer. Native cutthroat 6-10 inches are scattered throughout. Angling methods depend on the time of year and water conditions. Bait is best early in the year, when the stream is silty from glacial run-off. Good fly anglers should do well in summer and fall on the native flush.

There are two good campgrounds along the stream, Tollgate just east of Rhododendron, and Camp Creek is 2.5 miles further east. Both are off Hwy. 26.

CAMPERS LAKE A fairly consistent producer of brook trout located just east of the McKenzie Pass Highway 242 about one mile north of the Scott Lake turnoff. The lake has about 13 acres, mostly shallow, with the deepest area (the north end) about 15 feet. It's a

good fly fishing lake if you can get out beyond the shoal area, with fish to 14 inches, but it doesn't hold up well late in the season. There are no improved campsites at the lake, but there are campgrounds on the highway south.

CANBY POND About one acre, in Canby City Park at the western edge of the town off Hwy. 99E. No longer stocked with legal rainbow, it can be fished for largemouth bass, crappie, and bluegill.

CANIM LAKE An easy to find brook trout lake just north of Waldo Lake, south of the Taylor Burn area. Canim is 2 miles west of the North Waldo Campground on Trail 3590. The lake winterkills easily and is no longer stocked.

CARMEN RESERVOIR (a.k.a Beaver Marsh Reservoir) On the upper McKenzie River, built by the Eugene Electric and Water Board. Unlike a lot of power reservoirs, this one provides good fishing. It has about 65 acres and puts out a lot of fish.

Carmen is about 2 miles south of Clear Lake on Hwy. 126, about 21 miles north of the McKenzie Hwy. It's a scenic area and easily reached. Fishing is primarily for rainbow 7-12 inches, but larger trout show up. A few brook trout and cutthroat are also caught. Trolling takes most fish, but any method will work. You'll have to row, motorboats are prohibited. There is a nice campsite near the north end of the lake.

CAST CREEK A small trout stream in the Mt. Hood National Forest about 5 miles NE of Zigzag on Hwy. 26. It flows north from Cast Lake into Lost Creek. To reach it, take the Lost Creek Rd. FS 18 north from Zigzag about 5 miles to the Riley and McNeil campgrounds turnoff. Cast Creek is crossed by FS 382 about 1/2 mile past Riley Campground.

It provides fair fishing for native cutthroat and brook trout from 6-10 inches. There are three forest camps nearby, Riley, McNeil, and Lost Creek.

CAST LAKE A good hike-in brook trout lake on the west slope of Mt. Hood. From Hwy. 26 about 1 1/2 miles east of Rhododendron, take the Devil Canyon Rd. north about 5 miles to Trailhead 772. Hike to Devils Lake, about 1 1/2 miles, then take Trail 774 north 1/2 mile then west another 1/2 mile to the lake. Burnt Lake is just 1 1/2 miles east. It can also be approached from the north by Cast Creek Trail 773, which heads at Riley Campground on the Lolo Pass highway.

Dumbell shaped, this 7 acre lake is 17 Ft. deep at elevation 4450 ft. It has had some very good catches of trout from time to time, but can be slow. Brook trout here run 6-13 inches, averaging 9. All angling methods can be used, as the lake is easy to fish. Spinner and bait combinations do well in early season, and fly anglers take some large fish in late fall. There are no campsites at the lake, but Devils Meadow has a good camp. The lake is usually accessible in early June.

CEDAR CREEK A tributary of the middle Sandy River entering from the east, just north of the city of Sandy, about 27 miles from Portland. The upper stream is crossed by Hwy. 26 near Cherryville, and the lower section is followed for a way by county road.

There is a salmon hatchery is located near the mouth, and no angling is allowed on the

CLACKAMAS RIVER

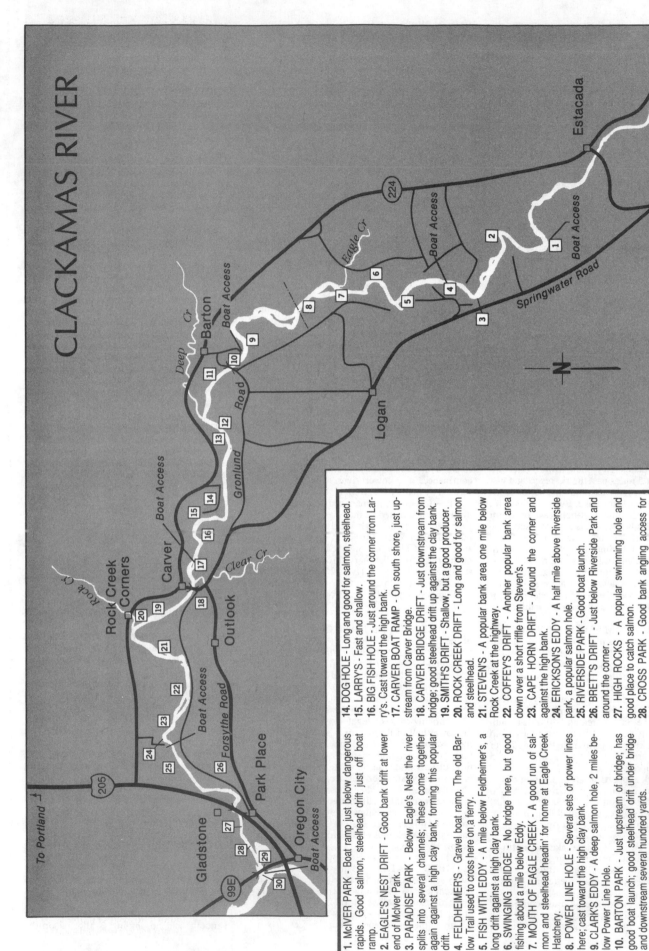

To Portland

To Colton

Estacada

Gladstone

Oregon City

Park Place

Outlook

Carver

Rock Creek Corners

Barton

Logan

Springwater Road

Forsythe Road

Gronlund Road

Clear Cr.

Rock Cr.

Deep Cr.

Eagle Cr.

Boat Access

2 Mi.

N

1. McIVER PARK - Boat ramp just below dangerous rapids. Good salmon, steelhead drift just off boat ramp.

2. EAGLE'S NEST DRIFT - Good bank drift at lower end of McIver Park.

3. PARADISE PARK - Below Eagle's Nest the river splits into several channels; these come together again against a high clay bank, forming this popular drift.

4. FELDHEIMER'S - Gravel boat ramp. The old Barlow Trail used to cross here on a ferry.

5. FISH WITH EDDY - A mile below Feldheimer's, a long drift against a high clay bank.

6. SWINGING BRIDGE - No bridge here, but good fishing about a mile below Eddy.

7. MOUTH OF EAGLE CREEK - A good run of salmon and steelhead headin' for home at Eagle Creek Hatchery.

8. POWER LINE HOLE - Several sets of power lines here; cast toward the high clay bank.

9. CLARK'S EDDY - A deep salmon hole, 2 miles below Power Line Hole.

10. BARTON PARK - Just upstream of bridge; has good boat launch; good steelhead drift under bridge and downstream several hundred yards.

11. LATOURETTE DRIFT - Best for steelhead and coho, about 1/2 mile below Barton.

12. RED BARN DRIFT - Several hundred yards long, a popular drift; cast towards south shore.

13. GRANT'S PARK DRIFT - Private property, once a park with good bank fishing. Get permission to fish.

14. DOG HOLE - Long and good for salmon, steelhead.

15. LARRY'S - Fast and shallow.

16. BIG FISH HOLE - Just around the corner from Larry's. Cast toward the high bank.

17. CARVER BOAT RAMP - On south shore, just upstream from Carver Bridge.

18. CARVER BRIDGE DRIFT - Just downstream from bridge; good steelhead drift up against the clay bank.

19. SMITH'S DRIFT - Shallow, but a good producer.

20. ROCK CREEK DRIFT - Long and good for salmon and steelhead.

21. STEVEN'S - A popular bank area one mile below Rock Creek at the highway.

22. COFFEY'S DRIFT - Another popular bank area down over a short riffle from Steven's.

23. CAPE HORN DRIFT - Around the corner and against the high bank.

24. ERICKSON'S EDDY - A half mile above Riverside park, a popular salmon hole.

25. RIVERSIDE PARK - Good boat launch.

26. BRETT'S DRIFT - Just below Riverside Park and around the corner.

27. HIGH ROCKS - A popular swimming hole and good place to catch salmon.

28. CROSS PARK - Good bank angling access for jack salmon and steelhead (winter and summer).

29. OLD STREET CAR BRIDGE - Popular summer steelhead and jack salmon drift.

30. CLACKAMETTE PARK - Where the Clackamas enters the Willamette; a very popular plunking area for spring chinook. Take a number.

grounds or below the dam to the mouth of the stream. There is a false outlet at the head of an island, so make sure you're not in the closed area. Watch for signs. Many unhappy anglers have been given tickets catching coho in what they thought was the Sandy River.

Cedar Creek isn't stocked, but wild cutthroat and rainbow 6-10 inches are caught in the upper stream. There is some private property along the creek, so watch trespassing. There's camping in Mt. Hood National Forest just east of Zigzag on Hwy. 26.

CERVUS LAKE A 12 acre brook trout lake in the popular Taylor Burn area, 2 miles north of Waldo Lake. From North Waldo Lake Campground, drive 7 miles north on a dirt road to Taylor Burn Campground. Cervus Lake is 1/2 mile south of Torrey Lake, which is just south of Taylor Butte, a tall pinnacle on the south side of the road as you enter the area. It can also be approached from Taylor Burn Camp by the Olallie Trail going south. Follow around the south side of Wahanna Lake and head 1/2 mile SE. The area is brushy, and you should have a forest map along, but there are good landmarks.

Cervus is lightly fished and shallow, and commonly winterkills, though some brook trout usually survive. The brookies run 6-14 inches, with an average of 10. All methods work, and fly fishing is excellent when the shadows hit the water. Bucktails and streamers will usually take fish. There are no campsites nearby, but there's a good camp at Taylor Burn. The lake is usually accessible by the end of June.

CHAMPOEG CREEK A small native trout stream about 12 miles long, flowing north from west of Woodburn into the Willamette near Champoeg State Park. About 8 miles from 99W at Newberg and 4 miles NE of St. Paul, the creek has been adversely affected by diminished water quality caused by development in the area, and is not stocked. There remains a small population of native cutthroat, best fished in early season.

CHEHALEM CREEK A small trout stream that heads in the Chehalem Mts. north of Newberg in Yamhill County. Tributary to the Willamette, it is crossed just above its mouth by Hwy. 99W at the east end of Newberg. Land development in the area has taken its toll on this small stream, though a few small native cutthroat can be caught early in the year. Adjacent property is all private, except for road crossings.

CHETLO LAKE A large, good brook trout lake one mile west of the north end of Waldo Lake. It's over a 4 mile hike from North Waldo Lake Campground. Take Trail 3590 west 2 1/2 miles to the outlet stream, which is the head of the Middle Fork of the Willamette. Some anglers take boats across the north end of Waldo Lake to this point. Here you pick up Trail 3583 and follow it south 1 1/2 miles to Chetlo.

Chetlo is about 19 acres and can be finicky about producing at times. Brook trout are stocked by air, and the catch generally runs 6-16 inches with an average of 11 inches, but a few larger have been reported. A rubber boat would be handy. Best angling is in August and September. Try a double blade spinner with a worm trailer fished slowly for the larger trout during the day.

In late spring mosquitoes in this area are awesome. Be prepared. There are natural campsites here and other good lakes within a mile or two. The area is usually inaccessible until late June.

CHIQUITO LAKE A fair size brook trout lake at the north end of the Eight Lakes Basin, SW of Mt. Jefferson. Chiquito is 1/4 mile NE of Bowerman Lake. Chiquito's fish are a naturally sustained population, with catches ranging from 6-11 inches. All methods are generally productive. There are good campsites near Jorn Lake and other good lakes to the south.

CINCHA LAKE A small brook trout lake south of the Duffy Lake Trail in the Mt. Jefferson Wilderness. Hard to find, it is lightly fished and has been known to put out some big fish. From North Santiam Hwy. 22 about 5 miles north of Santiam Junction, take FS 2267 to the Duffy Lake Trailhead. About 1 3/4 miles along the trail, a trail intersects from the north. Cincha is due south of the trail intersection about 1/4 mile. (Sounds easy, but its not).

It's a small lake and has a little sister just to the west. Cincha is about 2 acres and shallow, while Little Cincha is smaller but deeper. Both lakes are stocked by air every few years. There are good campsites at the larger lakes in the basin.

CLACKAMAS RIVER A favorite of anglers in the greater Portland area, always among the Top Ten producers of salmon and steelhead in the Columbia River system. Spring chinook, a large run of summer steelhead, coho, a small run of fall chinook, and a good run of winter steelhead come home to the Clackamas, a major tributary of the Willamette River.

The Clackamas heads in the Olallie Lake Basin, flowing over 80 miles through Mt. Hood National Forest to enter the Willamette just north of the I-205 Bridge at Oregon City. A beautiful mountain river, the Clackamas has carved high rock cliffs out of the steep Douglas fir forest, rushing past giant boulders, its shoreline strewn with smoothly tumbled river rock. The river has three major tributary streams, the North and Oak Grove Forks, and the Collawash River.

The Clackamas is followed for over 40 miles by Hwy. 224, from one mile north of Carver near Oregon City to Ripplebrook Ranger Station in the Mt. Hood National Forest. From there upstream, it's followed by FS 46 all the way to its headwaters in the Olallie Lake basin. Most salmon angling takes place in the lower river, while steelheading is best above the dams. The most popular spots on the river are within an hour's drive of Portland.

There are three dams on the Clackamas. The lowest, River Mill Dam below Estacada, was built around 1900 when there was little thought for fish passage. It destroyed bountiful native salmon and steelhead runs. The current river management plan calls for rebuilding those runs, a process which has been underway for some time.

Today there are two hatcheries on the stream, fish ladders at all the dams, and a downstream migration collection facility at North Fork that gathers in seaward steelhead and releases them below River Mill. For the past 10 years, the annual steelhead catch has been close to 10,000. The 1983-84 season brought in a landmark run with a catch close to 17,000. The 1985-86 catch of summer steelhead on the Clackamas was 6,580. About twice as many were caught above the dams as below. Summer steelhead are in the river the year around, but best angling in the upper river is June through October. The lower river season begins to pick up in April. The winter steelhead catch is usually around 5,000.

The spring chinook run has been developing nicely. It takes place from March through June, with fish holding in holes through fall. Only a small number of salmon are caught above the dams. The total spring chinook catch in 1986 was about 3000.

The coho fishery depends to a great extent on water level. In low water years the fish get to the Clackamas late and dark, but in high water years bright fish can be readily found. They show in the river as early as September, and bright fish are caught through December. The coho average 5-7 pounds. In 1986 about 2000 were caught. A small run of fall chinook is in the river from around mid-September through October, but they tend to spawn very soon after entering the river.

The good thing is that this angling takes place within an hour's drive of Portland. The bad thing is that, just an hour's drive from Portland, most of the land adjacent to the lower river is privately owned. Consequently, the lower Clackamas is primarily a boater's show. The river is suited to riverboats only (drift boats and jet sleds) except near the mouth and in the big pool at McIver Park near Estacada. From the mouth, anglers in standard motorboats can fish good water up to the first riffle above the Hwy. 99 Bridge. Be aware that spring chinook season typically brings on hoglines at the mouth, with boats anchored and tied in tight formation. At McIver, small motor boats can launch and fish the *big flats*, a 1/2 mile pool of relatively slow water below a major rapid, *the minefield*.

The most popular drifts on the Clackamas are below this rapid, named for the sharp protruding rocks that stud the riverbed there. Even experienced driftboat handlers, and jet boat operators who value their hull, avoid this stretch. From McIver to the mouth, the Clackamas offers fairly easy drifting, interspersed with rapids that are real enough, but not overwhelming for beginning driftboat operators. It is very popular with rafters.

There are 5 improved boat ramps on the lower river, and one natural gravel put-in. McIver Park, about 21 miles above the mouth, offers the last improved boat ramp upstream. To reach McIver, take I-205 to Hwy. 224 just north of Gladstone. Follow 224 east to Carver, turning right at Carver Store and crossing the bridge over the river. Turn left onto Springwater Rd., and drive about 7 miles to the park. Feldheimer's, the gravel bar launch, is off Springwater Rd. just 2 miles before you reach McIver (if you pass the tavern, you've missed Feldheimer's). The next ramp downriver is at Barton Park. Follow Hwy. 224 toward Estacada to Barton Store, then turn right onto Baker's Ferry Rd., which leads to the river. Carver Boat Ramp is immediately across the bridge from Carver store, down the first driveway on the left.

The last ramp above the mouth is at Riverside Park in Clackamas. Follow the merged Hwys. 212/224 east, one stoplight past the 82nd St. junction, turning right onto Evelyn St. (watch for the green ODFW sign. The Clackamas District headquarters is on this road, with some river frontage for bank angling). Follow Evelyn through an industrial warehouse district to the park.

At the mouth of the Clackamas is Clackamette Park, off Hwy. 99E at the north end of Oregon City. Clackamette has boat ramps both into the Willamette and Clackamas. This is where a 55 pound chinook was landed in 1983.

Bank angling on the lower river is restricted primarily to the parks and bridges. There's some bank angling at Clackamette Park, with good angling at Cross Park and High Rocks. To Reach High Rocks, a popular salmon and swimming hole, take the Park Place-Mollala Exit off I-205 and head west. The road ends at High Rocks on the east bank. There is a bridge across the river to Cross Park on the west bank. Riverside Park also offers a strip of bank for salmon and steelhead angling, and there is bank access on the south bank River Rd. just above the Gauging Station downstream from Carver.

The Oregon Dept. of Fish and Wildlife owns a strip of bank from Carver Bridge up to Clear Creek, purchased on behalf of Oregon anglers. There is bank angling at Barton Park, and at Bonnie Lure Park, off Hwy. 224 about 6 miles below River Mill Dam. Bonnie Lure accesses the fishery at the mouth of Eagle Creek. It is an undeveloped State Park. Park at the gate and walk in along a path to the river. The riverbank is also accessible from McIver Park to below River Mill Dam. From the dam up to Mt. Hood Forest most bank access is owned by Portland General Electric and is open to public trespass. Anglers pull off Hwy. 224 and fish at will.

Below River Mill Dam, salmon and steelhead are the primary quarry, though trout are stocked at many of the public sites in spring and summer. Above River Mill, angling is primarily for summer and winter steelhead. There's lots of good steelhead water in the upper river. There's a nice long steelhead drift accessible from the bank near Memaloose Log Scaling Station about 10 miles above Estacada, with some off-road parking available. Anglers also fish near the PGE Towers, a power line crossing about 2 miles further up.

Carter Bridge (not to be confused with Carter Store), about one mile above Big Eddy Picnic Area, offers access to nice pools and tail-outs downstream from the bridge, as does Lockaby Campground. Roaring River Campground features good holding water below a big cliff. At Three Links Power Station, about 22 miles above Estacada, there are good pools above and below the chute. Park off the road. And this is only the beginning. Steelhead run all the way up to the Big Bottom country above Austin Hot Springs, as well as into the Collowash and the forks.

The likelihood of catching fish on the Clackamas, as on many rivers in western Oregon, is heavily influenced by water level. Water level on the Clackamas is primarily affected by snow-melt in the mountains and by rainfall. To find out the water level prior to heading for the river, call (503) 249-0666 for a river gauge reading. The best reading for fishing the Clackamas is considered by many to be 4.5 cfs (cubic ft. per second), with readings as low as 3.6 and as high as 5.4 still worth the trip. Flood level on the Clackamas is 18 cfs.

Camping facilities are available below the national forest at Barton Park and McIver. Within Mt. Hood National Forest, campgrounds are numerous along FS 46, including many near good steelhead water (Lazy Bend, Carter Bridge, Lockaby, and Sunstrip to name but a few). Stocked trout are also available at most of these sites throughout trout season, as the river remains cold all summer long.

There are no stores or resorts in this part of the national forest. Supplies can be purchased at Oregon City, Estacada, and at Barton and Carver stores. For information about fishing the North Fork Dam pool, see North Fork Reservoir.

CLACKAMAS RIVER, NORTH FORK A good size tributary of the Clackamas, entering the river from the east about 15 miles SE of Estacada. FS 4610 follows the fork from the east end of North Fork Reservoir upstream, rarely straying more than 1/4 to 1/2 mile from the fork. FS 4613 crosses the stream near Whiskey Creek. There are many falls on the North Fork. Boyer and Winslow creeks, both good tributaries, join the North Fork at North Campground, about 9 miles upstream.

Fishing here is primarily for native cutthroat, which run 6-11 inches. Bait angling or bait and spinner is most productive early in season. Any method will work late in the year, with small dry fly patterns good in late fall. The road is usually open by late April. For information about fishing the reservoir, see North Fork Reservoir .

CLACKAMAS RIVER, OAK GROVE FORK A good size tributary of the upper mainstem Clackamas, affording fair trout fishing. About 25 miles long, it heads in the Big Meadows area in the NW corner of Warm Springs Reservation. It flows 7 miles to Timothy Lake, and 16 miles below the reservoir to its confluence with the Clackamas just above Ripplebrook Ranger Station, about 31 miles east of Estacada.

Both banks of the lower 5 miles are followed by forest roads east from Ripplebrook to Lake Harriet, a small reservoir on the fork. Above Harriet the roads meet, and FS 57 continues upstream about a mile beyond Timothy. Shortly thereafter, the river enters the reservation, where a tribal fishing permit is required.

The Oak Grove Fork is stocked with legal rainbow from April through July in the vicinity of Ripplebrook and Rainbow campgrounds. Above Harriet are good populations of native cutthroat, with native brook trout in the highest reaches. A few browns, spawners from Lake Harriet, are occasionally caught. Size range of all fish is 6-14 inches, with the larger fish taken within a few miles above the reservoirs.

Single eggs, caddis worms, and small bits of crawlers will work well on light leader. Fly angling is productive late in the year.

There are campgrounds at Ripplebrook, Rainbow, Lake Harriet, Shellrock Creek and in the Timothy Lake area. Supplies are available at Estacada and North Fork Reservoir.

CLACKAMAS RIVER, SOUTH FORK A nice stream entering the main river near Memaloose log scaling station at the east end of North Fork Reservoir. Long a water source for Oregon City and closed to all angling, the South Fork is now open, offering some exciting trout angling for the energetic. Most of the river flows through deep canyon, with a number of natural barriers. Best trout fishing is above these barriers. Memaloose Creek joins the South Fork just above its confluence with the mainstem Clackamas.

One way to approach the South Fork is by way of Trail 516. From Estacada, cross the Clackamas and head south along DuBois Creek toward Dodge. FS 45, the Hillockburn Rd., approaches and parallels the South Fork canyon. About 2 miles past the spur road to Hillockburn Spring (about 2 1/4 miles east of Dodge), Trail 516 leads down to the river. The 1956 USGS topographic quadrangle map shows this trail crossing the river and connecting with another trail that crosses over to Memaloose Creek and follows it to the mouth.

CLAGGET LAKE See Firecamp Lakes.

CLEAR CREEK (Clackamas System) A large tributary of the lower Clackamas River, flowing from the south into the main stream at Carver, about 6 miles east of Clackamas. The creek is about 24 miles long and heads in the low hills west of the Clackamas River south of Viola. It is followed by county roads south of Hwy. 2ll, and the upper end can be reached by going east from Hwy. 213 in the Mulino area.

Primarily a native cutthroat trout stream, a few steelhead do enter during January and February. Most fish are taken by bait in the lower end. Many of the small fish hooked early in trout season are young steelhead or coho moving downstream. These fish will produce a lot more excitement on their return journey if anglers will release them carefully, or better yet, fish heavier water and avoid them.

CLEAR FORK A tributary of the upper Sandy River which provides good late spring and summer angling in its lower stretch. From Portland, take Hwy. 26 east to Zigzag, a distance of 43 miles. Turn north on FS 18, the Lolo Pass Rd., which parallels Clear Fork about 1/4 mile or so to the north of it. Five miles north of Zigzag, at McNeil Campground, the road comes very close to the creek. It then follows the creek almost to the headwaters.

Small native cutthroat are present in good numbers. Because of its low temperature, it's not a good early stream. The natives start biting in late May. Some of the Sandy system steelhead get up here and can be caught, but the stream is closed to salmon angling.

Riley, McNeil, and Lost Creek campgrounds are all located near the midsection of the stream. Supplies are available in Zigzag and Welches.

CLEAR LAKE (Linn Co.) The very scenic and geologically fascinating headwaters of the McKenzie River, created *only* 3000 years ago by a lava flow that formed a natural dam on the stream. The impoundment inundated a standing Douglas fir forest, which the lake's cold waters have preserved. The Underwater Forest, as it is named on Forest Service maps, can be viewed by boaters through Clear Lake's crystalline lens.

The lake is just off Hwy. 126, about 3 miles south of the junction of Hwy. 126 with Hwy. 20.

Clear Lake contains a large self-sustaining population of brook trout and some native cutthroat, and is stocked with easier-to-catch rainbow trout. It covers 148 acres and is deep throughout, reaching 175 ft.near the south end. The only shallows are near Cold Water Cove. Still-fishing and trolling are the predominant angling methods here, with flyfishing near shore. There is a campground at Cold Water Cove on the east shore, and a resort with rustic cabins and rental boats on the west shore. The resort is run by the Santiam Fish and Game Association, a mid-valley sportsman's club, and is open to public use. There is a pole slide boat ramp at Cold Water Cove. Motor boats are prohibited on the lake.

CLEARY POND A 4 acre pond west of Neilson Rd. about 1/2 mile south of Hwy. 126. It contains largemouth bass.

CLIFF LAKE (Lane Co.) A 40 acre brook trout lake in the popular Mink Lake Basin of the Three Sisters Wilderness. It is off the Pacif-ic Crest Trail 1 1/2 miles east of Mink Lake (there is a trail between the two). The trail up to the PCT heads on Hwy. 46 at a turn-around between Elk Lake and the Hosmer Lake junction south of Elk.

The stocked trout in Cliff average 9-10 inches and run to 15 inches. Fished rather heavily, it still produces on all methods of angling. There are a lot of other good lakes close by. See Porky, Mink, Moody, Vogel.

There is a shelter at the lake, and other nice natural campsites. The area is usually accessible in late June, with angling good then, and again in late summer and fall. Closest supplies are at McKenzie Bridge and Elk Lake Resort.

COLLAWASH RIVER A beautiful tributary of the Clackamas River, flowing completely within the Mt. Hood National Forest, entering the Clackamas about 35 miles SE of Estacada. The Collawash and its tributary, the Hot Springs Fork, feature a nice size run of summer steelhead and fair to good trout angling.

The Collawash heads in Marion County north of the Breitenbush drainage and flows north to the Clackamas. From Estacada, follow Hwy. 224 to Ripplebrook Ranger Station, then head south on FS 46 to Two Rivers Camp at the confluence of the Collawash and Clackamas. A good road, FS 63, follows the stream south for 9 miles to Tom's Meadow. About 4 miles south of Two Rivers a branch road, FS 70, turns west and follows the Hot Springs Fork for about 7 miles. Trails access the upper reaches of both forks, as well as a number of lakes in the area.

Rainbow trout are the main catch in areas reached by road, with legal rainbow stocked in season. Upstream, the catch consists of rainbow and an occasional brook trout, with Dolly Varden scarce, but occasionally caught in all sections. A weighted Flatfish will take these in the deep holes.

Steelhead are available throughout the river, in the many pools carved by this rushing mountain stream. The annual summer steelhead catch has been as high as 600 in recent years, with best results in October or November. Only a few winter steelhead are taken. The river is closed to salmon angling to protect late steelhead spawners.

Plentiful trout of good size are taken by anglers willing to hike up the Hot Springs Fork to Bagby Guard Station and above. Trail 544 to Bagby Hot Springs and beyond heads about one mile south of Pegleg Campground. There is a large parking area at the trailhead, and it is well signed. The hot springs are a real treat after a day's angling. (Or before, or any time, actually. There is a good deal of inoffensive nudity here, so leave your hangups at home.)

The main river upstream from Tom's Meadow to Oh Boy Camp (about 5 miles south at the confluence of Elk Lake Creek, shown on topo but not forest map) is accessed by trail or bushwhack, and offers good fishing. Average size of fish caught is about 9 inches with a range 7-l5 inches.

Bait and lure angling will produce well, but there's beautiful fly water on both forks. In late summer and fall, dry fly anglers take big rainbow from the riffles using light leaders and small dries, (number 14 or smaller), with Blue Uprights, McGinty, and Mosquito patterns effective.

There are four campgrounds on the lower 4 miles between the Hot Springs Fork and the Clackamas River, and two campgrounds on the Hot Springs Fork.

COLLINS LAKE A tiny rainbow and brook trout lake of about one acre, just south of the old highway at the west end of Government Camp on Hwy. 26. The lake is formed by a block on one fork of Camp Creek. This is a private lake but it is open to public use. It is stocked with rainbow and has some wild brook and rainbow. Camping is not permitted at the lake.

COLORADO LAKE A 30 acre private lake 2 miles east of Corvallis, open to public use for a fee. The lake contains largemouth bass, white crappie, bluegill, and brown bullhead catfish.

COLUMBIA SLOUGH A long back eddy of the Columbia River which borders North Portland from Kelley Point to east of Parkrose, providing habitat for largemouth bass, crappie, bullhead, bluegill, perch, crawfish, and many species of rough fish that provide food for the bass. Occasional sturgeon and steelhead are also spotted, as well as salmon smolts.

Best fishing is in the lower slough, from just north of the intersection of North Lombard and North Columbia boulevards, across the railroad tracks. Best access is from NE 17th Ave. west to the mouth. Anglers can fish from the west bank here, or launch canoe, raft, or car-top boat. These can be slipped into the water at other points along the slough as well, all the way to Parkrose. Columbia and Sandy Blvds. parallel the slough, and many roads cross it, providing right-of-way access to the narrow shore. North Slough also contains good numbers of game fish, as do some portions of the upper slough. The Four Corners area between NE 158th and 185th avenues features a narrow channel with overhanging trees, shrubs, and submerged structures that are attractive to bass. Incidentally, the state record largemouth bass was taken out of the slough in 1915, and held that record for 52 years.

Because the Columbia Slough is an urban water, and a major drainage in a heavily industrial and densely populated area, there has been concern for the purity of fish taken from slough waters. Extensive sampling has determined that only the freshwater clams should be avoided. The agency also suggests that anglers avoid eating raw or undercooked fish caught in the lower slough during wet weather periods.

COPEPOD LAKE A good brook trout lake in the Mink Lake Basin at the head of the South Fork of the McKenzie River. The lake is just north of the Goose Lake/Corner Lake Trail 1/2 mile west of the the junction of that trail with the Pacific Crest Trail. See cliff lake for directions into the basin.

About 20 acres, Copecod has nice brook trout from 6-16 inches with the average 8-10 inches. Fly angling is good here, with wet flies working well most of the time. Bucktail coachman or caddis and most streamer flies will take fish. There are good natural campsites here and at other lakes in the basin. There is a shelter at Cliff Lake, a little over one mile south by trail. The lake is usually accessible in late June, but the mosquitoes can be fierce. Best angling is in the fall.

CORNER LAKE A 60 acre brook trout lake in the northern Mink Lake Basin, at the head of the South Fork McKenzie. It is about 2 trail miles north of Mink Lake and just north of Goose Lake, which flows into it. See cliff lake for directions into the basin.

Corner usually produces fair to good fishing through most of the season for naturally reproducing brook trout. The fish range from 6-18 inches, averaging 10 inches. All methods will take fish. Goose Lake, a shallow lake to the SE, has good angling early in the year, but gets very low in fall. There are many fine natural campsites throughout the basin.

COTTAGE GROVE PONDS Six bass and panfish ponds. Follow Rowe River Rd. to the truck scale, where the road crosses the Willamette River across from the car lot. A paved bicycle path leads to the first pond. Park near, but do not block, the scales.

COTTAGE GROVE RESERVOIR A large flood control reservoir on the Coast Fork of the Willamette River, managed primarily for bass and panfish, with catch-and-release regulations on trophy bass (over 15 inches). It is located about 6 miles south of Cottage Grove. Just south of town, a paved roads heads SW to the reservoir, and roads follow both shores. It covers about 1000 acres at high level, through the spring and summer months, and is drained down later in the year.

Catchable rainbow trout are stocked annually in the spring, but largemouth bass are the prime catch. Bluegill, black crappie, and brown bullhead catfish are also available. It should be noted that the reservoir's trophy size bass have been tested and shown to contain potentially toxic levels of mercury. Tests also indicate that consumption of smaller bass and other species in the reservoir pose no threat to public health.

The reservoir is popular for diverse recreational water activities, especially boating. Boat landings and ample parking space are provided. Overnight camping is available at Pine Meadow Campground (Corp. of Engineers) on the lake. There are three picnic areas here as well. Accommodations and supplies are available in Cottage Grove.

COTTONWOOD LAKE (a.k.a. Cottonwood Meadows Lake) Located south of the High Rock lakes area of the Mt. Hood National Forest, north of the Oak Grove Fork of the Clackamas River. From Estacada take Hwy. 224 to Ripplebrook Ranger Station, about 30 miles. From there, follow the Oak Grove Fork Rd. FS 57 to the Shellrock Creek Rd. FS 58. About 2 1/2 miles north of Shellrock Campground turn west onto FS 5830 and drive to Hideaway Lake. Continue on 5830 about 1 1/2 miles to the crossing of Trail 705, just past a creek crossing. The trail leads east about 1/2 mile to the lake. The creek also leads to the lake.

Cottonwood Lake is about 8 acres and shallow, ideal for fly angling if it doesn't get too low, and capable of growing good size fish. It has a lot of shoal area and deeper channels, and though it has its ups and downs, it's usually consistent for cutthroat 8-12 inches. In some years, fish up to 16 inches have been taken in good numbers. Primitive campsites are available. It's usually accessible in early June.

COUGAR LAKE (Clackamas Co.) A small brook trout lake near the headwaters of the North Fork Molalla River. Privately owned by Cavenham Forest Industries and maintained by them for their executives, it is no longer open to public enjoyment.

COUGAR RESERVOIR (Lane Co.) A large reservoir on the South Fork of the McKenzie River, 50 miles east of Eugene. Used both for power and flood control, it fluctuates considerably but provides good fishing for stocked rainbow trout. To reach it, take Hwy. 126 east from Eugene. Four miles past the community of Blue River turn south on the South Fork Rd., and follow it 3 miles to the lake.

Cougar covers about 1200 acres when full and is 6 miles long. The primary catch is rainbow trout, but a few Dolly Varden to 5 pounds are taken. Trolling with Ford Fenders or a silver or gold lure has been known to catch a lot of fish. Bank fishing at the upper end at the bridge also produces. Boat anglers should try fishing the coves, where there are usually large concentrations of trout.

Cougar Hot Springs is an added treat for visitors here, located on Rider Creek about 1/4 mile west of the reservoir. About 4 miles south of the dam, the west shore road bisects an embayment at the mouth of Rider Creek. There you will find a small parking area. Follow the trail along the north shore of the creek to the hot springs. Clothing is optional.

There are several forest campgrounds in the vicinity. Echo is on the East Fork Rd. FS 1993 near the lower end of the reservoir. Slide Creek is on the east shore near the southern end, and French Pete is one mile south on FS 19. There are additional campgrounds along the South Fork McKenzie.

CRABTREE CREEK A trout stream east of Albany, flowing from the Cascade foothills south of the North Santiam River into the South Santiam River near Scio. The lower end is crossed by Hwy. 226 about 9 miles north of Lebanon. Both paved and gravel roads follow and cross the lower end, and from Lacomb upstream a fair road follows it to the headwaters some 35 miles from the mouth. The extreme upper portion is sometimes closed to access by a logging concern during fire season.

A popular stream, it is stocked with rainbow trout, and has some native cutthroat. The success rate is high for trout 6-12 inches, with a few larger fish taken at times. All methods of angling will work, but bait is usually best in early season.

CRAIG LAKE This is a hard to find brook trout lake, though not a long hike. Because of its location, it's easily missed and lightly fished, but it puts out a lot of medium size trout. Craig is on top of Craig Butte at elevation 5300 ft. It is across the canyon west of the head of Lost Lake Creek, and is 3/4 miles due south of Lower Berley Creek.

Take the Pacific Crest Trail north 1 1/2 miles from the Santiam Lodge area to the junction of Trail 3491. Take 3491 about one mile north, and look for a fair trail which goes up the NE side of Craig Butte. It is about 1/2 mile to the lake by this trail.

Craig Lake is about 5 acres and is 14 ft. deep. Flyfishing is usually the best bet. There are good natural campsites at the lake.

CRESWELL PONDS Freeway ponds east of Creswell, containing largemouth bass, bluegill, brown bullhead, and black crappie.

CRIPPLE CREEK LAKE A very good 15 acre hike-in brook trout lake at the south end of the High Rock Lakes group in Mt. Hood National Forest. The lake is at elevation 4300 ft.

From Estacada, follow Hwy. 224 just past Ripplebrook Ranger Station, then turn NE on FS 4631 toward Silvertip. About 4 miles from Ripplebrook, FS 4635 cuts sharply back to the NW. Follow it 10 miles. Just after crossing Cripple Creek, the head of Trail 702 to Cache Meadow is on the east side of the road. (The road dead ends a mile or so beyond the trail-head, if you miss it.) Follow the creek upstream (NE) for one mile to the lake, an elevation gain of 300 ft.

By late June the High Rock Rd. is usually open, and the lake can also be reached by a 2 mile hike SW from Frazier Mt. From Frazier turn-around, take Trail. 517 to Cache Meadow, and follow the stream south for 1/2 mile.

Brook trout in the lake run 7-13 inches, averaging 9-10 inches. All methods can be used. At one time the lake was restricted to flyfishing only. It gets very heavy pressure in years when the fish are running large. Natural campsites are available.

CUNNINGHAM LAKE A 200 acre bass and panfish lake near the north end of Sauvie Island, NW of Portland. The lake is at the head of Cunningham Slough near the narrow neck of the island. Subjected to flood waters in the spring and affected by tides, it has a good selection of the warm water fish found in Willamette and mid-Columbia waters.

From St. Helens or Scappoose Bay the lake can be reached by boating up Cunningham Slough, which is just across Multnomah Channel from the Crown Paper Mill south of St. Helens. An alternate boat route is to go south 3 miles from the mouth of Scappoose Bay to the east side of the channel at a point opposite Jackson or Santosh Slough. Walk several hundred yards to the shore of the lake.

Brown bullhead angling is very good at times if you have a boat to get to them. Largemouth bass, crappie and perch move in and out of the lake with the tidal action. Best angling is in June and July when the water is up.

Tackle and boats are available at Brown's Landing just south of Scappoose Bay, and at St. Helens.

CUNNINGHAM SLOUGH A good bass and panfish fishery south of St. Helens on the north end of Sauvie Island. A boat is required to fish it. The slough is about 5 miles long and serpentines out of Cunningham Lake, flowing into Willamette Slough across from the mouth of Scappoose Bay. It has a double mouth with an island located at the entry. By boat from St. Helens, it's about a 2 mile run upstream. From the public ramp at Scappoose Bay north of Warren, it's 1 1/2 miles down the bay and across. Scappoose Bay is about 25 miles north of Portland (and offers good warm water angling itself).

The main catch in the slough is brown bullhead, which are very plentiful at times. These catfish run 8-12 inches with an occasional larger one. A number of good size perch are picked up in the lower slough, and crappie respond to cut bait, jig flies, and spinners. Best spots to fish are at the mouths of the smaller sloughs. Angling is best on the ebb tide, according to the experts, but some fish can be caught at any time.

Angling can be very good for bass to 5 pounds. Areas near the mouth and at the outlets of the smaller streams produce best results. All methods are used, a good spot to test everything in your tackle box. Bass seem to hit best at the tide changes.

Boats, tackle, motors, and supplies are available at Browns Landing on Multnomah Channel, along Hwy. 30, and in Scappoose.

DAIRY CREEK, EAST FORK. (Wash. Co.) A popular and heavily fished trout stream just 25 miles west of Portland, crossed by Hwy. 26. The stream flows from the north and joins West Dairy Creek, entering the Tualatin River near Cornelius.

Trout angling is largely confined to the area north of Hwy. 26. A good road turns north off the highway toward Mountaindale just before Hwy. 26 crosses the stream. A paved and gravel road follows the stream up about 10 miles. The lower creek has quite a bit of private property, so don't trespass.

East Dairy is managed as a wild cutthroat stream and is no longer stocked. Single eggs, worms, and caddis nymphs will all work well, and flies will take fish when the stream drops and clears. There is no camping in the area.

DAIRY CREEK, WEST FORK (Wash. Co.) A good native cutthroat stream in Washington County, tributary to the Tualatin River, with headwaters north of Hwy. 26. It flows south along Hwy. 47 out of Vernonia, then at Staleys Junction flows east along 26 to the Hillsboro junction at Banks. From there, it flows SE through farmland to join East Dairy Creek and the Tualatin River.

This is an excellent native cutthroat stream. Fishing usually holds up until early summer, but best catches are made early. The stream is fairly brushy and has a lot of cover for fish. Bait angling is best, but a small spinner/bait combination will work well. Black Gnats, brown hackles, and McGintys flicked off the brushy overhangs will take nice size cutthroat. Small crayfish tails will also attract the big ones. There's some private property along the stream, so avoid trespassing.

DALY LAKE Cupped in the headwaters of the Middle Fork of the Santiam River, 11 acres, with excellent angling for brook trout and cutthroat, and not too remote. From Hwy. 22, the North Santiam Rd., turn west on the Scar Mt. Road FS 2266 at a point about 22 miles SE of Idanha. Don't take the wrong turn and get onto 1164, which will take you too far north. FS 2266, about 4 miles from Hwy. 22, goes right between Daly and Parrish Lakes. Daly is on the north side.

Daly Lake has a lot of cutthroat 6-10 inches, with a few larger. A fair number of eastern brook trout are caught, from 6-14 inches. Both of these trout are sustained by natural reproduction. All methods will take fish, with flyfishing especially good in late summer and fall. The east side of the lake has the best fly water. There are good natural campsites here. Riggs Lake, also good for brook and cutthroat, is west along the same road. Parrish is also close by. The road may still be snowbound in early June.

DAVIS LAKE (Linn Co.) A lightly fished 3 acre brook trout lake between Marion Lake and the old Santiam Rd., located within the Mt. Jefferson Wilderness. It is 4 miles south of Marion Falls Ranger Station on North Santiam Hwy. 22. FS 2261 leads east to the Pine Ridge Scout Camp. From the camp, take Trail 3443 SE about 2 miles. The trail stays 1/4 mile south of the lake, crossing an inlet stream which can be followed to Davis.

The lake is very shallow, good for flyfishing, but it sometimes loses fish to winterkill. When it gets by for a few years without winter loss, it grows some good size brook trout. Fair natural campsites are available.

DEEP CREEK (Clackamas Co.) A native trout stream with a small winter steelhead run, tributary to the lower Clackamas River. The stream is about 15 miles SE of Portland and enters the Clackamas River near Barton. The upper North Fork is crossed by Hwy. 26 south of Orient, and the main upper stream is crossed by Hwy. 211 SW of Sandy. Other county roads cross and follow the stream from the mouth eastward.

Trout angling is good from late April through May and June, but the stream gets low in summer. It offers fair fishing for native cutthroat. Bait angling is most popular.

A few steelhead (less than 50) are caught on Deep Creek each year, from January through March. An occasional coho is taken in the early fall.

There's private property along the creek, but some owners will allow you to fish if you ask permission. There's no camping in the area.

DEER CREEK (Yamhill Co.) A native cutthroat stream about 17 miles long, flowing into the South Yamhill River about 3 miles east of Sheridan off Hwy. 18. The mouth is about 5 miles SW of McMinnville. The creek is crossed by the highway just east of Sheridan, and followed north by good roads for about 11 miles up Gopher Valley.

Fishing is best in the portion north of the highway, and angling holds up until June. Average catch is around 9 inches, with few larger. Bait is best here. There's a lot of private land along this stream.

DELTA PARK PONDS Offering bass and panfish opportunities in the Portland metropolitan area. From I-5 North take the Delta Park Exit, just after crossing Columbia Slough. The park is city owned, west of the freeway. Unfortunately, fishing seems to be losing ground to other park activities. The golf course ponds are closed to angling. However, there are a half dozen lakes and sloughs here, many of which are still accessible when the horses aren't running! The four largest lakes contain bass, perch, catfish and bluegill. All can be easily fished from the bank.

DELTA PONDS Offering 200 acres of bass and panfish water east of Delta Hwy. in North Eugene. Fish for largemouth bass, white crappie, brown bullhead, and bluegill.

DENUDE LAKE A scenic 9 acre brook trout lake in the Sisters Mirror Lakes Basin of the Three Sisters Wilderness, NW of Elk Lake near the Cascade summit. The Pacific Crest Trail crosses the basin, which is about 5 miles north-northwest of Elk Lake. One of several approaches begins at Elk Lake Lodge, about 35 miles SW of Bend on the Cascade Lakes Hwy. 46. Take the Horse Lake Trail 1 1/2 miles west to its intersection with the PCT, and turn north onto it. Hike 4 1/2 miles north to the Sisters Mirror area. Another route, about 3 miles to the lake, is by Trail 20, which leads NW from Hwy. 46 1/2 mile north of Sink Creek, which is about 2 miles north of the Elk Lake Lodge turn-off. Denude is the western-most lake in the basin.

The Mirror Lakes are on a picturesque plateau in an alpine setting. Most are quite shallow and don't provide much fishing. The brook trout in Denude average 9 inches, ranging 6-14 inches. They are easily fished from shore by all methods. Good natural campsites are available. This is designated wilderness, so no-trace camping guidelines should be followed.

DETROIT LAKE This large popular reservoir on the North Fork Santiam River has been providing good angling since it was first filled with water. It's about 100 miles from Portland, 50 miles east of Salem, off Hwy. 22. The town of Detroit is located near the upper (east) end of the lake.

Detroit Dam is used for flood control and power, so water level in the reservoir fluctuates during the year, though it's usually full in spring and summer, covering over 3,000 acres. In fall the water is lowered, but fishing can still be good in the pools and near the dam.

Catchable trout are stocked each spring and summer. As many as 20,000 legal rainbow are added to the pool prior to the spring opening. Heavy plants of small trout are made each fall, and these grow to good size the following summer. Detroit has a few wild brook trout and cutthroat from the Breitenbush and North Santiam Rivers as well as Blowout and Kinney Creeks and other minor streams, but stocked rainbow trout dominate the catch. Most of the fish caught are about 12 inches, though a good number of trout to 16 inches add to the excitement.

Brown bullhead, though not stocked by the state, have increased in number and provide quite a fishery. They run to 14 inches and are taken with nightcrawlers on the bottom. Some good places to find them are around Piety Island and in the tributary arms.

Kokanee are also stocked annually, and catches have been good. Anglers use downriggers to fish as deep as 80-100 ft. in July and August, or troll deep around the island and towards the dam.

All methods of fishing are used here, with trolling the most popular. One good hook-up is a rudder-flasher set-up with 2 ft. leader, followed by a small Flatfish or worm. Triple Teasers and small Spin-glos behind large flashers also work well, but remember to troll very slowly. Still fishing and lure casting also take lots of fish. Best angling is in the river arms and shoal areas. Catches have been good from opening through Labor Day, with the best fishing early and late in the year.

There is a boat ramp at Mongola State Park on the north shore near the east end of the lake. Mongola, and Lake Shore State Park offer camping facilities on the north shore off Hwy. 22. Hoover and South Shore Campgrounds are on the south shore, on FS 10. (From Hwy. 22 at Detroit, turn right onto FS 10.) There is also a boat-in campground on Piety Knob, an island in the main pool at the east end of the reservoir. Restaurants and supplies are available in Detroit.

DEXTER RESERVOIR A fair size reservoir on the lower Middle Fork Willamette River just downstream from Lookout Reservoir. Dexter is about 20 miles east of Eugene on Hwy. 58, about 140 miles from Portland. The community of Lowell is on the north side of the lake.

Dexter is about 3 miles long and is not very popular for angling. It is heavily infested with rough fish and used very heavily by waterskiers and sailboaters. There is a gravel boat ramp with parking on the south shore. The north shore features a campground, four good ramps, parking area, boat dock and picnic area.

DINGER LAKE A good little trout lake at 4000 ft. elevation, 2 1/2 miles NW of Timothy Lake (a reservoir on the Oak Grove Fork of the Clackamas) in the Mt. Hood National Forest. The lake is about 77 miles from Portland.

From Pine Point Campground on the SW arm of Timothy Lake, drive NW on FS 5820 toward Black Wolf Meadows Trailhead. About 3 miles from the campground a short spur road cuts back to the NE. If you see the trailhead for 724, you've gone 1/2 mile too far. Take the spur road to its end. From there the lake is a 1/3 mile bushwhack NW.

Dinger is very shallow and in some years loses fish to winterkill. This shallowness also makes it an excellent fly lake for trout 7-14 inches, average size 10 inches. There are good natural campsites and a spring at the lake. It is usually accessible in late May.

DIXIE LAKES A couple of small brook trout lakes at the southern end of the Eight Lakes Basin in the Mt. Jefferson Wilderness. Easy to find, they're fished lightly by anglers passing through on the way to more popular spots. See duffy lake for directions. From Duffy, take the trail leading SE toward Santiam Lake. At the meadow trail intersection about 1/2 mile down the trail, turn north toward Jorn Lake. The Dixies are about 3/4 mile from this junction on the west side of the trail.

North Dixie covers about 3 acres and is 8 ft. deep. The South lake is smaller, shallower, and is not stocked. It may or may not have fish. North has brook trout to 12 inches. There are lots of adequate campsites nearby.

DON LAKES These trout lakes are hard to find. In fact, the Forest Service map does not show their location correctly, which doesn't make finding them easier. Upper Don Lake is about 1/2 mile due north of Parrish Lake and 1/2 mile NW of Daly Lake. See daly lake for road directions. From Daly, it's about a 1/2 mile bushwhack to the Don Lakes, bearing NW and descending slightly. The maps show them closer, but you'll have to cross two stream beds on your way.

Riggs Lake is about 3 acres and over 20 ft. deep. Upper Don Lake is 1/4 mile or so north up the stream bed, and is smaller but also deep. Brook trout in both lakes grow to 12 inches, and there are lots of them. The lower lake also has quite a few cutthroat. There are good campsites in the area. A rubber boat would be handy but not necessary.

DORENA RESERVOIR A large reservoir on the Row River, 7 miles east of Hwy. 99 at Cottage Grove south of Eugene. Used mainly for flood control, it covers around 1800 acres of water when full and holds its water level pretty well throughout spring and summer. Two good roads follow the north and south shoreline.

The reservoir is stocked with rainbow trout and largemouth bass. It also has native cutthroat, brown bullhead, bluegill, and black crappie. Angling has been generally good here. The lake was treated for rough fish and restocked in 1985, and all species are now well established. It is open for year around angling and affords some good opportunities from September through January.

The trout range 6-14 inches, averaging 10 inches. Trolling accounts for most of the catch, but bait fishing from boats and shore is very popular. The upper end of the lake seems to be the most productive. There's good bass angling for fish to 8 pounds or more.

There are good boat ramps on both north and south shores, a picnic area, and sanitary facilities. The reservoir has a low-water boat ramp that permits launching year around. Boats, motors, and limited supplies are available at the reservoir. There are two parks with camping areas on the south side road.

DORMAN POND A 12 acre bass and panfish pond west of Forest Grove, at the junction of hwys. 8 and 6. The pond is on the south side of the road. It contains largemouth bass, bluegill, brown bullhead, and black crappie, as well as stocked legal rainbow. An old, high borrow pit,

its banks have returned to natural vegetation. Motors are prohibited on the pond, but anglers can launch car-top and rubber boats from the shore.

DUFFY LAKE One of the best lakes in the Eight Lakes Basin of the Mt. Jefferson Wilderness. From North Santiam Hwy 22, drive 3 miles east on FS 2267 to the Duffy Lake Trailhead. Turn off Hwy. 22 (sign says Big Meadow) just south of the Santiam River crossing, 8 miles south of the Marion Forks Ranger Station and about 4 1/2 miles north of the Santiam junction. Hike 3 miles east on the Duffy Lake Trail 3427. The old Pacific Crest Trail (the PCT has been relocated closer to the crest) meets here also, coming in from Santiam Pass on Hwy. 20. This trail is now numbered 3491 and passes Santiam Lake.

Duffy is 30 acres and a consistent producer of brook trout. The trout run 6-15 inches, averaging 10 inches. Rainbow have also been stocked and make up a quarter of the catch, running to 12 inches. The brookies are most easily taken while trolling, especially in early season, but you'll have to carry in that rubber raft. It's easy to fish from shore. Fly angling in fall is good for either species in late afternoon till dark. There are good small lakes in all directions. It is usually accessible by June, but it tends to get early snow.

DUMBELL LAKE One of the northern-most lakes of the Mink Lake Basin, holding stocked brook trout. From Elk Lake Resort take Trail 3517 west 2 1/2 miles to the Pacific Crest Trail, then hike south about 3 1/2 miles to the lake. An alternate approach is from the south by the Six Lakes Trail which heads one mile south of Elk Lake. This route will take you past Davis and Blow lakes. The Pacific Crest Trail touches the eastern shore of Dumbell, and the lake gets fished pretty hard.

Dumbell covers 6 acres and doesn't hold up well under the angling pressure. Its brook trout run 6-14 inches, averaging 9 inches. There are several unnamed lakes to the west of Dumbell that might provide surprises for the adventurous. Supplies are available at Elk Lake Resort.

EAGLE CREEK (Clackamas Co.) A very good trout, steelhead, and salmon stream, tributary to the lower Clackamas River. It has good angling and is a popular general recreation area. Eagle Creek enters the Clackamas River just west of the community of Eagle Creek on Hwy. 211, 5 miles north of Estacada. From Portland, take Hwy. 224 through Carver. From Eagle Creek, county roads follow the creek east. The upper 10 miles of stream is accessible only by trail.

The creek heads in the Cascade foothills near the Salmon River divide. Eagle Creek is heavily stocked with rainbow in the spring, and a few native cutthroat are also present. The catch rate is high for fish from 7-11 inches. Single eggs and worms will work best early in the season, and there's lots of good fly water.

Young steelhead about 10 inches long, which fail to go to sea, are also taken. Mostly males, they are already mature and will put up a good scrap, but they are dark like spawners. If they are released, they will probably go to sea the following spring.

Eagle Creek is a real producer of steelhead and salmon for its size, thanks primarily to a hatchery operation on the stream. There is an occasional down year, but the winter steelhead catch is typically 1000-2000. The coho catch often exceeds 1000, with 1986 a landmark year

with over 2000 coho caught. There are small spring and fall chinook runs (less than 100 of each generally caught), but there is some thought being given to discontinuing the chinook stocking program due to poaching and snagging.

Steelhead start up the creek in December and are available through March, with angling activity from the Scout Camp at the mouth up to the hatchery. Coho start to show in the stream in late September and peak around November. Coho jacks are picked up in good numbers in late fall. Bait or spinners and small Flatfish will take them. Spring chinook show in late April, May, and June.

Check the regulations for seasons and special closures, and stay within legal distance of the fish ladder 1/2 mile below Eagle Fern Park (fishing is prohibited within 200 ft. upstream and 300 ft. downstream). There are no overnight campsites on the creek, but Eagle Fern Park near the mouth has a nice picnic area.

EAST McFARLAND LAKE This is a lightly fished brook trout lake 2 miles north of Irish Mt. about 6 trail miles north of Irish Lake. About 10 acres and over 30 ft. deep, it's very difficult to get to. The best route is to hike north on the Pacific Crest Trail from Irish Lake about 6 miles, passing Dennis and Lindick lakes. About 1/4 mile north of Lindick, bushwhack about 1/2 mile west for 1/4 mile, and you'll find the lake.

It is stocked by air, and there is usually some carry-over each year. The lake is usually inaccessible until late June.

EASTERN BROOK LAKE A good 11 acre lake in the Taylor Burn area. It is very close to Taylor Burn Forest Camp, north of Waldo Lake. From Oakridge on Hwy. 58 drive 20 miles east, turning north on Waldo Lake Rd. FS 5897. When you get to North Waldo Campground, head north on the old road which meets the Taylor Burn Rd. in about 4 miles. From Bend, take the Cascade Lakes Hwy. to Little Cultus, or cut west off Hwy. 97 onto any of the roads to Crane Prairie or Wickiup Reservoir, and follow the signs to Taylor Burn. From Taylor Burn Camp, go south 1/2 mile on the Wahana Trail, then head west down a side trail through a meadow about 1/4 mile to the lake. There are good campsites and water at Taylor Burn Camp.

Eastern Brook Lake is deep and usually holds a lot of fish, but it has its slack periods. Alternate your methods for better luck. Spinner and bait fished slowly will usually produce. The brook trout run 6-18 inches, with most around 10 inches. The road in usually opens near the end of June.

EDDEELEO LAKE, LOWER A large brook trout lake in the Taylor Burn area of the Central Cascades, about 1/2 mile north of Upper Eddeeleo Lake. See Upper Eddeeleo for directions. Lower Eddeeleo covers about 160 acres and produces consistently.

It's a good deep lake suited to any angling method. It can be fished from shore, but a rubber boat would be very useful. Angling is for naturally reproducing brook trout from 6-14 inches with a 10 inches average. Rainbow are no longer stocked, but a remnant might show up.

Fly angling is good, early and late in the day. Bucktails fished wet with a slow retrieve have been successful on larger fish. Other good flies are the blue upright, mosquito, black gnat, spruce fly and the reliable gray and brown hackles. If things get dull, try Long Lake to the north of Upper Eddeeleo and Round Lake to the south. There are lots of good campsites in the area, usually accessible by late June.

EDDEELEO LAKE, UPPER A good brook trout lake 2 miles NW of Waldo Lake in the headwaters of the North Fork Willamette River. About 63 acres, the lake is approached from Taylor Burn Campground, 7 fairly rough road miles north of the North Waldo Lake Campground. The area is usually accessible in late June. The Indian sounding name for this lake is actually a combination of the first names of Ed Clark, Dee Wright, and Leo McMahon, three early forest service workers who first stocked the lake.

From Taylor Burn, take Trail 3553 west from camp, down through the Willamette canyon, and up to the Quinn Lakes Trail junction. Go south on Trail 3597 for 3 miles past Long and Lower Eddeeleo lakes.

Upper Eddeleo can also be reached from the Wehanna Trail 3590, which skirts the NW shore of Waldo Lake. Some anglers camp at North Waldo and take a boat across to the outlet at the NW corner of Waldo. From there it's only a 1 1/2 mile hike into the Eddeeleos.

The brook trout average about 10 inches and range 6-14 inches. The lake holds up well all season. The shore is quite brushy, making fly angling difficult from the bank. Flies work well early and late in the day, and bait and lures are effective any time. Other lakes close by are Lower Eddeeleo and Round Lake, and Chetlo Lake is about one mile to the south.

EDNA LAKE A small brook trout lake just a few hundred yards west of Taylor Burn Campground, 7 miles by rough road north of North Waldo Lake Campground. Take the Olallie Trail (leading to the Erma Bell Lakes) west out of Taylor Burn. In about 1/4 mile, the trail passes Edna Lake.

Edna is only 3 acres, but is lightly fished and holds up well. The brook trout range 6-10 inches. It's easy to fish from shore or from logs extending into the water.

ELBOW LAKE (Lane Co.) A 10 acre brook trout lake near the NW edge of Waldo Lake, about 1/2 mile south of Chetlo Lake. It's about 5 1/2 trail miles from Taylor Burn or North Waldo Lake campgrounds. The easiest way in is by boat from Waldo Lake. See Chetlo Lake for directions.

Elbow has its ups and downs from year to year. Brook trout average 10 inches and range 6-13 inches. It can be fished from shore, and all methods will work when the fish are hitting. Try a Mickey Finn, casting out and letting it lie, bringing it in with short twitches. If this doesn't work, use nymph patterns or lures.

ELK LAKE (Marion Co.) A lightly fished 60 acre brook trout and kokanee lake at the head of Elk Creek, one of the main forks of the upper Collawash River. It can't be reached by road from the Mt. Hood Forest. Best approach is from Detroit on Hwy. 22. Take FS 46 four miles NE from Detroit to FS 4696, which intersects from the north. Follow 4696 for one mile, then take FS 2209 left for 6 rough, steep miles to the lake. This road is usually impassable until late June.

Elk Lake usually provides good fishing for brook trout 7-10 inches. A population of kokanee has established itself, and the average fish caught is 8-9 inches. Though it's easy to fish from shore, a boat would be handy. All meth-

CRAWFISH
Bill Wagner, Photographer

ods are used, but bait angling and trolling are best in early season. Fly angling picks up in late August and September. There's a good size campground, but no room for trailers. This is a good base camp for pack trips to lakes to the north. See Twin Lakes, Pansy, Big Slide.

EMERALD LAKE A privately owned 4 acre trout lake 19 miles east of Molalla on the North Fork Molalla River. Owned by a logging company, the lake is now closed to public use.

ERMA BELL LAKES A series of three very good rainbow lakes in the northern part of the Taylor Burn area. The lakes are along the Olallie Trail 3563. The northernmost is Lower Erma Bell.

According to Lewis McArthur, these lakes are named for what must have been one of Oregon's earliest automobile victims. Miss Erma Bell, employed by the Forest Service as a *computer*, died in an automobile accident in April of 1918, and the Forest Service named these lakes for her.

The lakes can be approached from the north by driving to Skookum Creek Campground in the headwaters of the North Fork of the Middle Fork of the Willamette, by way of the North Fork Rd. Take Trail 3563 south 2 miles to Lower Erma Bell. An alternative approach is from Taylor Burn Campground, 7 miles by rough road north of North Waldo Lake Campground. Take Trail 3563 north about 2 miles to Upper Erma Bell.

Upper Erma Bell is the smallest of the three, covering 25 acres. Middle and Lower are each around 60 acres. Each of the lakes is fairly deep.

Lower and Middle have wild rainbow. Lower's rainbow run 6-15 inches with an average of 10 inches. They can be fished from shore. All methods will take fish, with fly angling good in mornings and evenings. Nymph patterns and deep fished wet flies should do well.

Middle Erma Bell is 1/4 mile south and slightly higher. It is a little larger and is very consistent for rainbow to 14 inches. All methods will work, and an occasional large trout is taken.

The upper lake is 1/2 mile further south and west of the trail. The fish here are brook trout, which average around 10 inches.

There are no improved campsites in the area, but there are good camps at Skookum Creek and Taylor Burn. Check current regulations for special season and catch information designed to protect spawning trout. The area is usually accessible near the end of June, depending on depth of snow pack.

ESTACADA LAKE The pool behind River Mill Dam on the Clackamas River at Estacada, reached from Hwy. 24. It is stocked with legal trout each season.

EUGENE REST AREA PONDS Five acres of bass and panfish water on the west side of Hwy. 99W between Eugene and Junction City, just north of Clear Lake Rd.

FAIRVIEW LAKE A bass and panfish lake, over 200 acres, north of Hwy. 30 and west of Troutdale. Adjacent to Blue Lake, it has a mixed population that includes a lot of rough fish. The lake is completely surrounded by private lands and currently closed to the public.

FALL CREEK (Lane Co.) This beautiful stream offers good trout angling and is quite popular. About 30 miles long, it heads in the Cascades between the McKenzie and Middle Fork Willamette drainages, and flows into Fall Creek Reservoir just NW of Dexter Reservoir. Above the reservoir it is followed by a hiking trail throughout much of its length.

From Eugene, drive SW on Hwy. 58 to Dexter Reservoir, then turn east onto the Lowell Rd. The reservoir is 3 miles past Lowell, and the creek empties into the eastern arm. Hwy. 126 from Springfield also leads to the reservoir, a 12 mile drive SE. From the town of Fall Creek, a paved road follows the stream east for 11 miles to the Willamette National Forest Boundary, where forest roads and a hiking trail following the creek to its headwaters.

Fall Creek is heavily stocked with rainbow trout and has some nice native cutthroat in the first 13 miles above the reservoir. Average size is about 9 inches with some going to 12. The best area for angling is from the head of the reservoir below the forest boundary to Sunshine Creek above Puma Camp. Bait and spinner are most effective in early season, with fly angling picking up in summer and good through the fall.

There are small runs of fall chinook and winter steelhead here. Angling for them is permitted only below the reservoir. Check current regulations for seasons and closures.

There's a lot of private land in the lower section, but the upper creek is all on public land. This is a fine recreational area, with four National Forest campgrounds in a 7 mile stretch. The upper creek has several good swimming holes favored by Eugene residents.

FALL CREEK RESERVOIR A fair size reservoir about 12 miles south of the Eugene/Springfield area. About 1800 acres when full, it is used mainly for flood control and is drawn down low in late fall. It is located just north of Lowell, which is reached from Hwy. 58 by crossing Dexter Reservoir. Two streams, Fall Creek and Winberry Creek, flow into it. The dam is just below the junction of the two streams.

Most angling is for stocked legal rainbow. The primary management objective for the reservoir is the rearing of juvenile chinook to smolt size. Consequently, no fingerling rainbow are stocked. Trout angling is best early in season and late fall, with trolling the best producer. There are several boat ramps and picnic areas on the reservoir. There are campgrounds on the Fall Creek Rd. All roads are good in this area.

FARADAY LAKE An easy, accessible, and popular 25 acre lake on the Clackamas River about 2 miles SE of Estacada by way of Hwy. 224. It is used for power purposes but provides fair angling. To reach it, turn off Hwy. 224 at the bridge, crosing the river.

The lake is stocked with rainbow, and occasionally gets some brood trout to create excitement. Most anglers use bait, but spinners and other lures will produce from the bank. Angling regulations say a fish over 20 inches will be considered a trout if caught here.

FAY LAKE A fairly good brook trout lake just off North Santiam Hwy. 22, in the Big Meadows camp area. About 4 1/2 miles north of Santiam Junction, take FS 2267 for approximately one mile, then go left on 2257 for 2 miles into Big Meadows. The lake is about one mile north of Big Meadows Campground on the east side of the road. There are more roads in this area than show on the current maps, but if you find Big Meadows, you'll find the lake.

Fay Lake is only about 7 acres but holds up well even with heavy pressure. Brook trout run 6-15 inches, averaging 9 inches. Stocked rainbow about the same size make up half the catch. Until recently, Fay was a *fly fishing only* lake but is now open to all methods. It's a hard lake to fish, shallow and clear, and if there is

no wind on the surface the fish spook easily. The Forest Service has felled and submerged a number of big trees to enhance fish cover. The lake is brushy and hard to fish from shore, but it is easily waded. A light car-top or rubber boat would be useful here. There are good campsites at Big Meadows.

FERN RIDGE BORROW PIT A 10 acre fishery on the north side of the main road immediately below Fern Ridge Dam. It contains white crappie, largemouth bass, bluegill, and brown bullhead.

FERN RIDGE RESERVOIR A large flood control reservoir on the Long Tom River, 12 miles west of Eugene. It covers 9000 acres when full. While mostly a warm water fishery, cutthroat trout are present. To reach it, follow Hwy. 126 west to the Territorial Rd. junction at Perkins Peninsula and Veneta. The Territorial Rd. passes through Elmira and leads to the dam at the north end of the reservoir.

Fern Ridge is very popular for general water recreation. There are 6 boat ramps, several boat docks, and 3 picnic areas as well as developments at Richardson Point on the NW shore and Perkin's Peninsula on the south. There is only one campground.

East of Perkins Peninsula Park, the Coyote Creek bypass leads to a lightly fished slough area that looks very promising for bass and panfish, with submerged trees and overhanging brush. To reach it, turn left just below the highway bridge. Crappie are plentiful at the inflow of the Long Tom River, and in the cement spillway structures below the dam (this area is especially good in winter). Bluegill are available in the shallows and the weedy areas. Largemouth bass can be found prowling the weedy slopes mornings and evenings.

FIR LAKE This lake was once a real sleeper, difficult to reach, with anglers in the know making terrific catches and keeping mum. It's not a big lake, only about 6 acres, but it's quite deep and puts out some really good brook trout. Most of the fish run 10-12 inches, but there are larger ones to 18 inches.

It used to be a brushy hike by compass to the lake, but there is now a blazed trail. To get there, first drive to Fay Lake. See Fay Lake for directions. Go north past Fay for about 1/4 mile to a turn-out. A blazed trail takes off to the east from here, and it's about one mile to Fir (past Pika Lake, which has brook trout in it). Fir is fairly brushy but can be fished easily from logs if you don't have a rubber boat.

FIRECAMP LAKES A group of three lakes NW of Mt. Jefferson, near the head of the South Fork of the Breitenbush River. From Detroit on Hwy. 22, take Breitenbush FS 46 for 10 miles (one mile past the Hot Springs), then take FS 4685 to road's end. Crown Lake, the largest of the group, is 2 miles east on Trail 3361, at elevation 4852 ft.

Crown is about 16 acres, quite shallow, and is no longer stocked due to a tendency to winterkill. The next lake, just a few hundred yards SE is Clagget Lake. This is a small but deep lake of several acres and is the most reliable lake of the three. The third lake is Sheep Lake, which usually produces only a few small size brook trout.

This is an old burned-off area, great for huckleberries in late fall. Just over the ridge to the east are three other lakes which have good fishing at times. See Slideout Lake.

FIRST LAKE A 3 acre cutthroat trout lake accessed by road just north of Olallie Lake. It is the first lake south of Lower Lake Campground. The Olallie Lake Basin is about 100 miles from Portland by way of highways 26 or 224 and a network of forest roads. First Lake is west of the road. See Olallie Lake.

First Lake is stocked every other year now. It doesn't have a large trout population, but cutthroat 8-13 inches are available, and it is lightly fished. Spinner and bait and small lures cast from shore are effective. Campsites are available at Lower Lake Campground to the north and all around Olallie Lake to the south.

FISH CREEK (Clackamas Co.) A 15 mile long tributary of the Clackamas River, completely within Mt Hood National Forest, offering fair to good trout angling. It joins the Clackamas from the south about 9 miles upstream from North Fork Reservoir. From Estacada drive SE 16 miles on Hwy. 224 past the reservoir. FS 54 crosses the Clackamas just past Lockaby Campground, immediately passes Fish Creek Campground, then follows the creek along its eastern bank for much of its length. Several trails lead down to the creek.

No longer stocked with rainbow, it offers fishing for wild cutthroat and a few brook trout. Wild rainbow also show up in the lower section. Average size of the catch is 8-12 inches. Bait works best early, with lures and flies effective later in the season. There's some nice fly fishing water in the upper stretch, but the fish are small. The Forest Service is currently studying the creek to determine how it can enhance the fishery through habitat improvement. There are four campgrounds near the mouth. Several lakes are located in the headwaters. See Skookum Lake, Surprise Lake.

FISH LAKE (Clackamas Co.) A 20 acres lake NW of Olallie Lake, featuring small stocked cutthroat and a few brook trout. From Lower Lake Campground on Olallie Lake Rd. FS 4220, follow Trail 717 NW just over one mile to the lake.

Though the trout only run 6-11 inches, good catches are made using all methods of angling. Bait, small lures, and spinners work well, with wet fly angling good in the evening. It's a very deep lake, and a rubber boat is useful. There are primitive campsites at the lake, but a power transmission line mars its scenic quality. There's a good camp at Lower Lake.

FISH LAKE (Hood River Co.) A small brook trout lake in the Mt. Hood National Forest about one mile by trail north of Wahtum Lake, 25 miles SW of Hood River. Trail 408 leads north from the Wahtum Lake parking area about 2 miles to the lake. When road conditions are suitable, you can follow a primitive road just over one mile around the east side of Wahtum then NW. This road intersects the trail and saves one mile of hiking.

Fish Lake is just 2 acres with few large fish. It is occasionally stocked with brook trout 6-12 inches, averaging 9-10 inches. The lake is shallow, and in severe winters the fish may all be lost to winterkill. Fly angling works best due to the shallowness of the lake. There are no good campsites here, but there are a few at Wahtum Lake to the south. The road usually opens late in spring.

FISH LAKE (Linn Co.) A shallow cutthroat lake north of Clear Lake, just off the South Santiam Hwy. 20. It's about 72 miles from Albany, 3 miles west of the Santiam junction.

About 50 acres, Fish Lake drains into Clear Lake. It has an unusually short open season (late April till June 1) because it tends to dry up, making its fish too vulnerable for sporting angling. Cutthroat from 6-14 inches are caught during the season, with flyfishing very effective. There's a small campground here, and supplies can be obtained at Clear Lake Resort. Motorboats are prohibited on the lake.

FISHER LAKES Two small lightly fished trout lakes in the Horse Lake area of the Upper McKenzie watershed. See Horse Lake for directions. From Upper Horse Lake, take the McBee Trail SW for 1 1/2 miles. The trail goes right by Fisher Lakes. The fish here are small, 8-10 inches, both brook trout and cutthroat.

East Fisher is about 2 acres and 20 feet deep. It's shaped like a dumbell and is easily fished from shore by standing on the logs that line its bank. There are many good campsites in the Horse Lake area.

FLYING M PONDS Two ponds on property owned by Flying M Ranch, a resort in the foothills of the coast range west of Yamhill. Both are stocked with catchable rainbow, and there are largemouth bass in the lower pond at the foot of the Flying M access road. The second pond is at the end of the airplane runway. The public is welcome to fish, but the ranch requests that all anglers advise the lodge of their intentions. For obvious safety reasons, the side of the pond bordered by the runway is posted. This pond is also used as the resort swimming hole.

FOSTER RESERVOIR A 1200 acre reservoir on the Santiam River near the town of Foster, about 3 miles east of Sweet Home, just north of Hwy. 20. It backs up the South and Middle Forks of the Santiam River, offering fishing for trout, bass, and bluegill.

Foster is stocked in April and May with catchable rainbow. Unauthorized plants of largemouth bass and bluegill have established themselves. Smallmouth bass appeared in the pool in 1988. Boat ramps are available at Gedney Creek Access, Sunnyside Park, and Calkins Park, and there are camping facilities at Sunnyside Park and Meare Bend Campground.

FRAZIER LAKE (Clackamas Co.) A 3 acre lake in the High Rock Lakes area, one mile NE of Shellrock Lake. From High Rocks Lookout (reached by the Squaw Mt. Road FS 4610 or by the Shellrock Creek Road FS 58 from the Clackamas River on the south) head west on FS 240 toward Frazier Mt. About 2 1/2 miles west there is a switchback from which the lake can be seen. It's a half mile hike from the road to the lake. There are other approaches to the lake as well. Check the Mt. Hood National Forest map.

Frazier is about 8 ft. deep, at an elevation of 4100 ft. It contains brook trout 6-11 inches. All methods seem effective, with bait best early in the season and flies in summer and fall. The road in is usually snowbound until late June.

FREEWAY PONDS Trout ponds along I-5 about 9 miles south of Albany. Take the State Police Exit and follow the frontage road south. The ponds are stocked with legal rainbow. Fishing holds up until the water warms in summer.

FROG LAKE RESERVOIR Given the redundant name to distinguish it from another Frog Lake in the Clackamas River drainage.

This Frog Lake is associated with the Three Lynx Power Station on the Oak Grove Fork of the Clackamas, and is notable for its population of rainbow and brown trout, both of which migrate to the reservoir through a pipeline from Harriet Lake. About 16 acres, it can be reached from the Three Lynx Rd., off Hwy. 224. Frog Lake Reservoir is on the right. Boats are prohibited. Parking is plentiful. This is an undeveloped recreation site, without camping or picnicking facilities, but Harriet Lake fish grow to nice size in this relatively uncompetetive environment.

GALES CREEK A steelhead and trout stream close to west Portland, major tributary of the Tualatin River, which it joins just south of Forest Grove. Gales Creek heads in the coast range near the headwaters of the Wilson River. The upper creek is followed by Hwy. 6, and the lower water by Hwy. 8 NW of Forest Grove. From Portland take Hwy. 26 west to the junction of Hwy. 6, then follow the highway to the stream.

Gales Creek is managed for winter steelhead, and the run has shown gradual improvement. The typical annual catch is over 300. It's a fairly early run, with the action starting around Thanksgiving and holding up through January. Native cutthroat trout are also available. The late trout opening on Gales Creek protects downstream steelhead migrants.

GANDER LAKE A fair size rainbow and brook trout lake at 5000 ft. elevation, 3 air miles NW of Waldo Lake. Forest roads have crept up on this lake and cut the hiking distance from 9 miles to a little over one, increasing the pressure and reducing the catch. Better have your forest map in hand when you set out for Gander, as you must navigate through a maze of roads to get to the trailhead.

From the south end of Oakridge on Hwy. 58, take the Salmon Creek road FS 24 east. (Watch for the salmon hatchery signs to locate the road). At about 11 miles, take FS 2417 east roughly 12 miles, almost to its end. At the last fork (about 3/4 mile before road's end) follow FS 256 to the left 1/2 mile to its end. Pick up a trail running due south. After 1/2 mile this trail intersects the Gander Lake Trail 3591. Take this trail to the right (west) and follow it 1/2 mile to the lake.

Gander covers 58 acres and is stocked with rainbow and/or brook trout. The average fish is around 10-11 inches, and they run to 16 inches. It's a good flyfishing lake and can be fished from shore, but you'll do better if you get out on the lake. Good natural campsites are available.

GIFFORD LAKE A small stocked rainbow lake in the Olallie area about one mile west of the Skyline Rd., just north of Olallie Lake. It's most easily reached by hiking from Lower Lake Campground, around the north shore of Lower Lake to the junction of Trail 706, then south 1/2 mile. Gifford is just east of the trail.

The lake covers about 8 acres and is quite deep. Easily fished from shore, all methods are effective. The rainbow run to 14 inches, averaging 10. A small lake of about one acre, is just north and has some good size brook trout. Gifford is set in rocky surroundings, and there are no campsites around the shore, but camping facilities are available at Lower Lake. It is not accessible until late June.

GILBERT RIVER A bass and panfish slough on Sauvie Island, about 10 miles NW of Portland. The property surrounding the slough is managed by the Dept. of Fish and Wildlife, and

angling is only restricted during duck season. Gilbert heads near the south end of the island and is crossed by Reeder Rd. near its upper end. Sauvie Island is about 10 miles NW of Portland off Hwy. 30. After crossing the Sauvie Island Bridge, turn left and drive west on Reeder Rd.

Gilbert River provides pretty good fishing for largemouth bass, crappie, bluegill, and brown bullhead.

The upper slough is followed by Oak Island Rd. several miles to Sturgeon Lake. The slough leaves the lake on the NW side and meanders another 5 miles NW, where it flows into Willamette Slough. The upper and lower ends are accessible by road and some walking.

To reach the lower slough area, continue on Reeder Rd. for another 8 miles along the Columbia until you see the waterfowl checking station. Turn left, and one mile west puts you at the main dike. In summer you can proceed over the dike and drive on dirt roads to McNary Lakes at the north end of Sturgeon Lake. In order to reach the Gilbert, leave your car on the east side of Pete's Slough, which parallels Gilbert, and cross on one of the footbridges. Gilbert is several hundred yards to the west.

The extreme lower end of the slough can be reached by going north past the checking station for 2 1/2 more miles and turning left on the dike road. This puts you at the mouth, where there is a gravel boat ramp is located.

GNAT LAKE A good 3 acre brook trout lake in the Mink Lakes Basin. Gnat is about 1 1/2 miles west of the Pacific Crest Trail near the Goose and Corner lakes trail. See Corner Lake and Cliff Lake. Gnat Lake is stocked with fingerling brook trout every few years. It provides good catches of 10 inch brook trout. You can fish from shore, but a rubber boat wouldn't hurt.

GOLD LAKE A very good trout lake for fly anglers. It's just north of the Willamette Pass summit off Hwy. 58, 23 miles SE of Oakridge. You can drive right to it. It is restricted to fly angling only, and no motorboats are allowed.

To reach Gold Lake, drive 23 miles SE from Oakridge on Hwy. 58. About 2 miles south of the Waldo Lake turn-off, FS 500 turns off to the east and leads 2 miles to the campground at the SW corner of the lake. The turn-off is signed. The road is usually open by June, but may be rough and muddy.

The catch in 1988 was running about 2 to 1 brook trout to rainbow. The lake isn't stocked, but holds up well because of the short season and restricted tackle. Trout taken here are all wild, ranging in size from 6-20 inches.

Gold is about 1/2 mile long and covers slightly over 100 acres. Although it can be fished from shore, it's pretty brushy, and a boat is strongly recommended. The shallower water at the NE end of the lake always seems to be livelier. Slow trolling a wet fly or nymph will stir up action when the hatch is off. Fly anglers will have a good time trying to match the hatch. Most standard patterns will do the trick if used at the right time. Bring plenty of tippet material.

There's a nice campground here, with boat ramp and shelter, and much waterfowl activity. Supplies are available at the Odell Lake resorts. The Marilyn Lakes, good for brook trout, are just south of Gold by trail. All tributaries of the lake are closed, and Salt Creek, the outlet stream, is closed down to the Hwy. 58 Bridge.

GOODFELLOW LAKES A series of three lakes in the closed area of the Bull Run Watershed, the water supply for the city of Portland. Gates on the roads leading to the area are locked. We mention it here to prevent anglers from walking into an illegal area.

GOOSE LAKE A 9 acre bass and panfish lake 7 miles north of Salem. Largemouth bass and white crappie are available.

GORDON CREEK This small tributary of the Sandy River provides interesting fishing for wild cutthroat and rainbow trout. The stream is about 12 miles long and joins the lower Sandy from the east. The Sandy River Rd. crosses its mouth about 7 miles south of Hwy. 30. No road follows the stream, but the upper reaches are accessible from several dirt roads that cut south off the Larch Mt. Rd.

The catch is primarily wild cutthroat in this rather steep stream. A few rainbow are also taken. The creek is not stocked. Average size is 9 inches with a few fish larger. Beaver ponds in the upper tributaries also have fair size cutthroat.

GORDON LAKES Two small cutthroat lakes south of South Santiam Hwy. 20, about 15 miles east of Cascadia. Take FS 2044 south from Hwy. 20 at House Rock Campground. It's a bit over 3 miles to FS 230, which cuts off to the SW. Follow 230 about 2 miles to road's end. The lakes are about 1/4 mile NW. The area is usually accessible in June.

These are wild cutthroat lakes, each about 7 acres and fairly deep. Both lakes have fish 6-15 inches, with an average length 10 inches. Bait angling with eggs or worms will take them early, and spinner and bait combinations should attract some large fish. Fly angling is good late in the season. The lakes are connected by stream and trail, with the further lake larger and at slightly lower elevation. It is also considerably deeper and with a brushy shore that makes casting difficult. An old growth log extending into the lake serves as a natural pier. Both lakes offer pleasant swimming.

GOVERNMENT ISLAND LAKE At the west end of state-owned Government Island, in the Columbia River just east of Portland. It supports a portion of the I-205 bridge across the river but can only be reached by boat. Upon landing on the south shore along NE Marine Dr., cross overland north. When the river is high you can take a boat up a slough on the north side of the island.

The 40 acre lake contains crappie, brown bullhead, perch and a few largemouth bass. Angling is usually fair before spring high water and again for a few months after. Bait, spinner, and plugs are all used with success, with bait most popular. The property and buildings on the island are owned by the Highway Commission. Please don't enter any buildings or litter the area, as it could be closed to use if vandalism occurs. Several other small sloughs and lakes on the island also contain fish brought in by high water.

GREEN PEAK LAKE A brook trout lake which is lightly fished and hard to find, located near the Eight Lakes Basin in the Mt. Jefferson Wilderness Area. Best approach is from Blue Lake. See Blue Lake for directions. Green Peak is a steep bushwhack one mile due west of Blue.

The lake is about 6 acres and 12 ft. deep. It puts out fair catches of 10-12 inch brook trout, but some large ones should show up due to light pressure. There are good natural campsites.

GREEN PETER RESERVOIR A flood control reservoir on the Middle Santiam River offering fishing for rainbow, kokanee, and largemouth bass. It is east of Sweet Home and Foster, north of Hwy. 20. Quartzville Creek and the Middle Santiam form a pool of over 3700 acres at high level.

A naturally reproducing population of kokanee is well established and drawing angler attention. Catches have been quite heavy, with fish usually closer to the surface than at Detroit Reservoir. Anglers jig Buzz Bombs at about 40 ft., going deeper later in the year. The Kokanee ran a little smaller than usual in 1988. The largemouth bass fishery here is growing in size and popularity. Catchable rainbow trout are stocked in April.

There is a boat ramp, but it's difficult to use at low water. When the reservoir is drawn down, car-top boats can be launched at Thistle Creek Boat Access and at Whitcomb Creek Park. There are overnight camping facilities at Whitcomb Creek.

GREEN POINT CREEK A small trout stream heading near Wahtum Lake, SW of Hood River, flowing into the West Fork Hood River near Dee. To reach Green Point, cross the West Fork downstream from Dee off Hwy. 281, and follow the signs west. The stream is about 10 miles long and is followed by a dirt road throughout most of its length. It has fair angling for wild trout.

HAGG LAKE (a.k.a. Scoggins Reservoir) A Bureau of Reclamation reservoir on lower Scoggins Creek about 7 miles SW of Forest Grove. Hagg is a popular water recreation area for communities SW of Portland. From Hwy. 47, just south of Dilley near Forest Grove, a paved roads runs about 7 miles west to the reservoir. A second road from Gaston also reaches the lake. The reservoir holds 1100 acres of water when full. It is drawn down in late fall.

There's a sel-sustaining population of cutthroat trout in Hagg which spawn in the tributaries. Illegally introduced smallmouth and largemouth bass, brown and yellow bullhead, and yellow perch are thriving and attracting growing interest among anglers. The perch, in particular, have been providing a lot of entertainment. The lake is also stocked with fingerlings and legal rainbow trout each April.

There are two developed recreational sites with picnic areas at the lake, each with a boat ramp, but no camping facilities. Check the current angling regulations for special boating information.

HALDEMAN POND A small pond on Sauvie Island built by the Dept. of Fish and Wildlife. It's on Oak Island in Sturgeon Lake. After crossing the Sauvie Island Bridge from Hwy. 30, turn left then right onto Reeder Rd. The Oak Island Rd. will be on the left.

The pond is only about 4 acres, but deep. Originally stocked with bluegill and largemouth bass, it now has rainbow trout as well. Best success is with single eggs. Rubber boats can be launched, but nothing larger. The trout average 10 inches and run to 15 inches. Try spinners with bait in early season. The pond is closed to angling during waterfowl season, but open the rest of the year.

HANKS LAKE A small scenic trout lake high in the Mt. Jefferson Wilderness south of Mt. Jefferson, west of Cathedral Rocks. Located in a cove-like meadow beside Hunts Lake. It is best reached by a short, steep trail from Pamelia. For cirections, see Hunts Lake. Hanks offers consistent fishing for rainbow trout. There are beautiful natural campsites at both lakes.

HARRIET LAKE A reservoir on the Oak Grove Fork of the Clackamas River, about 60 miles from Portland. Narrow and deep, it is 23 acres and contains 4 varieties of trout. Rainbow predominate, but some lunker brown and brook trout lurk here.

From Estacada, take Hwy. 224 SE into the Mt. Hood National Forest and continue to Ripplebrook Ranger Station. About one mile beyond the ranger station, follow FS 57 toward Timothy Lake. The road follows the south bank of the Oak Grove Fork. At about 6 miles, the road crosses the fork, and FS 4630 cuts back west a mile to Harriet Lake.

The fishing runs hot and cold at Harriet. It is stocked with legal rainbow in spring and summer and contains wild fish from the streams above. Best angling is at the upper end, where large rainbow and browns to 4 pounds are taken each spring by anglers who know the lake. Most of the catch consists of rainbow 8-15 inches. The action usually slows in summer and fall. Most fish are taken by trolling large spinners and worms. Anglers also cast small lures and spinners along the shore line.

There is a Portland General Electric campground and picnic area at the head of the lake.

HARVEY LAKE (Lane Co.) A brook trout and rainbow lake in the Taylor Burn area north of Waldo Lake. Harvey is 1 1/2 miles south of Taylor Burn Campground off Olallie Trail 3583, 1/4 mile south of Wahanna Lake and a bushwhack west of the trail. Taylor Burn campground is reached by 7 miles of rough road leading north from North Waldo Lake Campground.

The lake is 22 acres and up to 24 feet deep. It is stocked regularly with small rainbow. The fish do well and range in size from 6-18 inches, averaging 10 inches. Harvey can be fished from shore, and any method will take fish when they're hitting. There are no good campsites at the lake.

HEAD LAKE A 2 acre cutthroat trout lake off the Skyline Rd. just north of Olallie Lake. Head Lake is just west of the road, about 1/4 mile south of Lower Lake Campground.

It can be fished from shore and is fairly productive for fish ranging 7-14 inches, averaging 10 inches. Spinner and bait are usually best. Fly angling is generally good around evening later in the season. There is no camp at the lake, but camps are available all around Olallie Lake to the south. The road is rarely open before late June.

HEART LAKE (Linn Co.) A 13 acre brook trout lake south of South Santiam Hwy. 20, about 7 miles west of the Santiam Junction. About 3 miles west of Lost Prairie Campground on Hwy. 20, take FS 60, which cuts back sharply to the east. After 2 miles the road crosses Indian Creek and turns north. Stay on 60 and proceed east a mile over a mile to where the road dips to cross a stream. This stream is the outlet of Heart Lake, and the lake is upstream a steep 1/2 mile. A trail is currently under construction.

Heart Lake usually holds up well into the season. The brook trout average about 9 inches and run 6-12 inches. Heart is 13 acres and fairly deep. All methods of angling will take fish, with flies usually good in fall.

HELEN LAKE A 6 acre lake in the Taylor Burn area north of Waldo Lake, offering good rainbow trout fishing at times. A quarter mile trail leads north to the lake from the Taylor Burn Rd FS 517. The trailhead is at Taylor Butte, about one mile east of the Taylor Burn Campground.

Helen can be easily fished from shore. It's deep throughout, and lures or spinners cast and retrieved slowly bring up the fish. Flies work nicely in the evening. The trout average 8-10 inches with a few to 14 inches. The lake is usually accessible in late June.

HIDEAWAY LAKE A 12 acre lake stocked with cutthroat, in the upper Clackamas River area near the head of the South Fork of Shellrock Creek, elevation about 3800 ft. Once a dandy hike-in lake, it is now accessed by road and more heavily fished. From Estacada follow Hwy. 224 to the Timothy Lake Rd., turning north on Shellrock Creek. At about 3 miles, follow FS 5830 to the left. In 4 miles you'll be at the lake.

There's some natural reproduction of trout here, and the lake is stocked, but pressure is high. It's shallow enough to provide good fly fishing, but all methods work. The trout are 7-13 inches with most around 10. A nice campground has been provided courtesy of an Isaac Walton League chapter. Anglers can show their appreciation by helping to keep the grounds and facilities clean. The lake is usually snowbound until late May.

HIDDEN LAKE (Lane Co.) A good 11 acre wild cutthroat lake, 3 miles south of Cougar Reservoir. Not as well hidden as it was before the roads came in, it will still take your attention to find it.

From McKenzie Hwy. 126, take the South Fork of the McKenzie Rd. past Cougar Reservoir to FS 1980, 1/2 mile past French Pete Campground. Drive west on 1980 about 3 miles, crossing Buoy Creek to a right angle intersection with FS 231. Stay on 1980, which is the hard left, and you will again cross Buoy Creek, the outlet from Hidden Lake. There is no trail, and the lake is difficult to spot from the road, about 300 yards west, but you can always follow the stream. The snow usually melts by early June.

The cutthroat here are all wild and run 6-16 inches, averaging 10 inches. Bait or spinner combinations are best early in the season, and wet flies are effective. Supplies are available at Blue River or McKenzie Bridge on Hwy. 126. All tributaries are closed to angling.

HIGH LAKE (Clackamas Co.) A good place to get away from it all, on the Fish Creek Divide south of the upper Clackamas River. From Estacada drive SE on Hwy. 224 to where FS 4620 crosses the river and heads south. This cut-off is signed for Indian Henry Campground and is about 3 miles before Ripplebrook Ranger Station. Follow 4620 about 8 miles to FS 210 cutting west. Take this spur about 1/2 mile to an intersecting road. Turn north on this road and follow it to a hairpin turn about 3/4 mile distant. Ignore a fork to the left before the hairpin. Cold Spring Trail 541 heads north from the hairpin. This is a very steep trail which gains 1200 ft. in about 1 1/2 miles. Near the summit of Fish Creek Mountain, a trail drops down 1/4 mile or so to the lake. It is on the east side of the mountain.

High Lake has a lot of eastern brook trout 6-11 inches. The lake is about 3 acres and 12 feet deep. All methods can be effective. There

are some nice natural campsites here. It is accessible in early June.

HILLS CREEK (Lane Co., upper Willamette) A large tributary of the upper Middle Fork of the Willamette River, emptying into the Hills Creek Reservoir about 4 miles SE of Oakridge. About 18 miles long, the creek heads in Diamond Peak Wilderness. FS 23 follows it from the reservoir upstream.

The lower 3-4 miles are stocked with legal rainbow in summer. A few wild cutthroat show up in the catch, but rainbow predominate, running 10-12 inches. There are campgrounds at the reservoir.

HILLS CREEK RESERVOIR A multiple purpose reservoir 3 miles south of Oakridge, offering fair to good fishing for rainbow, cutthroat, crappie, and bullhead catfish. It was created by the damming of Hills Creek and the Middle Fork of the Willamette. To get there take Hwy. 58 SE from Eugene to Oakridge. About one mile beyond Oakridge, follow the signs. The reservoir is about 8 miles long and covers 2735 acres.

It is kept well stocked with rainbow and picks up cutthroat from its tributaries. Most of the rainbow are 8-12 inches, but quite a few get larger, with some to 20 inches. All methods can produce, through trolling is the most popular. Hills Creek Reservoir is heavily fished due to its easy access.

It has an excellent spring and early summer fishery for crappie, which now make up almost half the fish population. Crappie angling is concentrated in the Hills Creek arm, at the upper end of the reservoir.

The Forest Service and Corp of Engineers provide good recreational facilities here. Packard Creek Campground, on the west bank about 3 1/2 miles upstream from the dam, has a paved boat ramp, with trailer and picnic facilities. There is another ramp at the C.T. Beach Picnic area, about 2 miles from the dam on the Hills Creek arm. Supplies and accommodations are available in Oakridge.

HONEY LAKES A group of nice brook trout lakes in the Three Sisters Wilderness Area, 6 miles due west of South Sister and 6 miles south of Linton Lake. It's at least a 6 mile hike from the nearest road to this basin.

Just east of McKenzie Bridge Ranger Station on Hwy. 126, take the Foley Ridge Rd. FS 2643 about 12 miles to its end, where it meets the Substitute Point Trail 3511. About a 5 mile hike takes you past Substitute Point to the intersection of Trail 3520, which you follow south 1 1/2 miles to the basin. It's also possible to approach from the east by a side trail leading from the Pacific Crest Trail.

There are two main lakes in this group. Honey is the larger at about 12 acres. Brook trout here range 6-15 inches, averaging 10 inches. Kidney is the other good lake. It's 1/2 mile to the west of Honey, and is good for trout to 16 inches, averaging 10. Kidney Lake is about half the size of Honey. There are several smaller pothole lakes in the area, but they produce little but mosquitoes. This is a wilderness area, so there are no improved camps, but good natural sites. Users are urged to follow no-trace camping guidelines.

HORSE CREEK A large tributary of the upper McKenzie River, entering the river at the community of McKenzie Bridge on Hwy. 126. About 24 miles long, the stream heads in the Horse Lake area north of the Mink Lake Basin

and flows NW to McKenzie Bridge. FS 2638 follows the lower 10 miles of the stream to the boundary of the Three Sisters Wilderness.

Horse Creek has a population of native cutthroat. The water is clear, swift, and cold, and fishing can be slow. The average catch is 9-12 inches, with all methods of angling used. Horse Creek Campground is on the creek about a mile above McKenzie Bridge.

HORSE LAKES Several good hike-in trout lakes in the Three Sisters Wilderness Area at the head of Horse Creek, a tributary of the McKenzie River. Trails coming into the area from the west are all very long. Best access is from Elk Lake on the Cascade Lakes Hwy. 35 miles SW of Bend. Trail 3517 heads at the Elk Lake Guard Station and leads 4 miles west to Upper Horse Lake.

The upper lake covers 60 acres and contains naturally reproducing brook trout, including some of good size. It can be fished from shore, but more water can be covered from a raft. It offers good fly angling in late summer and fall.

Middle Horse Lake is about 1/2 mile west, but a little longer by the Horse Creek Trail, which is easier than beating brush. Middle Lake is about 5 acres, with small brook and cutthroat trout 6-10 inches.

Lower Horse Lake NW of Middle Lake, shallow and about 25 acres. It has a population of wild cutthroat and some brook trout. The cutthroat are small but eager, and are a lot of fun on light fly tackle. It really takes a rubber raft to fish this area decently.

There are many other smaller lakes in the area, such as Sunset, Moonlight, Herb, Park and Mile lakes. Most are stocked with brook trout.

HORSESHOE LAKE (Lane Co.) A good hike-in rainbow lake on the Pacific Crest Trail in the Mink Lake Basin west of Elk Lake. For trail directions, see Cliff Lake. Horseshoe Lake is about 1 mile south of cliff lake on the Pacific Crest Trail. The first lake you pass on the west side of the trail is Moody Lake. It has brook trout and rainbow. Horseshoe is 1/4 mile further south, on the east side of the trail.

Horseshoe is 60 acres and fairly shallow, with a population of rainbow trout 6-20 inches. All methods can produce, with flyfishing good in the evenings. There are good campsites nearby, and a shelter at Cliff Lake. Some of the many nearby fishable lakes include Mink, Mac, Cliff, Porky, Merrill.

FROGGER
Bill Wagner, Photographer

HORSESHOE LAKE (McMinnville area)
A classic oxbow lake formed when the Willamette river punched through a bend and shifted course. It offers a variety of Willamette species. The lake is about 40 miles SW of Portland between Dayton and St. Paul, 1/2 mile east of the Willamette River and 2 miles east of St. Paul by a good road. From Newberg on 99W, go south on Hwy. 219 to St. Paul. From 99E at Hubbard, turn west on Hwy. 214.

Horseshoe covers about 25 acres and is surrounded by private land. There's a small charge for parking, and boat rentals are available. It has good populations of crappie, bluegill, perch, brown bullhead and largemouth bass. A few large bass are taken on plugs each season. It's a good spot for some relaxed bait fishing during the summer.

HORSESHOE LAKE (Olallie Lake area)
A pretty, 14 acre brook and rainbow lake between Olallie and Breitenbush Lakes on FS 4220. You can drive right to this scenic beauty, and there is a campground here. A spit of land juts into the lake from the west shore giving the lake its characteristic shape. It's easy to fish from shore.

HUNTS LAKE A small scenic trout lake in the Mt. Jefferson Wilderness south of Mt. Jefferson, west of Cathedral Rocks. The Pacific Crest Trail passes above the lake 1/3 mile to the east. Best approach is from Pamelia Lake by taking the trail that follows Hunts Creek upstream (south) for 3 miles to the junction of Trail 3430. Follow this trail east past Hanks Lake and north to Hunts Lake, a total distance of about one mile.

Hunts Lake is about 6 acres and offers both rainbow and cutthroat. The cutthroat average 9 inches with a few to 12 inches. The rainbow average 8-10 inches. All methods of angling will work.

Hanks Lake, 1/4 mile south, is slightly larger and contains rainbow about the same size as those in Hunts. It's a beautiful alpine area with attractive natural campsites. Both lakes are consistent and easy to fish.

INDIAN PRAIRIE LAKE A good rainbow lake just outside the Willamette National Forest, south of the North Santiam Hwy. in the headwaters of Thomas Creek. The lake is between the head of Neal Creek and Indian Prairie Creek. The quality of roads in this area depends on logging status. No signs pinpoint the lake. Contact the State Forestry Department for the Linn County Fire Patrol District map. Indian Prairie lake is owned by a logging company, which allows access on foot only. There is a locked gate at the access road. The lake is 3/4 mile from the gate.

Indian Prairie is stocked with rainbow trout. Bait or spinner/bait combinations work well. Fishing from a motor propelled boat is prohibited.

INDIGO LAKE A high, fairly good hike-in trout lake in the SE corner of Willamette National Forest, 5 miles south of Summit Lake. This is a fine place to get away from the crowds. A good trail begins at the south end of Timpanogas Lake Campground and climbs 700 feet in 1 1/2 miles directly to the lake. See timpanogas.

Indigo is at 6000 feet in a basin directly below Sawtooth Mountain, which dominates the view when you reach the lake. The south end is a talus slope which offers plenty of backcasting room for fly anglers at the deepest end, over 30 feet just 100 feet from shore. The forest runs right up to the lake along the rest of the shore except at the extreme north end. The north half of the lake is under 10 feet deep.

Trout average 8-10 inches with some to 14 inches. Rainbow, cutthroat, and brook trout are often in residence. The lake isn't heavily fished, and almost any method will take fish when they're feeding. There are improved campsites at the south end of the lake. Timpanogas Lake has a fully developed campground. The road to Timpanogas usually opens in late June.

ISLAND LAKE (Mink Lake area) A 3 acre lake offering fair fishing for brook trout. It's located in the north Mink Lake Basin, east of Elk Lake. For trail directions, see Dumbell Lake. Island is 1/2 mile south of Dumbell on the west side of the Pacific Coast Trail.

The lake is stocked by air. Brook trout average 9 inches and run to 11 inches. Best fishing is early in the season and again in late fall. Though a little too accessible for good angling, it usually produces a few fish. There are natural campsites in the area.

ISLAND LAKES (Gold Lake area) Two small brook trout lakes which provide good fishing for a few months during spring and fall. About 14 miles SE of Oakridge on Hwy. 58, just past the railroad trestle crossing over the highway, FS 5883 cuts north. Follow 5883 about 9 miles to its end, where a short spur trail leads to the Fuji Mt. Trail 3670. A quarter mile north on 3670 brings you to an intersection with the Island Lake Trail, which you follow SE a bit over 1/2 mile to the intersection of the Waldo Lake Trail 3586. Hike 1/2 mile NE on 3586 to Island Lakes.

Lower Island is on the south side of the trail and is about 7 acres. Upper Island Lake, on the north side of the trail, is about 9 acres.

The trout average 10 inches, with a few to 13 inches and better. Some lunker brookies have been taken. All methods will work for the smaller ones, and fly angling is good in the evening. There are nice natural campsites at the lakes and a full-service campground at Gold Lake.

JEFFERSON JUNCTION BORROW PIT
A 5 acre pond north of Albany, west of Hwy. 99. It contains largemouth bass, bluegill, and brown bullhead.

JOHNSON CREEK (Multnomah Co.) An urban trout stream, popular with kids, which heads near Boring and flows 20 miles past Gresham on the south and through SE Portland, entering the Willamette River just north of Milwaukie. Roads follow the creek, and it's crossed many times by bridges.

Access is difficult because of private homes along the stream, but there is open water in the upper creek, and angling is possible downstream at the public road crossings. The city of Milwaukie owns land along the bank from the mouth upstream one mile, open to public access from Hwy. 99E.

The creek is stocked through May from Johnson Creek Park just west of McLoughlin almost to 82nd St. Unfortunately the stream's water quality drops too low to permit stocking later in the season. Some native cutthroat are also caught in the spring. An occasional coho is taken in fall.

Johnson Creek has a small (very small) run of winter steelhead, and several are caught each year. The stream is usually pretty high and muddy when the fish come up.

From summer through fall, bass and panfish are taken in the lower few miles. A few good sized bass are taken near the mouth each year. Waterfront Park Boat Ramp on the Willamette at the Johnson Creek confluence offers some access to the lower bass water. There are also two small city parks on the creek on 21 Ave. between Sherrett and Marion, and off SE Berkeley Way in Eastmoreland.

JORN LAKE A heavily fished lake in the Eight Lakes Basin of the Mt. Jefferson Wilderness. Take Trail 3422 four miles south from the western shore of Marion Lake to Jorn. This is beautiful hiking country.

The brook trout here average 10-12 inches with a few to 15 inches. All methods of angling will work at times, and the lake can be easily fished from shore. This 35 acre lake is hit hard because of its central location in the basin and pretty campsites. Flyfishing in the late afternoon and evenings usually pays off.

There are many good lakes in the basin. See Bowerman, Teto, Chiquito, Blue lakes. The area can also be reached from Duffy Lake to the south. It is usually accessible in early June depending on snow pack.

JUDE LAKE (Warm Springs Reservation)
One of a group of three hike-in brook trout lakes east of the Skyline Rd. and north of Olallie Lake. The trail begins at Olallie Meadow Campground, 3 miles north of Olallie Lake. It's a 1/2 mile hike to Jude.

Jude is about 2 acres and quite brushy. Bait or spinner and bait are effective early in the season, and fly angling works well later. The fish run 8-12 inches, averaging 10 inches. Though tribal fishing permits are required to fish most waters on the reservation, permits are not required to fish Jude, or nearby Russ and Brook lakes at this time. Overnight camping is prohibited at these lakes due to fire danger. The nearest campground is at Olallie Lake.

JUNCTION CITY POND An 8 acre pond on the west side of Hwy. 99 about 3 miles south of Junction City, 0.9 miles south of the Hwy. 36 junction. The pond contains crappie, brown bullhead, and largemouth bass. The bass were introduced in 1989.

JUNCTION LAKE A 50 acre hike-in brook trout lake in the Mink Lake Basin, west of Elk Lake. It is 1/2 mile NW of Mink Lake, and is at least 6 miles by trail from the nearest road. See mink lake.

Junction contains eastern brook trout from 8-11 inches, with a few to 15 inches. This is an on again, off again lake. Inquire at the Elk Lake Guard Station for current conditions. Good natural campsites are plentiful throughout the basin. Other good lakes in the basin include Mink, Porky, Corner, Cliff.

JUNE LAKE A shallow 11 acre lake in the headwaters of the Middle Fork Willamette, south of Summit Lake. It is no longer stocked with trout.

KIWA LAKE A good rainbow and brook trout lake in the heart of the Taylor Burn area north of Waldo Lake. To reach Taylor Burn Campground follow a rough road 7 miles north from North Waldo Lake Campground.

Kiwa is 2 miles south of Taylor Burn Campground by way of Olallie Trail 3583, on the east side of the trail. An easier drive, but slightly longer hike, begins at North Waldo Lake Campground. Hike west along the northern shore of Waldo Lake on Trail 3590, then north on Trail 3583 past the Rigdon lakes to Kiwa.

Consistent year after year for good size rainbow and brook trout, Kiwa covers about 40 acres and reaches a depth of 25 ft. The trout average 10 inches and run to 16. All methods of angling work, and you can easily fish from shore or raft. Bait angling is always good. Lures trolled or cast from shore work well. Fly-fishing with wet patterns produces mornings and evenings. There are good natural campsites here, and several other small fishable lakes nearby. Mosquitoes are fierce in spring. There are campgrounds at Taylor Burn and North Waldo Lake.

LAKE OF THE WOODS (Linn Co.) A 5 acre rainbow lake 2 miles NE of Marion Lake. Take the trail running north from the NE shore of Marion. It's about 2 miles to Lake of the Woods.

The lake is stocked with rainbow each year, and average catch is 8-10 inches, but a few get larger. All methods work well, with spinner and bait preferred early in the season. The lake is lightly fished and holds up well. It is usually accessible by mid-June.

LAMBERT SLOUGH A Willamette River slough 19 miles downstream from Salem. About 3 miles long, it contains bass and panfish. Most angelrs reach it from the boat ramp at San Salvadore Park near St. Paul.

LAYNG CREEK A native cutthroat stream, tributary of Row River SE of Cottage Grove. It joins Brice Creek at Disston, 22 miles from Cottage Grove. From Cottage Grove, take the highway leading east past Dorena Reservoir and Culp Creek. Logging roads follow Layng to its head about 15 miles up. Bait is most effective for taking fish here, with single eggs and nightcrawlers equally successful. There are no camping areas along the stream.

LENORE LAKE Shown on some maps as Leone Lake. This is a good hike-in brook trout lake tucked away in the Pansy Lake Basin, Bull of the Woods area of the upper Collawash River. A beautiful spot, Lenore offers good fishing for wild 7 inch brookies, overcrowded and hungry. It's about a 5 mile hike by trail from any road. The area is accessed by several trails, and there are other lakes worth visiting in the area. See Big Slide, Welcome, West lakes.

Hike in to Bull of the Woods Lookout (See Big Slide Lake for one approach), then take Trail 554 (Battle Creek and Welcome Lake) SE 1/2 mile to its intersection with Trail 555, which comes in from the NE. Follow 555 about 2 miles to Big Slide Mt. A short spur trail leads from the NE side of the mountain to the lake, which is due north of the mountain. Check at Ripplebrook Ranger Station for latest road and trail information.

Brook trout 7-10 inches are thick here. The lake is about 5 acres and shallow with a rocky shore, and can be easily bank fished. Flies will work best.

LEONE LAKE This is a good but difficult to find brook trout lake in the North Santiam area NE of Detroit Reservoir. Take FS 46 NE from Detroit to the Boulder Ridge Rd. FS 2231 at Breitenbush Hot Springs. Follow 2231 about 3 miles to a short spur road (S916) entering from the south 1/3 mile west of the Hill Creek crossing. Trail 3367 leads from the end of the spur west less than one mile to the lake. Bring your topo.

Leone brook trout average 9-12 inches with a few larger. An occasional brown trout is taken. Spinner and bait and still-fishing both work well, and flies are good mornings and evenings. There are good natural campsites in the vicinity.

LINTON LAKE A 75 acre trout lake off the old McKenzie Pass Hwy., easily reached, yet holds up well. It has wild brook, rainbow, and brown trout. The lake was formed when a wall of lava flowed across Linton Creek, perhaps as recently as 3000 years ago. The one mile trail to the lake leads through a classic lava field before diving into the forest.

To reach Linton drive 15 miles east from McKenzie Bridge on McKenzie Pass Hwy. 242 to Alder Springs Campground. A trail begins on the south side of the highway just before the campground and leads SE one mile to the lake. Linton covers 70 acres and reaches a depth of 82 ft.

It is one of the few lakes in the Oregon Cascades that has a reproducing population of brown trout. These fish are thriving and range 10-16 inches and larger. Small flatfish-type lures or flashing lures from one to two inches may fool them. A rubber raft is advisable for effective fishing.

In addition to the browns, there are brook trout and rainbow 10-14 inches. Bait is effective with any of these, and flies are especially good in the evening. The catch rate isn't high here, but the fish are worth the effort. There are nice natural campsites at the lake, and a campground at Alder Spring.

LITTLE FALL CREEK A fair trout stream flowing west from the Cascades, between the McKenzie and Middle Fork Willamette drainages. About 20 miles long, it flows into Big Fall Creek at the town of Fall Creek, 5 miles north of the community of Lowell at Dexter Reservoir. A good gravel road follows the stream east to its headwaters.

Cutthroat 6-10 inches make up the catch. The creek is only lightly fished and has some fair fly water. There are no camping areas along the stream.

LITTLE LUCKIAMUTE RIVER See Luckiamute River, Little.

LITTLE NORTH SANTIAM RIVER An accessible little river, fork of the North Santiam, with good winter and summer steelhead runs for its size, and fishing for native and stocked trout. There's some good fly water on the stream. It enters the North Santiam at Mehama, about 30 miles east of Salem off Hwy. 22. A paved road up Little North soon turns to gravel. This road follows the river into Willamette National Forest, where it becomes FS 2207. It runs close to the stream in many places. At Shady Cove Campground, Cedar Creek enters the stream, and Battle Ax Creek joins the flow about 6 miles higher. Road access ends at a gate about 4 miles above Shady Cove, locked due to a dispute involving commercial interests.

The Little North winter steelhead run arrives in November and provides fishing through March. The 1984-85 catch was 236. More than 500 summer steelhead were also taken from the river. Spring chinook enter in late May, but they seem to hold in water that is only accessed from private property closed to public use.

The river receives a good stocking of legal rainbow several times each spring, and angling holds up through July. All of the stocking, and most of the fishing, takes place below Elkhorn at the forest boundary. Within the forest, native cutthroat are available.

There are campgrounds at Shady Cove and Pearl Creek on the river road.

LONG LAKE (Lane Co.) Consistently good for both brook trout and cutthroat, 3 miles NW of Waldo Lake in the headwaters of the North Fork of the Willamette. From Taylor Burn Campground take Trail 3553 west about 2 miles to Fisher Creek, where you pick up Trail 3597 heading south to the Quinn Lakes. Long Lake is a bit over 1/2 mile from the trail junction, about 1/4 mile south of middle Quinn Lake.

True to its name, Long Lake is 3/4 mile long and only a few hundred yards wide, covering a total of 50 acres. It can be fished from shore. The trout range 6-16 inches, averaging 10 inches, and fishing holds up well through the season. There are good lakes north and south along the trail. The area is generally inaccessible until late June.

LONG TOM RIVER A long stream originating west of Eugene near Siuslaw Hwy. 36, and flowing south into Fern Ridge Reservoir. It offers a variety of angling. Downstream from the reservoir, it flows north past Junction City and along Hwy. 99W to join the Willamette about half-way between Corvallis and Monroe.

Above the reservoir Long Tom is primarily a trout stream. Below, trout, bass, and panfish are caught. Some nice cutthroat are taken above and below on spinner and bait, with early spring best for large trout. Largemouth bass, white crappie, and brown bullhead catfish are taken in the lower area. And there is reputed to be a sturgeon hole at the mouth.

There is a State Park picnic area on the upper stream, and many facilities are available at Fern Ridge Reservoir. There's no camping along the lower stream.

LOOKOUT POINT RESERVOIR This is one of the largest artifical impoundments in the state, stretching 14 miles along Hwy. 58 from 21 miles east of Eugene to within 6 miles of Oakridge. It is formed by a dam on the Middle Fork of the Willamette and when full, covers over 4300 acres.

The lake is heavily infested with rough fish, suckers, and squawfish but still produces good bank and troll catches of rainbow and landlocked chinook. Illegally introduced crappie are also present, as well as a small population of smallmouth bass.

There are four picnic areas along the lake and several boat ramps. An excellent ramp is located at the north end of the dam. Black Canyon Campground at the SW end has good camping facilities and a boat ramp, though the ramp is above the water line in winter.

LORIN LAKE A bushwhack brook trout lake in the Gold Lake area north of Willamette Pass. About 14 miles SE of Oakridge, and just past the railroad trestle over Hwy. 58, FS 5883 cuts north. Follow 5883 about 9 miles to its end, where a short spur trail leads to the Fuji Mt. Trail 3670. A one-quarter mile north on 3670 is

LOST LAKE, LINN CO.
Gerry Lewin, Photographer

the intersection with the Island Lake Trail, which you follow SE a bit over 1/2 mile to the intersection with Waldo Lake Trail 3586. A 1/2 mile hike NE on this brings you to the Island Lakes. Lorin Lake is 3/4 mile due east and slightly lower than the Island Lakes.

Ten acres and 17 feet deep, Lorin is at about 6000 ft. and rarely thaws before late June. It can be fished from shore, but a rubber raft would be handy. Try a Mickey Finn or bucktail caddis, and you might tie into a lunker. Natural campsites are available. Jo Ann Lake is below Lorin 1/2 mile to the SE and contains brook trout. Both Joann and Lorin can be tricky to find.

LOST CREEK (Clackamas Co) A tributary of the upper Sandy, joining it about 4 miles NE of Zigzag. From Hwy. 26, turn north at Zigzag on the Lolo Pass Rd. At McNeil Campground, about 4 1/2 miles, take FS 1825, which begins to parallel Lost Creek within 1/2 mile. About one mile upstream, at Lost Creek Campground, FS 109 branches south and continues to follow the creek another 2 miles upstream.

The creek has some nice native cutthroat and a few brook trout (probably migrants from Cast Lake in the headwaters). This is a good early season stream. It is stocked with legal rainbow during summer.

Lost Creek Campground provides fishing access for less-abled anglers. Riley and McNeil campgrounds are on the Sandy within 1/2 mile of the confluence.

LOST CREEK (Lane Co.) A native cutthroat stream about 15 miles long, joining the Middle Fork of the Willamette just below Dexter Reservoir. A paved road cuts SE off Hwy. 58 at Dexter and follows the stream for 10 miles. The stream is no longer stocked and flows primarily through private property There is no camping along the stream.

LOST LAKE (Linn Co.) A trout lake on the north side of Santiam Hwy. 20, two miles east of Santiam Junction. The lake is fed by several streams but has no visible outlet. The water disappears through lava cracks. In some years, such as 1987-88, it can get very shallow, and it always closes after Labor Day.

The lake generally covers about 50 acres at the beginning of the season. It is stocked annually with rainbow, and is currently being experimentally stocked with Atlantic salmon. It also contains wild brook trout 6-15 inches. The primary catch is rainbow 9-11 inches. Trolling and bait fishing work best early in the year, and fly-fishing is good in summer and fall. The fish tend to concentrate in two or three holes, so watch where the anglers bunch up.

Fishing from a motorboat is prohibited. The lake usually has a solid ice cover in early spring and provides good angling through the ice, but parking is scarce. There is a large developed campground on a spur road on the west shore of the lake. There is a possibility that the lake might become catch and release, so check current regulations.

LOWER LAKE A good cutthroat lake, very accessible, just west of the Skyline Rd. FS 4220 about one mile north of Olallie Lake. Take Hwy. 26 east then FS 4220 south to the area, about 100 miles from Portland.

Lower Lake is 14 acres and very deep. A lot of water can be covered from shore. Stocked cutthroat range 7-14 inches, averaging 10 inches. All methods of angling are used. Trolling with small lures or spinner and bait works well. Fly anglers will find good water along the north shore. Evening angling in late spring and fall produces nice fish. There is a good size campground at the east end of the lake. The road in is usually inaccessible until late June.

LUCKIAMUTE RIVER (a.k.a. Big Luckiamute) Pronounced *Lucky-mute*. A large trout stream heading in the coast range near Valsetz, flowing into the Willamette River at a point south of Independence. About 5 miles south of Monmouth it is crossed by Hwy. 99W, and further upstream by Hwy. 223, some 12 miles south of Dallas. A fair road parallels the river from Hoskins about 7 miles upstream, with several road crossings providing access. The river then flows about 10 miles through industrial forest land, with a private road paralleling the north bank. This road provides generally good angler access and is only occasionally closed during fire season.

Rainbow trout are stocked for 3 weeks in spring in the 7 mile stretch above Hoskins. There is a good population of native cutthroat throughout the river, with best fishing in the upper stretch. Rainbow dominate the catch 2 to 1, averaging 8 to 11 inches.

The Big Lucky is a good early season stream, with bait angling, and spinner and bait working well. Native trout are available well into summer for the persistent angler, with some good flyfishing possible after the crowd thins out. Some nice fish can be taken late in fall after the water cools.

The stream offers good steelhead habitat, but its early winter run receives little pressure (late January to early March). Large Willamette cutthroat migrating into the river to spawn in winter provide an additional fishery. A STEP program aimed at enhancing steelhead and salmon runs has been abandoned due to concern over the displacement of the river's strong wild trout population.

LUCKIAMMUTE RIVER (a.k.a. Little Luckiamute) Often a very good trout stream for the first 3 months of the season. Fished quite heavily, it produces well. The river heads in the coast range near Valsetz and joins the Big Luckiamute just south of Monmouth.

To reach it from Hwy. 99W at Salem, head east 16 miles to Dallas, then 5 miles south. Good roads follow the stream up through Falls City, but there is very limited access due to private property. A 4 mile stretch from Falls City upstream is easily reached from the highway and is stocked with rainbow in spring. Above this point, anglers can hike to the river from a logging road that follows about one mile north of the stream. This road is open, except during fire season. Native cutthroat are available in the upper waters. All fish run 6-13 inches, with rainbow dominating 3 to 1. Though it is primarily a bait or spinner stream, wet flies can be effective. Later in the season, try flies on the small cutthroat in the upper area.

Large trout from the Willamette migrate into the river below Falls City on an early spawning run in winter. The falls are a natural barrier to these fish. The Little Luckiamute has traditionally been open year around to permit anglers access to this winter fishery. Check current regulations for specifics.

MAC LAKE A rainbow and brook trout lake near the Pacific Crest Trail in the southern portion of the Mink Lake Basin, west of Elk Lake. Mac Lake is 1/2 mile SE of Mink Lake and 1 1/2 miles south of Cliff Lake and the Pacific

Crest Trail. It is one mile east of Packsaddle Mt. For a good overview of the basin, climb Packsaddle. You'll be able to pick out the various lakes from your map.

Mac Lake covers 70 acres and is stocked by air with fingerling rainbow and brook trout. Average size for both species is 10 inches, with some to 15 inches. The lake can be fished from shore using all methods, with flies effective mornings and evenings. There are good natural campsites available.

MARIE LAKE (Lane Co.) An eastern brook trout lake in Diamond Peak Wilderness NW of Summit Lake. Rainbow are also occasionally stocked. The lake is just north of what is known as the Diamond Rockpile south of Diamond Peak. Take the Pacific Crest Trail north from where it crosses the road just west of Summit Lake Campground. About 2 miles north, the PCT intersects Trail 3672. Follow this west about 1/2 mile to Marie.

Marie is easy to fish from shore. The brook trout run 6-14 inches, averaging 10 inches. In some years, larger fish have been taken. Spinner and bait usually work well any time, and late summer evening fishing with bucktails can be effective. There are good natural campsites available. The area is usually inaccessible until late June.

MARILYN LAKES Two good hike-in brook trout lakes near Gold Lake in the Willamette Pass area. These lakes are tailor-made for fly-fishing. They are about one mile north of Hwy. 58, 23 miles SE of Oakridge. Take the Gold Lake Rd. 2 miles to Gold Lake Campground, and follow the Marilyn Lakes Trail an easy 10 minute walk south.

The lakes are each about 25 acres. They drain into Salt Creek. Brook trout here run 6-16 inches, averaging 10 inches. They are lightly fished, as most fly anglers in the area are trying for Gold Lake's feisty rainbow. Late fall fly anglers can take some real lunkers here. There are no campsites near the lakes.

MARION CREEK Also known as the Marion Fork of the North Santiam, a cold, fast trout stream. Lightly fished, it flows from Marion Lake in Mt. Jefferson Wilderness. A good road, FS 2255, leaves Santiam Pass Hwy. 22 at the Marion Forks Ranger Station (about 15 miles south of Detroit at Detroit Reservoir) and follows the stream to Marion Falls, about 2 miles downstream from Marion Lake. Between the falls and the lake the stream is closed to angling.

Cold and clear, Marion is difficult to fish. Anglers might try single eggs or other bait, with flyfishing effective late in the season. The stream is seldom productive early in the year. If you are in the area pay a visit to the salmon hatchery on the south side of the stream near Hwy. 22. There's a good forest campground at the mouth.

MARION LAKE A large hike-in lake with large trout, both stocked and wild. It is at the head of Marion Creek within Mt. Jefferson Wilderness. Take Marion Forks Rd. FS 2255 SE from Hwy. 22 at Marion Forks Ranger Station, about 16 miles from Detroit. At the end of the road, follow Trail 3436 about 2 miles to the lake.

Marion is about 350 acres and holds some nice fish. The catch rate is not good, but size makes up for it. Brook trout and rainbow are equally plentiful, averaging 11-14 inches, with a good number of 3-4 pounders taken each sea-

son. A rubber boat is useful here, although the lake can be fished from shore. Bait angling and lures will take fish throughout the season. Cutthroat are also present and will put up a good fight on light gear. Other smaller lakes nearby offer good angling. See Ann Lake.

MARYS RIVER A fair trout stream flowing into the Willamette River at Corvallis. It heads on Mary's peak, highest point in the Coast Range, and flows over 30 miles to the Willamette. Hwy. 20 follows the river from Corvallis to Blodgett, where a good forest road heads north, accessing the upper forks. Private property restricts access in the lower river.

Mary's River has a good population of native cutthroat, typically from 7-12 inches. It is not stocked. Most angling takes place from Wren upstream. Early season fishing is best with bait, and small lures and spinners are effective as the water clears. Flyfishing with wet flies is good in late spring through fall in the upper area.

Mary's River has small salmon and winter steelhead runs, with angling for them permitted below the bridge at Blodgett. Big Willamette cutthroat (to 2 pounds plus) migrate into the stream to spawn in winter, providing an additional fishery. There's no camping along the stream.

McDOWELL CREEK A small native cutthroat stream entering the South Santiam River about 9 miles SE of Lebanon. Take Hwy. 20 south from Lebanon to McDowell Creek Rd., about 3 miles south of Hamilton Creek. A road follows the stream closely for about 5 miles.

Native cutthroat 6-12 inches make up most of the catch. Bait fishing is best in spring, with single eggs popular. There is no camping along the stream.

McFARLAND LAKE A 39 acre trout lake north of Irish Mt. about one mile west of the Pacific Crest Trail. You'll work to get here, but the hike sure does thin out the crowd. Take Trail 3307 west from FS 1958, a 4-5 mile hike.

Stocked with brook trout, McFarland is a good, deep lake for lure fishing, and all methods of angling will take trout when they're hitting. Some lunkers are taken each season. The catch runs 6-16 inches, averaging 13 inches. There are good natural campsites available. Several other small fishable lakes are nearby. It is usually inaccessible until late June.

McKAY CREEK (Washington Co.) A good early season trout stream only 20 miles west of Portland, crossed by Hwy. 26. The creek flows into the Tualatin River just south of Hillsboro, heading in the West Hills, north of North Plains near the Multnomah County line. From North Plains, the stream is followed north by gravel roads for about 9 miles. Most anglers fish the stretch north of the highway.

McKay is primarily a native cutthroat stream. Angling is good for a few weeks after opening, but slows up early. Bait is the most popular method. Some warm water species are taken near the mouth. Watch for private property along the stream.

McKENZIE RIVER One of the finest trout streams in Oregon, namesake of the McKenzie River drift boat, the boat that draws so little water it can float on dew, or over clawing rapids. The McKenzie River features plump and spunky *redside* rainbow trout, native brook trout, a good run of summer steelhead, and spring chinook. It flows past giant boulders and

through forested canyon at a grade that delights rafters, and with an iridescence that inspires poetry. It has, by the way, only one major (Class 4) rapids in its boatable stretch, and is a good river for less experienced riverboat anglers.

The McKenzie is one of those rivers that weaves its magic around an angler. In the last glimmer of light, an unexpected steelhead takes the fly. Out of mere inches of water, a big cutthroat suddenly materializes. Into the silence of an emerald pool, a huge spring chinook leaps and slams. Then there's the quality of sunset on shimmering water, the honey scent of cottonwood, a sudden storm of mayflies on a summer evening.

The McKenzie is 89 miles long and is followed for most of its length by Hwy. 126. The river heads in Clear Lake near the Santiam Pass, then flows south 14 miles to Belknap Springs, where it swings west. This upper water is very cold and swift, and the fishing is slow. By Blue River, 18 miles further downstream, the valley begins to open up and the slope is moderated. From here downstream to its junction with the Willamette River at the north end of Eugene, water conditions for trout fishing are excellent. Reaching the best water can be a chore without a boat, however, as the river runs through primarily private land in the lower 50 river miles. Most bank access is at the boat ramps.

There are almost 3 dozen public boat ramps on the McKenzie, with the lowest at Armitage State Park north of Eugene. To reach, it drive north from the city on Coburg Rd., or take I-5 to the first exit after the Belt Line Hwy., just south of the McKenzie. Most of the park stretches west of I-5. Anglers can also cross the McKenzie on Coburg Rd. and fish the north bank about 200 yds. upstream and down from the I-5 Bridge. Park on McKenzie View Drive and make your way down to the river, keeping an eye out for stinging nettles. Despite its proximity to one of Oregon's largest cities, not to mention the freeway, this is a rural spot, and an angler streamside is caught up in the world of the river. Be aware that this stretch of water is within the the catch and release portion of the McKenzie, with tackle restricted to barbless hooks and lures. These restrictions are in effect from the river mouth up to Hayden Bridge in Springfield.

There is also bank access at Deadmond Ferry Slide on the south bank at the end of Deadmond Ferry Rd. To get there take the Belt Line Hwy. east to Game Farm Rd. Turn left then right onto Deadmond. Harvest Lane is a potential boat ramp site in Springfield. Follow 6th St. north to Harlow Rd., turn right on Harlow, then left on 14th St. to Harvest Lane. Hayden Bridge in Springfield, Hendricks Bridge State Wayside north of Cedar Flat on Hwy. 126, Emmerich Co. Park just east of Walterville (bank access only, no boat ramp), and Greenwood Drive Ramp east of Leaburg all offer access to good water, as does Deerhorn Co. Park on the south bank. To reach Deerhorn, turn right onto Deerhorn Rd. before crossing Hendricks Bridge on Hwy. 126. Helfrich Landing on the north bank right below Marten Rapids offers interesting trout fishing, as does Ben and Kay Dorris State Park right above the rapids. Silver Creek, Finn Rock, and Forest Glen Boat Ramps (all off Hwy. 126) are good trout bank fisheries. Above Forest Glen (at Blue River) the river picks up speed, and bank fishing is more difficult.

The highest boat ramp on the river is at Olallie Campground, about 12 miles east of McKenzie Bridge, but the most popular fishing

NICE FISH!
Brian O'Keefe, Photographer

drifts are between Blue River and Leaburg Lake, a 17 mile stretch within which anglers can select a combination of put-ins and take-outs suitable to their time schedules.

In the following list of McKenzie River boat ramps, r.m. designates *river mile:* Armitage State Park r.m. 4, Deadmond's Ferry r.m. 6.4, Hayden Bridge r.m. 11.4, the Old EWEB Water Intake Slide r.m. 13.6, Bellinger Ramp r.m. 15.6, Hendricks State Park r.m. 20.6, Emmerich Landing Slide r.m. 23.8, Deerhorn Rd. Slide r.m. 26.4, Dot's Ramp r.m. 28.1 (private with public access), Deerhorn Bridge r.m. 28.8, Leaburg Town Landing r.m. 30.6, Greenwood Dr. Ramp r.m. 33.0, Leaburg Dam Slide r.m. 35.5, Leaburg Lake r.m. 36, Helfrich Landing r.m. 40.6, Dorris State Park Ramp r.m. 41.6, Rennie Landing r.m. 44.6, Silver Cr. Landing r.m. 46.4, Rosboro Bridge Slide r.m. 47.9 (private with public access), Sheppard Slide r.m. 49.2, McMullin Slide r.m. 49.8, Finn Rock Landing r.m. 50.8, Forest Glen Ramp r.m. 55.5, Hamlin Landing r.m. 56.1, Bruckhart Bridge Slide r.m. 58.9, Belknap Bridge Slide r.m. 61.4 (private with public access), McKenzie Bridge Campground Slide r.m. 64.6, McKenzie River Trail Slide r.m. 66.2, Paradise Campground Slide r.m. 69.1, Frissell Bridge Slide r.m. 72.9, Whitewater Slide r.m. 74.8, and Olallie Campground Slide r.m. 77.1.

The river below Leaburg Dam has a lower gradient that offers easy drifting, but the upper river is more challenging and includes one Class 4 rapids (Marten Rapids) between Dorris State Park and Helfrich Landing. All other runs on the McKenzie are rated class 1 or 2. This is good water for beginning drift boat operators, but it is always beneficial to follow a lead boat familiar with a river's peculiarities first time through. Licensed river guides are available through the Oregon Guides and Packers Association, and through Eugene and Springfield fly and tackle shops, many of which also offer informal streamside introductions to various fisheries on the river, and are glad to share practical tips and information about current river and fishing conditions.

Trout are plentiful throughout the season. The river is heavily stocked with hatchery rainbow from early spring through summer between Hayden Bridge and Paradise Campground. Over 126,000 are released annually at intervals. Above and below these points, anglers have a better chance of hooking the river's true prize, the native McKenzie rainbow, known as the *redside.*

In an effort to preserve these native beauties, regulations require that all rainbow over 14 inches must be released. These are the brood fish that keep the race going. Hatchery rainbow are marked with a ventral fin clip so that anglers can recognize and release even the smaller wild trout if they choose. Redsides are also distinguished by their bright orange spots.

Hatchery stocked trout rarely last through the season, with those not caught generally dying within a few months from the rigors of life on a wild stream. Most fish over 10 inches are natives. The average catch runs 7-11 inches, with many larger fish (2-3 pounders) in the river. Cutthroat and whitefish are also present throughout the system.

McKenzie River spring chinook enter the river in May, with peak catches in middle or late June. Anglers fish from boat and bank using bait and lures. Most chinook angling takes place in the 2 mile stretch from Leaburg Dam down to Greenwood Dr. Boat Ramp. Chinook anglers use the bank access at Greenwood and both banks below the dam. Watch for the deadline at the dam. The Hayden Bridge vicinity is popular with boat anglers, who use drift fishing and back bouncing techniques. Be aware of a deadline here, too, associated with a salmon aquaculture facility. About 500 spring chinook are caught each year, primarily in the lower river.

A hatchery program has built up a good summer steelhead run on the McKenzie, though the catch has fluctuated considerably. In most years over 1000 steelhead are taken, and 1986-87 saw a landmark catch of more that 3500. Steelhead are in the river May through October, with success considerably better from July on. They are fished primarily from Leaburg downstream.

The McKenzie has many special angling regulations related to each of its fisheries. Be sure to check the current synopsis for seasons, deadlines, limits, and special restrictions.

Developed camping and picnic sites are limited along the river below the National Forest. Armitage State Park north of Eugene offers camping, as does Ben and Kay Doris State Park just east of Vida. Above Blue River the McKenzie enters Willamette National Forest, where there are streamside campgrounds about every 5 miles. Delta, McKenzie Bridge, and Paradise are right on the McKenzie. Limberlost is about 2 miles up the Lost Creek Rd. just before Belknap Springs. Additional camps are available in the headwaters area from Trail Bridge to Clear Lake.

McKENZIE RIVER, SOUTH FORK A popular trout stream flowing into the upper McKenzie between Blue River and McKenzie Bridge. It joins the mainstem McKenzie about 3 miles upstream from the community of Blue River. The river is dammed to create Cougar Reservoir about 3 miles above the confluence. Cougar covers about 5 miles of stream channel. A good forest road, FS 19, follows the river upstream for the next 12 miles. Here the river splits into two forks, Elk Creek and Roaring River.

Elk Creek can be followed upstream 3 miles on FS 1964 to Trailhead 3510, which leads into the Mink Lake Basin. FS 19 follows Roaring River Creek then McBee Creek over a divide to the SW, then drops into the headwaters of the North Fork of the Willamette.

The South Fork is stocked with legal rainbow throughout spring and summer, and some native redside, cutthroat, and bull trout (Dolly Varden) are also available. The catch rate is high for such a popular stream, but the fish don't run large. Average size is 8-11 inches. Bait fishing will usually produce, and spinner and bait are effective when the water is clear. There's lots of good fly water, especially above the reservoir.

There are six campgrounds on the upper stream. Tributaries enter the fork at several of these camps, providing good fishing and additional angling opportunities along the creeks, accessed only by trail. Native cutthroat are the main fare in these creeks, with light leaders and stealth required. French Pete Creek, which enters from the east at French Pete Campground, offers many miles of hiking through superb old growth timber. The water in the creek is cold, swift, and clear—rough angling. Augusta Creek, which drains a considerable area, enters the river from the south at Dutch Oven Campground.

In the South Fork and its tributaries, rainbow over 14 inches must be released. They may be kept if caught in the reservoir.

When fishing the South Fork, a real treat for sore muscles or sagging spirits is Cougar Hot Springs. These are located about a 1/4 mile west of the reservoir near Rider Creek. There is a parking area on the reservoir side, and a short trail follows Rider to the hot springs. Clothing is optional.

McNARY LAKES Two warm water lakes at the north end of Sauvie Island, to which one can drive when the roads dry out. The lakes are about 2 miles north of Sturgeon Lake and are connected to it by Pete's Slough. Take Hwy. 30 NW from Portland 10 miles, then cross to Sauvie Island by the bridge. Follow Reeder Road (which crosses the island to the Columbia side) for about 11 miles to the waterfowl area checking station. Turn left onto a gravel road, and drive about one mile to a parking area. After July, and before the May high water, you can drive over the dike then follow dirt roads one mile north to the lakes. If the gate is locked you'll have to walk, as it's kept closed for your protection. The area is flooded each spring for several months.

There's lots of room to fish, either from bank or small boat. Brown bullhead are taken on worms is good. Bass anglers do well for a month or so once the high water starts dropping, but will do better in moving water after that. Plugs, Flatfish, and spinning lures all work at times. Crappie take small flashing lures, pork rind, and even maribou flies if retrieved very slowly.

For other waters close by, see Pete's Slough, Gilbert River, Haldeman Pond, Sturgeon Lake. No overnight camping is allowed. Fishing on Sauvie Island is restricted during waterfowl season. Check current regulations.

McNULTY CREEK A small trout stream, about 7 miles long, located in Columbia County south of St. Helens. It is crossed by Hwy. 30 about 25 miles NW of Portland. It is accessible primarily at road crossings.

The creek provides fair early season trout fishing, mainly for native cutthroat, but a few rainbow show up. It is not stocked, and the fish are mostly under 10 inches. Bait works best, or spinner and bait in the larger holes. The creek gets too low for angling after the first month or two. At the mouth of the river there is fair fishing for bass, perch, and brown bullhead.

MELAKWA LAKE A 35 acre brook trout lake west of the McKenzie Pass Hwy. 242, SW of Scott Lake. This lake is regulated for kid fishing (under 18 only, second childhood doesn't count). A scout camp is located here, and the boys fish it hard. The brook trout run 6-12 inches, averaging 9 inches.

MELIS LAKE A small brook trout lake midway between the Eight Lakes Basin and Marion Lake in Mt. Jefferson Wilderness. It is just

south of Jenny Lake, about 2 miles south of Marion, and the same distance north of Jorn Lake on the Jorn Lake Trail. See Jorn Lake for trail directions.

Not a very rich lake, its brook trout run small, 6-11 inches, averaging 9. Only 5 acres, the lake doesn't hold up long. It does have some fair natural campsites.

MERCER RESERVOIR On Rickreall Creek, 10 miles west of Dallas on Allendale Rd. It serves as the water supply for the city of Dallas but has been open to public angling. It was closed in 1987 following the Rock House Creek fire, and is scheduled for reopening in fall, 1990.

This 60 acre reservoir on Boise Cascade land is fished primarily for native cutthroat, which run to 12 inches. Boats are allowed, but no motors. There's lots of good bank angling

available from the road along the west shore. Largemouth bass have been illegally introduced and are thriving.

MERRILL LAKE A small brook trout lake in the south end of the Mink Lake Basin. Merrill is just south of the Pacific Coast Trail, 1/4 mile west of Horseshoe Lake and just east of Mac Lake. See Cliff Lake for trail directions.

Though only 7 acres, Merrill is consistent for brook trout 9-10 inches with some to 15, though not many. All methods will take fish when they're hitting. The area is usually accessible in late June.

MICKEY LAKE A lightly fished hike-in rainbow and brook trout lake in the Taylor Burn area, managed for large trout. Angling is restricted to barbless lures and flies only. To reach it, head south from Taylor Burn on Olal-

WILLAMETTE

lie Trail 3583, or north from Waldo Lake on the same trail. Mickey is 1/4 mile NE of Lower Rigdon. See Rigdon Lakes for trail directions. Mickey Lake is just a short way NW of Brittany, another good lake.

About 5 acres and deep, over 40 ft. in places, it has turned out some lunker rainbow. The trout don't spawn here, so it is stocked every few years. A good rocky shoal in the center of the lake is a consistent producer on flies. There are no good campsites here.

MIDNIGHT LAKE A good rainbow trout lake west of Odell Lake and south of Hwy. 58, just off the Pacific Crest Trail. Pick up the PCT from a spur road at the NW end of Odell, and hike about one mile SW to the lake.

Midnight covers about 12 acres and is quite deep. It is well stocked with rainbow 6-13 inches. It gets fairly heavy use but holds up well, best in early season and again in the fall. Camping and supplies are available at Odell Lake.

MILDRED LAKE A 3 acre brook trout lake in the headwaters of the Breitenbush River NW of Mt. Jefferson in the Mt. Jefferson Wilderness. Mildred is 1 1/2 miles NE of the Firecamp Lakes See Firecamp Lakes for directions. No trail leads to the lake, which is in a basin separated by a ridge from the Firecamps. Hike east-northeast from Crown Lake in the Firecamps, crossing the ridge at the saddle.

Mildred reportedly contains brook trout to 12 inches, with fall the best season. There are several other lakes nearby, including Slideout (just south) Swindle, and Bear. It's a good Huckleberry area and has natural campsites. Use no-trace camping methods.

MILE LAKE A 7 acre rainbow lake in the Horse Lake group NW of Elk Lake in the Three Sisters Wilderness. It is between Horse Mt. and Horse Lake Guard Station. A trail due west from Horse Lake reaches Mile in one mile, then continues on to Park Lake.

The rainbow here average 9-10 inches, with a 6-13 inch range. This lake has its ups and downs, hot one year and cold the next, but there are other lakes in the area to try if you catch this one on the off year.

MILK CREEK A fair trout stream for early season angling, flowing into the Molalla River SE of Canby. It is crossed by Hwy. 213 at Mulino, about 11 miles south of Oregon City. From Mulino a county road follows the creek east to Hwy. 211, which parallels the stream to near its headwaters in the Colton area. It is only accessible at the road crossings due to private ownership throughout. Milk Creek has a fair population of native cutthroat. Bait is most often used, but it's a good spinner stream. The best section to fish is west and east of Colton.

MILL CREEK (Marion Co.) A long stream with opportunities for viewing (but not fishing) a sizeable fall chinook run in the heart of Salem. The creek flows from the east near Stayton, and joins the Willamette River at the capital. Pringle Park, behind Salem Hospital, is a popular viewing area during the spawning migration in September and October.

The creek is closely followed by Hwy. 22 and the paved road from Aumsville to Salem. Private land throughout makes angling difficult, though it can be fished at road crossings. Mill Creek supports a small native trout population, and is lightly stocked with rainbow early in the season at Cascade Park. Most angling is with

bait or spinner and bait. The lower end of the creek below Turner offers some fishing for bluegill and crappie. The entire creek is closed during the chinook spawning season.

MILL CREEK (Yamhill Co.) A good rainbow and cutthroat stream, with winter steelhead and big Willamette cutthroat available. A tributary of the South Yamhill River, it joins the Yamhill from the south about half-way between Willamina and Sheridan. Hwy. 18 crosses the creek a short way above the mouth, and Hwy. 22 crosses it about 5 miles above that. Harmony Rd. follows the lower end, and Mill Creek Rd. parallels the creek south of Hwy. 22. About 20 miles long, its lower 10 miles pass through agricultural lands with limited access.

The upper end is on Willamette Industries property, which is open to the public. Here the creek runs through a wooded canyon, where most of the native cutthroat are taken. Legal rainbow are stocked in this upper area as well. Both rainbow and cutthroat run 9-12 inches. Fishing usually tapers off by late June. The creek supports a small winter steelhead run and is open for winter angling. An early run, the steelhead are usually in the river from late January to early March, seldom higher than one mile above Hwy. 22 due to a natural barrier on the stream. Big Willamette cutthroat spawners are also available in the creek during the winter season.

Willamette Industries has provided several day use facilities and a campground on the upper creek.

MILTON CREEK A fair size stream, entering the Columbia near the town of St. Helens, about 30 miles NW of Portland. It provides good early season trout angling and supports a small run of winter steelhead.

Eighteen miles long, Milton heads in the hills west of St. Helens and meanders east, flowing through the west end of town and into Scappoose Bay near its mouth. County roads access the upper waters. There's lots of private property along the stream near St. Helens, but open water above. When in doubt as to whether land is privately owned, be sure to ask. Some of the upstream farmers will give permission to trespass.

Milton is no longer stocked, but it has native cutthroat. Bait angling is the most commonly used method, but you can find good fly riffles in the upper area. Trout angling usually falls off in late June, and the water gets fairly low. The creek is open for winter steelheading, but the run is spread throughout the winter, and the catch is small. There is fair bass angling in the late spring near the mouth, though it seems to take a lot of casting to connect. There is no camping along the stream.

MINK LAKE The largest lake in the Mink Lake Basin, 180 acres at 6000 ft. elevation. Mink Lake is at the head of the South Fork of the McKenzie River.

Trails enter the area from all directions. To approach from the west, drive into the headwaters of the South Fork on FS 19. At Frissel Crossing Campground, head east on FS 1964 about 2 1/2 miles to a short northern spur which accesses Trail 3510. This trail leads about 7 miles to Mink Lake. Two popular eastern approaches are from Elk Lake on the Pacific Crest Trail, about 11 miles, or on the Six Lakes Trail by way of Blow Lake, about 8 miles. Trails surround the lake, and there are other good lakes in every direction.

Mink Lake is stocked with rainbow, cut-

throat, and brook trout, and it usually produces fair catches. The fish average about 10 inches, running 6-20 inches. A rubber boat would be handy, as the lake is large, and the fish are sometimes hard to find. All methods of angling are used. There are good natural campsites all around the lake. Mosquitoes are very fierce in spring.

MIRROR LAKE (Clackamas Co.) A popular lake reached by a short hike from Mt. Hood Hwy. 26, offering good brook trout angling despite heavy pressure. Most visitors are sightseers and hikers. The lake is about 53 miles from Portland, just west of Government Camp. Trail 664, the Tom, Dick, and Harry Mountain Trail, leads just over a mile to the lake. The trailhead is on the south side of Hwy. 26 at Yocum Falls, about one mile west of Multipor Ski area. It's fairly steep, gaining 650 ft. between the highway and lake.

Mirror Lake is stocked with rainbow and brook trout. Most of the catch runs 6-9 inches. Some larger fish remain each year, and good anglers can do well, especially on flies. Best fishing is early in June and again in fall, when the crowd thins out. The lake is 8 acres, with some improved campsites. A boat is not necessary.

MIRROR POND (Multnomah Co.) One of the I-84 ponds adjacent to the Columbia River, featuring bass and panfish. It is about 8 miles east of Troutdale, south of I-84 across from Rooster Rock State Park. The pond is directly under Crown Point State Park.

Mirror Pond is fed by several small streams and receives water from the Columbia during the freshet in May and June. It is almost one mile long and a 1/4 mile wide in spots. Largemouth bass 3-4 pounds have been taken on plugs or spinning lures. Weedless lures fished in the shallows in June are effective. There's a large population of crappie, and brown bullhead, perch, and bluegill are available. Bullhead fishing is best when the water drops.

There is limited parking at the pond off a dirt access road right before Rooster Rock. Camping is available at the state park.

MISSION CREEK RESERVOIR A 130 acre reservoir with good populations of bass and panfish north of St. Paul, 5 miles south of Newburg. Public access is limited to the south end of the reservoir, which can be reached by Hwy. 219 from Newbrrg. There is limited parking on the road shoulder, and car-top boats can be launched.

Most anglers fish from the highway shoulder. Good catches of bluegill to 8 inches are made in early spring, though weeds become a problem later in the season. After June you'll need a boat to get to open water. There's good bass water here if you can get to it.

MISSION LAKE A 19 acre oxbow lake along the Willamette River in Willamette Mission County Park, one mile south of Wheatland, about 8 miles north of Salem. Take the Brooks Exit off I-5 and drive towards Wheatland, or take the ferry from Wheatland to the east bank of the Willamette.

The lake has a good population of bass and panfish, including largemouth bass, white crappie, brown bullhead, and bluegill. There is a boat ramp in the park and a speed limit on the lake. A trail in the park leads to Goose Lake, a 9 acre oxbow offering the same species as Mission Lake.

MOHAWK RIVER A tributary of the lower McKenzie River, joining the main stream at Springfield. It provides fair fishing for native cutthroat early in the season.

The river is followed NE from Springfield by a paved road to Marcola, which is about half-way up the stream. From there, gravel roads access the upper river. Mill Creek, a fair tributary, comes in from the east, just north of Marcola. Most angling takes place in this area. The lower stream has much private land and almost no access. It is best fished early in the season, as the river gets pretty low by July. As on other McKenzie tributaries, anglers must release rainbow over 14 inches. There is no camping along the stream.

MOLALLA RIVER A 45 mile tributary of the middle Willamette, home river to many Portland area steelheaders. When the Molalla's good, it's very good. The river heads in the Cascades of the southern Mt. Hood National Forest and flows into the Willamette just up from Molalla State Park near Canby.

The lower stream is followed and crossed by paved backroads in the vicinities of Canby, Liberal, Union Mills, and Molalla. Above Molalla, a paved road closely parallels the river south and east. This road is through BLM property, and bank access is public.

The Molalla has a late steelhead run. Surprised trout anglers occasionally pick them up after trout season opens, some still bright. Just remember to turn loose the dark ones, which are better served as spawners than as table fare. The steelhead begin showing in December and generally run through April. The annual catch is around 1000. The summer steelhead catch has been improving, with 645 taken in 1986.

Drift boat fishing for winter steelhead is popular, with the best run from Molalla down to Canby. Keep your eyes open for sweepers (partially submerged fallen trees). From Canby downstream the river can be handled by novice boaters. The stretch from Liberal to the state park provides an easy day's drift, with a few steelhead holes and some classic slicks (watch for the Beaverhole) before the Pudding River muddies the water. If you take out at the state park, take time to enjoy the long easy trail along the river and the extensive heron rookery in the trees just back from water's edge. The take-out here is steep and often silted, so four-wheel drive with plenty of horse power is advisable.

Though there are few native trout in the main river, legal rainbow are stocked from the Liberal area 4 miles north of Molalla, to Horse Creek, about 20 stream miles south of the town. Native cutthroat are available in several tributaries. The lower 10 miles, west of Hwy. 213, are generally less productive than the upper waters, though nice fish are occasionally taken on spinner or bait. There's a lot of private land in this area, but paved and gravel roads access the stream in many places. Fishing holds up well into summer, and all methods of angling can be used with success.

Spring chinook from the early Willamette run show up from late January through March, and there are some fall run Tule stock chinook in the river, too. However, most Molalla chinook are taken in the Willamette just before they turn up their home stream.

Boats can be launched at Feyrer Park east of Molalla (gravel bar), the Hwy. 211 Bridge (pole slide), Hwy. 213 Bridge at Liberal (gravel bar), Goods Bridge just south of Canby (gravel bar), City Park just off 99E at the west end of Canby (gravel ramp), Knight's Bridge at the NW edge of Canby just outside the city limits (gravel ramp), and Molalla State Park on the Willamette about 1/2 mile below the Molalla mouth (paved ramp).

There are no campgrounds on the river.

MOODY LAKE A 5 acre brook and rainbow lake just west of the Pacific Coast Trail in the Mink Lake Basin. See Cliff Lake for directions. Moody is one mile south of Cliff Lake. The trout average 8-9 inches, but some go to 12. There are fish here, but they're hard to catch. They will take flies late in the day, with blue uprights and mosquitoes working well.

MOOLACK LAKE A good hike-in brook trout lake 2 miles SE of Moolack Mt. and west of the Taylor Burn area. *Moolack* was a chinook jargon word for elk. Shortest way in to this lake is from Taylor Burn Campground, which is best approached by the road from North Waldo Lake Campground. Hike west on the Blair Lake Trail 3553 about 2 miles, then take the Moolack Trail north 1/2 mile to the lake. This last trail is poorly marked, so keep a sharp eye. It's also possible to hike in from the west, starting on Trail 3594 just east of Etta Prairie on FS 2417 in the headwaters of Furnish Creek, a tributary of Salmon Creek. Bring your map.

About 14 acres, Moolack puts out some nice brook trout averaging 11-12 inches. All methods of fishing produce, and fly angling can be excellent in the fall. There are a few good natural campsites. The area is usually accessible by late June.

MOONLIGHT LAKE A very productive small lake with lots of brook trout, just under 2 miles NW of Horse Lake. It is lightly fished due to its location. The best route is by way of Bend and the Cascade Lakes Hwy. to Elk Lake. Take the Horse Lakes Trail 3517 west to Upper Horse Lake. From there, head NW on trail 3514, the Horse Cr. Trail, and continued 2 miles. Keep watch to the left, and you'll spot the lake.

Moonlight Lake covers 8 acres and reaches a maximum depth of 14 feet. There's a lot of brush along the edges, so a rubber boat or float tube will really help. The brook trout average 8-10 inches, but a few to 16 inches are caught. Any method usually works here. There are no good campsites here.

MOSBY CREEK A lightly-fished trout stream, over 20 miles long, located in southern Lane County. It enters Row River just below Dorena Reservoir, east of Cottage Grove. The headwaters are in the hills just west of the NW corner of the Umpqua National Forest.

From Hwy. 99 at Cottage Grove, turn east towards Dorena Reservoir, then south. A gravel road follows the stream closely for about 15 miles, then a dirt road takes over. A private timber company gate prevents vehicle access to several miles of the upper river, but anglers can continue on foot.

The creek has a fair population of native redband cutthroat with a fair catch rate, though there's a lot of private land even below the gate. There is no camping along the stream.

MOTHER LODE LAKES In the Pansy Basin area of the Collawash River headwaters, hard to reach but worth the effort for fine scenery and good fishing. The lakes are about half-way between Pansy Lake and the Twin Lakes. See Pansy Lake for trail directions. The Mother Lodes are west of the trail, on the east side of Mother Lode Mountain. Trail No. 558 will get you closest.

These are a series of 3 small lakes, each about an acre or two at an elevation of about 4000 ft. Currently only Ercrama Lake, the largest, is stocked. The state is using cutthroat now. It can easily be fished from shore, and bait or lures will take fish. There are no camp improvements.

MT. HOOD COMMUNITY COLLEGE PONDS Trout ponds on the Stark St. campus in Gresham, east of Portland. The ponds are stocked with legal rainbow in early season. Fishing falls off when the water warms in summer.

MOWICH LAKE A large and very good brook trout lake in the Eight Lakes Basin of Mt. Jefferson Wilderness. *Mowich* is the chinook word for deer. The largest lake in the basin, it covers 54 acres and reaches a depth of 45 ft. It is 1/2 mile north of Duffy Lake by Trail 3422, and can be reached from Marion Lake by good trail.

Its brook trout run 8-16 inches, averaging 12 inches. Bait fishing with worms, or eggs and lures will take fish almost any time, and flyfishing is effective early and late in the day. The lake is usually accessible by June.

MUDDY CREEK (Benton Co.) This stream lives up to its name during the spring. It is south of Corvallis, west of 99W, with headwaters in the hills west of Monroe. It flows over 20 miles north to join Mary's River at Corvallis. Many roads follow and cross the creek.

Muddy is a slow moving creek with a mud bottom. The stream is not stocked, but offers angling for bass, crappie, and a good population of native cutthroat averaging 8-11 inches. Single eggs or worms are most effective, with spinners working in the larger holes. Angling is good in early season and again when the fall rains begin. There's a lot of private land, and no camping along the stream.

MUDDY FORK (Sandy River) A small fork of the upper Sandy River which contains native cutthroat, joining the main Sandy and the Clear Fork about 5 miles NE of Zigzag and just north of McNeil Campground. To reach it, drive north from Zigzag on FS 18, the Lolo Pass Rd. Follow FS 100 from Lost Creek Campground about 2 miles to its end. There Trail 797 leads north about 1/2 mile to cross Muddy Fork. There is no road access to Muddy Fork.

Muddy Fork has some native cutthroat of fair size, and anglers can do well in spring after the water warms and before the glacial silt starts flowing. There are several forest campgrounds in the vicinity.

MULTNOMAH CHANNEL (a.k.a Willamette Slough) This long channel near the mouth of the Willamette carries a significant flow of the main river and offers spring chinook angling that rivals the popular Oregon City grounds. It forms the southern boundary of Sauvie Island, a large delta island about 9 miles NW of Portland, and flows into the Columbia River at St. Helens. See columbia river (st. helens to bonneville) for a map of the channel.

Hwy. 30 parallels the channel's west shore for most of its length, with plentiful bank access on Sauvie Island. Cross the Sauvie Island Bridge to pick up county roads that follow a good stretch of the channel's east bank. Much of the land along the channel on the island is publicly owned. Private land is well marked.

Anglers start fishing for salmon as early as mid-February if the water is clear, but few are

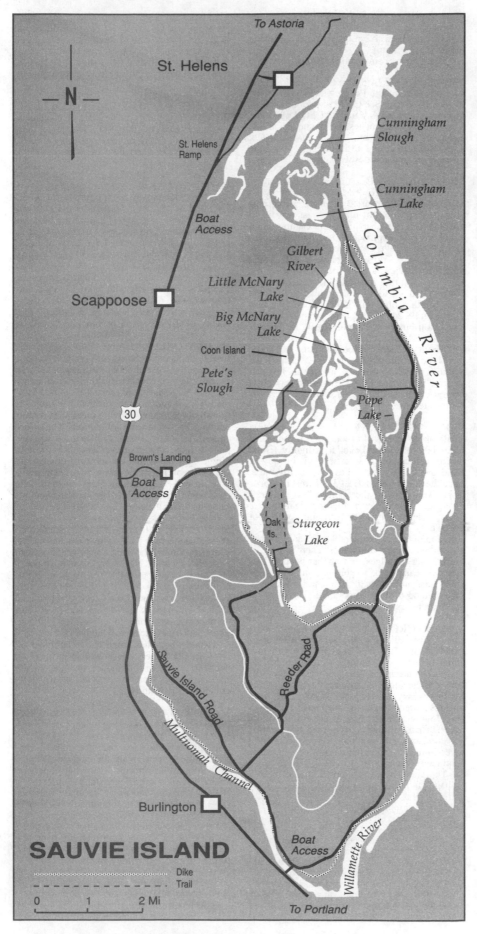

SAUVIE ISLAND

To Astoria

St. Helens

St. Helens Ramp

Boat Access

Scappoose

30

Brown's Landing

Boat Access

Burlington

Cunningham Slough

Cunningham Lake

Columbia River

Gilbert River

Little McNary Lake

Big McNary Lake

Coon Island

Pete's Slough

Pope Lake

Oak Is.

Sturgeon Lake

Reeder Road

Sauvie Island Road

Multnomah Channel

Willamette River

Boat Access

To Portland

········ Dike
- - - - Trail

0   1   2 Mi

caught until well into March. In late March and throughout May, the channel is literally filled with boats anchored or trolling for the elusive springers. Occasionally a steelhead is picked up, but if you hear *fish on* bellowing across the water, chances someone's got a hefty chinook in tow. The average catch weighs 18 pounds, but a few fish over 40 pounds are landed each spring. The middle of April is the best time to try.

Chinook anglers here are mostly trollers, although you'll find anchored boats at hot spots when the tide is running. Trollers move very slowly and fish the bottom, except in deep water, where they troll at 10-15 ft. Herring bait takes the overwhelming number of chinook, but lures have also proved worthy. When the water is murky, hardware trollers use good size spinners or wobblers (copper finishes are especially effective at this time), changing to smaller lures as the water clears. Plugs and Flatfish in silver, gold, and other light finishes are generally effective. Favorite spots include the mouth of Scappoose Bay, the Santosh Slough area, Coon Island, the Tank Hole, Rocky Point, and the head of the channel at the Willamette. Remember to keep an eye out for tow boats, whose vision is often impaired by barge loads.

From July through September, many anglers try for a mess of catfish, largemouth bass, perch, and crappie in the channel. A tremendous number of panfish are taken around the log rafts, pilings, and abandoned docks, and at the mouths of streams. Boat angling is easiest, but a number of these areas can be reached from road and bank on both sides of the channel.

The channel also offers western Oregon's greatest sport catch of crayfish. Try baiting these with shad, which are available near Coon Island in June. A few sturgeon are picked up in the lower and upper channel. In late fall some large cutthroat are taken by bait anglers. The cutthroat are heading for spawning grounds in the short mainland tributaries.

Moorages are located all along the channel, accessible from Hwy. 30. There are boat ramps on the channel at Burlington Ferry off Hwy. 31 across from Sauvie Island, at Brown's Landing 3 miles east of Scappoose on Dike Rd., and at the Gilbert River mouth on Sauvie Island. Channel boaters also put in at Cathedral Park on the Willamette, at Scappoose Bay, and at St. Helens.

Brown's Landing is one of several marinas on the channel that rent boats and carry supplies. Brown's rents bass boats, canoes, and touring kayaks and has supplies and tackle, as well as an RV park. They also keep the coffee hot and coming at a homestyle cafe with moorage in the channel, a good port to know about in case of a sudden squall.

MULTNOMAH CREEK A 7 mile stream in the Columbia Gorge, forming the beautiful Multnomah Falls east of Portland. It drains into Benson Lake at Hwy. 30. The only trout fishing is in the upper stream. Cut south off the scenic road at Bridal Veil, and a 6 mile drive brings you to the creek. A trail follows the creek both ways from the road's end. Native cutthroat 6-9 inches dominate the catch, with a few to 12 inches.

NASH LAKE A brook trout lake in the Three Sisters Wilderness, 6 air miles NW of Elk Lake. Best access is from the east side of the Cascades. Take the Cascade Lakes Highway to Sisters Mirror Lake Trailhead, about a 1/4 mile north of Sink Creek, which is about mid-way between Devil and Elk Lakes. Follow Trail 20 to the Sisters Mirror Lake group, then continue west 3 more miles.

Nash Lake covers 33 acres and is at 4900 ft. elevation. The lake is heavily fished for an isolated lake, but still produces consistently. The trout average 10 inches and get as large as 15. Fly fishing is exceptional here late in the year. There are good natural campsites.

NIGHTSHADE LAKES Two little brook trout lakes off the beaten path in the Mink Lake Basin, offering rather poor fishing. The west lake usually has the larger fish. There are no campsites available. If you still want to give it a try, bushwhack NW from the north end of Dumbell Lake. A half mile will get you to Krag Lake, and the Nightshades are just 1/4 mile west of there.

NORTH FORK RESERVOIR A large, accessible power reservoir on the Clackams River, covering 350 acres when full, located 7 miles south of Estacada off Hwy. 224. It's about 35 miles SE of Portland. The reservoir is formed by a PGE dam on the mainstem at the confluence of the North Fork of the Clackamas River.

The pool is 4 miles long, quite narrow and deep. It isn't very productive for wild fish, but it is stocked with legal rainbow every few weeks during the season and attracts a lot of anglers. Cutthroat, bull, brook and brown trout occasionally drop in from the river above the dam and are caught at times. Best fishing is at the upper end near the in-flow, and near the resort where fish are stocked. Best angling is with bait or troller/spinner combinations. Bank angling is possible in quite a few places.

PGE has provided boat ramps, picnic, and

FISH ON! MULTNOMAH CHANNEL
Steven Nehl, Photographer

camping facilities. There is a concession with supplies, tackle and boats at the upper end of the pool A portion of the reservoir 2.3 miles above the dam has a 10 mph speed restriction to protect angling in the resort and park area.

NOTCH LAKE A 4 acre brook trout lake in the headwaters of Hills Creek, just west of Diamond Peak Wilderness. Follow the Hills Creek road FS 23 to FS 2145, continuing 2 miles to Trail 3662, which follows the north bank of upper Hills Creek one mile to the lake. The brook trout and rainbow here run 6-11 inches. In most years the lake is accessible by early June. There are no improvements.

ONEONTA CREEK A small stream entering the Columbia River in the picturesque Columbia Gorge, dropping from the cliff between Benson State Park and Dodson several miles east of Multnomah Falls. Only 5 miles long, it is followed by trail through its own scenic gorge, and offers good fishing for small rainbow and a few cutthroat in the spring and summer.

OPAL LAKE (Marion Co.) A brook trout lake 6 miles north of Detroit Reservoir at the head of Opal Creek. Take the Little North Santiam River Rd. past the Pearl Creek Guard Station on FS 2207 to Shady Cove Campground. Cross the bridge on Cedar Creek Rd., taking the left fork uphill and switching back at the next right. Opal Lake is a half-mile bushwhack, at the bottom of the ridge. It is at elevation 3476 ft., covering 11 acres, and is 40 ft. deep, with a self-sustaining population of brook trout.

OSWEGO CREEK Once known as Sucker Creek, it flows out of Lake Oswego south of Portland and is crossed by the West Linn highway near the mouth. There is only about a mile of stream between the lake and the Willamette.

An occasional cutthroat is picked up during winter season, but most fishing here is for steelhead and coho which enter the stream in December. The runs are small, with two or three dozen fish caught in a typical year. Anglers fish from boat and shore, with minimal parking available at the mouth. A few bass and panfish are caught in the lower half mile.

OSWEGO LAKE A large private lake just south of Portland, whose outlet at the town of Lake Oswego drains into the Willamette River. The lake is about 3 miles long and 1/3 mile wide. It is fed by the Tualatin River and is privately stocked. There is no public access. A private corporation controls access and polices the lake against trespassers. The lake was originally called Sucker Lake, but the name offended the residents of this posh district, so they renamed it. You can fish the outlet stream, however, as long as you don't trespass.

OTTER LAKE A 17 acre trout lake at the north end of the Taylor Burn area, one mile NE of Erma Bell Lakes. Approach from the north from Skookum Creek Campground at the end of the Box Canyon Rd., FS 1957. The campground can be reached from the North Fork of the Willamette or the South Fork of the McKenzie. Head south 1/2 mile from Skookum Campground, then take Trail 3558 to the lake.

To approach from the south, take the Williams Lake Trail north from Taylor Burn Campground 3 miles to the lake. The Williams Lake Trail parallels the Olallie Trail, but is on the east side of Erma Bell Lakes.

Otter Lake is a consistent producer of rainbow and brook trout, with sizeable fish available. Late fall is the best time for success. The lake is very brushy around the shore, so carry in a rubber boat or float tube. There are good natural campsites and a small camp at Skookum Creek. It is usually accessible in late June.

PALMER LAKE A 15 acres lake NE of Larch Mt. on the Latourell Prairie Rd. It is in the closed area of the Bull Run watershed and is not open for angling.

PAMELIA LAKE A large lake with small cutthroat in the Mt. Jefferson Wilderness directly in front of the SW flank of the mountain. About 7 miles south of Idanha, take Pamelia Rd. FS 2246 east 4 miles to Trail 3439. The lake is 2 miles down the trail over easy terrain.

Pamelia covers about 50 acres but gets low in late summer and fall. It suffers from a classic case of overpopulation, teeming with stunted, eager cutthroat 6-8 inches. A special bag limit of 30 fish per day is an effort to encourage *catch and keep* angling in order reduce the population and increase average size. All methods will take fish here. The road is accessible dur-

SAUVIE ISLAND GEESE
Bill Wagner, Photographer

ing winter, and the lake open, so anglers could do a little snowshoe ice fishing.

There are several good natural campsites at the lake, and there are other good lakes in the neighborhood. See Hanks, Hunts. Supplies are available at Idanha or Detroit. The lake is often ice-free by late May, but there is usually lots of snow left.

PANSY LAKE In the Pansy Basin near the head of the Hot Springs Fork of the Collawash River. Take Hwy. 224 past Estacada 34 miles to the mouth of the Collawash. From there, follow FS 63 up the Collawash to Tom Meadows, then FS 6340 and FS 6341 to the Pansy Trail 551. Hike south for one mile to Pansy Basin. Bear right, and cross the meadow to the rock slide. Hike 1/2 mile up the ridge by trail. The lake is just west of Bull of the Woods Lookout, The trails are well signed.

Pansy covers about 6 acres and is very shallow. It is stocked with brook trout and supports some natural reproduction as well, offering consistent catches of 8-9 inch fish, with some to 12 inches. Fly angling or small lures work best due to the lake's shallow depth. Fall is the best season to fish here.

PANTHER CREEK A small trout stream flowing into the North Yamhill River, just north of McMinnville off Hwy. 18. The lower end of the stream is crossed by the paved road north from McMinnville to Carlton. A paved road west from Carlton accesses the upper stream.

Panther provides good angling the first few months of trout season, but gets low in the summer. A few fair size native cutthroat show up in the catch. Bait angling is the usual method in this small stream, although wet flies are effective. The creek flows entirely through private agricultural land, with public access only at road crossings.

PARRISH LAKE A good brook trout lake west of the North Santiam River, about 9 miles NW of Santiam Junction. From Hwy. 22, turn west 7 miles south of the Marion Forks Ranger Station onto FS 2266. Follow this road west about 5 miles. The road runs between Daly

Lake on the north, and Parrish Lake on the south.

Parrish is about 7 acres and produces brook trout 6-13 inches, averaging 9 inches. The lake is usually good early and late in the season. All methods are used to take fish. Spinner and bait are sure-fire in early season. There are good natural campsites available. It is usually accessible in late May.

PATJENS LAKES A group of three small lakes south of Big Lake along the Cascade Summit, south of Santiam Pass Hwy. 20. At Hoodoo Ski Bowl, turn onto FS 2690. It's 4 miles to Big Lake, and the Patjens are 2 miles south by Trail 3395. The upper and deepest lake covers about 3 acres and has brook trout 6-12 inches. The middle lake covers 6 acres and has rainbow trout. The lower lake is just a shallow pot hole and doesn't hold fish. The lakes are lightly fished. There's a good camp at Big Lake.

PENN LAKE A brook trout lake in the north Mink Lake Basin, at the head of the South Fork McKenzie, west of Elk Lake. See Corner Lake for directions. Penn Lake is lightly fished due to it's position in the basin. It is about 1/4 mile NW of Corner Lake by a good trail. About 26 acres and very shallow, it occasionally winterkills. Best fishing for brook trout is early in the year and again in fall.

PETE'S SLOUGH A Columbia River backwater on Sauvie Island at the north end of Sturgeon Lake, fished for bass and panfish. After crossing Sauvie Island Bridge 10 miles west of Portland off Hwy. 30, follow Reeder Rd. for 11 miles to the checking station. Drive left about one mile and cross the dike, where several dirt roads head west to the slough. The dike crossing is closed from late May through June, as the area is flooded.

Pete's Slough connects McNary and Sturgeon lakes and is fishable all along the shore. See mcnary lakes. Three or four footbridges cross it, and these are heavily used by anglers. Good catches of crappie, brown bullhead, and other panfish are taken. Bait is most popular, but small lures and streamer flies take large

crappie. An occasional largemouth bass is caught, but they're not numerous. Try plugging the few shallow oxbows. The entrances to the many duck lakes are also frequent bass hangouts. Overnight camping is not permitted in the area. Minimal supplies are available at the island store near the bridge.

PIKA LAKE A small brook trout lake, lightly fished but not too hard to reach. It's in the Big Meadows area off the North Santiam. See Fay Lake for directions. Continue past Fay for 1/4 mile, then follow a blazed trail south. It's 1/2 mile to the lake. Pika is very brushy and hard to fish, so a rubber boat is helpful. It's about 3 acres and shallow, and the fish bite well on almost anything once you get out to them. Brook trout here run 8-10 inches. There are no good campsites at the lake.

PINE RIDGE LAKE Also known as Pine Lake, adjacent to a heavily-used Scout camp. It can be reached from Marion Forks on Hwy. 22 by turning east onto Twin Meadows Rd. FS 2261 about 4 miles south of Marion Forks. From this point it's five miles to the lake. The lake is regulated for kid fishing, restricted to use by juveniles under 18 years. It's a fine lake for youngsters. Brook trout and rainbow run to 13 inches. Trails lead to other lakes in the area. See Temple, Davis. Public camping is prohibited.

PIPER LAKE A lightly fished 5 acre brook trout lake in the Irish Mt. area north of Irish and Taylor lakes. See Mcfarland Lake for directions. Piper is a few hundred yards west of McFarland. Although small, the lake has a maximum depth of 24 ft. deep. It's not very productive, but some nice brook trout catches have been reported. It's a good lake to try while in the Irish Mountain area.

PLATT LAKE An 8 acre trout lake in the Horse Lake area west of Elk Lake. See horse lake for directions. Platt Lake is 2 miles SW of Upper Horse Lake. Take the Horse Mt. Trail 3530, which goes right to the lake. Platt has some nice brook trout around 10 inches. All methods of angling will take fish at times, and the lake is easily fished from shore. There are good natural campsites at the lake. Other small lakes to the south are also stocked. See Mile Lake.

PLAZA LAKE A 5 acre hike-in brook trout lake east of Hwy. 224 near Squaw Mt., in a setting of rare old growth forest. The lake drains into the South Fork of the Salmon River from elevation 3650 ft. The hike in is about 20 minutes.

From Estacada follow Hwy. 224 about 6 miles to the North Fork Rd. FS 4610. At about 6 miles FS 4610 crosses Winslow Creek then cuts right sharply, while FS 4613 continues straight ahead to North Fork Crossing Campground. Stay on 4610 (known as the Squaw Mt. Rd.) 11 miles to Twin Springs Campground. About one mile past the camp, Trail 788 to Plaza Lake heads east. The trail is 3/4 mile downhill, although the lake is only 1/2 mile or less from the road.

Though small, Plaza produces a fair number of pan-size brook trout 6-10 inches. All methods of angling will take fish here. It's usually not open until late June.

PLUMB LAKE A brook trout lake in the Mink Lake Basin, 1/2 mile NE of Junction Lake on the trail to Corner Lake. See Mink Lake and Junction Lake for directions. One of the smaller lakes in the Mink Lake Basin, it covers 15 acres and reaches a maximum depth of 17 ft. Brook trout reproduce naturally here, and fishing for them is generally good. It's a good fly-fishing lake, with best catches late in the day.

POPE LAKE A Sauvie Island lake containing brown bullhead, crappie, bass, some carp, and chubs. To reach the lake, take Hwy. 30 north from Portland to the Sauvie Island Bridge. Cross to the island and follow Reeder Rd. for about 10 miles to a slough with moorage on the right. The lake is about 300 yards directly west. The surest way to find the lake is to proceed to the waterfowl checking station, then walk due south for 1/2 mile. This is Dept. of Fish and Wildlife property, which is open to public access except during duck season. A piece of land at the south end of Pope Lake is private property, so watch the signs.

Pope covers about 10 acres and is easily fished from shore. Fair size bass are taken on plugs and spinners, and crappie will hit the smaller lures. Angling for brown bullhead is fair throughout the summer. There is no camping in this area.

PORKY LAKE One of the most productive and consistent lakes in the Mink Lake Basin. See Cliff Lake and Mink Lake for directions. It covers about 38 acres, located 1/2 mile east of Mink Lake, half-way to Cliff Lake.

Porky is a very rich body of water with a lot of natural reproduction. It usually holds up throughout the season. All methods will catch fish, with flyfishing especially good in late summer. There are good natural campsites at the lake.

PRESLEY LAKE A shallow drive-in 3 acre lake 3 miles NW of Marion Lake. About 1/2 mile south of Marion Forks Ranger Station, turn east onto FS 2257. Follow this road about 2 miles to FS 515, a left fork which goes to Horn Creek Unit 2. At about 1/2 mile, you can see the lake to the north. A spur road runs down to Presley. The lake is stocked with catchable rainbow. There are no camping facilities.

PRILL LAKE A small brook trout lake in the Marion Lake Basin. See Marion Lake for directions. From Marion, follow the trail around the east bank to Mist Creek. Prill is about one mile east by very steep trail. It covers 8 acres and is 20 feet deep. Brook trout 8-14 inches will hit anything. There are few natural campsites.

PUDDING RIVER A fairly long stream with headwaters east of Salem, flowing through the center of Marion County north into Clackamas County, where it joins the Willamette River at Canby. It is crossed by Hwy. 99E just south of Canby. A number of paved and gravel roads in the Silverton, Mt. Angel, and Woodburn areas cross the stream. Most bank angling takes place at the road crossings.

The Pudding isn't stocked, but its main tributaries (Drift, Butte, Silver, and Abiqua creeks) keep the upper waters fairly populated with trout. Most trout anglers use bait or spinner/bait combinations. Cutthroat dominate the catch, with a few rainbow taken.

Winter steelhead, most of which are heading for Abiqua and Butte Creeks, are fished up to the mouth of Silver Creek, but only a few are caught in the Pudding each year. The lower stream offers fair bass angling on plugs or spinners, with panfish taken on bait. The extreme lower river can be drifted in small boats, and some anglers motor up from the Willamette

when the water is high. The lower river is sometimes navigable into June.

PYRAMID LAKE (Clackamas Co.) A cutthroat lake in the High Rocks area of the Clackamas drainage. At elevation 4000 ft., it is usually accessible several weeks earlier than the rest of the mountain lakes. It's only 1/2 mile by trail to this 4 acre lake.

From Estacada, take Hwy. 224 about 30 miles SE to Ripplebrook Ranger Station, and continue another 8 miles to the Shellrock Rd. FS 58. A little over 4 miles north past Shellrock Campground, FS 140 branches off to the left. Follow FS 140 about 2 miles to road's end at Pyramid Lake Trailhead.

Formerly stocked with brook trout, the lake is now stocked with cutthroat, which put on more size here. Fishing holds up well, producing fish 6-13 inches. Bait and spinner work best in early season, with good fly angling later on. There are natural campsites at the lake.

PYRAMID LAKE (Marion Co.) An up and down lake for brook trout, with occasional winterkills. Some years have produced fine, plump brookies. The lake is 1 1/2 miles west of Breitenbush Lake. See Breitenbush Lake for directions. The trail to Pyramid takes off south at the bridge over the Breitenbush Lake outlet, following the creek up 1/2 mile, then traversing a steep slope. Pyramid is on a flat, 1/2 mile west of Pyramid Butte.

The lake is about 5 acres and shallow. When the fish are there, flyfishing is excellent. There are some pretty, natural campsites.

QUARTZVILLE CREEK Also known as the Quartzville Fork of the Santiam. It enters Green Peter Reservoir from the north about 12 miles east of Sweet Home. From Hwy. 20, follow a paved road that runs north about 3 miles east of Foster. This crosses the upper end of Foster Reservoir and follows the north shore of Green Peter. Quartzville is about 25 miles long, and the paved road follows it most of the way, with gravel roads continuing to the headwaters.

The creek has a lot of excellent water, most on BLM or National Forest land. It's stocked with rainbow trout each spring and early summer, and some nice native cutthroat are present. All methods of angling are used, with light terminal gear usually necessary. Flyfishing can be good when the water warms. Best catches are from Canal Creek down to the Forks Canal.

Camping is available at Whitcomb Creek Campground, on the reservoir just west of the creek mouth, and at Yellowbottom BLM Campground about 6 miles upstream from the reservoir.

QUESTION MARK LAKE A good brook trout lake in the Mink Lake Basin. It receives a lot of pressure but still produces well. The lake takes its name from its unique shape, and not from puzzled fly anglers trying to match the hatch. The lake is on the east edge of the basin. From the junction of the Six Lakes Trail and the Pacific Crest Trail, which meet at Ledge Lake Meadow, it's 1/4 mile NW through the trees to Question Mark.

The lake is about 10 acres and deep in spots, but with a lot of shoal area for easy flyfishing. It's a very easy lake to fish. The trout run 7-12 inches, with a few larger. There are excellent campsites here. It's hard to reach before late June.

QUINN LAKES Two brook trout lakes west of Taylor Burn Campground across a canyon

carved by the North Fork of the Willamette. It's about a 2 mile hike, down and up, on Blair Lake Trail 3553. Lower Quinn is just south of the trail at the head of Fisher Creek. The Quinns can also be reached from North Waldo Camp or from the Oakridge area by the Salmon Creek Rd. and FS 2417. See Eddeeleo Lakes for trail details.

Lower Quinn is 12 acres and has good angling for both rainbow and brook trout. The shore is a little brushy, but it can be fished in places. A rubber boat would be handy. Upper Quinn Lake is 1/4 mile south, covering 17 acres. Upper has brook trout only and, like most brook trout lakes, it slows up for periods during the season. Both lakes are heavily fished.

RED BUTTE LAKE A scenic 6 acre lake in the Eight Lakes Basin of the Mt. Jefferson Wilderness. It is to the west of the trail running south from Jorn Lake, about 1/2 mile south of Jorn, 2 miles north of Duffy, on the east side of Red Butte, a prominent landmark. See Jorn and Duffy for directions.

Red Butte is long, narrow, and fairly deep for its size. Being on the trail, it's fished frequently. Stocked by the state every other year, the brook trout average 8-9 inches, with a few to 12 inches, it's easily fished from shore. There are a couple of good natural campsites at the north end of the lake, and additional sites at Jorn. There are other good lakes north and south.

RIGDON LAKES A pair of inconsistent trout lakes in the Taylor Burn area north of Waldo Lake, with both rainbow and brook trout. From Taylor Burn Campground, 7 miles north of the North Waldo Lake Campground by poor road, take the Olallie Trail 3583 south to Kiwa Lake, and turn east off the trail just south of Kiwa. The Rigdons are 1/2 mile east of the trail, just east of Rigdon Butte. From North Waldo, take the trail along the north end of Waldo Lake about 2 miles, then head north by trail about 1/2 mile to the Rigdons.

Upper Rigdon offers fair brook trout angling on its 50 acres. The fish run 6-13 inches, averaging 10 inches. Lower Rigdon is just a few hundred yards to the south. About the same size as Upper, it sometimes holds rainbow and brook trout to 15 inches. Both lakes can be fished from shore. Bait, lures, and flies can all work here depending on conditions. These lakes are at their best in late summer and fall.

ROARING RIVER (Clackamas Co.) A tributary of the upper Clackamas River, offering good hike-in angling for native trout, and summer steelhead in the lower river. About 15 miles long, it heads in the High Rock area of Mt. Hood National Forest about 4 miles NW of Timothy Lake. It joins the Clackamas just upstream from Fish Creek at Roaring River Campground on Hwy. 224.

Anglers must hike to reach the stream. Better plan on bringing your forest map. The canyon is very deep, and the hiking tough. Some anglers hike up from the forest camp at the mouth. The central creek can be reached by a 3 mile hike on a trail south from Lookout Spring Camp on the Squaw Mt. Rd. A dirt road, FS 4611, can be followed from about one mile south of North Fork Crossing Campground to a trailhead which takes at least 2 miles off this hike.

For rugged hikers, the upper river can be reached by a trek into the canyon about 2 miles by trail from Twin Springs Camp, which is several miles further east on Squaw Mt. Rd. Cutthroat run 6-12 inches. If you like fishing in solitude, this is the spot. Summer steelhead are in the lower 3 miles of river below the falls from June 1 to December 30.

There are several camps on the Squaw Mt. Rd. and near the mouth on Hwy. 224, and there are natural sites in the canyon.

ROARING RIVER (Linn Co.) A small trout stream, tributary to Crabtree Creek, 20 miles east of Albany. From Hwy. 99E, turn east at Jefferson, continue through Scio, then follow the Crabtree Creek Rd. Roaring River is only about 8 miles long, and most of it runs close to the road.

A hatchery near the mouth is a nice spot to visit. Bait is probably most consistently effective, but flies will work when the water warms up. Small spinners with bait should also do well. Some native cutthroat of small size are caught at times. A county park below the hatchery is stocked with legal rainbow from May through June. The catch runs 7-12 inches, with a few larger fish occasionally caught near the mouth. There are no camping areas.

ROBINSON LAKE A good brook trout lake on the western border of Mt. Washington Wilderness. To reach the lake take Robinson Rd. east from Hwy.126, the McKenzie River Hwy. The turn-off is about 2 miles south of Clear Lake. Follow this road about 4 miles to the end, where a trail leads 1/4 mile east to the lake.

Robinson is only 5 acres and mostly shallow, but runs to 20 ft. deep in spots. It offers good brook trout angling using any method with most fish averaging 12 inches, and some beauties to 16 inches. Campsites are available on Clear Lake Rd.

ROCK CREEK (Clackamas Co.) A fair early season native cutthroat stream, flowing into Butte Creek about 5 miles south of Canby and east of 99E. The head of the creek is about 10 miles south of Molalla. The stream is crossed by Hwy. 213 a few miles south of Molalla, and by paved and gravel roads throughout its length.

The cutthroat run 6-12 inches. Bait is the best method, with spinner and bait effective in the larger holes. Bear Creek, coming into Rock Creek near Marks Prairie, has some fair cutthroat angling, too. Best fishing is in May and June. Most land along the creek is privately owned, so get permission. There is no camping on the stream.

ROCK LAKES (Clackamas Co.) Three good lakes in the High Rock area, north of Hwy. 224, offering a variety of trout for the hiking angler. Upper Rock features cutthroat, Middle has rainbow, and Lower offers brook trout.

The lakes are just over 50 miles from Portland. The shortest hike in is by Trail 512, which heads between Frazier Fork and Frazier Turnaround campgrounds. Follow Hwy. 224 from Estacada to the Shellrock Rd. FS 58, and drive 7 miles to High Rock Springs Campground. Just north of the campground, take FS 240 five miles west to Frazier Forks Campground. The lakes are one mile west on Serene Lake Trail 512. Lower Rock Lake is to the north. Signs mark the trail junctions.

The lower lake is about 9 acres and 13 ft. deep. Middle Rock is 15 acres and 34 ft. deep. Upper Rock is only 3 acres, but 22 ft. deep. All the lakes have reproducing populations of eastern brook trout, as well as stocked fish. Average catch in all the lakes is 8-9 inches, and some brook trout over 12 inches are taken.

The lakes are fished rather heavily since they are so close to the road. One or more of the three is usually putting out catches. All methods of angling can be used, from boat or bank. Spinner and bait are usually good in early season, flyfishing in late summer and fall.

There are good campsites at the two larger lakes. They are usually inaccessible until early June, except by hiking west from Shellrock Lake. The road to Frazier Mt. is sometimes snowed in until late June.

ROCKPILE LAKE A scenic brook trout lake in Diamond Peak Wilderness at 6100 ft., just east of a peak called Diamond Rockpile. It is a few hundred yards SE of Marie Lake. See marie lake for trail directions.

This 6 acre lake is fished heavily, but it produces some nice brook trout. The fish average 10 inches and run to 14 inches. The lake is easily fished from shore, and all methods can be used. There are good natural campsites here, and a full-service campground at Summit Lake. It is usually snowbound until late June.

ROOSTER ROCK SLOUGH A Columbia River backwater, about 5 acres, north of I-84 at Rooster Rock State Park. The slough contains brown bullhead, yellow perch, white and black crappie, and largemouth bass.

ROSLYN LAKE A trout lake about 26 miles from Portland, 2 miles NE of Sandy. From Hwy. 26 at the east end of Sandy, turn north onto Dodge Park Rd. It's about 3 mile to the lake.

Years ago, before the Marmot power canal was screened, trout and steelhead moved into Roslyn Lake. Though fish can no longer migrate here on their own, catchable rainbow are stocked annually. Best fishing is on the east side, where the stream comes in.

There's a nice developed area with picnic and recreational facilities here. No motorboats are allowed, but car-top or rubber boats can be launched. A naturally flat bank permits access by less-abled anglers. The lake is controlled by PGE as part of the Bull Run Power Plant.

ROUND LAKE (Lane Co.) A good brook trout and rainbow lake in the Eddeeleo group south of Taylor Burn, NW of Waldo Lake. See Eddeeleo Lakes for directions. Round Lake is just east of Upper Eddeeleo, 100 yards from the trail to North Waldo.

The catch averages 8-11 inches, with some fish to 16 inches. All methods of angling are used with good results. The lake covers 20 acres and is easily fished from shore. There are good natural campsites available, and excellent fishing in other lakes north and south.

ROUND LAKE (Marion Co.) This is a good high lake in the southern Mt. Hood National Forest. Take Hwy. 224 from Estacada past Ripplebrook Ranger Station, then follow the Collawash River Rd. south to FS 6370. Follow this road to Round Lake Campground. It's an easy hike down to the lake.

Round Lake is 9 acres and about 20 ft. deep. It has naturally reproducing brown trout, supplemented by stocked brook trout. The brook trout have been running 8-14 inches, and the browns 8-16 inches, averaging 12 inches. It's a tough lake to fish from shore because of weeds along the shoals. Bring a rubber boat for best results. All methods will produce, but the browns are wary, so use light gear. There is a small campground above the lake.

ROW RIVER A good native cutthroat stream NE of Cottage Grove, a major tributary of the Coast Fork of the Willamette River. The river forms Dorena Reservoir, and a good road follows north along the lower stream, around the reservoir, and on up to the Forks at the confluence of Brice and Layng creeks. The distance from the mouth to this point is about 20 miles.

Average catch is around 10 inches with a range 6-13 inches. Fishing is best above the reservoir. Bait, or spinner and bait work well in early season, with some good flyfishing later. There are no improved camp areas along the stream, and access is difficult due to private property. Ask permission before entering.

RUSS LAKE (Warm Springs Indian Reservation) A 6 acre brook trout lake east of Olallie Meadows Campground on the Skyline Rd. A 1 1/4 mile easy going trail reaches the lake after passing two other small, good lakes. See Jude and Brook.

The fish run 6-15 inches, averaging 10 inches. The bank is brushy, and a rubber boat would be helpful. Angling with wet flies is usually good in the morning and late in the day. Spinner and bait will work well almost anytime.

The lake is on Warm Springs Reservation, but tribal fishing permits are not currently required here. Overnight camping is prohibited due to fire danger.

SALMON CREEK A good trout stream, tributary of the Middle Fork Willamette, flowing 26 miles from headwaters in Waldo Meadows to its confluence with the Middle Fork at Oakridge. Salmon Creek originates in Upper and Lower Salmon Lakes in the high lakes area west of Waldo Lake. It is fed by many small tributaries and two good size creeks (Furnish and Black), all of which contain native cutthroat. Salmon Creek itself has a lot of native cutthroat, some wild rainbow, and is stocked with rainbow in the lower 15 miles from the mouth to the Black Creek confluence. It has better trout habitat than nearby Salt Creek (less steep gradient, slower flow, more pools), and consequently has a better population of native fish.

The name *Salmon Creek* derives from a run of spring chinook that once spawned here, which was destroyed by the Army Corps. of Engineers' failure to construct fishways over Dexter and Lookout Point dams on the Middle Fork Willamette. To *mitigate* the loss, the Corps. has built a fish trap at Dexter Dam, where the Oregon Dept. of Fish and Wildlife collects salmon eggs for rearing in a hatchery on Salmon Creek.

To reach Salmon Creek, follow Hwy. 58 east from Springfield through Oakridge. The road to the hatchery, one mile east of town, joins FS 24, which follows the creek for about 10 miles. Logging roads access the upper stream and many of the tributaries. There is a Forest Service campground on the creek at Salmon Creek Falls.

SALMON RIVER (Clackamas Co.) A fine tributary of the upper Sandy River, with especially good water for steelhead flyfishing. The Salmon joins the Sandy from the south at Brightwood, on Hwy. 26 about 4 miles west of Zigzag.

At Wildwood on Hwy. 26, a road leads south to a BLM recreation area on the river, about 3 miles upstream from the mouth. Roads due south from Wemme and Zigzag Ranger Station join the Salmon about 6 miles from the mouth and continue south as FS 2618, follow-

SANDY RIVER DRIFT FISHING
Steve Terrill, Photographer

ing the river about 5 miles upstream to Trail 742, which keeps pace with the river for 11 miles in a wilderness-like setting. The upper river can be reached by trails which head from forest roads south of Trillium Lake. These are clearly shown on the Mt. Hood National Forest map.

The Salmon River heads on the upper slopes of Mt. Hood, carrying snow melt down from Palmer Glacier. It flows 31 miles, 24 through national forest. Thirteen miles above the mouth a series of scenic waterfalls form a barrier to salmon and steelhead passage. Above the falls there are good populations of native cutthroat. Some rainbow are stocked in the immediate vicinity of the campgrounds on the lower river.

The real thrill here continues to be the summer steelhead run, rebuilt in the late 1970s following decimation of the wild run by Marmot Dam. The average annual catch is over 2000, with seasons as good as 6400 (1984). Steelhead appear in numbers in June, and the catch continues through December. The stretch of river from the trailhead at Green Canyon Campground to the falls (about 4 miles) is regulated for flyfishing only. There are many fine pools in this charming wooded stretch, an overall quality angling opportunity.

The Salmon also contains spring chinook and coho, but all salmon angling is prohibited in order to protect spawning fish. Check current regulations for seasons, closures, and special information. Camping facilities are available at the Wildwood BLM Recreation Site on Hwy. 26, and at Green Canyon Campground on FS 2618 about 5 miles south of Zigzag. Supplies are available at general stores on Hwy. 26, and there is a fly shop in the shopping center at Welches.

SALMONBERRY LAKE A 3 acre put-n-take rainbow fishery near St. Helens, formerly a city water supply. From Hwy. 30 at St. Helens, head west on the Pittsburgh-St. Helens Rd. about 9 miles, turning left onto a gravel road

soon after the main road itself turns to gravel. The access road leads directly to the pond.

SALT CREEK A large and powerful tributary of the Middle Fork Willamette River. It flows 28 miles through Willamette Pass from its source at Gold Lake to its confluence with the Middle Fork at Oakridge. It is closely followed by Hwy. 58 to the Gold Lake cut-off and is a popular tourist fishery, due more to its proximity to the highway than to its productivity. Steep and tumultuous throughout much of its run, it offers little fish habitat and, consequently, has only a small native trout population. It is stocked with hatchery rainbow, however, from the mouth to South Fork Bridge (about 7 miles above Blue Pool Campground).

The most productive stretch for native trout is the few miles from Hwy. 58 Bridge down to Salt Creek Falls. Here the creek flows at a diminished gradient, meandering prettily through meadows. It is brushy and hard to fish, but wild rainbow and brook trout are plentiful. Salt Creek Falls is a handsome 286 ft. falls which can be viewed from a paved trail on the south side of Hwy. 58 about 20 miles east of Oakridge. From Gold Lake to Hwy. 58, Salt Creek is a rainbow spawning ground and is closed to angling year around.

Salt Creek flows within Willamette National Forest. There is a Forest Service Ranger Station at Oakridge and campgrounds on the creek at Blue Pool (a nice swimming hole), about 8 miles east of Oakridge, and at Salt Creek Falls. McCredie Hot Springs, an undeveloped natural hot spring pool beside the creek, is less than one mile from Blue Pool. There is a large gravel parking area above the springs, but no sign. Most bathers soak *au naturelle*. There are no facilities of any kind here, so users are urged to carry out all trash and respect the delicate sanitation situation. The nearest outhouses are at Blue Pool.

SANDY RIVER An excellent steelhead and salmon river, located conveniently close to Portland. The Sandy heads in the glaciers of Mt. Hood and flows 50 miles west to join the Columbia River at Troutdale. Too turbid throughout much of the season to provide good trout fishing, the river nevertheless offers angling every month of the year, and an impressive catch. More than 10,000 steelhead are landed yearly, and several thousand salmon. Most of these fish are caught within an hour's drive of Portland.

The majority of steelhead and salmon angling takes place between the river mouth, which can be reached from I-84 just east of Troutdale, and the town of Sandy on Hwy. 26, 23 river miles upstream. Good county roads cross and parallel the lower river, and Hwy. 26 follows it to its upper tributaries.

The spring chinook run is the largest of the three salmon runs. Springers enter the river in April, and fishing holds up through June. Fall chinook appear in late August and peak in October. These fish spawn in the lower river and are rarely seen above Sandy. Coho show in early September, with intense fishing through October. Small spinners, fluorescent wobblers, Flatfish, and Hotshots are all used here. Special hook and weight restrictions are in effect.

The Sandy's summer and winter steelhead fisheries are thriving. These big sea-run rainbow trout are in the river the year around, and not a month passes without a catch of at least several hundred. But winter steelhead are the big fishery. The average annual catch is in excess of 8000, with seasonal totals as high as 10,000 (1984-85). Fishing picks up in late No-

SMELTING ON THE SANDY RIVER
Steve Terrill, Photographer

vember and remains very good through April. Summer steelhead are caught in numbers from late May through August. The 1985-86 catch was about 2300. Sandy River steelhead average 6 pounds, but 15 pounders have been taken. Eggs, yarn, sand shrimp, and lures are all used, but check your pocketbook, as this boulder-strewn river is a real tackle-grabber.

For regulation purposes, the Sandy is divided into waters above and below Brightwood Bridge, about 12 miles east of Sandy at the confluence of the Salmon River. Check current regulations for fishery seasons, closures, tackle restrictions, and information relative to boat angling. There is a boat angling deadline (the lower end of Oxbow Park as of this writing). Few anglers bother with boats above this deadline, as plenty of good water is accessible from the bank. Those who do choose to use boats as a means of transportation should disconnect tackle while in transit.

The most popular boat drifts on the river are from Oxbow County Park to Dabney State Park, and from Dabney to Lewis and Clark State Park near the mouth, each a good day's run. The Sandy is only navigable by riverboats.

Excellent steelhead and salmon water is also accessible to bank anglers throughout much of the river. From the bank at Lewis and Clark, anglers can fish the Sandbar and Railroad Bridge Drifts. To reach Lewis and Clark, follow I-84 to the Lewis and Clark Exit just east of Troutdale. There is also a good hole above Troutdale Bridge (off Crown Point Hwy.) that can be fished from the west bank. Crown Point Hwy. crosses the river and follows the Sandy's east bank to Springdale, providing access to Chicken & Dumplin Hole, Pigpen Drift, Tippycanoe Drift, and Big Bend Drift. Anglers can park along the road. At Springdale, follow Hurlburt Rd. east to the road junction near Big Creek, turning onto Gordon Creek Rd. which follows the Sandy's north bank. Gordon Creek and Trout Creek drifts can be reached off this road.

The term *drift*, by the way, is used in several different ways when discussing steelhead fishing in the northwest. It is used to refer to the distance covered by a day's float downstream in a riverboat *(a good day's drift)*, or to a stretch of the river favored by steelhead *(Pigpen Drift)*, sometimes interchangeable with the term *hole*. It is also used to distinguish the steelhead angler who moves from place to place on the river *(drift fisherman)* from the angler who fishes one spot hour after hour *(plunker)*.

Dabney State Park offers bank access, and

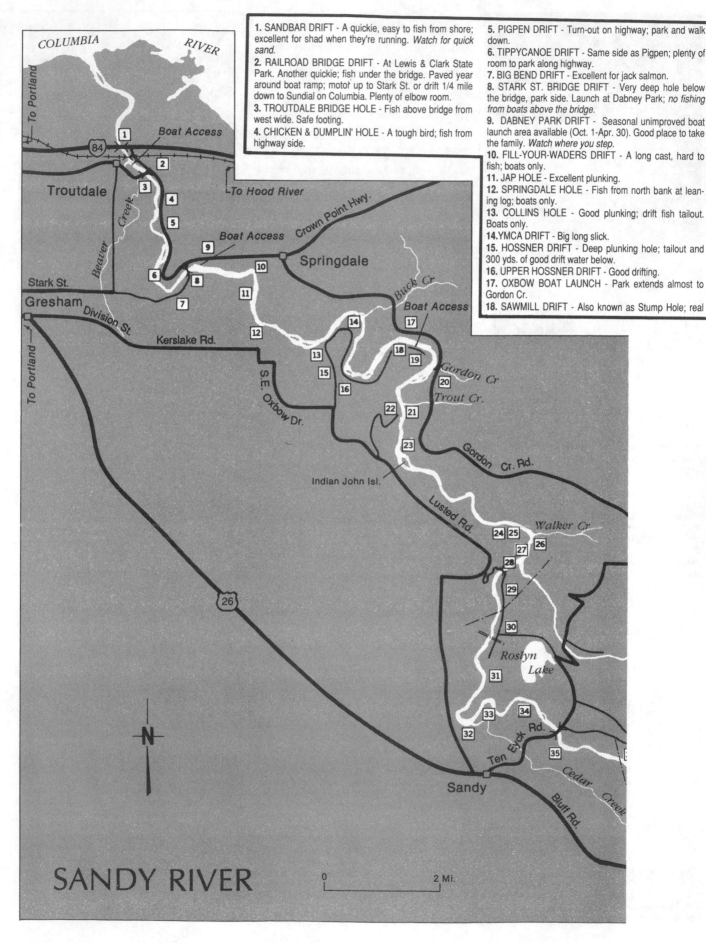

COLUMBIA RIVER

To Portland

84

Boat Access

Troutdale

Beaver Creek

To Hood River

Crown Point Hwy.

Boat Access

Springdale

Stark St.

Gresham

Division St.

To Portland

Kerslake Rd.

S.E. Oxbow Dr.

Buck Cr.

Boat Access

Gordon Cr.

Trout Cr.

Gordon Cr. Rd.

Indian John Isl.

Lusted Rd.

Walker Cr.

26

Roslyn Lake

Sandy

Ten Eyck Rd.

Bluff Rd.

Cedar Creek

0   2 MI.

SANDY RIVER

1. SANDBAR DRIFT - A quickie, easy to fish from shore; excellent for shad when they're running. *Watch for quick sand.*

2. RAILROAD BRIDGE DRIFT - At Lewis & Clark State Park. Another quickie; fish under the bridge. Paved year around boat ramp; motor up to Stark St. or drift 1/4 mile down to Sundial on Columbia. Plenty of elbow room.

3. TROUTDALE BRIDGE HOLE - Fish above bridge from west wide. Safe footing.

4. CHICKEN & DUMPLIN' HOLE - A tough bird; fish from highway side.

5. PIGPEN DRIFT - Turn-out on highway; park and walk down.

6. TIPPYCANOE DRIFT - Same side as Pigpen; plenty of room to park along highway.

7. BIG BEND DRIFT - Excellent for jack salmon.

8. STARK ST. BRIDGE DRIFT - Very deep hole below the bridge, park side. Launch at Dabney Park; *no fishing from boats above the bridge.*

9. DABNEY PARK DRIFT - Seasonal unimproved boat launch area available (Oct. 1-Apr. 30). Good place to take the family. *Watch where you step.*

10. FILL-YOUR-WADERS DRIFT - A long cast, hard to fish; boats only.

11. JAP HOLE - Excellent plunking.

12. SPRINGDALE HOLE - Fish from north bank at leaning log; boats only.

13. COLLINS HOLE - Good plunking; drift fish tailout. Boats only.

14. YMCA DRIFT - Big long slick.

15. HOSSNER DRIFT - Deep plunking hole; tailout and 300 yds. of good drift water below.

16. UPPER HOSSNER DRIFT - Good drifting.

17. OXBOW BOAT LAUNCH - Park extends almost to Gordon Cr.

18. SAWMILL DRIFT - Also known as Stump Hole; real

good drift water; the tackle snatcher on the river. Fish from north side.

19. CRUSHER HOLE - Also known as Turnaround Hole. Used to be an old rock crusher here. Long drift, good boat access. *Watch for quick sand below Buck Cr.*

20. GORDON CR. DRIFT - Large, long, deep riffle; drift it with floating lure. Easy access.

21. TROUT CREEK DRIFT - This one can be waded at low water.

22. BIG ROCK HOLE - Deep drift, good in low water; long walk in.

23. INDIAN JOHN ISLAND DRIFT - Good water above island, Oxbow side. Walk up from Oxbow Park.

24. BUTTLER'S EDDY - Walk here from Gauge Hole. Fish bottom of rough water.

25. BLUE HOLE - Below Gauge Hole; good for spring chinook; fish tailout for steelhead.

26. GAUGE HOLE - Walk from Pipeline Hole (road's rough). Fish deep water close to bank on pipeline side.

27. SWIMMING HOLE - Girl Scout Camp. Upper end is good.

28. PIPELINE HOLE - Large deep hole, excellent for plunking or drifting. Bull Run dumps in here. *Stay out of Bull Run.*

29. GARBAGE PIT HOLE - Plunking and drifting. Fairly easy access and good parking.

30. ALDERS HOLE - Long and deep; hard to get into.

31. SOAPSTONE DRIFT - Fairly deep hole drifts down to gravel bar. Walk up from Alders Hole.

32. MOUTH OF CEDAR CR. HOLE - Accessible from Cedar Cr. side. Plunking hole on Cedar Cr. side, drift fishing on opposite side. *Hatchery closure on Cedar Creek.*

33. OKIE DRIFT - Long, fast drift, good for floating lures, just above mouth of Cedar Cr.

34. REVENUE BRIDGE - Fish south side of stream below bridge.

35. LOWER CANYON HIKE - Park at bridge and hike up lower canyon.

36. AIRPORT HOLE - Park on road and walk downstream into canyon.

37. POWER LINE HOLE - Long walk in.

38. UPPER CANYON HIKE - Walk into canyon and fish to below dam. Road parallels stream to dam.

39. MARMOT DAM - Excellent bank angling access for winter steelhead; good for summer steelhead.

is a good place for non-fishing family members to play and relax. To reach Dabney, follow Stark Street east from Gresham, crossing from the south to the north bank on the Stark St. Bridge (a.k.a. Viking Bridge) just below the park. (There is a good deep plunking hole below Stark St. Bridge.) Above Dabney, Fill Your Waders Drift, Springdale Hole, and Collins Hole are accessible only to boat anglers.

Oxbow Park offers excellent access to many good holes and drifts, including the YMCA Drift, Hossner Drift, Upper Hossner Drift, Sawmill Drift, the Crusher Hole, and Big Rock Hole. To reach Oxbow, follow Division St. east from Gresham, turning right onto Oxbow Dr., then left on Oxbow Parkway.

Dodge Park also provides outstanding bank angling opportunities. To reach the park, follow Division St. east beyond Gresham, turning right onto Oxbow Drive, then right onto Lusted Rd at the Oxbow Parkway junction. Lusted follows the river along a high bluff, dropping down at Dodge and crossing to the Sandy's north bank. Buttler's Eddy, Blue Hole, Gauge Hole, Swimming Hole, and Pipeline Hole are all accessible from the bank at Dodge. Across the river from Dodge by way of Dodge Park Bridge, Lusted Rd. provides additional access.

There is also excellent steelhead water in the Revenue Bridge area north of the community of Sandy. From Hwy. 26 turn north onto Ten Eyck Rd., crossing Cedar Creek and following signs to the Oregon Dept. of Fish and Wildlife Hatchery. Park in the lot and walk down to the river to fish a good hole at the mouth of Cedar Creek (fishing is prohibited in the Creek itself), and Okie Drift just above the creek mouth. Anglers also fish the water below the bridge.

Upstream there is a lot of good water available for bank fishing off a private PGE road on the north bank. Cross Revenue Bridge, turning right onto Marmot Rd. and climbing Devil's Backbone, then dropping down onto the PGE road, which is usually open to public use. There is also good fishing above the Diversion Dam and below the road for anglers willing to do some hiking.

Shad occasionally come into the Sandy from the Columbia, usually in June if the Columbia is high. Most anglers fish for them from boats below I-84. Smelt come up into the river when they feel like it. Only the smelt seem to know exactly which years, and they aren't talking. Anglers can call the Clackamas Regional Office of the Oregon Dept. of Fish and Wildlife to check in March or April. When they do come in, smelt are caught by dipping hand nets from the bank in the area from Stark St. Bridge to the mouth, with heaviest concentration around the old Troutdale Bridge. Trout are not stocked in the Sandy, and the river is generally too turbid for good trout fishing. Trout anglers would do better to fish the Sandy's tributaries. See Salmon River, Camp Creek, Lost Creek.

The only campground on the lower Sandy is at Oxbow County Park. The other parks have picnic facilities only. Other campgrounds are located in Mt. Hood National Forest off Hwy. 26 east of Zigzag.

SANTIAM RIVER, MIDDLE The major tributary of the South Santiam, flowing about 30 miles to its confluence in the Foster Dam pool, where it forms the northeast arm of the reservoir. Only a few miles above Foster its flow is obstructed by Green Peter Dam to form Green Peter Lake with Quartz Creek.

Above Green Peter, the Middle Santiam flows free for about 20 miles, one of Oregon's

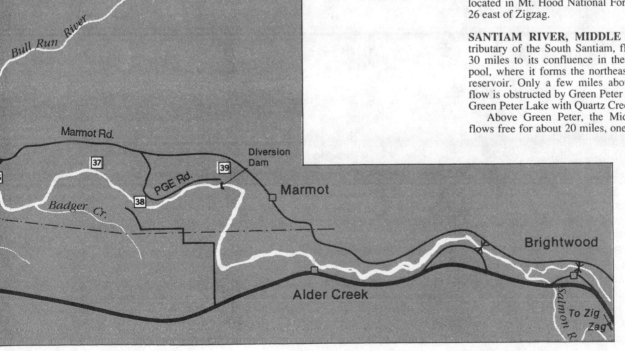

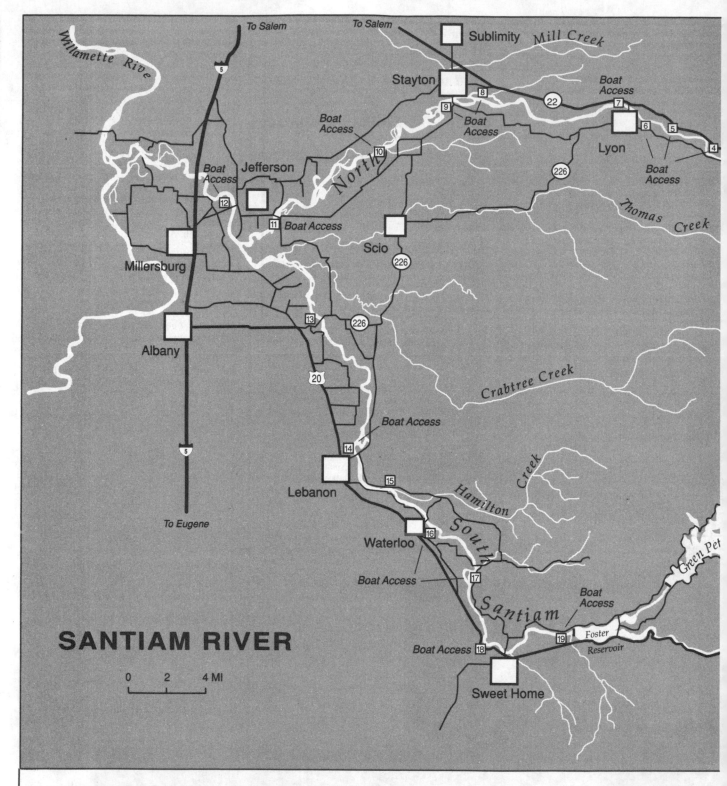

SANTIAM RIVER

0 2 4 MI

1. PACKSADDLE CO. PARK - Unimproved gravel launch for drift boats and rafts (ROUGH RAPIDS, EXPERIENCED BOATERS ONLY); next take-out 4 1/2 mi. at Kimmel on so. side; bank angling at lower end of park for summer steelhead, chinook in June & July. Check special regs.

2. MINTO CO. PARK - Good bank access for salmon & steelhead.

3. KIMMEL PARK - Pole slide put-in and take-out. Falls below boatable in high water only. Check spcial regs. for Mill City bridge area.

4. FISHERMEN'S BEND - BLM park, campground, gravel ramp. Prior to park opening, launch boats off bank west of park entrance. Drift 4 mi. to next take-out (moderately experienced boaters). Good bank access for summer steelhead, spring chinook, stocked rainbow.

5. NORTH SANTIAM STATE PARK - Unimproved launch from gravel road west of parking lot. Drift 1+ miles to Neal Park or 2+ mi. to Mehama Bridge (intermediate boaters). Good

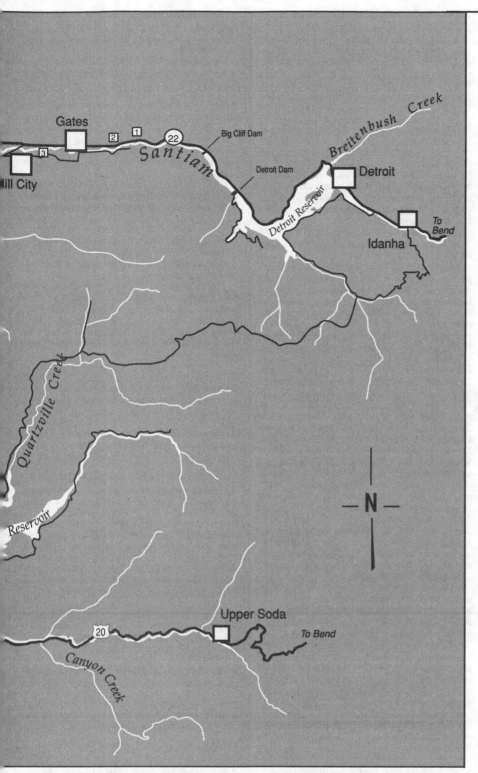

9. STAYTON BRIDGE - Improved public ramp at so. end of bridge for easy 5 mi. drift to next take-out. Good chinook holding water. Some bank angling on no. side.

10. BUELL MILLER BOAT RAMP - Improved ramp, limited parking. Beware of impassable log jam about 2 1/2 mi. down in main channel; right detour channel floatable only in high water; 7 mi. to next take-out.

11. GREEN'S BRIDGE - Public boat and bank access from gravel bar. Popular drift for winter steelhead in Mar. & April to confluence with and Jefferson ramp.

12. JEFFERSON BOAT RAMP - Improved ramp with good bank angling from bridge for chinook and steelhead amongst rock ledges.

13. SANDERSON'S BRIDGE - Gravel bar access at end of old hwy. right-of-way. Bank angling above & below bridge. Drift 10 mi. to Jefferson beyond N. Santiam confluence. Accesses smallmouth bass fishery at mouth of Thomas Cr.

14. GILL LANDING - Seldom used ramp above Grant St. Bridge; shallow drift over gravel bars.

15. LEBANON DAM - Popular bank angling for spring chinook mid-May to mid-June 200 ft. below dam.

16. WATERLOO-LINN CO. PARK - Last take-out before Lebanon Dam. Good bank fishing above bridge at rapids where fish hold below cascades and upstream from ramp.

17. MCDOWELL CR. - Private (fee pay) access to unimproved gravel bar upstream of bridge. Next take-out 4 mi. at Waterloo.

18. SWEET HOME BOAT RAMP - Steep improved ramp at so. end of Pleasant Valley Br. Next take-out a slow 6 mi. to McDowell Cr. Good bank fishing chinook hole downstream of bridge. Park along hwy.

19. WILEY CR. PARK - Intensive bank fishery for heavy concentrations of summer steelhead April-Aug.; winter steelhead Mar.-April; spring chinook May-Aug. Improved ramp accesses most popular drift on river.

bank access for summer steelhead, spring chinook, stocked rainbow.

6. JOHN NEAL CO. PARK - Easy 1 mile drift from improved ramp to Mehama. Good holes with bedrock ledges near mouth of Little No. Santiam. Good bank access for all fisheries.

7. MEHAMA BRIDGE - Fish above bridge on south bank and good water upstream 1/2 mi. Paved ramp on so. side accesses 7 mile drift to Stayton Is. with many holes and drifts. **VERIFY ACCESSIBILITY OF NEXT TAKE-OUT.**

8. STAYTON IS. - Tricky take-out. In high flows portage over dam on left and take-out at Stayton Br. Otherwise, check with City of Stayton Police for key to old water supply bridge access from right channel.

more productive wild trout fisheries. It offers good angling for large numbers of resident rainbow and cutthroat in the 6-9 inch range, with catches to 15 inches. The Willamette heads in the Three Pyramids area west of the southern Mt. Jefferson Wilderness, Willamette National Forest.

A private Weyerhauser road (open to public use except occasionally during fire season) follows the lower river from Green Peter through an old clear-cut. To reach it, head north off Hwy. 20 at a spot designated *Cascadia Damsite* on the Willamette National Forest map (about 1 1/2 miles west of Cascadia State Park). This road leads to the south bank of Green Peter. Turn east at the reservoir and continue about 7 miles before crossing to the north bank at the upper end of the dam pool. The Weyerhauser road closely follows the Middle Santiam about 6 miles upstream, providing access to good trout water.

Beyond this road, the Middle Santiam flows through a 7 mile roadless area, a wooded canyon that beckons the more adventurous angler. Near its headwaters, the river is again accessed by roads. FS 2041, which heads north from Hwy. 20 at Upper Soda (1 mile past Fernview Campground) crosses the Middle Santiam just above Pyramid Creek. There is some very nice flyfishing water near the crossing, with broad flat banks and good gravel. FS 2047 heads north from Hwy. 20 at House Rock Camp, following Sheep Creek and meeting the river just below Iron Mt. Lookout. This road follows the Middle Santiam about 3 miles downstream. These roads are snowbound until May or June.

The only developed campground on the Middle Santiam is on the north bank of Green Peter. Weyerhauser prefers no camping along the lower road due to fire danger. However, there are natural campsites in the national forest along the upper river.

SANTIAM RIVER, NORTH One of two equally productive and popular forks of the Santiam River, a Top 10 producer of summer and winter steelhead, with a fair run of spring chinook and plenty of trout angling. Over 60 miles long, this major tributary of the Willamette River is accessible from boat or bank, providing good angling the year around.

North and South Santiam meet near Jefferson, east of Hwy. 99E about 5 miles north of Albany, just 12 miles from the Willamette confluence. Most angling takes place from Jefferson upstream, with salmon and steelhead confined to the river below Big Cliff Dam. The lower river is followed east by the Jefferson to Stayton Rd. From Stayton it is tracked by Hwy. 22, which follows the river to within 8 miles of its headwaters at Santiam Lake in the southern Marion Lake Basin of Mt. Jefferson Wilderness, Willamette National Forest.

The North Santiam is fed by many good tributaries. See Breitenbush, Marion, Blow-out, Little North Santiam. Several dams obstruct the flow in the mid-section of the river, the largest one forming Detroit Reservoir.

Summer steelhead are in the river the year around, with good numbers taken May through October, and peak catches in June and July. The 1986 catch was over 5400. Winter steelhead enter the river in November, with peak angling in April and May. About 1500 were caught in 1986. Red and yellow fluorescent lures are popular with both boat and bank anglers. Spring chinook arrive in mid-May, with peak catches in June. From 500-1000 are caught each year, primarily in the area from Stayton to Mill City.

The North Santiam is a favorite river for flyfishing steelheaders. Anglers use a floating greased line, skating steelhead flies on the surface. Naturals on the river include stoneflies, caddis, green drakes, and mayflies. Popular imitations are Purple Matukas, Green-Butted Skunks, Macks Canyon, and Golden Demon. Bait anglers use eggs, sand shrimp, and nightcrawlers. Popular lures include Corkies (pink pearl, red, and chartreuse), No. 4 Bud's Spinner (gold or silver, especially effective in fast water), Wee Warts, Wiggle Warts, and Hot Shots.

There's fair angling for rainbow and cutthroat below Detroit Reservoir, with some big fish available (and the chance of incidentally hooking a steelhead). Rainbow are stocked several times each year between Mill City and Mehama. Catchables are launched in the river from boxes pulled behind drift boats, with releases made over several miles of stream. But the best trout fishing is above the reservoir. From Idanha to above Marion Forks the river is well stocked with legal trout, and there are good size natives as well. The water above Marion Forks is especially good for flyfishing. Above the last highway bridge in the Big Meadows area, small native cutthroat are available, as well as some eastern brook trout which have migrated from the lakes above. Late season angling in this section is usually productive.

Below Big Cliff Dam, the North Santiam offers a challenge to drift boat anglers. Boaters launch at Packsaddle County Park about 4 miles below Big Cliff Dam, Kimmel Park in Mill City, Fishermen's Bend BLM Campground just west of Mill City, North Santiam State Park 3 miles east of Lyons, John Neal County Park and Mehama Bridge in Lyons, Stayton Bridge, Buell Miller Access north of Shelburn, Green's Bridge east of Jefferson (natural gravel bar), and the Jefferson Boat Ramp. (See map for details). Popular one-day drifts are from Packsaddle County Park to Kimmel (rough rapids below Packsaddle), Fishermen's Bend to North Santiam State Park, State Park to John Neal Park or Mehama Bridge, Stayton Bridge to Buell Miller, and Green's Bridge to Jefferson. The river is laced with formidable rapids, and boating experience and advance scouting are recommended.

Bank anglers have good access to salmon and steelhead at Packsaddle Park, Minto Park, Fishermen's Bend, North Santiam State Park, John Neal, Mehama Bridge, Stayton Bridge, Green's Bridge, and Jefferson Boat Ramp.

Below Detroit Reservoir, camping facilities are available at Fishermen's Bend BLM Recreation Area west of Mill City. National Forest campgrounds are located at Detroit Lake, and off Hwy. 22 east of Idanha at Whispering Forks and Marion Falls.

SANTIAM RIVER, SOUTH FORK One of two equally popular and productive forks of the Santiam River, a Top 10 producer of summer and winter steelhead and spring chinook. The South Santiam joins the the North Santiam near Jefferson, about 5 miles north of Albany, just 12 miles from the Willamette confluence. It flows about 80 miles from its headwaters in the Cascades of Willamette National Forest, interrupted by two dams, at Lebanon and near Sweet Home. The dam near Sweet Home creates Foster Reservoir, one of whose major arms is the backwater of the Middle Santiam River. Green Peter Reservoir is on the Middle Santiam just a few miles upstream from Foster.

Hwy. 20 roughly follows the river from Albany to Sweet Home. River crossings are on Hwy. 226 just east of Albany, at Lebanon on the Grant St. Bridge, and at Sweet Home on the Pleasant Valley Bridge. Above Foster Reservoir Hwy. 20 follows the river very closely to its headwaters.

Summer steelhead offer the most popular sport on the South Santiam, a hatchery fishery that regularly produces annual catches in excess of 4,000. The 1986 catch was almost 5000. Summers are in the river year around, with heavy catches made from May through August. The run peaks in June and July. The winter steelhead are a wild run, in the river from January through May, with peak catches in April and May. The 1986 winter catch was about 1000.

Both summer and winter steelhead returning from sea after two years average 8 pounds, while three year salt steelhead weigh in at about 12 pounds. Sand shrimp and eggs are the common bait, with drift fishing techniques effective when the river is low. Flyfishing for steelhead continues to gain in popularity, with Green Butted Skunks and Muddler Minnows among the favorite patterns.

Most steelhead angling takes place in the Sweet Home and Foster Dam areas. The most popular bank fishery is at Wiley Creek Park just below Foster, where heavy concentrations of anglers fish heavy concentrations of summer run fish from April to August, and winter run in March and April.

The spring chinook catch is up to almost 1000 annually, with fish in the river from April through July, and peak catches in May. The most popular fisheries (with access from bank and boat) are at the Cable and Waterfall Holes below Foster Dam from May through August, downstream from the Pleasant Valley Bridge at Sweet Home, and below Lebanon Dam mid-May to Mid-June. The chinook average 13-17 pounds.

The South Santiam is a popular river for drift boats and jet sleds, with less challenging whitewater making it especially good for beginning boaters. As for angling techniques, back-bouncing eggs, or egg and shrimp combinations is very effective. Corkies or Spin-N-Glos help float the set-up, which usually includes 4-5 ounces of lead on about 8 inches of leader. Boat ramps are available at Wiley Cr. Park (accessing the most popular drift on the river), at Sweet Home on the south end of Pleasant Valley Bridge, and at Sanderson's Bridge 10 miles south of Jefferson. There is gravel bar access to the river at McDowell Cr. (across private property, fee pay), and a take-out at Waterloo-Linn Co. Park right before Lebanon Dam.

There's good fishing for trout in the river above Foster Dam. The stream is stocked with legal rainbow from mid-May through July, and native cutthroat are also available, with roughly 25% of the catch wild. Flyfishing is very good up here, and light gear is a necessity for all angling later in the season. The trout average 8-11 inches.

Smallmouth bass are available in the river from Thomas Creek to about 4 miles downstream. Bank angling for them is restricted due to private land holdings, but boat anglers reach the fishery in jet sleds, or by putting in at Sanderson's and drifting to Jefferson. The smallmouth average one pound.

Camping facilities are available at Foster Reservoir, at Cascadia 5 miles east of Foster, and at three campgrounds on Hwy. 20 in Willamette National Forest (Trout Creek, Fernview, and House Rock). Be sure to check current angling regulations for seasons, deadlines, and special closures. Above Foster Reservoir the steelhead fishery is catch and release only (if they make it past the dam, they deserve to live).

SANTOSH SLOUGH Good bass and panfish water convenient to the Portland area, a good family fishing spot. Santosh is off Multnomah Channel near Scappoose, NW of Portland. It can be approached from the Channel or by road, and successfully fished from boat and bank.

The Oregon Bass and Panfish Club has helped to make the grassy banks accessible to the public. Crappie to 3/4 pounds, largemouth bass to 2 pounds, perch, and bullhead catfish are available. To reach it, take Hwy. 30 north through Scappoose, turning right at the airport sign just beyond North Scappoose Creek. Turn left onto Honeyman Rd. at the 3-way stop sign and continue past the airport about 4 miles. At the metal gate on the dike near the pumping station associated with the slough, there is a dirt road that leads to the parking area. Stiles provide access through the fence to the public area. The slough bank is open to public use for 2,000 ft. The Bass and Panfish Club urges anglers to strictly obey the posted signs to insure continued access to the slough.

SCAPPOOSE CREEK A good early season trout stream in Columbia County, only 20 miles NW of Portland. Following Hwy. 30 from Portland to Scappoose, you'll cross the two forks of the stream just west of the town. They join just north of the highway, and the creek flows into Scappoose Bay a few miles downstream. To get to the upper North Fork, take the paved road south. This road crosses and follows the creek to its headwaters. The South Fork is reached by the Dutch Canyon Rd. which heads west from the highway just south of town. Lots of private property on the South Fork creates a real access problem, but the North Fork has plenty of available water.

The North Fork is stocked with catchable sea-run cutthroat. Some are caught immediately, and others migrate, returning as fat 12 inchers as early as fall of the same year. Both forks have a fair number of native cutthroat as well. Bait angling is effective, and flies and lures will work after early season when the water clears. A few large sea-runs are caught each year when the stream opens in April. Some good size cutthroat are taken in December by steelheaders.

Both forks are open for winter angling, with fair runs of steelhead in each. The fish enter the creek in December, and most of the fish are caught before March. The main stream is fished heavily below the forks. Bait plunking is standard, but spin casting takes fish above the forks and covers more stream. There are several picnic areas on the North Fork, but no campgrounds.

SCOGGINS CREEK This is a fair early season trout stream in the Tualatin River drainage south of Forest Grove. It heads at the Tillamook Co. line and flows east for 13 miles, paralleling and south of Gales Creek.

The upper section empties into Haag Lake Reservoir. This section is not stocked, but supports native cutthroat. A gravel logging road follows it upstream quite a ways. Angling usually slows up by June, and the creek gets quite low in late summer.

The lower section is crossed near the mouth by Hwy. 47, about 4 miles south of Forest Grove, and is followed upstream by a good road. This portion is stocked and has a fair number of native cutthroat as well. Most anglers use bait or small spinners and lures. Trout run 6-11 inches. See Haag Lake. There is no camping in the area.

SCOUT LAKE (Hood River Co.) A 3 acre lake in the Wahtum Lake area, just south of Wahtum on the same road. See Wahtum Lake for directions. Scout is stocked with brook trout. Fish caught range from 7-9 inches.

SCOUT LAKE (Marion Co.) A good lake in a beautiful natural alpine park at the base of Mt. Jefferson. See Bays Lake for trail directions into Jefferson Park. Scout Lake is 1/4 mile east of Bays Lake.

Seven acres and 30 ft. deep, it is stocked by air with fingerling brook trout. These fish are not easily caught, but they run to 3 pounds. Try a grasshopper in late August. Heavy use has impacted the land along the lakeshore, and the Forest Service is discouraging camping within 100 feet of the shore to allow regeneration of the vegetation. Please cooperate.

SEPARATION LAKE A relatively isolated 5 acre brook trout lake in Three Sisters Wilderness. From McKenzie Bridge on Hwy. 126 east of Eugene, take the Horse Creek Rd. FS 2638 SE 8 miles to Roney Creek. A trail from there leads about 7 miles to the lake.

Separation Lake is only about 5 acres but has had good angling for brook trout 10-14 inches. A few trout 18 inches or more have been taken. It can be easily fished from shore, and all methods can be effective. Natural campsites are available.

SERENE LAKE A 20 acre hike-in brook and rainbow lake at 4350 ft. in the western part of the High Rock area of the upper Clackamas watershed. Trail 512 begins at Frazier Forks Campground and winds past the Rock Lakes. For detailed directions to the trailhead see Rock Lakes. Signs point the way for the easy 3 mile hike west to Serene Lake.

Serene is stocked with brook and rainbow trout, which are usually present in good numbers. Fish run 6-15 inches, averaging 9-10. All methods can be effective depending on the season. Bait or lure fishing is best in early season, and flyfishing is best in late summer and fall. There are good natural campsites. Some pasture is available if you have a bronco. The road is usually not open until late June.

SHARPS CREEK This small trout stream flows into the Row River at Culp Creek, about 5 miles upstream from Dorena Reservoir. It's about 12 miles long. To reach it, turn east on the Row River Rd. from 99W at Cottage Grove. At the creek crossing, a gravel road follows the stream south to its head. The creek has a good population of native cutthroat, and it is currently stocked with rainbow early in trout season. It usually offers good bait fishing the first few months of the season.

SHEEP LAKE One of three brook trout lakes NW of Mt. Jefferson near the head of the South Fork of the Breitenbush River. See Firecamp Lakes for directions. Sheep has the poorest fishery of the three, producing poor catches of small brook trout. There are good huckleberries up here, though.

SHELLROCK CREEK A small accessible trout stream in the upper Clackamas drainage. Shellrock flows south from the High Rock area and enters the Oak Grove Fork several miles above Harriet Lake. From Estacada, follow Hwy. 224 to Ripplebrook Ranger Station. From there take FS 57 up the Oak Grove Fork. About 2 miles east of Harriet Lake, this road crosses the mouth of Shellrock Creek and turns north to

follow it upstream. At this point the road becomes FS 58, and you'll almost immediately pass Shellrock Creek Campground. It's 38 miles from Estacada to this point. Shellrock Rd. follows the creek on the east bank up to High Rock.

Not stocked, the stream has native cutthroat 6-10 inches, as well as a few brook trout that drift down from the lakes above. There are campgrounds at both ends of the creek.

SHELLROCK LAKE A very popular 20 acre brook trout lake in the High Rock lakes area., accessed by a good but steep trail one mile south of Frazier Forks Campground. The easier way to the lake is from Hideaway Lake to the south, which you can drive to. Shellrock is 1/2 mile north of Hideaway by Trail 700, which circles Hidaway Lake. For road directions see Hideaway Lake.

Both rainbow and cutthroat were previously stocked in Shellrock, but survival was poor. Brook trout hold up well, and that's what you'll find there now. The lake is fished hard, but manages to produce a lot of fish 6-13 inches, averaging 9 inches. Shellrock is a shallow lake, and flyfishing is very good mornings and evenings. Sunken wet flies retrieved slowly will usually work well. Bait angling is good at the start of the season. The lake is at 4200 ft., and snow usually limits access until mid to late June. There are good natural campsites at the lake.

SHINING LAKE A 12 acre rainbow trout lake in the High Rock area of the upper Clackamas watershed, about 55 miles from Portland.

The trailhead is a little over 3 miles west of Frazier Forks Campground on Indian Ridge Rd. It leaves that road on the north side, about 1/2 mile before the dead-end. The lake is an easy 15 minute hike. For road directions to Frazier Forks, see Rock Lakes.

Shining is stocked with rainbow trout averaging 6-13 inches, and there are usually plenty of them. The lake is 24 ft. deep, and all angling methods take fish. A lot of crayfish are present, and the tails attract big fish. This is a good fly lake in late fall, in fact, it is often a hot spot in general near the end of the season.

There is a campsite and spring at the lake, and a camp on the road above. This area is excellent for huckleberries.

SHORT LAKE A small but deep brook trout lake one mile north of Breitenbush Hot Springs. To reach it, follow the Breitenbush River Rd. from Detroit to Breitenbush Campground, take the first road to the left, then right. This is FS 46040. It heads north up the west side of Short Creek, and reaches Short lake in 2 miles. You can see the lake just south of the road. There used to be big brook trout to 18 inches here, but since the road came in, the size has dropped. It is stocked by air and truck.

SILVER CREEK (Marion Co.) One of the main forks of the Pudding River, about 25 miles long, heading east of Silver Creek Falls State Park. The 2 upper forks meet in the State Park, and the main creek joins the Pudding River east of Silverton after flowing through the city. From Silverton, Hwy. 214 follows the creek above the forks. The park is large and has camping and other improvements. Distance from Salem is about 25 miles.

A fair number of native cutthroat trout are taken in both the forks and mainstem below. It is not stocked. Most anglers use bait, but there is some lure and flyfishing. Fish range 6-11 inches.

SILVER CREEK RESERVOIR A 65 acre water supply reservoir for Silverton which drains into Silver Creek. It's stocked with legal size trout early each season. This one is hard to fish from the bank, so it helps to bring a boat. No motors are allowed.

SILVER KING LAKE A nice brook trout lake, still fairly isolated in the upper Collawash River headwaters west of Silver King Mountain. Shortest way in is by Trail 544 from Elk Lake. It's about 4 miles by ridge walk north to the lake. See Elk Lake for road directions.

A longer but interesting approach is by trail up the Hot Springs Fork of the Collawash River. You can look forward to a good soak in the waters of Bagby Hot Springs (clothing optional). Take Hwy. 224 to the Collawash River Rd. FS 63. Follow this to the Bagby Hot Springs Trailhead. The route up the Hot Springs Fork is fairly long, about 8 1/2 miles, but you can fish the stream. After 8 miles on Trail 544 south, you will reach a sign reading Silver King Mt. A quarter mile further, watch for a trail leading up to the lake.

The lake is only 4 acres and 8 feet deep, at about 4100 ft. There's good angling for brook trout 7-14 inches. All methods take fish here.

SKOOKUM LAKE (Clackamas Co.) A small trout lake with campground in the headwaters of Fish Creek, a bit over 30 road miles SE of Estacada. Skookum is at elevation 3800 ft. The lake covers only 4 acres but is fairly deep.

From Estacada drive SE on the Clackamas River Rd., Hwy. 224, into Mt. Hood National Forest. About 8 miles inside the forest, at Fish Creek Campground, FS 54 crosses the Clackamas River and heads south along Fish Creek. Six miles south, FS 5440 branches SW. Six miles down 5440, near Bracket Mountain, FS 5420 cuts back to the east. Follow this winding road a bit over 2 miles to FS 350, which turns SW and leads about 2 miles to the lake.

Skookum has good supply of brooktrout 6-12 inches, averaging 10 inches. The lake is stocked with fingerlings each year by air. All angling methods can work, and flyfishing is very good in late fall.

SKOOKUM LAKE (Marion Co.) A bass and panfish lake in northern Marion County, 3 miles south of Newberg, 1/2 mile south of Hwy. 219, which goes from Newberg to St. Paul. The road into the lake is private, and there's a charge for access. About 25 acres and lightly fished, it maintains the usual assortment of panfish, including bluegill, crappie, and brown bullhead. A few largemouth bass are also taken. There's a parking area and a few boats for rent.

SLIDEOUT LAKE A fair eastern brook trout lake high in the headwaters of the Breitenbush River, east of the Firecamp Lakes. See Firecamp Lakes for trail directions. Slideout is a mile bushwhack over the ridge to the east of the Firecamp area. It is downstream and north about 1/2 mile from Swindle Lake.

A fairly deep lake, Slideout is about 10 acres and lightly fished. The brook trout run 6-11 inches, but there may be a few sleepers in here. It can be fished from shore using any method.

SMITH LAKE (Lane Co.) An over-populated 8 acre brook trout lake one mile north of Irish Mt. Smith Lake is about 1/4 mile SW of McFarland Lake. See Mcfarland for trail directions. Fishing is very good for stunted brook trout 6-8 inches. Any method will take fish here almost any time. Natural campsites are available. McFarland Lake offers more exciting fishing.

SMITH LAKE (Multnomah Co.) A 60 acre fishery on North Portland Rd. It contains white crappie, brown bullhead, bluegill, yellow perch, and largemouth bass.

SMITH RIVER RESERVOIR A narrow deep reservoir in the upper McKenzie area. It can be reached by following the McKenzie Highway 71 miles to Carmen Bridge at Trail Bridge Reservoir. From there, FS 730 heads north for several miles, ending at the Smith Dam.

The lake is stocked with legal rainbow, and fishing is usually good. Most fish are taken by trolling or still-fishing. They run 9-13 inches, though a few good size cutthroat show up in the catch, and brook trout to 12 inches are occasionally taken.

A good boat ramp is available at the dam. A speed limit of 10 mph is in effect, so anglers get a break from speedboats. There is a nice camping area at the north end of the reservoir, but a boat is needed to reach it. There is good camping at Trail Bridge Lake just south.

SPINNING LAKE A good brook trout lake just off the road in the Breitenbush Lake area. The trail begins about 1 1/2 miles west of Breitenbush Lake, where the outlet of Pyramid Lake crosses FS 4220. It's 1/4 mile north to the lake. See Breitenbush Lake for road directions.

Spinning Lake is only 3 acres and shallow, but it's lightly fished and holds up well. Brook trout run big here, with most from 10-18 inches and some bigger. The lake loses fish in severe winters, but some fish usually survive. There are no campsites available, but there's good camping at Breitenbush Lake.

SPIRIT LAKE A good 12 acre brook trout lake in the headwaters of Salmon Creek about 5 miles west of Waldo Lake. From Oakridge, take Salmon Creek Rd. FS 24 all the way up to the Black Creek Branch road FS 2421. About 1/2 mile up 2421, FS 2422 cuts back to the north. Follow 2422 over 7 twisting miles to the Spirit Lake Trailhead. Trail 3584 offers an easy 1/4 mile hike to the lake.

The brook trout in Spirit Lake are in good shape and average about 10 inches, with some to 15 inches. All methods can be used.

SPY LAKE A small trout lake north of the Mink Lake Basin, well off the beaten track. See Corner Lake for directions. From Corner Lake, take Trail 3517 north one mile. Spy Lake is 1/4 mile to the east. Only 3 acres but 20 feet deep, the lake is lightly fished, with a population 6-9 inch brook trout or cutthroat. Nice natural campsites are available.

SQUAW LAKES (Clackamas Co.) A series of small brook trout lakes east of the Clackamas River near Squaw Mt. The three main lakes total only about 7 acres, and all are quite shallow. They are at elevation 3550 ft.

From Estacada, take Hwy. 224 SE 6 miles to North Fork Reservoir, then head east on FS 4610, the North Fork Rd. Follow 4610 about 14 miles east to the lakes, which are located just north of the road. Twin Springs Campground is about 2 miles further on 4610, so if you miss the lakes, backtrack from there. There is some private property in the area, which may be fenced. The western shore of the lakes is in the Mt. Hood National Forest.

The lakes have all produced well, with brook trout 6-14 inches. The lakes get slow in mid-summer, but fall angling is usually good. Squaw Lakes only run about 5 feet deep, so flyfishing can be effective. Sunken wet flies or nymphs have produced some big fish. There are a few natural campsites at the lakes, and a campground at Twin Springs.

ST. LOUIS PONDS A group of seven constructed ponds offering an interesting variety of panfish near the community of Gervais, south of Woodburn. From I-5 take the Woodburn Exit west to Gervais Rd. Head south, then west on Jenson Rd. This is a rural area well out of range of freeway sights and sounds. The ponds are in an attractive setting of natural undergrowth. They are located to the left of the railroad. A large parking area is provided out of sight of the ponds.

The seven ponds have a combined area of 55 acres and an incredible 7 miles of shoreline. They were excavated by of the State Highway Dept. in a maze design. This is strictly a bank fishery, as floating devices are prohibited. The ponds have been open to angling since 1980, and there is a little of everything in them, including bass, channel cats, bluegill, black and white crappie, and green and red ear sunfish. A map of the ponds is displayed in a central area a short hike in from the parking lot, along with information about the various specie mixes contained in each pond. A float on Pond #3 provides access for less-abled anglers.

The ponds are open all year except during pheasant and duck seasons. No camping is allowed here, but there is a small picnic area.

ST. PAUL PONDS The Oregon Dept. of Fish and Wildlife rearing ponds for bass and panfish. Not open to public fishing, but guided tours are available. Call (503) 633-4792.

STILL CREEK A fair native trout stream in Mt. Hood National Forest, flowing into the Zigzag River about 2 miles east of the community of Zigzag. The creek heads near Hwy. 26 in the Government Camp area and loops around south of the highway to meet the Zigzag. FS 2612 follows the creek quite closely throughout its length. The upper road is usually snowbound until late May. The creek is not stocked, but it offers fair fishing for wild cutthroat in a pristine mountain setting.

STRAWBERRY LAKE A privately owned trout pond, currently open to public access and stocked with legal rainbow. It is 8 miles from St. Helens on Patterson Rd.

STURGEON LAKE A 3500 acre bass and panfish lake in the center of Sauvie Island, so named because many years ago it was thought to be the spawning ground for sturgeon. Actually, very few sturgeon are found in the lake and surrounding water, and most are too small to keep. Roads almost encircle the lake, but you cannot drive around it because of the Gilbert River outlet at the north end. In recent years the lake has begun to silt in. Efforts are underway to collect funds to finance the construction of a new channel that will provide flushing from the Columbia.

From Portland drive NW 10 miles on Hwy. 30 to the Sauvie Island Bridge. Follow Sauvie Island Rd. north after crossing. Turn right on Reeder Rd. to reach the Oak Island access to the lake, or continue on Reeder about 1 1/2 miles past the Oak Island Junction to Coon Pt. where there is a parking area beside the road. The point offers good bank angling opportunities just over the dike. Reeder Rd. continues west to the junction with Gillihan Loop Rd., then turns north, following the Columbia River toward the north end of Sauvie Island. The west bank of Sturgeon Lake can be accessed through Game Management land at several points along Reeder. Anglers can also boat into the lake from the Gilbert River. There is a public boat ramp on Sauvie Island at the Gilbert River confluence with Multnomah Channel, and another at Brown's Landing (fee pay to park) just up the channel. It is about 5 miles from the Gilbert River mouth to Sturgeon Lake.

Crappie are the most abundant species in the lake, which also contains brown bullhead, perch, bluegill, and largemouth bass. Some fairly large bass are available in the shoal areas in June and July. Anglers seem to prefer using surface plugs. Other species are primarily taken on bait, with fishing best on the incoming tide, especially near the sloughs and streams. Help yourself to some expert tips from the folks at Brown's Landing, who rent bass boats. The crappie get big here and will hit spinner and bait or pork rind and feathered jigs.

There is no public camping on Sauvie Island, but there are many delightful natural picnic sites. The lake is closed to angling during duck hunting season. See also haldeman pond, gilbert river, and mcnary lakes.

SUNSET LAKE (Lane Co.) A good trout lake in the Horse Lake group west of Elk Lake. The easiest route to the lake is by the Island Meadow Trail from Elk Lake Lodge. The junction with the Pacific Crest Trail is about one mile west. Follow it west one mile to a side trail cutting to the north. This trail leads to Sunset Lake in about a mile, then continues to Horse Lake.

Sunset is about 40 acres and fairly shallow. It can be fished from shore using all methods. Rainbow and brook trout here average 9-12 inches. The lake has slow periods but is usually good. There are good natural campsites here and at other good lakes to the west. See Horse Lakes.

SURPRISE LAKE (Fish Creek Area) Mt. Hood National Forest has a few Surprise Lakes. This one is south of the Clackamas River on the west side of the Fish Creek divide. The lake is about 5 acres and contains a good supply of very nice rainbow. It is quite shallow, at elevation 4050 ft.

From Estacada, take Hwy. 224 16 miles SE to Fish Creek Campground. Follow the Fish Creek Rd. FS 54 for 6 miles to FS 5440. Follow 5440 about 8 miles to the lake. Distinctive Camelback Mountain is visible north of the lake across the canyon.

The fish here run 8-16 inches, averaging 10. This is a very shallow lake with little cover, so stealth is in order. The lake occasionally loses fish to winterkill, but produces consistently most years. There are fair natural campsites at the lake, and a good big camp at the mouth of Fish Creek.

SURPRISE LAKE (Olallie Area) A hike-in cutthroat lake in the Olallie Lake area, west of the Skyline Rd. The 2 mile trail to Surprise heads at Lower Lake Campground 1/2 mile north of Olallie Lake. Take Trail 717 north, reaching Surprise 1/4 mile past Fish Lake.

Cutthroat here range 6-12 inches and are feisty. There aren't many fish, but good anglers are successful. There are some fair natural campsites here, and a developed campground at Lower Lake. Skyline Road is usually snowbound until the end of June.

SWINDLE LAKE A 2 acre brook trout lake in the headwaters of the Breitenbush River NW of Mt. Jefferson. The lake is about one mile NE of Bear Point and due east of the Firecamp Lakes. See Slideout Lake for directions. Slideout is 1/2 mile north of Swindle. You'll need to bushwhack, so get out your topo map and compass. Very lightly fished, its eastern brook trout range 8-11 inches. Fall is the best season. There are good natural campsites here and at other lakes nearby. See Firecamp Lakes.

TANNER CREEK A short stream in the Columbia Gorge, flowing north into the Columbia River just below Bonneville Dam. It joins the Columbia about 41 miles east of Portland off I-84. The creek is about 8 miles long and is followed by a dirt road several miles, with a trail continuing up the creek beyond road's end. The upper creek has a few native cutthroat but is fished down quickly.

This little creek has two small steelhead runs. Most of the winter fish are caught in December, and the summer run peaks in July. Total catch is usually under 50 fish for each run. The mouth of Tanner offers one of the few bank access points for the Columbia system's shad fishery. Anglers walk down to the creek from the Bonneville Dam access road. Shad usually appear in May.

The stream below the railroad bridge is in the Columbia River Regulation Zone. Check current regulations for seasons and closures. Camping facilities are available at Eagle Creek, several miles east on I-84.

TEMPLE LAKE A good hike-in rainbow lake in the upper North Santiam area west of Marion Lake. Best access is from Pine Ridge Lake by FS 2261, the Twin Meadows Rd. south of Marion Forks. If the road is snowbound early in the season, you may have to hike up to the Scout Camp at Pine Ridge. Follow Trail 3443 east about 2 miles to a spur trail that leads north 1/4 mile to the lake.

Temple covers 7 acres and is quite shallow. It is stocked by air with rainbow, and they hold up well. Most fish caught run 9-11 inches, with some over 15 inches. Almost any method works, with flies a good bet early or late in the day.

TENAS LAKES Three heavily fished trout lakes 2 miles NW of Scott Lake Campground on the McKenzie Pass Highway. These are especially good lakes for a family outing, only a 2 mile hike from Scott Lake Camp. Take Trail 3502 and head north from Benson Lake.

One lake has brook trout, one cutthroat, and one rainbow. Damifino which is which. They all seem to produce lots of action for small fish. The first or Lower Tenas is about 3 acres and quite deep. The middle and upper lakes, just a bit north, are only an acre or so but are 15-20 ft. deep. They are usually inaccessible until late June.

TETO LAKE A fair brook trout lake at the northern end of the Eight Lakes Basin SW of Mt. Jefferson. Teto is about 1/2 mile NE and several hundred feet below Jorn Lake. See Jorn Lake for trail directions. Covering 12 acres,

Teto is just west of Chiquito Lake and has lots of small brook trout. It's a fairly deep lake, and all methods are used with success.

THOMAS CREEK (Linn Co.) A good size tributary of the South Santiam River, offering winter steelhead, smallmouth bass, and some native trout. It joins the South Santiam just south of the North Santiam confluence west of Scio. The creek is about 35 miles long and flows from the east slope of the Cascades south of Mill City. Hwy. 226 follows it from Scio to Jordan, and a gravel road continues east upstream about 10 miles further. A hiking trail follows the extreme upper end. Access is somewhat restricted.

Smallmouth bass are well established in the lower 8 miles below Scio. Quite a few native cutthroat are caught, and legal rainbow are stocked each spring. Thomas has a wild steelhead run, with around 50 caught each year, usually in March and April. A remnant chinook run spawns in this river, but angling for them is prohibited most of the season.

There's good flyfishing here when the water warms and clears. There is no camping along the creek. Supplies are available at Scio and Lyons.

TIMBER LAKE A 15 acre lake in the compound of the Timber Lake Job Corps. Center, open to public fishing for stocked legal rainbow and small brown bullhead. To reach it, take Hwy. 224 east from Estacada. The compound is just west of Ripplebrook Ranger Station.

TIMOTHY LAKE (Timothy Meadows Reservoir) A good 1400 acre reservoir featuring three varieties of trout, kokanee, and quantities of crayfish, located on the upper Oak Grove Fork of the Clackamas River. It's about 80 miles to Timothy from Portland by way of Hwy. 26 past Mt. Hood and FS 42 (the Skyline Rd.). It can also be reached from Estacada by Hwy. 224 along the Clackamas River, a route which appears to be shorter, but is slower.

For the Skyline route, follow Hwy. 26 about 11 miles east of Government Camp and turn west onto FS 42 about 2 miles past the Clear Lake turn-off. Seven miles south at Joe Graham Campground, FS 57 forks off to the west and leads 2 miles to the reservoir.

Timothy has brook, rainbow, and cutthroat trout. Brook trout are very plentiful, with some over 5 pounds and challenging to catch. Catchable rainbow are stocked. Kokanee provide good sport from spring through early summer. When the water warms they move down to the thermocline and the success rate drops off. The kokanee range 8-11 inches.

Most angling is from boats, with bait fishing and trolling both effective. Bank anglers favor spinning gear and small lures. Fly angling can be excellent near the mouths of the tributaries in late summer and fall. Although the lake gets heavy use, it maintains a high catch rate throughout the season, with catch rate increasing as the season progresses.

The reservoir supports a large population of crayfish. In fact, crayfish (a.k.a. crawdads, crawfish) are so plentiful here that the state licenses commercial fishing for them as long as the supply holds out. They are found in all the shallows, including right off the campgrounds. Fish for them with traps baited with pieces of fish or chicken. Crayfish tails can be very tempting to the lake's big brookies.

There are 5 large campgrounds around the lake, each within sight of a boat ramp. The Pine Point ramp is useable even when the reservoir is drawn down. Meditation Point Campground on the north side can be reached only by boat or trail. Several smaller lakes are within easy hiking distance. See dinger and buck.

TIMPANOGAS LAKE A very nice drive-to brook trout lake, headwaters of the Middle Fork of the Willamette. It can be reached by road from Oakridge or Crescent Lake. Neither of these approaches is open until late June in most years. The Crescent Lake approach is a bit rougher, but quicker if you can tolerate it.

From Oakridge, drive south on Hwy. 58 a mile or so to the Hills Creek Reservoir turnoff. Follow FS 21 around the west shore of the reservoir and up the upper middle fork of the Willamette about 33 miles (from the dam) to FS 2154. Take 2154 about 5 miles to its junction with FS 398/399, just before Opal Lake. Follow 399 1/2 mile south to Timpanogas.

From the town of Crescent Lake on Hwy. 58, follow FS 244 around the NW shore of the lake 6 miles to the junction with FS 211, the Summit Lake Rd. which enters from the NW. Take this road 6 miles to Summit Lake Campground, then head south on FS 398 about 4 miles to the lake.

Timpanogas is a pretty 40 acre lake at 5300 ft., in a setting of thick fir forest and abundant huckleberries. It's a little over 100 feet deep near the center, with most of its shoal water near the NW shore. It contains brook trout and is easily fished. Trolling is quite popular, but motors are prohibited.

There is a small but pleasant campground on the SW shore close to Lower (or Little) Timpanogas Lake, but mosquitoes can be awesome throughout much of the summer. Little Timpanogas, just west of the large lake, is 7 acres and offers fair fishing for brook trout. There are several hike-in lakes to the south, and Opal Lake is one mile north and 1/4 mile off the road. See also Indigo, June.

TORREY LAKE A large lake with fair angling for rainbow, brook, and cutthroat trout in the Taylor Burn area north of Waldo Lake. To reach it, follow a one mile trail from the trailhead on Taylor Burn Rd., 2 miles north of North Waldo Campground.

Torrey covers 70 acres and can be fished from shore, but a rubber boat would help. Brook trout averaging 10 inches make up the principal catch, with some to 16 inches plus. Rainbow are fewer but generally a bit larger. Cutthroat are also stocked. All methods are effective here, with fly angling good in the evenings. The nearest campground is Taylor Burn. It is usually accessible in late June.

TRAIL BRIDGE RESERVOIR A 90 acre reservoir in the upper McKenzie area. From Hwy. 126 about 14 miles south of the Santiam Junction, follow FS 730 around the northern shore of the reservoir. FS 2655 leads to the dam. The primary catch here is stocked rainbow 8-16 inches. A very few cutthroat and brook trout are also taken. Most anglers still fish or troll very slowly along the shoal areas. There is a boat launch at the north end beside a large campground.

TRILLIUM LAKE A trout lake on the south slope of Mt. Hood, just 3 miles from Government Camp. FS 2656 cuts south off Hwy. 26 opposite the road to Snow Bunny Lodge. The road leads directly to Trillium Lake Campground.

Trillium is formed by the damming of the headwaters of Mud Creek. It covers about 60 acres, with lots of shoal area. Pressure is very heavy on this drive-in lake so close to Portland. The lake is stocked with fingerling and legal rainbow, with a catch range 6-14 inches, averaging 9 inches. Flyfishing is quite good in late summer and fall. There is a large campground that accommodates trailers, and a boat ramp, but motors are prohibited on the lake.

TUALATIN RIVER The Tualatin is a meandering valley stream, about 75 miles long, flowing from the west across Washington County. It enters the Willamette River several miles above Oregon City. The Tualatin is fed by a number of good tributaries, including Gales Creek, Dairy Creek and Scoggins Creek. The main river is crossed and followed by many roads SW of Portland and in the Hillsboro-Forest Grove area.

Best trout angling is in the upper river above Gaston, which is on Hwy. 47 south of Forest Grove, but this part of the river is almost inaccessible due to private landholdings. For this reason, it is no longer stocked. Gravel roads follow the upper stream through the Cherry Grove area, west of Gaston.

The river below Gaston has some native cutthroat, but is primarily bass and panfish water. Most angling is confined to the bridges, though it is possible to boat stretches of the river in a small craft, with put-ins and take-outs at the bridges or with landowner permission. A few salmon and steelhead are taken in the lower river in November and December.

TUMBLE LAKE A fairly good 20 acre hike-in brook trout lake about 3 miles north of Detroit Reservoir at the head of Tumble Creek. Best approach is by French Creek Rd. FS 2223, leading north from Hwy. 22 at Detroit. About 8 miles from the highway take the Dome Rock Trail east, then hike south to the lake.

Tumble has naturally spawning brook trout 6-11 inches, averaging 9 inches. Trout are usually plentiful and can be caught using all methods. There are a few natural campsites around the lake. The outlet stream drops off a sheer cliff to the stream bed below.

TWIN LAKES (Marion Co.) Two good brook trout lakes in southern Mt. Hood National Forest near the head of the Collawash River. Best approach is by trail from Elk Lake north of Detroit. See Elk Lake for directions. The road is generally snowbound until June.

Twin Lakes are a pleasant 4 mile hike north from Elk Lake by Trail 544. The two 12 acre lakes lie in an east/west line just south of Mother Lode Mt. and are connected by a stream flowing east.

They have excellent natural reproduction and are occasionally stocked with brook trout. The fish range 6-13 inches, with most around 10 inches. Both lakes are deep, and all methods of angling can be effective. A rubber boat would be helpful. Fly angling is excellent late in the year, mornings and evenings West Twin is fished the heaviest. It has three campsites. East Twin has one campsite. The lakes can also be reached by about 12 miles of trail from the north by way of Bagby Hot Springs. See Mother Lode Lakes for trail details.

VEDA LAKE A 3 acre hike-in lake which produces consistently despite its small size and accessibility. It is on the south slope of Mt. Hood about 5 miles south of Government Camp. From Hwy. 26 turn south about 1/4 mile east of the Timberline Lodge turnoff onto FS 2613. From Fir Tree Campground about 5 miles

south, follow Trail 673 directly to the lake, an easy mile downhill.

Brook trout are stocked by helicopter, and there are a few wild trout. Size range is 6-13 inches, averaging 9-10 inches. All methods can be used, as the lake is easily fished from shore. Bait angling is best early in the season, with flyfishing is good in the fall, mornings and evenings. Wet flies or nymph patterns retrieved slowly are especially effective. There is a natural campsite at the lake. Roads usually open about the end of June.

VIVIAN LAKE An easily found 20 acre brook trout lake on the NW slopes of Mt. Yoran in Diamond Peak Wilderness. To reach it, hike south on Trail 3662 from Salt Creek Falls, about 4 miles.

The lake is fairly deep, at elevation 5500 ft. A rubber boat would be handy. The lake is stocked by air every few years. There are several good natural campsites. Bushwhacking 1/2 mile north along the lake's outlet creek will bring you to Lopez Lake, which also has brook trout and doesn't see a lot of traffic.

VOGEL LAKE A 25 acre brook trout lake in the Mink Lake Basin west of Elk Lake. For trail directions, see Cliff Lake and Mink Lake. Vogel is 1/4 mile SE of Cliff Lake, east of the Pacific Crest Trail. Quite shallow, it frequently winterkills. There is an island on the lake with the remnants of an old trapper's cabin, and good natural campsites around the shore.

WAHANNA LAKE A rainbow lake within short hiking distance of Taylor Burn Campground, north of Waldo Lake. Taylor Burn Camp is 7 miles north of Waldo Lake by rough road. Wahanna lies along Wahanna Trail 3583 about 1 1/2 miles south from Taylor Burn Camp.

About 60 acres, it generally offers good fishing for rainbow averaging 10 inches but up to 4 pounds. It can be fished from shore in places, but a rubber boat is helpful. All methods are effective at times. Try trolling a red and white flash bait for the large fish during the day. Fly angling is good in the evenings, especially late in the year.

WALDO LAKE A sparkling blue gem, a giant alpine lake whose water ranks among the purist in the world. It covers almost 10 square miles and is over 400 feet deep in places. The water is so clean that the bottom can still be seen at depths well over a 100 ft. Waldo is usually Oregon's second largest natural lake, following Upper Klamath. To reach it drive about 23 miles SE of Oakridge on Hwy. 58. At a well signed intersection, FS 5897 forks off to the NE and follows the east side of Waldo about one mile from the lake, with three spur roads leading west to the lake. The spurs at the south and north ends have lakeside campgrounds. From the east, FS 5897 leads to North Waldo Camp by way of various connecting roads from Crane Prairie, Wickiup and Davis Lakes. Trails lead into Waldo Lake from all directions.

Waldo has a fair supply of brook trout and an occasional kokanee, but in a lake of over 6,400 acres, it's a job to find them. It isn't easy fishing, but brook trout to 5 pounds are there for the angler who learns this lake's secrets. Fall is definitely the best time to try, and you'll beat the mosquitoes as well.

Waldo can be fished from shore, but most angling is done from boats. Speed limit is 10 mph. Trolling is probably the most productive method, but bait angling and flyfishing are profitable when feeding fish are located. Productive areas include the shoal areas at the north and south ends. The lake is very deep, so don't get below the fish. At times, fish seem to be working the shoal areas throughout the lake. Catching is usually confined to morning and evening hours. When the wind comes up, this water gets really rough. Small boats should stay near the shoreline.

There are beautiful campgrounds at north and south ends of lake, and many picturesque natural campsites on rocky promontories, but the mosquitoes of Waldo Lake are legendary, and throughout much of the season, the campgrounds are almost deserted. In spring and early summer, persistent campers often take to their boats to escape the blood thirsty hordes, as mosquitoes seldom attack beyond about 100 ft. offshore. Bring lots of repellent.

WALL LAKE A fairly good brook trout lake at the west end of the Olallie Lake group, about 100 miles from Portland by way of Hwy. 26 and the Skyline Rd. From Lower Lake Campground one mile north of Olallie Lake, take Trail 706 SW one mile to Trail 719. Follow 719 west 1/2 mile to Wall Lake. Averill and Red Lakes are further west on Trail 719. Easy to fish, Wall Lake brook trout run 6-13 inches, averaging 10 inches. Small lures or spinners usually work well, and evening fly angling is effective. There are good natural campsites here.

WALLING POND An old gravel pit that contains largemouth bass year around and is stocked with legal rainbow in spring. It is within Salem city limits west of I-5. To reach it, follow Turner Rd. or Mission St. The lake is south of Hines St. Most anglers use bait to catch the pond's 10-12 inch trout. There are no facilities of any kind here.

WALTER WIRTH LAKE A trout, bass and panfish lake on the east edge of Salem. It is fed by Mill Creek and is within Cascade Gateway Park, just west of I-5 at its junction with Hwy. 22. The lake can be reached from the airport road or Turner Rd. Largemouth bass, white crappie, and brown bullhead are available, as well as stocked legal rainbow and an occasional brood trout.

WALTERVILLE POND A 66 acre bass and panfish lake east of Springfield. It contains largemouth bass, black crappie, and brown bullhead.

WARREN LAKE A 5 acre brook trout lake at the head of Warren Creek. The creek flows north 3 miles into the Columbia River about 9 miles west of the community of Hood River. Warren is 1/4 mile by trail from the end of a primitive road SE of Mt. Defiance. You might want to walk the last mile of the road, too.

To reach the trailhead, follow the directions to Bear Lake, but take FS 2821 (to the left) at the forks, heading NE of FS 2820. Here is where you might bnegin to consider the capabilities of your vehicle. At the next T intersection, turn right, away from Mt. Defiance. The road ends in 1/3 mile, and the trail heads west to Warren Lake.

Warren Lake is about 5 acres and only 8 ft. deep. It is at an elevation of 3750 ft. and is fished quite heavily, yielding good catches of small brook trout. Most of the fish are 8-10 inches with a few to 12 inches. All methods can be used effectively, with flies working well in late summer and fall.

There is no camp at the lake. The nearest developed campground is at Rainy Lake, 3 miles west of the 2821 turnoff on 2820. It is normally accessible in June.

WAVERLY LAKE A panfish and trout lake along Hwy. 99E just north of Albany. The lake was formerly restricted to angling by children under 18 years old, but is now open to general public use. About 10 acres, it offers good angling for largemouth bass and bluegill, with crappie and catfish also available. The lake is easily fished from shore.

WELCOME LAKES Two brook trout lakes in the headwaters of the Collawash River east of Bull of the Woods Lookout. Several trail lead into this area. The most direct route is by way of Elk Lake Creek Trail 559 to Trail 554, which follows Welcome Creek to the lakes. This is a hike of 3 1/2 miles. To reach the trailhead, follow the Collawash Rd. FS 63 south a twisty four or five miles past Toms Meadow to FS 6380. Follow 6380 about 2 miles to a T intersection where a short spur road leads in from the south. Trail 559 begins at the end of this spur.

The largest lake, Lower Welcome, is about 6 acres, and West Welcome is about 3 acres. Both of these are shallow and rich. Upper Welcome Lake is only one acre and has no fish, campsites, or trail directly to it. Lower and West Welcome both have some natural reproduction, and Lower Welcome is stocked each year.

Brook trout in Lower and West run to 12 inches, averaging 8-9 inches. There are good populations of fish in both lakes. Flyfishing is the best method after early season. There are no campsites at West Welcome, but good campsites at Lower Welcome. The lakes are accessible in early June from the north, if you don't mind hiking through snow. Don't underestimate the challenge of sticking with a narrow trail that is intermittently obscured by snow.

WHIG LAKE A brook trout lake in an area well sprinkled with good lakes. Whig is located in the Taylor Burn area north of Waldo Lake. It is 1/2 mile south of Taylor Butte, a prominent landmark along FS 517 leading to Taylor Burn Campground. To reach the campground, head north from North Waldo Campground on FS 514 to its intersection with 517, then turn west on FS 517. Both roads are rough. If you park at Taylor Butte, circle the Butte and you'll come to long, narrow Whig Lake. It's at the west end of Torrey Lake.

Its shape makes it easy to fish from shore. The lake covers about 17 acres and is 10 feet deep. The catch ranges 10-16 inches. Lures and bait are usually effective, but fly angling mornings and evenings, especially in the fall, will really take fish. Bucktail coachman, caddis fly, mosquito, blue upright, and march brown are all good pattern choices. There's a good camp at Taylor Burn.

WIDGEON LAKE A good 3 acre eastern brook trout lake in the Big Meadows area east of Hwy. 22. See fay lake for directions. Go north past Fay for 1/4 mile and take the blazed trail east about 1/2 mile past Fir Lake. Widgeon is small but fairly deep and lightly fished. The brook trout run 8-13 inches. The shore is pretty brushy, so a rubber boat is useful. It is a good late season lake.

WILEY CREEK This is a just fair trout stream joining the South Santiam at Foster, east of Sweet Home. The creek is followed SE throughout its length by a gravel road. Not very productive after May, it is managed for wild steelhead and open to steelhead angling only in summer and fall, before the major run comes in. Native cutthroat are present in small numbers.

WILLAMETTE RIVER (Columbia R. to Oregon City) One of the few rivers in the world that provides salmon and steelhead angling in the midst of a major metropolitan area. The Willamette is the Number One producer of spring chinook in Oregon. Bass and panfish are also available near islands, log rafts, and the many structures in this section of the river (bridges, seawalls, docks, pilings), as well as in the sloughs. The largest slough in this section, Willamette Slough (a.k.a. Multnomah Channel, is treated separately in this book. See multnomah channel.

Salmon and steelhead taken in the Willamette are all just passing through, on their way to spawning grounds in its tributaries. The Clackamas River is the primary tributary of the lower Willamette, draining a section of the Cascade Range between Mt. Hood and Mt. Jefferson. It joins the Willamette just north of Oregon City, providing a popular fishery at its mouth. An impressive falls, Willamette Falls, which spans the river at Oregon City, creates another concentration of fish and fishing activity.

In this section, the Willamette flows 1/4 mile wide and quietly powerful. Its current is fed by 6 major tributaries—the Coast Fork, Middle Fork, North Middle Fork, McKenzie, North and South Santiams, and Clackamas— each a major river system in itself—and by many smaller rivers and streams. These drain the snow-melt of two major mountain ranges— the the Coast Range, and the Cascades, as well as the smaller Callapooya Mts. of Southern Oregon. The Willamette flows more than 200 miles to its meeting with the Columbia River just 4 miles north of Portland.

Best fishing on the Willamette is at river level 6.5 cfs (cubic ft. per second), with acceptable levels between 4 and 5.2 cfs. The current river level is available by calling the ODFW Portland Information line or the National Weather Service.

Chinook angling on the lower Willamette heats up in March, April, and May along a stretch of 25 river miles, from Willamette Falls at Oregon City to the Columbia confluence near St. Johns. Because Portland Harbor has been dredged to 50 feet from bank to bank to permit passage of commercial freighters, the main fishery in this stretch is from Sellwood Bridge up to the falls, and from St. Johns Bridge down to the Columbia. A major flow of Willamette water also enters the Columbia by way of Multnomah Channel, an important chinook highway that adds 33 additional river miles to the fishery.

Once feared to be a dying run, Willamette system spring chinook are back in force, thanks to increased hatchery production and vigilant efforts to limit losses at Willamette Falls turbines (the turbines are screened and shut down during peak passage). The 1988 run was estimated to be more than 104,000, and the catch reached 27,300.

The first spring chinook show up in February, with a few picked up at the mouth of the Clackamas. In March they come on steady, and the catch is good if the water isn't too murky. April is usually the hottest month for catches

near the Clackamas mouth, with best catches at Oregon City made in late April and early May. The average weight of a 3 year old Willamette springer is 15 pounds. The earlier arriving 5 year olds average 21 pounds. A 56 pounder was landed in 1983 at the Clackamas mouth, but fish that size are extremely rare here.

Most anglers fish from boats, but there are very popular chinook bank fisheries at Clackamette Park at the mouth of the Clackamas River on the east bank, and at Meldrum Bar just north of Gladstone on the east bank. Chinook are also taken from the catwalk behind the West Linn Municipal Building, from the seawall and fishing platform at Oregon City, at Dahl Park on the north bank of the Clackamas mouth, at the Swan Island Lagoon float in North Portland, and at Cathedral Park in North Portland.

The most popular boat fishery is from Meldrum Bar to Willamette Falls. This area includes the two major chinook gathering spots—the mouth of the Clackamas, and the pool below Willamette Falls. Always an imposition to salmon and steelhead, the falls became an obstruction when a concrete lip and power turbines were installed. A large fishway on the west side of the river now enables fish passage. The fish are observed and counted as they swim up the fishway. Anglers can obtain the daily count over the falls by calling the Oregon Dept. of Fish and Wildlife Information number. The schooling of fish at the base of the falls provides one of the most popular chinook fisheries on the river, and the most competitive.

When the chinook are in, boaters at the Clackamas mouth and at Willamette Falls traditionally anchor side by side to form a *hogline*. Near the falls, the water is swift and turbulent.

Anglers must use caution and observe posted deadlines. The turbulence of the water, the roaring of the falls, as well as the intense concentration of fish and anglers create a charged atmosphere here that may be unnerving to some. If you can't find a place in the line-up, or prefer a less pressurized environment, try your luck in Multnomah Channel, where the Coon Island fishery is reputed to be more relaxed, though equal in productivity to that at the falls. Throughout the Willamette, boating anglers are advised to *keep an eye out for tow boats*, whose vision is often impaired by loaded barges. When in doubt, weigh anchor.

Chinook boat anglers prefer to use herring and prawns as bait in early season, both fishing fat anchor and trolling. Most bank anglers seem to prefer prawns or Spin-N-Glos, frequently using double hook-ups with lots of weight. Both bank and boat anglers switch to hardware later on. Common lures include wobblers, plugs, Rainbow Spinners, and Flatfish. Effective trollers troll s-l-o-w-l-y. Some use a spinner to gauge correct motor speed. In deep water, they fish the 12-16 ft. level, just above cruising chinook. In addition to Multnomah Channel, the most popular trolls in this section are from Milwaukie to Sellwood Bridge, and from St. Johns Bridge to the mouth.

Salmon follow fairly definite current movements. Anglers try to locate these routes and troll through them, or troll an S-curve through water whose current is broken by tied up ships, log rafts, and bridge abutments. Salmon sometimes lie in the slack water pocket beside or just downstream from these obstructions.

The Willamette is strongly affected by tidal flows. Low slack to high tide provides the best fishing. Adjust Astoria tide readings (printed in the daily newspaper or available on cards at sporting goods stores) for the lower Willamette by adding 6 hours to the Astoria time for a correct Oregon City reading, 4 hours for Sellwood Bridge angling, and 2 hours for Multnomah Channel angling.

Sturgeon provide a year around fishery throughout the lower Willamette, with about 1000 legals landed annually. Quite a few are taken below the falls, and some are picked up by bank anglers casting from shore in the Sellwood to Oregon City section. A depth finder is helpful to identify the deep holes frequented by sturgeon. Bait up with smelt, eel, cut bait, or gobs of nightcrawlers, and keep it on the bottom.

The lower Willamette shad fishery is primarily a boat show, beginning in early May and extending through the July 4 weekend, with a peak in June. In 1988, 5,000 shad were taken in the main channel from the mouth of the Clackamas to Willamette Falls, and in the Coon Island vicinity of Multnomah Channel. There is some bank angling for shad at Clackamette Park.

Modest numbers of steelhead are taken in this stretch of the river, winter run from late December through early March, summer run from March till June. About 1000 winter and 700 summer steelhead are caught each year, primarily in the vicinity of the Clackamas mouth and near the falls.

The Willamette River provides excellent and extremely varied habitat for bass and panfish throughout its length. In this section in addition to islands and sloughs, there are manmade structures that attract concentrations of fish—bridges, seawalls, docks, pilings, and log rafts. Bass, crappie, perch, and crayfish are available from the bank at Oaks Bottom in Sellwood, particularly below the log booms (though standing on the booms themselves is extremely dangerous). Ross Island, with its blue heron rookery (mid-river in South Portland), Swan Island (north Portland), Elk Rock Island near Milwaukie, and Cedar Island north of Gladstone look intriguing for resident species. Swan Island Lagoon can be fished from floats there, with best catches downstream from the cross street between Basin and Lagoon Avenue. Bass and panfish are also fished at Cathedral Park, Willamette Park (plunk the shallow water south of the ramp), the harbor wall at Waterfront Park, and Milwaukie Boat Ramp (fish the bay). The mouth of Johnson Creek offers excellent crappie fishing and smallmouth bass, and can be reached from the Milwaukie Boat Ramp by wading during low water.

Fishing supplies are available in Sellwood, Oregon City, and at Brown's Landing on Multnomah Channel. There are boat rentals in Oregon City and at Brown's Landing. Public boat ramps are located at Sauvie Island on Multnomah Channel, Cathedral Park in North Portland, Swan Island, Willamette Park in SW Portland, Milwaukie off Hwy. 99E, Meldrum Bar Park, and Clackamette Park. There are numerous private moorages and boat ramps throughout this stretch, open to public use for a fee.

Locks at Willamette Falls, operated by the Army Corps of Engineers, enable passage for boats traveling upstream and down. The locks are open to public use at no fee from 7 a.m. to 11 p.m. daily. Boaters should tie up at the Corps. dock on the west bank, and pull the signal cord to alert the operator. Vessels should have protective fenders to protect their hulls from the lock walls. Allow about 35 minutes for passage through the 5 chambers.

1. MOLALLA RIVER STATE PARK - Steep paved ramps into Willamette also provide access to lower Mollala; fish for crappie, bass, bullheads, and occasional channel cats as well as trout, salmon, steelhead; also accesses lower Pudding for bass & panfish in spring.

2. MOUTH OF THE MOLALLA - Fish for winter steelhead late Jan. through Mar., chinook in April

3. ROCK IS. SLOUGHS - Fish submerged rocks, log booms & sunken trees for bass and panfish; explore inside and outside sloughs; park adjacent to 99E or launch boat at Willamette Park(West Linn).

4. WEST LINN MUNICIPAL BLDG. - Bank fish from catwalk for sturgeon & spring chinook; park behind bldg.

5. WILLAMETTE PARK(West Linn) - Good bank access at mouth of Tualatin for bass and panfish, occasional channel cat, steelhead, and coho; BOATERS BEWARE OF DRIFTING TOWARD FALLS.

6. OREGON CITY TO MELDRUM BAR - Three miles of intensive bank fishing; hoglines and trolling for summer & winter steelhead, spring chinoo, and sturgeon. Bank fishing in Oregon City from 99E seawall and platform 1/2 mi. below falls.

7. CLACKAMETTE PARK - Very popular improved boat ramp at south side of mouth of the Clackamas; intensive bank fishery for shad, summer steelhead, and chinook; boat access to lower Clackamas R.

8. DAHL PARK - North bank of mouth of Clackamas; bank fish for summer steelhead & spring chinook.

9. MELDRUM BAR - Improved boat ramp; largest bank fishery for summer steelhead & spring chinook; parking permitted on gravel bar.

10. MILWAUKIE BOAT RAMP - Improved public ramp with some bank angling for bass & panfish in the bay. Cast to submerged stub pilings, logs, and stumps. Wading access to mouth of Johnson Cr. during low water for smallmouth and excelent crappie fishing; intensive spring chinook trolling in deep water.

11. MILWAUKIE TO SELLWOOD BRIDGE - Very popular troll for spring chinook.

12. OAKS BOTTOM - Fish from bank for plentiful bass, crappie, perch, and crawfish. Fish water below log booms but DO NOT VENTURE ONTO LOGS.

13. WATERFRONT PARK - Plunk the length of harbor wall in downtown Portland for sturgeon, bass, crappie, perch, and occasional salmon and steelhead. Bass & panfish lurk close in here and at sea walls on east shore beneath freeway ramps.

14. WILLAMETTE PARK (Portland) - Fish weekdays and early to avoid motorized summer crowd, plunk the shall water south of ramp for bass and panfish. Use float to access deeper holds; popular launch for spring chinook trollers concentrating beneath Sellwood Bridge.

15. SWAN IS. LAGOON - Fish for crappie, bullhead, yellow perch, and numerous bluegill. Best fishing downstream from cross street between Basin and Lagoon aves. and in main Willamette from Channel Ave. BOATERS BEWARE OF HEAVY COMMERCIAL TRAFFIC. Floats and improved ramp at east shore of lagoon; popular access for lower river spring chinook & sturgeon fishing.

16. CATHEDRAL PARK - Improved public ramps, floats, bank access for salmon, sturgeon, bass, panfish, walleye, and channel cats.

17. ST. JOHNS BRIDGE to Mouth - Troll for spring chinook.

18. Multnomah Channel - Troll the length for spring chinook; anchor at hot spots; fish pilings and log rafts for largemouth and panfish.

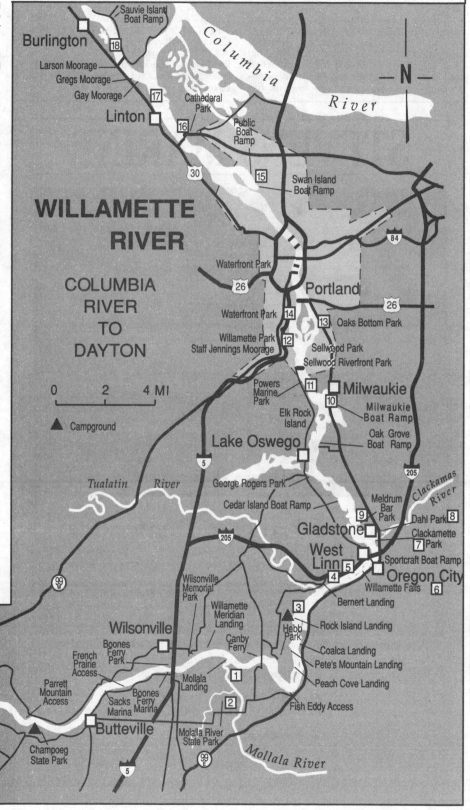

WILLAMETTE RIVER

COLUMBIA RIVER TO DAYTON

WILLAMETTE RIVER (Oregon City to Eugene) This portion of the Willamette offers more than 100 miles of freeway for thousands of migrating spring chinook and summer and winter steelhead, bound for their spawning grounds on the McKenzie, North and South Santiams, and the forks of the Willamette. Fished only lightly for these migrants, this section of the river is home to large numbers of largemouth bass and a growing population of smallmouth, as well as panfish, channel catfish, and sturgeon. Trout and whitefish grow more numerous from Harrisburg upstream.

The river can be reached by secondary roads off Hwy. 99E and Hwy. 99W throughout its length. It can be boated by all manner of craft launched from the many improved, primitive, and natural sites on both banks of the riv-er. Anglers commonly motor upstream from a ramp, and fish and drift their way back. Boat ramps popularly used by Willamette anglers in this section are located at Willamette Park in West Linn, Molalla River State Park off Hwy. 99E north of Canby, Willamette Mission State Park next to the Wheatland Ferry off Hwy. 221 between Dayton and Keizer, Wallace Marine Park off Hwy. 221 in West Salem, Independence Riverview Park off Hwy. 51 at Independence, Buena Vista Ferry south of Monmouth, Bryant Park in Albany, Hyak Park on Hwy. 20 west of Albany, Pioneer Boat Basin off 99W at Corvallis, Willamette Park off Hwy. 99W south of Corvallis, Peoria Park in Peoria, McCartney Park north of Harrisburg, Hileman and Whitely landings off River Rd. north of Eugene, Alton Baker Park in Eugene, and Island Park in Springfield. The river is used heavily by pleasure boat operators during the summer.

Salmon and steelhead are moving through this portion of the Willamette the year around, but they are difficult to locate in the big river and are more commonly fished in the tributaries. There are successful fisheries for them in the Willamette near the mouths of the Molalla, Santiam, and McKenzie rivers. In addition, summer steelhead are occasionally taken near Wheatland Ferry, and spring and fall chinook are fished at Wallace Marine Park (Salem) below the bridge.

The Willamette here is primarily the domain of resident bass and panfish Its shores are laced with sloughs that offer quiet refuge for largemouth and smallmouth bass, crappie, bluegill, and catfish. Its channel is broken by islands mid-stream that divide and slow the flow to either side. Look for largemouth in the sloughs under logs and brush piles, casting plugs or spinning lures along the shore where there's lots of cover to draw them out. Smallmouth are present in increasing numbers from Salem to Corvallis, found primarily at the mouths of the sloughs and at the edge of the main current. Best bass fishing takes place when the river drops in summer and fall.

This portion of the Willamette beckons the adventurous bass and panfish angler, for whom exploration is part of the sport. Try Rock Island Sloughs off 99E near West Linn, which offer good habitat among submerged rocks, log booms and sunken trees. There are two sloughs (inside and outside), and both can be productive. Lambert Slough, about 4 miles long, is 6-7 miles from boat ramps upstream or down, but nevertheless attracts a lot of interest among bass and panfish anglers. There is no bank access, and boaters should be wary of gravel bars throughout the slough. Best access is from Wheatland Ferry Boat Ramp, which is also used to reach Jackson Bend and Windsor Island sloughs.

One of the few slough areas in this section with bank access is Minto & Brown Island near Salem. There's a lot of good boatable bass and panfish water between Independence and Salem, including Murphy and Judson sloughs. Luckiamute Slough, just upstream from the Luckiamute River confluence, offers good boat fishing for largemouth, crappie, and bluegill until June. The 12 mile drift from Peoria Park to Corvallis offers many promising sloughs and holes, including the waters around McBee, John Smith, Kiger, and Fischer islands.

Sturgeon are available in the river above Oregon City, where a number were transplanted years ago. Use heavy gear, and fish the deep holes and eddies with bait well on the bottom. Large gobs of nightcrawlers, crawfish tails, or pieces of scrap fish make good bait. The area from Corvallis downstream to Newberg was stocked, so your best bet is in that section. There is reputed to be a sturgeon hole near the mouth of the Long Tom River.

Trout fishing in the Willamette is best from Harrisburg upstream, where the river is closer to its cool mountain sources, though there is some trout fishing in the Corvallis area for rainbow, cutthroat, and a cross-breed known as cuttbow. From Harrisburg upstream, trout and whitefish grow increasingly numerous, and grow to good size. cutthroat head up the tributaries each winter and return in early spring. The areas near the mouths of good cutthroat streams are usually best in April. Cutthroat are present all along the river throughout the summer, but are scattered. In the Eugene area, the river up and down from the I-5 Bridge offers

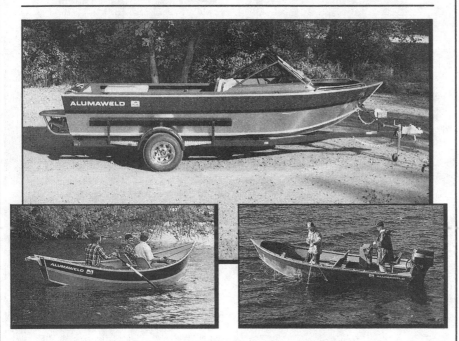

excellent flyfishing early in the season. Trout fishing drops off in this stretch as the water warms, and whitefish predominate by June.

Natural campsites are available on many of the islands in the river, and there is a developed campground on Wells Island below Buena Vista Ferry. Most of the parks that have boat ramps or fishing access do not have camping facilities, but there are campgrounds at Spring Valley Access on the west bank upstream from Wheatland Ferry, Sidney Landing on the east bank about 5 miles below Independence, American Bottom Landing on the west bank 2 miles above Sidney, Luckiamute Landing at the Luckiamute confluence, Riverside Landing on the east bank SW of Albany, Half Moon Bend Landing downstream about 4 miles from Corvallis on the west bank, Buckskin Mary Landing 4 miles above Peoria Park on the west bank, and Harkens Lake Landing 3 miles below McCartney Park on the west bank.

WILLAMETTE RIVER, COAST FORK
Least productive of the major Willamette tributaries, offering nothing but rough fish from Cottage Grove Reservoir to the mouth. It heads in the vicinity of Black Butte in the Calapooya Mts., flowing 7 miles to Cottage Grove Reservoir, closely followed by a road. This upper portion contains resident cutthroat trout. The lower river is stocked with rainbow trout in early season in the Cottage Grove area.

WILLAMETTE RIVER, MIDDLE FORK
The largest tributary of the upper Willamette, joining the Coast Fork to form the main river just south of Springfield and Eugene. Highways 58, 99 and 126 meet near it's mouth. From Springfield to Lowell (at Dexter Reservoir) a paved county road follows the north bank of the river's lower 18 miles. Hwy. 58 then follows it past Lookout Pt. Reservoir to just above Oakridge. About 3 miles SE of Oakridge, FS 21 cuts off to the south and follows the river past Hills Creek Reservoir and far into the headwaters. The river is easily accessible at most points.

This fork of the Willamette offers a variety of water. From Dexter Reservoir downstream it resembles the mainstem Willamette, flowing through mostly flat agricultural lands. Most anglers fish this stretch for summer steelhead and spring chinook, though some trout are present. Above Lookout Point Reservoir the Middle Fork is a fast, big river, much like the McKenzie, but the fishing is poor. Maybe its the dams. Above Hills Creek Reservoir the Middle Fork is a forested mountain stream, and a good one. For more on the reservoir angling, see Dexter, Hills Creek, Lookout Pt .

Above Hills Creek Reservoir the river is stocked with legal rainbow. Native rainbow and cutthroat trout are also in the river in fair numbers. All methods of angling are used, with bait and lures best the first few months of the season. There is excellent fly angling for trout through the summer and fall.

A fair chinook fishery has developed in the lower river between Springfield and Dexter Dam. Fishing with spinners or Flatfish lures is the usual method, but bank casting also takes fish. Most chinook are caught in June and July, close to 400 in 1986, nearly 1000 in some years. Boat ramps are available at Clearwater Lane in Springfield, Jasper Bridge, and there are 2 ramps below Dexter Dam on both sides of the river, 1/4 mile below the confluence of Fall Creek on North Bank. No angling is permitted from the concrete wing wall at the base of Dexter Dam (south shore). See the regulation book for special hook and weight restrictions in the dam area.

In 1981 in this lower river stretch, the Dept. of Fish and Wildlife began an experimental summer steelhead stocking program. Returns from this are looking good, with a catch of 500 in 1986-87.

Campgrounds are available at Lookout Pt. and Hills Creek reservoirs, on Hwy. 58 west of Oakridge, and roughly every 5 miles on FS 21. Check the current regulations for seasons, bag limits, deadlines, and restrictions. The river is

STURGEON, TOO BIG TO KEEP
Courtesy, Ray Beemsdorf, ODFW

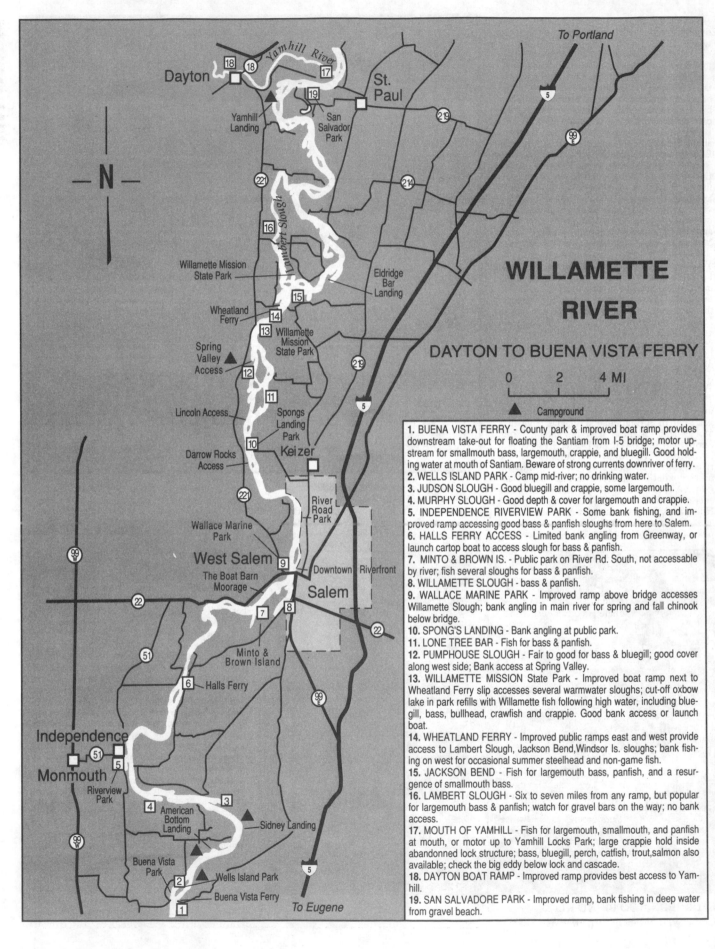

WILLAMETTE RIVER

DAYTON TO BUENA VISTA FERRY

0   2   4 MI

▲ Campground

1. BUENA VISTA FERRY - County park & improved boat ramp provides downstream take-out for floating the Santiam from I-5 bridge; motor upstream for smallmouth bass, largemouth, crappie, and bluegill. Good holding water at mouth of Santiam. Beware of strong currents downriver of ferry.

2. WELLS ISLAND PARK - Camp mid-river; no drinking water.

3. JUDSON SLOUGH - Good bluegill and crappie, some largemouth.

4. MURPHY SLOUGH - Good depth & cover for largemouth and crappie.

5. INDEPENDENCE RIVERVIEW PARK - Some bank fishing, and improved ramp accessing good bass & panfish sloughs from here to Salem.

6. HALLS FERRY ACCESS - Limited bank angling from Greenway, or launch cartop boat to access slough for bass & panfish.

7. MINTO & BROWN IS. - Public park on River Rd. South, not accessable by river; fish several sloughs for bass & panfish.

8. WILLAMETTE SLOUGH - bass & panfish.

9. WALLACE MARINE PARK - Improved ramp above bridge accesses Willamette Slough; bank angling in main river for spring and fall chinook below bridge.

10. SPONG'S LANDING - Bank angling at public park.

11. LONE TREE BAR - Fish for bass & panfish.

12. PUMPHOUSE SLOUGH - Fair to good for bass & bluegill; good cover along west side; Bank access at Spring Valley.

13. WILLAMETTE MISSION State Park - Improved boat ramp next to Wheatland Ferry slip accesses several warmwater sloughs; cut-off oxbow lake in park refills with Willamette fish following high water, including bluegill, bass, bullhead, crawfish and crappie. Good bank access or launch boat.

14. WHEATLAND FERRY - Improved public ramps east and west provide access to Lambert Slough, Jackson Bend, Windsor Is. sloughs; bank fishing on west for occasional summer steelhead and non-game fish.

15. JACKSON BEND - Fish for largemouth bass, panfish, and a resurgence of smallmouth bass.

16. LAMBERT SLOUGH - Six to seven miles from any ramp, but popular for largemouth bass & panfish; watch for gravel bars on the way; no bank access.

17. MOUTH OF YAMHILL - Fish for largemouth, smallmouth, and panfish at mouth, or motor up to Yamhill Locks Park; large crappie hold inside abandoned lock structure; bass, bluegill, perch, catfish, trout, salmon also available; check the big eddy below lock and cascade.

18. DAYTON BOAT RAMP - Improved ramp provides best access to Yamhill.

19. SAN SALVADORE PARK - Improved ramp, bank fishing in deep water from gravel beach.

currently open for salmon and steelhead angling the year around.

WILLAMETTE RIVER, NORTH FORK
The North Fork is a good size, very attractive trout stream. It is currently managed for wild trout and is, by regulation, flyfishing only upstream from the railroad bridge at Westfir. About 40 miles long, it joins the Middle Fork 2 miles west of Oakridge, about 35 miles SE of Eugene.

The river heads in Waldo Lake and skirts the Taylor Burn Lakes area. A good road, FS 19, follows the river from the community of West Fir far into the headwaters. The upper 8 miles to Waldo Lake are crossed once by a trail, but generally it is a bushwhack. FS 19 is gravel the last 10 miles to Box Canyon Guard Station, where it joins the South Fork McKenzie Rd.

There are good populations of native rainbow and cutthroat trout in the North Fork. The lower 12 miles offer excellent fly angling water from around July through the rest of the season. The fish run 8-10 inches. Angling pressure is generally light.

This is a lovely forest stream, and official recognition of this has won the North Fork state designation as a Wild and Scenic river. Its water is crystal clear and quite cold, too cold for good angling in the spring. But a sunny summer day on this sparkling river is inevitably memorable. The only campground on the river is Kiahane, about 20 miles north of Westfir on FS 19. Other camps are located on Hwy. 48 east and west of Oakridge.

WILLAMINA CREEK
A nice little trout stream on the east side of the coast range, flowing into the upper Yamhill River. From McMinnville on Hwy. 18 head north through Sheridan on the old highway to Willamina. From Willamina, at the mouth of the creek, a paved road heads north, and gravel roads follow the upper stretch.

Willamina has a small run of winter steelhead, and about 50 are caught annually. The fish are taken from late January through early March. Best steelhead water is in the lower portion where the creek runs through agricultural lands, but access is a problem here. The upper creek is on tree farm land, and public access is allowed. Some native cutthroat are available in the 7-11 inch range. There is no camping along the creek.

WILLAMINA POND
A 5 acre abandoned log pond in Huddeston Park in Willamina. Take the Hwy. 18 business loop through Sheridan into the community of Willamina. Turn left just past the Rocket Gas Station onto Polk (which runs behind the high school), and follow Polk to the park. It is stocked with catchable rainbow each spring and supports populations of largemouth bass, black crappie, brown bullhead and yellow perch.

WILLIAMS LAKE
A 4 acre brook trout lake just north of Taylor Burn Campground north of Waldo Lake. See Whig Lake for road and trail directions. The one mile trail heads north from the east side of the campground to Williams Lake. Williams is SE of Upper Erma Bell Lake. The trail goes on to Otter Lake. Williams is stocked with brook trout 6-12 inches. It is easily fished from shore, and all methods will take fish at times. The area is not accessible until late June.

WILSONVILLE POND
A 3 acre pond west of I-5, south of the Wilsonville Rest Area.

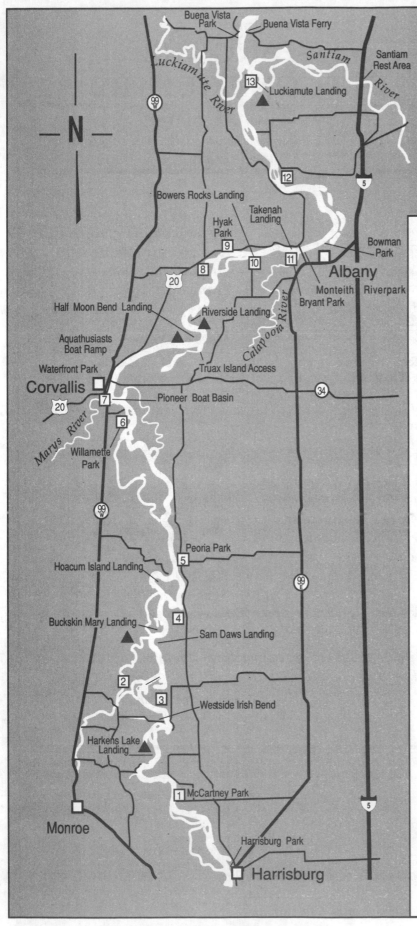

WILLAMETTE RIVER

BUENA VISTA FERRY
TO
HARRISBURG

0   2   4 MI

▲ Campground

1. MCCARTNEY PARK - Improved ramp accesses good bass & panfish sloughs from here to Peoria. Some early season native cutthroat.

2. MOUTH OF LONG TOM - Sturgeon hole at confluence; old mouth just upstream forms promising slough with deep water in lower half, good cover in upper for largemouth and crappie.

3. SLOUGH - Very promising, deep slough with good cover on east bank.

4. SLOUGH - Promising for bass & panfish, on east shore at the head of Hoacum Island.

5. PEORIA PARK - Many promising sloughs and holes between here and Corvallis, a 12 mile drift. Try the waters around McBee, John Smith, Kiger, and Fischer islands for the gamut of Willamette bass & panfish species. Improved ramp.

6. WILLAMETTE PARK (Corvallis) - Improved ramp with large bank angling access.

7. PIONEER BOAT BASIN - Take-out for 12-mile drift from Peoria

8. COLLINS BAY - Nearly circular slough with shallow neck holds abundant crappie, bluegill.

9. HYAK PARK - Improved ramp accesses nearby sloughs.

10. BOWERS ROCKS - Large slough with good ank cover good for crappie and lagemouth in spring, but shallow in summer.

11. BRYANT PARK - Improved ramp is difficult at low water; bank angling from dock.

12. BLACK DOG SLOUGH - Bluegill, largemouth, crappie.

13. LUCKIAMUTE SLOUGH - Just upstream from Willamette confluence. Good boat fishing until June for largemouth, crappie, bluegill.

From Butteville Rd., take Boones Ferry Rd. north about 1/2 mile. The pond contains large-mouth bass and bluegill.

WIND LAKE A small hike-in brook trout lake about 2 miles SW of Government Camp as the crow flies. You'll envy the crow when you hike this one. Wind Lake is on the south side of Tom Dick and Harry Mt. There are two ways to reach it. You can hike one mile to Mirror Lake on Trail 664, and then continue on this trail for an additional 1 1/2 miles, crossing the western flank of Tom Dick and Harry above timberline. From there hike about 3/4 mile due east, staying above timberline, and you will see the lake about 100 ft. below you. A trail leads down to the lake. This hike is about 4 miles and is strenuous.

The second route begins at the parking area of the Multipor ski area. A trail leads SW, following a ski lift to timberline. (Don't confuse this with the trail that follows another lift SE up Multipor Mt.) The trail crosses to the south side of the mountain and ends at Wind Lake. This route makes the lake in a little over 2 miles, but is even steeper than the first.

Wind Lake is stocked with brook trout by air and offers pretty good fishing for fish 6-12 inches. Flyfishing is the best method, as the lake is extremely shallow. In some severe winters most of the fish are lost, and it takes a year or two to rebuild the population. It is usually accessible in early June, with some snow left to struggle through.

WITHEE LAKE A fair warm water lake not far from McMinnville, just east of the Yamhill River. From Amity on 99W, head west about 2 miles. The state has an access agreement with the owner of the property, and if anglers act responsibly, the lake will remain open. A sign marks the area. Strictly a bank fishery, Withee sports good size largemouth bass and some crappie. After a big flood you can find all Yamhill species in here. The lake is usually good in spring and summer until the weeds get thick.

WOODBURN POND A highway borrow pit adjacent to I-5 north of Woodburn. Take the Woodburn Exit and head east on Hwy. 214 to Boones Ferry Rd., north on Boones Ferry about 2 miles, and west on Crosby Rd. Just before the Interstate overpass, turn north onto Edwin Road, which parallels the expressway and leads to the pond. There are 14 acres to fish for largemouth bass, bluegill, crappie, and channel cats to 18 inches. The water gets weed choked by late spring, though it has been treated with an herbicide to retard weed growth. Anglers can launch a car-topper here, but motors are prohibited.

There is a parking area, and anglers are encouraged to use it, hand carrying boats to the water. This pond has been badly abused by anglers who insist on driving right up to the bank, destroying the fragile lake-side vegetation that holds back erosion and provides habitat for insect life that, in turn, feed the fish. There is no garbage collection here either, so take home whatever you bring.

YAMHILL RIVER A pretty, rural stream, tributary of the Willamette, flowing 60 miles from the Coast Range to its confluence near Dayton. It offers good spring fishing for wild cutthroat in its upper forks, bass and panfish primarily in the mainstem, and big Willamette cutthroat spawners throughout the system in winter.

THE WILLAMETTE AT EUGENE
Dan Casali, Photographer

The river splits into two forks just east of McMinnville. The North Fork flows south from the mountains above Yamhill. The South Fork flows north from the Willamina area. Among the first Willamette tributaries to clear, the Yamhill is a good choice for the year's first trout outings.

From the lower end, the river can be reached by paved and gravel side roads leading south from Hwy. 99W and north from Hwy. 233. From McMinnville upstream, the South Fork is skirted on the north by Hwy. 18 and is followed through Sheridan and Willamina by the old highway. The North Fork is accessed by Hwy. 47 between Yamhill and Carlton, and is closely followed by a road NW of Yamhill in the vicinity of Pike.

The river and its forks are not stocked but have a good population of native cutthroat, plus the odd rainbow that drifts down from upper tributaries. There's good bank access for trout on the North Fork between Pike and the Flying M Ranch.

Bass and panfish angling is excellent from the McMinnville area down to the mouth. Some large crappie are caught each summer with spinner and bait, small flash lures, and streamer flies. The Yamhill is navigable by small motorboats from the mouth to the old locks above Dayton. There is also bank fishing at Yamhill Locks Park, where large crappie have been known to hold inside the abandoned lock structure. Check the big eddy below the lock and cascade as well. Bass, bluegill, perch, catfish, trout, and even salmon have been taken here on occasion. The sloughs in the lower river have excellent crayfish populations.

The Yamhill is open for winter angling, and a few coho and steelhead use the river, but do not spawn here. The reported catch is very low, and a better winter bet is to try for the big migrating Willamette cutthroat that head up the Yamhill in winter to spawn in its forks. Some anglers drift the upper river in pursuit of this quarry. A popular drift on the South Fork is

from Ft. Hill to Willamina, and on the North Fork, from Pike to the West Side Rd.

ZIGZAG RIVER A tributary of the Sandy River, flowing mostly within the Mt. Hood National Forest. About 12 miles long, the Zigzag joins the Sandy River at the community of Zigzag, which is located on Hwy. 26 about 43 miles east of Portland. Hwy. 26 follows the north bank all the way to its headwaters near Government Camp. It is not stocked, and little holding water is available. A few small native cutthroat are present.

CENTRAL ZONE

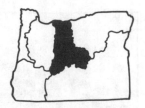

The Central Zone is all waters draining into the Columbia River from Bonneville Dam up to and including the Deschutes River.

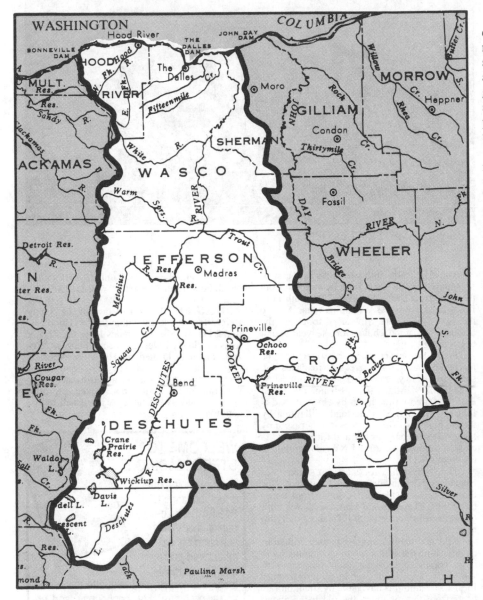

The central angling zone includes the entire watershed of Oregon's world famous Deschutes River. On the east slope of the high Cascades, over a mile above sea level, the Deschutes River begins its journey to the Columbia. It springs forth (literally) from a volcanic plateau south of the majestic Three Sisters Mountains, 30 miles south of Bend.

This plateau of lodgepole and ponderosa pine, lakes and lava, is entirely within the Deschutes National Forest. The forest map is an excellent trip planning aid. On the plateau are the fabulous Cascade Lakes: Crane Prairie, Lava, Hosmer, Sparks, Elk, Cultus, Twin, Davis, Wickiup, Odell, Crescent. And just east, high in Newberry Crater of the volcanic Paulina Mountains are Paulina and East Lakes. Taken together, this collection forms a mecca for trout anglers without equal in the state. Most of the major lakes are on or near the Cascade Lakes Highway, which runs south from Bend past Mt. Bachelor.

Surface drainage is noticeably absent in this area. Runoff and snowmelt rapidly percolate through loosely consolidated ash and lava fields, reappearing in numerous springs which feed many of the lakes. This rich source of groundwater creates entire rivers, such as Fall River and the Metolius, which spring from the earth fullblown.

Angling starts here in early May and continues right through October, throughout the year on the Deschutes and Metolius. This is high country, and the nights are cold. The sky is clear more often than not, even when valley dwellers are staring at gray.

The Deschutes swings north from Wickiup Reservoir and continues over a hundred miles to join the Columbia east of the Dalles. Once north of Bend it rapidly drops into a lava walled canyon that cuts north across high desert sagelands. Trout angling is excellent throughout its length. Below Pelton Dam there is angling for salmon and summer steelhead. See the text for more on this exciting blue ribbon river.

Patches of snow crunch under my wading shoes. Well, they say the best time to go fishing is any time you can. Still, this does seem a bit rushing the season. The 1986 regulations opened the Deschutes to year-around angling, and this is my first winter trip to the river.

The sky is clear, the air scented with sage. The sun is well over the canyon rim and warms my hands. Good to get out of the Portland rain. But what kind of flyfishing can I really expect this early in the season?

Hmmm. Was that a rise? And another. My gosh, that's a full blown hatch coming off. Do I have any little gray whatchamacallits? Maybe this will do. A rise over there. Easy cast, good drift. Gotcha.

ANTELOPE FLAT RESERVOIR A medium size reservoir in the Maury Mt. area of Ochoco National Forest, 30 air miles SE of Prineville. From Prineville take the highway toward Paulina, turning south onto FS 17 about 8 miles east of the community of Post. The reservoir is about 9 miles south at the head of Bear Creek, about 2 miles beyond Pine Creek Campground.

Antelope covers about 170 acres when full, but is sometimes drawn down to less than half that size. It's stocked annually with rainbow trout, and the fish grow rapidly. The average trout runs about 12 inches, with fish to 18 inches not uncommon. There is a campground with boat ramp at the west end of the reservoir, and there are additional campgrounds north at Pine Creek and east at Double Cabin and Wiley Flat.

BADGER CREEK A nice trout stream flowing out of Badger Lake on the SE slope of Mt Hood, entering Tygh Creek one mile west of the town of Tygh Valley. Tygh Creek empties into White River 3 miles to the east. About 25 miles long, the creek is accessible by road throughout its lower half. It is crossed by Hwy. 197 at Tygh Valley, and by secondary roads and FS 47 east of Tygh Valley. The upper 10 miles is reached by road only at Bonney Crossing Campground and at Badger Lake. A good trail follows the stream through this section.

There are native rainbow and a good annual stocking of legals at Bonney Crossing. Bait or spinner and lures will take fish early, and flies do well in summer and fall. A little hiking can result in good fishing. There are campgrounds at Bonney Crossing and at Little Badger Creek. FS 2710 connects the two camps.

BADGER LAKE A good rainbow trout lake on the lower SE slope of Mt. Hood. From Portland follow Hwy. 26 east 58 miles, then Hwy. 35 (the Mt. Hood Loop Road) to Bennett Pass. Take FS 3550 SE to Camp Windy. Turn east on FS 4860 then north on FS 140 to the lake. Watch for signs. Check with the Forest Service for road conditions. This route is usually inaccessible until late June. Two other routes generally clear 2 weeks earlier. From the east, heading into the forest from Wamic, follow the road to Rock Creek Reservoir, turning south of FS 48, then north to the lake on FS 4860 To reach the lake from the south, take Hwy. 26, Hwy. 216, then a network of forest roads. Keep the Mt. Hood Forest map open on the dash board.

Badger is stocked with rainbow, and there are native brook trout to 14 inches. There's fair fishing on bait or troll in early summer. Fly fishing is best in fall, and the fish are larger. Average size is 10 inches. There's a good camp at the lake. The Badger Lake Rd. is one-lane with no turn-outs. Trailers are prohibited from using it.

BAKEOVEN CREEK A small stream entering the Deschutes River just below Maupin, where Hwy. 197 crosses the river. The lower stretch usually contains some nice fish early in the year. The upper stream is accessible from hwys. 97 and 197. The lower stream is reached by the Eastside Deschutes Rd. Deep Creek, a tributary, also provides some good early fishing. A road follows Bakeoven a short way from the mouth. The stream gets dry in the summer and fall, but in spring, rainbow to 15 inches can be taken on bait or spinner combinations.

Bakeoven flows through mostly private land, and permission should be secured before trespassing. A note on the distinctive name of this creek and other features and sites in the area: according to Lewis McArthur, *Bakeoven*

derives from an incident in 1862, during Canyon City gold days. A Dalles trader with a pack train of flour was ambushed by Indians in the night. They drove off his horses but left his supplies. He built a rough oven of clay and stone on the spot, made bread, and sold it to the miners. The abandoned oven remained on the site for years.

BAKER POND A 4 acre pond 2 miles south of Bend in the Deschutes River Woods subdivision. A private lake with public access, it contains largemouth bass, small bluegill, brown bullhead, and a few small crappie. It's a popular kid fishery and swimming hole. Maximum depth is 25 ft.

BIBBY LAKE A 16 acre reservoir west of Hwy. 97 at Kent, in Sherman County. Used chiefly for irrigation, it supports a population of brown bullhead to 12 inches and is sporadically stocked with legal rainbow. A tributary of Buck Hollow Creek flows into the reservoir in winter only. Motor boats are allowed for transportation only. Regulations require anglers to shut off their boat motors while fishing.

BIG FINGER LAKE A 5 acre alpine lake in the Deschutes Forest, off the beaten path and lightly fished. Only 16 feet deep, it is air stocked with brook trout and sometimes winterkills. Shaped like a crooked finger, there are lots of fallen logs around the shoal area. To reach it from the Mink Lake Basin, head SE toward Cultus Lake by way of Trail 33, to Snowshoe Lake. From the west end of Cultus, head NW on Trail 16, cutting north on Trail 33 past Winopee Lake to Snowshoe. See Cultus for complete directions. Big Finger is 1/4 mile east of Snowshoe Lake. There is no trail between them. Little Finger Lake, about 2 acres, is another 1/4 mile east.

BIG HOUSTON LAKE An 88 acre lake near Powell Butte, privately owned with no public access. It contains largemouth bass, bluegill, brown bullhead, and channel catfish.

BIG MARSH CREEK A nice wild trout stream in south central Oregon, SE of Crescent Lake. It joins Crescent Creek just south of Hwy. 58, 14 miles NW of the junction of hwys. 58 and 97. FS 5825, which heads SW from Hwy. 58 just south of Odell Butte, follows the stream's marshy headwaters. FS 6020 crosses it east of the railroad crossing at Umli.

The upper creek runs through a large marsh, making the main channel hard to find in places. The stream is not stocked, but has predominantly brook trout and a good supply of brown trout. Don't expect too much size to the fish, but it's a pleasant stream.

The main fishery is in the east canal, one of two which were used to drain the main channel for grazing purposes. At this time, the Forest Service is planning to rehabilitate the original channel, which had more pools and natural cover for trout. Work should be underway in 1989-90. There is also good water above and below the marsh, including 1 1/2 miles of good dry fly water between the marsh and the railroad trestle, with lots of beaver ponding (watch for bank holes). The water below the railroad is good but brushy. This stream is in best shape between May and July, after which the water warms and fishing drops off.

BIKINI POND One of the I-84 ponds adjacent to the Columbia River, located at hwy. mile 75.7. Covering 4 acres, it is immediately west

of Mayer State Park's access road, between the railroad and the river. Access is from Exit 76. It may contain any of the Columbia River warmwater species.

BILLY CHINOOK RESERVOIR (a.k.a. LAKE BILLY CHINOOK) A large reservoir, partially administered by Warm Springs Reservation, in the scenic north-central canyon country east of the Cascades about 8 miles SW of Madras. Created by Round Butte Dam on the Deschutes River, it covers over 6 square miles and backs up three major Oregon rivers—the Deschutes, Metolius and Crooked. Long arms of slack water reach up each stream. The fishery on the Metolius Arm is administered by Warm Springs Reservation. The dam itself is regulated by Portland General Electric.

The major fishery here is kokanee, but brown, redband, and bull trout (formerly known as Dolly Varden) make up a portion of the catch. Good populations of bass, predominantly smallmouth, are now established in the reservoir, though the bass are apparently not growing to great size here. A few landlocked chinook are also present, but few are taken.

To reach Billy Chinook from Madras, drive south on Hwy. 97. Near Culver take the road west to Cove Palisades State Park. The route is well signed. A county road leads south from the park, crosses to the peninsula between the Crooked River and Deschutes River Arms, and crosses the Deschutes Arm to the community of Grandview.

Kokanee are thriving in Billy Chinook. There is, in fact, danger of overpopulation and a consequent drop in average size. To encourage harvest, a special season and bag limit have been in effect. Check current regulations. Kokanee are caught throughout the reservoir much of the year, with best fishing in late spring (May and early June) and again in August and early September when kokanee return to the tributaries to spawn. Popular fisheries are at the confluence of the Crooked and Deschutes rivers, and around the Island in the lower Metolius Arm in mid-summer. In late August and early September, the fish begin to school in the upper reaches of the tributaries, with the Metolius Arm turning in the greatest number of catches. (Kokanee in spawning condition are best eaten smoked). Angling methods include trolling flashers (the Ford Fender has been popular), and jigging in late summer with white corn and grubs. From mid-season through October, anglers find kokanee at deeper levels.

Good size bull trout are taken in the upper end of the Metolius Arm along with an occasional brown trout. The state record bull trout was caught here in 1988, weighing 20 pounds 8 ounces. To fish for these and the big browns, anglers commonly troll large lures that imitate the movement of crippled fish. A study is underway to learn more about the growth and habits of bull trout. Anglers catching tagged bull trout are asked to return the tag along with date caught, location, and length to the Oregon Dept. of Fish and Wildlife office in Prineville. The best trout habitat on the lake is upstream from the Island in the Metolius Arm.

Bass are caught near the shore, especially in the upper reaches of the Deschutes and Crooked River arms (be aware of a speed limit above the bridges in both arms). Some anglers troll for bass, but most cast plugs and lures toward the rocks. There is some bank angling opportunity for bass in the vicinity of the picnic area on the Deschutes Arm, and between the boat ramps on the Crooked River Arm.

The Metolius Arm is within the Warm Springs Reservation, and a tribal permit is required to fish it. Daily permits are modestly priced, cover fishing for the entire family, and are also valid on Lake Simtustus. Do not land on the (north) reservation shore. The island about midway up the arm is also tribal land, open for day use but closed to camping. Check current regulations for information about a special season on the Metolius Arm.

Most angling on Billy Chinook is from boats launched at Cove Palisades State Park on the Crooked River Arm (one ramp) and Deschutes Arm (two ramps). There is also a ramp at Perry South Campground on the Metolius Arm.

Camping facilities are available at Cove Palisades State Park, which has two campgrounds, one on the Deschutes Arm and one on the Crooked River Arm. It has a swimming beach, picnic areas, running water, and showers in addition to the two boat ramps. Supplies (grocery, tackle, gas) and boat rentals are available at a private marina on the lower Crooked River Arm.

Perry South Campground offers more primitive camping, situated in a shady draw at the Spring Creek inlet on the Metolius Arm, Deschutes National Forest. There is no drinking water. To reach it, follow signs toward Cove Palisades State Park, descending the Crooked River Canyon and crossing the Crooked then the Deschutes River, turning west then north toward Grandview. At Grandview, turn left onto County Rd. 64 toward Fly Lake, continuing past the lake and turning north into Fly Creek Canyon. After crossing Fly Creek, the road turns NW toward Perry. Monty Campground is about 5 miles further upstream from Perry South on the Metolius River.

Lake Chinook State Airstrip is on the west plateau above the Deschutes Arm. This is a 5000 foot dirt strip running north/south within walking distance of the arm about 700 feet below. Watch out for strong drafts from the canyon in the afternoon.

BINGHAM LAKES (Klamath Co.) A series of three hike-in lakes 2 miles south of Crescent Lake. See Crescent Lake for directions. The trailhead is 1/4 mile south of the entrance to Spring Campground on FS 60, which circles the NW edge of Crescent. It's about 2 1/2 miles to the lakes. The trail continues on past Oldenburg Lake to the Pacific Crest Trail. The Binghams lie close together in a northwesterly line. They are fairly good size lakes, varying from 10-20 acres, but fish survival has been poor, and stocking has been discontinued. There are good natural campsites at the lakes, but mosquitoes are bad until late summer.

SMALLMOUTH BASS CATCH AT LAKE BILLY CHINOOK
Deke Meyer, Photographer

BLACK LAKE A 4 acre brook trout lake in Mt. Hood National Forest which provides some good fishing. It's about 18 road miles SW of Hood River, one mile south of Rainy Lake, west off the Rainy Lake Rd. See Rainy Lake for directions..

This lake is small and fairly shallow but has some excellent brook trout angling. The fish are 7-14 inches, averaging 10 inches. Bait will usually produce well, especially early, and spinner-bait combinations work well for large fish if retrieved slowly. Flies, either wet or dry, are good late in the season.

BLOW LAKE A 45 acre brook trout lake about one mile off the road just south of Elk Lake. Take Century Drive (Hwy. 46) from Bend 37 miles south to Six Lakes Trailhead 14, about one mile south of Elk Lake. Blow Lake is an easy one mile hike to the west. The lake, which reaches a depth of 23 feet, is fairly productive for stocked brook trout 9-12 inches. All methods can be effective, with June and the fall months best. Adequate camping areas can be found around the lake.

BLOWDOWN LAKE A small, lightly fished hike-in brook trout lake one mile SE of Taylor Lake. Take the Taylor Burn Rd. (FS 600) from Little Cultus Lake to Irish and Taylor Lakes. This road is very rough, and often snowbound until June. From the Pacific Crest Trail crossing at Irish Lake, backtrack exactly one mile. Hike south from the road uphill 1/4 mile to the lake.

Blowdown is only about 4 acres, but has produced well. Stocked lightly by air, it has a good supply of brook trout 8-14 inches, averaging 12 inches. All methods work, but it's a good flyfishing lake. A rubber boat will be handy as the shore is brushy. There are no campsites here, but there are good camps at Irish Lake.

BLUE LAKE (Jefferson Co.) A very deep, pretty lake in the Deschutes National Forest about 16 miles west of Sisters. It lies just south of Hwy. 20 and can be seen from the highway as you approach Suttle Lake from the west. Take the Suttle Lake turnoff south from Hwy. 20, and proceed past Suttle to road's end at Blue Lake Resort.

The lake is 65 acres and 300 feet deep, its clarity and depth turning it an intense blue. Legal rainbow are stocked each year. Best fishing is in the warm months due to numerous cold springs and the depth of the lake. Rainbow run 10-12 inches with a few larger. Kokanee to 11 inches are plentiful. Most are caught by trolling.

Part of the lake shore is privately leased, and there is a fee to launch a boat. Some angling can be done from shore, but it's not easy. The resort at the east end has supplies, boat rentals, and a campground. Two Forest Service campgrounds are located on Suttle Lake and another at Scout Lake, all within 2 miles. Ling Creek, between Blue and Suttle Lake, is a spawning area and is closed to angling at all times.

BLUE LAKE (Warm Springs Reservation) An attractive pear-shaped 26 acre lake at the base of the northern slope of Olallie Butte. No longer stocked due to the natural acidity of the water, it is closed to public use.

BOBBY LAKE A very good brook and rainbow trout lake in the Deschutes National Forest about half-way between Odell and Waldo lakes. Although popular, the lake is far enough into the brush to produce consistently. From Hwy. 58 take the Waldo Lake Rd. FS 5897 north about 6 miles to the Bobby Lake Trailhead. This trail, 3663, leads east about 2 1/2 miles to the lake. The lake can also be reached from the east by way of FS 4652, which begins just north of Davis Lake across from North Davis Creek Campground. The trail follows Moore Creek 4 1/2 miles to the lake.

Bobby Lake, with 85 acres, has always been a good producer. There are brook trout to 16 inches here. Average size is 10-11 inches. It's a good fly lake, but lures and bait will work.

BONNEVILLE POOL The lowest of four reservoirs on the Columbia River in Oregon. About 20 miles long, it includes the stretch of the river east of Portland between Bonneville Dam and The Dalles Dam.

Most angling for fall salmon here (chinook and coho) occurs in the 20-mile stretch from just above Bonneville Dam to Hood River Bridge. In 1988, a total of 290,100 adult salmon and 72,700 jacks were counted as they navigated the fish ladders of Bonneville Dam. Favorite angling locations here are the mouth of Eagle Cr., in the old Cascade Locks, and at the mouths of the Wind and White Salmon Rivers on the Washington side. The mouth of the Klickitat River on the Washington side above Mosier is also popular. Most catches are made in September.

Steelhead reach this portion of the river in late June, and angling for them continues through late September. They are taken in the same waters as salmon. The catch is restricted to adipose fin clipped steelhead only. Most of the steelhead in this section of the river are just passing through, heading for the Deschutes River, John Day, Snake, and Eastern Washington streams. In 1988, the steelhead count over Bonneville Dam was 301,100, including 128,000 wild fish.

Sturgeon are fished from boat and bank in the pool. Favorite boat fisheries are between Cascade Locks and Stevenson WA, at the Dalles below the Interstate Bridge, and in a few scattered areas throughout the pool. Bank anglers fish from rocky points off I-84 where there are safe pull-offs on the highway shoulder.

Walleye and shad are surely present in the Bonneville Pool, but anglers have yet to locate them (or share their secrets!).

In this section of the river, most angling for bass and panfish takes place in ponds adjacent to the river. For a complete listing of from Hood River to the Deschutes, see map, Columbia River Ponds.

The Columbia is accessible from shore in many places throughout this section, but parking can be a problem due to the divided highway. Parking on the shoulder of I-84 is discouraged except in emergency situations. Alternative parking suggestions are included in the Columbia Ponds write-up. Public boat ramps are available at the Port of Cascade Locks, Port of Hood River, and Port of The Dalles.

BOOTH LAKE A fair brook and rainbow trout lake in the Mt. Jefferson Wilderness on the SE slope of Three Fingered Jack. Take the Pacific Crest Trail north from its crossing of Hwy. 20, one mile east of the Hoodoo Ski Bowl turnoff in the Santiam Pass area. A quarter mile north of the highway, Square Lake Trail 65 heads off to the east. Booth Lake is about 2 miles beyond and about 1 1/2 miles north of Square Lake on the left side of the trail.

The lake is about 8 acres and is usually accessible in June. Most of the fish are about 9 inches, with some to 12. An easy lake to fish.

BOULDER LAKE (Warm Springs Indian Reservation) A good hike-in brook trout lake 1/2 mile south of Trout Lake on the west edge of Warm Springs Reservation. The lake is accessible only by unimproved trail. The trail begins at the Trout Lake Rd., about 1/4 mile east of Trout Lake Campground.

Boulder is a round, 50 acre lake at elevation 4780 ft. It has a maximum depth of 29 ft., with about a third of its area shoals. There are just under 2 miles of shoreline, most of which is quite brushy. The lake is aptly named for the very large boulders that cover most of its bottom. It produces plump eastern brook trout. A tribal fishing permit is required for this lake. No overnight camping is allowed due to fire danger.

BOULDER LAKE (Wasco Co.) A fair brook and rainbow trout lake in the Mt. Hood National Forest on the SE slope of Mt. Hood. It's about a half mile hike to the lake from Bonney Camp, which is reached by 6 miles of poor road from Bennett Pass. The roads are usually snowbound until July. Approaches from the west are clear earlier.

Boulder Lake covers about 20 acres and is predominantly a brook trout fishery. A talus pile on the west side of the lake makes a good platform for flycasters. The fish here don't get large, averaging 8 inches. Little Boulder Lake, which is only half as big, is a half mile bushwhack SE, providing good angling at times. Both lakes are stocked with fingerlings. There are improved campsites at Boulder Lake.

BRAHMA LAKE A nice 10 acre brook trout lake on the Pacific Crest Trail in the Deschutes National Forest, north of Irish and Taylor lakes. From the south on Hwy. 58, take the Davis Lake Rd. past Crane Prairie to FS 600, the Little Cultus crossing of the Pacific Crest Trail at Irish and Taylor Lakes. Brahma is an easy 2 mile hike north.

It offers good angling for brook trout to 15 inches. Average size is around 10 inches. Flyfishing is good, as the lake is quite shallow. Wet bucktails fished with a slow retrieve can be effective. A few natural campsites are available. In early season the mosquitoes in this area are unbelievable. Be prepared. An army surplus mosquito helmet can be a godsend here.

CABOT LAKE A small lake in the Mt. Jefferson Wilderness on the northern edge of the Deschutes National Forest. Six acres and shallow, it is no longer stocked due to a tendency to winterkill.

CACHE LAKE A good trout lake in Deschutes National Forest SW of Suttle Lake on the Jefferson-Deschutes County line. From Hwy. 20, 2 miles east of the Suttle Lake turnoff, follow FS 2066 west 2 miles to FS 2068, and continue west on 2068 a bit over 2 miles to a short spur which leads to the lake. The spur is just before the road makes a sharp hairpin back to the east.

Cache Lake is just north of Cache Mountain. It's a shallow lake and offers excellent flyfishing throughout the season. Size of the fish fluctuates from year to year, but ordinarily eastern brook trout average 10 inches and get as large as 15 inches. A few rainbow of good size will show up now and then. It's usually accessible in early summer. There's no improved campground. Motorboats are prohibited.

CARL LAKE A good size brook trout lake in Deschutes National Forest on the eastern edge of Mt. Jefferson Wilderness. From Hwy. 20,

about one mile east of the Suttle Lake turn-off, take FS 12 north about 4 miles to FS 1230, which branches north at Jack Creek Campground. Follow 1230, the Abbot Butte Rd., 8 miles north to its end, where you will find Trailhead 68. The trail leads 2 miles west to Cabot lake. Carl Lake is about 2 miles beyond Cabot by way of Trail 68.

Carl is stocked, but is not rich in trout food. The brook trout caught here are 9-11 inches. A long deep lake, it can be effectively fished using any technique.

CELILO LAKE (a.k.a. Lake Celilo, The Dalles Pool) One of four power impoundments on the Columbia River east of Portland, offering the most productive angling of the four. Fairly shallow, and only about 15 miles long, Lake Celilo offers good habitat for its walleye, plentiful food sources for resident sturgeon, and features the powerful attraction (for salmon, steelhead *and* anglers) of the Deschutes River mouth.

The main salmon fishery here takes place immediately below the mouth of the Deschutes, where the big fish congregate in the cool water after their passage over The Dalles Dam. This is a boat fishery, with boats launched at Celilo Park downstream of the mouth, and at Heritage Landing just above the mouth on the Deschutes. Peak catches are in mid to late September.

Angling for summer steelhead in the pool begins July 4th weeken, primarily at the mouth of the Deschutes. There is also a small bank fishery just below John Day Dam.

Sturgeon are fished by boat throughout the pool, and there is a very popular sturgeon bank fishery at French Giles Park below John Day Dam. About 50% of the sturgeon catch for all the reservoirs is made in Lake Celilo.

Walleye are a big fishery here year around. Mostly a boat show, the best catches are made at the mouth of the Deschutes, and around Rufus up to the deadline below John Day Dam, a 3-4 mile stretch. There is a small bank fishery for walleye from French Giles Park below the dam down to the Rufus gravel pits.

Shad are taken at French Giles Park during June and early July. Most bass and panfish angling takes place in ponds adjacent to the river (See columbia river ponds, hood river to the deschutes) and in the Rufus gravel pit complex, a network of sloughs and ponds where anglers can walk out on the flats at low tide from access roads off French Giles Park.

CHARLTON LAKE A large brook trout lake on the Pacific Crest Trail 2 miles east of Waldo Lake. Best reached by the Waldo Lake Rd. FS 5897, a paved road leading north from Hwy. 58 about 3 miles west of Odell Lake. Near the north end of Waldo Lake, the road turns sharply to the east and gives way to gravel. This is easy to miss, as a paved road continues north to North Waldo Lake Campground. The 1/4 mile trail into the lake is within one mile of the transition to gravel.

Charlton is big, and sometimes the fish are hard to find. Watch out for rough water during the day. Brook trout here average 10-12 inches with some to 16 inches. Spinners or lures do well, but fly angling will out fish both in fall. Peak fishing is just after ice-out and late in the season. The former is hard to catch, as snow often blocks the roads. There are excellent blueberries around the lake in late summer and some improved campsites. Motorboats are prohibited.

CHENOWETH CREEK A small, lightly fished stream, about 10 miles long, entering the Columbia at the west end of The Dalles. It is followed by gravel road west to the headwaters. Not stocked, it offers fair cutthroat fishing in late fall and early spring. Bait angling or spinner/bait combinations work well. There's a lot of private property, so watch your trespassing.

CLEAR CREEK (Wasco Co.) A fair trout stream flowing from Clear Lake east into the White River in Mt. Hood National Forest. The creek is crossed by Hwy. 26 about 14 miles SE of Government Camp. Several forest roads follow and cross the stream as well.

Clear Creek is not stocked but has good populations of rainbow and brook trout, some from Clear Lake. Fishing is usually good from early season through the summer in the upper section. Irrigation water is diverted from the lower stream. Bait is usually the best trout producer, with fish 7-12 inches. A small portion of the creek is on Warm Springs Reservation land and is signed to that effect.

CLEAR LAKE (Wasco Co.) A good trout lake in Mt. Hood National Forest, drained by Clear Creek of the White River system on the east side of the Cascade Range. The lake is 67 miles from Portland by Hwy. 26. Turn off at a well signed intersection to the right, about 11 miles past Government Camp. It's a short mile to the lake. A good road follows the lakeshore about half-way around.

Clear Lake covers just under a square mile most of the season, but is drawn down heavily in the fall. It's stocked with rainbow trout, which are supplemented by a healthy self-sustaining population of brook trout. The rainbow show up about 5 to 1 in the catch. Both species average 8-12 inches, with some fish to 18 inches. Trolling and bait fishing take a lot of fish, and flies are good early and late in the day. There is a nice campground with boat ramp on the east shore of the lake.

CLIFF LAKE (Wasco Co.) An I-84 pond adjacent to the Columbia River, located at hwy. mile 74.6. Only one acre, it is immediately east of McClures Lake south of the freeway. There is limited unimproved parking for eastbound traffic only at the east end of the lake. The pond may contain any of the Columbia River warmwater species.

CODY PONDS Three small ponds offering bass and panfish west of Tygh Valley off Hwy. 197 south of the Dalles. From 197 head west 5 miles to the community of Wamic. From there continue west 4 miles on Rock Creek Reservoir Rd. Between 2 small ponds on the right, a road turns off north. Follow this a short way to the first 5 acre pond. For the second pond, stay on the main road to Rock Creek Reservoir, and head north on FS S466. After one mile, turn right to the pond, which covers 6 acres. The third pond is on the north edge of the Reservoir road, about 1 1/2 miles from Rock Creek, about 5 acres.

The ponds are all on Dept. of Fish and Wildlife land, but the second has only a 10 foot public easement around the shore. All are shallow, with good populations of bluegill and bass. The bass are rather small, with an occasional 16 inch fish tops. A rubber boat would be handy on the lakes, but they're easily fished from shore. There are no facilities here, but there's a campground at Rock Creek Reservoir.

CRANE PRAIRIE RESERVOIR A large, unique, and very rich reservoir, fed by the waters of the upper Deschutes River. This is one of Oregon's premier trout lakes, and beautiful, too. It offers consistently outstanding trout fishing and plentiful, big trout. Relatively shallow water, abundant cover, and dense insect populations make this a fly angler's paradise. The waters of the prairie cover over 5 square miles, with many interesting arms and embayments. A fairly constant water level throughout the year further enhances the fishery.

When Crane Prairie was flooded in 1928, most of the timber was left standing. Much of it still stands, silver skeletons rising from the water, their bark long since weathered away. The fallen timber forms intricate and extensive log jams. Approximately ten percent of the lake is covered by these stands, which provide excellent fish habitat and, with the bottom ooze and pond weed, produce an endless supply of mayflies, water beetles, scuds, damselflies, dragonflies, and other trout delights. Average depth of the reservoir is 11 ft. at full pool, and maximum depth in the old river channels is 20 ft.

Crane Prairie is a Wildlife Management

WEIGHING ANCHOR AT CRANE PRAIRIE
Steven Nehl, Photographer

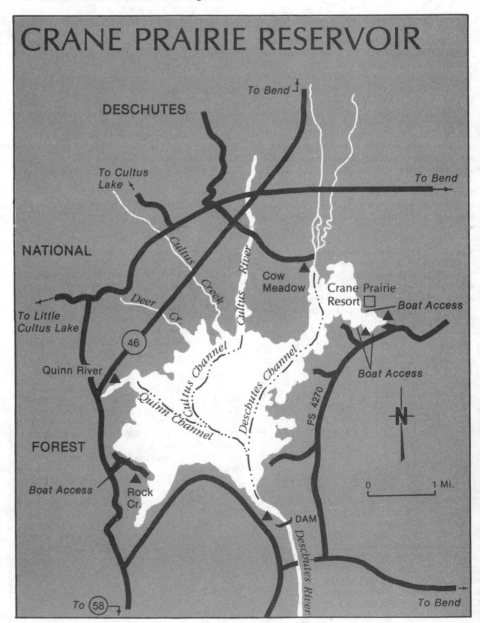

CRANE PRAIRIE RESERVOIR

DESCHUTES

NATIONAL

FOREST

To Bend

To Cultus Lake

To Bend

To Little Cultus Lake

Quinn River

46

Deer Cr.

Cultus Creek

Cultus River

Quinn Channel

Cultus Channel

Deschutes Channel

FS 4270

Cow Meadow

Crane Prairie Resort

Boat Access

Boat Access

Boat Access

Rock Cr.

DAM

Deschutes River

To 58

To Bend

N

0   1 Mi.

Area. Osprey, Canadian geese, great numbers of assorted ducks, grebes, blue heron, bald eagles, and an occasional sandhill crane are among the many birds that frequent the area. The osprey and eagles nest in the snag forests and do their own share of fishing with consumate skill. Around the lake deer, elk, mink, porcupine, and otter can be seen.

Crane Prairie is just east of Century Drive about 46 miles from Bend, a beautiful drive on paved road past other fine Cascade lakes. Alternately, one can drive south from Bend about 18 miles on Hwy. 97 to County Rd. 42, the Fall River Rd. Turn off 2 1/2 miles past the Sunriver junction, and continue west approximately 20 miles to FS 4270, which is signed for Crane Prairie. Turn right. It is only 4 miles to the east side of the lake. From the Willamette Valley, Eugene offers good access by way of Hwy. 58 to the Davis Lake cutoff (Hwy. 61), which is 3 miles south of the Crescent Lake junction. Take Hwy. 46 north past Davis Lake to the junction with Hwy. 42. Here one may go east to reach Crane Prairie's eastern shore, or proceed north to the campground on the west or the resort on the north shore.

The reservoir offers excellent angling for both amateurss and experts. These waters are very rich, and trout put on poundage quickly here. In good years, fish average 12 inches, with many big fish taken daily. Rainbow to 18 3/4 pounds and eastern brook to 6 pounds have been landed. Five pounders don't even raise eyebrows at the resort.

In 1987 and 1988 Crane Prairie felt the effect of drought. The water was low, and fishing was off. It takes about a year of good snowpack and rainfall to recharge the springs that feed Crane Prairie's tributary streams (the upper Deschutes, Quinn River, Cultus River, and Snow Creek). Anglers might look forward to 1990 for a full Crane Prairie comeback.

Although Crane Prairie rainbow dominate the fishing interest here, fair numbers of brook trout can be found in the areas near creek mouths. A kokanee population is well established but isn't heavily pursued.

Largemouth bass were illegally introduced 5-6 years ago and are now an established population, though not a big fishery yet. Look for them along the eastern shore and its backwater, along the southern shore, and near the dam. Bass will avoid the cold water inlets. Check with ODFW's Bend office, or Crane Prairie Resort, for information about possible bass tournaments.

Crane Prairie offers outstanding conditions for all types of angling, and two or three methods may be producing fish at the same time. Many of the large rainbow are taken on trolled wooly worms or big streamers, including some developed especially for Crane Prairie (available at the resort store and at area fly shops). Anglers handy with nymphs do well with gold-ribbed Hare's Ears and other small nymphs, especially in spring. Orange-bodied Caddis, Green Damselfly, and Orange-bodied Bucktail Coachman are popular. Smaller mayflies are about throughout the season, and healthy rises occur from late spring on.

Fish of all sizes may be taken with a variety of bait fishing methods (either on the bottom or with a bobber). A live dragonfly nymph is a favorite for still-fishing, using a bobber or quill float to detect the soft bite. Spin fishermen favor Panther Martins, Flatfish, Roostertails, and spinner and worm combinations. Check in at the resort store for advice on tackle and hot spots.

Fish the area close to shore and among the submerged trees in spring and early summer, or during high water. Later in the year, as the water lowers, head for the channels. The biggest fish are usually landed in May and June. But really, there is no *off* season here.

Kokanee concentrate in the Quinn and Cultus River channels in late summer and can be taken on bait or by spinfishing.

Crane Prairie is so large it can be a bit overwhelming at first, but the cover is obvious (though the channels aren't). Looking for other concentrations of boats is a legitimate scouting tactic. Fishing guides are available through Eugene and Bend fly and tackle shops and at the resort on the north shore.

Crane Prairie is primarily a boater's show only because a boat givers anglers mobility to go where the action is. Trolling is rarely the best method here. A canoe does well, though you must keep a weather eye out. A 10 mph speed limit is in effect. Boats, motors, and canoes are rented at the resort, and gasoline is available there. There's a good boat ramp at the resort, at Rock Creek. and at Quinn River Campground. A new campground just south of the resort has 2 boat ramps. A very poor ramp (not recommended) is available at Browns Landing by the dam.

There are 4 campgrounds on the reservoir. Rock Creek and Quinn River campgrounds on the west shore are large and have boat ramps. A small campground, Cow Meadow, is located on the north shore. The road into this is a bit rough, and there is no ramp, though you can slip in a shallow draft car-topper or canoe. A campground shows up on the forest map at the dam, but there are no developed sites there. The bad news is that all these camping areas get crowded, and individual sites are not very secluded. The new campground just south of the resort features 140 additional spaces. Cow Meadow sometimes offers the best bet for solitude, and there are natural campsites elsewhere around the lake.

CRESCENT CREEK A good trout stream which meanders 40 fishing miles through Deschutes National Forest from Crescent Lake to the Little Deschutes River. It produces some of the largest stream trout in the area, especially big browns. Though moderately swift, it's an easy stream to fish using any method.

Crescent Creek flows east out of Crescent Lake and away from any roads for its first 2 miles. The creek then swings south, paralleling Hwy. 58 for about 3 miles, where it flows through mostly private land. It then turns east again, crossing and leaving Hwy. 58, entering a steep valley which is National Forest land. Here the creek is followed from above by County Rd. 61, the shortcut to Lapine and main route to Davis Lake. Crescent Creek crosses this road just past the Davis Lake turn-off and trends east through mostly private land until it joins the Little Deschutes River about 5 miles north of the town of Crescent on Hwy. 97.

The creek is not stocked but has nice populations of brown and rainbow trout. The browns run 8-14 inches and are found throughout the stream. Rainbow run a bit smaller. The best fishing on the creek is in the steep valley. It isn't easy to get down there, and the bank is brushy, but the fish are there. You can park anywhere along the road and climb down, or bull your way in from either road crossing. Fly angling wet or dry can be effective. Evening fishing is red hot when a good hatch is on. There is a campground at the stream crossing on FS 61, and lodging on Hwy. 58.

CRESCENT LAKE (Klamath Co.) A large deep lake in the Deschutes National Forest, 3 miles south of Odell Lake, offering good fishing for hefty Mackinaw lake trout, brown trout, and rainbow, as well as kokanee and whitefish. Just under 6 square miles, with a depth of 280 ft., it's a popular general recreation area, with clear sparkling water and miles of wooded shoreline.

Crescent Lake is about 75 miles SE of Eugene by Hwy. 58, about 18 miles NW of the junction of hwys. 58 and 97. A small community, Crescent Lake Junction, is on Hwy. 58 at the turnoff to the lake, FS 60. The forest road reaches the lake in about 2 miles and hugs the western and southern shore for about 5 miles. Another road, FS 6015, follows the eastern shore.

This big, deep lake grows big, deep bodied

CROOKED RIVER AT SMITH ROCKS
Courtesy, Oregon State Highway Dept.

lake trout from 5-10 pounds, with some over 20 pounds occasionally landed. Ice-out finds the big trout cruising the shallows, and anglers have good success casting spoons from shore, particularly in the Simax Beach area on the NE side of the lake. Fly anglers participate in the action at this time of year using big leach patterns and dragonfly nymphs. The trick is spotting the fish and casting directly to them. Wearing polaroid glasses helps.

By July, the Mackinaw have begun to school and are running in deep water. Deep trolling with downriggers and lead line along the summer home area (NW shore), and along the ledges off Spring and Contorta Point campgrounds (southern shore), is often productive. A depth finder is useful to locate the ledges. If you don't have one, the area offshore from the scout camp, one mile east of Contorta Point, sports a straight ledge at 80 feet that is easy to track. Trollers favor Flatfish type lures or fish-imitation plugs like Rebels and Rappalas. Fly anglers use big streamers. In spring and fall, trollers often work at depths of 20-30 ft. In summer, they go deeper.

A big lead jig, like the Luhr Jensen Nordic, might be effective here, as they have been at nearby Odell. With these jigs, anglers can avoid all the special downrigging gear. The only catch is, of course, being (and knowing you be) directly over the fish in order to get results.

Large numbers of fingerling kokanee are planted in Crescent Lake annually (150,000 in 1989) in a continuing effort to better establish that fishery. Kokanee survival seems to be related to the amount of run-off feeding the lake, as the lake water is too pure to be very productive. Kokanee are generally taken by trolling spinner and bait. Average size is about 12 inches, with a range 9-15 inches. Kokanee have soft mouths, and hooks have a tendency to pull loose unless fish are handled carefully. Best kokanee areas are off the resort and near the island at the south end. Success is usually best in May and June.

Brown trout continue to be stocked and grow to respectable size in Crescent. Fish to 12 pounds have been taken. Rainbow reproduce

naturally here, and additional Deschutes red-sides are stocked each year. All angling methods are used, with good success near the creek inlets on the southern shore. Whitefish also show up in the catch. Some anglers regard them as a nuisance, but they make fine eating, especially if smoked.

Crescent Lake Resort is located at the northern tip of the lake. This is one of the most charming forest resorts in Oregon, with open, sunny views of the lake, neat green lawns, large old firs, and tidy cabins. The resort provides boat rentals, supplies, accommodations, and has a small restaurant. Supplies are also available on Hwy. 58 at Crescent Lake Junction.

There are three Forest Service campgrounds on the lakeshore—Crescent Lake, Spring, and Contorta Point. Each has a boat ramp. Picnic facilities are available at Simax Beach, Tandy Bay, and Tranquil Cove.

CROOKED RIVER A large tributary of the Deschutes River, whose two major forks carve canyons through the central Oregon desert. The Crooked joins the Deschutes in Lake Billy Chinook. The North Fork heads in the Ochoco Mts. about 75 miles east of Prineville. The South Fork heads in the high desert NE of Brothers on the G.I. Ranch. Spring fed, the Crooked remains consistently cool despite the desert heat, growing good size trout and smallmouth bass. Southeast of Prineville the river is dammed to form Prineville Reservoir.

The river above the reservoir is followed for some distance by the Post-Paulina Hwy. Below the reservoir, Hwy. 27 follows the river to Prineville.

The upper South Fork flows through several large ranches which limit access. But best fishing is between the Westmoreland Ranch and the Post-Paulina Hwy., almost all of which is bordered by BLM land. To reach the river here, take Camp Creek Rd. to the canyon rim and hike down to the river, following any of several dirt foot tracks. The Dept. of Fish and Wildlife in Prineville will provide specific route information and direct anglers to an un-signed dirt road that leads to the river off the Post-Paulina Hwy, about 7 miles east of Camp Creek Rd.

This section of the Crooked has provided outstanding fishing since the early 1980's. It was poisoned in 1981 to eliminate rough fish, and was restocked with rainbow and smallmouth bass. Fingerlings here grow to 18 inches in a single season. Trout average 12-18 inches, and fly fishing is excellent. The fishery here might be down temporarily as a result of the 1987-88 drought. It takes about a year for spring-fed rivers to feel the effects of drought, and a year for them to recover once good snowpack and rainfall resume. Keep an eye out for rattlesnakes in the canyon in summer, or avoid the area in that season. Best fishing is in spring anyway. This is, by the way, a wilderness study area.

The confluence of the North and South Fork Crooked is on the Les Schwab Ranch about 25 miles east of Prineville Reservoir. Best fishing on the North Fork is in the canyon where the river flows through BLM and Ochoco National Forest land. To reach the river, follow FS 42 to Deep Creek Camp, then get out your map. The North Fork carves a narrow deep canyon and offers fair trout angling in spring.

Below Prineville Reservoir the river is cooled by the waters of Lake Billy Chinook, and fish grow to good size. However, large fish are not as common as they were in the 1970s

shortly after Lake Billy Chinook was constructed. There's more competition for the food supply today, rough fish have begun to re-populate, and there is increased sediment in the river. Rainbow average 8-18 inches, with a few 2-3 pounders occasionally taken. There are some Lahontan cutthroat in the river from previous stocking. A good road runs along this stretch, and the first 8 miles below the dam have good access across public land. Angling is best in early and late season.

Campsites are scattered along the lower river, and there are a couple of campgrounds in the Ochoco National Forest in the vicinity of the North Fork. Deep Creek Campground, near the creek's confluence with the Crooked, is on FS 42.

CULTUS LAKE, BIG A large deep lake with excellent fishing for Mackinaw (lake trout), located in central Oregon, about 50 miles SW of Bend in Deschutes National Forest. Take Century Drive (Hwy. 46) south from Bend to the Cultus Lake turn-off, about 10 miles past Elk Lake. FS 4630 leads west 2 miles to FS 4635, which shortly reaches the lake. Both roads are paved and well signed. From the Willamette Valley, take Hwy. 58 SE from Eugene to the Davis Lake cutoff (Hwy. 61), which is 3 miles south of the Crescent Lake junction. Then take Hwy. 46 north past Davis Lake and Crane Prairie to the Cultus turn-off.

Cultus covers 785 acres and is exceptionally deep and sparkling clear. In places its blue waters reach a depth of 200 feet. Lurking in these depths are hefty Mackinaw. Fishing for these lunkers is as good here as anywhere in the state, but the pressure is fairly light. In the first few weeks after ice-out you can find them in the shallows, and even tempt them with a fly (try big dragonfly nymphs and leach patterns). Mackinaw fishing is best in May before the fish seek deeper waters, and again in fall, from mid-September on. In July and and August, waterskiers dominate the lake.

During the summer, be prepared to go deep for Mackinaw. Trolling flashers with U20 Flatfish-type lures near dropoffs is a good method. Trollers use lead core line or 6 ounces of lead to get down to the fish, and a fish-finder really helps. The deepest areas are from about 1/2 mile west of the lodge on the west shore, right down the middle of the lake.

Typical Mackinaw here run 3-8 pounds, but some monsters have been landed. If you want to try this fishery without a lot of special gear, you might look into a leaded jig, like the Luhr Jensen Nordic. With this you can effectively take fish without an elaborate rig. There is some indication that these jigs are taken more readily than a trolled lure *if* you're over the fish. With a fish finder, that's not hard to accomplish.

Cultus also offers fair fishing for rainbow trout, which are stocked annually. Most run 8-12 inches, but a few reach 18 inches. Trolling accounts for most of the rainbow. The SE shoreline is a popular area, and sticking near shore is good advice anywhere on the lake. You might also try working the shelves along the NW shore. Fly casting along shore can be effective in late summer and fall. A few brook trout show up around the mouth of Winopee Creek. There are a lot of whitefish in this lake, which are tasty when smoked.

Cultus Resort is a pleasant place, with restaurant, boats and motors, cabins, supplies and gas at the east end of the lake. This is a good family lake, with nice swimming areas and

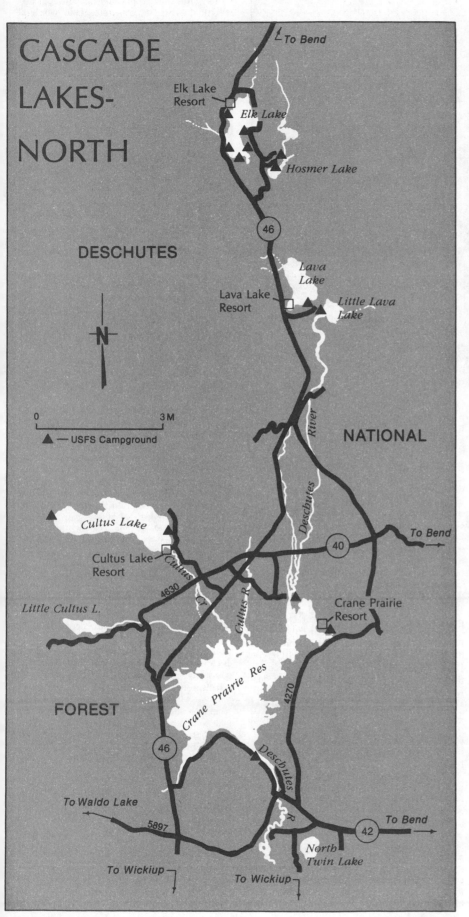

CASCADE
LAKES-
NORTH

DESCHUTES

N

0   3 M

▲ — USFS Campground

NATIONAL

FOREST

beautiful water. It is one of the few lakes in the area without a speed limit, so water skiing and large boat cruising are popular here. A campground with boat ramp is located just north of the resort. There is also a boat or hike-in campground at the west end of the lake, 3 miles by water from the resort. There is no road access to the westside camp. The trail to the westside camp heads at Deer Lake, one mile south.

CULTUS LAKE, LITTLE A good trout and kokanee lake in the Deschutes National Forest, SW of Bend on the east slope of the Cascade Range. Don't let the *little* fool you. The lake covers 170 acres. About 50 miles from Bend by Century Drive (Hwy. 46), it is 2 miles south of Big Cultus Lake on the south side of Cultus Mt. Take the Big Cultus turn-off (FS 4630) 2 miles beyond Big Cultus, and pick up FS 600, which leads to the lake in one mile. By late June you can come in from the west by this road, taking the Waldo Lake Hwy. to North Waldo Campground, then going north on FS 20031 to FS 600, on past Irish and Taylor Lakes. This road is rough when coming from the west, so take it easy.

Little Cultus offers good angling for brook trout, with a few rainbow available. The lake is fairly shallow, with shoal area predominating, although the deepest spot is 60 feet. Best fishing is in the spring, trolling for brook trout. They don't run big, averaging 9-10 inches, with a few fish to 14 inches taken late in the season. The rainbow are generally a bit smaller. Nymphs, or bucktails fished wet will take lots of fish, especially late in the season.

There is a good campground at the eastern end of the lake, but it lacks a boat ramp. There is a speed limit on the lake.

SUNSET AT DAVIS LAKE
Deke Meyer, Photographer

CULTUS RIVER A very short stream in the Deschutes National Forest, about 50 miles SW of Bend. The river rises from a large spring about 2 miles north of Crane Prairie Reservoir and flows into the north end of the reservoir. The road to Cultus Lake crosses it about midway, near Round Mountain. It is rather brushy but carries a lot of water. There are very few trout of legal size in the stream. Not recommended for angling except where it enters Crane Prairie.

DARK LAKE (Warm Springs Indian Reservation) The middle lake in a chain of five, which also includes Trout, Island, Long, and Olallie. It is accessible only by unimproved trail from either Olallie Lake on the east, or Trout Lake on the west. From Trout Lake Campground, it's about a 1 1/2 mile hike. The first 1/4 mile of trail is a fairly steep uphill grind, but the remaining distance is more easily traveled, passing Island Lake on the way in. The trail from Olallie Lake begins at the SE end of Olallie, and is most easily reached from Olallie Peninsula Campground.

With a maximum depth of 52 feet, Dark Lake is the deepest lake in the chain. It occupies a glacial cirque, its west and south shores abutting a steep talus slope 200 feet high. The shadow of this cliff over the lake and its depth are responsible for the name Dark Lake. It is at 4690 ft. and has a surface area of about 22 acres. There isn't a lot of shoal area around the lake. It contains eastern brook trout. A tribal permit is required to fish this lake. No overnight camping is allowed due to fire danger.

DARLENE LAKE A small, deep hike-in brook trout lake in the Windy Lakes area SW of Crescent Lake. See crescent Lake for road directions. The trail is 1/2 mile west of the entrance to Spring Camp, sharing a trailhead with the Windy Lake Trail. It is about 4 miles to Windy, where the trail forks, and Darlene is about one mile further on Trail 46. The trail continues east to eventually meet the Pacific Crest Trail.

Darlene covers 11 acres and is 48 feet deep. All angling methods can be used, and the size of some of the rainbow may surprise you. There are some fair natural campsites at the lake.

DAVIS CREEK Inundated by Wickiup Reservoir, a major cold water entry to the lake, attracting large numbers of whitefish. See wickiup reservoir.

DAVIS LAKE (Deschutes Co.) Regulated for fly fishing only, a large, handsome, shallow lake in Deschutes National Forest that has a proven capacity to grow large and abundant trout. The Davis management plan calls for development of a fishery where average angler success would be one fish for every three hours of effort, and where most fish landed would exceed 15 inches. Davis has often met, and exceeded this goal in past years. But the 1987-88 drought had a very severe effect on the lake, which is fed primarily by snowpack. Trout habitat and food sources were drastically reduced. And the large numbers of big trout that once schooled at the Odell Creek inlet pool just haven't been there. In fact, currently the pool isn't there.

The lake could recover in one year, given a good winter. But the fishery at Davis has other problems less easily solved. For reasons unknown, Davis Lake trout are susceptible to disease. For some years now the Oregon Dept. of Fish and Wildlife has been seeking a trout strain that is disease resistant. The current stock, the Deschutes redside rainbow, resists infection but does not take advantage of Davis's primary food source, an abundance of rough fish. ODFW may next try stocking Klamath Lake rainbow and landlocked coho. If tests in 1989 prove successful, stocking may begin in 1990.

As if this were not enough, Davis was also afflicted with a plague of beetles that attacked its lodgepole pine stands. This scourge, which affected much of the Deschutes National Forest in the mid-1980's, at least has run its course. Since lodgepole are shallow rooted, The Forest Service has removed many of the damaged trees. Large trees have been replanted in the campground areas, and natural reseeding will begin to fill in relatively quickly. Fortunately, lodgepole is a fast grower.

Inspite of these problems, Davis Lake is still productive for good size fish, worth at least one visit each season, if only to keep tabs on its recovery. Davis Lake is located about 8 miles south of Crane Prairie in Deschutes National Forest, about 60 miles south of Bend by way of Century Drive (Hwy. 46). From the Willamette Valley it is best reached by taking Hwy. 58 from Eugene to County Rd. 61, which joins the highway from the east about 3 miles south of Crescent Lake Junction. Three miles down 61, Hwy. 46 joins from the north. Follow Hwy. 61 six miles or so north to signed turn-offs for Davis Lake. It's about 220 miles from Portland to Davis.

Davis Lake was formed when recent (less than 3000 years ago) volcanic action sent a wall of lava, 100 feet high and over a mile wide, across the bed of Odell Creek. This natural dam has formed a roughly round lake almost 3 miles across, but quite shallow. It offers about 5 square miles of fishable water, all of it under 25 feet deep even during high water. Water from Davis seeps through the lava dam at a fair rate. The lake is rich with vegetation and consequently, thick with insects. It is also rich with a small shiner-like rough fish called roach. Roach love the vegetation, which they use as spawning grounds.

This lake is ideally suited to fly angling. There's too much vegetation for effective trolling. It's not deep enough for dependable stillfishing. And it has rich insect populations. This was recognized as far back as 1939, when the lake was first designated fly-only by an act of the State Legislature. It has remained so for all but 5 of the past 45 years.

Davis presents many challenges to the fly angler. Five square miles is a lot of water to cover. Regulations prohibit fishing while using a motor, though anglers may motor from spot to spot. Summer winds can rapidly turn the center of the lake into a character building outdoor experience. The fish can be wary since most anglers here practice catch-and-release, and many of these trout have tasted a fly in the past. In addition, the pros here use long, fine leaders, upon which big trout often practice their own brand of catch-and-release.

In good water years fish are scattered throughout the lake. As the season progresses and the water warms, they seek out the cooler water near the inlets and in the depths near the lava dam. Under current conditions, the lava dam area may have the only productive fishery on the lake. By late June, dragonfly and damselfly nymph patterns would normally be effective near the reed beds along shore. A black leech pattern is usually effective anywhere on the lake, and roach imitations may take some large trout.

There are three campgrounds on the lake, each with a boat ramp—West Davis, East Davis, and Lava Flow. Supplies can be purchased at Twin Lakes or Crane Prairie resorts to the north.

The size of the Davis rainbow has always been due in part to the voluntary catch-and-release practices of anglers here. Your support is encouraged.

DEEP CREEK (Crook Co.) A nice stream in the upper Crooked River drainage in Ochoco National Forest, about 45 miles east of Prineville. The stream is about 12 miles long and flows from the east into the North Fork of

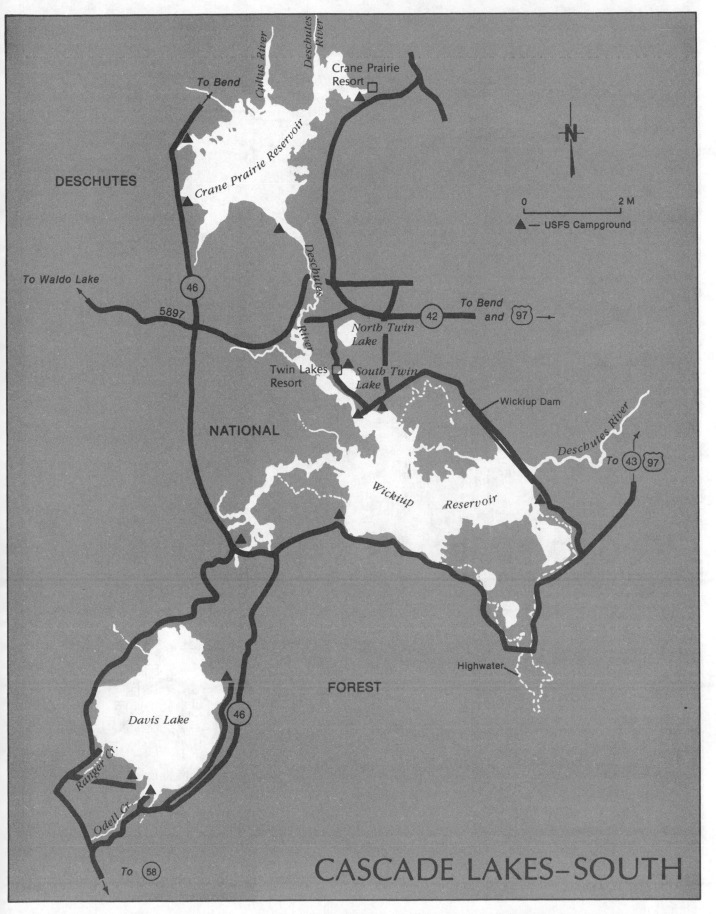

To Bend

Cultus River

Deschutes River

Crane Prairie
Resort

DESCHUTES

Crane Prairie Reservoir

Deschutes River

To Waldo Lake

46

5897

North Twin
Lake

To Bend
and 97

42

Twin Lakes
Resort

South Twin
Lake

Wickiup Dam

NATIONAL

Deschutes River

To 43 97

Wickiup Reservoir

Highwater

FOREST

46

Davis Lake

Ranger Cr.

Odell Cr.

To 58

CASCADE LAKES–SOUTH

N

0   2 M

▲ — USFS Campground

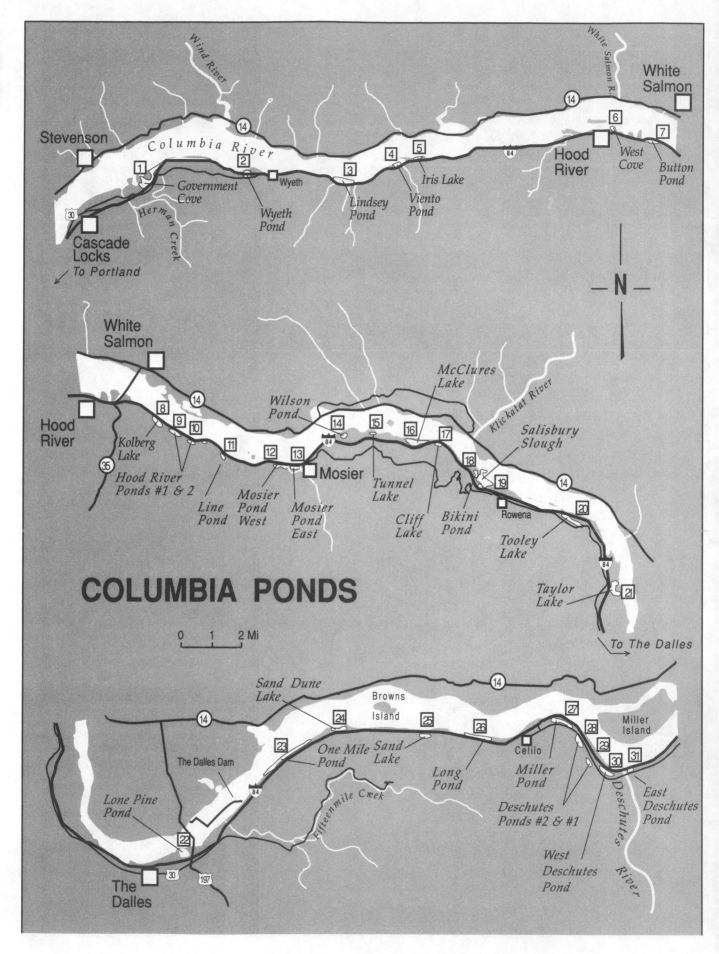

Stevenson

Columbia River

Wind River

Cascade Locks

To Portland

Herman Creek

1

Government Cove

2 Wyeth

Wyeth Pond

3

Lindsey Pond

4

5

Viento Pond

Iris Lake

Hood River

6

West Cove

7

Button Pond

White Salmon

White Salmon R.

14

84

30

—N—

White Salmon

Hood River

14

35

8

Kolberg Lake

9

10

Hood River Ponds #1 & 2

11

Line Pond

12

Mosier Pond West

13

Mosier Pond East

Mosier

14

15

Tunnel Lake

Wilson Pond

McClures Lake

16

17

Cliff Lake

Bikini Pond

18

19

Rowena

Salisbury Slough

Klickatat River

Tooley Lake

20

84

14

Taylor Lake

21

To The Dalles

COLUMBIA PONDS

0   1   2 Mi

14

Sand Dune Lake

Browns Island

24

25

23

One Mile Pond

Sand Lake

26

Long Pond

Celilo

27

28

29

30

31

Miller Island

Miller Pond

Deschutes Ponds #2 & #1

West Deschutes Pond

East Deschutes Pond

Deschutes River

The Dalles Dam

Fifteenmile Creek

Lone Pine Pond

22

84

30   197

The Dalles

COLUMBIA RIVER BACKWATER PONDS
Bonneville Dam to Deschutes River

From Bonneville Dam to the Deschutes River, the Oregon shore of the Columbia is dotted with small to medium-sized backwater ponds. Since most of these waters are connected directly to the river, they may contain any fish found in the Columbia. However, most anglers fish them for largemouth and smallmouth bass, crappie, yellow perch, pumpkinseed sunfish, bullhead catfish, and some channel catfish.

Unfortunately, access to many of these ponds is complicated by the proximity of both I-84 and the Union Pacific Railroad. Motorists are discouraged from parking on the freeway shoulder except in emergency situations.

1. GOVERNMENT COVE (hwy. mile 47) A 90 acre pond located two miles east of Cascade Locks, with access from I-84 at the Herman Creek exit.

2. WYETH LAKE (hwy. mile 50.6) A 6 acre pond located between I-84 and the railroad. One of the few waters in this series that can be reached by boat from the Columbia River.

3. LINDSEY POND (hwy. mile 54) Covering 60 acres at the mouth of Lindsey Creek. Best parking and access is for westbound traffic at the truck weigh station.

4. VIENTO LAKE (hwy. mile 56) Four acres at the mouth of Viento Creek, with good access from Viento State Park at freeway exit 56.

5. IRIS LAKE (hwy. mile 56.2) Also at Viento State Park, a 5 acre pond at the eastern end. Take exit 56.

6. WEST COVE (hwy. mile 62.3) Ten acres at the west end of the Hood River Industrial Park, accessible from freeway exit 63.

7. BUTTON POND (hwy. mile 65) One acre immediately south of the freeway, with limited vehicle parking on an unimproved road paralleling the freeway. Access is from exit 64, but pond is located at mile 65.

8. KOLBERG LAKE (hwy. mile 65.8) Five acres directly across I-84 from the Kolberg Beach State Rest Area. Park at rest area.

9. HOOD RIVER POND #1 (hwy. mile 66.3) Four acres, south of I-84. Access probably limited to eastbound vehicles only, with parking in a limited unimproved area.

10. HOOD RIVER POND #2 (hwy. mile 67) A 3 acre pond located south of I-84. Limited unimproved parking for eastbound traffic only.

11. LINE POND (hwy. mile 68) This 1 acre pond at the Hood River/Wasco County line has unimproved and limited parking for eastbound traffic only.

12. MOSIER POND, WEST (hwy. mile 68.7) An 8 acre pond bisected by the Union Pacific Railroad south of the freeway. There is limited unimproved parking for eastbound freeway traffic at the west end of the pond. Also accessible from Hwy. 30 via freeway exit 69.

13. MOSIER POND, EAST (hwy. 69) Six acres located immediately east of freeway exit 69 between I-84 and Hwy. 30. There is no parking along freeway.

14. WILSON POND (hwy. mile 71.4) Five acres on private property between I-84 and the Union Pacific Railroad. Access from Hwy. 30 with landowner permission only.

15. TUNNEL LAKE (hwy. mile 72.6) One acre located immediately west of Memaloose State Park between I-84 and the railroad. Best access is for westbound traffic.

16. McCLURES LAKE (hwy. mile 74) Fifty acres immediately east of Memaloose State Park and Rest Area. Best access is for westbound traffic, with parking available at the rest area.

17. CLIFF LAKE (hwy. 74.6) One acre immediately east of McClures Lake, south of the freeway. There is limited unimproved parking for eastbound traffic only at the east end of the lake.

18. BIKINI POND (hwy. mile 75.7) A 4 acre pond immediately west of Mayer State Park access road, between railroad and river. Access from freeway exit 76.

19. SALISBURY SLOUGH (hwy. mile 76) A 50 acre stretch of backwater located at Mayer State Park, with concrete boat ramp and ample parking. Access from freeway exit 76.

20. TOOLEY LAKE (hwy. mile 79) Thirty acres located south of the freeway, with limited unimproved parking at the west end of the lake for eastbound traffic only. Most of the north shore is private property.

21. TAYLOR LAKE (hwy. mile 80.2) Covering 50 acres east of I-84 between railroad and river, Taylor offers good angling for trout, bass, crappie, channel catfish, and bullhead catfish. There is limited unimproved parking for westbound traffic, but best access for parking and boat launching is from freeway exit 83, north and west on Frontage Rd. to the Taylor Lake Rd.

22. LONE PINE POND (hwy. mile 86.6) A 5 acre pond located north of I-84, immediately west of Hwy. 197. Parking is difficult, and the east shore of the pond is private property.

23. ONE-MILE LAKE (hwy. mile 90-91) Nine acres, located between the east and westbound lanes on I-84. There is no parking for westbound traffic, and parking for eastbound traffic is unimproved and limited.

24. SAND DUNE LAKE (hwy. mile 92.3) A one acre pond situated between east and westbound freeway lanes. There is no parking for westbound traffic, limited parking for eastbound.

25. SAND LAKE (hwy. mile 94) One acre south of I-84, with limited unimproved parking for eastbound traffic only.

26. LONG POND (hwy. mile 94) Twenty-seven acres between east and westbound freeway lanes. Best access is from exit 97 at Celilo, then follow a gravel road west from Celilo Park.

27. MILLER POND (hwy. mile 97.5) Eight acres between I-84 and Hwy. 30. No parking on I-84. Best access is from freeway exit 97, then proceed east on Hwy. 30 for one mile.

28. DESCHUTES POND #2 (hwy. mile 98.5) A 5 acre pond located south of Hwy. 30, with good off-road parking.

29. DESCHUTES POND #1 (hwy. mile 99) An old paved road bisects this 3 acre pond, providing excellent vehicle access. Located south of Hwy. 30.

30. DESCHUTES POND WEST (hwy. mile 99-99.8) Ten acres between I-84 and Hwy. 30. Park along Hwy. 30, not along freeway.

31. DESCHUTES POND EAST (hwy. mile 99.9) One acre immediately east of the Deschutes River between

Crooked River about 4 miles east of Big Summit Prairie. Take Hwy. 26 east from Prineville about 16 miles to FS 42, which follows Ochoco Creek to the Ochoco Guard Station, then swing SE to Big Summit Prairie, about 12 miles beyond the guard station. Three miles after leaving the prairie you will reach Deep Creek Campground, which is at the confluence of Deep Creek and Crooked River. FS 42 continues east, closely following Deep Creek.

The stream is stocked by the state and has some native rainbow. The catch runs 8-12 inches, but there aren't many large trout. Bait is the usual method, but small lures and flies will also work. There's a good campground at the confluence.

DEER LAKE (Deschutes Co.) A very good early season brook trout and cutthroat lake in the Cultus Lake area SW of Bend. The lake is about one mile NW of Little Cultus Lake, which is about 55 miles from Bend by way of Century Drive. Go north about 25 miles from Hwy. 58, three miles past Crescent Lake Junction. From Big Cultus Lake Rd. 4630 take FS 600 west one mile to Little Cultus Lake. Here FS 640 branches off, skirting the northern shore of Little Cultus and leading 2 miles to Deer Lake.

The lake covers 70 acres but is only 20 feet deep at most. It is stocked with cutthroat and brook trout. The majority caught are 8-12 inches. Bait or cast lures are good in spring, and fly angling is good in fall. There are good campgrounds at Big and Little Cultus Lakes, and supplies and accomodations at Cultus Resort.

DENNIS LAKE (Deschutes Co.) Here is a real jewel of a brook trout lake, a scenic blue beauty one mile past Irish Mt. on the Pacific Crest Trail. Best route in is to pick up the PCT at Irish Lake. See irish lake for road directions. Head north for about 5 miles on the PCT. Dennis is about 1/4 mile west of the trail. There is no trail leading to the lake. The PCT reaches Blaze Lake about 1/2 mile past Irish Mt. A quarter mile beyond, it crosses a spring creek. From this point, Dennis Lake is 1/4 mile to the NW and a steep 400 feet above the trail. Carry the Irish Mt. topo map for this one.

Dennis has 11 acres and is 42 feet deep. Any method will take fish. If you're fishing from shore, your best bet is with flies cast just outside the shoal area. Fly anglers won't have trouble with their backcasts here. With a rubber boat or raft, bait fishing between 15 and 30 feet deep can be very effective. There are fair natural campsites nearby.

DESCHUTES POND #1 One of the I-84 ponds adjacent to the Columbia River, located at hwy. mile 99. It may contain any of the Columbia River warmwater species. An old paved road bisects this 3 acre pond, providing excellent vehicle access. It is south of Hwy. 30.

DESCHUTES POND #2 One of the I-84 ponds adjacent to the Columbia River, located at hwy. mile 98.5. It covers 5 acres and is south of Hwy. 30, with good off-road parking. It may contain any of the Columbia warmwater species.

DESCHUTES POND EAST One of the I-84 ponds adjacent to the Columbia River. It is between hwy. miles 99 and 99.8. It covers 10 acres between I-84 and Hwy. 30. Park along Hwy. 30, not along the freeway. It may contain any of the Columbia warmwater species.

DESCHUTES RIVER (Mouth to Pelton Regulating Dam) One of the world's most productive trout waters and a top producer of summer-run steelhead, managed primarily for wild fish. This 100-mile stretch of the river slices through high desert country, carving a canyon out of ancient volcanic rock. Brown palisades rise on either side of the wide stream, and brown hills roll to meet the horizon. The dry air, characteristic of the Cascade rain-shadow, is fragrant with sage, offering a happy alternative to western Oregon's wet-weather angling. Pungent junipers cluster in the draws. This is a land of cliff swallows, meadowlarks, hawks, snakes, and ranging cattle—a dominating landscape guaranteed to restore the perspective of world-weary anglers.

The Deschutes is wide and strong in this stretch, but it offers a variety of fishing environments. There are long slow runs, deep pools, spring creek-like weed beds, gravel bars, boulder pockets, and white water—including 12 major rapids and an impassable falls (Shears). Here you'll find a chain of legendary steelhead holes, in the 42 river miles below Shears Falls, as well as spring and fall chinook. Above, there is good shelter, feeding, and spawning ground for the Deschutes *redside* (rainbow) trout, as well as additional steelhead territory.

The Deschutes empties into the Lake Celilo impoundment of the Columbia River about 12 miles west of The Dalles, only a 2 hour drive from Portland. Deschutes River State Park, off I-84, affords access to angling at the mouth. From the west, take I-84 exit 97 at Celilo and follow Hwy. 206 east to the park. From the east, take I-84 exit 104 at Biggs. Follow Hwy. 97 south and 206 west. There is a boat launch at the park. Some anglers use jet boats to reach the upper waters from this point.

There are no public roads leading from the mouth to the upper canyon, but anglers can follow the banks for 12 miles upstream through public property, thanks to the 1983 purchase of river frontage by the Oregon Wildlife Heritage Foundation, who gave it in trust to the people of Oregon following an emotional grass-roots campaign to *Save the Deschutes* from out-of-state speculators and private sport clubs. The trust specifies continuance of the *no motor vehicles* policy in the lower canyon.

Highways 197 (on the west) and 97 (on the east) flank the river for 30 miles upstream but do not enter its canyon. The only secondary roads into the lower canyon head east from Hwy. 197 to the sites of Kloan and Sinamox, at river miles 7 and 25. Overland access to the upper waters of the lower canyon is provided by 27 miles of gravel road along the east bank of the river, from Maupin to Macks Canyon. It is 9 miles from Maupin to Buckhollow Creek below Shears, 18 miles from Buckhollow down to Macks. Most of the land along the Deschutes through this stretch is open to public access. To reach this road from the west, follow Hwy. 197 to Tygh Valley. Turn east on Hwy. 216, crossing the river on Shears Bridge just below the falls. From the east, take Hwy. 97, turning onto Hwy. 216 at Grass Valley, about 15 miles from Shears.

The river below Shears Falls is primarily steelhead water. In 1986, about 5500 summer steelhead were landed in this section. An additional 1200 were landed in the upper river. Of these, an estimated 75% were natives (adipose fin *unclipped*) and, as specified by the regulations, were released. Since 1979, Deschutes steelhead management has focused on protection of the native stock. The wild run is currently estimated to be 6900 strong. When that figure reaches 10,000, the Dept. of Fish and Wildlife will consider a recommendation to allow harvesting.

Steelhead begin moving into the Deschutes in July, and the run continues through October with a peak in August or September. When the Columbia water temperature is high, additional steelhead (those bound for home waters in Idaho) slip into the lower Descutes to cool off, some wandering as far up as Pelton Regulating Dam. This Clearwater strain of steelhead weighs up to 22 pounds. Most of these eventually drop back out of the Deschutes and continue moving up the Columbia system. Steelheading at Maupin is generally prime mid-September through October. Average catch rate for this section is 3/4 fish per angler trip. Deschutes steelhead average 5-10 pounds.

Much of the Deschutes is accessible only by boat. Anglers drift to a likely spot and beach their craft before beginning pursuit, since *angling from a floating device is prohibited*. Popular steelhead drifts are from Warm Springs (r.m.97) to Trout Creek (r.m. 87), Maupin (r.m. 51) to a take-out just below White River before Shears. (r.m. 46); from just below the twin railroad tressels (r.m. 41) to Beavertail Campground (r.m. 31); from Beavertail Campground (r.m. 31) to Macks Canyon (r.m. 24); and from

Macks Canyon to the mouth. From Maupin to the mouth, boaters will encounter three Class 4 rapids, as well as many lesser whitewater stretches and the impassable Sherars Falls.

There is, however, much good water that can be reached by a combination of motor vehicle, hiking, and wading. From Sherars Falls to Macks Canyon, anglers can simply park along the road and walk down to the river through the sagebrush. Beavertail Recreation Site, about 12 miles below Sherars, has good water and natural campsites.

Check current regulations for season, bag limits, deadlines, and special regulations. On the Deschutes, all rainbow trout over 20 inches are considered steelhead. *Only adipose fin clipped steelhead may be kept. Others must be released unharmed.* Use of bait is allowed only from Buckhollow Creek a short .9 miles upstream to Sherars Falls. Elsewhere, anglers must use artificial flies and lures with barbless hooks only.

A number of wet and dry flies have been developed especially for the Deschutes steelhead fishery, including Doug Stewart's black and orange Macks Canyon and its subtle variants (judged to be one of five top producers on the stream). Other classics are Don McClain's Deschutes Demon (yellow, orange and gold), his Deschutes Skunk, and the purple bodied Dr. Gillis. Randall Kaufmann's Freight Train and Coal Car (variations on the Skunk) are also popular. Most fly-caught steelhead are hooked on a tight, floating line on or just below the surface. Be prepared for a powerful hit. Popular lures include wobblers of various colors, Bear Valley spinners, Hot shots, Tadpollies, Glogo's, and corkies.

Angling for both spring and fall chinook is concentrated in the area from Sherars downstream, with most angling taking place in the area between the falls and Buckhollow Creek, where bait fishing is allowed. Salmon eggs are the bait of choice. The spring run begins in late March, peaking between mid-April and mid-May, and continuing to mid-June. The number of springers caught here in 1988 was 1500. The most popular chinook fishery is at Sherars Falls. It runs from end of May to end of July, when the fall chinook begin passing through. The fall run extends to the end of October, but the fish begin to deteriorate about October 1. Most successful salmon fishing occurs from mid-August to September 30. The 1988 fall chinook catch was 700. The fall chinook population is estimated to be 4000-5000 and is composed entirely of natives, while the spring run has been augmented by a hatchery program since the decimation of upper Deschutes natives following construction of Pelton Dam. The precarious-looking platforms constructed over the edges of Sherars falls, by the way, are for use by Warm Springs tribal members only.

The Deschutes trout fishery is outstanding. Year around residence in this big, powerful river grows fish of superior strength. It is estimated that there are currently more than 1700 trout over 7 inches *per mile* in the river between Sherars Bridge and Pelton Regulation Dam. These fish range 8-15 inches and there are many larger, with catches over 20 inches subject to steelhead regulations. Hatchery-produced rainbow trout were last stocked in the Deschutes in 1978. A subsequent reduction in native trout encouraged the Dept. of Fish and Wildlife to abandon that program and work, instead, to promote the native redside, a program which has been enormously successful.

Trout fishing is best above Sherars. Rainbow trout predominate in this section of the riv-

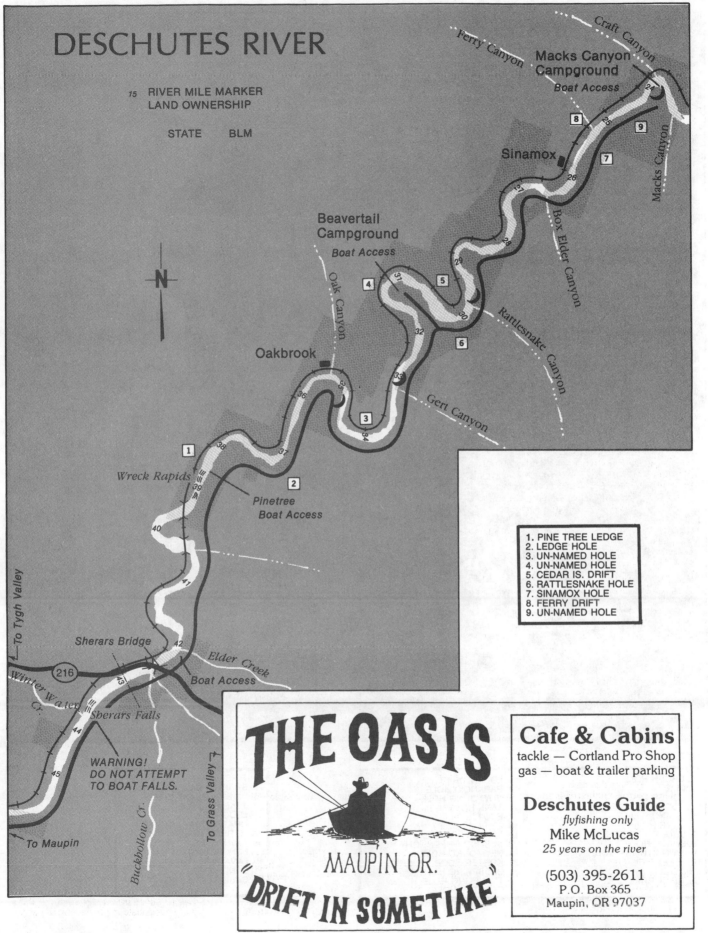

DESCHUTES RIVER

15 RIVER MILE MARKER
LAND OWNERSHIP

STATE   BLM

N

Craft Canyon

Ferry Canyon

Macks Canyon
Campground
Boat Access

Sinamox

Box Elder Canyon

Macks Canyon

Beavertail
Campground
Boat Access

Oak Canyon

Rattlesnake Canyon

Oakbrook

Gert Canyon

Wreck Rapids

Pinetree
Boat Access

1. PINE TREE LEDGE
2. LEDGE HOLE
3. UN-NAMED HOLE
4. UN-NAMED HOLE
5. CEDAR IS. DRIFT
6. RATTLESNAKE HOLE
7. SINAMOX HOLE
8. FERRY DRIFT
9. UN-NAMED HOLE

To Tygh Valley

Sherars Bridge

Winter Water Cr.

216

Elder Creek
Boat Access

Sherars Falls

*WARNING!
DO NOT ATTEMPT
TO BOAT FALLS.*

Buckhollow Cr.

To Grass Valley

To Maupin

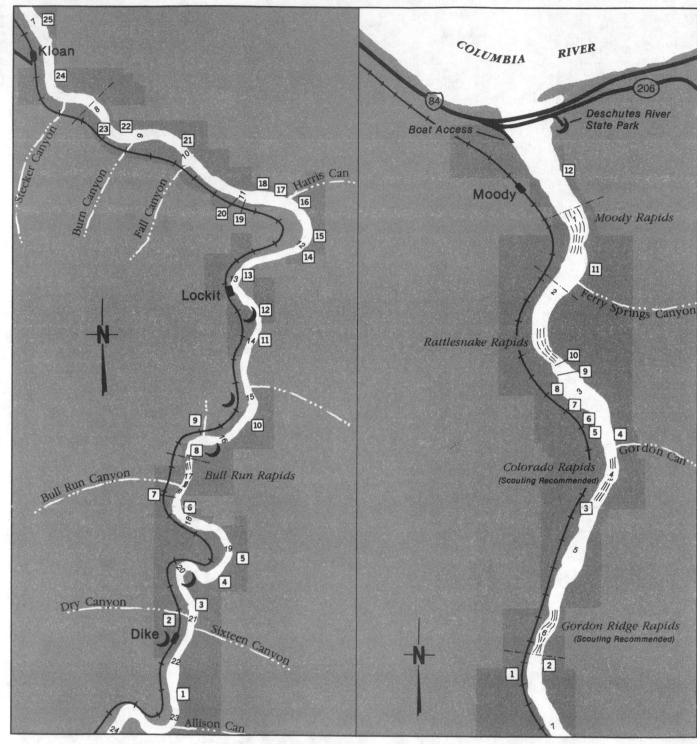

CENTRAL

COLUMBIA RIVER

Deschutes River State Park

Boat Access

Moody

Moody Rapids

Ferry Springs Canyon

Rattlesnake Rapids

Colorado Rapids
(Scouting Recommended)

Gordon Can

Gordon Ridge Rapids
(Scouting Recommended)

Kloan

Stecker Canyon

Burn Canyon

Fall Canyon

Harris Can

Lockit

Bull Run Canyon

Bull Run Rapids

Dry Canyon

Dike

Sixteen Canyon

Allison Can

1. BRUSH HOLE	13. LOCKIT DRIFT
2. DIKE	14. PARANOID HOLE
3. LOWER DIKE	15. COW DUNG HOLE
4. NOOKIE ROCK	16. TANK HOLE
5. ISLAND RIFFLE	17. EDDIE'S RIFFLE
6. DOVE HOLE	18. AIRPORT DRIFT
7. BULL RUN RIFFLE	19. GRAVEYARD HOLE
8. SHADE HOLE	20. SECOND GREENLIGHT HOLE
9. TWIN STUMPS HOLE	21. NEWFOUND HOLE
10. STEELIE FLATS	22. KORTEGE CORRAL DRIFT
11. DEAD COW HOLE	23. BEDSPRING HOLE
12. TIE CORRAL HOLE	24. TRAVELING HOLE
	25. BATHTUB HOLE

1. FIRST GREEN LIGHT HOLE
2. SHARP'S BAR
3. WAGON BLAST DRIFT
4. ZEKE'S RIFFLE
5. LEDGE HOLE
6. GRASSHOPPER HOLE
7. MERRILL HOLE
8. TWIN IS. DRIFT
9. FENCE HOLE
10. LAVA ROCK DRIFT
11. SAND HOLE
12. CABLE CROSSING

DRIFTING THE DESCHUTES - A SPRING TRADITION
Courtesy, Oregon Dept. of Fish and Wildlife

er, though there are a few bull trout (Dolly Varden). Browns grow numerous at Pelton Dam and above. Whitefish are also abundant.

Motor vehicle access to this section of the river is limited, but adequate. From Maupin, a right turn across from The Oasis Resort leads to the property of the Deschutes Club. The public is welcome, but leave your vehicle at the locked gate and proceed on foot to enjoy 14 miles of productive trout water. An old railroad bed follows the riverbank, providing easy hiking and several primitive BLM campsites. It is possible to continue on foot as far as South Junction, along the railroad right of way, where there is a mix of BLM and private land, and about 15 miles of excellent water. To reach South Junction by car, take Hwy. 197 south from Maupin to the junction with Hwy. 97 (Shaniko). A gravel road heads west to the river. BLM maintains a campground at South Junction and at the Trout Creek confluence north of Gateway.

The old railroad bed trail follows the river from Trout Creek 10 miles upstream to the Mecca site. The trail proceeds through some private land where BLM has easement. There are outhouses at intervals along the path. To reach Trout Creek by motor vehicle, follow Hwy. 97 to Lyle Gap, turning west toward Paxton at the first paved road south of Willowdale. Just north of Paxton, a gravel road leads to and through Gateway to Trout Creek, and follows the creek 3 miles to its confluence with the Deschutes.

Other popular bank fisheries are on the east bank between Sherars and Maupin City Park, including a fishing platform at about r.m. 48, built over good trout water, that accommodates 15 wheelchairs. The site was constructed by BLM and the Western Rod & Reel Club. On the west bank, anglers can fish upstream and down from the Oak Springs Hatchery for trout and steelhead. To reach the hatchery, take Hwy. 197 south from Tygh Valley, turning left onto the hatchery road about 2 miles south of the White River crossing. Be prepared for a spectacular drop down into the Deschutes canyon. There is also east bank public access on Warm Springs Reservation at Dry Creek Camp-

ground. Anglers can hike and fish downstream about 6 miles. Tribal permits are required, and overnight camping is allowed.

Many anglers drift this portion of the river, putting in at Warm Springs for a day's drift to Trout Creek. Immediately below Trout Creek, boaters must contend with a class 3 rapids and are committed to the long trip to Maupin (at least 2 days drifting) which includes much heavy water. There is no boat ramp at South Junction. *Angling from a floating device is prohibited* in this section, as elsewhere on the Deschutes, but boats do provide access to otherwise inaccessible waters.

The richness of Deschutes insect life is legendary. Giant salmon flies (Deschutes stoneflies) become active in mid-May, hatching in late May, and continuing on the water surface through late June—a cycle that produces what some consider to be the best fly fishing west of the Mississippi (including Montana). Weighted stonefly nymph patterns are a staple for Deschutes anglers, and will produce year around. Caddis and cranefly hatches also occur during this time. Grasshopper, stonefly, mayfly, and caddis are thick in August, with many big fish ignoring these morsels in maddening favor of miniscule midges.

Often, hatches of small mayflies occur simultaneously with caddis and stonefly, and fish reluctant to go for imitations of these more visible insects may be feeding selectively on Baetis hors d'ouvres. Evenings on the river often produce excellent spinner falls. Oregon fly tiers and anglers have long been studying ways to match and anticipate the river's hatches. The complex picture remains inscrutable, however, so wise anglers will come prepared with a range of insect, stage, and color imitations. And patience. Popular lures include Roostertail, Flatfish, and Mepp Spinner.

A word of warning to all Deschutes anglers: this is a big, swift, dangerous river, and wading it must be approached with proper re-

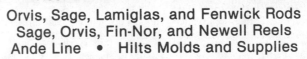

DESCHUTES RIVER RETRIEVER
Brian O'Keefe

presides. Furthermore, the coffee's good, Virginia's home-style meals are great, and the walls are covered with historic Deschutes photos and momentoes. The Oasis also has tackle, gas, cabins, and long-term vehicle parking for those using the Maupin City Park launch. Kaufmann's Streamborn of Portland maintains a house in Maupin, available by advance reservation, which comes complete with food, guide, raft, local transportation, and a well-stocked fly-tying bench. Gas and lodging are also available at Madras.

The only established campgrounds from Maupin to the mouth are at Maupin City Park, Beavertail and Macks Canyon. Campgrounds upstream from Sherars include South Junction and Trout Creek. Only Maupin City Park has drinking water. There are natural campsites at many points along the river. Users are urged to camp lightly, using wilderness (no trace) camping methods. Open fires are discouraged, and are prohibited between June 1 and October 1 due to fire danger. For environmental protection, there are outhouses up from the river bank at frequent intervals, even in areas accessible only by boat. Cattle with BLM grazing permits don't seem to bother with such niceties, unfortunately. This here's cow pie country, partner. If watching herds of large animals upsets your casting, you might prefer the stretch above Sherars Bridge.

DESCHUTES RIVER (Warm Springs Indian Reservation) Warm Springs Reservation follows the west riverbank from 16 miles south of Maupin to the Metolius confluence. Daily and seasonal permits are sold, allowing anglers to fish a fairly small segment of the Deschutes from tribal property on the west bank, as well as

spect. It can kill. If you wear waders, be sure to wear a wading belt. A wading staff and properly surfaced wading shoes are both prudent precautions.

The Deschutes is currently open for trout angling all year (though the stretch from Pelton to the North edge of Warm Springs Reservation might be withdrawn; check current angling regulations). Fishing is generally excellent throughout the year. Fall fishing is probably best, enhanced by the reduced number of anglers. The recent regulatory change opening the waters to trout angling in winter lets rain maddened Willamette valley anglers escape for weekend dry fly action for prolific mid-winter Baetis hatches. The action starts around midday and can be excellent.

The Deschutes offers a popular challenge for whitewater enthusiasts as well as anglers, and maps and literature on drifting the river are readily available both commercially and through the Oregon Department of Transportation's Parks and Recreation Division. But this

is not novice water, and boaters are urged to use caution. A boater pass system in effect throughout the river requires a daily use fee, but does not limit the number of boaters. Passes may be purchased from the State Parks Department at 525 Trade St. S.E., Salem 97310, from their regional office in Portland, and at tackle and supply stores along the river and in all metropolitan areas. The Deschutes fishery is affected by water discharges from Pelton Dam, which are variable in spring. Heavy discharge can put the fishery off for several days. To keep in touch with the dam discharge, anglers can telephone PGE-FISH (503-743-3474) for a reading on the river flow and anticipated discharge plans.

Experienced Deschutes angling and river guide services are available through fly and tackle shops in all Oregon metropolitan areas, by contacting the Oregon Guides and Packers Association, and at Madras and Maupin. The Oasis Resort in Maupin is an unofficial information center for angling this portion of the river. Long-time Deschutes guide Mike McLucas

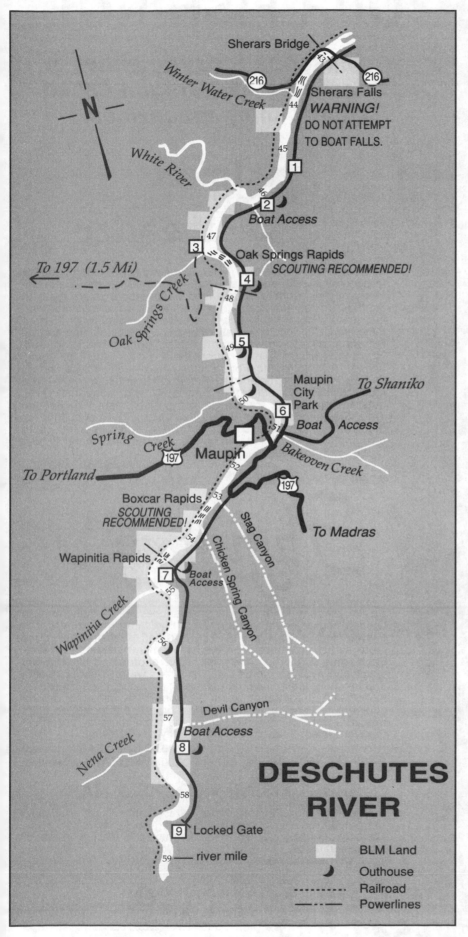

Sherars Bridge

216

216

Winter Water Creek

Sherars Falls
WARNING!
DO NOT ATTEMPT
TO BOAT FALLS.

43

44

45

White River

1

46

2

Boat Access

47

3

Oak Springs Rapids
SCOUTING RECOMMENDED!

To 197 (1.5 Mi)

4

48

Oak Springs Creek

49

5

Maupin
City Park

To Shaniko

50

6

Boat   Access

51

Spring   Creek

197

Maupin

Bakeoven Creek

To Portland

52

197

Boxcar Rapids,
*SCOUTING
RECOMMENDED!*

53

To Madras

54

Wapinitia Rapids

Stag Canyon

7

*Boat
Access*

Chicken Spring Canyon

55

Wapinitia Creek

56

Devil Canyon

57

Boat Access

Nena Creek

8

DESCHUTES
RIVER

58

9 Locked Gate

59 — river mile

☽ Outhouse

········· Railroad

—·—·— Powerlines

BLM Land

DESCHUTES STONEFLY
Steven Nehl, Photographer

1. SANDY BEACH PULL-OUT - floaters encouraged to take out here to avoid Sherars congestion. Plentiful parking & good fishing during raft off-season.

2. CAR-PARK/CAMPSITE - Public access to undeveloped tribally owned peninsula.

3. OAK SPRINGS HATCHERY - Fish up and down for trout and steelhead. Narrow access road off Hwy. 197 features spectacular last mile.

4. HANDICAPPED ACCESS - Fishing platform accomodates 15 wheelchairs accessing good trout water, built by Western Rod & Reel Club. Accessible restrooms, paved car park.

5. BLM LAND - undeveloped car pull-offs & campsites scattered along road to Maupin provide public access to good trout and steelhead water.

6. MAUPIN CITY PARK - Improved boat ramp with take-out fee, camping, long-term parking for drifters of upper river. Shuttle service in Maupin.

7. WAUPINITIA CR. BOAT RAMP - Primitive raft put-in accesses popular whitewater. Primarily for day use down to Sherars.

8. NENA CR. BOAT RAMP - Last launch below locked gate. Small ramp, camp sites on narrow flat, fewer rafters.

9. DESCHUTES CLUB GATE - Vehicles prohibited, but public welcome to hike and fish 14 miles of prime trout and steelhead water. Abandoned railroad grade trail leads to North Junction. Includes several boat-in campsites.

other tribal waters. For information, contact the Dept. of Natural Resources, Box C, Warm Springs, OR 97761. Permits can be purchased in the community of Warm Springs at the Warm Springs Police Station, the Information Center, Rainbow Market, and Macy's Store.

To access the open portion of tribal riverbank, drive 3 miles north from Warm Springs on the paved road to Kahneeta Hot Springs, then 2 miles east to Dry Creek Campground. The river is accessible by unimproved road along the bank for about 4 miles downstream. There is no drinking water at the camp.

DESCHUTES RIVER (Pelton Dam to Bend)

Three river miles above Warm Springs, Pelton Dam backs up the Deschutes creating Lake Simtustus, which is managed by Warm Springs Indian Reservation. For a description of this reservoir, see simtustus. Above Lake Simtustus, Round Butte Dam backs up the waters of the Deschutes, Metolius, and Crooked rivers to form the three-pronged Lake Billy Chinook. A tribal permit is required to fish the Metolius Arm. See billy chinook.

Above Lake Billy Chinook the Deschutes flows through an extremely scenic, narrow gorge. The river is too shallow here for summer drifting due to irrigation withdrawals, but there is good angling for wild rainbow and brown trout. Landlocked salmon from lake Billy Chinook also wander into this section of the river. Trout regulations apply to this fishery.

From Round Butte Dam to Big Falls, the gorge cuts through BLM and National Forest land. There are access tracks into the gorge and un-named trails, some of which show up on the USGS topographic map of the area. The Steelhead Falls vicinity below Big Falls is especially unique.

Upstream, the river flows through much private land, but landowners are tolerant of anglers who stop in to ask permission to cross over to the gorge. From about 15 miles north of Redmond, the river is again accessed by secondary roads. Lower Bridge, Odin Falls, Tetherow Bridge, and Cline Falls State Park are popular angler access sites. Between Redmond and Bend, the Deschutes can be fished at Tumalo and Sawyer State Parks on Hwy. 97. There is excellent trout fly water in this section of the river. Angling from a floating device is prohibited, but there are no bait and tackle restrictions in this section of the river at this time. Check current regulations. There are no steelhead in this portion of the Deschutes.

DESCHUTES RIVER (Bend to Crane Prairie)

A rich, dark, powerful stream, 20-100 feet wide, characterized by deceptively smooth but powerful slicks broken by sharp rapids. The Deschutes is a big river from its release from Crane Prairie on, but its character here is distinctly different from the lower canyonland. Here its power is easily missed under the deceptively smooth surface, but at the base of Pringle Falls lie the shards of many a careless canoeist's pride. The river runs through fairly open ponderosa pinelands for much of this stretch, and the banks are often sand or tall grasses. The river is drawn down substantially in winter to fill Crane Prairie and Wickiup Reservoirs.

The Deschutes flows through the heart of the high desert community of Bend, which is at the edge of the forest, the largest metropolitan area within the river's drainage. For 15 miles beyond the city, the stream is easily fished from shore, and local anglers drive out the Mt. Bachelor road to try their luck on the evening rise.

To reach the river beyond the metropolitan area, take Hwy. 97 south from Bend. Secondary and forest roads access both sides of the stream at several locations. In the stretch between Lava Butte and the Lapine State Recreation Area the river flows through much private land, including Sunriver Resort.

Rainbow and brown trout predominate. The average fish is only 9 inches, but big browns are frequently taken. Anglers work the pockets and undercut banks of the meandering stream. Bait fishermen sometimes take the big browns on crayfish, while hardware angles favor Flatfish lures in size ranges F-3 to F-7, silver and gold Rapallas, and crayfish-finish Rebels.

Fly casting, however, is the preferred angling method throughout this stretch of the river. Hatches take place throughout the year. An excellent hatch of yellow mayflies occurs in June. Wet flies seem to work best during the days, dries best in the evenings. Favorite dry fly patterns include stone fly, dun, caddis, and mosquito imitations, with small patterns best in late summer. Most successful wet flies imitate the small trout relished by big browns. Whitefish are also plentiful and susceptible to all angling methods.

Angling from a floating device is permitted in this stretch. Bank and boat angling are both effective. The river is driftable starting about 1/4 mile below Wickiup Dam. There is some flow through private property, and permission should be obtained to bank fish there. There is a good 8 mile drift from below Wickiup to the Pringle Falls area. To reach Pringle Falls from Hwy. 97, turn west on County Rd. 43 just north of LaPine.

Pringle Falls is not boatable, and the current gets very strong quickly. Keep a sharp watch for warning signs on the river. One of the finest drifts on this section is the 17 miles from just below the log jam at Pringle Falls to Big River (a.k.a Colonel Patch) Bridge. Another nice drift is from Big River Bridge to the Spring River area. From there to Bend much of the river is boatable, but it's advisable to check locally for trouble spots. In addition to Pringle, boaters should avoid Benham, Dillon, and Lava Island Falls. Guides for boating the upper river are available. Contact the Oregon Guides and Packers Association, or check locally in Bend, LaPine or at the area resorts.

Campgrounds are plentiful along the river beginning at Meadow Camp just 4 miles south of Bend. Other National Forest campgrounds are Lava Island, Slough Camp, and Benham Falls near the Lava Butte Geological Area, Session Camp near Spring River, Big River Bridge, LaPine State Recreation Area, Pringle Falls, Wyeth, Bull Bend, and Wampus. The Deschutes runs through Sunriver, a popular Oregon resort, about 12 miles south of Bend. This resort offers just about every recreational activity one could desire, and up-scale vacation homes are usually available for short-term rental. There is an airstrip at the resort.

DESCHUTES RIVER (Crane Prairie to Headwaters)

The Deschutes begins its life in the high Cascades, draining Lava Lakes just below Three Sisters Wilderness, Deschutes National Forest. These lakes have no inlet streams, but are fed by springs whose source is snowmelt percolating into the porous lava underlying the region. From Lava Lakes the river flows south, first as a slow, clear slough, then as a

THE DESCHUTES ABOVE CRANE PRAIRIE
Steve Terrill, Photographer

sparkling meadow creek, flowing into Crane Prairie Reservoir in about 8 miles.

Whitefish predominate in the slough waters from Lava Lake downstream about 2 miles. The meadow stretch below that, however, is a wonderful stream. with firm, small resident rainbow and brook trout, as well as hatchery rainbow which are stocked every 2 weeks throughout the season. This is classic small stream water, and fishing is rarely disappointing. The river is generally less than 10 feet across and can be waded at almost any point. Fly angling is the best method here,with dries almost always effective. Watch your backcast. The small pines along the shore eat flies.

The Cascade Lakes Hwy. parallels much of the stream. About 2 miles below the Deschutes Bridge Guard Station the road curves west, away from the river. FS 40 crosses the river a mile or so below that point, and a mile above the outflow into Crane Prairie. Upstream from this bridge the river flows through a delightful setting of green meadow grass, waist-high lupine, and small pines, with Mt. Bachelor looking on.

There is a delayed opening on this stretch of the river to protect spawning rainbow trout. Forest Service campgrounds are available at Little Lava Lake, Deschutes Bridge, and Cow Meadow where the river joins Crane Prairie. Supplies are available at Lava Lake, Cultus Lake, and Crane Prairie Resorts.

DEVILS LAKE (Deschutes Co.) A nice trout lake on Century Drive about 30 miles SW of Bend. It stretches along the south side of the road about one mile west of Sparks Lake.

Devils Lake is about 40 acres and only 9 feet at its deepest point. Brook trout reproduce naturally here, and catchable rainbow are stocked annually. Fed primarily by a spring creek one mile west, the lake is remarkably clear, which can make fishing tough. It also indicates a lack of nutrients, so fish don't grow quickly, ranging 8-11 inches. Very light terminal tackle is needed. Fly angling is good in shoal areas when there's a bit of wind to rough up the water. There's an improved campground at the lake, and others just to the east. No motors are allowed on the lake, but rowboats can be launched.

DORIS LAKE (Deschutes Co.) A large hike-in lake in the Cascades west of Elk Lake, about 35 miles SW of Bend. Deep and cold, it provides only fair fishing for brook trout. Take Century Drive (Hwy. 46) from Bend about 2 miles past the turn-off to Elk Lake Resor,t to Six Lakes Trailhead 14 on the west side of the road. Follow Trail 14 about 3 miles west to Doris Lake, passing Blow Lake at about the half-way point.

Doris covers about 90 acres, and has a maximum depth over 70 ft. The lake is stocked annually with brook trout which average 9-14 inches. Best method varies with the season, with bait popular early, and fly angling best in late fall. There are no improved campsites at the lake.

EAGLE CREEK (Multnomah Co.) A very popular trout stream, with salmon and steelhead runs, located near Bonneville Dam about 43 miles east of Portland, entering the Columbia just above the dam. Eagle Creek flows 15 miles north from the slopes of Mt. Hood. It is not accessible by road except at the mouth and at the extreme headwaters. The upper stream is encircled by the forest road that runs from Larch Mountain to Wahtum Lake. A good trail follows the stream, and it is a popular hiking area.

A state salmon hatchery is located on the creek just above its mouth and provides an interesting spectacle during the fall run. Check current regulations for special closures related to salmon and steelhead angling. The stretch of

EAST LAKE

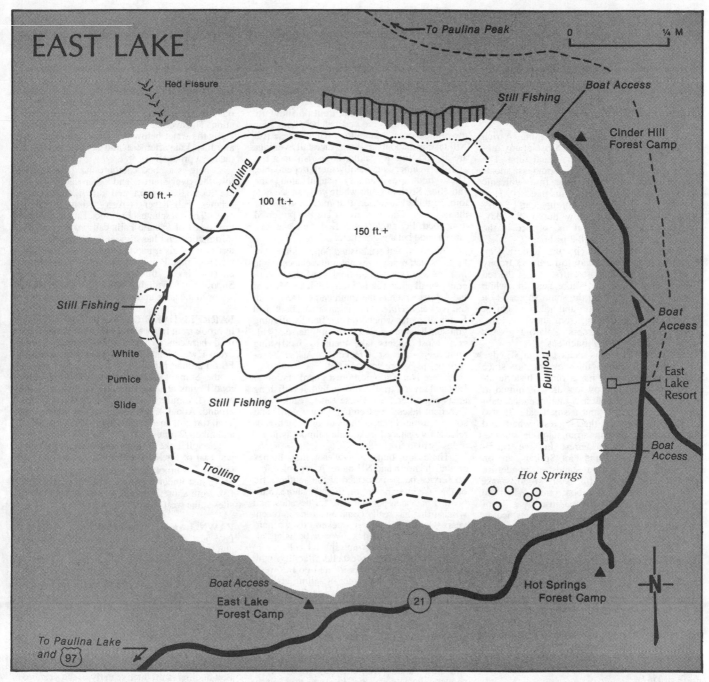

To Paulina Peak

0   ¼ M

Red Fissure

Still Fishing

Boat Access

Cinder Hill
Forest Camp

Trolling

50 ft.+

100 ft.+

150 ft.+

Still Fishing

Still Fishing

Boat
Access

Trolling

East
Lake
Resort

White

Pumice

Slide

Boat
Access

Trolling

Hot Springs

Boat Access
East Lake
Forest Camp

21

Hot Springs
Forest Camp

N

To Paulina Lake
and 97

lower creek from the railroad bridge to the mouth is within the Columbia River regulation zone.

A fair summer steelhead run shows up in the creek in July and is fished up to the special season closure. Fishing is only fair due to angler pressure. Check current regulations. The upper stream has good angling for native rainbow and cutthroat trout. A few eastern brook trout are also taken in the upper reaches. Both bait and fly angling will take fish, although fly fishing is difficult. There is a large campground near the mouth.

EAST LAKE Here is a truly unique fishery—a prime trout lake in the maw of a dormant volcano in central Oregon, about 25 air miles SE of Bend. East Lake is one of two lakes within Newberry Crater in the Paulina Mountains of Deschutes National Forest. The other lake, sep-

arated from East by a high ridge, is Paulina. Both lakes offer very good fishing, but the trout in East Lake reach trophy size and are more easily taken on a fly. Rainbow trout predominate here, and there are a lot of good size brook trout as well.

From Bend, drive south 20 miles on Hwy. 97 to the Newberry Crater turnoff. Turn east on FS 21, and wind upward about 14 miles to Paulina Lake, then continue east another 3 miles to East Lake.

East is one of the most consistent large lakes in Oregon. It was totally unaffected by the 1987-88 drought. In fact, fishing here in 1988 was exceptionally good. It offers slightly over 1000 acres, with broad shoal areas and a maximum depth of 175 feet. This is high country, over 6,300 ft. in elevation, and it isn't unusual to find snow on the ground in June. It gets cold up here at night.

The catch has been averaging 80 percent rainbow, with size range 10-14 inches, though some get larger—as much as ten pounds larger! Brook trout show up in the catch primarily in early or late season, and in recent years 4 pounders have not been uncommon. As for the browns, expert Jim Teeny developed his famous nymph while stalking monster browns in the shallows here. Browns over 20 pounds have been grudgingly dragged from the lake.

With this variety of fish and water conditions, almost any technique will have its day and place. In terms of popularity, trolling and still-fishing are probably tops, though fly anglers do well here, too—very well.

Still-fishing takes a lot of rainbow and brook trout. In early season when the fish are close to the surface, a bobber rig is effective. The north side and near the east campground are consistently the first areas to produce. Later it pays to go deeper, and the north and south edges of the lake are popular spots. Bait anglers do best in early season.

Trollers generally work slowly around the shoreline of the lake, going deeper in the warm weather months. Flatfish and flasher-bait rigs are always in evidence here. Dark colored wooly-worms or Teeny nymphs can be effective on a troll. S-l-o-w-l-y is the key here. Incidentally, there is a 10 mph speed limit in effect on the lake.

This is a great lake for flyfishing. A rich insect population can turn on a rise at any moment, though evening is the usual time. The shorelines produce well. The southeast shoals get an influx of warm water from volcanic springs that might serve as a magnet to browns in early season. The east shoreline can be very good at evening, but slow during the day. Watch for feeding fish at the surface in the shoal areas along the southern shore.

Stalking big fish which cruise at dusk is an exciting and effective way to tie into a trophy trout. Try the north shore cliffs, east of the red fissure, along the west shore near the white pumice slide, and along the south shore. Try a Teeny nymph in sizes 4-6 and hold on tight. A partner on shore spotting from above will improve the odds of success. Polaroid glasses will make fish spotting much easier.

East Lake Resort is located at the SE edge of the lake. In roughly the same location since the 1920's, the resort has a rustic, historic atmosphere which the owners are committed to retaining. It offers boat and motor rentals, cabins, tackle, supplies, and a small cafe. It also provides a free map that suggests where and how to fish, and can arrange guide service. Two very attractive Forest Service campgrounds, East Lake and Hot Springs, are on the south shore within stands of ponderosa pine. A third, Cinder Hill, is on the NE shore. Each campground has a boat ramp. When the lake opens in spring, there is usually a lot of snow around the camps and, sometimes, ice on the lake, but ice-out fishing can be terrific. Bring plenty of cold weather gear.

Check the regulations for special bag limit, designed to encourage better carry-over, and bigger catches.

EIGHTMILE CREEK Much longer than its name, this stream flows east for about 30 miles from the east edge of Mt. Hood National Forest, crosses Hwy. 197, and joins Fifteen Mile Creek to enter the Columbia near The Dalles. Followed for most of its length by gravel and dirt roads, it is crossed by Hwy. 197 about 12 miles SE of The Dalles, 6 miles north of Dufur.

Used quite a bit for irrigation, it doesn't provide much angling, but there is some fair fishing early in the season for native rainbow trout. While roads follow the stream closely, there is a lot of private land. The best bet is along the upper stream in early season, with worms, eggs or grasshoppers for bait. There are no camping areas along the lower stream, but several in the upper headwaters in the forest, about 17 miles west of Dufur on FS 44.

ELK LAKE (Deschutes Co.) A scenic large lake in the Cascades west of Bend, in the heart of a popular recreational area. Brook trout and kokanee will occupy the fisherman, but sailing, wind surfing and swimming are a big part of the action here. The lake is just east of Century Drive (Hwy. 46), about 32 miles SW of Bend. It can also be reached from the south by forest roads branching off from Hwy. 97 to the east, and by Hwy. 58 from the south.

Elk Lake is in a picturesque setting, with the Three Sisters towering over the north end of the lake and Mt. Bachelor dominating the eastern horizon. It is about 1 1/2 miles long from north to south, and 1/2 mile wide, covering 250 acres. Most of it is fairly deep, with maximum depth 65 ft.

Fishing here is not the major activity, but it can certainly be good. Brook trout generally range 7-14 inches, but large trout do show up. Early season offers the best catches, with June the prime month. After a long winter, these fish will take just about anything. Late fall evenings are a good time for taking large fish on a fly, and the weather is generally more dependable. These trout are primarily caught along the shoreline. Stick to water where you can see bottom. In this clear water, that means no deeper than 20 feet. Caddis nymphs are the preferred trout food. Fly anglers will find dark wet patterns a good bet anytime here.

Elk has a well established population of kokanee which reproduces naturally. Success rate in 1988 was very high, though the fish are generally small since Elk is not a rich lake. Most of the fish are taken at the south end of the lake at the *Kokanee Hole.* This is an area about 100 feet in diameter which you can find by aligning yourself between a rockslide and the road culvert. Most anglers take them by baitfishing quite deep—at least 50 feet down. Ask at the resort for tips before you start out.

There is a National Forest guard station at Elk, and several trails to prime high lake fishing areas begin here. See Horse Lake, Mink Lake. Excellent lakes line Century Drive, north and south. Hosmer Lake, with its unique catch-and-release fly fishery for Atlantic salmon, is just 3 miles by road from Elk Lake.

There are quite a few summer homes around the north and NE shore. A very nice forest service beach is located at the southern tip of the lake and another on the NW shore. Sailboating has been popular here for decades, and windsurfing has really come on strong in recent years. On a fine summer weekend over a hundred sails will dot the lake. Power boats are allowed, but there is a 10 mph speed limit.

Elk lake Resort, an excellent facility, with cabins and trailer sites, is located on the western shore. This is the center of sailing activity. The resort offers boat rentals, gas, tackle and supplies, and has a snack bar. There is a boat launch at the resort and at two additional forest service campgrounds, Little Fawn and Point, along the south shore of the lake.

Elk Lake opens in late April with regular size and bag limits. In most years, the roads are still snow-blocked until late May. If you have a snowmobile you can get in some good early fishing.

FALL RIVER A nice flyfishing only stream in the Deschutes National Forest SW of Bend. Clear and cold, it springs full-blown from the ground about 2 miles NW of Pringle Falls on the Deschutes River, and winds its way NE 8 miles to join the Deschutes about 6 miles below the falls.

The upper waters are paralleled by FS 42, which follows the north bank of the river from Fall River Hatchery to the river springs at the Fall River Guard Station. FS 42 can be reached from Hwy. 97 by taking the Sunriver turn-off, or you may come in from the south from Pringle Falls by FS 4352. The lower river is an easy hike from Fall River Hatchery, which is at about the mid-point of the river, or from FS 4360, which turns south off FS 42 and crosses the river one mile above the confluence with the Deschutes. In the lower 4 miles the river flows through a lot of private property.

Fall River is not large, averaging 50-75 feet across, but it provides some interesting flyfishing. Spring-fed, it is crystal clear and requires very light tackle techniques. Native rainbow, eastern brook trout, and brown trout are present, and the state stocks aggressively with weekly releases of catchable rainbow throughout the season. Angling holds steady throughout the entire season, as there is no water fluctuation. The average catch runs 7-12 inches. Best bet is the water below the hatchery in late June and July. Late afternoon and evening angling is the most productive.

There is a good campground 1/2 mile below the river source, and other campgrounds are located upstream and down on the Deschutes. Fall River is restricted to flyfishing only. The Deschutes Fly and Tackle Shop 5 miles east of Pringle Falls can provide current information and has a great stock of local patterns for the river and the high lakes. Their Davis and Crane Prairie Specials have been proven on lakes throughout central Oregon. Supplies are available there, at other general stores in the area, and in Bend.

FARRELL LAKE One of a pair of good hike-in brook trout lakes about one mile north of the road between Crescent and Summit Lakes. From Hwy. 58 at Crescent Lake Junction take FS 60 around the NW shore of Crescent Lake to the Summit Lake turn-off, FS 6010. This road begins at the west end of Crescent Lake about 1/4 mile south of Tandy Bay Campground. About 4 miles west, at the Meek Lake Trail turnout, head north (opposite Meek Lake) and hike 1/2 mile on Trail 43 to Farrell.

Farrell Lake is long and narrow, and lies just east of Snell Lake. Four acres and mostly shallow, its brook trout run 8-14 inches and average just under a pound. The lake is easy to fish from shore. There are good natural campsites at the west end of the lake.

FAWN LAKE A good hike-in brook trout lake just east of Diamond Peak Wilderness, about midway between Odell and Crescent Lakes. From the highway junction at Eugene, it's about 70 miles to the Odell-Crescent area. Trails lead to Fawn Lake from the east end of Odell Lake and from Crescent Lake Resort, which is 2 miles south of Hwy. 58. It's about a 3 mile hike from Odell by Trail 44, a little shorter from Crescent Lake.

At elevation 5680 ft., the lake covers 43 acres, with a maximum depth of 27 feet. Brook trout average 12 inches and run to 16 inches. Bait angling is productive early in the year, and flies do best in summer and fall. There are natural campsites. The lake is usually accessible in late June, depending on snow pack.

FROG LAKE A small trout lake, heavily fished, just off Hwy. 26, 9 miles SE of Government Camp. The turn-off is well signed. The lake is east of the highway, with a road directly to it, though a short hike is required in spring before the snowdrifts clear. Fishing is for hatchery rainbow plants. All methods are used. Boats can be launched to fish this shallow 11 acre pond, but motors are prohibited.

GIBSON LAKE (Warm Springs Indian Reservation) A 6 acre brook trout lake 1/4 mile north of Breitenbush Lake by a trail that starts across from the Breitenbush Lake entry road. Maximum depth here is 14 feet. The lake is stocked annually with brook trout. Although on the Reservation, no tribal permit is currently required, and overnight camping is permitted.

GOVERNMENT COVE One of the I-84 ponds adjacent to the Columbia River. Government Cove is 90 acres, located at hwy. mile 47, two miles east of Cascade Locks, with access from I-84 at the Herman Creek Exit. As with all the ponds in this series, Government Cove may contain any of the species found in the Columbia, including largemouth and smallmouth bass, crappie, yellow perch, pumpkinseed sunfish, bullhead catfish, and even channel catfish.

GREEN LAKES (Deschutes Co.) A series of three lovely glacial lakes in the Three Sisters Wilderness west of Bend. The lakes are nestled between South Sister and Broken Top Mountains, with South Sister dominating the skyline. They are most commonly reached by a 5 mile hike on a well marked trail north from North Century Drive (Hwy. 46). The trail begins at a turn-out across from Sparks Lake about 28 miles west of Bend. This trail has an elevation gain of 1000 ft.

An easier, but less well known approach is possible from Crater Ditch Creek north of Todd Lake. It's still a 5 mile hike by well marked, scenic trail, but there is almost no elevation gain. Take the Todd Lake turn off Century Drive, but continue past Todd Lake on FS 370 (a fair dirt road) about 3 miles to FS 380, which branches north toward Broken Top and ends in 1 1/2 miles at the head of Trail 10. There's an impressive view of the blown away south face of Broken Top from the trailhead. Follow Trail 10 an easy 5 miles to Green Lakes.

Middle Green is the largest, covering 85 acres, and it has the best angling. Both wild brook trout and rainbow are available, and run to good size. The rainbow range 10-14 inches, the brook trout a shade smaller. North Green is the next largest, about 10 acres, just north of the main lake. South Green is the smallest at 8 acres, and is the first one you see from the trail. South is stocked with rainbow.

The setting here is breathtakingly scenic, a high rocky saddle which is mostly unforested. Fly anglers will have no trouble with their backcast here. At elevation 6500 ft., the snow rarely clears before mid-July. By late August this area really draws sun worshippers. Don't be startled by backpackers wearing boots and pack—period. A fine setting for nude fly angling if you stick to small flies and avoid strong winds. Pack sun screen, for at this altitude you'll roast in no time. Good natural campsites are available.

HAND LAKE A 4 acre trout lake in the Cache Lake Basin, Deschutes National Forest. See Island Lake, Link Lake for directions. From Hwy. 20 north of Sisters, take FS 2068 west, then turn right on FS 600 to Hand Lake. The lake is 16 ft. deep and is stocked by ground and air with cutthroat and brook trout.

HANKS LAKES (Deschutes Co.) A series of 3 good trout lakes one mile east of Irish and Taylor Lakes, a short hike from the road. The trailhead is on FS 600 about 1 1/2 miles east of the Pacific Crest Trail crossing at Irish Lake. FS 600 can be reached from the west from Waldo Lake, or from the east from Little Cultus Lake. Trail 15 leads north from the road about 1/3 mile to the west shore of Middle Hanks Lake. West Hanks is just to the west, and East Hanks is slightly SE of Middle. The current Deschutes National Forest map shows the lakes and the trail, but fails to give their names. Mid-

dle Hanks is the first lake the trail encounters. The lakes are usually accessible by the end of June.

East Hanks is about 8 acres, and middle and west lakes are about 6 acres each. All the lakes contain rainbow trout. West and East also contain brook and cutthroat trout. Angling is comparable in all three lakes, with the west lake probably the best. All are good on bait or lures most of the time, and fly angling can be excellent. Fish here range 10-14 inches, with some larger.

In the area to the north are many lakes and potholes, some of which have been stocked, and there's good angling in several of them. There are campgrounds at Irish and Taylor Lakes. Mosquito repellent and head nets are useful in late spring when the fish may or may not be biting, but hordes of skeeters can be depended upon.

HARVEY LAKE (Warm Springs Indian Reservation) A scenic, lightly fished hike-in brook and cutthroat trout lake occupying a narrow flat step between two very steep slopes, about 4 miles south of Olallie Lake. A former road from Warm Springs to the trailhead has been closed. The lake is now only accessible by trail from Breitenbush Campground. The trail begins at the south end of the camp near the inlet. It is a 3 mile hike to Harvey Lake.

Harvey is at elevation 5400 ft. and covers 27 acres. It is located in a cirque at the base of a 300 ft. talus slope, very similar to Dark Lake to the north, and rivals Blue Lake for beauty. The inlet stream tumbles down from Lake Hilda, 300 feet above. The outlet flow shoots over a 200 foot sheer cliff into Shitke Creek. It has a maximum depth of 40 feet with limited shoal area. The lake has some eastern brook trout along with residual cutthroat trout from earlier stocking. A tribal permit is required to fish this lake. No overnight camping is allowed due to fire danger.

HAYSTACK RESERVOIR A fair size reservoir 9 miles south of Madras in Crooked River

National Grassland, not especially attractive, but with plentiful bank angling opportunity and an unusually wide choice of fisheries for this area. It is used as a storage reservoir, and though there can be considerable daily fluctuation in water level, it is not drained. It grows good size fish and supports fair angling for kokanee, largemouth bass, black crappie, brown bullhead, and a few stocked legal rainbow. From Madras drive 8 miles south on Hwy. 97, turning east onto a county road about one mile south of the Culver turn-off. From there it's about 2 miles to Haystack.

Kokanee 10-18 inches attract the most angling attention, with best catches in spring and fall. Anglers have success both trolling and bank fishing. Legal rainbow are lightly stocked, with best fishing in spring and fall near the south shore. Crappie are small but plentiful, especially near the inlets. There is a boat ramp at the west end of the reservoir and no speed limit. Consequently the summer fishery is, for the most part, sacrificed to waterskiers. A primitive forest service campground is located on the east shore of the reservoir. The reservoir is open year around, but is sometimes frozen over for short periods in winter (though not thick enough for ice fishing).

HERMAN CREEK A trout stream with small steelhead and chinook runs, entering the Columbia River about 2 miles east of Cascade Locks. It heads about 12 miles upstream in several small lakes in the Wahtum Lake area and is crossed by I-84 just above the mouth. The lower stretch of the creek from the railroad to the Columbia is under Columbia Zone angling regulations.

You must hike in if you want to fish this stream. A good trail begins at the Columbia Work Center, joining the Herman Creek Trail, one mile up the hill. The Herman Creek Trail parallels the mainstem of the creek to the forks, then follows the east fork to the headwaters. Small native cutthroat can be taken all along this stretch. It has some big holes where nice size trout are taken.

FALL RIVER FALLS
Bill McMillan, Photographer

Herman Creek has a fall chinook run, and there is a hatchery is near the mouth, just off I-84. The run usually makes the creek in late August, and fish are caught through November. Check current regulations for special closures related to the hatchery.

There is a small summer steelhead run in the stream from June through October.

HICKS LAKE A small brook trout lake in Mt. Hood National Forest north of Wahtum Lake, about 25 miles SW of Hood River. Hicks Lake is 1/2 mile NW of Wahtum at the head of Herman Creek. Only about 2 acres and shallow, it has frequently winterkilled, and stocking has been discontinued.

HIDDEN LAKE (Deschutes Co.) A 13 acre lake, sometimes confused with Found Lake, way off the beaten path in the Deschutes Forest east of Waldo Lake. The lake has a small population of little brook trout. It is on the western slope of Gerdine Butte, about 1 1/2 miles south of Charlton Lake.

HOOD RIVER A large stream with a very good steelhead run, flowing into the Columbia River at the town of Hood River in the Columbia Gorge, about 50 miles east of Portland. The river's source is the glaciers on the north and east slopes of Mt. Hood. The main forks of the river join near the community of Dee, about 14 miles upstream from the Columbia. The lower river provides most of the steelhead angling, and there is opportunity to take fish any month of the year.

Hood River supports both winter and summer steelhead runs. The total annual catch varies between 1000 and 4000 fish. The 1986 summer steelhead catch in the mainstem was 2115, with 362 picked up in the west fork and 159 in the east fork. The winter steelhead catch was 570 in the mainstem, with only a few caught in either east or west fork. Most steelhead angling takes place on the lower 3 miles of the river, but good numbers of fish are taken upstream as far as the punchbowl. Bank angling produces quite a few fish.

There is some boat angling at the lower end near the mouth, mostly in the short stretch between I-84 and the Columbia. The boat ramp is at a park on the river's east bank. Above, the river is too rough for boating. The upper waters are fairly clear, requiring light leaders and stealth. The stream offers excellent possibilities for fly anglers. A special fly-only area in the upper West Fork would be a good place to start. See Hood River, West Fork.

Trout angling is fair in the lower river for both native and stocked fish. There are no camping areas on the lower river.

HOOD RIVER, EAST FORK A stocked rainbow trout stream, heading on the SE slopes of Mt. Hood and flowing over 20 miles to join the main river about 2 miles north of Dee. It also has a small run of summer steelhead, and some winter steelhead. The fork is closely followed by Hwy. 35, which is clear of snow in late spring. Prior to that, access is from Hwy. 30 at Hood River. Hwy. 281 follows the stream south from Dee, where it joins Hwy. 35 at Parkdale.

Legal rainbow trout are stocked annually from Parkdale upstream throughout the spring and summer. Fishing is usually good through the summer months. About 150 summer steelhead were caught here in 1986, and fewer than 20 winter steelhead.

There are three campgrounds along the river in Mt. Hood National Forest—Polallie, Sherwood, and Robinhood.

HOOD RIVER, LAKE BRANCH A tributary of the West Fork of the Hood River, beginning as the outlet creek for Lost Lake on the NE slope of Mt. Hood. It is now used as a steelhead spawning sanctuary and is not open to angling except in the headwaters. The branch is followed closely by FS 13 all the way to Lost Lake.

The open area is found above the Sawtooth Spur Rd. (FS 700/1300). Angling above this point is for wild trout, and a fair number of native cutthroat and rainbow are taken with some hard work. Bait works best, but flies will produce later in the season. The *color* (turbidity) of the water usually determines methods. There is a large campground and resort at Lost Lake.

HOOD RIVER, WEST FORK The West Fork of Hood River joins the mainstem about 1 1/2 miles north of Dee. The stream heads near the east boundary of the Bull Run Reserve and flows NE for about 5 miles to the confluence. It offers fair angling for wild trout in the upper waters, and steelhead fishing below the Punchbowl. About 350 summer steelhead were caught here in 1986. The West Fork is a designated steelhead sanctuary, and is no longer stocked with hatchery trout. There are campgrounds at Lost Lake and about 5 miles west of the crest of Lolo Pass.

HOOD RIVER POND #1 One of the I-84 ponds adjacent to the Columbia River. Located at hwy. mile 66.3, this 4 acre pond is accessible to eastbound vehicles only, with parking in a limited unimproved area It may contain any of the Columbia River species, including largemouth and smallmouth bass, crappie, yellow perch, pumpkinseed sunfish, bullhead catfish, and channel catfish.

HOOD RIVER POND #2 One of the I-84 ponds adjacent to the Columbia River, located at hwy. mile 67. It covers 3 acres south of I-84, with limited unimproved parking for eastbound traffic only. It may contain any of the Columbia's warmwater species.

HOOD RIVER POND #3 A 3 acre pond south of I-84 adjacent to the Columbia River at hwy. mile 67. There is limited unimproved parking for eastbound traffic only. It may contain any of the Columbia River species, including largemouth and smallmouth bass, crappie, yellow perch, pumpkinseed sunfish, bullhead catfish, and channel catfish.

HORSESHOE LAKE (Olallie Lake area) A pretty, 14 acre brook and rainbow trout lake between Olallie and Breitenbush lakes on FS 4220. You can drive right to this scenic beauty, and there is a campground here. A spit of land juts into the lake from the west shore, giving the lake its characteristic shape. It's easy to fish from shore.

HOSMER LAKE One of the richest lakes in the Deschutes National Forest, one mile SE of Elk Lake on Century Drive, 34 road miles SW of Bend. It offers fishing for very large brook trout, and a catch and release fishery for landlocked Atlantic salmon. Angling is restricted to fly fishing only, with barbless flies.

The lake is composed of two large main pools connected by a long channel through which Hosmer 's big fish glide. The pools are thick with submerged weed, and water lillies hover at the surface. The channel is lined with bullrushes, but weed free. Even when the bite is off, there is some satisfaction in boating the channel, where big fish are clearly visible at all times. A mid-day tour on the channel is like cruising an aquarium.

Hosmer's dumbbell shape offers many views to the boater. Red Crater (a forested cinder cone) looms over the main pool, Bachelor Butte provides a handsome backdrop to many of the campsites. The Three Sisters guard the-back pool. In one cove the waters slip into a lava field and disappears. Wildlife abounds, and osprey will put your best fishing efforts to shame. The early riser may slip through the fog and surprise otter, mink, or deer along the shore, while countless marsh birds grumble in the rushes.

To reach Hosmer Lake drive south from Bend on Century Drive. The turn-off to Hosmer is about 3 miles past the entrance to Elk Lake Resort and is well marked. The road reaches the lake in about one mile. Century Drive (Hwy. 46) can also be reached from the Willamette Valley by driving SE from Eugene on Hwy. 58 to the Davis Lake turnoff 3 miles past Crescent Lake Junction. Following the signs to Davis Lake will put you on Hwy. 46 heading north. Hosmer is 10 miles north of the Crane Prairie junction.

Hosmer is a large shallow lake, the channel connecting its two main pools extending north to south. The southern pool is the deeper of the two, yet its maximum depth is only 10 ft. It has two campgrounds on its western shore. The richly organic water limits visibility to about 6 ft. depth. Fish are found throughout this portion of the lake. Try the bullrushes along the western shore.

A winding channel almost a mile long leads to the northern pool. By anchoring, standing, and using polaroid glasses you can watch the movement of these fish and cast accordingly. A short channel branches off towards the northeast, ending at a floodgate which regulates the flow of water into a natural lava sink.

The northern (back) lake covers more area but is generally shallower. Here, a cold, clear, spring fed stream, Quinn Creek, joins Hosmer from the north. Many heather covered islands dot this portion of the lake. Fishing activity is concentrated along its southern and eastern shores.

The rich waters of Hosmer have long grown the largest brook trout in Oregon. For some time it has also been home to a good population of planted Atlantic salmon which average around 15 inches and go to over 20. Brook trout are periodically stocked here to maintain the fishery, and they reach very impressive size. These old hawgs (which can live to be 10-20 years old) are hard to fool.

The salmon are a catch-and-release fishery, and most anglers treat the occasional trout hooked here similarly, though you can legally keep them. Tackle is restricted to barbless flies only. Standard flies with pinched barbs are sufficient. The salmon are eager risers but present their own unique problems. These fish are enthusiastic. In fishing to a rise you have to decide whether to cast to the circle that marks where the fish left the water, or the circle that marks where it landed. Standard trout tactics are effective.

The lake has good insect hatches in the spring. and leaches and water boatmen are a staple in the salmon's diet throughout the season. Stalking fish in the channels is a favorite method, but slow trolling in the lower pool and the channels will work if nothing else seems effective. Late June through mid-July seems to be the best time. Fall can be good.

There are two excellent forest campgrounds are located on the southern pool, and there is a boat ramp at the southern tip. This is a great lake for canoes, and Mallard Marsh Campground at the north end of the lake has a little canoe slip through the bull rushes. There is a 10 mph speed limit on the lake.

HUSTON LAKES Two bass and panfish lakes in the Powell Butte area about half-way between Redmond and Prineville in central Oregon. The lakes are on private land, and neither is currently open for public access.

INDIAN CREEK (Hood River Co.) A small stream which flows right through the town of Hood River. Used for agricultural drainage, it no longer supports life.

INDIAN FORD CREEK (Deschutes Co.) A small creek flowing about 11 miles through mostly private land into Squaw Creek just north of Sisters. The upper stretch is crossed by Hwy. 20 about 5 miles NW of Sisters. The stream flows to the east then south to Sisters. Its north bank is followed fairly closely by a forest road. The creek supports a few small native trout, averaging 6-10 inches. There is a nice campground on the upper end at the Hwy. 20 crossing 5 miles west of Sisters.

IRIS LAKE One of the I-84 ponds adjacent to the Columbia River, located at hwy. mile 56.2. It covers 5 acres at the east end of Viento State park. Take Exit 56. It may contain any of the Columbia's warmwater species.

ISLAND LAKE (Jefferson Co.) An 8 acre lake just south of Suttle Lake in Deschutes National Forest west of Link Lake. See Link Lake for directions. Eighteen feet deep, Island contains cutthroat and brook trout.

ISLAND LAKE (Warm Springs Indian Reservation) Island Lake is the fourth downstream lake in the five lake Olallie-to-Trout Lake chain. The oval lake's name is derived from a one acre island located in the middle of it. It is accessible only by unimproved trail from either Olallie Lake east or Trout Lake west. From Trout Lake, it's about one mile to Island Lake. The first 1/4 mile of trail is a fairly steep uphill grind, but the remaining distance is more easily traveled. The trail from Olallie Lake begins at the SE end of the lake, and is most easily reached from Olallie Peninsula Campground.

Island covers about 26 acres at elevation 4650 ft. It is the shallowest lake of the chain, with a maximum depth of only 10 feet. Most of the lake is 3 feet deep or less. Eastern brook trout are stocked here. The lake is difficult to fish without a boat or raft. A tribal fishing permit is required. No overnight camping is allowed due to fire danger.

IRISH LAKE A scenic trout lake near the summit of the Cascades that you can drive to if you're careful and have a high center vehicle. The access road is not quite a jeep trail, but not a lot better. Irish Lake is about mid-way between Waldo and Cultus Lakes, SW of Bend in Deschutes National Forest. The Pacific Crest Trail follows the western shore of the lake.

Irish can be approached from either the east or the west. Access from the east is usually available first. From Bend follow Century

HOSMER LAKE WITH MT. BACHELOR
Dan Casali, Photographer

Drive (Hwy. 46) SW past Lava Lake to the Cultus Lake turn-off. Take FS 4630 about 2 1/2 miles to FS 600, passing the Cultus Resort turn-off and following signs for Little Cultus Lake. Irish Lake is 6 fairly rough miles to the west from this point. Drive slowly. From the east, FS 20031 leads north from North Waldo Lake Campground towards Taylor Burn. It intersects FS 600 one mile west of Irish Lake. This last mile is even worse than the stretch from little Cultus. Irish Lake is at 5500 ft., and the snow lingers until late June most years. This usually blocks the western access.

Irish has 28 acres of clear water and is mostly shallow. The lake is a consistent producer of large eastern brook trout, and is currently being stocked with cutthroat trout, because they are known to take the hook more readily. At this time, however, brook trout predominate at Irish. Trout here are typically 8-12 inches, but quite a few run to 16 inches or better. Bait angling or lures will work most of the time, but fly angling in the early morning and evening hours will give best results. Brook trout feed in the shoal areas after the sun goes down, and some evenings any fly will entice them. Fishing

is best as soon after ice-out as you can get in.

Taylor Lake, just 100 yards south of Irish, is bigger but less productive. Other smaller fishable lakes can be reached by hiking the PCT north, or by taking Trail 15 (Deer Lake) north from FS 600 1 1/2 miles east of the PCT crossing. This area is riddled with lakes and tarns, and hordes of mosquitoes breed in them, especially in early season. Bring repellent and consider head nets.

There is a rustic improved camping area at the lake (no drinking water). Motors are prohibited on the lake, and there is no boat ramp.

JACK LAKE A small, easily reached but, unfortunately, probably fishless lake in the Deschutes National Forest west of the Metolius recreational area. Jack is 5 air miles NW of Hwy. 20 at Suttle Lake, about 14 miles west of Sisters. Only about 7 acres and quite shallow, it is no longer stocked due to frequent winterkills. There is a good campground at the lake.

JEAN LAKE A 6 acre rainbow trout lake 1/2 mile NW of Badger Lake on the SE slope of Mt. Hood. To reach Jean Lake, drive east from

Government Camp on Hwy. 26, and take Hwy. 35 toward Hood River. Six miles from the intersection at Bennett Pass, take FS 3550 SE about 3 miles to the Camp Windy Rd. 3530, which leads NE. Take this a little over one mile past Camp Windy to the trail, which descends about 240 feet in 1/2 mile to the lake. These roads are high and rough. Don't expect to get in before late June.

Jean Lake is about 1/2 mile NW and 800 feet above Badger lake. It isn't heavily fished (after you drive the road you'll understand why) and provides very good angling for a small lake. Formerly stocked with eastern brook trout, it now contains predominantly rainbow trout. Anglers usually find a good population of 8-9 inch fish, with some to 13 inches. Any method seems to produce fish. There are no campsites at the lake, but there are facilities at Camp Windy.

JEFFERSON CREEK A small, pretty stream that heads on the SE slopes of Mt. Jefferson and flows into the Metolius River at Candle Creek Campground north of Sisters. Jefferson serves as a rearing stream for Metolius bull trout (Dolly Varden). Drive north from Hwy. 20 just west of Black Butte on the Camp Sherman road, FS 14, continuing north about 8 miles past Camp Sherman to Candle Creek Campground. Jefferson Creek joins the Metolius about 1/4 mile downstream from the confluence of Candle Creek and the Metolius. It follows the northern edge of a lava flow and forms the southern boundary of Warm Springs Indian Reservation.

The lower few miles of the stream can be reached from the road, and the rest requires hiking. This is a cold stream, and the fish run small. There's a good campground at Candle Creek and several others along the Metolius to the south.

JOHNNY LAKE A brook trout lake in the center of a triangle formed by Waldo Lake, Davis Lake, and Crane Prairie. From the intersection of Century Drive and Hwy. 42, take FS 5897 heading west towards Waldo Lake. Follow this road west about 3 miles, then take FS 200 south for one mile. A trail leading south 1/2 mile to the lake begins where FS 200 cuts sharply back to the east. Johnny covers about 20 acres and is fairly deep. There is a good campsite at the lake, but no improvements.

KERSHAW LAKE A 4 acre, lightly fished lake in the Irish Lake area, a good producer for those who find it. It is within a group of small lakes between Little Cultus Lake and Irish. Starting from the trail along the west shore of

Middle Hanks Lake, hike north on the trail about 1/2 mile. See hanks lakes for road directions. The lake is east of the trail, and you will cross a depression with a small creek connecting a chain of ponds just before reaching it. Bring the Irish Mt. topo map with you. Total hike from the road is just under one mile.

The lake is 4 acres and 13 feet deep. It has a drop-off ledge along the east side. Try casting just over this ledge to bring up the biggest fish. Brook trout average 8-10 inches here. Mosquitoes are terrible in spring.

KINGSLEY RESERVOIR (a.k.a. Green Point Reservoir) One of the largest lakes in the Hood River area, this 60 acre impoundment offers fishing for stocked rainbow trout. It is about 11 miles by road SW of Hood River. Two roads lead west to the reservoir over 6 rough miles. The rainbow run 6-13 inches, averaging 10 inches, and there is usually a good supply of catchables. Bait angling or trolling are the most popular methods.

There is a good campground with sanitary facilities here, but the camp is closed to use by trailers.

KOLBERG LAKE One of the I-84 ponds adjacent to the Columbia River. Kolberg is at hwy. mile 65.8, covering 5 acres directly across I-84 from the Kolberg Beach State Rest Area. Anglers should park at the rest area and walk across the highway. Kolberg may contain any of the Columbia River species, including largemouth and smallmouth bass, crappie, yellow perch, pumpkinseed sunfish, bullhead catfish, and channel catfish.

LAKE CREEK (Jefferson Co.) A short creek flowing out of Suttle Lake and into the Metolius River just south of Camp Sherman. The stream is crossed near the lake several times and again near the mouth, but no roads follow it. There is some private land along the lower creek.

The creek behaves most peculiarly about a mile below Suttle Lake, dividing into three braids which parallel each other about a half mile apart. These are known as the North, Middle, and South Forks, with the middle carrying the most water. They rejoin about a mile up from the mouth. The South Fork flows through a private resort, Lake Creek Resort, located near the lower end. Another private resort, The Pines, includes 27 acres on the lower North Fork. This portion is stocked with rainbow by the owners of the resort and is open only to resort guests. Some of these rainbow run to 16 inches. The main creek has wild rainbow and browns, which slip in from Suttle Lake. Lake Creek is usually worth a try on bait or fly. There are forest camps at Suttle Lake and along the Metolius River. Supplies are available at Camp Sherman.

LAURANCE LAKE A small irrigation reservoir on the Clear CreekBranch of the Middle Fork of Hood River. Motor boats are prohibited on the lake, which covers about 104 acres 19 miles south of the city of Hood River. From Parkdale School drive about 3 miles south to FS 2810, Clear Creek Rd. This road swings west and reaches the reservoir in another 3 miles.

Laurance is stocked with catchable rainbow and contains a population of wild cutthroat. Anglers also pick up an occasional bull trout (Dolly Varden). The dam appears to cut off what might once have been good steelhead and salmon spawning water. There is no fishway.

There is a very small campground on the lake with a paved boat ramp, and several unimproved campsites on the creek above the pool.

LAVA LAKE, BIG An excellent trout lake in the Deschutes National Forest, 38 miles south of Bend on the Cascades Lakes Highway. The lake is about 20 miles beyond Mt. Bachelor. For early season access it is usually necessary to approach from the east. Drive south from Bend on Hwy. 97 to the Sunriver turn-off, Hwy. 42, which can be followed east to its eventual junction with the Lakes Highway, about 13 miles south of Lava Lake.

Big Lava is a scenic lake with much of the character of Hosmer Lake to the north. Mt. Bachelor dominates the horizon. A wealth of wildlife adds to the enjoyment of its mountain setting. Although the lake is spring fed, the water is rich with organic material. This forms a food base that grows big fish quickly. Lava is about 1/2 mile square and 30 feet at its deepest point. Bullrushes line much of the shoreline, and a good deal of shoal water can be effectively flyfished.

In 1980 the Dept. of Fish and Wildlife poisoned the lake to remove rough fish and restocked with brook and rainbow trout. At this time, rainbow are the predominant catch, ranging 12-24 inches, averaging 12-15 with many 16-17 inchers taken. Brook trout currently run smaller, averaging 12 inches, but some 19 inchers are taken. Big Lava has grown trophy brook trout in past years, and there's good reason to suspect the current population will eventually include a good number of challenging old lunkers. (Brook trout can live and grow 20 years). Best fishing for brook trout is just after ice-out and again in fall, though the fall fish are in spawning condition, and catch and release is recommended (they don't taste their best at this time, and will serve us all better in the redd than in the pan.).

Unfortunately, some of the rough fish escaped the treatment and are staging a slow comeback, but angler success continues to be excellent. Bait is best from ice-out through June. Favorite baits are cheese and worms, with marshmallows used as floats to keep the bait just off the bottom. So popular is Velveeta cheese as a bait here, that a prominant penninsula on the NE shore is popularly known as Velveeta Point. Trolling picks up in July and August, with spinner-bait combinations effective. Spinning and small Flatfish type lures are both popular. In late summer and fall, flyfishing can really pay off, both trolling bright streamers and fishing to the shoreline shelves. Grasshopper imitations are occasionally just what the fish are waiting for.

Lava Lake Resort, on the west shore, offers boat and motor rentals, including canoes and paddleboats. They also have moorage, tackle, groceries and gasoline, as well as a full hook-up RV park (with most sites providing a good view of the lake), RV dump station, showers, and laundromat. There is a Forest Service campground and boat ramp is located across the street from the resort, and another camp at nearby Little Lava Lake. There is a 10 mph speed limit on the lake.

LAVA LAKE, LITTLE A fair trout lake 1/4 mile SE of Big Lava Lake, headwaters of the Deschutes River. See big lava for road directions. Little Lava is 110 acres and offers angling for stocked rainbow, wild brook trout, and whitefish.

The brook trout are self-sustaining and go to 12 inches or better, with 20 inchers taken by skilled and patient anglers. Rainbow are stocked each year. They run 6-15 inches and make up most of the catch. All methods of fishing are used, with trolling very popular and trolled flies extremely effective. Most fish are caught near the shoreline. There's a small attractive campground with boat ramp at the lake, and a resort with supplies at nearby Big Lava.

LEMISH LAKE A very good hike-in lake 3 miles south of the west end of Cultus Lake, SW of Bend. It's about a 1/2 mile hike south to the lake on the Lemish Lake Trail, which takes off about 3 miles west of the Little Cultus Lake Rd. junction. The lake is 1/2 mile due west of Lemish Butte, after which it is named. Lemish is the Klamath Indian word for thunder.

Some nice brook trout are taken in this 16 acre lake, with catches 8-16 inches. The lake is usually good in early season before the Waldo road opens up, and again in late fall. There's good fly angling in evenings. The nearest campground is at Little Cultus.

LILY LAKE (Deschutes Co.) A nice hike-in rainbow lake just off the Pacific Crest Trail on the north side of Charlton Butte, 2 miles east of the northern end of Waldo Lake. Shortest approach is from the south, taking the PCT north from Charlton Lake a bit over one mile to Trail 19, which leads east a short way to the lake. Charlton Lake is on the east-west stretch of FS 5897, the Waldo Lake Rd., one mile east of the North Waldo Lake Campground turnoff. FS 5897 intersects the Cascade Lakes Highway one mile south of Crane Prairie.

This 15 acre lake is fairly rich and has good shoal areas and cover. The deeper water is over 40 feet. Lightly fished, it is a consistent producer, with all methods effective. Average catch is about 10 inches, with some to 15 inches. It is air stocked with rainbow fingerlings, as the lake is not conducive to spawning. Lily is usually not accessible until late June.

LINDSEY POND One of the I-84 ponds adjacent to the Columbia River at hwy. mile 54, covering 60 acres at the mouth of Lindsey Creek. Best parking and access is for westbound traffic at the truck weight station.

LINE POND One of the I-84 ponds adjacent to the Columbia River at hwy. mile 68, just one acre at the Hood River/Wasco County line. It has limited unimproved parking for eastbound traffic only.

LINK LAKE A good trout lake 2 miles SW of Suttle Lake in Deschutes National Forest. From the Corbett snow-park west of the Suttle Lake turnoff on Hwy. 20, drive west about 2 1/2 miles to FS 2076, which leads south. Link is about 2 miles south and about 1/8 mile west of the road. A fire road, which may not be marked, leads to the lake.

Link covers 18 acres and reaches a depth of 20 feet maximum. It has had cutthroat, rainbow and brook trout, with brook trout predominant. The fish run 8-16 inches, averaging 12 inches most years. There are several good campsites at the lake.

LITTLE CULTUS LAKE See Cultus Lake, Little.

LITTLE DESCHUTES RIVER A good brown trout stream which flows almost 100 miles from its headwaters near Miller Lake in Klamath County to its confluence with the Deschutes River about 15 miles south of Bend.

The upper stream, south of Gilchrist, flows thorugh Deschutes National Forest, but much of the lower river flows through private property. County roads cross and parallel much of the stream however, and road easements provide public access.

The upper stream is crossed by Hwy. 58 about 15 miles SE of Odell Lake. From this area, forest roads follow the stream up to its headwaters. Other roads branching off hwys. 58 and 97 cross and follow the river to Bend.

The Little Deschutes is a meandering, slow-moving stream with deeply undercut banks and a sandy bottom. Big browns to 5 pounds often lurk in the undercuts, and stealth is adviseable as you approach the bank. Casting from as far back as 15 ft. might be necessary, as browns can detect bank vibrations from their cavern hideaways. There are also some rainbow trout in the river, primarily in the faster water upstream from Lapine.

Little Deschutes Campground, the only camp on the stream, is about 15 miles east of Odell Lake.

LITTLE THREE CREEKS LAKE See Three Creeks Lake, Little.

LIONS PONDS A one acre kid fishery 1/4 mile east of Hwy. 97 at the south end of Redmond. It contains largemouth bass, bluegill, and brown bullhead, and is restricted to fishing by children 14 years or younger.

LONE PINE POND One of the I-84 ponds adjacent to the Columbia River at hwy. mile 86.6. It covers 5 acres, north of the freeway and immediately west of Hwy. 197. Parking is difficult, and the east shore of the pond is privately owned. It may contain any of the Columbia's warmwater species.

LONG LAKE (Jefferson. Co.) A 16 acre cutthroat and rainbow trout lake in Deschutes National Forest on the Cascade slope east of the Santiam summit. Long lake is the middle lake in a chain that begins with Square Lake and ends at Round Lake. The best hike in begins at Round Lake. Take FS 12 one mile east of the Suttle Lake junction on Hwy. 20. This road leads in a mile to FS 1210, which goes to Round Lake. It is accessible in June in most years.

Long Lake is 1/3 mile long but quite narrow. It will yield trout almost any time, though the catch is generally small, averaging about 8 inches with some to 12 inches. All methods can be used, but bait and lure are best in early season. There is a small improved tent campground at Round Lake.

LONG POND One of the I-84 ponds adjacent to the Columbia River, located at hwy. mile 94. It covers 27 acres between east and westbound freeway lanes. Best access is from Exit 97 at Celilo, then follow a gravel road west from Celilo Park. It may contain any of the Columbia's warmwater species.

LOST LAKE (Hood River Co.) A large, very scenic, and very popular lake on the NW slope of Mt. Hood. Located at 3100 ft., Lost Lake offers a picture postcard view of the mountain. Clear and deep, covering almost a square half mile, it contains three varieties of trout plus kokanee, but you must leave your boat motor behind. A prohibition against use of motors on the lake contributes to the tranquility of the setting and docs little harm, if any, to angler success here.

Lost Lake must be approached from the east side of Mt. Hood. Take Hwy. 35 to the community of Dee, about 16 miles south of Hood River. From Portland, cross Mt. Hood on Hwy. 26 to reach Hwy. 35 at its southern end, or take I-84 east through the Columbia Gorge to Hood River and catch Hwy. 35 at its northern end. From Dee, follow FS 13 nine miles west to the lake. The route is well signed, and the snow is usually clear in June. Check with Mt. Hood National Forest or Lost Lake Resort for early season road conditions.

Fishing is generally good in the summer and fall. The lake supports natural reproduction of rainbow, brown, and brook trout, and is stocked with additional legal rainbow. Rainbow are the most frequent catch, averaging 10 inches and running to 16. The browns go to 18 inches.

The lake was last stocked with kokanee 15 years ago, and they are well established. Kokanee here run about the same size as the rainbow.

Trolling with flasher and worm is the most popular fishing method, though trolled flies work well on the edge of the shoal areas. Troll s-l-o-w-l-y for best results. Much of this lake is quite deep —up to 200 feet—but there are good shoals in the western lobe of the lake across from the campground. Single eggs and worms are usually effective. Lures will take some of the larger fish, with small Flatfish, Hotshots and flash-type artificials working well.

A pretty trail encircles the lake (about one mile). This is a pleasant place, and if you're lucky, you'll get to see otters shucking crayfish while you tempt the wiley trout. Lost Lake Resort, offering cabins, boat ramp, boat rentals, and supplies, is located at the north end of the

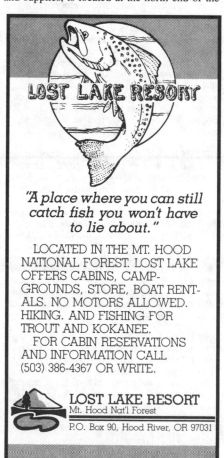

lake. The resort also manages a large Forest Service campground along the eastern shore of the lake. There is a parking fee.

LUCKY LAKE A pretty good hike-in lake for brook trout, one mile west of Lava Lake in Deschutes National Forest. Take the Cascade Lakes Hwy. south from Bend for about 40 miles to the Lava Lake turn-off, about 5 miles past Elk Lake. Lucky Lake Trail 148 heads on the west side of the highway about 1/4 mile past the turnoff. It's about a 1 1/2 mile hike to the lake. Lucky covers 30 acres and is over 50 feet deep. Brook trout run 8-16 inches. No motors are allowed, so don't pack in your outboard. There are fair natural campsites here.

MAIDEN LAKE A small, deep hike-in brook trout lake on the south slopes of Maiden Peak, a familiar landmark in the Odell Lake-Davis Lake area. From Crescent Lake Junction 2 miles south of Odell Lake on Hwy. 58, drive south on Hwy. 58 about 3 miles to County Rd. 61, which branches off to the east and leads to Davis Lake at the southern end of the Cascades Lakes Hwy. At the Davis Lake turn off FS 61, turn north and drive about 3 miles to FS 4660, which leads NW. Follow signs to Maiden Lake Trail, about 5 miles from the turn. Trail 41 leads west about 3 miles to the lake. The trail continues west about 2 miles to the Pacific Crest Trail, just north of Rosary Lakes.

Only 6 acres but over 20 feet deep, Maiden Lake offers fair fishing for brook trout 6-10 inches. The lake is usually accessible in late June, though there is often still some snow.

MARKS CREEK A fair trout stream heading in the Ochoco National Forest and flowing into Ochoco Creek 7 miles above Ochoco Reservoir, about 17 miles east of Prineville by Hwy. 26. The creek is crossed by Hwy. 26 at the Ochoco confluence, then followed closely by the highway NE to its headwaters.

Marks Creek is stocked with rainbow averaging 8-11 inches. Bait angling is the usual method, but lures and flies will also produce. The upper section is good late in the season. In some years this stream almost dries up. There is a Forest Service campground at Cougar and Ochoco Divide on the upper creek.

MARTIN LAKE A 4 acre hike-in brook trout lake, 2 miles south of Three Fingered Jack and a few miles north of Hwy. 20, east of the Santiam Pass summit. Take the Pacific Crest Trail north from Hwy. 20, 1/2 mile east of Hoodoo Ski Bowl, and hike a short distance to Square Lake Trail 65. About 3 miles on the trail gets you to Booth Lake. Continue 1/4 mile north on the trail, and head due west up a draw. Martin is about 1/3 mile west of the trail.

Martin is deep for its size and has brook trout 6-12 inches. It's a nice flyfishing lake and a fairly consistent producer. Bait and lures can be effectively used. It is usually accessible in late June.

MATTHIEU LAKES These hike-in lakes are on the east edge of an impressive lava field south of McKenzie Pass near the Dee Wright Observatory. This lava looks like it spilled out yesterday, an enormous field of grey rubble stretching as far as the eye can see. Take the Pacific Crest Trail south from Hwy. 126 at the Observatory, and hike about 3 miles to the lower (North) lake. The upper (south) lake holds no fish.

North Matthieu Lake, about 6 acres and not very deep, has been a steady producer of good

size rainbow. There is some spawning here, but the lake also gets airdrops of fingerlings.

McCLURES LAKE One of the I-84 ponds adjacent to the Columbia River at hwy. mile 74. It covers 50 acres and is immediately east of Memaloose State Park and Rest Area. Best access is for westbound traffic, with parking available at the rest area. It may contain any of the Columbia's warmwater species.

MEADOW LAKE A good trout lake in the Deschutes National Forest SW of Suttle Lake and south of Hwy. 20, on the west side of Cache Mountain. From the Suttle Lake turn off Hwy. 20, drive west about 2 1/2 miles to FS 2076, which leads south. Meadow Lake is about 3 miles south and 1/4 mile west of the road. Many fire roads were built in this area, but most have been closed, including the one which leads to the lake. You'll have to hike a short way in.

Meadow Lake covers about 16 acres, a consistent producer of nice trout 10-16 inches. Rainbow, brook, and cutthroat are all stocked. Fly angling is especially good, with best results late in the year. The lake is usually accessible in June, and early season angling is good. There are several nice natural campsites at the lake. Motors are prohibited.

MEEK LAKE A brook and cutthroat trout lake in Deschutes National Forest about midway between Crescent and Summit Lakes. From Crescent Lake Junction on Hwy. 58 SE of Oakridge, take FS 60 around the western shore of Crescent Lake to FS 6010, the Summit Lake Rd. Drive about 5 miles west, and watch for Meek Lake Trailhead on the south side of the road. The lake is just 1/2 mile off the road by Trail 43.

Rather deep for its 11 acres, it offers fair angling for brook trout and cutthroat, which seem to do better than a previous rainbow stocking. All methods can be effective, although bait angling is probably best. Fish to 14 inches have been taken here.

In late summer, try flyfishing in Summit Creek, which you must cross on the trail. Larger brook trout sometimes wander in from the lake. The nearest campground is at Summit Lake. Meek is usually accessible in late June.

METOLIUS RIVER A beautiful spring fed stream in central Oregon, which gushes full blown from a fern carpeted hollow at the base of Black Butte, managed primarily for wild trout. Tackle restrictions and a catch and release fishery for these wild beauties throughout the mainstem have successfully restored the Metolius' reputation as world class trout water.

To get there, take Hwy. 20 NW from Sisters, or east from the Willamette Valley. Follow signs to Camp Sherman, a small resort community near the Metolius headwaters about 3 miles east of Suttle Lake. From Sisters, turn off Hwy. 20 at FS 14, and skirt the west flank of Black Butte, reaching Camp Sherman in about 5 miles. The Metolius flows about 9 miles through a handsome pine forest before entering a canyon, joining the Deschutes River in Lake Billy Chinook 20 miles further. Its source is a large spring at the north base of Black Butte, which can be viewed from a paved stroll-in path about one mile south of Camp Sherman, just off FS 14. The spring site is well marked.

At this time, the Metolius is restricted to fly angling with barbless hook on the mainstem above Bridge 99, and to barbless flies and lures only (no bait) below the bridge. The river is

currently open for year around angling above Bridge 99. All wild trout (adipose fin intact) must be released unharmed. The adipose fin is the small fin located behind the dorsal fin.

The Metolius supports wild rainbow, bull (Dolly Varden), brown, and brook trout, as well as whitefish and a spawning run of kokanee. Hatchery rainbow are heavily stocked in spring and summer near the campgrounds, but these all migrate into Lake Billy Chinook by winter. The river maintains a constant temperature year around, shows no more than a few inches of fluctuation, and always runs clear.

Water clarity is only one of the challenges confronting anglers here. Matching the hatch is another. Though its water temperature remains constant, the river flows through a wide variety of mini-environments, each of which produces its own insect hatch on its own time schedule. The three general environments are from Lake Creek to Gorge Campground, Gorge to Bridge 99, and Bridge 99 to Lake Billy Chinook. But within each of these sections there is great variety. To check on the status of the major hatches, anglers might call or stop by The Fly Fisher's Place in Sisters. The general store at Camp Sherman may also be helpful.

Some of the best fly fishing occurs in early May and early July, when anglers match the big green drake hatch, followed by the golden stonefly. Caddis and mayfly hatches occur throughout summer. A second hatch of smaller green drakes takes place in fall, along with hatches of smaller caddis and mayflies. Insect hatches continue throughout the winter, including small Baetis mayflies, small caddis, midges, and a tiny blue winged olive mayfly November through February. Nymphing produces most consistently, with stonefly nymphs, tied-down caddis, hares ear, and green drake patterns frequently used.

Because the use of lead or split shot is illegal on the Metolius, some anglers tie on a large stonefly to weight their line, then add one or two dropper nymphs, casting upstream and fishing the nymphs dead-drift close to the bottom in a drag-free presentation. Retrieving with short jerks can also be effective. Many anglers use a strike indicator to better detect the take. Small dry flies (size 16-18) will take fish when they are feeding on the surface.

The Metolius is primarily a bank fishery, with some wading possible. Though the river appears fairly smooth in the campground area below Gorge Campground, whitewater and downed timber make it treacherous for boats of all kinds. Easiest wading is in the stretch between Lake Creek and Gorge Campground. Below Gorge, wading is trickier, since the river is powerful, rife with holes, and very cold. Wading becomes very difficult in the Gorge itself, and the canyon. However there are many good bank casting spots all along the river. Below Bridge 99, these spots are a secret well guarded by local anglers. You can look for pull-offs along the road, but trails down to the river are not obvious.

From its source, the Metolius flows due north, with FS 14 following its eastern bank for about 9 miles to Bridge 99. There is some private property on the west bank in the Camp Sherman area, but beyond that the river flows through national forest, with only two small private land holdings, one below Gorge Campground, the other just above Pioneer Ford Campground. At Bridge 99, the pavement ends where the main road crosses the Metolius. Candle Creek Campground is on the west side of the river about 2 miles downstream from the bridge on a good gravel road.

Below Bridge 99 and Lower Bridge Campground, which is right below the bridge on the east side, a rough gravel road follows the river's east bank downstream. This road is best suited to 4 wheel drive vehicles with good tires. From Candle Creek downstream, the Metolius forms the southern boundary of Warm Springs Indian Reservation, and the west bank of the river is closed to public access.

The gravel road continues to follow the east bank till the river bends east, and the road ends. A trail follows streamside for the next 2 miles, providing access to many nice pools and rapids. At its east end, the trail is met by FS 64, which leads west from Perry South Campground on the Metolius Arm of Lake Billy Chinook. Monty Campground is on the Metolius half-way between the east end of the trail and Perry.

The most popular angling area on the Metolius is from Lake Creek (2 miles below the source) to Bridge 99 (just before the river reaches the Reservation), about a 10 mile stretch. Here the river is stocked frequently throughout spring and summer with rainbow trout reared at the Metolius' Wizard Falls Hatchery. These rainbow average 9-12 inches, with an occasional catch to 15 inches.

The Gorge is within this area, a 2 mile stretch of river away from any roads. It offers good fishing for wild trout, since hatchery plants are not made in this section of the Metolius. You can fish a short section of the upper Gorge near Gorge Campground on the main paved road from Camp Sherman, FS 14. Access downstream from Gorge Campground is limited by the private grounds of House on the Metolius, a private resort. Access to most of the Gorge, however, is available from a trail that follows the river's west bank. Lower Canyon Creek Campground is at the upper end of the trail, and Wizard Falls Hatchery on FS 14 is at the lower end. There is also some trail access on the east side of the river in the Gorge area upstream from Wizard Falls.

Smaller wild rainbow can be taken in the waters above Gorge Campground, where the river is shallow and offers easy wading. Larger rainbow are more prevalent below Canyon Creek, where wading is more difficult. There are a number of deep holes in the river's mid-section where large trout sulk, including the Canyon Creek confluence and the water near Allen Springs Campground. Canyon Creek is on the west bank. To get there, take FS 1217 about 1/4 mile west of Camp Sherman, then turn north on FS 1420. Allen Springs is below Wizard Falls Hatchery off FS 14.

Bull trout 5-20 pounds lurk beneath bank cover and submerged structures throughout the river, and may be enticed by sculpin, mouse imitations, and streamers. Brown trout are numerous in the Metolius but are not popularly fished. Brook trout are the least plentiful breed here, and are primarily taken in fall. Kokanee come into the Metolius in the fall on their spawning run up from Lake Billy Chinook.

There are 10 developed campgrounds along the road between Camp Sherman and Candle Creek, each in an attractive setting of huge ponderosa pine. The fee-pay camps have drinking water. Supplies and gas are available in Camp Sherman, where there are also a number of motels and low key resorts. A short closure exists near the Camp Sherman store, where large trout are clearly visible, cruising for bread and other trifles tossed by tourists, but the area is clearly marked. Check current regulations for other closures, seasons, and special restrictions.

MILL CREEK (Wasco Co.) A fair-size trout stream entering the Columbia River at the west edge of The Dalles, crossed by Hwy. 30 near its mouth. It heads at the eastern edge of Mt. Hood Forest and flows NE about 20 miles through The Dalles. The creek is followed by paved and gravel road for most of its length.

It offers fair angling for wild trout in the upper area. The Dept. of Fish and Wildlife stocks the creek with legal rainbow near the outskirts of The Dalles. There is no camping convenient to the stream.

MILLER POND One of the I-84 ponds adjacent to the Columbia River at hwy. mile 97.5. Covering 8 acres between I-84 and Hwy. 30, it may contain any of the Columbia's warmwater species. Best access is from Exit 97, then proceed east on Hwy. 30 for one mile. Parking on the freeway is prohibited.

MONON LAKE A large trout lake adjacent to Olallie Lake north of Mt. Jefferson. It is just south of Olallie, about 35 miles south of Hwy. 26. Take FS 42 south from Hwy. 26 about 2 miles past the Clear Lake turn-off, and follow the signs to Olallie Lake. Monon is just beyond Olallie on the same road. It can also be reached from the south by about 28 miles of forest road from Detroit. It's usually late June before the north road is open, and the road from the south rarely opens before July.

Monon is over 90 acres, fairly deep, and lightly fished in comparison to its popular neighbor. It is stocked with Montana black spotted cutthroat, a breed which is supposedly easier to catch than rainbow (which were stocked previously) or the more challenging brook trout, which were last stocked here in 1983. The cutthroat are disappointingly small. Brook trout here run 7-18 inches and are only occasionally taken. All methods work on the cutthroat, with bait angling the most consistent producer. Trolled lures or spinner-bait combinations should work, and flies can be effective.

Motors are prohibited on the lake, and there is no developed campground. There is a full service campground at Olallie on the peninsula that separates the two lakes, and there is one top notch campsite on a rocky point that juts into the center of Monon, accessible only by boat. Monon offers a good escape from the crowds.

MORAINE LAKE A pretty but fishless lake in a very scenic area on the south flank of South Sister in Three Sisters Wilderness. Stocking of this lake was discontinued a number of years ago due to frequent winterkill.

MOSIER POND EAST One of the I-84 ponds adjacent to the Columbia River at hwy. mile 69. It covers 6 acres and is immediately east of Exit 69 between I-84 and Hwy. 30. Parking along the freeway is prohibited. The pond may contain any of the Columbia's warmwater species.

MOSIER POND WEST One of the I-84 ponds adjacent to the Columbia River at hwy. mile 69. Covering 8 acres, it is bisected by the Union Pacific Railroad south of the freeway. There is limited unimproved parking for eastbound freeway traffic at the west end of the pond. It is also accessible from Hwy. 30 by way of I-84 Exit 69. The pond may contain any of the Columbia's warmwater species.

MUSKRAT LAKE An 8 acre hike-in trout lake in the Cultus Lake area SW of Bend. The lake is 1 1/2 miles NW of the west end of Big Cultus Lake and is reached by a 5 mile hike on the Winopee Lake Trail 16 from the east end of Big Cultus Lake. Boating across Big Cultus Lake to the campground at the west end of the lake and picking up the trail there will save you 3 miles of hiking. See Cultus Lake for road directions.

Muskrat is a difficult lake to fish. The brook trout average 8 inches and run to about 15 inches. Fly angling can be good late in summer and fall. An old trapper's cabin survives in good repair here. Please help preserve it. Natural campsites are available. It is usually accessible in late June. Mosquitoes can be devilish.

NAP-TE-PAH LAKE (Warm Springs Indian Reservation) A deep 2 acre lake between Olallie and Monon lakes, reached by trail from Peninsula Campground at the south end of Olallie. Maximum depth is 25 feet. Both this lake and a smaller neighbor, Mangriff Lake, are stocked with brook trout. Although located on the Reservation, no tribal permit is required at this time.

NORTH LAKE A 6 acre hike-in brook trout lake, 3 miles south of the Columbia Gorge in the NE corner of Mt. Hood National Forest. It can be reached by a strenuous hike up from the gorge on Trail 411, which heads at the Forest Service campground at Wyeth, 12 miles west of Hood River. The trail ascends 3800 ft. in about 4 miles. For you Sunday morning fisherman who can't make the grade, as it were, the alternative is to approach the lake from the south. Trail 416 heads at Rainy Lake Campground and gets you there in 1 1/2 miles. (Had you worried there, eh?) See Rainy Lake for road information. North Lake is at 4000 ft.

Fly anglers do well here, as the lake is only 8 ft. at its deepest point. Brook trout average 9 inches, but an occasional 16 incher is taken. There are some fair natural campsites around the lake and a good improved camp at Rainy Lake. The road is usually snowbound until mid-June. Check with Mt. Hood Forest Service for early season conditions.

OCHOCO CREEK A good size stream flowing into Ochoco Reservoir from the east. It is followed closely by Hwy. 26 for 6 miles upstream from the reservoir, then by FS 22 to it's source at Walton Lake, 14 miles to the NE. It is accessible for most of its length, but there is some private land in the lower stretch, and permission must be obtained.

The creek has native rainbow trout and is stocked with catchable rainbow in the area around Prineville. Angling is usually good early in the season and again in the fall, with bait the most popular method. The trout range 7-12 inches, and the catch rate is good. There are two campgrounds on the upper creek, one at Ochoco Guard Station and the other at the source at Walton Lake.

OCHOCO RESERVOIR A large reservoir with good fishing for rainbow trout 5 miles east of Prineville. Ochoco covers over 1,000 acres and is a popular recreational area. To reach it, drive east from Prineville on Hwy. 26, which follows the north shore.

The reservoir is well stocked annually, and rainbow average 10-12 inches with some to 15 inches. Large fish are available some years, and limits are common. The reservoir was poisoned in the fall of 1988 and restocked in spring. The trout fishery during the next few years should be better than average. The lake is open year around, and fish are caught in every season, with best catches in spring and fall. Bank an

gling and trolling are both popular, with most bank anglers working the north shore below the highway. Ice fishing is sometimes popular.

There is a good state park with camping facilities at about mid-point on the reservoir off Hwy. 26. Trailers are prohibited, but a modern trailer court is located across the highway from the park. Several resorts with rental boats, motors, and supplies are also on the highway.

ODELL CREEK The outlet stream from Odell Lake, flowing NE 6 miles from the SE tip of Odell into Davis Lake. Forest roads parallel it without coming too close for the first 4 miles.

The creek has a small population of native rainbow and bull trou. Kokanee move through from Odell to Davis, but few are caught here. This is a good creek for whitefish in the fall, but not much of a trout stream.

ODELL LAKE One of the largest mountain lakes in Oregon, 5 miles long with about 3300 surface acres, offering outstanding fishing for trophy size Mackinaw trout and some of the best kokanee fishing in the state. Odell also contains bull trout (Dolly Varden) and and a good population of rainbow. Angler success rate for all species is extremely high.

Odell stretches along the east side of Willamette Pass just south of Hwy. 58, distracting drivers with glimpses of sparkling water or churning whitecaps through the dark firs that surround it. Diamond Peak stands guard just 5 miles away on the western horizon. More than thirty creeks and a number of springs feed the lake, keeping its water level constant to within a foot throughout the year. Glacially scoured to over 280 ft. deep near the east end, Odell provides a rich and variable environment for its residents, all of which are self-sustaining.

Odell Lake is about 70 miles SE of Eugene by Hwy. 58, and 23 miles NW of the junction of hwys. 58 and 97. Hwy. 58 follows its NW shore for about 5 miles, and secondary roads lead partially around the east and west shores.

The lake was first stocked with Mackinaw trout (also known as lake trout), in 1951, and stocking continued through 1965, at which point the mackinaw took over and have been successfully propagating the species here ever since. Lake trout can live to be over 20 years old and exceed 40 pounds. The state record Mackinaw was caught here in 1984, weighing 40 pounds, 8 ounces. Most run 10-20 pounds.

Though Mackinaw have always preyed on Odell's whitefish and chubs, in recent years they have been especially enjoying the growing population of tasty kokanee. One of the tricks anglers use to locate Mackinaw (which often hunt in groups) is to first find the kokanee. The bottom of Odell is a varied landscape, with many submerged buttes (or shoals), around which the kokanee cower and dart in schools. Groups of mackinaw tend to hover atop these buttes, including those east of Princess Creek boat ramp, east of the Hwy. 58 viewpoint, east of Chinquapin Point boat ramp, near the railroad slide on the south shore east of Serenity Bay, and off Burly Bluff near West Bay. Use a depth finder to locate these shoals (at 60-90 ft.), or ask the folks at Shelter Cove to point out landmarks that can line you up. They can also usually tell you where Mackinaw and kokanee have been schooling lately. Electronic depthfinders and fish locators are also valuable.

The best way to go after schooled mackinaw seems to be by jigging. The Luhr Jensen Nordic jig has been especially successful here. Most jiggers use the No. 060 in silver and fluorescent green with a very sharp treble hook. They locate a likely spot, and lower the jig on an 8 pound line, working it vertically, raising it up several feet and letting it flutter down on a slack line. Trolling is effective for picking up single Mackinaw cruising through deeper water. Trollers work *off* the shoals rather than over them, using leaded line with sinkers or downriggers to get to 60-90 ft., trailing big Flatfish or Rapalas. (White and blue lures are supposed to look very kokanee-like down in the depths.) Average angler success rate for Mackinaw is about 2 fish per day.

For better numbers and faster action, try for the kokanee. Kokanee are a delicious tasting landlocked sockeye salmon, now a very large and self-sustaining population in Odell. So numerous are they, in fact, that average size is beginning to drop from 12 to 9-10 inches, though 20 inchers are also caught. Because of their fine taste, abundance, and ease of catch, most kokanee are sought by anglers as meat for the table rather than angling sport. Some anglers still-fish for them early in the season using shelled caddis fly larvae, single eggs, or worms. Most anglers troll, using a small flasher, followed by a snubber, 18 inch leader, and a small kokanee lure tipped with a piece of worm and a kernel of corn. Kokanee have soft mouths, and the rubber snubber absorbs some of the shock on the initial hookup.

Jigging is also effective and growing in popularity, especially using the Nordic in pink pearl or fluorescent green. However, kokanee can also provide good sport to anglers who use a downrigger (rather than heavy hardware) to get to the kokanee level, and light gear—a light, sensitive rod, light line (6 pound test monofilament, 4 pound leader), and light terminal tackle (a few fluorescent beads, a tiny spinner with the blade removed, a No. 6 hook, and a single kernel of white corn). The downrigger usually has to be manually released, since the kokanee bite is more subtle than most tension mechanisms can detect.

In early season, kokanee schools can generally be found within 8-20 ft. of the surface. But kokanee prefer water temperatures 50 degrees or

colder, and as the lake warms in June they descend to about 50 ft., then to around 75 ft. in July, and down to 100 ft. in August. Towards fall, they move closer to shore, seeking spawning inlets. Electronic fish finders can locate where and at what depth the schools are holding, though looking for congregations of boats on the lake and asking other anglers what depth they're fishing is just as effective. Kokanee anglers tend to be generous with information, since there are plenty here for all. Best fishing is in early morning and late in the day, which suits Odell's temperament perfectly.

Odell Lake is aligned with a major mountain pass and, at elevation 4788 ft., the wind can really whip through, churning up the water. When it does, you want to be safely ashore, perhaps sipping coffee beside the big stone fireplace at Odell Lodge on the east end of the lake, or cleaning fish and talking shop with the knowledgeable owners of Shelter Cove Resort on the west end. The weather can change quickly in spring and late fall, so keep a weather eye out. Typically, the lake is calm in the morning, and boating even by canoe can be quite pleasant. (There is, in fact, an annual canoe race on Odell). Afternoons, the wind can be counted on to pick up, a fact which sail boarders have taken note of in recent years. Most anglers pack it in afternoons, or move over to Odell Creek or nearby Crescent Creek. The lake generally calms again by early evening.

Other species available in Odell include bull trout (formerly known as Dolly Varden) and rainbow. Both reproduce naturally here and reach good size, but neither are very actively sought by anglers. Bull trout are taken incidentally by anglers fishing for Mackinaw, and they are still-fished by some anglers, especially among the weed beds off Trapper Creek. Bull trout average 12-14 inches. The rainbow typically range from 8-16 inches with many to 20 inches and better.

They can be taken by all method, though trolling with lure or spinner/bait combinations is most common. Rainbow anglers work the shorelines from mid-June throughout the season, with best catches in fall.

There are excellent campgrounds at the east and west ends of the lake and along the north shoreline. Princess Creek, Trapper Bay, and Sunset Cove campgrounds have boat launches. Pebble Bay Campground is a small tent camp on the west shore, accessible only by boat.

There are two excellent resorts on Odell, one at each end of the lake, each offering accommodations, supplies, tackle, boats and motors. The resorts have telephone service. The fireplace at Odell Lake Lodge is worth a visit, and you can get an excellent meal there. Shelter Cove Resort has especially attractive modern cabins (some of locally hewn logs) and a general store. If you get by there in October, be sure to look for the kokanee in scarlet spawning colors along the shoreline near the marina.

OLALLIE LAKE A large popular trout lake north of Mt. Jefferson. Olallie is the largest lake in the Olallie Lake Scenic Area. Olallie is at one end of a chain of 5 trout lakes that drain east into Warm Springs Reservation. The others must be reached by hiking. See Trout, Island, Dark, Long.

The best routes to Olallie are from Hwy. 26 from the north, and from Detroit Reservoir from the west. From Portland, continue from Government Camp south on Hwy. 26 to FS 42, about 2 miles south of the Clear Lake turn-off. It's about 35 miles from the intersection to the lake, the last 12 miles or so unpaved but good when dry. At Warm Springs Meadow, leave FS 42 and pick up FS 4220. The way in is well signed.

From Salem south, the best route is by way of Detroit, on the east side of Detroit Reservoir. Drive east on FS 46 past Breitenbush Campground and on up the North Fork of the Breitenbush River. In the upper reaches of this river the road turns sharply to the north upslope. Just after passing beneath a power transmission line, FS 4220 turns off to the east. It is signed for Breitenbush Lake. This road is the shorter but rougher way in to Olallie, which is 3 miles beyond Breitenbush Lake. The first 4 miles of road are the worst, but no problem if you take it slow and easy.

From June through October you can expect good rainbow fishing at Olallie, along with a few nice brook trout that wander in from the higher lakes. Olallie is shallow but does have some deep spots. The lake is over a mile long and covers 240 surface acres. Trout average 10-14 inches, with a few to 20 inches. Motors are prohibited on the lake.

The Pacific Crest Trail follows the northern tip of the lake, and other good trails lead west from the north end to a number of small trout lakes. See Red, Averill, Fish, Lower, Gifford. A trail east from the Peninsula Campground follows the creek that links the five lake chain. The downstream lakes are on Warm Springs Indian Reservation, and a tribal fishing permit is required. Monon Lake, a good size lake just south of Olallie, contains small cutthroat and some brook trout.

There is a boat ramp at Peninsula Camp. There are two other smaller campgrounds—Paul Dennis and Camp Ten. Paul Dennis is a boat or hike-in camp on the NE shore. There are also good campgrounds north and south of the lake on FS 4220. A resort at the north end has cabins, boats, food and tackle.

OLDENBERG LAKE A 28 acre hike-in brook trout lake in Deschutes National Forest 3 miles south of Crescent Lake. From Crescent Lake Junction on Hwy. 58, take the Crescent Lake Rd. south about 7 miles to Oldenburg Lake Trail

head, 1/2 mile west of the entrance to Spring Campground. Its about a 3 mile hike to the lake past the Bingham Lakes. The trail continues south to Windigo Pass on the Klamath-Douglas County line.

The typical brook trout caught here is 8-10 inches, with some fish to 14 inches. Good natural campsites are available, and there are campgrounds at Crescent Lake.

ONE-MILE LAKE One of the I-84 ponds adjacent to the Columbia River at hwy. mile 90-91. It covers 9 acres and is between the east and westbound lanes on I-84. There is no parking for westbound traffic, and parking for eastbound traffic is unimproved and limited. It may contain any of the Columbia's warmwater species.

OTTERTAIL LAKE (a.k.a. Otter Lake) A 2 acre lake at the head of Green Point Creek, 1/2 mile east of Wahtum Lake on the opposite side of the ridge. Follow FS 2810 from Punchbowl Falls, one mile north of Dee, to the lake. Ottertail supports a population of brook trout.

PAULINA CREEK Outlet stream for Paulina Lake in the Newberry Crater of Paulina Mt. SE of Bend. The creek is stocked, and there can be fair angling for migrants from Paulina Lake. The creek flows down the western slope of the mountain, and enters the Deschutes River about 6 miles south of Bend. Much of the lower creek flows through private lands. It is followed upstream from Prairie Campground by Trail 56.

Prairie Campground is on FS 2120 three miles east of Hwy. 97. McKay Crossing Campground is 2 miles further east.

PAULINA LAKE A large, very popular lake in the crater of a dormant volcano in the Paulina Mountains, about 20 air miles SE of Bend. Paulina shares its handsome setting in Newberry Crater with East Lake, from which it is separated by a high ridge. Paulina is a consistent producer of good size rainbow trout, and is managed for trophy browns and kokanee. Its kokanee are the egg source for kokanee fisheries throughout the Northwest.

To reach Paulina, drive south from Bend on Hwy. 97 about 19 miles to County Rd. 21, which leads east about 12 miles up the slope of Paulina Mountain to the Crater and its lakes. Plan a stop at Lava Lands Visitor Center, a Forest Service interpretive center 8 miles south of Bend on Hwy. 97. The Center is located atop a cinder cone and presents a good overview of this interesting area.

Newberry is actually a double crater, for both Paulina and East have their own lava dome. Paulina has very little shoal area; its over 200 ft. deep almost throughout. The lava dome comes to within only 60 feet of the surface. The cream colored tuft crater walls are clearly visible around the perimeter, and these, combined with the great depth, color Paulina's waters an unusual turquoise. The lake is at elevation 6331 ft. It is about half again larger than East Lake, about 2 1/2 square miles. The lake's only shoal areas are on the SW edge near the resort, and directly across from the resort at the black slide.

Rainbow trout are predominant, with most from 9-14 inches. The lake has some lunkers over 5 pounds, but they're hard to hook. Trolling and bait fishing are a toss-up for popularity. Rainbow anglers work the shorelines, usually keeping within depths of 20 ft. or less. Popular trolling and still-fishing areas are off the rocky points on the mid-eastern shore and off the western shore between Green Slide and Paulina Resort. Trollers also work the area SE of Big Point (the rocky point near the main campground). There is good still fishing in the little cove between Red Slide and the warm springs. Most of the fly action is over the moss beds near the warm springs and

Black Slide in the NE, between Green Slide and Big Bay in the NW, and north of the Clay Banks in the SE.

Kokanee make a good contribution to the mid-summer catch. They can be found all over the lake. These fish run to 22 inches, which is large for the species. The state record kokanee was taken from Paulina, weighing 3 pounds 6 ounces.

The record brown trout, at 35 pounds 8 ounces, was caught at Paulina in 1965. A 12 pounder was caught here in 1988.

There are three nice campgrounds on the lake—Chief Paulina, Paulina Lake and Little Crater Campgrounds. Paulina and Little Crater have boat ramps. There is a resort with attractive restaurant, cabins, boats, motors, and supplies at the west end of the lake. A few summer homes are located on the south shore. Boaters should observe the 10 mph speed limit on the lake and keep a weather eye out, as Paulina gets rough in a blowWinter holds on long up here, and the campgrounds are often blocked with snow at season's opening. Things are pleasant by late June in most years, but bring warm clothes.

PINE HOLLOW RESERVOIR An irrigation reservoir which has turned into a fine fishery for trout, bass, catfish, and bluegill, located near Wamic south of the The Dalles. From Hwy. 197 at Tygh Valley go 5 miles west to Wamic. The reservoir is one mile NW of Wamic by county road.

At high water the reservoir covers 240 acres. The state has bought a 10 ft. access above the high water line all around the lake. The public is entitled to use this easement, despite occasional landowner contentiousness.

Pinehollow is stocked with catchable rainbow and fingerlings. A largemouth bass and brown bullhead fishery is developing as well. There are two public boat ramps on the reservoir and, at the NE end of the lake, a private campground with store, boat rentals and restaurant. There is concern that the lake may be becoming overpopulated with trout, so come help out.

PRINEVILLE RESERVOIR A large reservoir stocked with a variety of game fish, formed by a dam on the Crooked River 12 miles SE of Prineville. Hwy. 27 reaches the dam about 15 miles south of Prineville, and gravel roads up Bear Creek and Birch Canyon reach points on the south shore. These roads lead in from Hwy. 27, several miles south of the dam.

Best bank access is along the NE shore, where Prineville Reservoir State Park roads follow 3 miles of shoreline. The park is accessed by the paved Juniper Canyon Rd., which cuts south from the Post-Paulina Hwy. near Prineville city limits.

Prineville Reservoir was created for flood control and irrigation, and varies considerably in water level during the season. At maximum water the reservoir covers almost 5 square miles, at low water, under 4 square miles.

The state currently stocks about 170,000 rainbow fingerlings annually in the reservoir, and fishing is good throughout regular trout season. Lahontan cutthroat, holdovers from an abandoned stocking program, are still occasionally taken. When the ice is thick enough, ice fishing can be excellent here.

In addition to trout angling, the reservoir supports populations of brown bullhead, largemouth, and smallmouth bass. Bullhead angling takes off in spring when the water warms above 55 degrees, and slows down once it gets over 60. Catfishing picks up again in mid-September. These bullhead have generally run big, with fish to 17 inches caught. But the reservoir currently appears to be overpopulated with bullhead, resulting in smaller average size. Worms are the popular bait. Bass angling is good from May through September.

A boat is really handy here, though there are excellent bank fishing opportunities off any of the roads. The most popular bank angling spots are at Jasper Point, the state park, and at the dam. There are good ramps at the state park and at Jasper Point. Another ramp is located about one mile south of the dam, and there are ramps at the Crook County Park and Prineville Resort east of the state park. The resort also rents boats and motors.

Camping is available at the state park, which accepts reservations, and at a private campground run by the resort. Supplies are available at the resort and in Prineville.

RAFT LAKE A lightly fished brook trout lake in the Deschutes National Forest, one mile west of Little Cultus Lake. No trails lead to the lake. To reach it, go west on FS 600, the Irish Lake Rd., a little over 2 miles. Then head north cross country for 1/2 mile. The Irish Mt. topo map will come in handy. You may hit Strider or Lois Lake first, but they are smaller. Both have fish, incidentally.

Raft Lake is 10 acres and about 30 ft. deep. It has good shoal areas which provide fine fly fishing in the evenings. It takes a raft to get out to the deep spots, and it's not too far (if you find it) to carry a rubber boat. There are brook trout in good supply here, 8-16 inches averaging 11 inches. There are also a few good size cutthroat. There are some fair natural campsites at the lake. Mosquitoes are fierce in spring.

RAINY LAKE A 10 acre brook trout lake you can drive to in Mt. Hood Forest SW of Hood River. From the community of Dee, drive north about 2 miles toward Punchbowl Falls, and pick up FS 2820, which twists and winds its way west about 10 miles to the lake campground. Rainy is just a short walk north of the road. This road can be a bit rough in wet weather. The lake is usually accessible in June.

Rainy is a shallow lake, not over 10 feet deep, and provides good flyfishing. Bait and lures can also be used. The brook trout run from 6-15 inches, but the average fish runs 8-10 inches. Rainy is fished heavily but produces well. There is a nice Forest Service camp at the lake.

RED LAKE (Marion Co.) A good small rainbow trout lake in Mt. Hood Forest west of the Olallie Lake area. From Lower Lake Campground, head south on Trail 719 past Wall and Averill Lakes. Red Lake is about 3 1/2 miles from Lower Lake. It is south of the trail about 1/4 mile past Averill Lake. The approach from the west is only 1 1/2 miles. See Averill Lake for directions. There are good natural campsites at the lake. It's usually inaccessible until June.

RED SLIDE LAKE A small, difficult to find brook trout lake 1 1/2 miles north of Irish Lake, about 1/4 mile south of Brahma Lake, which is on the Pacific Crest Trail above Irish Lake. No trail leads to Red Slide. You might get lost for awhile, as this is tricky terrain with potholes and lakes all about. Happily, many of them hold fish. Some that you may stumble across are Timmy, Brahma, Lady, Gleneden, and Pocket. Hiking due west will get you back on the trail anywhere in here. Bringing along the Irish Mt. topo map will help some.

Red Slide covers only 2 acres but is deep. There aren't a lot of fish here, but the brook trout present reach good size. Mosquitoes in this area are fierce in early season.

ROCK CREEK RESERVOIR A small reservoir with trout, bass, and brown bullhead in eastern Mt. Hood National Forest, about 10 miles west of Tygh Valley. From Tygh Valley, follow the paved road to Wamic, continuing west on this road for about 5 miles to the reservoir. It can also be reached from Hwy. 26 by cutting north from Wapinita, crossing the White River at Smock Crossing, then following the signs north to the lake.

Part of the White River drainage, Rock Creek Reservoir has about 100 surface acres when full. It is stocked annually with legal rainbow trout. The average catch is 9-13 inches, with some to 18 inches. All fishing methods are effective, with bait fishing most common. Trollers do well using Flatfish, Triple-Teasers, or spinner-worm rigs. Brown bullhead and largemouth bass populations have steadily gained ground here, with bass currently up to 5 pounds.

Rock Creek Campground is located on the south shore of the reservoir. It is well shaded with pine trees. Motors are prohibited on the lake, but there is a boat ramp at the campground. Use of this ramp can be affected by a draw down of the reservoir. Most anglers here launch car-top boats. The west shore of the reservoir, disfigured by fire in the late 1970's, is coming back nicely.

ROSARY LAKES A series of three hike-in trout lakes on the Pacific Crest Trail one mile north of Odell Lake. Lower Rosary Lake is 2 1/2 miles by trail from the PCT crossing of Hwy. 58 at Willamette Pass. The lower lake is 42 acres, the middle 9 acres, and the upper lake 8 acres.

The lower lake has rainbow and brook trout 8-12 inches with some to 16 inches or better. The other two are stocked with brook trout that run a little smaller. Lures or bait work well early in the season, but all three lakes are easily fished with a fly. In early season, come prepared for mosquitoes. The trail is snowbound into June most years.

ROUND LAKE (Jefferson Co.) A trout lake in the Santiam Pass area NW of Suttle Lake. Take FS 12 north from Hwy. 20 one mile east of the Suttle Lake turn-off. FS 1210, a loop road, leads to the lake. Ignore the first crossing of this road one mile from the highway, and continue a bit over one mile to the second intersection. From there it is about 4 miles to the lake.

Round has only 22 acres but is fairly deep and holds up well. Brook trout and rainbow are stocked, and a lot of trout are caught here averaging 8-12 inches, with quite a few to 18 inches. There is a small improved campground on the east side of the lake. The Forest Service grants a use permit to church groups for an area on the west side. Motors are prohibited on the lake.

SALISBURY SLOUGH A backwater of the Columbia River, off I-84 at hwy. mile 76. It covers about 50 acres and can be accessed at Mayer State Park, where there is a concrete boat ramp and ample parking. Take Exit 76. The slough may contain any of the Columbia River species.

SAND LAKE One of the I-84 ponds associated with the Columbia River, located at highway mile 94. Just one acre, it is south of I-84, with limited unimproved parking for eastbound traffic. It may contain any of the Columbia's warmwater species.

SAND DUNE LAKE One of the I-84 ponds adjacent to the Columbia River at hwy. mile 92.3. This one acre pond is between east and westbound freeway lanes. There is no parking for westbound traffic, and only limited parking for eastbound. It may contain any of the Columbia's warmwater species.

SCOUT LAKE (Jefferson Co.) A small lake 1/2 mile south of the west end of Suttle Lake. This lake is currently not stocked and is probably barren. A campground is located on the east shore.

SIMTUSTUS RESERVOIR (a.k.a. Lake Simtustus, Warm Springs Indian Reservation) A reservoir created by Pelton Dam, a power dam on the Deschutes River west of Madras. Most fishing here is for kokanee, but huge rainbow trout are occasionally taken. This is the smaller of two major impoundments on the Deschutes. The second, Lake Billy Chinook, is just upriver.

To reach the reservoir's western shore, take the Pelton turn-off about 3 miles south of the community of Warm Springs. A paved road leads to Pelton Park, where PGE maintains a boat launch. East shore access is from Indian Park, a campground on the Warm Springs Reservation. Best bet here is to ask for directions at Warm Springs Information Center when you stop to pick up your fishing permit.

The dam backs up about 8 miles of river, all the way to Round Butte Dam. Angling is almost exclusively by boat, as there is no access to the canyon much above the dam. The lake is stocked with rainbow, kokanee, and most recently with brown trout. Angling is generally only fair, with most fishing in the upper part of the lake, although early and late in the season anglers have good luck throughout the reservoir.

Trolling is the most popular method, with bait angling the next choice. Rainbow trout average 10-12 inches, but some go larger—much larger. Trout 25 pounds have been taken here. Not many anglers know about or go after these large fish, and anglers must use different tactics to attract them. Big fish want big lures, and stay fairly deep throughout most of the season. Here's a chance to see if that fish finder was worth what you gave that friendly fellow at the boat show.

Bull trout (Dolly Varden) are infrequently taken on troll and bait, averaging 10-12 inches, with a very few 3-4 pounds.

Lake Simtustus is within the boundaries of Warm Springs Indian Reservation, and a tribal permit is required to fish it. A daily permit is modestly priced and covers the whole family. Permits can be purchased at the grocery store in Warm Springs.

A 10 mph speed limit is in effect on all but the lower 3/4 mile of the reservoir. Boat landing on the western shore is allowed only at Indian Park. Boats may be launched at Pelton Park and Indian Park, with camping allowed at Indian Park only. Supplies are available at Pelton Park. Simtustus was named after a Warm Springs warrior who served as a US Army scout in the Piute wars of the 1860s and lived on the reservation to his death in 1926.

SISTERS MIRROR LAKE A very scenic lake with only fair angling for rainbow trout in the Wickiup Plains area north of Elk Lake, south of the Three Sisters. It is best reached by Trail 20, which heads north from Century Drive near Sink Creek, 2 miles north of Elk Lake. It's about 4 miles by trail to the lake. The Pacific

Crest Trail from the Horse Lake area approaches the lake from the south.

Though stocked with rainbow trout, it is not a rich lake and doesn't produce well. Fish run 6-10 inches but are fished down early. Flyfishing is the best method on this shallow, 16 acre lake. There are good campsites all around the lake, and better lakes are nearby. See Denude, Burnt Top, Nash.

SNELL LAKE A nice 9 acre hike-in trout lake in the Deschutes National Forest between Crescent and Summit Lakes. Snell can be reached by trail 1/8 mile NW of Farrell Lake, less than one mile from the Summit Lake Rd. See Farrell for detailed road and trail directions.

Both brook and rainbow trout are stocked, but brookies dominate the catch. Brook trout average 10-12 inches, and fish up to 18 inches have been reported. Snell Lake is fairly shallow, and fly fishing is good late in the year. Nearby Farrell Lake also contains trout.

SNOW CREEK A small, clear trout stream which joins the upper Deschutes River just above Cow Meadow on the north shore of Crane Prairie Reservoir. Snow Creek flows only about 5 miles from springs NE of the Deschutes Bridge Guard Station on the Cascade Lakes Hwy. It offers difficult fishing for rainbow and brook trout. Spring fed, it is very clear and cold, and light tackle is a must. The fish here will take a fly. No good trail follows the stream, and the banks are very brushy. The upper portion is crossed by FS 4270 south of Deschutes Bridge. FS 40 to Cow Meadow crosses the creek one mile above its mouth.

SNOWSHOE LAKES Three remote hike-in trout lakes roughly half-way between Big Cultus Lake and Mink Lake in Three Sisters Wilderness. The area is at least a 7 mile hike from the nearest road. The lakes are north of Winopee Lake on a trail that runs from the west end of Big Cultus Lake to Mink Lake. The trail is usually clear of snow by late June, but bring dry footwear, as the snow melt tends toi pool along the Winopee Trail. Unless you are camped in the Mink Lake Basin, you will probably approach from Big Cultus.

First chore is to reach the western end of Big Cultus. Your choices are to hike around the north shore on a good trail, to hike north from road's end near Deer Lake, or to boat across to West Cultus Lake Campground. The latter will save about 3 miles of hiking. From the west end of Big Cultus Lake take Trail 16 north about 5 miles to Winopee Lake. Here the trail splits. Follow Trail 35, the eastern fork. Lower Snowshoe Lake is about 1/3 mile north of Winopee on the east side of the trail.

This fairly shallow lake is 18 acres acres, with a rocky ledge that runs along the west shore. Infrequently visited, it has some nice brook trout 8-12 inches, with some to 16 inches. All methods of angling can be effective, but this is a great flyfishing situation.

Middle Snowshoe Lake, 1/4 mile west of the north end of Lower, is only 3 acres. It's stocked with rainbow trout. Continuing north on the trail 1/2 mile brings you to Upper Snowshoe Lake, the largest of the group, covering 30 acres. It is also the shallowest, with a maximum depth of only 8 ft., and will occasionally winterkill. Upper Snowshoe produces medium-size brook trout.

From Upper Snowshoe the trail continues north into the rich Mink Lake Basin, reaching Mink Lake in about 2 1/2 miles. There are many opportunities for anglers willing to explore with map and rod from Winopee north.

SPARKS LAKE A large fly-only brook trout lake just off the Cascades Lakes Hwy. directly south of the Three Sisters. The lake is visible from the highway, about 28 miles SW of Bend and 3 miles beyond the Mt. Bachelor ski area. A spur road leads to the east shore of the lake. Sparks Lake campground was recently closed. A trail leads from Soda Creek Campground south 2 miles to the south end of the lake.

Sparks Lake covers a lot of area, about 400 acres, and none of it is more than 10 feet deep. Its water is a rich nutrient broth that produces plump trout. A narrow extension of the lake winds south about one mile from the campground into a lava field. Here you will find the deepest water and, as soon as the lake warms, the most action. Hiking along this rocky shoreline is almost impossible due to rock walls and crevasses.

Brook trout here average 8-13 inches, with some 16-17 inches. Use streamers during the day and small dry flies in evening. Bucktails and Mickey Finns are favored for trolling. The fishing is tops right after ice-out if you can fight your way in through the snow. A low snowpack year augurs great fishing here.

The lake's waters seep into the lava field, and at one time the seepage was so extreme that in fall it was often necessary to drag boats 50-200 yards to deeper water. The Forest Service and the Dept. of Fish and Wildlife have plugged many of the lava leaks and stabilized the summer water level, but it can still be a problem to boaters.

Motors are allowed for transportation on the lake, but fishing is prohibited while the motor is operating. This still allows trolling a fly while rowing or wind drifting.

The campground on the lake's east shore is currently closed. Check with forest service for an update. There are a few RV sites along the road. Soda Creek Campground is on the main road about one mile from the water. A small campground no longer shown on the forest map is still available at the NW corner of the lake. The road to the camp turns off the highway 1/2 mile east of Devils Lake. There is no boat ramp here, but a canoe or raft can be launched in the creek and paddled into the lake.

SPOON LAKE (Warm Springs Indian Reservation) A shallow 2 acre lake on the west side of the Skyline Rd. between Horseshoe and Breitenbush Lakes. A small population of brook trout is present but subject to winterkill. The lake is on the reservation, but no tribal permit is required at this time. Overnight camping is permitted here. See breitenbush lake for road directions.

SQUARE LAKE A hike-in trout lake one mile NE of the Santiam Pass on Hwy. 20. Take the Pacific Crest Trail north 1/4 mile from its crossing of the highway 1/2 mile east of the entrance to Hoodoo Ski Bowl. Trail 65 takes off to the east and leads a bit over one mile to the lake.

Square lake is 55 acres and fairly deep. It's fished pretty hard, but continues to produce good catches. Brook and cutthroat trout are stocked. Most fish are 8-11 inches, with some to 14 inches. A rubber boat will come in handy here. Bait angling is good in spring, and lures and flies will also work. Following the trail along the outlet creek will bring you to Long Lake, 1/2 mile to the east, where there is also good fishing. Good natural campsites are available.

SQUAW CREEK (Jefferson Co.) Heading on the eastern slopes of the Three Sisters and flowing through the town of Sisters into canyon country to the NE. It joins the Deschutes about 3 miles upriver from Lake Billy Chinook. Below Sisters, Squaw Creek flows through its own canyon. Unimproved roads drop down to it at Camp Polk and at several points to the north. These roads are shown on the Deschutes National Forest map.

Much of the creek goes dry during irrigation season, as water is removed from above. Except in early spring, there is little or no fishing in the upper creek. There is good early angling at the lower end.

STRIDER LAKE A seldom-fished, deep 3 acre lake above Little Cultus, just off the road to Taylor Burn. See directions to Little Cultus lake. At Little Cultus Lake Campground, follow the primitive Irish and Taylor lakes road, FS 600, west about 2 miles. Strider is about 3/4 mile past the Lemish Lake Trailhead, on the north side of the road. There is no trail to the lake, but it's a fairly easy 1/2 mile bushwhack north.

You will be rewarded with some very sporting brook trout. There are a few logs to cast from, and the fishing's generally good along the rock slide, but a raft or float tube would come in handy.

SUMMIT LAKE (Klamath Co.) A large alpine lake on the summit between the Willamette and Deschutes River drainages. From Crescent Lake Junction on Hwy. 58, drive around the NW shore of Crescent Lake to FS 6010, the Summit Lake Rd. This road leads west about 1/4 mile south of Tandy Bay Campground. Summit Lake is a bit over 5 miles by good dirt road. Diamond Peak stakes out the northern horizon, and Sawtooth Mountain the southern. This is a beautiful lake, surrounded by spruce and pine, but like Waldo Lake to the north, the fish come hard here. At an elevation of 5553 ft., the lake is usually snowbound until late June.

Summit is about 500 acres but is not a rich lake, and fishing is only fair. Some anglers do well, but locating the fish here is a problem. Brook and rainbow trout are stocked, and a population of Mackinaw is self sustaining. The altitude and extremely clear water lead to slow growth of the stocked fish. Brook trout average about 10 inches, get up to 18, and are plentiful if you can locate the schools. Trolling in different areas is the best way to do this. Not many large fish are seen. Most rainbow caught are 8-10 inches, but fish to 20 inches are present. Both rainbow and brook trout can be taken by flyfishing in early morning and evening. Few anglers try for the Mackinaw, but they do show up occasionally on deep trolls. Summit Lake Mackinaw rarely exceed 8 pounds.

Bring lots of mosquito repellent! There's a good campground at the N W corner, and Summit makes a nice base camp for exploring other smaller lakes. See Windy Lakes, Suzanne, Darlene. The Pacific Crest Trail touches the SW corner of Summit and crosses the road 1/4 mile west of the camp.

SUTTLE LAKE A popular multi-use lake in the Deschutes National Forest just off Hwy. 20 NW of Sisters, featuring both kokanee and waterskiing. Follow Hwy. 20 (from Albany or Bend). The lake is just 7 miles east of the Santiam Pass summit.

Kokanee (landlocked salmon) are the main feature for anglers on this 240 acre lake. Late

May and June are most productive, but fish are taken throughout the season, with bait the favored method. Bait anglers fish perrywinkles or caddis fly larvae as one would a single egg. Kokanee here run 7-12 inches, with a 10 inch average. Though generally smaller than Kokanee in other Cascade lakes, the Suttle Lake population is numerous, outnumbering rainbow three to one. Check current regulations for a special generous bag limit.

Legal rainbow are stocked in spring, and there is a reproducing population of browns. Browns to 16 inches and an occasional 4-5 pounder are taken on lures or bait. Lake Creek and nearby Blue and Scout lakes offer additional angling opportunities.

A good family lake, Suttle offers pleasant swimming and opportunities for recreational boating, with an area roped-off for waterskiing. Mosquitoes, for some reason, are a rarity here. FS 2070 circles the lake, and there are four boat ramps on the south shore. Four USFS campgrounds are located at NE and SW ends of the lake and on the south shore. Equipment rentals, lodging, and supplies are available at a resort on the NE end and at Blue Lake Resort.

SUZANNE LAKE One of a pair of good hike-in trout lakes above Crescent and Summit Lakes. The Trailhead is 1/2 mile west of the Spring Campground entrance road at Crescent. It's about a 3 mile hike to the junction with Trail 46. Hike about 1/2 mile east on 46 to reach Suzanne and her neighbor Darlene. From Summit Lake it's about a 5 mile hike on Trail 46, past Windy Lakes, to Suzanne. The trailhead is off the south side of FS 6010.

Suzanne covers about 14 acres and is very deep. Rainbow average 12 inches, with an occasional 18 incher. Brook trout are also stocked, with catches to 16 inches. Flyfishing is good except at mid-day.

TAYLOR LAKE (Deschutes Co) The larger, but slightly less productive, of a pair of closely nestled Cascade summit lakes known as Irish and Taylor. These are scenic trout lakes that you can drive to if you're careful and have a high center vehicle. The road in is not quite a jeep trail, but not a lot better. Irish and Taylor are about mid-way between Waldo and Cultus Lakes SW of Bend in the Deschutes National Forest. The Pacific Crest Trail follows the west shore. (See irish lake for complete directions.)

Brook and cutthroat trout in Taylor average 9-12 inches, with a few to 16. The fish in Taylor usually run slightly smaller than those in Irish, but are generally easier to catch. There's good fly angling here, but be warned—the mosquitoes can be ferocious, especially in spring. Try fishing the ice-out or early fall to avoid these pests. Motorboats are prohibited on the lake, so plan to row or paddle if you want to troll. There are good primitive campsites here and at Irish, and the Pacific Crest Trail leads north to other high lakes. See Brahma, Red Slide. The roads in are generally snowbound till late June or early July. Check with the Forest Service for road conditions.

TAYLOR LAKE (Wasco Co.) One of the I-84 ponds adjacent to the Columbia River, offering good angling for trout, bass, crappie, channel catfish, and bullhead. There is limited unimproved parking for westbound traffic, but best access for parking and boat launching is on Taylor Lake Rd. Take Exit 83, north and then go west on Frontage Rd. to the Taylor Lake Rd. Taylor covers 35 acres.

The lake was long managed for bass and panfish, but several years ago fingerling steelhead were added to feed the bass. These rainbow trout thrived. Since then, trout have been stocked, and trout anglers currently outnumber bass anglers. There's no boat ramp, but it's easy to launch car-top boats. There are no improvements or campsites here.

TEDDY LAKES North and South Teddy Lake are two good hike-in lakes, far enough away to take the pressure off but close enough (if you have a boat) for an easy day hike. The lakes are in the Cultus Lake area about 50 miles SW of Bend. The Cultus to Mink Lake Trail runs between the lakes about one mile north of the west end of Big Cultus. Start at Big Cultus Lake Campground, and follow Trail 16 along the north shore. At the west end of the lake the trail heads north, and South Teddy is one mile up on the west side of the trail. From the campground it's about 4 miles to the lake. Many anglers use a boat to get to the west end of Big Cultus, then hike the remaining mile.

South Teddy, at 17 acres and 10 ft. maximum depth, is smaller and shallower than North. It provides brook trout 7-18 inches with the average 11-12 inches. The north lake is 1/4 mile NE of South Teddy, and is twice as large and deep. It is stocked with rainbow to about 13 inches. Both lakes offer excellent flyfishing, but bait and lures are also used. There are nice campsites at Big Cultus Lake.

THE DALLES POOL (a.k.a. Lake Celilo, Celilo Lake) See Celilo.

THREE CREEKS LAKE A 28 acre trout lake in the Deschutes National Forest on the north slope of the Cascades west of Bend. It's cupped in a depression in the mountains, at elevation 6500 ft. and receives one of the heaviest snowfalls in the forest. To reach the lake, take FS 16 about 15 miles south from Sisters about 15 miles to the lake. The road is paved to within 1/2 mile of lake, and the rest is rough. From Bend it's 24 miles by way of Tumalo Creek Rd. west, then FS 4601, following the NW spur. The last 8 miles of this approach are rough. These roads usually open in mid-June or, in heavy snowpack years, around July 4.

The lake has rainbow trout and a sustaining population of brook trout. The trout run 8-15 inches. All fishing methods are used with success. There are two camping areas on the lake, and a third one mile north on FS 16. A trail leads west from Driftwood Campground, on the north shore of the lake, to Little Three Creeks Lake. This lake is about 1/2 the size of Big Three Creeks and has nice brook trout to 14 inches.

THREE CREEKS LAKE, LITTLE A wild brook trout lake just beyond Big Three Creeks Lake. About 14 acres and 10 feet deep, it can be reached by Trail 97 from Big Three Creeks. Its brook trout are self-sustaining and reach 14 inches. See Three Creeks Lake for directions.

TIMBER LAKE A hike-in lake in the Olallie Lake area north of Mt. Jefferson, about 100 miles from Portland. It is about one mile west of the south end of Olallie Lake. Take the trail west from the north end of Olallie, which meets the Pacific Crest Trail, and at 1/2 mile, head south on Trail 733 to Timber. The lake is less than 1/2 mile from the trail junction.

Timber is about 10 acres and fairly shallow. It's stocked by air every few years with brook and rainbow trout. The fish don't get large because of fairly heavy pressure, but fly angling in late summer and fall can net some nice fish. Besides, the setting's real pretty, and the hiking is easy. The road into Olallie Lake usually opens in late June. There are many other small hike-in lakes south and west.

TIMMY LAKE A tiny brook trout lake on the west side of the Pacific Crest Trail in the area north of the Irish-Taylor Lakes group. It's a bit over one mile NE of the north end of Irish Lake, and 1/3 mile south of Brahma Lake. See brahma for trail directions. The lake is on the top of a knoll and is hard to spot.

Timmy is easy to fish from shore. Only 3 acres but fairly deep, it has produced some big fish in the past. You can expect eager medium size brook trout if you can find the lake. There are other good lakes close by. See Red Slide, Gleneden, Lady, Brahma. A maze of potholes in the area breed confusion and a wretched excess of mosquitoes in spring.

TODD LAKE A brook trout lake 2 miles due north of Bachelor Butte in Deschutes National Forest west of Bend. Take Hwy. 46, the Cascades Lakes Hwy., about 2 miles past the Bachelor Ski Resort parking area to FS 370, which joins from the north. At 1/2 mile, the Todd Lake Rd. heads east. This is blocked to motor vehicles, so you'll have to hike in, but the lake is only 100 yards from the main road.

Todd Lake is 45 acres and provides angling for brook trout to 15 inches. For a week or so after the ice melts fishing is hot, but during the rest of the year the fish are hard to catch. There is a small tent campground on the west shore of the lake, as well as a picnic area.

TOOLEY LAKE One of the I-84 ponds adjacent to the Columbia River, located at hwy. mile 79. It covers 30 acres south of the freeway, with limited unimproved parking at the west end of the lake for eastbound traffic only. Most of the north shore is privately owned. It may contain any of the Columbia's warmwater species.

TROUT LAKE (Warm Springs Indian Reservation) Trout Lake is the lowest of a chain of five good lakes which begins with Olallie Lake. It gets its name from an amazingly self-sustaining population of trout which has maintained a fishery in the lake without any additional stocking for at least 20 years. It is 6 1/2 miles NW from Warm Springs by way of Hwy. 26, then 18 miles west on a good gravel road.

Trout is at 4600 feet and covers 23 acres, about 1/3 in shoal area. It is a pear-shaped lake with a maximum depth of 28 feet. A tribal fishing permit is required for this lake. There is a campground here. The lake's outflow is the source of Mill Creek

TUMALO CREEK A trout stream about 20 miles long which heads on the east slope of the Three Sisters west of Bend. It flows east and north to join the Deschutes River north of Bend. It is the municipal water supply for Bend. Several good roads follow the stream and cross it several times. FS 4601, which runs west from the west end of Bend, picks up the creek about 7 miles from town and parallels it for several miles to Tumalo Falls Campground. Here trails follow the major tributaries of the creek west.

The creek has a fair population of small wild trout averaging 7-9 inches. Bait, lures, or flies can all be used. The creek is a nice close-in recreation area for Bend residents. Shevlin City Park is located on the creek 3 miles NW of town.

TUNNEL LAKE One of the I-84 ponds adjacent to the Columbia River, located at hwy. mile 72.6. Just one acre, it is immediately west of Memaloose State Park between I-84 and the railroad. Best access is for westbound traffic. It may contain any of the Columbia's warmwater species.

TWIN LAKE, NORTH (Deschutes Co.) A good size trout lake one mile north of Wickiup Reservoir in the Deschutes Forest SW of Bend. South Twin, similar in character and productivity, is one mile south. North Twin is a little over 45 miles from Bend by way of the Cascade Lakes Hwy. 46. For directions, see south twin.

North Twin is about 130 acres and 60 feet deep. It is stocked heavily with rainbow, and the catch averages 10 inches, with some larger. A kokanee stocking program has been discontinued. Bait angling and trolling are both good, and flyfishing is excellent at times. There is a good campground with boat ramp on the north shore of the lake. Motorboats are prohibited.

TWIN LAKE, SOUTH (Deschutes Co.) A good trout lake 1/2 mile north of the main body of Wickiup Reservoir, about 40 miles SW of Bend. Many people fishing Wickiup camp here. From Bend you can drive to the lake by the Cascades Lakes Hwy., taking the Wickiup turn-off (County Rd. 42) east one mile south of Crane Prairie. The Twin Lakes turn-off is one mile past the Deschutes crossing.

Alternately, you may drive south from Bend on Hwy. 97. Take the Sunriver turn-off, which is the east end of County Rd. 42, and follow it to the Twin Lakes turn-off, following signs to Crane Prairie or Wickiup Reservoir. From the Willamette Valley, drive SE from Eugene on Hwy. 58 to the Davis Lake turn-off, 3 miles past Crescent Lake Junction. Follow Davis Lake signs to the south end of the Cascades Lakes Hwy., and drive past Davis to the Wickiup turn-off, County Rd. 42.

South Twin is about 120 acres and reaches a depth of 55 feet. It is stocked with both fingerling and legal rainbow in the spring. The fingerlings grow to size by late season. The catch average is 9-10 inches, and trout to 15 inches are taken.

South Twin is suitable for all methods of angling. Bait fishing is popular, but doesn't seem to produce any better than other methods. Many anglers fish too deep, below the oxygen layer, so stay shallow.

There is a resort just south of the campground where supplies and boat rentals are available. If fishing on South Twin is slack, an arm of Wickiup Reservoir is only 200 yards west. There is a good Forest Service campground, West South Twin, on this arm directly across from the resort. The resort keeps boats here for use on Wickiup. And if Wickiup is slow, there is always Crane Prairie 3 miles north.

South Twin Campground, on the west shore, has a boat ramp. Motorboats are prohibited on the lake

TWIN LAKES (Wasco Co.) Two good hike-in brook trout lakes 6 miles south of Government Camp on the south slope of Mt. Hood, reached by way of the Pacific Crest Trail. The lower lake covers 12 acres, and the upper or north lake about 10 acres. Follow Hwy. 26 four miles south from its junction with Hwy. 35 to the crossing of the Pacific Crest Trail 1/2 mile north of Frog Lake (watch for a road sign). The lower lake is an easy mile hike east and north on the PCT. The upper lake is 1/2 mile further north.

These lakes are well stocked with fingerling brook trout. They are fairly deep (lower, 40 feet; upper, 50 feet) and usually have some holdover fish of good size. The lakes see a lot of angling pressure. There is an improved camp at lower lake and a full-service campground at Frog Lake south of the trailhead.

UPPER LAKE An easy to reach hike-in brook trout lake in the Olallie Lake area, about 100 miles from Portland. See Olallie Lake for road directions. Take the Pacific Crest Trail west about 1 1/2 miles from the north end of Olallie Lake.

Upper is stocked by air with brook trout fingerlings every few years. The lake covers 8 acres and is of moderate depth. It's a good fly-fishing spot for brook trout 6-12 inches. There are fair natural campsites at the lake.

VIENTO LAKE One of the I-84 ponds adjacent to the Columbia River, at hwy. mile 56. It covers 4 acres at the mouth of Viento Creek, with good access from Viento State Park at Exit 56. It may contain any of the Columbia's warmwater species.

VIEW LAKE Offering a good view of the large and small lakes within the eastern half of the Olallie Lake area. This 10 acre lake is one of many which are a short hiking distance from the Skyline Rd. at Olallie Lake. See Olallie Lake for road directions. To reach View, take the cut-off trail to the Pacific Crest Trail from the north end of Olallie (about 1/2 mile) and go south past Timber Lake for another 1/2 mile, or head due west from the Skyline Rd. at about the middle of Monon Lake, for a half mile uphill bushwhack.

View is stocked by air with brook trout fingerlings. Covering 7 acres, it offers good fishing for trout 8-12 inches, but no large fish. Fly angling is good, but bait and lure are also effective.

WAHTUM LAKE Next to Lost Lake, Wahtum is the largest lake in the northern Mt. Hood area, and some nice fish are taken out of it each year. It is 6 miles north of Lost Lake, about 25 miles from Hood River. From the community of Dee SW of Hood River, drive 3 miles west to FS 13, the Lost Lake Rd. At about 10 miles, take FS 1310 to the right and follow it about 6 miles to Wahtum Lake Campground. The lake is to the west, at the bottom of a quarter mile trail which descends about 200 ft. from road level.

Wahtum covers 57 acres and is exceptionally clear and deep. Mid-lake, the bottom is 180 ft. below, and the depth and clarity give the lake a deep blue hue. It sits in a depression and is often sheltered from the wind. In the morning calm a fly line seems to hang suspended in air as it floats on the lake surface.

Wahtum is more easily fished from a boat than from shore. A canoe can be (has been) lugged down to the lake, but it's a chore on steep switch-back terrain. A rubber boat or float tube would be easier. Fishing is best in the 10-30 ft. shoal areas. Brook trout here average 10 inches, with a few to 15. Once in a while the lake will turn up a real lunker.

There are several nice natural campsites here, and huckleberries in season. Bring your rain gear and warm clothes when you come. Maybe it's just the luck of the draw, but Wahtum seems to have its own private cloud. If the weather is crummy anywhere within 200 miles, it'll be cold and crummy at Wahtum. For other fishing lakes nearby, see hicks and scout.

WALTON LAKE A 25 acre lake created by damming a spring creek in the headwaters of Ochoco Creek, a contribution of Isaac Walton League members in the Prineville area. Take Hwy. 26 east of Prineville 35 miles to the Ochoco Cr. Rd. FS 22, which leads to the lake, about 6 miles from the junction.

Walton is at elevation 5150 ft. and is 25 ft. deep maximum. Each year it is stocked with legal rainbow, and catches 8-10 inches are taken on bait and lure. A few reach 16 inches. There is a large campground at the lake.

WARM SPRINGS RIVER (Warm Springs Indian Reservation) The Warm Springs River is open to fishing only in the vicinity of Kah-Nee-Ta Resort. To reach it, drive north from Warm Springs about 10 miles. The way is well signed. The open area is between Kah-Nee-Tah Village Bridge and the marker at the east end of the golf course. A paved road follows the northern bank of the fishing area.

The river is well stocked with rainbow trout. Anglers are prohibited from using cluster eggs, spinners, wobblers, or any attractor blade or device. A tribal permit specifically for this area is required.

WARREN LAKE A 5 acre brook trout lake at the head of Warren Creek, which flows north 3 miles into the Columbia River, 9 miles west of the town of Hood River. The lake is 1/4 mile from the end of a primitive road SE of Mt. Defiance. You might want to walk the last mile of road. To reach the trailhead, follow the directions to Bear Lake, but take FS 2821 when it forks NE off 2820. The road forks after 2 miles. Take the left (west) fork. (Here is where you should begin to consider the capabilities of your vehicle.) About 3/4 mile beyond, the road makes a T intersection with the Mt. Defiance Rd. Turn right, away from Mt. Defiance. About 1/3 mile ahead the road ends at a trail crossing. The trail west leads to Warren Lake.

WASCO LAKE A good brook trout lake below the Pacific Crest Trail 2 miles NE of Three Fingered Jack in Mt. Jefferson Wilderness. The most direct approach to the lake is 1 1/2 miles by Trail 65, which heads at Jack Lake. The trail passes along the west shore of the lake 1/2 mile before joining the Pacific Crest Trail just north of Minto Pass. See jack lake for road directions.

Wasco is at elevation 5150 ft. and covers 20 acres. The lake is over 20 ft. deep, and all methods will take fish. A hike up to the PCT and back south 1/2 mile will take you to Catlin and Koko lakes, two small brookie lakes that are lightly fished.

WEST COVE One of the I-84 ponds adjacent to the Columbia River, located at hwy. mile 62.3. It covers 10 acres at the west end of the Hood River Industrial Park and is accessible from Exit 63. It may contain any of the Columbia's warmwater species.

WHITE RIVER A good size tributary of the Deschutes, flowing almost 50 miles from its glacial origin on Mt. Hood's south face to its confluence with the Deschutes north of Maupin.

To reach it from Portland, follow Hwy. 26 to Mt. Hood, then Hwy. 35, which crosses the upper end of the river. FS 48 heads south from Hwy. 35 just beyond the crossing and parallels the river's Iron Creek tributary, reaching the river itself at Barlow Crossing Campground. The primitive Old Barlow Rd. also accesses the river at Barlow Crossing. FS 3530 follows the stream's west bank for about 4 miles from Barlow Crossing past White River Station Campground. Other campgrounds on and near the stream include Keeps Mill, Forest Creek, Grindstone, and Devil's Half Acre Meadow. This middle section of the river is stocked with rainbow at the campgrounds and has some native trout.

East of Mt. Hood National Forest, the river cuts a deep canyon. Anglers can reach the canyon in the Smock Prairie area. Take Hwy. 216 to a north-bound county road about mid-way between Wapinita and Pine Grove. The canyon is about 2 1/2 miles past the Oak Grove School. This road crosses the river and continues north to Wamic. Hwy. 197 crosses the river east of Tygh Valley, and there is pretty good early season fishing in the flatland stretch from there to the series of three falls about 3 miles above the Deschutes confluence. Rainbow average 7-11 inches.

Bait produces best and is legal above the first fall above the Deschutes. Below the first falls, angling is currently restricted to the use of artificial flies or lures with barbless hooks. Check current regulations for other information and restrictions on fishing the river.

WICKIUP RESERVOIR One of Oregon's largest and most productive artificial impoundments, created by a dam on the upper Deschutes River in Deschutes National Forest, about 40 miles SW of Bend. Wickiup is a fertile lake with large self-sustaining populations of brown trout, kokanee, and coho salmon. Coho and some rainbow are also stocked annually, though efforts to get a naturally reproducing population of rainbow started in the reservoir have failed. Wickiup is most successfully fished by anglers who have dedicated their weekends and vacations to learning how the fish respond to discreet changes in water level, temperature, and time.

To reach Wickiup from Bend, take Hwy. 97 south to County Rd. 43, just north of LaPine. Turn south onto FS 4380 about 2 1/4 miles beyond Pringle Falls. This road follows all but the west shore of the lake. Paved forest roads connect the reservoir to all the major lakes in the area, including Odell, Crescent, and Davis lakes to the south.

Wickiup covers nearly 10,000 acres when full. Much of the reservoir is under 20 ft. deep, but the old Deschutes channel carves an arc in the lake bed from the Deschutes arm in the north to the southern end of the dam in the east. The river had cut a steep rocky channel, and this now provides a cool deep water refuge for fish in late summer. The water in this channel is over 60 ft. deep in places, with much irregular structure. A shallower channel leads east from the Davis Creek arm. Deepest water in the reservoir is at the intersection of a line drawn out from the Deschutes and Davis channels. Wickiup is significantly affected by drought. In 1988 the reservoir was severely drawn down, and the fishery was poor. Heavy draw-down is also probable in 1989. These severe draw-downs destroy many juvenile coho and kokanee, but the brown trout are not affected.

Wickiup is very large and difficult to fish. Its fishery changes as the water level changes even during a normal season. At high water, fish are generally widely scattered. As drawdown occurs, they move into the channels. In spring the water temperature is uniform, and catches can be made in as little as 10 ft. of water.

Coho and kokanee provide the most popular sport here. They are taken beginning with the spring opener. Throughout the summer, bait fishermen and trollers work the main channels

and the dam area. Bait fishermen seem to fare better, offering a concoction called the *Wickiup sandwich*—a pinch of crawdad tail, a chunk of nightcrawler, and a kernel of white corn on a size 8 hook. Trollers use kokanee hardware tipped with nightcrawler or corn. Near the end of August, kokanee assume spawning colors and move into the waters of the Deschutes channel, which are closed to angling.

Coho are schooling fish and tend to feed in concert. If the splashing itself doesn't alert you to the performance, look for the cluster of boats and follow the whoops and hollers. The coho fishery lasts through early October, with fish feeding actively in the channels and in the Gull Point area through September and early October. Salmon spawning grounds are protected by a September 1 closure of the Deschutes from the ODFW marker below Brown's Creek up to Crane Prairie Dam.

Wickiup's browns are imposing, if less numerous, than the salmon, and anglers who pursue them here are a dedicated lot. The typical Wickiup brown is 10-20 inches, weighing an average of 2-3 pounds, with 9 and 10 pounders available and a rumor of grandfolks to 20 pounds. A state record brown taken here (now deposed by a Paulina catch) weighed 24 pounds, 14 ounces. Unlike the salmon, browns survive their annual spawning migration to grow another year, and another, and ... Look for big browns in the old channels where the water is cool and the current serves up the meal. Trollers work at about 15 ft. depth, trolling shallower as the weather cools. They troll quickly, attempting to imitate the bait fish and cover greater area. Anglers also cast to the edges of drop-offs and along channel ledges.

Browns are nocturnal feeders. As evening approaches, they venture into the shallows where they are available for flyfishing. Fly anglers also work the points and ledges. Early morning and dusk are said to be the best times to catch the big trout, whose many years in the lake have increased their savy as well as their girth. Fish before and after the sun hits the water. Cloudy days can also be good. In September browns begin to gather along the Deschutes channel and off Gull Point, feeding enthusiastically prior to their late (November or December) spawning. In addition to whatever insects are available, they gorge on crayfish and on Wickiup's hearty population of chubs. Gold or bronze finish minnow imitations (Rapalla, Rebel, Bomber) do a good chub imitation. Flatfish and large streamers are also popular. Crayfish (whole or tails only) are hard to beat.

Tasty native whitefish are also available in quantity in the reservoir and shouldn't be ignored. Averaging 2 pounds and running to 4, they are good eating, especially smoked. Look for them in the clear cold water (such as the Davis Creek Arm, where they gather prior. to spawning). Schools may also congregate in creek coves, flats, and riffles where they feed on aquatic insects. Because they favor clear water, whitefish must be approached with light line. They have small mouths, so use small bait (natural insect larvae on small egg hooks) or imitations (small dark patterns size 14 to 18). A light, flexible rod will allow you to play the fish to a satisfactory conclusion without breaking the line.

Wickiup is primarily a boat fishery, though early season anglers do well at the dam and along the channel. There are good boat ramps at Gull Point and North Wickiup campgrounds at the mouth of the Deschutes Arm, at West South Twin Campground on the lower Deschutes Arm, and at Reservoir Campground on the SW shore. Boats can also be launched at Wickiup Butte Campground on the SE shore.

The resort at Twin Lakes keeps a fleet of rental boats on the Deschutes Arm. There is a 10 mile per hour speed limit there and in the Davis Creek Arm. Watch out for the pumice flats when the lake is low. It's easy to get stuck.

There are Forest Service campgrounds on the Deschutes Arm (Gull Point and North Wickiup), at Wickiup Butte near the east spillway, and at Reservoir Camp on the SW shore. Supplies, gas, a restaurant and accommodations are available at Twin Lakes Resort.

WILSON POND One of the I-84 ponds adjacent to the Columbia River, located at highway mile 71.4. Privately owned, it covers 5 acres between I-84 and the Union Pacific Railroad. Access is from Hwy. 30 with landowner permission only.

WINDY LAKES A group of 4 hike-in lakes not far from the Pacific Crest Trail SE of Summit Lake, SW of Crescent Lake. The trail begins on the road about 1/2 mile south of Tandy Bay Picnic Area on Crescent Lake, and it's a fairly steep hike in.

The Windys haven't been very productive, perhaps due to their location at 6000 ft. They are currently all stocked with eastern brook trout. South Windy has cutthroat, too, but they haven't shown well in the catch. The lakes range from 5-16 acres and are close together. The best bet is the south lake.

WINOPEE LAKE A fairly remote 40 acre hike-in lake between Mink Lake Basin and Big Cultus Lake. Winopee is a fair producer of good size brook and rainbow. It is about 8 miles by trail from the end of the road at the east end of Big Cultus. Some anglers run a boat to the west end of the big lake, cutting the hike in half.

Winopee has a lot of marshy shoals along the shoreline, and a rubber boat comes in handy. (Old Paint comes in handy for lugging a boat this far.) There is deep water, too, as the lake goes to 30 ft. in places, and many wild fish. Brook trout and rainbow 8 to 14 inches are available, and its a good flyfishing set-up. You can get through the snow in June in most years. There are other good lakes in the vicinity. See Snowshoe. Mosquitoes are fierce here in spring.

WYETH LAKE An I-84 pond adjacent to the Columbia River at hwy. mile 50.6. It may contain any of the Columbia River species. Covering 6 acres, it is located between I-84 and the railroad and is one of the few ponds in the series that can be reached by boat from the Columbia.

YAPOAH LAKE A small high lake that turns out good rainbow trout for the few who hike to it. Yapoah Lake is at 5800 ft., one mile east of Yapoah Crater in the McKenzie Pass area north of North Sister. To reach the lake you can take an unusual hike on the Pacific Crest Trail, heading south from the Dee Wright Observatory's lunar-like lava flow area. Hike a little over 2 miles south to the Matthieu Lakes, then take Trail 95, the Scott Trail, east one mile. From that point the lake is a 1/4 mile bushwhack due south. The trail in begins high, so there's not a lot of climbing. Better bring your Three Sisters Quadrangle topo map.

Rainbow stocked here run to 15 inches. The lake covers 10 acres and is 25 ft. deep. This is fairly open country, and the lake is easy to fish from shore. It's in a scenic area, worth the hike for the view of North Sister.

NORTHEAST ZONE

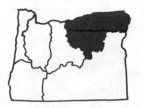

The Northeast Zone is all waters draining into the Columbia River east of the Deschutes River, including the Snake River system up to Hells Canyon Dam.

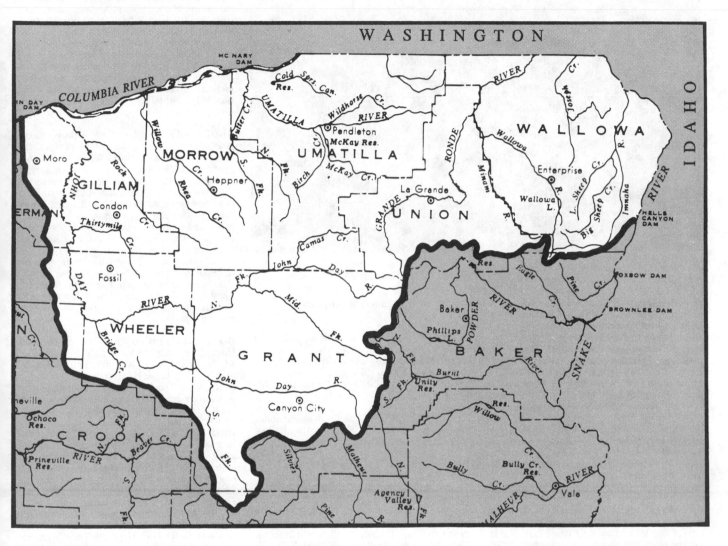

Our base camp is a small dome tent erected on a pillow of granite about 200 ft. above Moccasin Lake. This is wilderness, high in the Eagle Cap of Wallowa-Whitman National Forest.

We are comfortable in our eyrie, perched like a pair of eagles with the lake spread out below and the gray and chocolate peaks of the Wallow-as above. It's a scramble down to Moccasin, and we only go a few times each day—to fish, bathe, or fetch cooking water. Our map shows Pocket Lake a mile or so above and southwest of Moccasin, a glacial cirque ringed by ridges, unusually deep for its small acreage. We have heard rumors of nice size trout. We pack minimum supplies for a day trip and, rods in hand, begin the trek. It isn't a difficult climb, over large boulders, the ascent marked by rock cairns, though we remark that we wouldn't want to negotiate the descent in the dark...or the rain.

I love the look of these high mountain cirques, like fire opals set in rocky filligree, or a full teacup adrift on granite waves. We walk the lip of

the cup, admiring the view. And there are fish, too. I stand quietly back from water's edge watching one of good size sip the surface with a nonchalance that suggests she knows little of anglers. I select a fly, tie it on, check my back cast. I watch her feeding pattern and calculate where she will surface next.

So intent am I on the fish, I have lost track of the weather. A cloud is suddenly pouring through a notch in the peaks, like fake fog pumped onto a Hollywood set. I look up and see the cloud—then down as my fish sips just where I knew she would. She's making a slow circuit of a little cove.

"We should get out of here," whines my more prudent interior voice. "I know where she's going to rise next," whispers the other. I cast just as the cloud closes in, obscuring my partner on the nearby shore, the Wallowas, my fish, and the way back. I am alone on a rock in a world engulfed in white. Then she takes the fly—like a force reaching up out of the void.

The Northeast Zone is defined by the watersheds of the John Day, Grand Ronde, and Snake rivers. The John Day is a typical desert canyon stream in its lower stretches. The Grand Ronde is a wild stream, with much of its waters difficult to access. The Snake is as wild as they come, and you'll see little of it without a float or long hike.

Although the region is a long way from most of the northwest's population centers, a major interstate highway crossing through its heart (I-84) makes getting there simple. Two mountain ranges lift the terrain high enough to support timberlands. These ranges, the Blue and Wallowa mountains, receive more than twice as much precipitation as the Southeast Zone.

The Wallowas are unique in Oregon, being of granitic origin (as are the Rockies) rather than volcanic. These high peaks have been deeply carved by glaciers, and their rugged appearance has earned them the nickname "Oregon's Alps." Much of the range is within Eagle Cap Wilderness, and there the avid hiker will find unparalleled mountain vistas and darn good fishing, too.

WALLOWA MOUNTAINS
Steve Terrill, Photographer

ANEROID LAKE A large hike-in lake in Eagle Cap Wilderness, Wallowa-Whitman National Forest, with good angling for eastern brook and rainbow trout. The lake is cradled among high peaks and ridges at 7520 ft., six miles by good trail from the southern end of Wallowa Lake. Elevation gain is 2320 ft. Trail 1804 heads south from Wallowa Lake State Park at the south end of Hwy. 82, about 5 miles south of Joseph. Snow may block access until July.

Covering 39 acres, the lake supports populations of brook and rainbow trout to 14 inches, averaging 10 inches. Fly angling is good in August and September. As this is a wilderness area, there are no developed campgrounds, but there are good campsites at the lake. Campers are urged to use no-trace camping methods.

BALM CREEK RESERVOIR A good size reservoir near the head of Balm Creek, a tributary of the lower Powder River NE of Baker. Follow Hwy. 203 about 25 miles north to Medical Springs, then take FS 70 east about 10 miles to the reservoir. Another gravel road, FS 7040, comes in from Hwy. 86 to the south. The turn-off to the reservoir is about 22 miles east of Baker. Other roads come in from the east and north.

The reservoir covers about 110 acres when full and affords good angling for rainbow trout. It's usually stocked with fingerlings, and there is some carry-over, with fish to 15 inches. Bait is the most popular method.

Motors may be used to get around, but cannot be operating while fishing. Fishing usually holds up well into mid-summer when the water level drops. There are no improved campsites at the lake, but there is space for trailers. There are two campgrounds on FS 67 north and east of the reservoir. Follow FS 475 north to the junction with 67.

BARTH QUARRY POND In Umatilla County, a little pond whose bass and panfish fishery has been ruined by onions. *(Ask the locals to explain.)*

BATES POND An 8 acre former mill pond about 30 miles NE of John Day, just west of Bates. It is currently closed to public access due to work on the spillway and dam. For an update, check with the Dept. of Fish and Wildlife at John Day.

BIBBY RESERVOIR A 16 acre impoundment 5 miles west of Kent on Buckhollow Creek. It contains largemouth bass.

BIG SHEEP CREEK A tributary of the Imnaha River, lightly fished and supporting excellent populations of wild rainbow and bull (Dolly Varden) trout. It flows 25 miles to its confluence at the town of Imnaha, 32 miles east of Enterprise or Joseph on Hwy. 82. A primitive road follows the lower 12 miles. There is a 2 mile trail at road's end. To reach the headwaters from the west you'll need a map. Wallow-Whitman National Forest map, north half, shows the network of gravel and dirt tracks that take off from Little Sheep Rd. east of Joseph.

Trout here average 9-12 inches. Bait and flies are both productive, with angling best from August until October. There are no improved campsites streamside.

BILLY JONES LAKE A 6 acre hike-in lake near the top of Hurricane Divide in Wallowa-Whitman National Forest, well-stocked and supporting a population of fine rainbow to 14 inches. From Joseph, take the Hurricane Creek Rd. south to Hurricane Creek Campground. Follow Hurricane Creek Trail 1807 south about 7 miles to Trail 1824, a steep 3 mile switch-back to Echo Lake. Billy Jones can be reached by hiking south one mile from Echo Lake. There is no trail, and snow may block access until July.

Worms or eggs will work well in summer, with flies best in September. Try black ant, red ant, mosquito, and similar patterns. Angling season is determined by trail conditions, generally open July through September.

BIRCH CREEK A tributary of the lower Umatilla River which joins the river at Pendleton. About 30 miles long, it heads in the Pine Grove area south of Pilot Rock. It is followed closely by Hwy. 395 and by secondary roads from Pendleton to Pilot Rock. Most access is through private property. Ask permission to fish. South of Pilot Rock the creek is followed by paved and gravel roads up both the east and west forks. Fishing for wild rainbow is fair to good in early season. There are no campgrounds in the area. The creek has steelhead runs but is closed to steelhead and salmon angling.

BLUE LAKE (Wallowa Co.) A deep 30 acre hike-in brook trout lake, headwaters of the Minam River, in Wallowa-Whitman National Forest. From the community of Lostine, east of Enterprise, follow the Lostine River Rd. to the end. The trail to Blue heads south from Two Pan Campground. Follow the Lostine River Trail 1670 about 5.7 miles to Minam Lake. Blue Lake is .9 mile south of Minam's southern tip. Take the right fork at the trail junction. Snow may block access until July.

Blue Lake derives its rich color from its 62 ft. depth. It supports a large population of fair-size brook trout, which take flies and bait. Trout season is determined by trail conditions. August and September are generally the best angling months.

BOARDMAN POND #2 A 1/4 acre pond on Umatilla National Wildlife Refuge south of I-84. Turn right at the Boardman Exit. When the road dead-ends, work your way over to the pond. It has excellent bluegill, and reportedly contains crappie and walleye. Pond #1, also on the Refuge, is said to be inaccessible.

BRIDGE CREEK A scenic stream both near its source and confluence, offering fair trout angling. It flows through a variety of interesting eastern Oregon terrain, including a forest wilderness (Bridge Creek Wilderness, created in 1984), and the Painted Hills of the John Day Formation, a geologic study area.

Bridge Creek originates in springs near Mt. Pisgah in the Ochoco Mountains south of Mitchell, which is on Hwy. 26. There is an undeveloped campground (Carroll Camp, Ochoco National Forest) at the head of the creek near Pisgah Springs. The main attraction of the wilderness is North Point, a 600 ft. cliff overlooking central Oregon and the Cascade peaks. The wilderness itself, through which Bridge Creek flows 4 miles, is a mix of fir, larch, lodgepole, and ponderosa pine, with clearings of sagebrush, grass, and mountain mahogany typical of Oregon's high desert plateau.

Carroll Campground is accessed by two primitive roads off FS 22 south of Mitchell, about 39 miles east of Prineville. FS 22 is a paved road off Hwy. 26. A primitive road also meets the creek as it flows out of the Wilderness. To reach this track, turn south off Hwy. 26 at Mitchell. The track to Bridge Creek cuts off on the right about 1 3/4 miles south of town.

About 4 miles west of Mitchell, a road heads north from Hwy. 26, following Bridge Creek through the Painted Hills toward its confluence with the John Day near Burnt Ranch.

The Painted Hills are handsome red and yellow layered volcanic formations that are studied for their wealth of fossils and for the gologic story they tell—of volcanic eruptions, oceanic inundations, and climatic changes over the past 75 million years.

Bridge Creek provides fair trout angling in May and June after the spring run-off. Other than Carroll Camp in the headwaters, there is no camping streamside. There is a State Picnic Area on Bridge Creek Rd. about 10 miles NW of Mitchell at the beginning of the Painted Hills, a very pretty spot.

BULL PRAIRIE RESERVOIR Good trout water within easy reach, offering year-round angling. It's located about 35 miles south of Heppner, about 15 miles north of Spray, in the Umatilla National Forest. From Heppner, drive south on Hwy. 207 to FS 2039, which leads 2 1/2 miles east to the reservoir.

The 27 acre reservoir was built cooperatively by the Forest Service and Dept. of Fish and Wildlife in 1961. Fishing has been good for rainbow and brook trout 8-13 inches, and some to 16 inches are occasionally caught.

There is a campground with boat ramp on the lake. Motors are prohibited. Ice fishing is popular, but snow depth can make it a snowmobile or ski trek to get in. Bring your ice drill and camp stool, and join the fun. Don't forget that holes cut in the ice must be 12 inches or smaller in diameter by regulation.

BURNT RIVER Outlet of Unity Reservoir, featuring some large trout and a smallmouth bass fishery. The river flows east 77 miles, joining the Snake just east of Huntington on I-84. It is followed east by paved county roads from the reservoir downstream 30 miles to Bridgeport. This stretch is cross-ditched for irrigation purposes. From Bridgeport to Durkee on I-84, the river flows through the Burnt River Canyon and is followed by a gravel road. At Durkee the river turns south and is followed by I-84 to Huntington. There are lots of rough fish in this section. Much of the river flows across private lands, so get permission prior to crossing fences.

Trout angling just below Unity Reservoir Dam can be excellent at times. Some large trout are scattered through the lower river. Smallmouth bass are available near the mouth in the Huntington area.

Farewell Bend State Park just south of Huntington, and Unity Lake State Park north of Unity, offer complete camping facilities. Other campgrounds are available in the national forest along the South Fork 8 miles south of Unity.

BURNT RIVER, SOUTH FORK A trout stream heading on the east slope of the Blue Mts. SW of Baker, a major tributary of Unity Reservoir. The South Fork is only about 12 miles long and is paralleled by gravel FS 6005 to its headwaters. It's crossed by Hwy. 26 about 3 miles above the reservoir. Several roads lead from Unity to the upper South Fork, which flows within Wallowa-Whitman National Forest.

The upper stream is good for trout in spring and summer, as are several of its tributaries, including Elk and Last Chance Creeks. Its water gets low in fall, and fishing falls off. The South Fork has a good population of wild trout and is stocked with rainbow catchables. Bait fishing is the most popular method. Four campgrounds are available on FS 6005 within a 3 mile stretch, beginning about 8 miles SW of Unity.

BURNT RIVER, NORTH FORK A 25 mile long trout stream, major tributary of Unity Reservoir, located in the southern Wallowa-Whitman Forest. County Rd. 507 leads NW about 2 miles east of Unity Dam and picks up the North Fork about 2 miles above the reservoir. Dirt roads follow it downstream from this crossing to the pool. County Rd. 507 closely follows the river upstream into the forest to Whitney, where County Rd. 7 and then a forest road continue to the headwaters near Greenhorn. Other forest roads branch out to the upper tributaries, which can be good for small native trout.

The North Fork has a good supply of wild trout in spring. During summer, the river gets quite low, and fish drop down into the reservoir. Rainbow here typically range 6-10 inches. Fourth Creek Campground is on County Rd. 507 about 10 miles above the highway. Unity Lake State Park near the dam also provides camping facilities.

BUTTE CREEK (Wheeler Co.) A tributary of the lower John Day River, entering the river near the county line between Gilliam and Wheeler counties. The creek, 27 miles long, heads SE of Fossil at Butte Creek Summit on Hwy. 19. The upper waters of the creek are crossed and followed by Hwy. 218 in the vicinity of Fossil. The lower creek is approached by a gravel road leading NW from Fossil. The road roughens after about 3 miles. After another 2 or 3 miles it can hardly be termed a road.

Irrigation withdrawals from the creek lower it considerably in summer. In early spring it's too high for good fishing due to run-off. But in late spring and early summer it offers good angling for wild rainbow. Bait fishing with worms, eggs or grasshoppers is the most common approach. There are several state picnic areas on Hwy. 19 north and south of Fossil, but no camping.

CANYON CREEK (Grant Co.) A popular 27 mile long trout stream, tributary to the upper John Day River, which joins the river at the city of John Day. The creek is closely followed by roads throughout most of its length. Hwy. 395 follows it south from the town of John Day about 11 miles. FS 15 continues along the creek for another 8 miles, and FS 1520 picks up the final 3 miles to Canyon Meadows Reservoir. The few miles of water above the reservoir are followed by a logging road on the slope to the north.

The creek below the reservoir is heavily stocked with rainbow in spring and summer. There's good angling for wild trout in the headwaters above the reservoir. Bait fishing is best until water drops in late spring.

Camping is available at Starr Campground on Hwy. 395, 3 miles south of its intersection with FS 15. Wickiup Campground is on FS 15 about 8 miles upstream from the highway intersection, and there is a campground at Willow Meadow Reservoir.

CANYON CREEK MEADOWS RESERVOIR A 25 acre impoundment of upper Canyon Creek in Malheur National Forest. For directions, see Canyon Creek. The reservoir is stocked with rainbow and has native brook trout and cutthroat. The dam leaks, and the pool drops to low levels during July, August, and September. Angling is good in spring and late fall. All fish run to good size, and winter fishing through the ice takes lots of nice ones. There is a campground here with tent sites, piped water, and a boat ramp.

CARPENTER POND A private, one acre pond near John Day, offering mediocre fishing for largemouth bass and bluegill.

CARTER SLOUGH A 2 acre pond NW of Cove, offering mediocre fishing for largemouth bass, crappie, bluegill, and brown bullhead.

CATHERINE CREEK A good trout stream, flowing into the upper Grande Ronde River north of Union. It heads on the SW slope of the Wallowa mountains and flows about 32 miles below its forks. It's closely followed by gravel roads SE from Union for about 10 miles. FS 7785 follows the North Fork and FS 600 follows the South Fork.

Angling is good for rainbow in the upper stream through summer and into late fall, with a good supply of wild fish as well as supplemental hatchery trout. Bait and flies both produce. The trout range 8-12 inches. Camping is available at Catherine Creek State Park 8 miles SE of Union. Another campground is located at the end of the North Fork Rd.

CATHERINE CREEK SLOUGH A privately owned 10 acre fishery east of LaGrande, offering mediocre catches of largemouth bass, brown bullhead, crappie, yellow perch, bluegill, and smallmouth bass.

CHESNIMNUS CREEK A wild rainbow trout stream, flowing 25 miles through a remote section of NE Wallowa-Whitman National Forest west of Troy. Coming in from the west, it joins Joseph Creek near its confluence with Crow Creek, about 15 miles above Joseph Creek Canyon.

From Enterprise, follow Hwy. 3 north 13 miles, then turn east on FS 46. This road follows Elk Cr., then Crow Creek briefly, before heading up Chesnimus. FS 46 follows Chesnimus quite closely past Vigne Campground, about 12 stream miles, to a dirt road east of Hilton Ridge, FS 4695, which follows the stream to its forks near Thomason Meadow Guard Station.

Best angling is in early spring and late fall, for trout averaging 8-12 inches. Larger fish are available in the deep canyon in early summer.

CHEVAL LAKE A 10 acre brook trout lake in Eagle Cap Wilderness, accessed from the Lostine River Trail. To reach the trailhead, follow the Lostine River Rd. south from the community of Lostine on Hwy. 82. At road's end (about 18 miles), follow Lostine Trail 1670 for 2.8 miles, then take the Elkhorn Creek Trail 1656 five miles to its junction with Trail 1681. Follow this trail south and west to the lake, 2.3 miles. Elevation gain is 3095 ft. over 10.1 miles. Snow may block access until July.

Trout run to 12 inches, with angling best in August and September. You'll want a fly rod or your spinner outfit here.

CHIMNEY LAKE A very good 30 acre lake beneath Lookout Mountain in northern Eagle Cap Wilderness, Wallowa-Whitman National Forest, reached by Hwy. 82. Follow the Lostine River Rd. south about 16 miles to Lillyville Horse Camp. Follow Bowman Creek Trail 1651 west 3.6 miles, climbing a steep saddle, then follow Trail 1659 about one mile to Chimney Lake. Snow may block access until July.

Brook trout to 11 inches are plentiful and bite eagerly at anything. There are good campsites here, and Chimney Lake makes a nice base camp for exploring other lakes in the area. See Hobo, Wood. As this is a wilderness area, campers are urged to follow no-trace camping guidelines.

COLD SPRINGS RESERVOIR A large reservoir about 4 miles east of Hermiston, in Cold Springs Wildlife Refuge. It usually fluctuates from about 1,000 acres in spring to less than 500 at the end of irrigation season. Best access is from Hermiston. Head east from town, then north to the Refuge.

Cold Springs offers excellent fishing for crappie 8-11 inches, and very good populations of largemouth bass and brown bullhead. Most of the crappie are caught on jigs by anglers wading deep and jigging in the bushes. Bait fishing is popular near the inlet. The reservoir has proven itself capable of growing 5 pound bass and bullhead to 18 inches. There has been a fair carry-over following the drought of 1987-88. There is some possibility that the reservoir may be drained in 1991 to allow work on the dam. Check locally or with ODFW Pendleton.

The Cold Springs boat ramp has been upgraded so that it can now be used with any vehicle when the reservoir is full. However, only electric motors may be used on the lake. There's no camping in the area. The reservoir is closed during waterfowl season.

CRACKER CREEK A short tributary of the Powder River, entering the mainstream at Sumpter, about 30 miles west of Baker. It offers angling for stocked rainbow and small wild trout. From Baker, take Hwy. 7 south and west along the Powder River, following the river to Sumpter. A gravel forest road follows Cracker Creek north about 4 miles, and dirt roads follow its forks.

Fishing in the main creek and its forks is quite good after the spring thaw, and holds up well into summer. Stocked annually with rainbow trout, it also has lots of natives, though they seldom run over 10 inches. The nearest campground is at McCully Forks, west of Sumpter.

CRAWFISH LAKE A 15 acre brook trout lake near the Grant-Baker County Line, a short hike from the road. It is reached from the Baker County side by a 20 mile drive west from the town of North Powder, which is on Hwy. 30 south of La Grande. Follow the signs for Anthony Lake Ski Area. From the ski area, continue west on FS 73 about 3 miles to the trailhead, which is on the east side of the road. The lake is a mile hike in. The brookies here are small but plentiful. There are several campgrounds near Anthony Lake.

CRESCENT LAKE (Wallowa Co.) A small but very productive lake in the lake basin SW of Wallowa Lake. From Joseph drive around Wallowa Lake to the end of Hwy. 82, one mile south beyond the lake. Hike up the Wallowa River on Trail 1820 for about 6 miles, to the intersection of Trail 1821, which leads west and climbs into the Lake Basin. In 3 miles you'll reach Horseshoe Lake, and the climbing is over. Douglas Lake is 1 1/2 miles beyond, and Crescent is just north of it. Total hike is about 10 1/2 miles, elevation gain 2600 ft.

The basin can also be reached from the upper Lostine River by a hike of about the same distance, up the East Fork Lostine River. From the end of the Lostine Rd., hike upstream along the East Fork Trail 1662. It's 6 1/2 miles to the west end of the Lake Basin at Mirror Lake. Snow may block access until July.

Crescent covers 24 acres and is about 20 feet deep. It puts out good catches of brook trout and holds up well through the season, with fish 7-13 inches. There are several good campsites around the lake, and other lakes nearby provide good fishing as well. Flies and lures are the preferred methods here. Tackle and supplies are available in Enterprise.

CULVER LAKE An 8 acre brook trout lake in southern Eagle Cap Wilderness, about 6 trail miles from Boulder Park, elevation gain about 2050 ft. From Baker, follow Hwy. 203 then FS 67 to Boulder Park, about 45 miles. Take Eagle Creek Trail 1922 into the wilderness, then follow 1921 and 1921A to Culver. Other lakes nearby include bear, lookingglass. Trails are generally accessible by July 4, and fishing is good through September.

DEER CREEK (Baker Co.) A small native rainbow trout stream, tributary to the upper Powder River west of Baker. It flows about 8 miles from the north into Phillips Lake. Hwy. 7 crosses the stream at Mowich Park, a picnic area. FS 6550, west of Mowich Park, leads to Deer Creek Campground, and roads 6540 and 220 follow the creek to its head. Deer Creek offers good angling for wild rainbow averaging 8-9 inches, running to 12 inches. All methods can be used here from late spring through summer.

DESOLATION CREEK A nice trout stream, tributary to the North Fork of the John Day, entering the river near Dale on Hwy. 395. This is about 15 miles south of Ukiah. The creek flows about 40 miles, counting the upper forks.

FS 10 follows the creek from Dale upstream over 20 miles to the creek fork, then follows the North Fork to its headwaters, continuing several more miles to Olive Lake. From Dale, an unimproved road also follows the east bank of the lower creek closely for about 6 miles before joining FS 10. The South Fork has no direct access. FS 45 approaches the upper creek area from Susanville.

Desolation Creek has wild trout and is stocked each year. Most trout caught are 8-11 inches. The creek is fished fairly heavily in late spring and summer, and good catches are made on bait, lures and flies. Heavy run-off slows the fishing early in the spring.

Tollbridge Campground is located near the mouth of Desolation Cr., and there are camping facilities at Olive Lake. A ranger station at Ukiah can provide additional information.

DIAMOND LAKE (Eagle Cap Wilderness) A remote brook trout lake just north of Tombstone Lake, near the southern border of Eagle Cap Wilderness. The lake is about 20 acres, and its outlet flows into Elk Creek, a small tributary of the upper Minam River. From any direction, it can only be reached by a considerable hike.

Best approach is by Trail 1944, the Middle Fork Trail, which can be reached from FS 7787. From Hwy. 203 south of Union take FS77 east about 3 miles to the Catherine Creek turn-off. Follow FS 7785 about one mile up the creek to the Buck Creek Rd., FS 7787, and head up Buck Creek about 4 miles to the trailhead, which is on a hairpin turn. Hike north 1/2 mile on Trail 1944A to the main trail, then head east upslope. The trail follows the middle fork to its head and crosses a saddle north of Burger Butte, about 4 miles from the trail junction. It's another 3 miles, downhill, to Diamond Lake, and Tombstone Lake is just .4 miles further along. Total elevation gain is about 1500 ft.

At elevation 6900 ft., Diamond Lake is 11

acres and has a maximum depth of 24 feet. Angling is usually good for brook trout to 12 inches. August and September are the best months. Flies and lures work are equally effective. There's fishing in nearby Tombstone Lake as well. Snow may block access until July.

DODD POND A small privately owned pond east of Hermiston and McNary Dam, containing largemouth bass and brown bullhead. It is closed to public access.

DOLLARHIDE POND A one acre pond at Mitchell, off Hwy. 26, between Prineville and John Day. It's stocked with legal rainbow trout several times each season. The trout run 8-10 inches and are fished from the bank. Fishing slows down after the first month or so in spring.

DOUGLAS LAKE A 44 acre brook trout lake in the popular lake basin at the headwaters of the West Fork Wallowa River. Douglas is about half-way between Eagle Cap and Matterhorn mountains. From Joseph drive around Wallowa Lake to the end of Hwy. 82, one mile south beyond the lake. Hike up the Wallowa River on Trail 1820 for about 6 miles to the intersection of Trail 1821, which leads west and climbs into the lake basin. In 3 miles you'll reach Horseshoe Lake, and the climbing is over. Douglas Lake is 1 1/2 miles beyond, and Crescent is just north of it. Total hike is about 10 1/2 miles, and the elevation gain is 2600 ft. Snow may block access until July. These trails get chewed up by the pack horses, so be prepared for a bit of mud.

The basin can also be reached by a hike of about the same distance up the East Fork Lostine River. From the end of the Lostine Rd., 18 miles south of the town of Lostine, hike upstream along the East Fork on Trail 1662 6 1/2 miles to the west end of the basin at Mirror Lake. Horses and packers are available at Joseph. You'll want to make reservations for guided trips. Supplies and tackle are available in Enterprise.

Fishing for brook trout can be very good here in August and September. The lake covers about 44 acres and has a maximum depth of 80 ft. Trout run to 12 inches and are plentiful. Flies and lures are best. Other nearby lakes offer good angling. See crescent, moccasin, mirror, unit, horseshoe.

DUCK LAKE A low elevation, hike-in trout lake, about 20 acres, above the Imnaha River in Hells Canyon National Recreation Area. It sees little angler pressure.

From Joseph, head east 8 miles on the road to Imnaha, then go south about 30 miles on the graded gravel road that becomes FS 39. Turn west on (dirt) FS 3960 across from Ollokot Campground. Trail 1875 heads south from Indian Crossing Horse Camp, about 8 miles from Ollokot. The trail passes the lake and continues to the southern wilderness trailhead on FS 66. To access the lake from the Baker area to the south, follow Hwy. 86 east to FS 39. Turn west on FS 66 to its junction with FS 3960. The trail heads north from the junction. It's a 2 mile hike from either trailhead.

Duck Lake is stocked every other year with brook trout, which are here in abundance, averaging 10 inches, running to 13. There are also some rainbow, with few over 10 inches. The lake is open all year and, at elevation 5366 ft. (lowest of all natural lakes in Wallowa-Whitman National Forest) Duck Lake provides an early opportunity for hike-in angling.

EAGLE CREEK (Baker Co.) A many-pronged, 35-mile tributary of the lower Powder River, draining a number of the southeastern lakes of Eagle Cap Wilderness, and entering the Powder River Arm of the Snake River's Brownlee Reservoir near Richland. Wilderness trails follow its upper waters, and good roads access the lower stream. It supports a population of native rainbow and is heavily stocked. Angling is good from June to September for trout to 12 inches.

Hwy. 86 crosses Eagle Creek at Richland, and the paved northbound road to Newbridge follows the creek into the Wallowa-Whitman National Forest, becoming FS 7735. From Eagle Forks Campground (the confluence of Little Eagle Creek with the mainstem 7 miles north of Newbridge) Trail 1878 follows the main creek about 5 miles.

FS 77 follows 26 miles of the creek and its west fork. To connect with this road, turn east off Hwy. 203 about 4 miles south of Catherine Creek Guard Station east of Union. West Eagle Creek Trail 1934 follows the fork to its head at Echo and Traverse lakes. Main Eagle Creek Trail 1922 follows the mainstem to its head at Eagle Lake.

In addition to Eagle Forks Campground on the lower stream, there are camps beside the stream on FS 77 at the end of the East Fork Rd. (7740) and south of the Main Eagle Trailhead.

EAGLE LAKE A fair size, deep lake at the head of Eagle Creek in the Eagle Cap Wilderness of Wallowa-Whitman National Forest, featuring Mackinaw as well as brook trout. It's a 7 mile hike up the main Eagle Creek Trail 1922 from Boulder Park, with an elevation gain of 2609 ft. From Hwy. 203 east of LaGrande and Baker, follow FS 77 or 67 to the trailhead.

There are brook trout here to 12 inches, and lake trout to 16 inches. The brookies respond well to flies. The Mackinaw are best taken with deep lures or spinner and bait. The lake is 104 ft. deep and covers 37 acres. At elevation 7400 ft., the lake is generally only accessible from July through September.

ECHO LAKE (Eagle Cap Wilderness) A small brook trout lake high in the Hurricane Creek watershed of Eagle Cap Wilderness, just a ridge to the east of the upper Lostine River. From Joseph, take the Hurricane Creek Rd. south to Hurricane Creek Campground. Follow Hurricane Creek Trail 1807 south about 7 miles to Trail 7775, a steep 3 mile switch-back to Echo Lake. Snow may block access until July.

Echo is at elevation 8320 ft. near the top of Hurricane Divide and is the source of Granite Creek. The lake is only 7 acres, but almost 50 feet deep. Fair size brook trout are taken from late July through September. Bait, lures, or flies can all be effective. Billy Jones Lake, a 1/2 mile bushwhack south-southeast, also contains trout.

FISH LAKE (Baker Co.) An 86 acre drive-in brook and rainbow trout lake just south of Eagle Cap Wilderness in the Wallowa-Whitman National Forest. The lake is north of Halfway on Hwy. 86, 55 miles east of Baker. From Halfway drive due north on FS 66 and follow this road a long 36 miles to the lake. Early in the summer, verify access with the Forest Service at Pine Creek Ranger Station SE of Halfway.

Fish Lake is at elevation 6640 ft. and is usually accessible only from July through September. The lake has a maximum depth of 50 f. Trout are plentiful here, but on the small side.

GLACIER LAKE, EAGLE CAP WILDERNESS
Courtesy, Oregon State Highway Dept.

Brook trout outnumber rainbow about 2 to 1, and you'll be lucky to find many over 12 inches. There's a guard station at the lake and a good campground with boat ramp. Several interesting trails head at the campground, including those heading east into the Hell's Canyon Recreation Area.

FRANCES LAKE (Wallowa Co.) A large scenic lake within Eagle Cap Wilderness, Wallowa Whitman National Forest. The lake is cupped on a bench of the Hurricane Divide east of the Lostine River, and is reached by about 4 miles of steep trail from the Lostine Rd. The trail takes off east 3 miles south of Lostine Guard Station. Although it's only 4 miles in, be prepared for a very strenuous climb, as the elevation gain is about 1000 ft. *per mile* for the first 3 miles.

Frances Lake covers 30 acres and is 21 ft. deep. The water is very clear and not very rich. However, it's well stocked with brook trout, which average 10-12 inches and occasionally reach 15 inches. All methods will take fish, and flyfishing is tops in September. The scenery is beautiful in this alpine terrain.

FRAZIER LAKE (Wallowa Co.) A fairly shallow lake in the headwaters of the West Fork Wallowa River, within Eagle Cap Wilderness. From Joseph drive around Wallowa Lake to the end of Hwy. 82, one mile south beyond the lake. Hike up the Wallowa River on Trail 1820 for about 10 miles to Frazier Lake. This is an easy trail with a total elevation gain of about 1800 ft., much of it spread out along the first 8 miles. The last 2 miles are fairly steep. These trails get chewed up by pack horses, so be prepared for a bit of mud. Little Frazier Lake is above Frazier but holds no fish.

Frazier covers about 16 acres and offers good fishing for brook trout 7-10 inches and larger. Glacier and Prospect lakes to the west also offer good fishing. Horses and guides are available at Joseph.

GLACIER LAKE A scenic deep lake, high in Eagle Cap Wilderness at the head of the West Fork Wallowa River. Glacier Lake is cradled in a cirque on the east slope of Eagle Cap, which towers above it.

From Joseph on Hwy. 82, take the road to the south end of Wallowa Lake, where Trail 1820 begins. It's a 12 mile hike up the West Fork Wallowa River to the lake. You can also hike in from the north following the East Fork of the Lostine River. Horses and guides are available at Lostine and Joseph.

Glacier is at elevation 8200 ft. in a beautiful alpine setting. Fishing for brook trout can be excellent in August and September. The trout run 7-15 inches, averaging 10 inches. All methods can be used effectively. Be prepared for sudden snow squalls in late September. For other fishable lakes in the area, see Prospect, Frazier. Supplies and tackle are available in Enterprise.

GRAND RONDE LAKE A trout lake in the Anthony Lake area of the Elkhorn Mountains, within the southern Wallowa-Whitman National Forest. The lake outlet flows north into the Grand Ronde River. From the town of North Powder, on Hwy. 30 south of La Grande, drive west on County Rd. 411 and FS 73 to Anthony Lake. About one mile past the lake on FS 77, take FS 43 one-half mile to Grande Ronde Lake.

This 10 acre lake has both rainbow and brook trout, and the fishing is good on almost anything after the lake becomes accessible, usually in late June. Maximum depth is 20 ft. There is a campground on the lake and other good campgrounds at Anthony Lake.

GRAND RONDE RIVER (Below La Grande) The Grande Ronde flows over 200 miles, heading in the mountains SW of La Grande and running NE through Union and Wallowa counties, crossing into Washington and entering the Snake River 5 miles north of the state line. The lower 35 miles of the river are in Washington. The Grand Ronde has been designated a Wild and Scenic River, hopefully saving it from further degradation by dams, which decimated its salmon and steelhead runs.

Efforts to restore these runs through hatchery plants and restricted angling (the Lower Snake River Compensation Plan) have begun to show modest success, though the salmon run is still below harvestable level. Returns of hatchery reared steelhead have been good since 1986, and the lower river is now open for restricted steelhead angling from the mouth to Beaver Creek above LaGrande. Check current regulations for seasons. Summer run returns have been less consistent than winter, and at this time the season is only open from September to mid-April. Anglers must used barbless hooks and release all wild steelhead before removing them from the water. Hatchery steelhead can be identified by their clipped adipose fin. Flyfishing for steelhead is popular in this stretch.

Below La Grande the Grand Ronde follows a meandering course through agricultural and marshlands, dropping into forested canyons as it nears the border. Hwy. 82 follows the river from La Grande to Elgin, and county roads follow at some distance from there to Palmer Junction. From Palmer Junction to Wildcat Creek, the river can be accessed only by riverboats. (The Grand Ronde is popular with rafters.) From the junction of Wildcat Creek, about 4 miles south of Troy, county roads follow the river closely to the state border.

Trout, bass, and panfish are found throughout the river. Panfish are primarily in the river valley from La Grande to Elgin. Some large native rainbow are landed in the lower stream, usually below Elgin. Bass, crappie, catfish, perch, and bluegill are taken in good numbers in the stretch between Cove and Elgin.

Camping is available at a state park at Hilgard, on Hwy. 30 west of La Grande, and at several campgrounds in Umatilla National Forest between Palmer Junction and Troy. River guides are available at Troy.

GRAND RONDE RIVER (Above La Grande) The Grand Ronde above La Grande offers about 40 miles of good trout angling. La Grande is on Hwy. 30 about 50 miles south of Pendleton. The river marks the city's northern boundary, flowing from the west from its headwaters in Umatilla National Forest. Hwy. 244 follows the stream for 23 river miles west from La Grande. Paved FS 51 follows south another 12 miles, and FS 5125 continues upstream, where a dirt track leads to the river's headwaters at Grande Ronde Lake near Anthony Lake.

Angling on the upper river is good in late spring, summer, and fall for both native and stocked rainbow. Most fish run 8-12 inches, with a few larger. There's lots of good fly water.

Campgrounds are plentiful along the upper stream, and there is camping at Hilgard Junction State Park just west of La Grande. Red Bridge State Park, on Hwy. 244 west of Hilgard, offers only picnic facilities.

HAINES POND A one acre pond 1/4 mile north of Haines. It contains largemouth bass.

HIGHWAY 203 POND A 10 acre pond north of Baker at the junction of Hwy. 203 and I-84. It contains largemouth bass.

IMNAHA RIVER Like the Grand Ronde, and other streams of the Snake River System, the Imnaha once hosted sizeable runs of chinook salmon and steelhead. These native runs were all but destroyed by hydroelectric dams. Recent efforts to restore the runs, through mitigation efforts at the dams and plantings of hatchery reared salmon and steelhead, have met with some success. Like the Grand Ronde, the Imnaha is now open for a restricted steelhead season. A harvestable population of salmon is still some years away. Check current regulations for season and restrictions.

The Imnaha flows 75 miles from its headwaters in Eagle Cap Wilderness to its confluence with the Snake River about 22 miles north of Imnaha, east of Joseph. From Hwy. 82 at Joseph, it is 32 miles to the Imnaha by way of the paved Little Sheep Creek Rd. From there, a dirt road follows the river upstream for about 45 miles and downstream to within 3 miles of the Snake. The Imnaha River Rd. is also accessible from Baker and La Grande by way of Hwy. 86 east and FS 39 north.

The river supports a large population of native rainbow and is heavily stocked with hatchery trout. Angling is excellent during summer and fall above and below the town of Imnaha. Bait is always a sure thing, but the river has some good fly water. It also has a large population of good size whitefish (to 16 inches), with best fishing in late fall. Supplies, tackle, and local information are available at Enterprise.

GREEN LAKE (Wallowa Co.) A solitary brook trout lake high in the North Minam River drainage, within Eagle Cap Wilderness. Green Lake sits pretty much by itself, 2 miles south of (and about 1800 feet above) the North Minam. There really is no easy way to get to the lake, although a good trail leads in.

The easiest hike is probably up the Minam River from Red's Horse Ranch, but you have to fly or pack into the ranch. Most backpackers approach from the lakes east of the river. The Bowerman Trail 1651 leads west from the Lostine Rd. about 2 1/2 miles south of Lostine Guard Station. Take 1651 past John Henry Lake and down into North Minam Meadows, then ascend the steep Green Lake Trail 1666 to the lake. The total hike is over 12 miles, with many steep, long pitches. Naturally, you won't suffer from a lot of company once you get in here.

The lake is at elevation 7000 ft., in a glacial cirque on the north side of Hazel Mt. It covers about 15 acres and has abundant brook trout to 16 inches. Flies and lures can both be effective. August and September are the best time to be up here. If the walk sounds daunting, horses and guides are available at Lostine.

HOBO LAKE A small lake high on the east side of Lookout Mt., west of the Lostine River within Eagle Cap Wilderness. Head south 15 miles from Lostine on Hwy. 82 to the Bowman Creek Trail 1651, about 2.5 miles south of Lostine Guard Station. Climb east on this trail for 3.6 miles to the junction of Trail 1659, which you follow north 1.2 miles to the short spur trail that leads west to Hobo Lake, passing Chimney Lake one mile before Hobo. Total trail mileage is 5.4 miles, and total elevation gain is over 3000 ft., so fuel up before hitting the trail.

Hobo is at 8320 ft and covers 8 acres. It is quite deep for its size, stocked with rainbow trout. Bait is usually the most productive method, but a wet fly or nymph can do well in the late fall.

HORSESHOE LAKE (Wallowa Co.) A brook trout lake at the east end of the of Eagle Cap Wilderness lake basin. Horseshoe is the first large lake approached by the trail from the east. From Joseph, drive south around Wallowa Lake to the end of Hwy. 82, one mile south beyond the lake. Hike up the Wallowa River on Trail 1820 for about 6 miles to the intersection of Trail 1821, which leads west and climbs into the basin. In 3 miles you'll reach Horseshoe Lake, and the climbing is over. Douglas Lake is 1 1/2 miles beyond, and Crescent Lake is just to the north. The total hike is about 9 miles, with an elevation gain of 2400 ft.

You can also approach from the north along the East Fork Lostine River, Trail 1662. It's 6 1/2 miles from the end of the Lostine River Rd. to the west end of the basin at Mirror Lake. Snow may block access to either route until July. All these trails can get muddy.

This is a fair size lake, 40 acres with maximum depth over 70 ft. Brook trout are abundant and fairly easy to catch, but average size will be small. The larger fish are taken in fall, usually on flies and lures. For other lakes in the vicinity, see Douglas, Crescent, Moccasin, Lee, Mirror. Horseshoe can usually be reached in early July, and fishing holds up well throughout the season. Supplies, tackle, and local information can be obtained at Enterprise.

ICE LAKE A deep lake high in the Eagle Cap Wilderness of Wallowa-Whitman National Forest. The lake is perched above the West Fork Wallowa River north of a ridge that separates the river valley from the lake basin. From Joseph, drive around Wallowa Lake to the end of Hwy. 82, one mile south of the lake. Hike up the Wallowa River on Trail 1820 for 2.8 miles to the intersection of Trail 1808, which climbs west. Grit your teeth, and start switch-backing upslope for 5.1 miles to the lake. Total elevation gain for this stretch is 2300 ft., but the trail is well laid out.

Ice Lake is nestled on the east side of Matterhorn Mt. at elevation 7900 ft. Its basin was carved from rock by a glacier, and the setting is spectacularly alpine. The lake is over 190 feet deep, the deepest lake in the wilderness, and it covers about 46 acres.

The lake is loaded with brook trout 7-11 inches, with some larger. Bait is best in July, and lures and flies work best by September. Horses and guides are available at the south end of Wallowa Lake. Call ahead for reservations.

JOHN DAY ARM OF LAKE UMATILLA See Umatilla, Lake (John Day Arm).

JOHN DAY RIVER (Below Kimberly) One of Oregon's Top Ten summer steelhead rivers, with an annual steelhead catch as high as 6,000 some years, and an excellent smallmouth bass fishery. The John Day enters the Columbia River about half-way between Biggs Junction and Blalock on I-84, about 25 miles east of The Dalles. It's crossed by the highway just above its mouth. John Day Dam backs the Columbia 9 miles into the lower John Day Canyon, forming a productive pool that can only be approached from the Columbia due to an impassable falls.

The 185 river miles between Kimberly, on Hwy. 19, and the mouth offer fine fishing for smallmouth bass from May through July, and steelhead from September to mid-April. Much of the river flows through a canyon carved out of lava bedrock. The canyon has weathered in a manner similar to that of the Deschutes, with great round hills roughly carpeted with desert grass, sagebrush, and juniper. Much of the water here is accessible only by riverboat.

The 160 miles of river below Service Creek has been designated a Scenic Waterway. Rafting is an exciting and practical way to fish it. For a day's drift, anglers can put in at Service Creek (r.m. 157, at the junction of Hwys. 19 and 207) and drift 12 river miles to Twickenham (r.m. 145). A popular longer drift is from Twickenham to Clarno Rapids (r.m. 110 off Hwy. 218 west of Fossil Beds National Monument).

Another good day's drift is from Cottonwood Bridge (r.m. 40, at the crossing of Hwy. 206) to the mouth of Rock Cr. (r.m. 22, east of Wasco). Gravel roads from Wasco to the west, and Rock Creek to the east, reach the river at Scotts Ford. A gravel road leading west from Mikkalo follows Hays Creek down into the canyon and parallels the river from r.m. 30 to r.m. 27. Much of this land is private, though there are a few parcels owned by BLM. Ask permission to fish at the nearest ranch if you're in doubt as to ownership. The next 65 miles upstream are in private ownership with little or no public access.

Access improves near Clarno Rapids. There is BLM river access from just below Clarno Rapids to 1/2 mile above Butte Creek, about 12 river miles. Fished for both smallmouth and steelhead, this is a classic stretch of John Day water, shallow riffles alternating with deep pools. An unimproved road follows the river's east bank. To reach it, head west from Fossil along the Butte Creek Rd.

Hwy. 207 parallels the river from the Hwy. 26 junction in Picture Gorge all the way to Service Creek. Angler access is excellent throughout this stretch, with the road always within 100 yards of the river. Anglers fish this section for both smallmouth bass and summer steelhead, as well as trout in early season. Picture Gorge is the upper limit for most smallmouth activity.

Steelhead fishing fluctuates yearly, dependent on river flow here as elsewhere. In many years, steelhead enter the John Day in late August, and don't spawn until the following May. Fishing for them can be good from September through April, with early steelhead activity best below Clarno. By February and March, anglers begin to take steelhead above Service Creek.

Smallmouth bass are in the river in abundance from Picture Gorge downstream. Most smallmouth angling takes place in spring and summer. In early spring, smallmouth can be found in the deeper pools. During their spawning season they head for the backwaters and linger along the rimrock ledges. After spawning, they can be found throughout the river, feeding and holding.

Tumwater Falls, about 10 miles from the mouth, marks the beginning of the John Day Arm of Lake Umatilla. Approachable only from the mouth, this portion of the river contains crappie, brown bullhead, channel catfish and smallmouth bass, as well as steelhead. See Umatilla, Lake (John Day Arm).

The John Day runs through a patchwork of private and BLM lands. Check with landowners along the lower river for access permission. There are no developed campground on the river, though camping is permitted on BLM land. There is a campground at Sheldon State Park about 10 miles north of Service Creek, and in Ochoco National Forest to the south.

JOHN DAY RIVER (Above Kimberly) The John Day heads just east of Strawberry Mt. Wilderness in Malheur National Forest and flows over 100 miles before it reaches Kimberly. It can be fished for steelhead later in the season, and for trout. Its flow within national forest is brief and spotted with private land holdings. There are two camps on the river here, Crescent and Trout Farm. Good roads parallel the river downstream, but much of it flows through the private ranchlands of the John Day Valley.

From Kimberly upstream, the river is followed by Hwy. 19 to Dayville, by Hwy. 26 to Prairie City, and by County Rds. 61 then 14 to its headwaters. In the last 15 miles, the roads turn to dirt and gravel.

These upper waters have a rough fish problem, last treated in 1979. The river was restocked with rainbow trout and continues to be stocked annually. Wild rainbow are available in the headwaters. Steelhead are present in this stretch later in the season, with best fishing here generally in November and December. The river is closed to steelhead angling upstream of Indian Creek.

Clyde Holliday State Park east of Mt Vernon provides camping facilities and access to good steelhead water. Though the park is officially closed in winter, and camping is prohibited then, anglers can park and walk in to fish. Trout Creek Campground is near the headwaters about 16 miles south of Prairie City on the road to Drewsey.

JOHN DAY RIVER, MIDDLE FORK A major tributary of the John Day system, joining the North Fork 15 river miles west of the community of Ritter. The Middle Fork flows through Ritter, which is about 10 air miles SW of Dale. It offers steelhead and trout angling and has good road access for all but its lower 9 miles. The Middle Fork is 75 miles long, and heads near Hwy. 26 east of Prairie City. More riffle than pool throughout most of its run, the Middle Fork has a narrow flood plain and flows through a shallow rimrock canyon below its headwaters. The head of the Middle Fork, in the Bates area, is a meandering meadow stream at about 4800 ft.

The lower 9 river miles have no road access. Paved and gravel roads follow the river closely from a few miles below Ritter, to its headwaters above Austin Junction on Hwy. 26 east of Prairie City. The river is crossed by Hwy. 395 about 7 miles east of Ritter, 12 miles south of Dale, and 15 miles north of Long Creek. A good road, County Rd. 20, follows the stream from Hwy. 395 SE past Susanville, and all the way to Austin Junction, where it joins Hwy. 26. Landowners are generous along the Middle Fork, and the riverbank is currently accessible for angling throughout.

Hwy. 395 is the legal deadline for steelhead angling on the Middle Fork. The annual steelhead catch varies from 100-500. Most of these are taken in March. Rainbow trout 9-14 inches are the primary fishery. They are taken in good numbers from June through late fall in the upper river. Fly angling can be good in summer and fall, with bait best early.

Middle Fork Campground is at river mile 60, about 6 miles north of Hwy. 26. Dixie Campground is about 6 miles SW of the upper river on Hwy. 26, about 12 miles east of Prairie City.

JOHN DAY RIVER, NORTH FORK A large tributary of the John Day River, joining the mainstem at Kimberly on Hwy.19. Rich in good habitat and food resources, the North Fork has historically been a natural rearing stream for steelhead. Resident rainbow are scarce, however bull trout (Dolly Varden) are present in the upper stream.

JOHN DAY RIVER
Dan Casali, Photographer

The North Fork is about 113 miles long, heading in the Elkhorn Mountains 20 miles west of Baker. The upper waters of this fork flow through Umatilla National Forest. This is a big river with a strong flow, yet more riffle than pool throughout most of its run. The best pools are below the confluence of the Middle Fork.

The North Fork has an adequate flow for riverboats, and there is some boat angling. Boaters put in at the mouth of Wall Creek and drift to Monument, about 6 miles, or from Monument to Kimberly, about 15 miles.

Much of the river is accessible from nearby roads, though private property may present a problem below Dale. From the North Fork's confluence with the mainstem at Kimberly, a paved road follows the northern bank 15 river miles upstream to Monument. A gravel road continues upstream from Monument as far as r.m. 28 at Birch Creek. The next 11 miles, to Potamus Creek, are roadless. A gravel road follows the river downstream from Dale to Potamus Creek. Dale is on Hwy. 395 south of Ukiah at about the mid-point of the river. Desolation and Camas Creek, both good size tributaries, join the North Fork at Dale.

The North Fork above Dale is followed by paved and gravel forest roads 55 and 5506 to r.m. 7, just below Simpson Creek. For the next 23 miles the stream flows within the North Fork Wilderness, Umatilla National Forest, and is accessed only by trails. Several trails lead in from the north and south. The main trail is adjacent to the river, which is in a steep forested canyon. The river flows at a moderate gradient over a boulder strewn bed. Here, most angling is for juvenile steelhead. This is their natural habitat, and their historical predominance here means that there are few resident rainbow of any size. By the time the steelhead approach good size, they are ready to move out. Bull trout are available, however. Look for the big bulls in the deeper pools. The extreme upper waters are approached by gravel roads in the vicinity of Granite.

There is fair steelhead angling in the lower river from the mouth up to the Hwy. 395 Bridge at Dale, the steelheading deadline. Annual catches have varied greatly, but generally about 300 steelhead are landed each year. Steelhead may appear in the North Fork as early as October, but generally steelheading begins in November and continues until mid-April. The river usually carries plenty of flow, but it can get very low and clear during winter cold spells, even freezing over. In fact, ice chunks in the river can be a problem to winter anglers.

There is no improved camping on the river below Dale, although you can squat on BLM land. Ukiah Dale State Park offers camping facilities on Hwy. 395, about 8 miles north of Dale. There are four campgrounds on the river in Umatilla National Forest upstream from Dale. Tollbridge Campground is just one mile east of Dale. Trough Creek is about 4 miles further east on FS 55. Two primitive camps, Gold Dredge and Oriental Creek, are further upstream on FS 5506.

JOHN DAY RIVER, SOUTH FORK A large tributary of the upper John Day River, entering the main stream from the south at Dayville on Hwy. 26, about 30 miles west of John Day. The South Fork heads in the Snow Mountain area south of Izee and flows about 60 miles through high desert country. It has fair road access along its entire length. You can pick up this road at its intersection with Hwy. 26 at Dayville, or by taking the Post-Paulina Hwy. east from Prineville and continuing east 29 miles to the upper river, just north of Izee. (This tiny community took its name from a ranch brand, I Z).

The fork has some native trout and is stocked annually with rainbow. Bait fishing is the preferred method. There is a lot of private property along the river, but public access is available on Murders Creek Wildlife Management lands which are scattered along the stream. Nearest campgrounds are in the national forest to east and west.

JOSEPH CREEK Formed by the confluence of Chesnimus, Crow, and Elk Creeks about 25 miles north of Enterprise. It flows through a big, deep, picturesque canyon north of Joseph Creek Ranch, offering good early and late season angling for native rainbow. About 23 miles north of Enterprise, Hwy. 3 offers a view of the canyon from the west rim, but access to the creek is from the east.

From Enterprise, follow Hwy. 3 north about 15 miles, turning east on FS 46, which leads to the head of Joseph Creek near the M. Davis Ranch. A road follows the creek downstream to Joseph Creek Ranch. There is a public trail along the creek whose trailhead is on Table Mt. The trail may also be reached from Joseph Creek Ranch, but permission is required. The route into the canyon from Table Mt. is a steep 4 mile hike. To reach it, continue north on FS 46 to Coyote Campground, turning west on FS 4650 to Table Mt. Joseph Creek enters the Grande Ronde near its confluence with the Snake River in Washington. The creek has a self-sustaining native steelhead run, but is closed to steelhead angling.

JUBILEE LAKE A 97 acre impoundment which provides good angling in an area where lakes are scarce. Jubilee is about 60 miles NE of Pendleton in Umatilla National Forest at the head of Mottet Creek, about 12 miles north of Tollgate, which is on Hwy. 204. Take FS 64

north from Tollgate directly to the lake. Jubilee reaches a depth of 55 ft. Its rainbow are small but numerous. The Forest Service maintains a large campground here with boat ramp. Motors are prohibited on the lake.

KINNEY LAKE A 20 acre catfish and rainbow trout lake in the upper Wallowa Valley 5 miles due east of Wallowa Lake. From Joseph on Hwy. 82, drive about 5 miles east on paved road S393, the Little Sheep Creek Rd. Turn south onto a gravel road and drive 1 1/2 miles to Pleasant Center. A dirt road leads east to the lake, one mile from Pleasant Center School.

Kinney offers good fishing for brown bullhead and stocked rainbow trout. The rainbow are plentiful and average 9-13 inches. There are also a few bull trout (Dolly Varden). The bullhead average 9 inches. Bait fishing is most popular here. There is no campground.

LANGDON LAKE A fair size lake on Hwy. 204 about half-way between Elgin and Weston at the community of Tollgate. It is privately owned and operated as part of a resort, with angling for patrons only.

LITTLE SHEEP CREEK A nice little trout stream with good road access, heading about 10 miles SE of Joseph and flowing NE to join Big Sheep Creek at the town of Imnaha. From Joseph, on Hwy. 82 just north of Wallowa Lake, a paved road goes east for about 8 miles to meet FS 39 and the creek. The forest road follows the creek south to its headwaters, and the paved road follows it closely north all the way to Imnaha. Most of the upper waters and some of the lower flow within the Wallowa-Whitman National Forest.

Best catches are made in late summer and fall. Native fish provide the action. Campgrounds are available at Wallowa Lake State Park, south of Joseph, or at Lick Creek Campground south of the creek on FS 39.

LEE LAKE One of the better lakes in the NE lake basin of Eagle Cap Wilderness above the west fork of the Wallowa River. It's about 10 miles by trail to the lake, which is 1/3 mile west of Horseshoe Lake. See Horseshoe Lake for directions.

Lee Lake is only 9 acres, but is 80 ft. deep. It provides excellent angling for brook trout averaging 10 inches. Any method will take fish here, though bait seems to be best in the early season. The lake offers good fishing from July through September, and later if the weather holds. There are no campsites at the lake.

LITTLE STRAWBERRY LAKE See Strawberry Lake, Little.

LONG CREEK A tributary of the Middle Fork of the John Day River, about 30 miles long, entering the Middle Fork near Ritter. It heads north of Magone Lake about half-way between the communities of Long Creek and John Day. Hwy. 395 crosses it about 15 miles above its mouth, just north of the town of Long Creek. The creek is inaccessible downstream from the highway, flowing across private, roadless ranchland. Good gravel roads parallel the upper creek SE into Malheur National Forest.

The creek supports a fair population of native rainbow and is lightly fished. There's a forest service campground at Magone Lake. Several unimproved campsites can be found along the stream.

LONG LAKE (Wallowa Co.) A fair size lake in the headwaters of the North Fork of the Minam River. From the town of Lostine on Hwy. 82 drive south to the end of the road. Take the Lostine River Trail 1670 2.8 miles to the junction of the Elkhorn Trail 1656, which forks SW. Follow 1656 about 5 miles to a trail junction above Swamp Lake. Drop down by trail to Swamp Lake, and take Trail 1669, which follows the outlet stream about one mile NW to Long Lake. Its a 10 mile hike on moderately steep trails.

Long Lake is 25 acres, stocked with brook trout 6-12 inches. Fishing is best in August and September. There's also good fishing in Swamp and Steamboat lakes one mile due east of Swamp.

LOSTINE RIVER A pretty, pretty good trout stream heading at Minam Lake, high in the Eagle Cap Wilderness of Wallowa-Whitman National Forest. Crystalline and idyllic within the wilderness, tranquilly majestic in the valley below with its mountainous backdrop, the Lostine flows 31 miles north to join the Wallowa River 2 miles east of the town of Wallowa on Hwy. 82, about 45 miles east of La Grande. The stream is followed 24 miles south by FS 8210. The upper river is followed to its source by Trail 1670. Its major tributary, the East Fork, is followed by Trail 1662. Both trails head at Two Pan Campground at the end of the Lostine River Rd. The Lostine Rd. is the jump-off point for several key trails into the Wallowas.

Lostine provides good angling for small trout in summer and fall. The stream is well stocked with rainbow and has some natives, particularly in the upper stretches. The average trout here is 7-11 inches, with a few larger. Bait is most commonly employed, but flyfishing is good in late fall. The Lostine is not open for salmon and steelhead.

There are five forest campgrounds along the Lostine River Rd. from the forest boundary south to road's end. These are *heavily* used by horse packers—dusty, noisy, crowded with vehicles and unsuitable for long stays. Don't expect solitude down below. There are many attractive natural campsites along the upper stream, however. No trace camping is urged within the wilderness.

McNARY CHANNEL PONDS Six ponds and connecting channels, covering about 25 acres below McNary Dam on the Columbia River off I-84. They contain largemouth bass, channel catfish, bluegill, and stocked trout. Fishing is good in early spring and summer. A flat terrain and gravel trail provide accessibility for less-abled anglers. The pond area is pleasantly shaded with cottonwoods and willows. To reach them, drive west beyond the Fish Viewing Window.

McCORMACH SLOUGH A 2 mile stretch of Columbia backwater just west of Irrigon on the Umatilla National Wildlife Refuge, featuring good fishing for smallmouth bass and brown bullhead. Access from the refuge is a bushwhack, so most anglers approach by boat from launches on Lake Umatilla at Irrigon or Boardman. The narrow neck of the slough is characterized by shifting sandbars, so enter cautiously. Most boaters go in only about 1/2 mile, then fish around the many islands in the slough.

MAGONE LAKE A popular trout lake in Malheur National Forest, about 10 air miles due north of the town of John Day. The lake can be reached by several routes. About 9 miles east of John Day County Rd. 18 leaves Hwy. 26 and runs NE to the lake. FS 36 leaves Hwy. 395 to the east about 15 miles north of Mt. Vernon, and winds about 10 miles to the lake.

Covering 50 acres at elevation 4900 ft., the lake is very rich and quite deep, about 100 ft. It is heavily fished for nice size rainbow and brook trout. Fish up to 16 inches are taken. The north end of the lake has good shoal areas where flies will take large fish in the fall.

Magone is open all year, and ice fishing is popular and yields good catches. There is a campground at the lake. Boats can be launched, but fishing from a motor propelled craft with the motor running is prohibited. There is a 10 mph speed limit on the lake.

McKAY CREEK (Umatilla Co.) The outlet stream of McKay Reservoir, a tributary of the Umatilla River. Hwy. 395 leads to the area from Pendleton, and several secondary roads follow the creek from the reservoir and the Pilot Rock area. Only about 5 miles of creek above the reservoir are outside the Umatilla Reservation. For angling on reservation lands, check with the agency at Mission.

There is very little angling in the creek below the reservoir because of water fluctuation. The upper creek offers good fishing, with nice riffles and pools. The catch rate is generally high in spring and early summer. The creek has been stocked with rainbow, and fish move into the creek from the reservoir. Unlike most streams in this district, McKay Creek opens with the early trout opener at the end of April. There are no camping areas nearby.

McKAY RESERVOIR A large reservoir, usually providing excellent crappie fishing and doubling as a goose and duck refuge. The reservoir is about 4 miles due south of Pendleton, just to the east of Hwy. 395. A good gravel road cuts in from the highway to the north end of the reservoir.

When full, McKay covers about 1200 acres, but it's not unusual for this lake to be drawn down to almost nothing in the fall. The drought of 1987-88 appears to have had no noticeable effect on the reservoir's inhabitants. Fishing continues to be excellent for black crappie 6-10 inches, with some to 12 inches. Largemouth bass are present, as are yellow perch, brown bullhead, and channel catfish. The unofficial state record channel cat was caught here in 1980, weighing 36 pounds 8 ounces. Of its two boat ramps, one is useable only at full pool.

MEACHAM CREEK A 30 mile tributary of the Umatilla River with good angling, accessible to strong hikers. It heads near Meacham, SE of Pendleton and winds through canyons to the east and south. Meacham joins the Umatilla at Gibbon, about 26 miles upstream from Pendleton. The creek is quite inaccessible. Forest roads leave the Meacham area to the east and stay high on the ridge above the creek. A Union Pacific railroad line follows the creek from Meacham downstream, and anglers can walk the railroad right-of-way to access the creek. It offers good fishing for native trout. The lower 5 miles flow within the Umatilla Indian Reservation, and tribal permits are required.

MEACHAM LAKE A private 12 acre lake in the Blue Mountains, one mile SW of Meacham. The area around it has been developed, and there is no longer public access.

MEADOW CREEK A 24 mile long trout stream entering the upper Grand Ronde River about 10 miles west of Hilgard, a community on I-84 about 8 miles west of La Grande. Hwy. 244 follows the lower stream from the Grande Ronde confluence to Starkey, 6 miles upstream. The upper stream flows within Wallowa-Whitman National Forest, and the portion followed by roads is a designated study area, currently closed to angling. This stretch is followed by FS 2120 and 21 for much of its length. Trail 1855 leads up the final 6 miles of creek, above Smith Creek, which are open for angling.

Meadow offers good trout angling in the lower creek late in spring and again in fall. Native rainbow provide most of the fishing. The trout run 7-11 inches, with a few larger. The stream closure is from the forest boundary just above Bear Creek to the end of the road at Smith Creek, in the headwaters. Nearest camping is at Camas Campground on Hwy. 224, about 12 miles south of Starkey.

MESSNER POND #2 About 12 acres, one mile east of Boardman north of I-84. It is a rich pond, with good potential for growing nice size bass and crappie. It's fished primarily for these, but since a culvert connects it to the Columbia, it might hold anything. It does have lots of carp at this time, though there are some plans to add a screening device to keep the carp out. To reach the pond, take the Port of Morrow Exit off I-84 and drive due north.

MILL CREEK (Umatilla Co.) A trout stream in extreme northeast Oregon with headwaters in Washington. It flows through Oregon for about 7 miles before doubling back to Washington, where it enters the Walla Walla River about 10 miles east of Milton Freewater, which is on Hwy. 11. Mill Creek is just north of the North Fork Walla Walla River. Fishing in Mill is for wild trout in fast water, with lots of brush to hang you up. But the creek does have a lot of good riffle areas, and it abounds with rainbow and bull trout (Dolly Varden).

MINAM LAKE A fair size brook trout lake in Eagle Cap Wilderness at the head of the Lostine River. While near the head of the Minam River, it does not drain into that watershed. From the community of Lostine, east of Enterprise, follow the Lostine River Rd. about 18 miles to its end. Follow the Lostine River Trail 1670 upstream from Two Pan Campground 5.7 miles to Minam Lake. The total elevation gain is about 2000 feet, but it's spread out along the entire hike, making this one of the easier trails in the Eagle Cap. Snow may block access until July.

The lake is at elevation 7400 ft. and covers 33 acres. Maximum depth is 30 ft. Fishing for brook trout is terrific from late July through September, with all methods taking 6-14 inch fish. Blue Lake is one mile beyond Minam, and also offers good fishing.

MINAM RIVER A major tributary of the Grand Ronde River, heading at Blue Lake, high in Eagle Cap Wilderness, and flowing north-northwest 50 miles to join the Wallowa River at the town of Minam. Designated a scenic waterway, the Minam has limited road access throughout its length. It is a favorite of rafters and hikers.

The town of Minam is 15 miles east of Elgin, 12 miles west of Wallowa on Hwy. 82. The lower 9 river miles from the mouth to Meads Flat are followed by roads south from

Minam. Secondary roads upstream of the Flat are a mile or more from the river, and trails must be used to approach the stream. Trail access is excellent. Trail 1673 follows the river all the way from Meads Flat to Blue Lake, a distance of over 40 miles. See the North Wallowa-Whitman National Forest map for details.

Red's Wallowa Horse Ranch offers unique access at about the midpoint of the river, just outside the wilderness boundary at the notch above Jim White Ridge. Red's has an airstrip deep in the canyon, and private flyers can literally drop right in. If you don't fly, you can charter a flight at Enterprise Municipal Airport. If you do pilot your own craft, stop at Enterprise anyway for a briefing on the approach, and plan your flight for early morning. Red's only other access is by an 8 mile pack or hike from Horse Meadow on FS 62.

Angling on the Minam is excellent in late summer and fall. The stream is not stocked but has a good native population, with rainbow 8-15 inches and a few brook and bull trout as well. Bait, flies, or lures will all take fish. As you might expect, the best fishing is away from the roads. Fishing gets underway as soon as the run-off drops, usually in June. Fishing on the lower river slows by August, but picks up again in September.

A sad note. At one time, not so very long ago, there was a salmon and steelhead run to write about as well. A variety of man-made ills, primarily dams, have reduced the runs to the endangered point, and angling for the few remaining fish is strictly prohibited. Camping is available at Boundary Campground on Bear Creek about 8 miles south of Wallowa, along Lostine River Rd., and at natural campsites throughout the wilderness. Supplies, tackle, and local information are available at Enterprise.

MIRROR LAKE (Wallowa Co.) A scenic trout lake only one mile north of Eagle Cap, highest peak in the Wallowas at 9595 ft. Mirror is at the west end of the NE lake basin within the Wilderness. The most direct route to it is from the north by way of the East Fork of the Lostine River. From the end of the Lostine Rd., 18 miles south of the town of Lostine, hike upstream along the East Fork on Trail 1662, 6 1/2 miles to the lake. Total elevation gain is 2000 ft. You can also hike in from Wallowa Lake south of Joseph, taking Trail 1820 and 1810 into the eastern basin, crossing west to Mirror. This route covers about 14 miles.

Mirror Lake is 26 acres with a maximum depth of 77 ft. Brook trout here average 10 inches and range from 6-13 inches. Other lakes in the basin to the NE provide good angling as well. You can usually get in by July, but fishing is best in August and September. There are quite a few good campsites.

MOCCASIN LAKE A fair size brook trout lake in the NE lake basin of Eagle Cap Wilderness. The hike in can be made from either Wallowa Lake or Two Pan Campground on the Lostine River. The distance is almost identical. See mirror lake for directions. Moccasin is just NE of Mirror. Total trip is about 11 miles, with elevation gain 2400 ft.

Moccasin doesn't have very large fish, but there are lots of them. These brook trout run to 10 inches, and they can be taken easily on bait, lures or flies. Spinner and bait combinations retrieved very slowly will take the largest fish. Other lakes in the basin provide good angling as well. See Mirror, Douglas, Unit, Lilly, Cres-

OPENING DAY AT MORGAN LAKE
Courtesy *LaGrande Observer*, Phil Bullock, Photographer

cent. There's one improved campsite at this centrally located lake, and several other good sites nearby.

MORGAN LAKE Managed for public trout angling, just 5 miles SW of, and above, La-Grande. The city is on Hwy. 84, and a gravel and dirt road leads from the highway to the lake, where there is a city park with picnic and camping facilities. Formerly a private water supply, the 60 acre lake was acquired under a plan by the city of La Grande and the Dept. of Fish and Wildlife.

The catch rate is very good for trout to 15 inches, with rainbow averaging 9-12 inches and a few brook trout of good size. Crappie to 10 inches are also taken. Fishing is best in early summer, and bait is the most popular method. The lake is restocked annually.

OLIVE LAKE A good trout lake of 160 acres near the headwaters of Desolation Creek in Umatilla National Forest, about 30 miles west of Baker. This lake is worth the trip when it's hot. Gravel and dirt roads approach it from several directions. FS 10 leads west about 11 miles from Granite to the lake. Granite can be reached by State Rd. 220 from Hwy. 7 south of Baker. From Dale, on Hwy. 395, take FS 10 SE up Desolation Creek to the lake. It can also be reached from Susanville to the south.

Olive sits at a cool 6200 ft. elevation. It's over 100 ft. deep. Good catches of rainbow trout to 15 inches can be made here. Brook trout of the same size make up about half the catch. An occasional cutthroat is also taken. Trolling and bait fishing are both popular methods here.

Olive also has lots of kokanee, with some to 12 inches, but most a little smaller. Best method for taking kokanee is trolling with spinners trailing a small baited hook. Kokanee tend

to school, so when you get a strike, stay in the same area. Fall is a good time for both rainbow and kokanee, with flies taking the larger rainbow. There's a campground and boat ramp at the lake.

PENLAND LAKE A trout lake in Morrow County about 25 miles SE of Heppner. It was built by local private interests, but offers public access. Take County Rd. 682 along Willow Creek for 17 miles, then continue south on FS 53 and 21 to Butcher Creek, then east 2 miles on FS 2103 to the lake.

Penland covers 67 acres and is fairly shallow. Winterkill is often a problem, but trout have been known to grow large here. Legal trout are stocked following severe winters. Fall fishing is especially good here.

There is a campground with boat ramp, however motors are prohibited on the lake.

POCKET LAKE A small brook trout lake in Eagle Cap Wilderness, perched in a glacial cirque 700 ft. above Moccasin Lake. No trail leads directly to this lake. It is 1 1/2 miles SE and 700 ft. above Moccasin. See Moccasin Lake for directions. Follow Lake Creek, the outlet of Moccasin Lake, about 1/2 mile to a tributary which enters from the south, then bushwhack up this creek to Pocket Lake. Though only 9 acres, Pocket is very deep for its size. There's not a lot of traffic up here, and the lake produces well for small to medium brook trout.

POWER CITY PONDS On Power City Wildlife Area, 4 miles north of Hermiston. The ponds contain largemouth bass and brown bullhead catfish.

PROSPECT LAKE A good, small rainbow lake at the very head of the West Fork Wallowa River in Eagle Cap Wilderness. It sits below a

ridge that separates it from Glacier Lake, 1/2 mile south. There is no trail to the lake. Hike to Little Frazier Lake (See Frazier Lake) and follow the inlet stream up to Prospect Lake, 1/2 mile NW. It's about a 12 mile trip.

Prospect is at 8380 ft., so be prepared for cold nights and the possibility of snow showers in September. The lake has been known to have some nice rainbow trout for a small rainbow, possibly because of its great depth. Though only 14 acres, the lake is over 100 ft. deep. Average size is 10-12 inches, with some fish to 20 inches taken in August and September.

PRAIRIE CREEK (Wallowa Co.) A small trout stream near Enterprise. About 18 miles long, it heads a couple of miles east of Wallowa Lake and flows NW, joining the Wallowa River at Enterprise. Gravel roads leading east and south from Hwy. 82, between Enterprise and Joseph, follow and cross the stream.

The creek is stocked with hatchery rainbow and has a fair native trout population. Bait is the best method early in the year, and flies are good in late summer and fall. Fish here range 7-15 inches, with the average 10 inches.

RAZZ LAKE A small but interesting brook trout lake high in Eagle Cap Wilderness just to the north of the popular lake basin south of Wallowa Lake. Razz is about one mile north of Horseshoe Lake at 8100 ft., about 900 ft. above Horseshoe. See Horseshoe Lake for trail directions. Follow Horseshoe's inlet stream upslope one mile to the lake. Change your pacemaker batteries before starting out.

The lake is about 14 acres and 26 ft. deep. The brookies here average 10 inches with some to 13 or better. Fishing is good in August and September.

RHEA CREEK A good wild trout stream about 35 miles long, flowing into Willow Creek, 2 miles east of Ione about 15 miles north of Heppner. Most of its flow is through private property, so ask permission before you fish. Ione is on Hwy. 74, which intersects I-84 east of Arlington. The creek is followed upstream by 20 miles of paved and gravel roads from Ione to the crossing of Hwy. 207 at Ruggs, 10 miles SW of Heppner. From there, gravel roads follow the creek to its headwaters.

ROCK CREEK (Gilliam Co.) A 40 mile tributary of the lower John Day River, with native rainbow in its upper stretches. It enters the John Day about 15 miles above the mouth, just above the bridge on the road from Wasco to Rock Creek, and is followed by roads for most of its length. It is followed east by a gravel road from Rock Creek to Olex on Hwy. 19, the Arlington-Condon Rd., and crossed again further south by several gravel roads and Hwy. 206, the Condon-Heppner Rd..

There are a lot of irrigation withdrawals on the creek, and trout fishing is confined mainly to the upper areas, where there's a fair native rainbow population. There are a lot of rough fish in the lower end.

ROWE CREEK RESERVOIR A 30 acre impoundment south of Hwy. 19 about 17 miles south of Fossil. From Hwy. 19 about 10 miles SE of Fossil, turn south onto the gravel road going SW to Twickenham. The turn is just west of Sheldon Wayside.

Although a private lake, the public has gained access through an agreement made between its owner and the Dept. of Fish and

Wildlife. A 50 ft. strip around the shore is reserved for anglers. It is stocked with legal rainbow trout and fished very hard by local people. Still, it generally holds up well through spring. The rainbow range 8-11 inches.

Supplies are available at Fossil. The reservoir is open to fishing all year. Motors on the lake, open fires, and camping are prohibited.

SERVICE CREEK A small creek, tributary to the lower John Day River. It enters the John Day at the community of Service Creek at the junction of Hwys. 19 and 207, between Fossil and Mitchell. It is followed closely by Hwy. 19 north from Service Creek to Sheldon Wayside. The creek is only 9 miles long, but it offers fair trout fishing in spring. It gets very low in summer, but will produce on bait until low water conditions. There is no camping nearby. Sheldon Wayside has a nice picnic area.

SLIDE LAKE (Grant Co.) A small lake high in the Strawberry Mt. Wilderness south of Prairie City. The wilderness is a handsome counterpoint to the arrid John Day Valley over which it towers, with its snowy peaks and cool coniferous forest. Follow Main St. (County Rd. 60) south from Prairie City to Malheur National Forest. FS 6001 continues to the trailhead at Strawberry Camp. The upper road is usually poor in early spring. Trail 375 leads south into the wilderness, meeting Trail 372 about 1/2 mile in. Take this trail about 2 miles to the east, and swing south on Trail 385 to the lake. It's a 4.3 mile hike.

Slide Lake is 13 acres and only 8 feet at its deepest point. It fills a glacial cirque at 7200 ft. but has plenty of aquatic vegetation and grows nice trout. It's not stocked, but has a good self-sustaining population of brook trout. Flyfishing is enjoyable here late in fall, but bring your long johns if you plan to stay for the evening rise. Just south of Slide Lake is Upper or Little Slide Lake, a 3 acre cup that holds a lot of brook trout. It's a bit deeper than the lower lake. Both can usually be reached in June.

SNAKE RIVER (Northeast Zone) That stretch of the river from the Oregon/Washington border upstream to the Hell's Canyon Dam, carving the boundary between Idaho and Oregon. One of the state's original Wild and Scenic Rivers, the Snake has some of the best fishing to be found anywhere—when you can get to it. Access is the tough part, as the river here runs through spectacular Hells Canyon, an awesome gorge over 6,000 ft. deep in places.

Hells Canyon is contained within Hells Canyon National Recreation Area in Wallowa-Whitman National Forest, and a good portion of it has been protected by Wilderness status as the Hells Canyon Wilderness Area in both Oregon and Idaho. This is one of the few places civilization hasn't reached yet, and the fishing shows it. If you have the time and/or money—not all that much—you're in for the angling experience of a lifetime.

Access is very limited. From the west side, the river is reached by road only at Hells Canyon Dam, Dug Bar, and at the mouth of the Grande Ronde River, in Washington. From the Idaho side, roads reach the river at Pittsburg, Wolf Creek and Dry Creek. There is trail access for much of the canyon, and commercial rafting operations will take you the whole length of this wild river. Dug Bar is at the confluence of the Imnaha and Snake, and is reached from Joseph, on Hwy. 82, by going east on the Sheep Creek Rd. to the community

AN ALPINE LAKE, EAGLE CAP WILDERNESS
Steve Terrill, Photographer

of Imnaha, then following the river road downstream. Hells Canyon Dam is reached by taking Hwy. 86 from Halfway to Copperfield, crossing to Idaho, and following the river downstream on the Idaho side. There is no trail access from the dam.

For trail access, check the Wallowa-Whitman National Forest map, north half. Most of the trails begin on spur roads leading east from the Imnaha River Rd. Several good trails begin at Hat Point, which is reached by FS 4240 leading SE from the town of Imnaha.

The river below the dam is full of feisty smallmouth bass that reach 3 pounds and more. They'll take almost any lure thrown to them. Rainbow trout are numerous and range 8-20 inches. They can always be found where a tributary enters the main river, but actually you can hook them anywhere in the canyon.

Steelhead angling has been improving over the past few years as a result of an intense program of hatchery plants, mitigation programs to offset losses caused by dams, and restricted angling throughout the Snake system. Most are caught by trolling hotshots or casting lures. Be sure to check current regulations for steelhead seasons, deadlines, and restrictions.

If you like channel catfish, this is the place. Almost any bait hook-up will work, and the bigger the bait, the bigger the fish. Channel cats to 20 pounds have been taken here. There are also mighty big sturgeon in the river, some in the 8-9 ft. class, but the fishery for them is currently restricted to catch and release only. Sturgeon are to be released without removing them from the water.

Really, unless you've got plenty of time and are a strong hiker, horse packing or rafting are the only ways to get in here. This is water for the expert rafter only. Jet boats are available for hire in Lewiston, ID and Clarkston, WA. Guides and outfitters are available in Oxbow, Enterprise, and Joseph, as well as other areas of

the state. Write the Oregon Guides and Packers Association, PO Box 3797, Portland Or. 97208, for a complete listing of professional guides.

STEAMBOAT LAKE A fair size lake in the headwaters of the North Fork of the Minam River. See long lake for directions to Swamp Lake. From Swamp Lake, follow the trail that leads across a saddle to the east, dropping down to Steamboat. It's a 10 mile hike, and the trails aren't too steep.

Steamboat is 30 acres and just over 100 ft. deep. It has a good population of eastern brook trout, but the fish don't get large. Most are 7-10 inches with a few larger caught in the late fall. Bait and flies are both productive methods here. Long Lake is just one mile west and can be reached by a trail leading down from Swamp Lake.

STRAWBERRY LAKE The largest lake in the Strawberry Mt. Wilderness, south of Prairie City. The Strawberry Mountains, compact and distinct from other Oregon ranges, rise stately and cool above the arrid John Day Valley. Their slopes are covered in dense conifer forest, meadows are carpeted with wildflowers in June, the forest floor with wild strawberries in July. Strawberry Lake is one of several glacially created lakes in the Wilderness, extremely scenic with a backdrop of snowy crests. It was formed during glacial retreat when steep valley walls collapsed, blocking Strawberry Creek. See also Little Strawberry, Slide.

County Rd. 60 leads south from Prairie City into Malheur National Forest, and FS 6001 continues to the trailhead at Strawberry Camp. The upper road is usually poor in early spring. Trail 375 leads south into the wilderness area and skirts the eastern border of Strawberry Lake. The trail continues south past Strawberry Falls, a 40 ft. cascade, and on to Little Strawberry Lake.

Strawberry is at 6320 ft. and covers 31 acres, with a maximum depth of 40 ft. The lake offers good angling for brook trout, and some rainbow are taken. Brook trout outnumber rainbow here about 3 to 1. Both tend to grow nice and plump and run to 16 inches. Flyfishing is best in the southern half of the lake. There are some good deep holes in the center and at the north end. Fishing is best in early spring and again in late fall. These fish seem to sulk during the middle of the summer. There is a camping area just north of the lake between Strawberry and Little Strawberry.

STRAWBERRY LAKE, LITTLE A small high lake 1/2 mile south of Strawberry Lake in Strawberry Mt. Wilderness. See Strawberry Lake for directions. Trail 375 leads south into the wilderness, skirts the eastern border of Strawberry Lake, and climbs 1.1 miles to Strawberry Falls. Here a side trail leads east .6 mile to Little Strawberry Lake, cupped in a glacial cirque.

Little Strawberry is at elevation 6960 ft. with a handsome craggy backdrop. It covers 4 acres and is 10 ft. deep. It contains large numbers of brook trout, small but easy to catch. There is a camping area to the north between Little Strawberry and Big Strawberry Lakes.

SWAMP LAKE A very good lake with golden and rainbow trout in Eagle Cap Wilderness, Wallowa-Whitman National Forest. It is west of the head of the Lostine River, above and south of Steamboat and Long Lakes. See Long Lake for directions. It's a 9 mile hike on moderately steep trails.

The lake covers about 43 acres and is 23 ft. deep. This is one of the few lakes in Oregon stocked with golden trout, a beautiful fish native to the high Sierras of California. Fishing is generally excellent in August and September on flies or lures. Still fishing with worms or eggs will take fish almost anytime. The rainbow average 8-12 inches with a few to 15 inches. The goldens run a bit smaller. Both Long Lake and Steamboat Lake are less than one mile away and offer good fishing.

THIRTY-MILE CREEK A native rainbow creek, tributary of the lower John Day River, actually 39 miles long. It enters the John Day at river mile 84, about half-way between Hwy. 206 and 218. Trout angling is confined to the upper portions of the creek, where there are quite a few native rainbow. The upper creek is reached from Kinzua just east of Hwy. 19 and south of Fossil.

UMATILLA, LAKE (John Day Pool) One of the four dam pools in Oregon's chain of Columbia River reservoirs. In 1989, the Oregon Department of Fish and Wildlife, Umatilla District, gently chided us for calling this section of the Columbia a biological wasteland. We should have known better. Nature abhors a vacuum.

Though salmon and steelhead no longer linger here, other species have made themselves at home in the old channel, on the submerged gravel bars, amidst the drowned islands and rocky structures. Today, Lake Umatilla offers excellent smallmouth bass angling, one of the best walleye fisheries in the state, some sturgeon opportunities, fair channel catfish, and an abundance of crappie, bluegill, pumpkinseed, yellow perch, and brown bullhead.

Angling for smallmouth bass is a recent sportfishing phenomenon here, adding an Oregon link to the national bass tournament circuit. The first smallmouth open tournament on Lake Umatilla took place in 1988, sponsored by the Blue Mt. Bass Club of Pendleton. Tournament catches have reportedly been on a par with the best in the country.

Most smallmouth are caught in the mid-pool area from Fulton Canyon to above Irrigon. Using plugs and jigs, anglers start taking fish in May and continue throughout the fall. Smallmouth to 6 pounds have been taken, and 3 pounders are not uncommon. A growing number of anglers are practicing catch and release.

Though walleye are present in the lower Columbia, nowhere are these monster perch more enthusiastically sought than in Lake Umatilla. Since 1984, growing numbers of out-of-state anglers are joining the locals in this fishery, drawn by the potential for a trophy catch, over 10 pounds. Walleye are year around residents of the lake, their reproduction regulated by the spring flow. If the flow is high, reproduction that season will be low, and vice versa. A schooling fish, walleye tend to inhabit submerged structures. Depth finders and navigational charts showing the contours of the lake are useful for locating likely walleye environments.

The major walleye fishery takes place between the base of the dam and Boardman. The fish concentrate upstream in spring, then move downriver throughout the summer to spawning areas on submerged gravel bars. Though walleye are available year around, most angling effort is concentrated in March and April, then picks up again from August to November. Anglers troll large plugs near the bottom, or jig with 4-inch Twister Tails. Some use night crawlers and minnows. This is a boat fishery. Bank anglers have had little success. The catch rate on walleye in Lake Umatilla is not high at present, but a size range from 3-12 pounds makes this an attractive sport, and the walleye population density here, still on the thin side by midwest standards, is expected to increase.

The sturgeon population here appears to be down and is currently under study. Anglers should anticipate fluctuating regulations over the next few years. At present there is a catch and release fishery for over-size (7-9 foot) sturgeon just below McNary Dam.

Angling for fall chinook and summer steelhead is on the increase here, with most effort concentrated at the upper end of the pool around McNary Dam. The shad run is fished only at Umatilla at this time.

Crappie fishing is popular in fall, particularly in the boat basins, where there's good fishing from the docks. Additional bass and panfish angling is available on McCormach Slough. For complete information on this water, see McCormach Slough.

Public boat ramps are available at the mouth of the John Day River, Blalock Canyon, Arlington, Patterson Ferry, Irrigon, and Umatilla. Bank access is limited due to the proximity of I-84 and the Union Pacific railroad tracks. Best bank access is at the boat basins, excepting Blalock and Patterson Ferry. There is good bank access for crappie, smallmouth bass, and brown bullhead at Three-Mile Falls, a park on the Umatilla River.

Complete camping facilities are available at Boardman City Park, and at Umatilla. Supplies are available in Boardman, Umatilla, Irrigon, and Arlington. There is also a developed boat-in campground on the John Day Arm of the lake.

UMATILLA, LAKE, (John Day Arm) Cut off from access above by a major falls, accessible only by boat from Lake Umatilla, the last 9 miles of the John Day offer fine fishing in a stunning environment—a narrow canyon with sheer rock walls, and the added attraction (for some) of a full service boat-in campground complete with running water, picnic tables, grassy lawn, and two boat docks. It can get crowded in here, but fishing is excellent for summer steelhead, very good for smallmouth bass, good for channel catfish and brown bullhead, and fair for crappie.

Steelheaders fish the upper 2 miles, where their quarry congregate at the base of Tumwater Falls. Bass and panfish angling takes place throughout.

UMATILLA RIVER A good steelhead and trout stream. The Umatilla enters the Columbia River about 3 miles below McNary Dam at the town of Umatilla. It heads in the northern Blue Mts. and flows west past Pendleton and Hermiston. From Pendleton to the Columbia the stream is easily reached by a paved road that follows it from Rieth to Echo, both of which are on I-84. East of Pendleton paved and gravel roads follow the stream for another 30 miles, mostly through Umatilla Indian Reservation lands.

Steelhead are taken from December through March in the water below the deadline at the Hwy. 11 Bridge in Pendleton. Bait fishing with eggs or nightcrawlers produce most of the fish. Annual catch for the past 5 years has been less than 200, though prior to that, the catch generally exceeded 500.

The river is well stocked with rainbow in the areas above the reservation boundaries, and by the Federal government within the reservation. Tribal permits, required to fish from Indian land, are available at Mission. Some good catches of native trout are made in the Bingham Springs area, upstream from Pendleton.

The river is closed to salmon its entire length, and closed for steelhead above Pendleton.

UMATILLA RIVER, SOUTH FORK A rather short stream, tributary to the upper Umatilla River, which it joins about 32 miles east of Pendleton upriver from Bingham Springs. FS 32, Umatilla National Forest, which is reached by driving east from Bingham Springs, follows the lower 3 miles of the fork. Trail 3076 continues up the fork an additional 2 miles. FS 3128 follows the upper waters along a ridge about one mile west of the river and could serve as a jump-off for the bushwhacking enthusiast.

The Fork provides good trout angling for both native and stocked trout. Bull trout (Dolly Varden) and rainbow are found in its upper waters. Camping is available at Umatilla Forks Campground, about 3 miles above Bingham Springs, and at Elk and South Fork Campgrounds 3 miles south.

UNIT LAKE A 15 acre lake in the popular lake basin about 10 trail miles south of Wallowa Lake. It is 1/2 mile NE of Horseshoe Lake by trail. See horseshoe lake for directions. Unit has brook and rainbow trout, with brookies to 11 inches predominant. Rainbow reach 14 inches.

WALLA WALLA RIVER A fair steelhead stream just south and east of Milton Freewater in the northeast corner of the state. The river heads in Oregon and flows NW into Washington, meeting the Columbia River a few miles above the Oregon border. About 12 miles of the river flow through Oregon up to the forks, which are about 5 miles SE of Milton Freewater. Milton Freewater is about 32 miles NE of Pendleton on Hwy. 11.

The river flows right through Milton Freewater, and is open for steelhead up to the forks. However, there is no public access to the river. Ask permission to access the river through the orchards. Marie Dorian County Park about 4 miles upstream from Walla Walla accesses good steelhead water.

A few trout are picked up in the mainstem, but most angling for them takes place on the upper forks. There is no camping in the area.

WALLA WALLA RIVER, NORTH FORK
A tributary of the Walla Walla joining it about 5 miles east of Milton Freewater. The stream is about 20 miles long, but a road only follows it up about 8 miles through private property, which is closed to public access. Forest Trail 3222 follows the river to its headwaters, offering the only public angling opportunity. You can reach the trail from FS 65 about 4 miles below Deduck Campground off Tiger Canyon Rd., or from the end of a dirt road which follows the lower fork above Milton Freewater. Check the Umatilla National Forest map.

The fork below the forest is heavily used for irrigation, and water gets very low in summer and fall. The North Fork contains native bull trout (Dolly Varden) and rainbow, with best fishing in early season. Camping is available at Deduck Campground.

WALLA WALLA RIVER, SOUTH FORK
A large tributary of the Walla Walla River joining the North Fork about 5 miles east of the city of Milton Freewater. The South Fork is about 30 miles long, although roads only parallel the stream for about 12 miles upstream. It heads 3 miles south of the upper corner of the state and arcs south through Umatilla National Forest, emerging SE of Milton Freewater. In the forest it can be fished from Trail 3225, which begins at Bear Creek Guard Station and follows the river to its head near Deduck Campground.

The South Fork carries more water than the North Fork, and angling holds up well into summer. Trout fishing is good from opening through August. The river below the forest is well stocked with rainbow trout. Native bull trout and rainbow can be caught in the upper waters. Bait fishing is the most common method, but a good fly angler can out-produce bait on this steam. Camping is available at Deduck Campground. A Umatilla National Forest map will be useful.

WALLOWA LAKE
The largest natural lake in northeast Oregon, just south of Joseph at the foot of the Wallowa Mts. The lake was formed by the terminal moraine of a glacier that carved out the Wallowa River Valley. The moraine forms an immense natural dam on the Wallowa River and towers over 400 ft. above the surface of this 1600 acre lake. To reach the lake drive to Joseph, south of Enterprise on Hwy. 82, and follow 82 south to the lake. This highway follows the lake's eastern shore to its southern tip.

Wallowa is a clear, deep lake, with ideal conditions for kokanee and Mackinaw, and the state has stocked accordingly. The kokanee average 9-10 inches, but there are some 15-20 inches. Large numbers of fish are present, and

WALLOWA LAKE
Steve Terrill, Photographer

angling is excellent, with best catches in May, June, and the first part of July. These are wonderfully tasty freshwater fish. The Mackinaw are caught by deep trolling with spinners and lures, or combinations, but they haven't been heavily pursued.

The lake also provides good angling for both native and stocked rainbow trout averaging 9 inches, with a few reaching 16 inches. Rainbow are taken both by trolling and by bank fishing with bait. Fishing around the edges in the fall will produce nice catches.

To protect spawning fish, all angling in the tributaries of the lake (up to the falls on the West Fork and the PP&L intake on the East Fork) is prohibited from September 1 through October 31.

Boats are available for rent at the lake, and private boats can be launched. There is a resort at the south end of the lake with accommodations and supplies. Wallowa Lake State Park, also at the south end, has a full-service campground. This is a jumping-off place for many high lakes in Eagle Cap Wilderness. Horses and guides are available.

WALLOWA RIVER Once host to large runs of salmon and steelhead, now primarily a popular and accessible trout stream. It does have a limited steelhead season. The river flows 80 miles from headwaters in the central lake basin of Eagle Cap Wilderness to its confluence with the Grande Ronde River about 16 miles downstream from Elgin. The river feeds Wallowa Lake, skirts the eastern edges of Joseph and Enterprise, and absorbs Lostine and Minam rivers on its journey north and west. Hwy. 82 follows the river from Wallowa Lake to the Minam confluence. Trails 1820 and 1804 follow the West and East forks from South Park Picnic Area at Wallowa Lake into Eagle Cap.

Trout angling is excellent from late spring through late fall. The stream is heavily stocked with hatchery rainbow and has a good supply of native brook trout, rainbow, and bull trout. The average catch runs 8-14 inches, with some onative rainbow and bull trout to several pounds. Flyfishing is excellent in September and October.

There is currently a limited steelhead season on the river, restricted to hatchery steel-

head (adipose fin-clipped) only. Wild steelhead must be released without removing the fish from the water. Minam State Park downstream from Minam, and two waysides offer bank fishing opportunities. Anglers also pull off the highway and fish throughout the canyon, which is easily accessible and quite good, especially for late season rainbow.

The nearest campgrounds are within the National Forest south of the community of Wallowa, and along the Lostine River.

WALLULA, LAKE (McNary Dam Pool) The easternmost pool in Oregon's string of four Columbia River reservoirs. Most angling effort in Lake Wallula is devoted to smallmouth bass. Smallmouth are taken near the islands on both Oregon and Washington sides, with catches up to 6 pounds. Walleye, sturgeon, and channel catfish are all present in the lake, but anglers here are still trying to figure out how, when, and where to catch them.

Fall chinook and summer steelhead are both fished immediately behind McNary Dam at the buoy line, from boats launched at the dam. Summer steelhead are taken from the end of July into January, with peak catches in November. Fall chinook angling is best in September. A second boat ramp is located at Hat Rock State Park, where there are also camping facilities. Bank fishing for salmon occurs at the Corps. park behind the dam as well as at a scattering of points along the shore to Hat Rock.

WENAHA RIVER A good native trout stream that originates in the Blue Mountains of Wenaha-Tucannon Wilderness in Oregon's extreme northeast corner. The river flows east about 35 miles and enters the Grande Ronde River at the community of Troy, about 30 miles north of Wallowa. There are no roads near the stream, except for the lower few miles, but trails follow the main stream for more than 31 miles through the wilderness. See the U.S. Forest Service's Wenaha-Tucannon Wilderness map for best trail information, supplemented by the Umatilla National Forest map.

The Wenaha-Tucannon Wilderness is a huge canyonland, especially popular with horse packers, and with hunters. It has the nation's highest density elk population. The Wenaha River valley is lined with old growth cottonwoods, fir, and ponderosa pine. The south facing canyons are covered in the bunchgrass and sage typical of eastern Oregon, while the north slopes are thick with conifers and sumac that burns a brilliant red in autumn. The name Wenaha is Nez Perce for *ha* (domain) of Wenak, a Nez Perce chief (as Imnaha was ha of Chief Imna).

Trout angling is excellent here in summer and fall. Native rainbow run to 15 inches, with the average 10 inches. Bull trout are also present and may go to several pounds. The bull respond to bait fished deep in the holes.

The Wenaha now also has a limited steelhead season, currently restricted to catch and release with barbless hooks only. Flyfishing for steelhead is popular here, with favorite patterns including the Skunk, Macks Canyon, and Silver Hilton. Check current regulations.

As the river runs almost entirely through designated wilderness, there are no developed campgrounds, and campers are urged to use no-trace methods. Check with Forest Service guard stations for camping permits during fire season.

WILLOW CREEK (Morrow Co.) An 80 mile stream that flows NW from the area around Arbuckle Mt. Ski Area, Umatilla National Forest, SE of Heppner. There is a reservoir on the creek just above Heppner. Willow Creek was devastated, in the 22 miles above the reservoir, by a massive pesticide spill in the spring of 1983. This spill killed every living thing in the creek from the spill site to the reservoir. The fishery in the stream has since been rebuilt.

The creek flows through Heppner on its way across the wheatlands to the Columbia, which it joins about 11 miles east of Arlington. The creek is followed from its mouth to Heppner by Hwy. 74, and SE from Heppner by county road.

There's no camping in the area. There's quite a bit of private property, so watch your trespassing, or get permission.

WILLOW CREEK RESERVOIR (Morrow Co.) An impoundment on Willow Creek just south of Heppner in Morrow County, with maximum pool 110 acres. A gravel road leads SE from Heppner along the creek to the reservoir. The reservoir offers good fishing for smallmouth bass, largemouth bass, crappie, and pumpkinseed sunfish. It has excellent boat ramps, and motor boats are allowed. The reservoir is popular with water skiers in summer.

WOOD LAKE (Wallowa Co.) A very good lake in the northern Eagle Cap Wilderness west of the Lostine River. It sits about one mile north of Hobo Lake. From Lostine on Hwy. 82, head south to the Bowman Creek Trail 1651, about 2.5 miles south of Lostine Guard Station. Climb east on this trail for 3.6 miles to the junction of Trail 1659, which leads north past Chimney Lake and Hobo Lake, reaching Wood Lake 1 1/2 miles beyond Hobo. The total hike is just over 6 miles, with elevation gain over 3000 ft.

Wood Lake contains brook and golden trout. The goldens, native to the high Sierras of California, are beautifully colored. This is one of the few waters in Oregon where golden trout are stocked. They run 8-12 inches, with brook trout generally smaller. Bait works well for both throughout the season, and flies will take fish in late summer and fall.

SOUTHEAST ZONE

The Southeast Zone is all waters of the Snake River System above Hells Canyon Dam (including impoundments and tributaries); the Silvies River drainage in Grant County; all waters in Malheur, Harney, and Lake Counties; and all waters of the Klamath Basin in Klamath County.

You can't fish in a blizzard. That thought crossed my mind as I strained to make out the edges of the road behind the swirling snow illuminated by my headlights. A 2 a.m. crossing of Steens Mt. to reach Mann Lake for early spring fishing for large cutthroat trout.

"Wow. Did you see the wind topple that cow?"

"What cow? I can't even see the road."

Long drive from Portland. At 3 a.m. the three of us struggle mightily against the wind to pitch a tent. The campground looks like a war zone, with tents blow down and refugees huddled in the cabs of their trucks. Exhausted, and perhaps slow learners, we crawl into our sleeping bags as the wind howls and the tent flaps and bows.

When I awake, my companions are already up. I peer out the tent but see only a lead gray sky spitting flurries of snow. Then I spot the abominable snowman hulking around the lake. With fish rod. Soon it's skulking back toward me. Could that be Bob? He was so young. This looks like a survivor of the Scott Antarctic party.

"I caught one," he croaks triumphantly. "I'm freezing. Let me in. Gosh, it doesn't get any better than this."

The southeast zone includes over one third of Oregon. Its western extreme is typical of the eastern high Cascades, but as one moves further east, the high desert of the Great Basin quickly predominates. Be prepared for hot days, cold nights. At least four fifths of this region is federal land, with the BLM holding the majority.

The western waters of the region fall within the Klamath River watershed and are arguably the richest trout waters in the state. Rainbow trout in Klamath Lake are capable of growing to 20 inches in only three seasons. The Klamath, Williamson, Sycan, and Sprague Rivers are all premier trout waters.

To the east is basin and range country, a land of desert lakes, where shallow waters and sunshine grow big fish quickly. From Lakeview east, prepare for desert conditions and dirt road travel if you plan to leave the main highway. These waters are usually best in spring and fall; it gets right warm in the summer. If you don't like crowds, you'll love the southeast zone.

In the north, the Malheur, Powder, Burnt, and Owyhee River drainages carry water to the Snake River Canyon. The quality and kind of angling opportunities varies greatly throughout each.

The southeast region. Wide open spaces, coyotes and antelope—and big trout. Old west fishing at its finest.

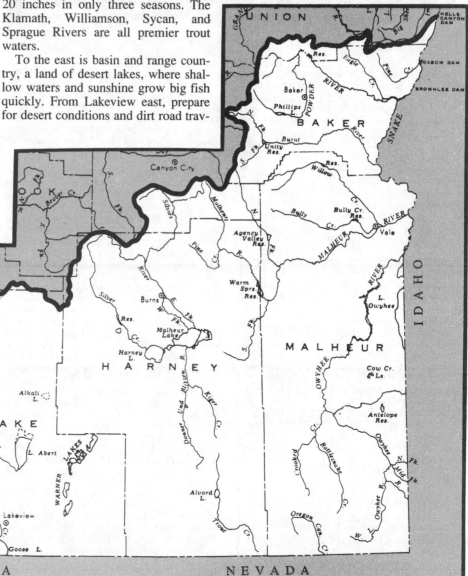

ANTHONY LAKE
Steve Terrill, Photographer

AGENCY LAKE The large northern pool of Upper Klamath Lake, separated from the main body by a narrow natural channel, offering excellent opportunities for large rainbow and brown trout. From Klamath Falls take Hwy. 97 north to Modoc Point, then the old Hwy. 162 NW to Agency Lake, about a 23 mile drive. From Bend, follow Hwy. 97 south to Chiloquin, then take the Klamath Agency cut-off south of town, about a 115 mile drive. Hwy. 162 follows Agency's east shore closely. A secondary road south of Klamath Agency crosses the northern narrows and follows the Wood River tributary.

Like the Upper Klamath, Agency is primarily a trout fishery, with even larger rainbow and browns. The big fish migrate through Agency's main tributaries, Wood River and Sevenmile Creek. In early spring, anglers troll slowly near the mouths of these streams at the north end of the lake, and in the narrows. As the lake warms in June, they troll closer to the Wood River mouth. Angling usually slows by July. Large lures seem to be most successful, with bait paying off more slowly. Rainbow average 12-18 inches, with some 20 pounders taken in the north. Fishing is traditionally best in the early morning. Large perch and brown bullhead are also available, primarily at the north end of the lake.

Boats can be launched at Henzel Park in the south, at Petric Park on the Wood River, and at the resort on the NE shore. Agency can get rough, so stay close to the shore. The lake is open year around for panfish, with no limits on bullhead and perch.

ALTNOW LAKE An 8 acre bass and panfish lake in Harney County, its largemouth bass and bluegill populations restored following a dam break-down. It is located NE of Drewsey, just off Hwy. 20 about 47 miles east of Burns. Though the fishery is stable, it is not as productive as it was years ago.

Though privately owned and stocked, the lake has been open to the public. A user fee (currently $6) was instituted due to occurrences of vandalism and excessive littering. Anglers are urged to respect the owner's generosity and help keep this lake available for all. Small boats can be launched here. There is no camping at the lake.

ANA RESERVOIR A 60-acre reservoir north of Summer Lake, offering year-round, ice-free fishing for stocked legal trout. The lake is in a popular waterfowl hunting area. It is about 2 miles east of Hwy. 31 and 5 miles north of the community of Summer Lake.

Most angling is from the bank. Bait, lures, and flies are all effective, but bait anglers have some problem with chubs taking their offerings. The lake also contains sterile hybrid bass (white crossed with striped), which were experimentally stocked to forage on the reservoir's excessive chub population. At this time, anglers are allowed to keep one of these hybrids per day. Hybrids 10-12 pounds have been taken here.

Ana was not effected by the drought in 1987-88, as it is fed by underground streams whose flows remain constant. Their temperature remains constant as well, 58 degrees, which keeps the reservoir ice free for winter fishing.

ANA RIVER A short but excellent fly fishing stream flowing south from Ana Reservoir into Summer Lake Marsh. Flowing parallel to Hwy. 31 about 2 miles east of the highway, this 7 mile stream is approached near its outlet by a road east from the community of Summer Lake or, at its head, by way of the Ana Reservoir Rd. north of town. The river is about 75 miles north of Lakeview. From Bend, a 100 mile drive, take Hwy. 97 south to the Hwy. 31 junction just south of LaPine, and continue south.

The river maintains a stable, clear, cool flow and a constant 50-60 degree water temper-

ature that produces insect hatches throughout the season. Planted rainbow fingerlings rear in the stream, averaging 8-12 inches, with 16-18 inch fish common and some to 5 pounds. Small dry fly patterns work best, though streamers imitating chubs may take the larger fish. There is a state park picnic area at Summer Lake, but no designated campground in the vicinity.

ANDERSON LAKE See Warner Valley Lakes.

ANNIE CREEK A spring-fed trout stream heading in Crater Lake National Park, tributary to the Wood River. Hwy. 62 follows the creek closely from its headwaters about 5 road miles south of the lake, to its confluence with the Wood just north of Fort Klamath. Fort Klamath is near the junction of hwys. 62 and 232, about 40 miles north of Klamath Falls.

Annie Creek is about 14 miles long and offers good angling for wild rainbow, brown, and brook trout, especially in the lower end. It is not stocked. Fly angling is good in the evenings. The stream has a high pumice content and retains a milky color throughout the year. There is a good campground at its head, off Hwy. 62, with the Pacific Crest Trail passing just to the west of camp.

State licenses are not required to fish in the national park. Fishing permits may be obtained at park headquarters on the south rim.

ANTELOPE RESERVOIR A large trout reservoir in extreme SE Oregon near the Idaho line, about 15 miles west of Jordan Valley. From Burns follow Hwy. 78 to Burns Junction, then go east on I-95 to the reservoir.

This 2000 acre impoundment grows trout very well in good water years, though it has problems with rough fish populations from time to time. The reservoir leaks badly, and when water levels are low, fish production suffers. There is a BLM campground here with toilets and tables.

ANTHONY LAKE High in the Elkhorn Mountains of Wallowa-Whitman National Forest NW of Baker. This 19 acre lake is one of many located about 20 miles east of the town of North Powder, which is on Hwy. 30 between LaGrande and Baker. A good paved road heads west from North Powder, connecting with Hwy. 411, which becomes FS 73 and leads to the lake. Hwy. 411 can also be picked up in Haines. Other good forest roads lead in from Ukiah (on Hwy. 395 between Pendleton and John Day). Anthony Lake is the site of a popular ski resort.

Fishing is good for stocked rainbow to 14 inches from early summer through fall. There are also wild brook trout to 10 inches. Flyfishing can be good, but most anglers troll or cast bait. The lake is 30 feet at its deepest point. There is a boat ramp, but motors are prohibited.

A large campground at the lake has kitchen facilities, and there are camps at tiny Mud Lake and at Grande Ronde Lake to the north. Other lakes in the area include hike-ins Van Patten, Black, Crawfish. There is a resort at Anthony with accommodations, supplies, and boat rentals. At elevation 7100 ft., ice-out is generally around July 4.

ARRITOLA RESERVOIR A 200 acre reservoir on the Jaca Ranch 20 miles south of Jordan Valley. It has contained largemouth bass, bluegill, and bullhead, but the lake went dry in 1988 and the fishery was lost. The Jaca Ranch has not been allowing public access.

ASPEN LAKE A 500 acre marsh area west of Klamath Falls, with rumored catches of brown bullhead. To get there, take Lake of the Woods Hwy.140 north from Klamath Falls about 16 miles, turning south onto Aspen Lake Rd. one mile past Rock Creek Ranch. There are no campgrounds in the vicinity.

AUGUR CREEK A small wild trout stream, tributary to Thomas Creek, about 10 miles NW of Lakeview. You'll need a map to find this one. A gravel road follows much of its 7 miles from the Hotchkiss Ranch area to Lucky Lass and White King mines. It's accessible by circuitous route from Hwy. 140 west of Lakeview, and from Hwy. 395 north of the community.

This stream contains native brook trout to 10 inches and native Goose Lake Basin rainbow. In the spring it hosts a spawning run of large Goose Lake fish. There are campgrounds west of the headwaters in the areas of Cox Flat and Ranger Station Spring. Check current regulations for special restrictions on Thomas Creek tributaries.

BACA LAKE A 300 acre irrigation reservoir for the Malheur Wildlife Refuge north of French Glen. It is closed to angling.

BEAR CREEK (Harney Co.) An eastern Oregon trout stream entering the upper Silvies near the community of Seneca, on Hwy. 395 between John Day and Burns. About 25 miles long, it is followed east from Hwy. 395 (about 26 miles south of John Day) by FS 16. FS 1530 and 1640 access the waters upstream from Parish Cabin.

Lightly fished, the creek produces an average catch for this country. Bait angling is the usual method, but flies will work for anglers with know-how. May, June, and July are the best months, but fish can be taken later. Parish Cabin Campground is located streamside, about 11 miles east of Seneca.

BEAR CREEK (Lake Co.) A small tributary of the Chewaucan River in the Winema National Forest, joining the main stream near the community of Paisley. You'll find Paisley on Hwy. 31 (Bend to Lakeview) south of Summer Lake. To reach the creek's confluence with the Chewaucan, follow the Chewaucan River Rd. FS 330 south about 6 miles from town. A north-bound gravel road just west of town, FS 331, crosses the upper stream, as does FS 348.

The stream flows about 9 miles and offers good rainbow fishing in late spring and early summer. Its trout run small but are numerous, as the creek is lightly fished. Bait is usually best.

BECKERS POND A small lake within the city limits of Ontario, stocked with bluegill, channel catfish, and largemouth bass. It doesn't have many channel cats, but its bluegill and bass populations are thriving. The shoreline is developed, but anglers can reach the pond through the city park.

BENDIRE CREEK A little known, lightly fished trout stream, tributary to Beulah Reservoir, which flows into the reservoir's NE arm. See Beulah Reservoir for directions from Burns and Vale. Flowing about 12 miles from spring-fed headwaters north of Bendire Mountain, its lower waters are primarily within the Butler Ranch, though it is crossed several times by roads. Ask permission to fish on ranch property.

Native trout make up most of the catch, averaging 9-12 inches, with a few to 16 inches. Bait is most frequently used. Beulah Reservoir has the only improved campground in the area.

BERT LAKE A small, hike-in brook trout lake, in the south Sky Lakes Area of the Winema National Forest. The lake is off-trail, about 1/4 mile north of Trail 3712 to Island Lake. To reach the area, follow Lake of the Woods Hwy. 140 NW from Klamath Falls towards the lake. Just past the junction with Hwy. 53, take the first right and, in less than one mile, a left onto FS 3455. At the next fork, take the left road FS 3458, and left again at the next junction onto FS 3659 heading toward Big Meadows. Trailhead 3712 is at the apex of the next hairpin turn. The trail leads to Island Lake. Bert is south of the trail, just 1/3 mile in.

Covering only 2 acres, it usually has good numbers of brook trout 10-11 inches. Though the lake is accessible in late June, fishing is best in fall. In addition to Cold Springs Campground, there are nice campsites at Island Lake, one mile west of Bert.

BEULAH RESERVOIR (Agency Valley Res.) A large irrigation reservoir in north Malheur County which is severely drawn down during drought years. In 1988 the reservoir was dry by mid-July, its newly planted fingerlings washed into the Malheur. The fishery may be adequately re-established by fall, 1989. From Juntura, on Hwy. 20 mid-way between Burns and Vale, a gravel road leads north about 15 miles to the reservoir. Juntura is about half-way between Burns and Vale. Roads also lead in from Drewsey on the west, and from Hwy. 26 at Ironside to the north.

The reservoir covers almost 2000 acres when full, with bait most effective for taking the larger fish, when they're available. Ice fishing is also popular. Open all year, the lake makes a convenient base camp for deer hunters. A hot spring is located near the NE arm just west of Bendire Creek between the lake and the road.

There are generally quite a few campers and trailers here. There's no drinking water, but there are outhouses just above the dam. Supplies and gas are available at Juntura, Burns, or Vale.

BIG CREEK (Grant Co.) A fair, mostly wild trout stream in the Logan Valley of Malheur National Forest, tributary to the Middle Fork Malheur River, with headwaters in the Strawberry Mountains. From John Day, follow Hwy. 395 south 9 miles to Seneca (about 45 miles north of Burns). Turn east on FS 16. Big Creek Camp is 18 miles east on FS 16, only 2 miles from the creek's mouth. Trail 377 follows Big Creek to its headwaters in the Strawberry Mountain Wilderness. To reach the trailhead, turn north off FS 16 one mile west of Big Creek Camp, then follow FS 21 to road's end.

The creek is stocked below Big Creek Campground, but above the stream the fishery is wild. The trout run small (7-10 inches) but are plentiful, due to light pressure. In addition to Big Creek Campground, there are other Forest Service camps on FS 14 to the east.

BLACK LAKE A small mountain lake above Anthony Lake in the Wallowa Whitman National Forest NW of Baker. The lake contains wild brook trout. Anthony Lake is on FS 73, which heads into the forest off Hwy. 411. The trailhead to Black heads east from Anthony Lake Campground. It reaches the lake in less than one mile.

BLITZEN RIVER See Donner And Blitzen River.

BLUE JOINT LAKE See Warner Valley Lakes.

BLUE LAKE (Lake Co.) A large, deep rainbow lake in the Gearhart Mt. Wilderness of Fremont National Forest. It's the only lake in the wilderness, though spring-fed creeks are plentiful. The wilderness covers 18,709 acres and is accessed by the 12-mile Gearhart Trail 100, with trailheads at the north-central and southeast boundaries. Blue Lake is near the northern border at elevation 7031 ft. It's a 2 mile hike to the lake from the northern trailhead, with a 600 ft. elevation gain. The 10 mile hike to the lake from the SE trailhead involves a 760 ft. climb over 3 miles, followed by a spectacular ridge walk among the volcanic spires of Gearhart Mountain, with views of the area's many meadows, of the distant Cascades, and of Steens Mt..

From Lakeview, follow Hwy. 140 west to Quartz Mt. Pass, turning north onto FS 3660, which leads to the SE trailhead. To reach the northern trailhead, cut north off Hwy. 140 about 4 miles west of Lakeview onto County Rd. 2-16. Turn west onto 2-16A, which follows Thomas Creek into Freemont Forest, becoming FS 28. Turn west onto FS 3428 at Dairy Pt. Campground and, at the next junction, head north on FS 3372 along the Sprague River. A primitive track leads south to the trailhead about 8 miles from the junction.

Blue Lake covers 20 acres and is stocked, with trout averaging 11-12 inches, running to 15. Bait fishing is most common, and success rate is high, but fly angling is good later in the season, mornings and evenings.

Trails into the Wilderness are generally clear by mid-June, July in wet years, and stay clear until November. In keeping with its wilderness designation, there are no established campgrounds, and users should practice no-trace camping methods. Campgrounds are available in the surrounding forest.

BOSENBERG CREEK A short tributary of the Middle Fork of the Malheur River offering fair trout angling. It flows near Big Creek in the Malheur National Forest south of Strawberry Mountain Wilderness. From John Day follow Hwy. 395 south, turning east onto County Rd. 65 (following Canyon Cr.) which becomes FS 15 beyond Wickiup Campground. Beyond Parish Cabin Campground, turn left onto FS 16, which crosses the creek at Kimberling Cabin just east of the turnoff to Big Creek Campground. Forest roads north of the cabin follow the creek into its headwaters.

Bosenberg is not stocked, and its wild trout, mostly brookies, run to 12 inches, averaging 9-10 inches. Bait fishing is good in May and June.

BOYLE RESERVOIR A 450 acre impoundment on the Klamath River, used to store water for power generation. Fluctuation is heavy, as much as 3 ft. daily. Nevertheless, it is fished from boat and bank.

Boyle contains largemouth bass, black and white crappie, brown bullhead, and yellow perch. The bass population is modest, and the catch average is 2 pounds, though some 6 pounders have been taken. The reservoir is lightly fished, and bank anglers seem to stick close to the boat ramps and picnic areas.

There is a boat ramp and parking area on the east shore where Hwy. 66 crosses the maintenance bridge. On the west side of the bridge is

CATFISH CAMP AT BROWNLEE RESERVOIR
S. John Collins, Photographer

a picnic area. Topsy Campground and Boat Ramp are on the south shore of the reservoir, south of Hwy. 66 on Topsy Rd.

BRIDGE CREEK (Harney Co.) A fair trout stream flowing off the west slope of Steens Mt. into the Blitzen River in the southern Malheur Wildlife Refuge NE of Frenchglen. Frenchglen is at the south end of the Blitzen valley and is reached by Hwy. 205 about 55 miles south of Hwy. 20 from Burns. To reach the creek, drive toward Page Springs Campground from Frenchglen. Just after crossing the Blitzen River, take a dirt road that leads north. The creek flows out of a low canyon about 3 miles down this road, which leads through mosquito infested marshlands, home to many aquatic birds.

Bridge Creek has native redband trout that average 10 inches. Occasionally much larger fish are taken, probably spawners from Baca Lake. Most anglers bait fish here, but flies or lures will work. Page Springs BLM Campground is located nearby. The mosquitoes seem to stay pretty much in the marshland.

BRIDGE CREEK (Lake Co.) A shallow stream flowing about 20 miles from the northern edge of Fremont National Forest into Paulina Marsh, just north of the community of Silver Lake. The stream is crossed by Hwy. 31 NW of town, and by County Rd. 650-N beyond the forest service landing strip SW of town. Dirt roads south from 650-N access the upper waters.

Rainbow trout predominate in the lower stretch, brook trout in the upper, with the upper waters most productive. Trout go to 10 inches. Best time to fish is spring and early summer. Bait is most effective, but flies dropped off the vegetation along the pools often find takers.

BROWNLEE RESERVOIR A generally turbulent 51 mile impoundment of the Snake River, formed by dams west of Baker—Oxbow at the lower end, and Brownlee, the uppermost

dam on the Snake. The dams also back up the Powder River near Richland, and the Burnt River near Huntington. Most angling is in these arms and at the upper end near Weiser, Idaho. The reservoir provides angling for channel cats, crappie, smallmouth and largemouth bass, sturgeon, and rainbow trout.

To reach the Powder River arm from Baker, follow Hwy. 86 to Richland. A road follows the reservoir south to the Burnt River arm at Huntington. To access the lower reservoir, continue north on 86 to Oxbow Dam. A paved road follows the reservoir up to Brownlee Dam. The two roads along the reservoir do not connect. From Burns, follow Hwy. 20 east to Ontario, then head north on Hwy. 30 to Huntington.

Drought conditions work wonders on the fishery here, providing a more stable environment than usual. All species prospered in 1987 and 1988. Some of the best crappie fishing ever known here occurred in the summer of 1988, with fish to 14 inches taken.

Catfish are the reservoir's most popular fare. Channel cats run fairly small, averaging 12 inches, but some very large ones have been caught. Flathead catfish also grow to good size here. In 1974, a 27 pounder caught in June held the record until September, when a monster weighing 33 pounds was caught. Dead minnows, cut bait, or nightcrawlers work well.

Smallmouth bass are present in numbers, with fishing best in the western arms at the upper end of the lake. There are also a few largemouth. Some sturgeon are taken, including a very occasional monster. Rainbow trout are stocked as soon as possible after ice-off, as early as January or November. Though rainbow average 10-14 inches, trout to 3 pounds have been taken here in recent years.

The reservoir is big and gets rough. Most anglers stick to the shallow areas and around the islands. There are boat ramps at Richland, Farewell Bend State Park south of Huntington, and at Idaho Power Company's McCormick

Park, just below Brownlee Dam on the Idaho shore (there's a bridge just below the dam). There are campgrounds at the above sites, and at Copperfield Park just north of Oxbow Dam. Supplies are available at marinas on the reservoir.

BUCK CREEK A good eastern Oregon stream, about 20 miles long, heading in the Yamsay Mt. area and flowing into Paulina Marsh near the town of Silver Lake. From La-Pine on Hwy. 97, drive about 43 miles SE on Hwy. 31. The creek is crossed by Hwy. 31 two miles west of Silver Lake. One mile closer to Silver Lake, County Rd. 660 runs west, following the creek. It leads to Forest Service and logging roads that follow the creek to its source.

The upper creek has some nice water. It's small, but supports a good population of small brook trout. Redband trout are found in the lower reaches, but most of the land there is private. There are no improved camps, but lots of nice natural campsites.

BULLY CREEK RESERVOIR A multiple purpose reservoir with bass and panfish, located about 8 miles west of Vale. Vale is about 12 miles west of Ontario by way of Hwy. 20. From Vale, drive west on Hwy. 20 about 8 miles, and take a road leading north at Hope School. The reservoir is about 7 miles north. The road continues along the northern shore of the reservoir then west up Bully Creek.

White crappie, yellow perch, and largemouth and smallmouth bass are all present. Crappie fishing is best near the upper end where the lake is shallower. There is a nice county park with camping and boat ramps about one mile above the dam. There are two hot springs near the upper end of the reservoir. One is near the road at the upper end of the pool, and the second, O'Neal Hot Spring, is one mile further west along the road.

The reservoir was severely drawn down during the drought of 1987-88, and many fish died. It may take as many as 5 years for the fishery here to return to its former strength.

BUMPHEAD RESERVOIR A 100 acre irrigation impoundment in Klamath County, east of Klamath Falls near the California line. It is located 10 miles NE of Langell Valley, which is 18 miles south of Bonanza and 3 miles north of Willow Valley Reservoir. The reservoir dried up during the 1987-88 drought. It will be restocked with crappie and largemouth bass in summer 1989, and should offer good fishing in 2-3 years.

BURNT CREEK A short trout stream about 5 air miles, (but many more road miles) SE of Lakeview. An unpaved shortcut road leading east from Lakeview has washed out in past years, but may be available. Check locally. The creek may also be approached from the north. From Lakeview drive north on Hwy. 395 about 5 miles to the intersection of Hwy. 140. Take 140 east about 7 miles to FS 391, which leads a bit over 3 miles to the creek, then parallels it south. Fishing here is for native trout to 12 inches.

CACHED LAKE A tiny but productive trout lake off the trail to Eagle Lake, in the Eagle Cap Wilderness of Wallowa-Whitman National Forest. Only 2 acres, it supports a lot of small brook trout. From Boulder Park on FS 7755, follow the Eagle Creek Trail 1922 north 5.7 miles towards Eagle Lake, gaining 1649 ft. elevation. One mile south of Eagle Lake, turn east on Trail 1931 for a fairly easy (600 ft.) mile to Cached Lake. Snow may block access until July.

Campgrounds are available on Eagle Creek Rd. To reach this area from Baker or LaGrande, follow Hwy. 203 east. From Baker, follow FS 67 NE to the trailhead. From LaGrande, follow FS 77. Both are all-weather roads. Trout season is determined by trail conditions, with best fishing in August and September.

CALAMITY CREEK A small trout stream in the upper Malheur system. It enters the Malheur south of Van, which is on County Rd. 306 east of Silvies. To reach the upper waters, follow County Rd. 309, a primitive track, west from Van. The creek heads in the Malheur National Forest near Calamity Butte. It has a population of native trout (up to 10 inches) that don't get to see a lot of anglers. Rock Springs Campground is off FS 17 about 10 miles west of Van.

CAMAS CREEK One of the best trout streams in the Lakeview area. It heads in the Fremont National Forest about 6 miles east of Lakeview and flows east about 15 miles into Deep Creek. From Lakeview head north 4 1/2 miles on Hwy. 395, turning east onto Warner Canyon Rd. 140. At the junction of FS 391, 7 miles east, the highway hits the creek near its head and follows it east. Several other roads cross it at points where it leaves the main road. It can be reached from Warner Valley by going west from Adel.

Camas Creek is usually good after the spring run-off, and holds up through early summer. Fishing picks up again in fall. The creek is well stocked with legal rainbow and supports good numbers of larger natives. Most fish caught will be around 12 inches, but a few go to 16 inches. Beaver ponds along the creek are worth exploring for larger rainbows. Bait angling is most popular, but flies take fish in late afternoon and evening. Spinners and small lures work well in the larger holes.

CAMP CREEK (Grant Co.) A fairly good trout stream, about 14 miles long, entering the Silvies River between Seneca and Silvies near Hwy. 395. Silvies is on Hwy. 395 about 32 miles north of Burns. The creek flows out of Malheur National Forest to the west and joins the Silvies River about 3 miles north of Silvies. FS 37, which leaves the highway 4 miles north of Silvies, follows the creek about 6 miles, and FS 370 continues to the headwaters.

Camp Creek has a fair number of native rainbow trout 9-12 inches. Most angling takes place in May and June on bait or flies.

CAMPBELL LAKE A fair high mountain rainbow lake in Fremont National Forest, 34 air miles NW of Lakeview, about half-way between hwys. 140 and 31. The lake, a little over 20 acres, is reached by fairly good graded roads. From Paisley on Hwy. 31 it's about 23 miles by forest roads, primarily FS 331. From Bly on Hwy. 140 it's about 35 miles by FS 348 NE to FS 331. Other forest roads come in from Lakeview and the Sycan Marsh area to the NW. Campbell is one mile east of Dead Horse Lake. The time period in which the lake is accessible is fairly short, from July through October. The Forest Service locks the road gate in spring and doesn't open it until the road is passable. Check with the Ranger Stations at Bly, Lakeview, or Paisley.

Campbell has the best catch rate in the district for stocked trout, but little carry-over. This is a good flyfishing lake, but lures or bait also work. Troll slowly with a lot of line. Small boats with trailers can be launched, but motors are prohibited. There is a good camp here. Dead Horse Lake, one mile west, offers similar angling opportunities.

CAMPBELL LAKE, UPPER See Warner Valley Lakes.

CAMPBELL LAKE, LOWER See Warner Valley Lakes.

CAMPBELL RESERVOIR A 200 acre reservoir 8 miles NE of Bly which has contained largemouth bass. The reservoir is mostly on private land, though there is some public access across BLM property. It went dry in 1988, and the status of the fishery is uncertain at this time.

CHERRY CREEK A nice trout stream west of Upper Klamath Lake. When Hwy. 140 turns west toward Lake of the Woods, continue north on FS 3459 about 4 miles, then west on 3450. Trail 3708 at road's end follows Cherry Creek for several miles towards its headwaters, then leads to Horseshoe Lake in the Sky Lakes Basin.

Cherry Creek offers very good angling for wild brook trout and doesn't get a lot of pressure. Though not a large stream, it's worth the effort. Use stealth, as these trout are spooky.

CHEWAUCAN RIVER The largest and one of the best trout streams in Fremont National Forest. About 50 miles long, it flows NW from the mountains SW of Lakeview, past the town of Paisley, and into the Chewaucan Marsh. The lower end near Paisley is crossed by Hwy. 31. At this point you are about 130 miles SE of Bend. From Lakeview, drive north on Hwy. 395 then turn NW onto Hwy. 31 at Valley Falls. The stream is followed south from Paisley by FS 330, a good graded road. The upper stream and tributaries are followed and crossed by forest roads branching from FS 351, which is reached by 330. From Bly, on Hwy. 140, follow FS 348 to Paisley.

The river is well stocked with rainbow in all the upper areas, and they make up most of the catch. There has been some attempt to improve fish habitat here. Cut junipers were wired in along the banks in places to stop bank erosion, reduce siltation, and provide cover. The result should be more and larger fish, so work around the clumps.

The stream is large enough for all types of fishing. Drifted worms are always a sure bet, but wet and dry fly anglers can do well. There are catfish in the extreme lower stream. Check locally.

There is a good campground at Marster's Spring, about 8 miles south of Paisley, and other camps are available in the headwater area.

CHICKAHOMINY RESERVOIR A desert reservoir near Burns, created especially for anglers by the Oregon Department of Fish and Wildlife, known for growing big rainbow trout. It can be counted on for catches 16-20 inches (up to 5 pounds). Drought conditions in 1987-88 lowered the reservoir to 10 ft. at its deepest point, and a lot of fish were lost. Though the fishery will certainly be off in 1989, it could easily make a good recovery by 1990.

The 530 acre reservoir is just north of Hwy. 20 about 32 miles west of Burns, 100 miles from Bend.

Chickahominy is stocked with 60,000-80,000 rainbow fingerlings each spring. In good years, the fingerlings grow about 2 inches per month during the summer. Anglers use all methods to fish here. There's a boat ramp, and many anglers troll or cast bait. It's an excellent float tube lake, and fly anglers take advantage of float tube mobility to fish for the big trout that cruise near the weed beds. The reservoir has good hatches of dragonflies and damselflies.

It should be noted that Chickahominy sits among the sagebrush, its banks and the landscape for miles around entirely devoid of trees. The wind can really pick up here in a hurry, and the summers are very hot. Fishing is best in spring.

BLM maintains a primitive campground here, with pit toilets, drinking water, a fish cleaning station, and a few shaded picnic tables. Camp anywhere in the parking lot or sagebrush. In 1989 BLM began charging a fee to camp. Money collected will be used to upgrade the Chickahominy site.

CLOVER LAKE A small, lightly fished brook trout lake in the southern Mountain Lakes Wilderness in Winema National Forest. It's a 2 mile hike by trail north from the end of the Buck Peak Lookout Rd. Buck Peak is about 12 miles SW of Lake of the Woods Resort.

The lake is in a basin of potholes at the head of Clover Creek. It's only a couple of acres, but offers good angling for brook trout to 12 inches. The lake is stocked with fingerlings by air. Fairly shallow, it's an easy lake to flyfish. Some of the other small lakes in this area just might offer surprises.

COMO LAKE a very nice lake in the Mountain Lake Wilderness of the southern Winema National Forest. From Hwy. 140, about 7 miles east of Lake of the Woods, take the Varney Creek Rd. FS 3610 south about 1 1/2 miles, turning left onto FS 3637 and right on FS 3664. Varney Creek Trailhead 3718 is at the end of the road. It's about a 4 mile hike to Como Lake.

The lake is 7 acres and quite deep. It's stocked with brook and rainbow trout averaging 10-14 inches, with a few larger. Bait is best in spring, and all methods can be effective in fall. For other good lakes in the area see Harriet, Echo, South Pass.

COTTONWOOD CREEK (Lake Co.) A fair trout stream NW of Lakeview. The lower stream offers little if any trout angling. The

BAKER LICENSE PLATE
S. John Collins, Photographer

upper waters, above Cottonwood Reservoir include 6 fishable miles. This section is reached by FS 387, which leads NE from Hwy. 140 about 20 miles west of Lakeview. This approach takes you by Cottonwood Meadow Lake, a small impoundment on the upper creek, and follows the creek fairly closely to the reservoir.

The creek has populations of native brook trout and rainbow. Good catches are made by local anglers, with most trout 6-8 inches and a few to 14 inches. Most local anglers use bait, but flies should produce as well.

Both Cottonwood Meadow Lake and Cottonwood Reservoir have rainbow and brook trout. There are two campgrounds on Cottonwood Meadow Lake.

COTTONWOOD CREEK (Malheur Co.) A fair, lightly fished trout stream near Westfall, about 56 miles west of Ontario. Follow Hwy. 20 to Harper Junction, then go north to Westfall and the confluence of Cottonwood and Bully Creeks. A graded gravel road heading SW from town follows a good portion of the stream. The creek is also accessible north of Drewsey (on Hwy. 20). A road follows the stream above and below Cottonwood Creek Reservoir.

Bully Creek does not offer any fishing, but Cottonwood has native trout and a pretty good catch rate due to little angling pressure. Trout average 9-10 inches and run to 12 inches. Bait or flies are effective. There is no camping along the stream.

COTTONWOOD CREEK RESERVOIR (Harney Co.) An impoundment north of Drewsey in Harney County which has offered only fair trout fishing in the past and which is scheduled for management as bass and panfish water beginning in 1989. Drewsey is reached by paved road north from Hwy. 20, about 47 miles east of Burns. A gravel road leads north from town to the reservoir. Watch for a sign. The reservoir covers about 120 acres.

COTTONWOOD MEADOWS LAKE (Lake Co) In the Fremont National Forest, about 22 miles NW of Lakeview, created by the Forest Service and the Dept. of Fish and Wildlife. From Lakeview, take Hwy. 140 about 20 miles west to FS 3870. Follow 3870 about 6 miles NW to the lake. Do not confuse it with Cottonwood Reservoir, a much larger impoundment near Lakeview on lower Cottonwood Creek.

The Meadows Lake is a nice body of water, with about 42 acres of good fishing. Rainbow fingerling are stocked each year, and the catch rate is high. The rainbow have averaged 9-12 inches with a lot up to 15 inches. Brook trout here run larger, with most 14-16 inches. All methods work, but there's always a slack period in late summer because of algae. Late fall produces good fly fishing. There are two campgrounds on the lake. Motor boats are prohibited. The road in is usually open by May.

COTTONWOOD RESERVOIR (Lake Co.) A 900 acre reservoir on lower Cottonwood Creek, about 8 air miles NW of Lakeview. It offers slow bait fishing in fairly turbid water, but rainbow 14-20 inches are taken. There is a large annual draw-down for irrigation. The reservoir is located 8 miles downstream from Cottonwood Meadows Lake on Cottonwood Creek. See Cottonwood Meadows Lake for directions.

COW LAKES Two large panfish lakes near the Idaho border south of Ontario, only the upper of which is providing angling. Roads approach the lakes from Hwy. 95 just south of Sheaville, from Jordan Valley, or the Northbound Danner Rd. The access road is gravel.

Covering almost 1000 acres, the upper lake maintains a population of brown bullhead and white crappie. There is a BLM campground and boat ramp, but no drinking water. Fishing's best at the west end near the lava bed.

CRATER LAKE (Baker Co.) A good brook trout lake high in the SE corner of Eagle Cap Wilderness in the Wallowa Mountains. Crater Lake is at the head of Kettle Creek, a tributary of the upper East Fork of Eagle Creek, and you'll work hard to get to it. Best route to the lake is from the south from Baker or Halfway. Snow may block access until July. From Baker take Hwy. 203 north to Medical Springs (hot springs) and pick up FS 67, which leads to Eagle Creek, meeting it at Tamarack Campground. From here, follow the creek downstream on FS 77.

You have your choice of two trails, one a steep but somewhat shorter punishment, and the other a bit longer but not quite so steep. For the aggressive hiker, Trail 1945 will get you there quickest. Turn up the East Fork of Eagle Creek on FS 7740, and follow it about 5 miles north to its end at Kettle Creek Campground. Trail 1945 grinds east following Little Kettle Creek for about 6.6 miles to the lake, switch-backing most of the way and gaining 3000 ft. in elevation—a killer.

The better route in is by Trail 1946. About 6 miles beyond the East Fork junction on FS 77, take FS 7732 NW to its end. There Trail 1946 leads NE towards Pine Lake and eventually Crater Lake. This hike is 7.7 miles long, but it's over an interesting ridge route. Total elevation gain is still at least 3000 feet.

Crater Lake covers 12 acres and is only 10 feet at its deepest point. The lake is cupped in a high saddle between Red Mountain and Krag Peak at an elevation of 7500 feet. It produces good catches of brook trout 8-13 inches. This is a good place to give your fly rod a workout. The scenery is grand and the fish are willing.

CRATER LAKE (Klamath Co.) This is a great scenic attraction, but it doesn't attract many anglers. Located in the maw of a dormant volcano, Crater Lake is the showpiece of Crater Lake National Park. The lake is reached by Hwy. 62 from Medford, and by Hwy. 97 from Klamath Falls or Bend. The park shows up on every map.

The lake is about 5 miles in diameter, and 2000 ft. deep. It is stocked at times by the Federal government, as the state has no jurisdiction here. State fishing licenses are not required within the park, but anglers must abide by current park regulations.

Some rainbow trout are caught, as well as a few kokanee, Dolly Varden and brook trout. Best fishing is in the few shoal areas, such as around Wizard Island. The lake doesn't provide much feed, so productivity is low.

Boats are available at the landing below Rim Village at the SW side of the lake. Park headquarters is also located here, and you can check on current regulations and fishing conditions. Three campgrounds are available during the summer. This is high country, and the snow lingers long.

CRATER LAKE (Harney Co.) A 2 acre lake in Malheur Wildlife Refuge that has contained largemouth bass and white crappie. The lake periodically winterkills and has not been restocked recently.

CROOKED CREEK (Klamath Co.) A short tributary of lower Wood River flowing south of Fort Klamath. Only about 5 miles long, it has some fair angling for rainbow, browns and brook trout. The creek is closely followed north by Hwy. 62 from the junction of the Chiloquin road and Hwy. 97. A state hatchery is located on Crooked Creek about 2 miles north of Klamath Indian Agency. The creek is closed on the hatchery grounds. Bait or fly angling is good in spring and early summer. Mosquitoes are a problem in spring. Much of this creek is on private land, so ask permission to fish.

CROOKED CREEK (Lake Co.) A fair trout stream, easily reached, located between Lakeview and Valley Falls. It flows into the lower Chewaucan River just north of Valley Falls. The creek is followed south by Hwy. 395 and is accessible from the west by Hwy. 31. The upper creek is only 10 miles north of Lakeview. Fishing is good for a short time in spring and early summer. The creek is quite small, and bait fishing produces best. Chandler State Park is on the creek about 5 miles south of Valley Falls.

CRUMP LAKE A large shallow lake at the south end of Warner Valley, due south of Hart Mountain. To reach it, take the gravel road north from Adel to Plush. You'll hit the west shore of the lake in about 7 miles. Covering 3200 acres, the lake provides a lot of 10 inch bullhead catfish in spring, and both black and white crappie to 12 inches. An occasional bass is also taken. Supplies are available at Adel. This is remote country, so check your gas gauge.

DAIRY CREEK (Lake Co.) A nice creek in Fremont National Forest NW of Lakeview. It heads on the east slope of Gearhart Mt. in the Gearhart Mt. Wilderness Area, and flows east into the upper Chewaucan River. It enters the river about 18 miles south of Paisley, forming a major western fork of the river. A network of forest roads follow and cross the creek, and a Fremont Forest map will come in handy. An easy way in is to take Hwy. 140 west 3 miles to a paved road leading north. About 5 1/2 miles north, turn west onto FS 2823, which follows Thomas Creek to its headwaters and eventually reaches Dairy Creek Guard Station. From their you can follow the creek east or west by forest road.

Dairy Creek is stocked each spring with rainbow trout. Native rainbow and a few brook trout are also present. Average size is 9-10 inches, with some to 12 inches or better. Bait angling is the preferred method, but there's a lot of nice fly water. There are several good forest camps along the creek.

DEAD HORSE LAKE A pretty good trout lake in the Fremont National Forest just north of Dead Horse Rim. The lake is about 45 miles NW of Lakeview on a fairly good road. From Paisley on Hwy. 31, the lake is about 23 miles by forest roads, primarily FS 331. From Bly, on Hwy. 140, it's about 35 miles. Take FS 348 NE from Bly to FS 331. Other forest roads come in from the Sycan Marsh area to the NW. Follow the signs. Dead Horse Lake is accessible for only a short period, from July through October. The Forest Service locks the road gate in spring and doesn't open it until the road is passable. Check with the Ranger Stations at Bly, Lakeview, or Paisley.

About 20 acres, Dead Horse is stocked with legal size rainbow trout and brook trout fingerlings. Trolling is popular as well as still fishing with bait, but any method will produce fish. The success rate is pretty high, but few large fish are caught. Rainbow and brook trout average 10 inches.

Boats can be launched and effectively used, but motors are prohibited. There is a small campground at the lake, and hike or boat-in camping units are available on the shoreline for a more remote experience.

DEE LAKE One of the hike-in lakes in the Island Lake area of Rogue River National Forest, about 10 miles north of Lake of the Woods. Drive about 5 miles east of Lake of the Woods on Hwy. 140, then north on FS 3561 to the Big Meadows spur road FS 3659. This leads west a bit over one mile to a hairpin turn north, on which you will find the Lost Creek Trailhead. Take that trail, 3712, west about 3 1/2 miles to Island Lake. Dee Lake is just west of Island Lake.

Dee is not heavily fished, and has some nice brook trout. The average size is 10 inches, with some fish to 18 inches taken occasionally. The lake is 14 acres and fairly shallow, stocked by air. It's an excellent fly fishing lake, with best results in August and September. It's usually accessible by late June. There are good campsites at Island Lake to the east. Others of the Island Lake group are also worth fishing. See Red, Pear, Camp.

DEEP CREEK (Lake Co.) A very good eastern Oregon trout stream SE of Lakeview, flowing into Warner Valley near Adel. The creek heads near the California state line SE of Lakeview in the Fremont National Forest. The upper water is reached by FS 391, which runs south from Hwy. 140 about 6 miles east of its junction with Hwy. 395 north of Lakeview. The creek flows out of the forest into Big Valley, and the Sage Hen Creek Rd. picks it up for about one mile as it leaves the valley. The creek then plunges into a canyon and has no road access until it reaches Hwy. 140 about 5 miles west of Adel. The highway closely follows it into Adel.

Deep Creek fishing is very good in late spring and summer. The creek is stocked with hatchery rainbow and has natives to 15 inches. There is excellent flyfishing water on the stretch west of Adel along the highway after the water clears, usually around the beginning of July. Bait, small spinner-and-bait, and small lures are all successful. Willow Creek and Deep Creek Campgrounds are located on FS 391 in the headwaters.

DEEP LAKE (Klamath Co.) A fairly good hike-in brook trout lake in the Sky Lakes Wilderness, Winema National Forest, 10 miles NW of Upper Klamath Lake. A popular route into the area begins at Cold Springs Campground. From Hwy. 140, about 5 miles east of Lake of the Woods, take FS 3651 north to Cold Springs Campground, about 11 miles. From the campground take either Trail 3710 or 3709 north to Heavenly Twin Lake, then continue north on Trail 3762 to Trapper Lake. From here Trail 3734 leads past Donna Lake to Deep Lake. The hike to Deep is about 6 miles. Other approaches from the east, west, and north are possible. Take along a topographic map (USGS or Sky Lakes Wilderness).

Deep Lake is lightly fished and has large numbers of brook trout averaging 9 inches. The lake is 4 acres and is not too deep. It's an easy lake to fish, best in late summer and fall. All methods will take fish, with spinner-and-

bait or wet flies very effective. Other lakes in the area include Trapper, Donna, Sonya, Marguerette. The Pacific Crest Trail passes about 1/2 mile to the west.

DEER LAKE (Klamath Co.) A small brook trout lake at the SW end of the Sky Lakes area of the Winema National Forest, 10 miles NW of Klamath Lake. A popular route into the area begins at Cold Springs Campground about 6 trail miles from the lake. See Deep Lake for road directions. From the campground, hike 2 miles on Trail 3710 to the junction, then 1/4 mile on Trail 3762 west, to Deer Lake. Continuing 1/2 mile on this trail brings you to the Pacific Crest Trail.

Deer Lake is a fairly shallow 5 acre lake that receives brook trout fingerlings by air. The average fish runs about 11 inches, with few big ones. This situation can change from year to year, as in most other high lakes. Flyfishing is usually good here in late summer and fall.

DELINTMENT LAKE A popular 50 acre trout lake in Ochoco National Forest NW of Burns, featuring large rainbow. The lake and its surrounding ponderosa pine forest are a welcome oasis on a summer trip across hot, dry eastern Oregon. From Burns, travel south on Hwy. 20 to Hines, then NW on FS 47 to its junction with FS 41, about 15 miles from Burns. FS 41 reaches the lake in about 35 miles. Additional forest routes access the lake from all directions. Refer to the forest map.

There's usually good angling for large rainbow here, with an annual supplement of fingerlings to replace those lost during the winter. The lake is deep and rich, and fish grow well. Efforts have been made to keep the water level high enough to allow more big fish to survive. Trout average 10-14 inches, with some 3-4 pounds. It has a good shoreline for bank casting.

The campground is large and attractive, with many flat grassy sites tucked discretely among the tall pines. There is a boat ramp here with a 5 mph speed limit.

DEVIL LAKE (Klamath Co.) An irrigation reservoir with bass and panfish 7 miles SE of Bly, which is located on Hwy. 140 (Klamath Falls to Lakeview). Drive south on Fishhole Creek Rd. to the lake, which is on the west side of the road.

The reservoir normally covers about 100 acres. It was once stocked with trout, but they've all but disappeared, and no more trout plants are planned. Current fishing is for brown bullhead to 14 inches, yellow perch, and largemouth bass. Boats are allowed, but there is no ramp. Fishing here is generally best in the fall. There is no campground nearby.

DOG LAKE A large lake in Fremont National Forest about 25 miles SW of Lakeview. Good roads approach the lake from Hwy. 140 west of Lakeview. Head south from 140 either east or west of Drews Reservoir. Dog Lake is about 6 miles south of Drews on the road to Yocum, which is just north of the California line. The land around the lake was purchased by the Nature Conservancy in 1978 and was recently acquired by the Forest Service.

About 500 acres, Dog Lake provides fair fishing for perch, brown bullhead, black crappie and largemouth bass. Experienced anglers can take trophy-size bass, but few small bass are present. There are 2 campgrounds, Cinder Hill and Dog Lake. Dog Lake Campground has a boat ramp.

DONNA LAKE A small brook trout lake in the northern end of the Sky Lakes Wilderness of the Winema National Forest, 10 miles NW of Klamath Lake. A popular route in begins at Cold Springs Campground. See Deep Lake for road directions. From Cold Springs follow either Trail 3710 or 3709 north to Heavenly Twin Lake, then continue north on trail 3762 to Trapper Lake. From there Trail 3734 leads to Donna Lake. Donna is just east of the trail, slightly north of Trapper and Margurette Lakes. Other approaches from the east, west, and north are possible. Bring a topographic map (Sky Lakes Wilderness or USGS).

Only 2 acres and 9 ft. deep, Donna doesn't provide very large fish. Brook trout here range 8-14 inches. The lake is stocked every other year. There are good natural campsites, and fishing at larger lakes to the south.

DONNER UND BLITZEN RIVER (a.k. Blitzen River) A good trout stream in its upper waters, flowing 40 miless off Steens Mt., through Malheur Wildlife Refuge, and into Malheur Lake. Hwy. 205 (Burns to Frenchglen) follows a portion of the lower stream, as do secondary roads within the wildlife refuge. Within the refuge, however, from Bridge Creek downstream, the river is closed to angling. This is of little concern since there are almost no trout below Bridge Creek due to heavy irrigation ditching.

The stream above Frenchglen offers fairly good angling and is approached by a maze of primitive mountain roads and by the Steens Mountain Loop Rd. The Loop Rd. heads east from Hwy. 205 about 4 miles north of Roaring Springs Ranch, crossing the river in about 13 miles at Blitzen Crossing just below the Indian Creek confluence. There is no longer a campground at the crossing. Poor dirt roads lead north between the crossing and Roaring Springs to access points at Tombstone and Burnt Car. The other end of the Loop Rd. is at Page Springs Campground just south of Frenchglen. The Loop Rd. is generally snowbound until mid-June.

The river is stocked with hatchery rainbow below the dam at Page Springs Campground east of Frenchglen. This dam isolates the fish population of the upper stream, which is made up of a hardy race of truly native fish, the redband trout. The redband is a desert-adapted fish that can withstand water temperature extremes fatal to other trout, silted bedding gravel, and extremely alkaline waters.

This river becomes extremely turbid during spring runoff, and in heavy snowpack years it may not clear until mid-July or later. Spring angling requires bait, but wet and dry flies work well in summer and fall in the upper stretch. Trout average 10-12 inches, with fish 20 inches and larger sometimes taken.

Though remote for most anglers, the Blitzen can be fished in conjunction with other waters in the area. See fish lake and krumbo reservoir. Or it can be enjoyed as one activity in an exploration of this fascinating corner of the state. In addition to a lush assemblage of wildlife on the refuge, there is the historic Frenchglen Hotel, ghost towns, lava tube caves, hot springs, and other geologic phenomena (from the curious Diamond Craters to the majestic fault-block Steens Mountain itself). Mosquitos, by the way, are a curse along the stream into July, particularly near the marshlands of the refuge. *Donner und Blitzen* is German for *thunder and lightning*. The river was named in 1864 by army troops who crossed it during a thunder storm. Storms in the high Steens (wind, rain, and snow), are legendary and often come up suddenly.

In addition to the campground at Page Springs, there are camps at Fish Lake and Jackman Park on the upper Steens slope. The Frenchglen Hotel (part of the National Park system) offers home-style food and lodging. Supplies and gasoline are also available in Frenchglen. Bunks and cooking facilities are available for a modest fee at Malheur Field Station, which is located on the Refuge about 32 miles south of Burns, half-way to Frenchglen. Facilities include mobile homes and dorms with kitchens ($9/night) and dorms without kitchens ($8/night). Reservations must be made in advance. Dinners are also available at the Field Station by advance reservation. The Station is open year around, with limited lodging in winter.

DRAKE CREEK A good small creek east of Lakeview, tributary to Deep Creek, which flows into Warner Valley at Adel. From Hwy. 395, about 6 miles north of Lakeview, the Warner Canyon Rd. north joins Deep Creek about 6 miles west of Adel. The creek heads on the east slopes of Drake Peak to the NW, but the upper stream flows through mostly private property, limiting fishing to the stretch from the bridge to the mouth, which is less than one mile.

Drake Creek is not stocked, and native trout aren't large, averaging about 10 inches with some to 14. Bait fishing is most effective.

DREWS CREEK A fair early season trout stream, crossed by Hwy. 140 about 23 miles west of Lakeview. The creek heads in Fremont National Forest NW of the highway. FS 3733 leaves Hwy.140 just east of the crossing and follows the creek to its headwaters. Drews flows east about 6 miles to Drews Reservoir. This stretch is mostly on private land. The creek below the reservoir drains into Goose Lake.

Drews is not stocked but there is some fishing for wild rainbow trout in the upper areas in spring. The creek below the reservoir picks up spawning trout from Goose Lake and has a late May opener to protect them.

DREWS RESERVOIR A large reservoir, lightly fished by local anglers, located about 18 miles west of Lakeview on Hwy.140. The reservoir is encircled by gravel and dirt roads.

When full, Drews covers about 4500 acres, but it is used for irrigation and in some years gets very low. It contains a lot of rough fish, but there are fair numbers of white crappie 6-10 inches, brown bullhead to 12 inches, and some nice yellow perch to 13 inches. Though no longer stocked, channel catfish were introduced in 1978 and still make it into the catch. Most run 3 pounds or better. An occasional large rainbow is also taken. There is a boat ramp at the south end of the reservoir.

DUNAWAY POND A one acre borrow pit on the east side of the highway south of Nyssa, containing bluegill, largemouth bass, and brown bullhead. The pond is about mid-way between Nyssa and Owyhee Junction. Pull off the highway and walk over.

DUNCAN RESERVOIR A small impoundment about 2 miles SW of Silver Lake which has produced nice size trout. From the town of Silver Lake, 40 miles east of LaPine, it's about 6 miles by good gravel road SE to the reservoir.

Duncan covers about 33 acres. In the late '70s it put out some fine large rainbows, but by the end of the decade a flourishing population of chubs was crowding them out. In 1980 the reservoir was poisoned by the Dept. of Fish and Wildlife and has since received annual stockings of Eagle Lake rainbow fingerlings. Currently the lake is still clear of rough fish and raising nice trout. Bait, lures, and flies all take fish here.

In 1984 Duncan Creek was opened to year around angling to give anglers the opportunity to take trout that leave the reservoir in the spring water release. The creek dries up completely in summer. There are some camping facilities at the reservoir.

DUTCH FLAT LAKE A small wild brook trout lake in the southern Wallowa-Whitman National Forest west of North Powder. The trail to the lake follows Dutch Flat Cr. west from an unimproved road that heads south from Hwy. 411 just beyond a Forest Service campground.

ECHO LAKE (Eagle Creek Watershed) A brook trout lake at the head of Eagle Creek's West Fork, in the southern Eagle Cap Wilderness, Wallowa-Whitman National Forest. From Hwy. 203 east of LaGrande and Baker, turn east on FS 77 about 4 miles south of Catherine Creek Guard Station. The turn-off to the trailhead is about 30 miles from the junction.

Trail 1934 heads north from FS 77, gaining 1500 feet elevation in 5 miles. The trail continues north 1.6 miles to Traverse Lake and connects with other wilderness trails, including an arduous 12.7 mile connection to the lake group at the head of the main Eagle Creek Trail. Echo covers 28 acres and has a maximum depth of 19 feet. At 7100 ft. it is one of the lower lakes in the wilderness. It has an abundant population of small eastern brook trout, with good fly angling in August and September.

ECHO LAKE (Mountain Lakes Wilderness) A small, fairly good hike-in brook trout lake in the Mountain Lakes Wilderness of Winema National Forest, east of Lake of the Woods. From Hwy. 140 on the west shore of Klamath Lake, turn west into the forest just NW of the southern entrance to Odessa Campground. Follow FS 3637, turning left onto FS 3664 to Varney Creek Trailhead 3718. At the trail junction, about 4 miles in, turn left (east) onto Trail 3127, which reaches Harriet Lake in about 1 1/2 miles. Echo is just a short walk NE.

Echo is only about 5 acres and is lightly fished for brook trout 7-2 inches, and a few that run larger. Some good size lunkers are reported from time to time. Flies or spinner/bait combinations work well. There are fair campsites along the trail near Harriette Lake. Most of the other small lakes in this area are too shallow to shelter fish.

ELDER CREEK A small trout stream south of Paisley, flowing into the upper Chewaucan River. Paisley is about 130 miles SE of Bend by way of hwys. 97 and 31. The creek enters the river about 18 miles south of Paisley. It contains native redband and some brook trout, with few over 8 inches. Several campgrounds are located a few miles south of the creek, west of Dairy Creek Guard Station.

ELIZABETH LAKE A small brook trout lake in the southern Sky Lakes area of Sky Lakes Wilderness, Winema National Forest. A popular route in begins at Cold Springs Campground. See Deep Lake for road directions. From the campground, take Trail 3710 about 3 miles to Elizabeth Lake, which is 1/4 mile north of Natasha Lake.

Elizabeth is only about 5 acres, but it's lightly fished and a steady producer of brook trout to 11 inches. Quite shallow, it is best suited to fly angling. Fishing is best in early spring and in fall.

EMIGRANT CREEK A better than average trout stream flowing 30 miles from the Delintment Lake area in southern Ochoco National Forest, entering the Silvies River 20 miles NW of Burns.

From Burns, follow Hwy. 20 south to Hines, then turn onto FS 47, which crosses Emigrant Creek at the road 's junction with FS 43. FS 43 follows the creek to its headwaters. Primitive roads access the lower stream near the Silvies confluence.

The fishing is good in late spring and summer, with a catch rate considerably better than that of other streams in the area. Stocked annually with legal rainbow, there are also natives up to 15 inches. Average size is 10 inches. Bait is a sure bet, but fly fishing is effective. In addition to several camps at and near Delintment, there are Forest Service camps creekside on FS 43.

FISH LAKE (Harney Co.) A remote but popular lake high on the west slope of Steens Mt. Deer hunters like to camp here in fall. The lake is on the Steens Mt. Loop Rd., which is usually snowbound at its upper elevations until July. Take Hwy. 205 from Burns south through the Malheur Wildlife Refuge to the tiny community of Frenchglen, a 55 mile trip. To reach the Loop Rd., drive east from Frenchglen towards Page Springs Campground, turning north immediately after crossing the Blitzen River. The road is blocked by a gate until the snow has cleared. It climbs the mountain for 15 or so rough miles to Fish Lake.

The lake is tucked withinin a sparse aspen grove near the rim of Steens Mt, at 7200 ft. Winter hangs on hard here, and there are snowbanks and cold nights into early July. The lake is stocked annually with legal rainbow trout, and you might hook an eastern brook trout from previous stockings. The lake is only about 20 acres, but lots of fish are caught. The rainbow are typically 8-10 inches, brook trout reach 3 pounds. Flyfishing can be excellent here, especially in the fall.

If you drive up here, be sure to continue the extra 4-5 miles to the rim for a spectacular view of the Steens escarpment and the desert below. There are a number of nice BLM campsites around the lake. Occasionally a strong, steady wind comes up here, and there is little to break it. When that happens, you'll wish you were elsewhere. Storms in the high Steens (wind, rain, and snow), are legendary and often come up suddenly. A second campground, at Jackman Park (a natural meadow), is located a mile further east on the Loop Rd., and Page Springs Campground is at the base of the mountain near Frenchglen.

Fish Lake is ideal for a rubber raft or canoe. Motors are prohibited on the lake. Supplies and limited accommodations area available in Frenchglen.

FLAGSTAFF LAKE See Warner Valley Lakes.

FORT CREEK A short tributary of Wood River, south of Fort Klamath, crossed by Hwy. 62 about 2 miles south of town near Fort Klamath Park and Museum. It's a very clear, spring-fed creek, accessible by road for most of its 3 mile length. A dirt road takes off just north of Klamath Junction and follows the headwaters of the creek to the east.

Fort Creek has primarily small brook trout in its upper waters. The lower stream has good-size brown trout, but flows through land owned by two resorts with access only for guests (Take-It-Easy Ranch and Fort Creek Resort).

FOURMILE LAKE A large lake on the east edge of Winema National Forest, 9 miles west of Klamath Lake. It contains kokanee, brook and rainbow trout. The lake is on the divide between the Rogue and Klamath basins, high in the Cascade range. To reach it, take FS 3661 north from Hwy. 140 at Lake of the Woods Visitor Center. See Lake Of The Woods for complete directions.

Fourmile covers 740 acres and has a maximum depth of 170 ft. At 5744 ft. elevation the winters are long and the growing season short. Nevertheless, kokanee are doing almost too well here, with a large self-sustaining population holding the size range to 6-10 inches. Kokanee are taken by trolling with large spinners trailing a small baited hook, and by still fishing with eggs on the bottom. They can also be taken on small wet flies and nymphs on sinking lines.

Naturally reproducing brook trout reach 15 inches here and are present in good numbers. Trolling and flies take these speckled trout. Best time to go for the larger ones is in September and October. Stocked rainbow trout reach 14 inches. Best rainbow fishing is in spring and fall.

The lake is open all year but doesn't get much play in winter. There is no boat ramp, but you can launch from the beach at the campground. Fourmile gets awfully rough at midday, so be careful when boating. A Forest Service campground with limited facilities is located at the southern tip of the lake. Trails leading to nearby small lakes begin near the campground. See Badger, Long, Squaw.

FRANCIS LAKE (Klamath Co.) A small brook trout lake north of the Pelican Butte Lookout about 4 miles NW of Point Comfort on the west shore of upper Klamath Lake. You'll have to bushwhack in to this lake, which is one mile north and 1500 ft. below the lookout. You won't have a lot of company. From the north end of the Lake of the Woods on Hwy. 140, take the Cold Springs Campground Rd. north almost to the campground, then cut west on the Lookout Rd. The lookout is at 8000 ft. and provides a great view of the country. From the lookout, backtrack about 1 1/2 miles by road, and trek north around the butte at constant elevation. You'll reach the lake in 1 1/2 miles. Francis is within a draw that runs NE from the butte. Don't confuse it with Gladys Lake 1/4 mile NW.

Francis is 3.5 acres and is stocked periodically with brook trout. The typical fish here runs 8-10 inches. Other small lakes nearby hold no fish.

GERBER RESERVOIR A large reservoir in south central Oregon between Lakeview and Klamath Falls, fished for bass, panfish, and nice size trout. The state record white crappie came out of Gerber Reservoir at 4 pounds 12 ounces.

To get there from Klamath Falls, take Hwy. 140 east 19 miles to Dairy, then County Rd. 70 SE about 17 miles to Bonanza and Lorella. Head NE about 8 miles to the reservoir. From Lakeview, take Hwy. 140 west to Bly, and follow FS 375 and FS 381 south 10 miles to the lake.

Gerber covers over 3800 acres when full, but the water level fluctuates. Some fair size bass are caught, but most anglers are after crappie and perch. The crappie run 7-14 inches, and perch about the same, though the average perch will be smaller. A lot of nice brown bullhead are also available. Rainbow are periodically stocked, and in recent years trout 18-20 inches have been caught. Gerber has been popular for ice fishing.

The BLM provides 2 campgrounds with boat ramps, one at the dam and another about 2 miles north.

GOOSE LAKE A very large lake on the Oregon-California border about 8 miles south of Lakeview. Covering about 46 square miles, it is mostly very shallow water. Hunters come here primarily for ducks and geese, but a few large trout are taken in spring. Most angling is concentrated near the inlets along the east side.

Hwy. 395 leads south from Lakeview and parallels the east shore of the lake from a distance. A road runs to the lakeshore at the border town of New Pine Creek. A road closely follow the western shore on the California side. This road can be reached by secondary roads leading south from Hwy. 140 towards West Side, about 4 miles west of Lakeview.

HARRIETTE LAKE The largest lake in the Mountain Lakes Wilderness of SE Winema National Forest. It's in a very scenic area, surrounded by tall peaks, with small lakes and potholes close by. See Echo Lake for directions. Harriet is about 5 miles from the trailhead.

The lake is at 6750 ft., covers 70 acres, and is 63 ft. deep. It's popular and heavily fished. Good catches of brook trout and rainbow are made, with the average about 10 inches. A few larger fish to 15 inches show up from time to time. Any method can be effective, with bait angling from the west shore popular. Best angling occurs in spring and fall. Other fishable lakes in the area include Echo, Como, South Pass.

HART LAKE (Lake Co.) A large lake in Warner Valley north and downstream from Crump Lake. The rugged face of Hart Mt. rises 3000 feet above the lake to the east. Hart Lake is due east of the tiny town of Plush on Hwy 140, 18 miles north of Adel. Adel is 31 miles east of Lakeview. Dirt roads lead north and east from Plush over a dike along the north edge of the lake. A jeep road runs along the east shore and eventually leads back to Hwy. 140. The SW shore is reached by a jeep road that first follows the north shore of Crump Lake. This road leaves the Plush Rd. about 9 miles north of Adel.

Hart Lake covers 10,000 acres in wet years, but has even gone dry in the past. See Warner Valley Lakes for additional information.

Hart is primarily fished for catfish and crappie. The cats are numerous and of good size. Average weight is one pound, but some tip the scale at 2-3 pounds. A favorite area in the spring is the narrows near the inlet from Crump Lake.

Fishing for white crappie is popular off the SE shore, with peak activity in July. Sometimes this lake really turns on for crappie, with thousands taken on jigs in a few days. The crappie run to 14 inches, averaging 8-10. There's not much in the way of trout fishing, although a few large rainbow are caught. Largemouth bass have been stocked but aren't thriving. The Warner Sucker, a fish unique to the Warner Valley, is protected.

This is pretty remote country, so check your rig, gas and supplies before you head out.

HEART LAKE (Eagle Cap Wilderness) A small lake in the southern Eagle Cap Wilderness, part of the upper Eagle Creek drainage. The trail to Heart begins at Boulder Park, which is reached by about 15 miles of gravel road heading east from Medical Springs on Hwy. 203, between La Grande and Baker. Take Trail 1922 up the creek from the resort and branch west in about 2.5 miles onto Trail 1937. This trail is steep, climbing over 1500 feet in just 1 1/2 miles.

Heart Lake is at the head of Bench Canyon south of the main trail at 7300 ft. Though only 3 acres, it is quite deep. It contains rainbow trout to 15 inches, although the average size is about 9. It provides good bait and fly angling in August and September.

HEART LAKE (Lake Co.) A 25 acre kokanee and rainbow lake in Fremont National Forest about 28 miles west of Lakeview. Follow Hwy. 140 to Quartz Mt. Pass. Turn south on FS 3715. Heart Lake is about 9 miles from the junction. A primitive road on the right circles through a small lake basin that includes Spatterdock Lake, Tule Pond, and Heart Lake, the southernmost lake on the circle.

Small kokanee 8-10 inches provide good spring angling on single eggs. Rainbow to 10 inches make up the bulk of the catch in summer and fall. Bait is best in early season, with flies effective in summer and fall. The nearest campground is at Lofton Reservoir across the road from the Heart Springs turn-off.

HEAVENLY TWINS LAKES Two nice lakes in the Sky Lakes Area near the border between Rogue and Winema National Forests. From Hwy. 140 about 5 miles east of Lake of the Woods, FS 3651 leads to the trailhead at Cold Springs Campground. Trails 3710 and 3709 both access the lake basin. Trail 3710 follows a steeper route up Imagination Peak before dropping into the basin. The trail crosses a small ridge between the two lakes. Trails are usually accessible in late June, with good fishing then and in late summer and fall.

The larger of the two lakes covers about 25 acres and is fairly shallow, a good fly fishing lake. Heavily fished, it is an excellent producer of rainbow and brook trout averaging 10 inches, but fish over 5 pounds have been taken. A rubber boat would allow you to troll lures for the big ones. The smaller lake covers about 7 acres and is deeper, providing mostly brook trout to 12 inches with larger brookies taken rarely. There are good campsites around the lakes near the trail, and at Isherwood Lake just east of Big Twin. The season here is limited only by the weather.

HELLS CANYON RESERVOIR The lowest reservoir on the Snake River, 21 miles of harnessed flow between Oxbow Dam at Copperfield, Oregon, and Hells Canyon Dam at the southern boundary of Hells Canyon Wilderness. Below Hells Canyon Dam, the river runs free through its magnificent gorge, accessed only by trails and intrepid river runners.

To reach the reservoir from Baker, follow Hwy. 86 to Copperfield. From Weiser, Idaho, take I-95 north to Hwy. 71. There's a boat ramp at Copperfield Park, just downstream from Oxbow Dam. A gravel road then a dirt track parallel the Oregon shore for about 8 miles. Trail 1890 continues downstream another 7 miles. A paved road follows the Idaho shore from Oxbow

DESERT LAKE
Gerry Lewin, Photographer

to Hells Canyon Dam. There is a boat launch on the Idaho shore at Hells Canyon Park, about 5 miles downstream from Oxbow. The road crosses Hells Canyon Dam to the Oregon shore, leading to Hells Canyon Creek Boat Ramp, access to the lower river.

The impoundment contains channel cats averaging 10-14 inches, but running to 20 inches. Anglers use bait, fishing from both bank and boats. Smallmouth bass are taken on lures and spinners. Bluegill and a few crappie are caught on jigs or cut bait. There are also sturgeon present, but the Snake River and its impoundments are closed to sturgeon angling.

There are campgrounds at Copperfield Park on the Oregon shore, and at Hells Canyon Park and McCormick Park (near Brownlee dam) in Idaho. There are also 4 hike or boat-in camps on the Oregon shore between road's end and Hells Canyon Dam.

HIDDEN LAKE (Union Co.) A brook trout lake high in the Eagle Cap Wilderness, about 50 miles NE of Baker. The outlet from the lake flows into the East Fork of Eagle Creek. The lake is about 1 1/2 miles NE of Eagle Lake on the opposite side of a ridge. Best approach is from the south by East Fork Trail 1910, which starts at the Kettle Creek Campground, a hike-in camp at the end of FS 7740, which heads north from Main Eagle Bridge Camp. To get there from Baker or LaGrande, turn east into the forest at Medical Springs on Hwy. 203, taking FS 67 to Tamarack Campground, then FS 77 to Main Eagle Bridge Camp. The trailhead is about 15 miles from Medical Springs.

Hidden Lake has lots of brook trout and produces well. Best fishing is August through September, using flies or bait.

HIGGINS RESERVOIR A 100 acre impoundment on Camp Creek NE of Unity. An unimproved road less than one mile east of town heads north off Hwy. 26 toward the reservoir, a 5 mile drive.

Higgins has been stocked with rainbow trout, and there are frequent catches 14-15 inches, with 20 inch fish available. Trolling and bait fishing with eggs or worms are most productive. The reservoir is open year around, and ice fishing is good. There's a state park with picnic facilities and campground at Unity Reservoir on Hwy. 7.

HIGH LAKE (Grant Co.) A 10 acre lake, highest in the Strawberry Mt. Wilderness of Malheur National Forest. It's nestled just above timberline in a glacial cirque. Spring fed and not too deep, it's a good fly fishing lake, especially in fall.

The shortest route to the lake is from the south. At Seneca on Hwy. 395 north of Burns, turn east onto FS 16, and drive east about 13 miles to the intersection of FS 1640. Drive north on 1640 to a short spur road leading NE about 2 miles beyond Indian Springs Campground. Trail 385 begins at the end of this road and leads to the lake in about 1 1/2 miles, losing about 600 ft. of elevation in the process. If you are coming on Hwy. 395 from John Day to the north, take FS 15 east about 9 miles south of Hwy. 26. FS 15 and 16 meet at Parish Cabin Campground, about 3 miles west of the FS 1640 junction.

Alternately, you may hike in from the north by way of Strawberry and Slide Lake. Trail 385 leads from Slide Lake to High Lake, following a scenic route near timberline. Access in early spring may be impossible due to snowbound roads.

HOLBROOK RESERVOIR A 40 acre reservoir on Fishhole Creek 2 miles downstream from Lofton Reservoir. Holbrook is south of Hwy. 140 at Quartz Mt. Pass, about 28 miles

west of Lakeview. The reservoir is managed for public fishing through a cooperative agreement between a private landowner, the Dept. of Fish and Wildlife, and the Forest Service.

The lake was originally stocked with rainbow and has been productive for trout to 12 inches. However, an expanding population of brown bullhead catfish is diminishing the trout fishery. Check with ODFW in Lakeview for information about its plans for dealing with the bullhead.

HOME CREEK A short eastern Oregon stream, originating on Steens Mt. and flowing 9 miles east into the Catlow Valley. It can be reached from Burns by way of Hwy. 205 south, about 21 miles south of Frenchglen. The creek crosses the road at Home Creek Ranch, about 7 miles south of the change from pavement to gravel. It flows mostly through BLM land, but the area near the highway is on private land. The BLM land touches the highway about mid-way through the kinked section, about 1/10 mile north of the creek crossing. Dirt roads cross the upper creek in at least two places. You'd better have a BLM map in hand to find your way in the upper creek area.

Home Creek is not stocked but has a fair native rainbow trout population, best fished in spring and early summer. Rainbow to 14 inches are taken, with bait fishing the most common method. There are no improved campgrounds in the area.

HONEY CREEK A good trout stream which heads on Abert Rim in Fremont National Forest. Its headwaters can be reached from FS 3615 or FS 3720 before the creek flows into a canyon then down through private ranchland, which is closed to public access (due to past vandalism). The lowest waters enter a small canyon that begins on the ranch, and through which the creek flows toward Plush. Plush is in Warner Valley on Hwy. 140 east of Lakeview.

Best fishing on Honey is in the lower stretch, for wild redband and brook trout. However, we have been advised that lower Honey Creek Canyon is particularly rattlesnake infested. *(It's so bad that most people never go back twice, even though the fishing is tremendous!)* Our source assures us that this isn't a rumor propagated by the local folks to keep outsiders away from a good thing.

ISHERWOOD LAKE A very good 18 acre hike-in lake in the Sky Lakes group of Sky Lakes Wilderness, Winema National Forest. It's a 3 1/2 mile hike north by trail 3710 from Cold Springs Campground. See Deep Lake and Heavenly Twin for directions. Near the north end of the largest Heavenly Twin, the Isherwood Trail branches west. Isherwood is on the west side of the trail.

Eastern brook trout and rainbow 12-14 inches can be found here. All methods may be used successfully, but fly angling early and late in the day is especially productive. Mosquitoes, March Brown, Caddis or almost any standard pattern will do. Campsites are currently limited due to efforts to rehabilitate the lakeshore following years of heavy use.

ISLAND LAKE (Klamath Co.) The largest lake in the Island Lake group of Sky Lakes Wilderness, Winema National Forest. It's 3 miles north of Fourmile Lake. For directions, see Deep Lake. Island Lake can also be reached by longer trails from Fourmile Lake and the Blue Lake area on the Rogue side.

At elevation 5906 ft., Island covers 40 acres but is only 17 feet deep at its deepest point near the northern end. Fishing from shore is easy and, more often than not, excellent.

The lake is stocked with brook trout and has natural reproduction. The average fish is 11 inches, with some to 18 inches. Flyfishing is the preferred method here, but bait and trolling will also produce. Try tossing a fly into the shoal areas of the island around evening. Campsites are currently limited due to lakeshore rehabilitation efforts.

J.C. RESERVOIR A 450 acre reservoir 15 miles west of Klamath Falls. The reservoir is just off Hwy. 66. It contains white crappie, brown bullhead, largemouth bass, Sacramento perch, and pumpkinseed sunfish.

JENNY CREEK A good trout stream heading south of Howard Prairie between the Rogue and Klamath drainages, 16 miles east of Ashland. Rainbow 8-10 inches make themselves at home throughout the creek, and brook trout are present in the lower stream.

The creek flows south, crossing Hwy. 66 at Pinehurst, and skirts the eastern border of the Siskiyou Mountains, finally reaching Iron Gate Reservoir on the Klamath River about 3 miles south of the California line. A fair stretch of the upper river is followed by the Jenny Creek Rd. south from the southern tip of Howard Prairie. Moon Prairie Rd. follows the creek from about one mile to the east from the end of Jenny Creek Rd. to Hwy. 66.

Jenny Creek provides good angling in early spring and again in the fall. Bait fishing is most popular with anglers here, but lures and flies work well. There are no improved campgrounds along the creek, but Tub Springs Wayside, about 4 miles west of the crossing on Hwy. 66, has a nice picnic area.

JONES LAKE See Warner Valley Lakes.

KILLAMACUE LAKE A small high lake in the Elkhorn Range of southern Wallowa-Whitman National Forest west of Haines. The lake contains small Mackinaw trout. To reach it from Haines, take Hwy. 411 west to Rock Creek, continuing west past Rock Creek Power Station into the forest. The road becomes an unimproved track, FS 5520 and follows the North Fork Rock Creek. About 2 miles from the paved road, Trail 1617 leads NW to Killamacue, following Killamacue Creek to the lake.

KLAMATH LAKE See Upper Klamath Lake.

KLAMATH RIVER An outstanding trout stream, one of America's best, and one of Oregon's best kept secrets. The river is born in Oregon of enormous Upper Klamath Lake, but flows free only briefly within Oregon borders. To our discredit as an environmentally aware state, only 18 free-flowing river miles remain. The other 22 miles are captured by dams. Yet the river continues to produce good numbers of large, powerful rainbow here, testifying to the vitality of the Klamath—and to its lost potential.

Since 1978 Oregon has managed the Klamath as a wild trout stream, with encouraging results. Still, it's distressing to see how much of this extremely productive river (certainly among the top 3 in the state) is lost to power impoundments. Steelhead and salmon runs were eliminated by California's Copco Dam in 1917. And power interests continue to push proposals for additional dams in Oregon.

The Klamath River once began at Upper Klamath Lake. A dam at Keno, 17 miles downstream, created Lake Ewauna, a pool that backs up to within a mile of Klamath Lake. The outlet of Keno Dam is where trout action begins. The river flows past one additional dam in its remaining 23 miles north of the California border. From there it wanders over 200 miles before reaching the Pacific.

The most productive stretch of Oregon's Klamath today is the flow between Keno Dam and Boyle Reservoir, only 6 miles. Highway 66 parallels this stretch from the south, and Weyerhauser forest roads follow on the north. The river pours through a relatively steep canyon and features a series of runs and deep holes with intermittant shallow riffles over a bedrock base. The average fish here is 14 inches, with many to 20 inches, weighing 2-4 pounds. This is heavy water. Fly anglers use big weighted nymphs on sinking or sink tip lines. Spin casters favor Rooster Tails, and bait casters use a heavily weighted worm rig. A number of trails drop into the canyon. You can also enter the canyon at Keno Dam. Check in at the Keno store for additional information and directions.

This stretch has a special closure from mid-June until the beginning of October, related to the effects of rising water temperature on the trout. As the water climbs toward 70 degrees and the river fills with algae, the fish acquire an unpalatable taste. Trout also lose much of their strength when the water warms, and would suffer high mortality if catch and release were practiced here.

Below the reservoir, the river flows south of Hwy. 66. A road closely follows its west bank to 3 miles below Boyle Powerhouse, then crosses to the east side, following the Klamath into California. From the reservoir to Boyle Powerhouse, a run of 5 miles, the river is cool and stable, though its flow is much reduced by diversion into a sluice that carries water to the generating station. In this 5 mile stretch, the Klamath runs its clearest, and trout are abundant. Resident trout here are only 8-12 inches, but larger fish move through. The flow is augmented by spring outflows from the reservoirs. The riverbed here is much the same as in the Keno stretch. Best fishing is from the end of May until mid-June. From the reservoir to the Oregon border, angling is restricted to catch and release with barbless flies and lures from June 15 to Oct. 1.

Below the powerhouse the river regains its size, and so do the fish, averaging 12-15 inches. This section is called the *Frain Ranch*, named for Martin Frain who settled the valley in the late 1800's. The few remaining buildings and the original Frain orchard have been named an Oregon Historical landmark. Fishing in this section is characterized by very unstable water conditions resulting from Boyle Power Plant. The water usually drops in late evening and rises at 7 or 8 a.m. Once the river rises and stabilizes, good fishing generally resumes. The fish here are larger than those in the Boyle section, but smaller than the Keno trout. Peak fishing in this stretch is from the end of May until mid-June. In early spring and summer stonefly nymphs are generally most effective. Try Polly Rosborough's Golden Stone and Dark Stone Bucktail, or the yellow Bucktail Caddis.

Currently, the City of Klamath Falls is still seeking permission to construct a dam on the river below Boyle Powerhouse. We encourage anglers to visit this great river and learn its ways, then be ready to help block further damming efforts. Support for the Klamath has been coordinated by Klamath Country Flycasters, P.O. Box 1956, Klamath Falls, OR 97601.

The only campground on the Klamath is Topsy Campground, a BLM campground with boat ramp, located at Boyle Dam. Boaters are advised to inquire locally before attempting to run the river.

KRUMBO RESERVOIR A reservoir on lower Krumbo Creek in the Malheur Wildlife Refuge, stocked with a mix of trout, bass, and panfish. To reach it, drive south from Burns on Hwy. 205 toward Frenchglen. About 20 miles south of the Malheur Refuge Headquarters turnoff, a road leads east 4 miles to the reservoir.

Krumbo covers about 150 acres and is capable of growing fair fish. Over-population by roach has been a recurring problem, and the reservoir has been poisoned and restocked. The creek above the reservoir has a fair population of wild trout. For other fisheries in the vicinity, see Donner Und Blitzen River, Fish Lake.

Camping is available at Page Springs BLM Campground east of Frenchglen. While in Frenchglen, visit the historic Frenchglen Hotel, which is included in the state park system. Accommodations, good family style meals, and the most pleasant sereened front porch for a hundred miles are available there. Don't neglect a visit to the beautiful Refuge Headquarters.

LAKE CREEK (Grant Co.) A fair wild rainbow and brook trout stream flowing south out of Strawberry Mt. Wilderness into the Malheur River. The creek begins as the outlet of High Lake, 7400 ft. above sea level, and flows through the Malheur National Forest. Its trout reach 11 inches, averaging 9-10 inches.

Trail 378 follows the creek closely from High Lake to FS 924, which continues along the creek to FS 16 about 20 miles east of Seneca. Lake Creek and Big Creek enter the Malheur River together about 1 1/2 miles south of Big Creek Camp. The campground is on a short spur road just north of FS 16, less than 2 miles west of the FS 924 junction.

LAKE OF THE WOODS (Klamath Co.) A large, popular lake near the summit of the Cascade range west of Klamath Lake, offering fair angling and varied recreational opportunities. The lake is a very popular spot with summer boaters and offers good fishing for kokanee, rainbow, and largemouth bass.

Direct routes access the lake from east, south, and west. From Medford, follow Hwy. 140 east. From Klamath Falls, follow 140 west. From Ashland, follow signs to the airport then turn north just beyond the runway onto (ugh) Dead Indian Rd., which becomes FS 363 after entering the Rogue River National Forest. Lake of the Woods is about 35 miles from both Ashland and Klamath Falls, about 45 miles from Medford. It covers 1113 acres and is circled by roads, as well as many homes.

Lake of the Woods has never been very productive, though it has substantial shoal area, primarily at the north and south ends. The east shore has gravel beaches that are used by kokanee as spawning beds. The west shore is steep and rocky. A population of stunted brown bullhead, most about six inches long, still make up over half the population in the lake, though legal rainbow are stocked annually

Kokanee are also stocked in large numbers and are well established, the best fishery in the lake at present. The catch rate is low, though the fish are present in good numbers, and the lake isn't deep—only 50 ft. maximum. The kokanee average about 9 inches at maturity.

Trout stocking programs here have not been satisfactory. Past strains have consistently failed to winter over, possibly due to disease. ODFW is planning to experiment with stocking Klamath Lake rainbow. At present, most rainbow caught here are 9-14 inches.

Fishing is best early in the morning and late evening, when the water-skiers are otherwise occupied. There are campgrounds with boat ramps at the north end and near Rainbow Bay on the east. A large resort at the north end offers accommodations, supplies, food, and boat rentals.

LITTLE MALHEUR RIVER A good trout stream, tributary to the North Fork of the Malheur River. The Little Malheur joins the North Fork about 5 miles NW of Beulah Reservoir north of Juntura. It runs generally north-south, draining the south slope of the Blue Mts. Much of the creek shows up on the Malheur National Forest map, as it runs near or in the east edge of the forest. It offers fair fishing for wild rainbow and brook trout to 11 inches, averaging 9-10 inches.

From Juntura on Hwy. 20, 23 miles of gravel road follow the river north to the forest. FS 16 crosses the upper river, and FS 457 follows it north 2 miles from that point. A primitive road leads south from FS 16, following the river from a short distance for several miles, and other tracks access it in the forest as well. Trail 366, which heads at Elk Flat, follows Elk Creek down to the Little Malheur's headwaters.

LOFTON RESERVOIR A 40 acre impoundment on upper Fishhole Creek, 30 miles west of Lakeview and about 5 miles NW of Drews Reservoir. Take Hwy. 140 west from Lakeview to Quartz Mt. Turn left (south) onto FS 3715, which reaches the Lofton access road in about 5 miles.

Lofton has been treated several times for rough fish. Its dam was rebuilt cooperatively, and reasonable water levels are now maintained. Rainbow fingerlings are stocked each year, providing good angling for 8-12 inch fish, with some trout to 16 inches available. It's easy to fish from shore, but a rowboat or raft could be useful. Most anglers here use bait, but flies and lures can be equally productive. In late summer flies have the edge, as weed growth makes bait angling difficult. There is a Forest Service campground here. Several other small lakes in this area might be worth investigating.

LOOKINGGLASS LAKE A nice glacial cirque lake just within the southern border of Eagle Cap Wilderness, Wallowa-Whitman National Forest. This is one of the easier lakes to hike to in this physically challenging wilderness. It's about 6 miles north and east of Boulder Park at the end of the Eagle Creek Rd. FS 7755. From LaGrande or Baker, follow Hwy. 203 to Medical Springs, then head east for about 15 miles on gravel roads to Boulder. Take Trail 1922 north 4 easy miles, then cut back south on Trail 1921, climbing 1300 feet in 2.2 miles to the lake.

Lookingglass is 31 acres and 45 ft. deep at elevation 7500 ft. In addition to good numbers of brook trout, it probably still has carry-over Mackinaw (lake trout), from a stocking in the early 1970s. Bait fishing or flies will take brook trout easily, while lures fished deep work best for the lake trout. Best months are August and September.

LOST LAKE A small high lake in the Elkhorn Range west of Haines. It contains wild brook trout. See Red Mt. Lake for directions to North Fork North Powder River Rd. At road's end, follow Trail 1632 west less than one mile, then turn left (north) onto Trail 1621, which leads first to Meadow Lake then to Lost in about 1 1/2 miles.

LOST RIVER A slow stream with fishing for bass and panfish east of Klamath Falls. The river originates in California, draining Clear Lake, and flows NW in a great arc through the Langell Valley, Bonanza, Olene, and Merrill, finally re-entering California and flowing into Tule Lake. In the upper stretch from California to Bonanza the stream is split and channelized extensively for irrigation. Hwy. 140 parallels the river for a short way at Olene, and county roads follow it for most of the distance from Bonanza downstream. Klamath County has provided a public parking area and bank fishing access. There is public access for boat and bank anglers south of Olene on Crystal Springs Rd.

Lost River offers fishing for brown bullhead, crappie, perch, and bass. The bass range 2-7 pounds. Sacramento perch are common in addition to yellow perch, pumpkinseed sunfish, and crappie. The state record black crappie, at 4 pounds, was caught here in 1978. A few trout show in the catch but are not common.

Spring is probably the best time here, but fishing is good the year around. There are no campsites along the stream.

LUCKY RESERVOIR A 6 acre desert reservoir on BLM land SW of Adel. Take Hwy. 140 west from Adel 3 miles, and turn south, fording Deep Creek and following the powerline road 4 1/2 miles to the reservoir. You'll go through four gates. Please leave them as you find them. The creek isn't fordable until the spring runoff has dropped, usually in June.

The reservoir is stocked with rainbow, which grow to 18 inches here, but the water is quite turbid and fishing is usually slow. Bait is the normal method, although fly anglers take fish at times.

MALHEUR RESERVOIR A large popular reservoir capable of growing good size trout. It is north of Hwy. 26 between Ontario and John Day, approached by 15 miles of dirt road north from Ironside or Brogan, both located on Hwy. 26. The reservoir covers 1300 acres when full. In 1988 it was treated to remove rough fish and is currently scheduled for restocking with rainbow and Lahontan cutthroat. Development of a trophy fishery for Lahontan has been proposed and may be implemented in 1990. Check current angling regulations.

In past years, Malheur has grown trout 10-12 inches. But these desert reservoirs are often capable of doing much better. Lahontan are a strain of trout especially adapted to desert conditions and capable of good growth. With effective regulations, nature will take her course here.

MALHEUR RIVER, UPPER Formerly referred to as the *Middle Fork*, but now officially recognized as the mainstem of the river system. It flows 50 miles from Logan Valley, just south of the Strawberry Mountains in Malheur National Forest, to its confluence with North and South Forks at Juntura, on Hwy. 20 east of Burns.

To access the upper river and its tributaries (See Lake Creek, Big Creek, Bosenberg Creek), follow Hwy. 395 to Seneca (about 24 miles

south of John Day, 45 miles north of Burns). Follow FS 16 east about 18 miles to the Big Creek area. Forest roads south of the main route approach and cross the river many times. From Big Creek Campground you can follow the creek south about 2 miles to the confluence of Big, Bosenberg, and Lake creeks.

Gravel roads follow the river's mid-section between the communities of Drewsey and Van. To reach this area from Burns, follow Hwy. 20 east to the northbound graded gravel road just beyond the community of Buchanan. Take the right fork at Pine Creek School. This road follows the river south to Drewsey. Beyond Drewsey, the river flows into Warm Springs Reservoir from the north, outflows at the south, then doubles back north to its confluence with the forks at Juntura. No roads access this stretch. There is an easy 12 mile boat drift from Hwy. 20 to the reservoir.

The Malheur has a good population of native redband trout and bull trout (Dolly Varden) in the headwaters above the reservoir and is stocked with hatchery rainbow in the Logan Valley area. Fish average 10 inches, but the natives run to 16 inches. All methods can be effective, but bait angling is most popular. Spring, after the runoff recedes, is the best time to fish. Smallmouth bass are also common in the stream below Warm Springs Reservoir.

A note on the river's name, French for *unfortunate river*: According to Lewis MacArthur, the river was so named by a Hudson's Bay trader in 1826, whose cache of furs and trade goods, hidden near the river, was discovered and stolen by natives.

MALHEUR RIVER, LOWER An accessible 90 mile stretch of water that is capable of providing excellent angling for trout to 20 inches. Hwy. 20 follows it closely from Juntura (about an hour east of Burns) to Vale, and secondary roads approach the river in the Ontario area, where it empties into the Snake River at the Idaho border. Much of the river flows through public BLM land, but there are some posted areas. Watch for signs.

Plagued with rough fish, the river is now treated periodically and restocked with trout. The last treatment was in the fall of 1987, but a spring of '88 restocking with rainbow fingerlings and yearlings showed less growth than would normally occur due to drought conditions. Largest trout in the river in 1988 seemed to be 12 inches.

There are many pools and riffles in the lower Malheur, and trout will grow large here. Fall offers the best angling. During irrigation season the water runs high and murky, but drifted bait will still take large fish. There are no camping opportunities along the stream.

MALHEUR RIVER, NORTH FORK Another productive branch of the upper Malheur system, heading in the Blue Mountains of Malheur National Forest and joining the mainstem at Juntura. It flows 41 miles south before its impoundment as Beulah Reservoir, about 15 miles north of the confluence.

A graded gravel road follows the stream north from Juntura, on Hwy. 20, to the reservoir. Forest roads follow and cross the upper stream. From John Day, take Hwy. 26 east to Prairie City. Cross the John Day River, and follow FS 14, then FS 13, to the North Fork headwaters, about 25 miles from Prairie City. The river may also be approached from Seneca, on Hwy. 395, by way of FS 16.

The North Fork is stocked heavily with rainbow trout each spring and summer. Angler success rate is very high in comparison with other streams in the area. Trout run 9-13 inches, with a few to 20 inches. Best angling is in the upper area. There are a number of forest camps near the river on FS 16 and 14.

MALHEUR RIVER, SOUTH FORK A short stem of the Malheur, with headwaters in Virginia Valley east of Malheur Lake, flowing east to the Malheur Cave area and north to Juntura, where it joins the North Fork and mainstem. Hwy. 78 follows a section of the upper stream about 10 miles SE of Princeton, an hour's drive from Burns. An eastbound cut-off at Crane approaches the river's mid-section. The lower stream flows through a deep canyon to Juntura, but it's accessible in a few spots. Most of the land along the river is private property. Check in at the nearest ranch for permission to fish.

The South Fork is stocked annually with rainbow fingerlings. Angling is only fair, with fishing best during the first month after trout season opens. There are no camping opportunities along the stream.

MANN LAKE A fair size lake with very good angling for big Mann Lake cutthroat, a strain especially adapted to life in the lake's high elevation alkaline waters. Mann sprawls at the summit of a gentle saddle in the rain shadow east of Steens Mt. Fishing is restricted to barbless flies and lures. This is a wild and wonderful place if you love open spaces and the vast scale of a desert. Keep an eye to the slopes of Steens Mt. and you are very likely to see antelope during your stay here.

Mann Lake is due east of Frenchglen, but there is no direct route from there. You'll have to drive around the mountain. It's about 100 road miles to Mann Lake from Burns. From the north, take Hwy. 78 SE from Burns, crossing over Steens Mt. east of New Princeton, and turning south at Folly Farm onto the east side Steens road to Fields. The lake is just west of the road, about 25 miles south of Folly Farm. Tencent Lake and Juniper Lake are sometimes mistaken for Mann Lake, but both are much closer to Folly Farm. Juniper Lake has also been stocked and in wet years shows good results.

Mann Lake covers about 275 acres, except in dry years. Water levels are currently still high from the heavy precipitation of the early 1980s, its access road still partially inundated. The lake is fairly rich and quite shallow, with an average depth of 8 ft. and a maximum depth of only 15 ft. Reeds encircle the lakeshore, and aquatic vegetation flourishes. The water is often somewhat turbid. There is no forage fish in Mann, but a rich and varied population of aquatic insects thrive here, and trout grow quickly grazing upon them. Algal blooms tend to give the fish an off flavor by mid-summer.

The lake has been managed as a brood supply for high desert cutthroat trout, with eggs taken annually, raised to fingerlings in hatcheries, and used to continue this fishery and stock other high desert waters. Special regulations are in effect to preserve both the quality of the fishing and a steady supply of eggs for these unique native trout. The stock preserved here is officially recognized as Mann Lake cutthroat, and (along with Lahontan) are among the largest and most predacious trout native to western North America.

Most trout landed here are in excess of 12 inches, with fish up to 20 inches. Fishing is restricted to the use of artificial flies or lures with barbless hooks, and any fish under 16 inches

must be released unharmed. Fishing in the tributary streams is prohibited. The fly angler can do very well here, despite the poor water clarity. By July there are swarms of dragon and damsel flies hatching, and big nymphs will bring in the fish if retrieved in short jerks on a sinking or sink tip line through the shallows. Fishing drops off in August due to water temperatures in the '70s, but picks up again in fall.

The lake is on BLM land, and the area on the west side is used as an unimproved campground. There is no drinking water here. A raft or canoe can be used but isn't necessary. The lake is at the top of a low pass, and the wind can really howl through on occasion. The water doesn't stir up much, but it makes fishing either unpleasant or impossible. When it gets like that, drive north towards Fields to Alvord Hot Springs, on the left side of the road around the midpoint of the Alvord Desert. Supplies and the best burgers for fifty miles around are at Fields. This is exceptionally remote country, so top up your gas and water tanks prior to heading out.

MARGURETTE LAKE A good hike-in brook trout lake, about 15 acres, located in the Sky Lakes group of Sky Lakes Wilderness, Winema National Forest. From Hwy. 140 at Pelican Guard Station, north of Lake of the Woods, continue north about 10 miles, past Crystal Springs Roadside Rest, turning west on FS 3450. At the end of the road, Trail 3708 follows Cherry Creek into the lake basin. At the trail junction about 4 miles in, turn right onto Trail 3762 past Trapper Lake to Margurette, which is 1/8 mile NW of Trapper. The trail loops west around the north end of Trapper and leads to Margurette.

You'll find good fishing in Margurette for medium size brook and rainbow trout. Most fish will run 8-11 inches, with a few larger. Any method will take fish, except in mid-summer when they are finicky. A good trick to try is casting a large-blade spinner with a worm trailing, retrieve very slowly a yard at a time, and let settle. This usually wakes them up. Campsites are limited here, as elsewhere in the basin, due to shoreline rehabilitation efforts. For other good fishing opportunities nearby see Donna, Deep, Trapper.

McCOY CREEK A tributary of the Blitzen River, flowing NW off Steens Mt. It joins the Blitzen on Malheur Wildlife Refuge about 14 miles south of the southern border of Malheur Lake. The creek enters the refuge through Diamond Valley, and several miles have been channelized for irrigation.

To reach it, take Hwy. 205 south from Burns toward Frenchglen. The turn-off to Diamond is about 16 miles south of the Refuge Headquarters turn-off, and the road reaches the creek about 5 miles to the east. Dirt roads south of the Diamond area follow the creek east for many miles.

McCoy is about 25 miles long and has some good size trout, but it is lightly fished due to its remoteness. Much of the stream flows through private property, and permission to fish is hard to get. The native trout here reach 15 inches. Bait is probably the best method.

MILLER CREEK A small but good trout stream, outlet of Miller Lake, west of Hwy. 97 at Chemult. The creek is followed west from Hwy. 97 by the Miller Lake Rd. FS 9771, which intersects the highway 6 miles south of Chemult. The entire creek is only 10 miles long. It ends in Beaver Marsh and percolates into the ground, as do most of the creeks in this area.

The upper 4 miles flow within Winema National Forest.

The stream is not stocked, but solid populations of brown and rainbow trout are well established here. The nearest campground is at Miller Lake.

MILLER LAKE A deep, clear lake of over 600 acres between Chemult on Hwy. 97, and Diamond Lake. It is reached by 14 miles of good road north of Chemult.

Kokanee are present in abundance, have in fact overpopulated the lake, and average size has declined accordingly. They currently run 6-9 inches. Rainbow trout are stocked annually, and there are a few nice browns. Slow trolling with a long line can be effective. Fly angling along the shores and near inlet streams is good in evenings.

A nice campground with boat ramp and picnic facilities is located on the NW shore at Digit Point. Supplies are available at Chemult.

MOON RESERVOIR A 619 desert reservoir SE of Riley 25 miles SW of Burns. It was treated for rough fish in 1987, and has been filled and restocked with largemouth bass and black and white crappie. It should provide good fishing in a couple of years.

MUD LAKE RESERVOIR (Lake Co.) A 170 acre BLM desert reservoir NE of Adel. Take Hwy. 140 about 12 miles east of Adel, and turn onto a dirt road heading north. The reservoir is about 10 miles north, and you'd best get a county or BLM map before setting out for it.

The reservoir has been stocked with rainbow, and most are in the 8-14 inch range. The fish are of excellent quality but slow biters in this muddy water. Bait is best here. The reservoir is undeveloped, and there are no camping facilities or shade trees here.

MURRAY RESERVOIR A rainbow trout lake just off Hwy. 26 in western Baker County SE of Unity. From Baker, follow hwys. 7 then 26 south, about 9 miles beyond the community of Unity. The 45 acre lake is on the north side of Hwy. 26.

Bank angling is good for rainbow averaging 10-12 inches. Most anglers use bait. The reservoir is on private property, generously opened to public use without fee. Users are urged to carry out their own trash and to be considerate of waters, grounds and facilities in order to encourage continuance of the *open* policy. Angling from a floating device is prohibited.

MYRTLE CREEK (Harney Co.) A small stream flowing into the Silvies River north of Burns. The creek is within Malheur National Forest and joins the Silvies about 25 miles north of Burns, about 12 miles west of Hwy. 395. To reach it take Hwy. 395 north from Burns about 18 miles to FS 31, which cuts west from the highway one mile north of Idlewild Campground. FS 31 hits the creek about 12 miles NW, crossing it 7 miles above the Silvies. Forest roads follow it closely to its headwaters. Downstream, Trail 308 follows the creek almost to the Silvies River, providing the only access.

Myrtle produces a lot of small native redband trout. They are caught in spring and summer, averaging 10 inches. Bait fishing is popular. Campground are located north and south of the intersection of FS 31 and Hwy. 395.

SUNSET ON OWYHEE RESERVOIR
S. John Collins, Photographer

NATASHA LAKE A hike-in brook trout lake in the southern Dwarf Lakes area of the Sky Lakes group, Sky Lakes Wilderness. See Deep Lake for road directions to the trailhead at Cold Springs Campground. Trails 3709 and 3710 lead from Cold Springs to the basin. Trail 3709 is less steep. Pass between the Heavenly Twins, then turn north onto Trail 3729. Lake Natasha is on the west side of the trail. At about 6 acres, it's a steady producer of brook trout 6-9 inches. There are good campsites off the trail to the east, at Heavenly Twins, and at Isherwood, though camping throughout the basin is currently limited due to rehabilitation efforts along the shorelines. The angling season is determined by the weather.

NORTH PINE CREEK A wild rainbow stream, tributary to Pine Creek of the Snake River system, flowing mostly within Hells Canyon National Recreation Area of Wallowa-Whitman National Forest. It can be reached from Baker by taking Hwy. 86 east 51 miles to Halfway. Continue about 9 miles past Halfway to the mouth of North Pine Creek. The mouth is mid-way between the town of Copperfield, where Pine Creek enters the Snake River, and Halfway. From the south, take Idaho Hwy. 11 north from Robinette, crossing the Snake at Brownlee Dam, and continue north to Copper-

field. A paved road, FS 39, follows the creek north to its headwaters.

North Pine offers 16 miles of water with good road access. Fishing is fair for native rainbow to 12 inches. Bait is best, but spinner and bait will take fish in murky water. North Pine Campground is located 5 miles up from the mouth, and Lakefork Campground is 3 miles further upstream. A good trail leads west from the latter, following Lake Fork, a good tributary of North Pine.

NORTH POWDER RIVER A rainbow stream, flowing west from the Blue Mountains, entering the Powder River just east of the town of North Powder at the junction of hwys. 84 and 237. North Powder is 20 miles north of Baker. The main stream is followed by paved road for about 7 miles SW from North Powder. Forest roads access its North Fork and Anthony Fork headwaters north of Anthony Lake. See the Wallowa-Whitman National Forest map, south half, for details.

The stream and its tributaries offer fairly good angling for native and stocked rainbow in late spring and summer. Bait angling (nightcrawlers, eggs, or hoppers) will produce best. The nearest campgrounds are in the Anthony Lake area, with an unimproved camp at Rocky Ford, where the stream flows from the south toward the main road.

OBENCHAIN RESERVOIR A 40 acre reservoir 10 miles NE of Bly on Hwy. 140 Privately owned but open to public use, it contains a dense population of small largemouth bass. It offers good active fishing for the family. Camping is permitted. From Bly, follow FS 34 toward Campbell Reservoir, turning left at the road junction before Dutchman Flat. Obenchain is less than 4 miles NW of the junction.

OWYHEE RESERVOIR A long, narrow reservoir near the Idaho line, with excellent angling for bass and panfish. The reservoir was formed by an irrigation dam on the Owyhee river about 25 miles SW of Nyssa, 40 miles from Ontario. It fills a deep, scenic canyon with a pool about 40 miles long that has over 300 miles of shoreline. This canyon cuts through colorful volcanic rocks—a raw, wild place that can be reached, for the most part, only by boat. The reservoir is mighty remote for western Oregonians, but it's a popular area for southeasterners and Idaho anglers.

An excellent road, 4 miles west of the town of Owyhee, which is south of Nyssa and Vale, follows the river south to the dam and Lake Owyhee State Park, on the east shore near the dam. Other unimproved roads enter from Vale, Adrian and other towns along the Snake River near the border. Other access areas are at the end of the Dry Creek Rd. on the west side of the lake about 10 miles up from the dam, and at Leslie Gulch, coming in from the Succor Creek Rd. on the east side of the lake. These and other unimproved roads are shown on the Vale District BLM map.

Owyhee Reservoir State Airport, a dirt strip 1840 ft. x 30. ft which shows on the sectional, is located at Pelican Point, over 20 miles south of the dam. This strip sees a surprising amount of use. Pilots should low pass the runway to check for ruts before landing.

Owyhee's largemouth bass have attracted a lot of anglers in the past. Catches averaged 1-2 pounds, but reached 5 pounds. Currently the largemouth are running small and slender, 1 1/2 pounds maximum, and no big fish are being caught. Over-fishing and low water years in 1987-88 might be the culprits. Low water has been hard on all the reservoir's population, and recovery could take several years. Bass anglers here traditionally use both sinking and surface plugs, but almost any method can be effective at times. Bombers, Sonics, plastic worms, and black eels are the most popular lures.

Black crappie, which have run 7-9 inches and weigh 5-8 ounces, still seem to be present in abundance. They are taken on bait, spinner, jigs, flies or almost anything. The water in the center is deep, so most anglers work the shorelines. The area around Leslie Gulch has been providing channel cats to 15 lbs. Smallmouth and cat fishing is best at the head of the reservoir. Rainbow trout aren't stocked, but some drift in from elsewhere in the basin. Big rainbow occasionally show up in the catch.

Cherry Creek Resort, about 5 miles east of the dam, offers boats for rent, supplies, accommodations, dining room, and trailer parking. A nice State Park between resort and dam has 4 boat ramps, picnic facilities, and toilets. BLM campgrounds are located below the dam and toward the upper end at Leslie Gulch. Cherry Creek State Recreation Area also has a campground. All the recreation sites above have boat ramps. A hot spring is located near the south end of the reservoir on the south shore just west of the narrows, north of Red Rock Spring.

There has recently been some gold exploration underway on the west side of the reservoir.

There is some danger of pollution associated with the cyanide leach process used to withdraw the gold. Local anglers might want to keep track of these developments.

OWYHEE RIVER Flowing 205 miles from headwaters in the Owyhee Mts. of northern Nevada, through the remote and rugged canyonland of Idaho and southeast Oregon. It is fished primarily for channel catfish and smallmouth bass. The Owyhee joins the Snake River just south of Nyssa on the Oregon shore, across the river from Nampa, Idaho. Below Owyhee Reservoir (a 42-mile impoundment described above) the river is approached and closely followed by gravel roads all the way to the Snake.

The upper river is extremely remote, and much of it flows through deep canyons. It is crossed by Hwy. 95 at the community of Rome (about 135 miles SW of Ontario, Oregon), and is approached by unimproved roads in the backcountry (check Malheur County maps). A popular access point is Three Forks, approached by 28 miles of gravel road from Hwy. 95. Turn south off the highway about one mile east of the cut-off to Danner.

The upper canyon is best fished by float trip, and best floated with experienced Owyhee guides. Float trips usually take 3-5 days. The 60-mile stretch of canyon from Rome to the reservoir is rated advanced intermediate, with a Class 4 rapids and several Class 3s. Prime floating takes place during spring runoff from April to June. About 2000 people make the trip yearly, encountering some of the nation's most difficult white water and some of its most breathtaking canyonland scenery. Permits to raft are not required, but users are asked to register with the BLM.

Owyhee water runs murky year around, with best visibility in early fall. The entire upper river was treated for rough fish in 1970 and restocked with rainbow trout, smallmouth bass, and channel catfish. Angling has been very good for bass and channel catfish, but few trout are taken above the dam. Best catfishing is in the lower 50 miles from Rome to the reservoir.

OXBOW RESERVOIR A 12 mile impoundment of the Snake River between Oxbow and Brownlee dams, offering bass, panfish, and stocked rainbow. From Baker take Hwy. 86 east 70 miles to the community of Copperfield, at the huge bend in the Snake from which the dam gets its name. A paved road follows the reservoir closely from Oxbow upstream to Brownlee.

Quite a few channel cats are taken, and rainbow 10-15 inches and are caught in good numbers. There have been coho in the reservoir, which drift in from an Idaho stocking program. These may be counted in the daily trout limit. Boats may be launched at McCormick Park on the Idaho shore at the south end of the reservoir, just below Brownlee Dam. The Idaho Power Company maintains a campground there with good trailer sites. There is also a campground at Copperfield Park just below Oxbow Dam.

PELICAN LAKE See Warner Valley Lakes.

PHILLIPS RESERVOIR A large reservoir, with trout, coho salmon, largemouth and smallmouth bass on the upper Powder River about 5 miles east of Sumpter, SE of Baker. It was created by Mason Dam, built in 1967. From Baker, head south on Hwy. 7 to Salisbury and

TAKING IT EASY ON OXBOW RESERVOIR
S. John Collins, Photographer

about 9 miles east toward Sumpter. The reservoir usually covers about 2400 acres, though it got quite low during the 1987-88 drought and may take several years to completely refill and recover.

Trout angling at Phillips is usually good, with the average catch 12-15 inches and some larger. Trolling or still fishing near the dam is often effective. The state has been stocking coho salmon, and these are coming in around 16 inches now. The lake is open all year, and ice fishing is very popular. Winter efforts are generally well rewarded.

There are two campgrounds on the lake, one at the dam and the second at Union Creek, about 2 miles west of the dam. Both are easily reached from the highway, and each has a boat ramps. Supplies are available at Baker or Sumpter.

PINE CREEK (Baker Co.) A good stream, though rather isolated, entering the Snake River below Oxbow Dam. The stream heads in the SE corner of Eagle Cap Wilderness, flowing SE 15 miles to the town of Halfway, then swings east to the Snake. The stretch from Halfway to the Snake River at Copperfield is closely followed by Hwy. 86. Halfway is 51 miles east of Baker on Hwy. 86. A gravel road follows the creek upstream from Halfway to the headwaters, about 11 miles. Cornucopia, a ghost town, is located near the end of this road. Most of Pine Creek runs across private lands, so access may be a problem.

The stream is well stocked with rainbow trout, and fair catches of natives are made. The fish aren't large, to 12 inches or so. Best trout water is upstream from Halfway. Bait or flies will take fish in spring and summer. There are

no camping opportunities on the creek, but McBride Campground is only 4 miles west of Carson, mid-way between Halfway and Cornucopia.

PINE LAKES (Baker Co.) Two small, fairly deep brook trout lakes in the southern Eagle Cap Wilderness, Wallowa-Whitman National Forest. The lakes are about 3 air miles NW of Cornucopia, which is 10 miles NW of Halfway by County Rd. 413. Drive as far north on 413 as you can, and you'll reach the Pine Creek Trailhead. Follow Trail 1880 along Pine Creek all the way to the lake, about 7 miles of steady uphill hiking, elevation gain about 2400 ft.

The lakes are side by side and quite deep. Upper Pine is the larger, 14 acres with a depth of 70 feet. Lower is only 3 acres, but is 35 feet deep. Each has a good supply of brook trout. Bait, flies, and lures all work. These fish aren't fussy. Average size is 10 inches.

POISON CREEK An 18-mile trout stream originating in Malheur National Forest, followed by Hwy. 395 for about 7 miles north from Burns. The upper waters are accessed by westbound forest roads in the vicinity of Joaquin Miller and Idlewild campgrounds. It offers fair angling for native trout in spring, with bait most effective. The stream is fairly sluggish and gets low in summer.

POWDER RIVER A long tributary of the Snake River, heading near Sumpter and winding over 140 miles to the Snake near Richland, which is on Hwy. 86 south of Halfway. The lower 10 miles below Richland are actually part of the pool from the Snake's Brownlee Dam. Highway 86 follows the next 25 miles, and

ICE FISHING ON PHILLIPS
S. John Collins, Photographer

county roads north from 86 provide access up to the crossing of Hwy. 203 at river mile 58 NE of Baker. There really isn't much access from that point north to Thief Valley Reservoir. Highway 30 parallels the river from North Powder to Baker, with many roads leading east to cross or follow the River. From Baker to Phillips Reservoir, the river is followed by Hwy. 7.

The Powder provides a diversity of angling. In the lower 10 miles from Richland to the Snake, bass, channel cats, crappie and perch predominate. Trolling, casting lures from shore, or bait fishing from boat or bank take fish throughout the season. The upper river is stocked heavily with rainbow, and a few natives are also caught. Best angling is in the tailwaters of Mason Dam (Phillips Reservoir) and Thief Valley Dam. Trout in these stretches reach 20 inches, with most around 10-14 inches. On the rest of the river the fish run smaller, with average around 10 inches.

Above Phillips Reservoir the river has been devastated by gold mining. Hewitt County Park, 2 miles east of Richland, provides boating access to the lower river. Camping is available at Thief Valley and Phillips Reservoirs.

PRIDAY RESERVOIR Covering about 100 acres, located in Warner Valley, about 57 miles NE of Lakeview. From I-395 follow Warner Canyon Rd. 140 east to Adel, then turn north toward Hart Lake and the community of Plush. The reservoir is on the west side of the road about 12 miles beyond Adel. It is stocked with Lahontan cutthroat, which run 10-17 inches. Largemouth bass are also present from an unauthorized introduction. The water is generally turbid, and the catch rate is slow even with bait.

PUCK LAKES Two fair fishing lakes on the east slope of the Cascades, set off by themselves between the Sky Lakes Area to the south, and the Seven Lakes Basin to the north, accessible by trail from either lake group. For direct access from the east, follow Upper Klamath Lake's westside road, County Rd. 531, to

FS 3484, 2 miles north of Crystal Springs Campground. Follow 3484 to the end. Trail 3707 (Nannie Creek Trail) reaches the lakes in less than 6 miles.

The larger southern lake covers about 25 acres, and the north lake covers 10 acres. Fishing is fair for brook trout averaging 10 inches. There are no improved campsites. The lakes are usually accessible in June or earlier and are open as long as trail and weather conditions permit.

RATTLESNAKE CREEK A small desert stream east of Burns, with native rainbow to 10 inches. It flows about 12 miles from headwaters in Malheur National Forest. From Burns follow Hwy. 20 east about 13 miles, turning north at the cut-off to Harney. A graded gravel road follows the stream from just north of Harney (near the Ft. Harney site) to its headwaters. Late spring and early summer are the best times to fish. Worms, grasshoppers, and wet flies do well. Trout average 8 inches and smaller. There are no campsites in the area.

RED LAKE (Klamath Co.) A shallow lake in the Island Lake group of the Sky Lakes Wilderness, Winema National Forest, about one mile north of Island Lake. Due to frequent winterkill, it will no longer be stocked, though fish may wander in from Island Lake.

RED MT. LAKE A small lake below Red Mt. in the Elkhorn Range west of Haines. It contains wild brook trout. To reach it, head west from Haines, turning north at Muddy Creek School. About one mile from the school, a road heads west toward Bulger Flat and the North Fk. North Powder River beyond it. Follow the North Fk. North Powder River Rd., FS 7301, into the forest. The trail to Red Mt. Lake is about 3 1/2 miles into the forest on the south side of the road. The lake is about one mile up the trail.

REYNOLDS POND A 5 acre reservoir SE of Alfalfa, containing largemouth bass and pumpkinseed sunfish.

ROCK CREEK LAKE A hike-in trout lake on the Elkhorn Ridge NW of Baker, in Wallowa-Whitman National Forest. The lake is the source of Rock Creek, which flows NE to the Powder River through Haines. The trailhead is reached from Haines, on Hwy.30, by driving west for 10 miles on gravel and dirt roads toward the community of Rock Creek. It's about a 3 mile hike SE from road's end, following Trail 1626. Another trail, somewhat shorter, approaches from the east from Pine Creek Reservoir west of Wingville.

Rock Creek Lake is at elevation 7600 ft. Although only 35 acres, the lake is over 100 ft. deep. It has a good brook trout population, and Mackinaw (lake trout) have been stocked. The Mackinaw run to 20 inches but are not numerous. You'll have to go deep for them, except right after ice off.

ROUND VALLEY RESERVOIR 150 acres 15 miles east of Lovella just south of Gerber Reservoir. It has contained pumpkinseed sunfish, yellow perch, and largemouth bass. The reservoir got very low in 1988, and the status of the fishery is currently unknown. The reservoir is on BLM land and is open to public access.

SAWMILL CREEK A short tributary of Silver Creek, 29 miles east of Burns, with fair early season fishing for native trout. Only about 10

miles long, it flows into Silver Creek about 12 miles north of Riley. From just west of Riley, on Hwy. 20, follow the Silver Creek Rd. north about 20 miles. Sawmill comes in from the NW and is followed and crossed by FS 45 in Malheur National Forest. The stream has a fair population of small native rainbow averaging 6-8 inches.

SEVENMILE CREEK An excellent fly stream, major tributary of Agency Lake, with headwaters in the Cascades SW of Crater Lake National Park. Despite its name, it is about 18 miles long.

From Sevenmile Forest Station on Klamath Lake's Westside Road, paved FS 3334 follows about 8 miles of the stream to Sevenmile Marsh. To reach this section from Hwy. 62, turn west onto Nicholson Rd. at Fort Klamath. The lower creek flows into Agency Lake, with an unboatable water level dam at the mouth of the creek.

Most of the lower stream is a canal, and is not fished. Above the canal, fishing is good for rainbow and brown trout. Brook trout are further upstream. Ask permission before fishing in areas where cattle are grazing.

SHERLOCK GULCH RESERVOIR A 10 acre desert reservoir on BLM land NW of Plush. Turn north onto the Sunstone Rd. from Hogback Rd., which runs between Plush and Hwy. 395. The reservoir is about 4 miles NW of the Sunstone Area. Get local directions before seeking this one out. The reservoir is stocked annually with rainbow fingerlings and holds trout 8-18 inches. The water is always turbid, making bait the most popular method here. Fly angling is occasionally productive. Winter ice-fishing can be good here.

SID LUCE (SID'S) RESERVOIR A natural lake converted to irrigation reservoir in Warner Valley east of Lakeview. Its excellent rainbow population is lightly fished due to long, difficult access over rough roads. Though only 15 air miles from Lakeview, the drive is over 75 miles one way.

From Lakeview, follow Hwy. 140 east to Adel. Turn north following the road toward Hart Lake and the community of Plush. Just north of Plush, head west toward the Fitzgerald Ranch. The road from Plush to Fitzgerald's is suitable for pick-up trucks. The road through the Fitzgerald property (which is open to public use) is very rough and turns into a power line access road shortly after the ranch buildings. If there have been recent rains, this road is impassable to all but off-road vehicles. There are 6 gates on the ranch road. Be sure to leave each as you found it. There are 2 creeks to ford after leaving the ranch, first Snyder (one mile past the ranch) then Colvin (shortly before Sid's).

The 50 acre lake sits in a bowl between Honey and Colvin creeks. It's rich with trout food (similar to Mann Lake in this respect), and stocked rainbow fingerlings show rapid growth, averaging 10-14 inches, nice and fat. Crayfish will eat fish left on stringers in the water, or can be trapped and eaten themselves. Most anglers use bait and fish from the shore, but a rubber boat would come in handy. There is no camping here. Be advised, too, that Sid's is at the beginning of snake country. Rattlesnakes are abundant.

SILVER CREEK (Harney Co.) A long stream NW of Burns, with trout in its upper waters. It heads in southern Ochoco National Forest a few miles north of Delintment Lake, and winds south through forest and high desert, finally emptying into Harney Lake. Hwy. 20 crosses the creek about 28 miles west of Burns near Riley. A paved road leads north from Riley, becoming FS 45 upon entering the Ochoco Forest. This road leads to Delintment Lake, and crosses and parallels the creek near the lake. It first parallels Sawmill Creek, which also has fish.

Most fishing takes place in the upper creek, north of Delintment and near Allison Ranger Station. Rainbow trout provide good catches in late spring until the water gets low and warm. The fish, mostly caught on bait, are generally 8-11 inches.

There are three forest campgrounds near the stream in the vicinity of Delintment Lake. Buck Spring Campground is located just west of FS 45 near Sawmill Creek, SW of Delintment.

SILVER CREEK (Lake Co.) A good trout stream, flowing north from Fremont National Forest west of Hager Mountain, into Paulina Marsh near the community of Silver Lake. The stream is about 16 miles long. It is crossed near its mouth by Hwy. 31, and is followed by graded roads and logging roads to its headwaters. FS. 288 from Silver Lake takes you to the upper reaches.

Very low winter flows below Thompson Reservoir practically eliminate any wild trout production. There is a stocked redband fishery in summer, when irrigation releases from Thompson keep the creek flowing high and cool while other streams are flowing low and warm. Best angling is in June and July. The West Fork (above Silver Creek Diversion Reservoir) is lightly stocked and contains a good population of small native rainbow (6-10 inches).

There is a campground at Silver Creek Marsh on FS 288 south of Thompson Reservoir, and two campgrounds at the reservoir.

SILVER CREEK DIVERSION RESERVOIR (Lake Co.) A 30 acre lake that rears big drop-out trout from the Silver Creek system. From the community of Silver Lake on Hwy. 31, drive south about 4 miles on County Rd. 4-12 toward Thompson Reservoir. The land at the north end is privately owned, but the SE arms are surrounded by BLM land, and you can fish from shore. Average fish taken exceed 14 inches.

SILVIES RIVER Flows 95 miles from headwaters in the southern Blue Mountains of Malheur National Forest south of John Day, to Malheur Lake, south of Burns. Trout fishing is best in the upper waters from Seneca downstream about 20 miles to the confluence with Trout Creek.

Hwy. 395 follows the stream closely through most of this stretch. The catch rate is high, but the fish run small, 8-11 inches. Bait fishing is most popular, but other methods will produce. About 8 miles south of the community of Trout Creek (16 miles north of Burns), FS 31 heads NW towards Myrtle Park Meadows and the ice caves, crossing the Silvies at its Stancliffe Creek confluence. Since 1970 this confluence area has been stocked with smallmouth bass, and they appear to be doing well.

The Silvies flows through Burns from the NW. A road heading due north beyond the city limits crosses and follows the river, deteriorating to ungraded gravel but sticking with the stream all the way to its confluence with Myrtle Creek. The Five-Mile Dam area, 5 miles NW of

Burns, affords some good fishing. The lower 20 miles from Burns to Malheur Lake offers no trout fishing.

SLIDE LAKE (Lake Co) A 3 acre lake in an interesting geological area of Fremont National Forest, about 12 miles west of Paisley. Follow Hwy. 31 north from Paisley, then turn south on FS 29 at the south end of Summer Lake. The road to Slide Lake cuts west after about 4 miles. Follow signs to Slide Mt. Geologic Area. It's about 8 miles to the lake. The road is not maintained for low clearance vehicles.

Slide Lake has some small trout, but they don't hold up long. The real interest here is the opportunity to view volcanic geology and resulting earth movement. Slide Mt., once a large dome-shaped volcano, has been scarred by a giant prehistoric slide. The slide can be seen from Hwy. 31 on the way in. Withers Lake, a 5 acre lake about 2 miles to the east, also holds fish. Best access is a mile bushwhack up Withers Creek from FS 3360.

SNAKE RIVER (Southeast Zone) This portion of the river runs from about Brownlee Dam, east of Baker, upstream to a point about 20 miles south of Nyssa, where the river swings east into Idaho. On the Oregon side, Hwy. 201 and county roads parallel the river from Adrian north to Ontario and the bridge at Weiser, Idaho. I-84 follows the river from Ontario north to Huntington, with county roads at exits leading east to the river. A county road closely follows the river for about 40 miles from Huntington north.

Most popular angling in this area is for channel catfish, although smallmouth bass are taken in growing numbers. Most of the cats are in the 2 pound range, but fish over 5 pounds are not unusual. Crappie are also available. This is primarily a bait show, with the best spots near the mouths of tributary streams. Local tackle shops can direct you to the current hot spots.

Boats can be launched at Nyssa, Ontario, Payette, Patch Island (south of Weiser), Oasis (north of Ontario), Farewell Bend State Park, Burnt River (east of Huntington), Spring Recreation Site (NE of Huntington), and Whiskey Rapids (same). Farewell Bend is a large park with complete camping facilities.

SOUTH PASS LAKE A good hike-in lake, excellent on flies, most productive of all the lakes in Mountain Lakes Wilderness. It is on the eastern edge of the wilderness and may be approached from the west (Lake of the Woods, 9 miles), north (Varney Creek Camp, 7 miles), or south (Clover Creek Rd., 7 miles). From Harriette Lake on the main basin-circling trail, it's a steep 2 mile hike to South Pass Lake on an unmaintained track.

Covering 7 acres, the lake is quite shallow. It is stocked bi-annually with brook and rainbow trout. Fish average 8-10 inches with a few larger, and the lake has been known to grow some lunkers. Fly fishing is good here, with fall and early spring best. As this is a wilderness, there are no improved camps, and users are urged to follow no-trace camping guidelines. The entire basin has suffered from heavy use in recent years, and many good campsites are currently closed due to efforts to rehabilitate lakeside vegetation. The season is limited only by the weather and trail access.

SPALDING RESERVOIR A 20 acre desert reservoir on BLM land 85 miles east of Lakeview. Turn north from Hwy.140 about 20 miles east of Adel, onto a dirt road that skirts the east-

ern edge of Guano Valley. The reservoir is 19 miles from the highway. This is remote country. Be prepared.

In 1988, Spalding went completely dry. It has since refilled and been restocked. In the past, trout grown here averaged 10-14 inches. Given normal rainfall, good fishing should be restored by 1990. The water here is clearer than in most desert reservoirs, and flies or lures can be very effective.

SPENCER CREEK A very good trout stream, tributary of the Klamath River. It flows 18 miles from spring-fed headwaters south of Lake of the Woods into John Boyle Reservoir on the Klamath west of Klamath Falls. The main creek and its tributaries are followed north by good graded roads from Keno on Hwy. 66, west of Klamath Lake.

Spencer Creek is managed as a wild trout stream. Fair numbers of large rainbow come into the creek from the Klamath River. The fishing is good on both bait and flies. The larger trout are usually taken early in season on lures or spinner/bait combinations. A late opening on the stream protects spawning fish.

SPRAGUE RIVER A long, good trout stream, with some bass, flowing into the Williamson River at Chiloquin, about 30 miles north of Klamath Falls. This river, which is managed for wild trout, flows over 100 miles from east to west. In its central stretch there is good fishing for largemouth bass.

The Sprague heads on the west slope of Gearhart Mt. and the rimlands to the south, about 30 miles west of Lakeview. Two major forks and Fishhole Creek combine near the town of Bly to form the main stream. Hwy. 140 (Lakeview to Klamath Falls) follows the upper half of the river west from Quartz Mt. Pass to the town of Beatty at river mile 70 on the mainstem.

The north fork provides excellent fly fishing for rainbow, brook, and brown trout in its upper reaches near Sandhill Crossing. The south fork has abundant small brook trout. There are some nice browns in the lower stretches of this fork also. Fremont National Forest roads leading north and west from Bly and north from Quartz Mt. pass provide access to these upper waters. Better bring a map.

Largemouth bass are available in the Sprague River valley section between the town of Sprague River and Beatty, where the river meanders. Bass fishing is best in mid-summer. A secondary road runs east from Hwy. 858 just north of its crossing of the river at the town of Sprague River, and follows the north bank to a point north of Beatty.

Five miles west of Beatty, Hwy. 858 cuts NW from Hwy. 140 and follows the river all the way to Chiloquin. Chiloquin is on Hwy. 97, a good distance south of Bend and 30 miles north of Klamath Falls. Access to much of the lower stream is prohibited by landowners, but some grant permission to fish.

The lower Sprague has many rainbow to 3 pounds or better, and good-size browns take a fly nicely. Large streamers and bucktails can do the trick. Bait and lures are also effective. Best time for trout on this river is late spring and early summer. The final mile of river below Chiloquin Dam is restricted to artificial lures or flies.

Sprague River Picnic Area, 5 miles east of Bly, is a nice lunch spot, but camping is prohibited. Several forest campgrounds are on or near the upper forks, including Sandhill Crossing, Lee Thomas, and Campbell Lake. S'Ocholis Campground is on the river 12 miles east of Chiloquin, along Hwy. 858.

SPRAGUE RIVER
Steve Terrill, Photographer

SPRING CREEK (Klamath Co.) A very short tributary of the Williamson River, offering good spring and summer angling. Only 2 miles long, it flows into the Williamson at Collier State Park, accessible from Hwy. 97 about 4 miles north of Chiloquin. It's primarily a put-and-take fishery with most angling pressure from Crater Lake tourists.

Spring is stocked with 16,000 fish annually near the headwaters and in the area above Collie. In addition to these, some sizeable rainbow and brown trout wander into the stream from the Williamson.

Collier State Park is a very attractive full service park beside the river, with trailer hookups, tent sites, and showers as well as a picnic area. For other good fishing in the area, see Sprague, Williamson.

SQUAW LAKE (Lake Co.) A 10 acre natural desert lake about 5 miles from Hwy. 31 north of Picture Rock Pass between Summer and Silver Lakes. A road leaves the highway to the east about 4 miles north of the community of Summer Lake. Squaw Lake is very turbid and receives little use. It is stocked periodically with rainbow fingerlings. The typical fish caught here is in the 8-10 inch range. Bait is the most effective method.

STONE CORRAL LAKE See Warner Lakes.

SUMMIT LAKE A small mountain lake in the Elkhorn Range west of Haines. It contains wild brook trout. See Red Mt. Lake for directions. The trail to Summit is a little more than one mile beyond the Red. Mt. Lake Trailhead, on the south side of the road. It's about a one mile hike to the lake.

SWAMP LAKE See Warner Valley Lakes.

SYCAN RIVER A fair tributary of the Sprague River, located north of Beatty in Fremont National Forest. It heads on the west slope of Winter Ridge and flows NW about 20 miles into Sycan Marsh. Leaving the marsh, it flows about 30 miles south to the Sprague at Beatty. In this stretch it forms the border between Fremont and Winema National Forests. The river is only lightly fished, probably due to its remoteness and rugged access roads. But the upper river offers very good fly angling for small wild brook trout in a very pretty setting.

The Sycan has reproducing populations of brown, rainbow, and brook trout. It is managed as a wild trout stream, so no stocking takes place. Rainbow are found throughout the stream, but brook trout are mostly in the upper river above the marsh, and the browns are strictly in the waters below the marsh. Bull trout reside in Long Creek, a tributary of the upper river.

The Sycan enters the marsh at its SE corner. Upstream from this point, the river is reached and crossed by many forest roads. Use the Fremont National Forest map to locate road access and crossings. Angling for brook and rainbow trout is good throughout most of the season in this stretch. Most fish are 6-10 inches, but larger fish to 20 inches plus are occasionally landed. Some of the finest fly fishing in the area is on the upper Sycan River and its tributaries.

A maze of rough forest and county roads provide access to the river below the Sycan Marsh. Follow County Rd. 1193 north from Beatty. At the first junction, FS 347 (to the left) leads to the river and crosses it below Teddy Powers Meadow, a popular take-out for drifters from the marsh. If you continue north instead of left onto FS 347, you will reach Sycan Ford, a rough crossing. A Fremont Forest map will come in handy. Most of the lower 12 miles of river is on private land, and you will need permission to fish.

The waters below the marsh have suffered from overgrazing and excessive water withdrawals for irrigation. Recent designation as a Federal Scenic River might protect the Sycan from further degradation. Most of the fishing in this stretch is concentrated between Torrent Spring (2 miles above Sycan Ford) and the mouth. Early season angling can be quite good for rainbow 10-18 inches, and for some good size browns. These fish are probably spawners from the Sprague River. By summer the stream flow has dropped to the point where water temperatures make fishing unproductive.

There are quite a few good campsites along the stream in the upper area. Campgrounds to the south are available at Lee Thomas Meadow and the Sandhill Crossing of the North Fork of the Sprague.

TAFT MILLER RESERVOIR A large irrigation reservoir in the desert country east of Hart Mt. National Antelope Refuge. The reservoir is about 85 miles south of Burns and 85 miles east of Lakeview. It can be reached by the Hart Mt. Road from either direction.

The reservoir normally covers about 350 acres and is loaded with white crappie 6-10 inches. In 1988 the reservoir almost went dry, and some effect on the fishery is inevitable. However, crappie are a very hearty species with a history of survival. Since the reservoir was becoming a little crowded, with a consequent drop in average crappie size, some thinning out might actually improve fishing.

Effects of the drought on the largemouth bass population here, which had been growing nicely for several years, are unknown at this time. If necessary, largemouth will be restocked in 1989. Large wild rainbow, spawned in Rock Creek, are also taken here on occasion.

Camping is available near Frenchglen and on the Hart Mt. Refuge, both about 25 miles from the reservoir.

THOMAS CREEK (Lake Co.) A fair stream for resident redband trout, flowing about 20 miles from Fremont National Forest south of Gearhart Mt. Wilderness into Goose Lake. Hwy. 140 crosses the lower stream about 2 miles west of Lakeview. About one mile west of the crossing, turn north to join FS 28, which follows the stream for about 10 miles. FS 100, an unmaintained road, follows the creek to its headwaters. The upper stream is also accessible from Hwy. 140 at Quartz Mt. Pass east of Bly.

In the past, the main activity on the lower stream has been a spring fishery for Goose Lake spawners. Due to a decrease in that run, the stream has been given a late opening to protect the spawning fish. This restriction applies to the entire stream and its tributaries except Cottonwood Creek. The headwaters offer fair fishing throughout the season. There is a primitive camp on FS 2823 about 16 miles NW of Lakeview.

THOMPSON VALLEY RESERVOIR A large impoundment capable of providing very good angling for large trout, about 12 air miles SW of Silver Lake in northern Lake County. The reservoir is in the headwaters of the upper east fork of Silver Creek in Fremont National Forest. It is about 14 miles south of the town of Silver Lake, which is on Hwy. 31. Several roads lead south from the highway near the town, so just follow the signs to the reservoir.

Thompson has a continuing problem with chub overpopulation. It was treated for chubs in 1977, 1981, and 1988. It will be restocked gradually as the reservoir refills following the 1987-88 drought, and should be back in business with good size fish by 1990.

UNITY RESERVOIR
Tom Ballard, Photographer

Thompson Valley has covered as much as 2500 acres when full. With a maximum depth of only 30 ft. and lots of sunshine, trout food is abundant. The current stocking program uses Eagle Lake rainbow and Lahontan cutthroat, both well adapted to desert lake conditions. The rainbow usually reach 12-24 inches and about 5 pounds maximum. The cutthroat are smaller, about 3 pounds, ranging 8-18 inches.

With fish this big, fly fishing the shallows can provide some real thrills. Trolling with spinner and worm is productive, as is still fishing with worms, cheese or eggs. The reservoir could stand a lot more use than its getting.

Thompson is open all year, and lots of anglers fish through the ice during winter season. If the snow's too deep, you may have to hike a short way. Winter anglers stick to bait fished just off the bottom.

There are two Forest Service campgrounds on the reservoir, each with a boat ramp.

THREE MILE CREEK A small native trout stream, heading near Puck Lakes in the Cascades, west of Fort Klamath. The lower end is crossed by the Westside Upper Klamath Lake Highway, about 10 miles out of Fort Klamath. A road heads part way up the stream, and a trail follows along the rest of the way. There are about 5 miles of productive water with lots of rock-hard brook trout, not big, but tasty and full of scrap. Three mile offers a good chance for a mess of pan-size natives and not much company. There is no camping along the stream.

THIEF VALLEY RESERVOIR A large irrigation reservoir on the Powder River, about 15 miles north of Baker, about 5 miles east of I-84. It can be reached from the road between Telocaset and Medical Springs. Telocaset is on Hwy. 237 eight miles south of Union and 7 miles NE of the North Powder Exit on I-84, south of La Grande.

The pool covers 890 acres when full. Fishing success varies with the water levels. The reservoir is stocked every year with rainbow trout fingerlings and grows trout to a good size. A few get up to 20 inches, with the typical trout 10-14 inches.

Quite a few brown bullhead 9-12 inches are available, as well as crappie, largemouth and smallmouth bass. Bait fishing from the bank is popular, with the dam a favorite spot. The reservoir is open for angling all year around, and ice fishing is popular, with the success rate high. The county maintains a small park with boat ramp on the reservoir.

TRAVERSE LAKE A nice brook trout lake in the SW Eagle Cap Wilderness. It is at the head of the East Fork of Eagle Creek, one mile above Echo Lake on the same trail. Take FS 77 east from Hwy. 203 about 16 miles south of Union, and drive about 30 miles to the crossing of the East Fork of Eagle Creek. A spur road leads north 1/2 mile to the trailhead. Take Trail 1934 north 6 1/2 miles to the lake, 1100 feet above the trailhead.

Brook trout are numerous and of good size. Fly angling is excellent in August and September, and bait will produce fish at any time. This lake doesn't get much pressure.

TROUT CREEK Want to get away from it all? This creek is about as remote as any you can drive to in Oregon. Located in the far southeast, the creek heads high in the Trout Creek Mts. near the Nevada border and flows north into the desert country SE of the Steens Mts. About 30 miles long, it is so remote it is hardly ever fished. Small, unique Alvord cutthroat inhabit its bracing upper waters.

Only the upper waters are available for fishing. The lower stream is all in private ownership. You'll want a good map before heading in here. The BLM Steens Mt. map covers the area well. Four-wheel drive or at least a high center vehicle is strongly recommended, along with a good stock of supplies. Inquire at the State Patrol office in Burns for road conditions prior to attempting this. (We once had to rebuild a section of the road to get out.)

A graded road leads east toward Whitehorse Ranch from the Fields to Denio Rd., about mid-way between them and one mile north of Tum Tum Lake. This road reaches a gap formed by lower Trout Creek about 6 miles to the east, and follows the lower waters about 8 miles. Unfortunately, the creek flows across private land here.

To reach the upper waters, take the Whitehorse Rd. 5 miles east of Fields to the Denio Rd., and turn south on a graded road which loops on to Denio. A bit over one mile later, turn SE onto a road which will meet Oreanna

Creek in about 3 miles. Stay on this road and follow it SE and up about 13 rough miles to a ford through Trout Creek. The road follows the creek for a mile or so. You'll have to hike for further access. You can continue on this road and loop north and back down to Whitehorse Ranch.

Trout Creek offers fair fishing for rainbow trout on bait or flies in the lower waters if you can get permission to fish. There's not a lot of water in the upper creek, and the trout above are generally under 8 inches and darkly speckled. There are natural campsites in the aspen groves and plenty of wide open spaces.

TWENTYMILE CREEK A pretty good desert trout stream, flowing east and north from springs near the California line into Warner Valley, about 7 miles south of Adel. Adel is on Hwy. 140, about 30 miles east of Hwy. 395. Twentymile is followed by a gravel road that leads south from Adel to California. The upper stream is accessed by graded roads running NW from this road toward Big Valley and Big Lake, then on to Hwy. 140.

Between the Big Lake Rd. and the Adel-to-California Rd., the stream flows into a canyon. Most of the fishing takes place here, for native rainbow. Angling is good in spring and summer for trout to 15 inches, but the average is 9-10 inches. Bait or wet flies are best.

TWIN LAKES (Baker Co.) Two little lakes below Elkhorn peak in the Elkhorn Range NW of Baker. The trail to the lake is at the end of the Lake Cr. Rd. FS 030, which heads north from Deer Creek Campground. Trail 1633 reaches the lakes in about 2 miles.

UNITY RESERVOIR A large reservoir on the upper Burnt River south of Baker, 3 miles north of the town of Unity. It offers good angling for rainbow trout. Just west of Unity, Hwy. 7 runs north to the reservoir.

Over 2000 acres when full, Unity Reservoir is stocked with rainbow trout and provides good catches. The maximum size is about 16 inches, with the typical fish 9-12 inches. Trolling and bait fishing are both popular, but bait anglers fare better early in the season. There is lots of angling pressure here, but good success. South of the dam, a state park provides boat ramps and camping facilities.

UPPER KLAMATH LAKE Often the largest lake in Oregon (vying with Malheur), shallow and extremely productive, featuring big native rainbow trout. Covering about 64,000 acres, Upper Klamath is connected by a natural strait to 8200 acre Agency Lake. Its primary tributary is the rich Williamson River system, and from it flows the great Klamath River. From its southern tip within the town of Klamath Falls, the lake stretches north almost 25 miles.

I-97 provides direct access from Bend and from Redding, California and follows a good portion of the east lakeshore. Hwy. 140, a direct route from the Medford area, follows the more popular west lakeshore from Pelican Bay to Klamath Falls. There are no bridges or opportunities to cross the 10 mile swath of water and wetland between Klamath Falls and the northernmost reach of Agency Lake. Motorists on I-97 should continue on to Chiloquin, then take Hwy. 62 to Ft. Klamath. Secondary roads east from Hwy. 140 access boat ramps and popular fishing areas on the west shore, including Pelican Bay, Odessa Creek, Ball Bay, Shoalwater Bay, and Howard Bay.

Of Klamath Lake's 100 square miles, all but 2% is less than 25 ft. deep. This shallow water is high in nutrients and provides a food-rich environment that grows fish quickly. Large rainbow, over 20 inches, are the main attraction in the Upper Klamath, with the *average* catch a whopping 18 inches. Studies have shown that rainbow trout in this lake reach 20 inches in only 3 years, and by 5 years have reached a length of 26 inches. A few 17-20 pound rainbow are occasionally taken. The lake's trout population is entirely dependent on natural reproduction, since past fish stocking programs failed. Hatchery trout proved to be susceptible to a disease organism present in the lake.

By mid-summer the main lake becomes too warm for trout, and the fish move into spring-fed pockets and toward the mouths of tributaries, including the Pelican Bay area and Recreation Creek. Most fishing during the heat of the summer is catch and release, since annual summer algae blooms on the lake tend to give fish caught during the summer an off taste.

Bank angling is popular in winter, spring, and fall in Klamath Falls at Moore Park, Pelican Marina, and the Link River outlet. Anglers also fish along Howard (Wocus) Bay, in the SW and near springs on the east shore, just north of Hagelstein County Park off Hwy. 97. In early spring, a boat fishery develops near Eagle Ridge and in Howard (Wocus)and Shoalwater bays. In late April the northern lake opens and there are active troll fisheries out of Rocky Point and Harriman resorts, at the Recreation Creek inlet of Pelican Bay, and in the narrows between Upper Klamath and Agency lakes. In late summer fish gather in the Fourmile Creek inlet of Pelican Bay, which is cooled by springs, and at the mouths of cooler tributaries.

Klamath Lake has a large chub population, and bait fishing with chub chunks is popular. *(Note that fish bait is not legal in most of Oregon's waters. Klamath Lake is an exception.)* Bait is available at local shops. Trollers use large flasher-type lures or Flatfish and the standard spinner/bait set-up. The Andy Reeker No. 4 has been a standard lure here for years, and Rapalas are popular. Trolling with dead minnows behind a flasher is effective and legal here.

Other fish available in Upper Klamath include brown bullhead, yellow perch, sculpin, and sturgeon. Largemouth bass have been introduced, but have not thrived. Mullet (Lost River suckers) are now a protected species.

Boat anglers are generally cautious and keep close to shore. Klamath Lake is mighty big and can kick up in even moderate wind. There is a public boat launch at Moore Park in Klamath Falls. Westshore ramps are located at Howard Bay just off Hwy. 140, at Odessa Creek Campground just south of Pelican Bay, at Rocky Point near the Pelican Bay inlet off County Rd. 531, and at Shoalwater Bay. The only public ramp on the east shore is at Hagelstein Park and Campground. There is a 10 mph speed limit in the channels and resort areas.

Supplies, lodging, boat rentals, and private launches and marinas are available near the prime fisheries around the lake. Williamson, Wood, Sprague, and Klamath Rivers offer outstanding angling alternatives in the immediate area. Lake of the Woods, Fourmile Lake, and Mountain Lakes Wilderness offer additional angling, camping, and hiking opportunities nearby.

UPPER MIDWAY RESERVOIR 40 acres about 18 miles east of Lorella. Located on BLM land, the reservoir contains largemouth bass which are small, but plentiful and willing. Camping is permitted.

VAN PATTEN LAKE A hike-in rainbow trout lake in the Anthony Lake area west of Haines on Hwy. 411. From Haines, go west on 411, which becomes FS 73. Trail 1634 to Van Patten Lake takes off south from FS 73 two miles east of Anthony Lake Guard Station.

The lake covers 23 acres and generally offers excellent angling for rainbow to 12 inches from late spring through fall. All methods can be used to take fish. The lake is stocked with fingerlings bi-annually. Supplies and accommodations are available at Anthony Lake Resort, 3 miles to the west. There are campgrounds at Anthony Lake and at Grande Ronde Lake.

VEE LAKE A 13 acre lake in Fremont National Forest that was created by a small dam to provide fish and goose habitat. The lake is in the North Warner Mts. NE of Lakeview. Drive east from Lakeview on Hwy. 140 about 15 miles to the North Warner Road (FS 3615), and follow this north about 25 miles to the lake.

It's a shallow, weedy lake with lots of natural food to grow trout quickly. Most of the rainbow are 12-16 inches. Bait, lures and flies all produce well here. Boats without motors are allowed on the lake. Several forest service campgrounds are nearby.

WARM SPRING RESERVOIR A large reservoir SW of Juntura, a town on Hwy. 20 between Burns and Vale. From Juntura, the reservoir is 20 miles south. Another road leads there from Crane on Hwy. 78.

Warm Springs covers about 4500 acres when full, but is used for irrigation and gets pretty low in the fall some years. It's stocked with rainbow trout, and fishing is fair for 10-20 inchers in spring and fall. Smallmouth bass here run to 4 pounds and take small lures, spinners and small rubber worms with enthusiasm. Streamers with a lot of color will work, too.

This is one of the few lakes in the state with channel catfish. A fair number are caught, with some to 24 inches. Brown bullhead are taken in larger numbers, but run only to 14 inches, most just under a pound. There are no improvements at the reservoir. In dry years, it's hard to put a boat in late in the season, but bank fishing at the dam will produce.

WARNER VALLEY LAKES Eleven highly alkaline but life-supporting lakes in an eerie setting of desert vastness. They form a north-south chain across the floor of Warner Valley west of Hart Mountain. From north to south they are Blue Joint, Stone Corral, Lower Campbell, Upper Campbell, Flagstaff, Swamp, Jones, Anderson, Hart, Crump, and Pelican. All are interconnected during high water, and contain crappie, brown bullhead, and a few largemouth bass.

The most dramatic approach is to drop down into the valley from Hart Mt. From Burns, take Hwy. 205 south, turning east toward Hart about 6 miles south of Frenchglen. Hart Mt. Antelope Refuge Headquarters is 51 miles from the road junction. Take time to visit the headquarters, which has a small museum and informative literature related to this incredible landscape and its wildlife. There is also a rustic hot spring south of the headquarters which can be refreshing after the long drive through the desert, though one can't float and take in the view, since the pools are walled (less for modesty's sake, we have concluded, than to to thwart the wind). Head down the west slope of Hart Mt. for a stunning vista of Warner Valley.

SOUTHEAST

The first lake that comes into view is Big Upper Campbell, which has been known to cover 4 square miles. Its depth ranges from 10 ft. to less than 4 ft. All the Warner Lakes have been dry at one time or another. During high water their populations intermingle. The lakes were originally stocked in 1961 and have been self-sustaining since that time. Four-five years of good water lead to outstanding crappie catches in 1987, especially in Lower and Upper Campbell, with fish 16-18 inches and up to 2 1/2 pounds taken. The lakes were severely affected by the 1987-88 drought, and it is doubtful that lakes north of Hart Lake will refill before 1990.

They are all quite alkaline, and aquatic weed growth is heavy in mid-summer. Most angling takes place from the roadside since bank fishing is very good. Frequent high winds across the lakes also discourage boating. This is a wonderful area for aquatic bird watching. See also Hart Lake, Crump Lake.

WEST SUNSTONE RESERVOIR A small desert reservoir 2 miles east of Sherlock Gulch Reservoir. For directions see Sherlock Gulch Reservoir. The reservoir covers 8 acres when full. It got quite low in 1987, and some fish were lost. It had refilled by spring of 1989. The reservoir is stocked annually with rainbow fingerlings, and the catch generally runs from 8-16 inches. Turbid water makes bait the preferred method.

WILLIAMSON RIVER (Lower) A long, meandering river, major tributary of Upper Klamath Lake, with a national reputation for fine fly water and large rainbow in the lower section. It was one of the first rivers in Oregon to be selected for wild trout management. The Williamson wanders over 70 miles from the Yamsey Mt. area of Winema National Forest, flowing west through Klamath Marsh, then south into Upper Klamath Lake, entering from the NE. Its headwaters are in Winema National Forest, but after only 1/4 mile the river flows through private ranchland. Access is limited by extensive private landholdings both in the upper and lower river.

The section below the marsh covers 38 miles and is quite different in character from the upper river. Most of the lower river flows through private property, so check locally for permission to fish. The Klamath Agency Junction Rd. crosses the river 5 miles above the mouth, and Hwy. 97 crosses 7 miles above the mouth. Just below Chiloquin, 11 miles above the mouth, the cooler spring fed waters of the upper river are joined by the warmer waters of the Sprague River at a point known as Blue Hole. This mixing generally results in water temperatures in the lower river that are ideal for trout. Chiloquin is about 25 miles north of Klamath Falls, a mile east of Hwy. 97 on the Sprague River Hwy. 858. There are opportunities to fish at Chiloquin from the Sprague confluence downstream for a mile or so.

About 5 miles north of Chiloquin, just north of the confluence of Spring Creek, the river flows through the Winema National Forest. It can be fished at Williamson River Campground on FS 9730, which leaves Hwy. 97 just north of Spring Creek. About 2 miles north, FS 9734 leaves Hwy. 97 and follows the west bank of the river for several miles. FS 4502 follows the east bank east of Kirk (on Hwy. 97). Above Kirk the river again enters private lands, and access is limited. Refer to the Winema National Forest map.

The river below Kirk Canyon provides exceptional angling for large native rainbow. Much of the credit for the preservation of this marvelous fishing must go to the efforts of the Klamath County Fly Casters, organized by Polly Rosborough and Dick Winters to counter a trend of declining fishing that occurred in the late '50s and early '60s when access to the river increased due to transfers of lands from the Klamath Indian Reservation. Their efforts, and those of the Dept. of Fish and Wildlife, have reversed the trend and preserved a true trophy trout fishery here.

These large rainbow are apparently growing to size in the incredibly productive waters of Klamath Lake, where 3 year old fish normally reach 20 inches or better. The cycle of migration is poorly understood, probably tied to both spawning and avoidance of warm lake temperatures in summer, but the fact is that large fish are in the river in good numbers from late June through fall. By late August many of these fish have moved into the upper stretches of the river.

Eighteen inch rainbows are ho-hum here, and fish that go well over 10 pounds have shocked many an angler. Available in smaller numbers are good size browns, particularly in the river below the mouth of Spring Creek. The Williamson remains high through June, with *big fish* fishing best in August and September. Fishing remains good through October, and there are few anglers on the water in late season.

From Agency Lake Rd. to Kirk Bridge, angling is restricted to use of artificial flies or lures. From Chiloquin Bridge up to Kirk Bridge, flies and lures must also be barbless. Large flies and streamers are most popular. Try black and white patterns such as the maribou leech and muddler, or a bucktail coachman. There are good mayfly and caddis hatches in June and July, and large October caddis are present in fall. Check with local tackle shops, resorts and Klamath Lake marinas for fly and tackle recommendations.

In addition to trout, the Williamson hosts a population of Lost River suckers, locally called *mullet*. These are now a protected species, and taking them is illegal.

Access to the Williamson is a problem. There is fair bank access immediately below Chiloquin, as mentioned above. A boat can be put in at Blue Hole to float the river below the Sprague confluence. This is flat water. A canoe is sufficient. Above Chiloquin there is fair access in the national forest where a boat is handy. Check current regulations for restrictions relative to angling from a boat.

There are no public camping areas below Chiloquin, though there are some RV parks off Hwy. 97. Above Chiloquin there is the Williamson River Campground east of 97, Collier State Park north of Chiloquin, and Kimball State Park at the source of Wood River 3 miles north of Ft. Klamath. There's a nice picnic area on the Wood River at Ft. Klamath.

Accommodations in the area offer pretty slim pickings—a couple of very expensive fishing resorts, and a couple of roadside motels. There is a good cafe in Fort Klamath, a truck stop near Chiloquin, and a cafe with great pies on Hwy. 97 near its crossing of the river. A small state airstrip at Chiloquin is within an easy walk of accessible stretches of the lower river. More plentiful supplies and accommodations are available in Klamath Falls, 20 miles or so to the south.

WILLIAMSON RIVER (Upper) Above Klamath Marsh the Williamson offers spring fed water, native rainbow and brook trout 8-15 inches, and good bank access in the Winema National Forest, where the river begins its 86 mile journey to Klamath Lake.

To reach the upper river from Chiloquin, follow the Sprague River Rd. 858 east to Braymill, then take the Williamson River Rd. 600 (the left fork), which crosses the Williamson at Yamsay Guard Station. Head of the River Campground is just north of the station. The river flows north 27 miles to the marsh and is accessed by a number of forest roads. Refer to the Winema National Forest map.

WILLOW CREEK (Malheur Co., Trout Creek. Mts.) A remote stream, with a rock for everybody to stand on. Only about 12 miles long, Willow Creek runs out into the desert at White Horse Ranch and dries up. It is reached by gravel and dirt roads. For directions see Trout Creek.

Native cutthroat run 6-8 inches, and an occasional catch reaches 14 inches. These fish are unique to Whitehorse and Willow Creek, descendents of Lahontan cutthroat. Bait is best, but the stream can be fished with flies in late spring and summer.

WILLOW CREEK (Malheur Co., Vale area) A long stream in extreme eastern Oregon, flowing into the lower Malheur River at the town of Vale. Only the upper reaches are good for trout angling. Below Malheur Reservoir the creek is heavily infested with rough fish.

The upper creek flows into Malheur Reservoir about 15 miles NW of Brogan and has a good population of native trout. It is followed by dirt roads above the reservoir and crossed by Hwy. 26 near Ironside. Secondary roads follow South Willow Creek south from Ironside, and Middle Willow Creek south from the highway about 3 miles west of Ironside.

Willow is not stocked, but has a large number of native rainbow as well as trout that move up out of Malheur Reservoir. Most of the catch runs 9-10 inches, but some fish to 15 inches are landed. Anglers don't put much pressure on this creek. Bait is the most common method, but flies or small lures can also produce well. There is no camping along the stream.

WILLOW VALLEY RESERVOIR A 500 acre irrigation reservoir 50 miles east of Klamath Falls, featuring fine bass fishing. Located right above the California line, it's a long drive for most people in the state, but if you're a bass bug, you'll want to take a look at these good size largemouth. From Klamath Falls follow Hwy. 140 to Dairy, then turn right on County Rd. 70 to Bonanza, continuing SE on the Langell Valley Rd. through Lorella and south toward California. As you near the border, watch for the sign to the reservoir, which is east of the State Line Rd. The reservoir is about 5 miles from the turn-off on BLM land, open to the public.

Willow Valley harbors good populations of bass, white crappie, a few brown bullhead and bluegill.

WOOD RIVER A spring-fed, crystal-clear, productive little stream in the Fort Klamath area north of Agency Lake, about 35 miles from Klamath Falls. Hwy. 62 crosses the river at Ft. Klamath. Much of the lower stream flows through grazing land, so ask permission to fish.

This is a delightful spring creek, generally under 30 feet wide and not too deep. It runs through lush meadowland and has undercut banks, log jams, and occasional deep pools. Perfect fly water. Though stocked, it has a fair population of native rainbow that go to 4-5 pounds, as well as some large browns of similar size. There are also some brook trout. You'll need a light, long leader here to be successful. The stream flow is consistent throughout the year. Good boating water is available below Kimball State Park. Boats can also be launched and taken out at the Ft. Klamath Picnic Area, Loosley Rd. crossing, and Weed Rd. crossing. The river is best suited to canoe, raft, or a small driftboat. The float from Kimball to Petric park on Agency Lake is a long day's trip (about 17 miles.).

Jackson F. Kimball State Park is located at the source spring of the river, above the intersection of hwys. 232 and 62. It has an earthen put-in suitable for raft or canoe. Boats must be hand carried to the water's edge. There is a small tent campground here. Mosquitoes can be thick in summer.

YELLOWJACKET LAKE A 35 acre impoundment on upper Yellowjacket Creek in Malheur National Forest south of the Blue Mountains, about 40 miles NW of Burns. To get there, cut west off Hwy. 20, just south of the Hines Mill south of Burns, and follow FS 47, watching for a road sign. The lake covers about 35 acres and contains good size rainbow. It's stocked with rainbow each year. Most anglers fish from shore, but small boats can be used. There is an improved campground at the lake.

BASS AND PANFISH WATERS

ADDITIONAL SOURCES OF INFORMATION

Bureau of Land Management
PO Box 2965, Portland, OR 97208
(503) 231-6281
Four-color maps of land holdings including Lower Deschutes, John Day, Steens Mt., Central Oregon; index available.

Oregon Dept. of Fish and Wildlife (ODFW)
Headquarters
506 SW Mill St.,
Portland OR 97201
(503) 229-5400

ODFW NW Region
NEWPORT	(503) 867-4741
SALEM	(503) 378-6925
FLORENCE	(503) 997-7366
SPRINGFIELD	(503) 726-3515
CORVALLIS	(503) 757-4186

ODFW SW Region
ROSEBURG	(503) 440-3353
CHARLESTON	(503) 888-5515
GOLD BEACH	(503) 247-7605
CENTRAL POINT	(503) 776-6170

ODFW Central Region
BEND	(503) 388-6363
THE DALLES	(503) 296-4628
KLAMATH FALLS	(503) 883-5732
PRINEVILLE	(503) 447-5111
MADRAS	(503) 475-2183

ODFW NE Region
LAGRANDE	(503) 963-2138
JOHN DAY	(503) 575-1167
PENDLETON	(503) 276-2344
ENTERPRISE	(503) 426-3279

ODFW SE Region
HINES	(503) 573-6582
LAKEVIEW	(503) 947-2950
ONTARIO	(503) 889-6975

ODFW Columbia Region
CLACKAMAS	(503) 657-2058
SEASIDE	(503) 738-7066
TILLAMOOK	(503) 842-2741

ODFW Marine Region
NEWPORT	(503) 86704741
ASTORIA	(503) 325-2462

Oregon Dept. of Tourism
595 Cottage St., NE
Salem, OR 97310
(503) 378-3451

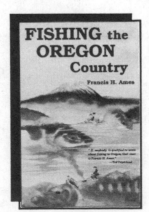